*Rhode Island
in Rhetoric
and Reflection*

Rhode Island in Rhetoric and Reflection

Public Addresses and Essays

Patrick T. Conley

Rhode Island Publications Society
East Providence · 2002

For information write:
    The Rhode Island Publications Society
    1445 Wampanoag Trail
    East Providence, Rhode Island 02915
    TEL: (401) 272-1776
    FAX: (401) 273-1791

Printed in the United States of America
ISBN 1-930483-00-7
Library of Congress Control Number 2002094991

Book design, composition, and image processing by Clifford Garber
Cover design by Patrick T. Conley

Printed by the E. A. Johnson Company, East Providence, Rhode Island
Bound by Acme Bookbinders, Charlestown, Massachusetts

DEDICATED TO

The Reverend Cornelius Philip Forster, O.P.

Inspiring Teacher, Lifelong Mentor,

Challenging Colleague, and Steadfast Friend

Acknowledgements

THIS BOOK was conceived in November 2001 during discussions about its propriety and contents with my wife Gail, whose counsel continued through completion. Its period of gestation has been considerably less than a year.

A successful delivery was due in great measure to the typing and computer talents of my legal secretaries Linda M. Gallen and Anna Maria Loiselle, the editorial expertise of Dr. Hilliard Beller, and the design skills of Cliff Garber. This book is their creation too.

Forewords

P ROVIDENCE COLLEGE OFFERED A DOCTORAL DEGREE in history for several years. I entered the part-time program in 1982, while I was still a bus driver for the Rhode Island Public Transit Authority. It had been ten years since I finished a master's degree. I was still trying to understand the world around me, as well as change it from the bottom up as a labor activist.

I enrolled in Dr. Patrick T. Conley's historiography course, my first foray into academia in a decade. I never fully understood the discipline of history until I attended his lectures and read the accompanying assignments.

Pat Conley seamlessly joined the historical temper of the times with various schools of interpretation. Patricians from the dawn of American scholarship dotted our venerable workload: Jared Sparks, George Bancroft, Francis Parkman, John Fiske, and the farsighted Henry Adams. We also waded through the scientific historians, the Progressives' New History, the Consensus School, and the New Left.

Dr. Conley's piercing lectures and keen intellect left nothing murky in history's shadow box. He graced his powerful lectures with entertaining anecdotes and insights about the great masters. He provided his students with a firm grasp of American history instead of the usual end-of-the-year gasp at a comprehensive exam question on the subject. He spoke at a fast pace, and we took our notes even quicker. We often felt like that old television series, "You Are There," which tried to recreate important historical events—but never as successfully as Pat Conley.

If the good professor held himself and his own writings to a skyscraper standard, his exams offered a not so subtle reminder that we had better at least strain for respectability under his critical care. In another course he once returned a preliminary outline to his star student with a caustic note that translated into "Shape up or ship out." I never embarrassed myself again.

Dr. Conley did more than provide a key to unlock the secrets of historical interpretation. I also took his two-semester course on the history of Rhode Island, "our mini-paradise," as he gently mocked it. Only he could stretch the history of the nation's most diminutive state into a year-long joyride through primary material that took us behind the scenes to witness the state's incredible background, much of which appears in this omnibus volume.

If Dr. Conley demanded much of us, most students actually responded well to a higher academic bar. Most of his seminar papers, master's theses, and doctoral dissertations address local topics. He may have done more individually to cover the spectrum of Ocean State history than anyone else. Even the undergraduate papers he assigned over the years are valuable guides to the recesses of local history. More than a few of his students have published scholarly articles and stately monographs—not bad for a part-time doctoral program in a state that national publishers usually shun because it is such a small market, yet another testament to Dr. Conley's own prodigious publications. Many other of his students have also found success, some entering politics and the judicial community. I have heard Congressman Patrick Kennedy, another pupil, pay homage to Dr. Conley's teaching influence and rigorous standards.

The classroom was never large enough to contain Pat Conley's desire to spread the historical message to just about any group or organization that was willing to listen. He celebrated the nation's bicentennial with a profusion of talks and events that rivaled the energy and influence of the original revolutionaries. He helped make the Dorr War the state's seminal event in the nineteenth century through his writings and activities. His fingerprints are all over the Rhode Island Irish Famine Memorial and display at the forthcoming Heritage Harbor Museum in Providence. He helps choose inductees to the Rhode Island Heritage Hall of Fame and annually hosts a Law Day convocation that reflects his own personality: good food, wry humor, and inspiring lectures.

More than anything, first and foremost, the sage of Bristol Point is a friend and mentor.

DR. D. SCOTT MOLLOY
Professor of Labor Relations and Human Resources
University of Rhode Island

THESE ARE WONDERFUL ESSAYS on the history of Rhode Island by the premier historian of Rhode Island. With wit, clarity, and an extraordinary command of historical information, Patrick T. Conley has covered all aspects of Rhode Island history from its earliest origins in the seventeenth century to the beginning of the twenty-first century. There are essays on Rhode Island constitutionalism (Conley's specialty), on immigration and ethnicity, on Rhode Island sports, on Catholicism, and on a wide variety of the Ocean State's local scenes and colorful characters. The beauty of collections like this is that they preserve what otherwise might be lost. And Conley's writings are worth preserving. He is a treasure.

DR. GORDON S. WOOD
Alva O. Way Professor of History, Brown University
Winner of the Pulitzer Prize in History

WHATEVER PATRICK T. CONLEY SETS OUT TO DO, he does masterfully—whether that be teaching, public speaking, practicing law, developing real estate, performing on the athletic field, volunteering his expert organizational skills, ghostwriting political position papers, or writing history. The latter is his passion. He has a profound grasp of American history and his bibliographic knowledge is breathtaking. In this, his latest volume, Conley is at his best in offering an astonishing array of Rhode Island history. This tiniest of states has played a significant role in the country's development, much of which is analyzed with great insight in the varied pieces in this volume.

With his usual fidelity to the highest standards of scholarship, Conley examines here constitutional history from colonial and Revolutionary times, to the nineteenth-century upheaval of Dorr's Rebellion, to Rhode Island's twentieth-century constitutional conventions. He deftly investigates religious history, nativism, ethnic studies, sports history, local history, and biography. Throughout these offerings Conley's charm, wit, and humor shine through. Many of these pieces were either delivered as speeches or printed in out-of-the-way publications. This volume pulls together these disparate "words...written on the wind" and makes them readily available to a broad audience. Undeniably, Pat Conley is the greatest historian of Rhode Island ever. This book helps prove that fact.

DR. JOHN P. KAMINSKI
Director of The Center for the Study of the
American Constitution and Editor of *The Documentary
History of the Ratification of the Constitution*

A STATE IS FORTUNATE INDEED which can boast a native scholar who devotes his or her talents, as Patrick Conley has, to recording and making available to its citizens the richness of the heritage which they enjoy. A scholar who can illuminate the state's historical past performs an invaluable service. A scholar who is a student of the law, who can elucidate and bring to life the state's legal and constitutional evolution, performs an equally valuable service. Rhode Island enjoys the perhaps unique advantage of having a scholar who is skilled both in the study and writing of history, but also can convey an understanding of her constitutional development. The stream of works written by Pat Conley (listed in his bibliography), with their wealth of commentary on the state from almost every imaginable perspective, is truly a treasure trove. The table of contents reveals the volume of his contributions but also the extraordinary range of subject matter that flowed from his pen over the years. We his contemporaries, but also generations to come, will find this wealth of material indispensable to an understanding of what Rhode Island was and has become. We owe him a great debt.

DR. ELMER E. CORNWELL, JR.
Professor of Political Science, Brown University

DR. PATRICK CONLEY, the dean of Rhode Island historians, has gathered together into one volume sixty of his occasional writings and speeches on the history of the colony and state. They display great erudition and learning, and, what is just as important, an accessible writing style that will engage every type of reader from the scholar to the lay resident interested in the history of the state. Providing many insights into crucial events, developments, and personalities in Rhode Island's profoundly interesting and often unique history, this volume stands as yet another example of Dr. Conley's many contributions to the public life of this state.

DR. JACK P. GREENE
Andrew W. Mellon Professor in the Humanities
Johns Hopkins University

IN *RHODE ISLAND IN RHETORIC AND REFLECTION*, Dr. Patrick Conley releases the reader from a foggy appreciation of Rhode Island roots to a vivid understanding of the basis of the very tenets we hold most dear in twenty-first century life in the Ocean State.

The authoritativeness of the essays, the pithy observations, and Pat's remarkable word craftsmanship make this read a joy. Over the years, I have been privileged to be enlightened, fascinated, and often amused by attending many of Dr. Conley's public speeches from the Newport Courthouse to Warren's Veterans Park to Independence Hall in Philadelphia. The fact that every one of these experiences has been uplifting punctuates for me the extraordinary value that will result from Pat's making the presentations and their perorations available to all in print.

Halsey C. Herreshoff
President, America's Cup Hall of Fame;
President, Herreshoff Marine Museum, Bristol

This book is a thoughtful compilation of the works of Dr. Patrick T. Conley—our foremost Rhode Island historian and my former professor at Providence College. Through his essays and public addresses, Dr. Conley has masterfully chronicled the social and cultural milestones in the state of Rhode Island's development. No one has a more complete and thorough understanding of the characters and culture that compose our state's unique history. Dr. Conley is not only a Rhode Island treasure; his writing and teaching about all aspects of American history, especially our Constitution, make him a national treasure.

Patrick J. Kennedy
Member of Congress

Introduction

I T SHOULD NOT BE SURPRISING to anyone that while the craft of writing Rhode Island's history stretches back more than 250 years, there have not been very many people who have taken up that craft. With a few notable exceptions, history writing that includes reflective analysis, in addition to the mere setting down of facts in chronological sequence, is a relatively recent development in Rhode Island. There are several explanations for this. One is Rhode Island's diminutive size; another is that Rhode Island, unlike some other states, has not made the study of its history a publicly funded, public-education priority. In other states, teachers' colleges and university presses have been the usual producers of works of state and local history. Sometimes this function has been performed by state-funded historical societies, as in Wisconsin and Minnesota. In Rhode Island, on the other hand, writing the state's history has largely been the avocation of clergy, attorneys, and amateur scholars (in the best sense of that term).

As a result of this arrangement, Rhode Island has served as no more than a foil or exception, in a substantial part of the written history of New England. Surprisingly, however, a remarkable amount of the history of the nation stems from unique contributions that originated here. From concepts embodied in our Bill of

Rights, like the idea of the First Amendment entitlement to religious liberty, to innovations in technology, government, design, architecture, music, art, theater, manufacturing, and national defense, Rhode Island has had a national impact far beyond other geographical areas of comparable size—usually the equivalent of a county in a midwestern state. Consequently, the need has always existed to write about and to spread the Rhode Island story, even if the financial resources required for publication have not always been available.

One person who has recognized that acute need, and who on more than one occasion has personally supplied the required resources, is Patrick T. Conley. As a professor of history and constitutional law at Providence College, chairman of the Rhode Island Bicentennial Commission and the state Bicentennial of the Constitution Foundation, and founder of the Rhode Island Heritage Commission, the Rhode Island Publications Society, and various commemorative bodies for the city of Providence, Pat Conley has devoted his considerable intellectual skills and energies to the cause of Rhode Island history for nearly a half century. He has also brought to this labor of love a competitive vigor learned from the many playing fields where he excelled by dint of discipline and determination.

The result has been a prodigious parade of book-length works of history and large-format pictorial books. During the course of this career (of which historical research has been only a part), there have been many addresses, articles, and reviews that have never been published, or that have appeared in scattered, isolated formats. The current work pulls them all together in a comprehensive presentation, as outlined by Dr. Conley in his preface.

The chief usefulness of these essays is the sheer volume of new information set in the context of truly insightful analysis. The collection of writings is, admittedly, not a complete beginning-to-end history of Rhode Island, but it casts a very wide net, catching important facts and personalities encompassing the full canvas of Rhode Island history. From Anne Hutchinson to the issues surrounding Rhode Island's adoption of the United States Constitution to the little-known aspects of the life of reformer Thomas

Wilson Dorr to the historical roots of the current controversy over separation of power, Conley's writings are full of vitality and valuable, well-considered conclusions.

Here are important book reviews of standard works of academic scholarship, as well as a series of essays that clearly establish Conley as the forerunner of all of the current local interest in ethnic history and cultural diversity. His town sketches and sketches of Rhode Island figures from Henry Bowen Anthony to Lloyd Griffin attest to his breadth and his grasp of the fact that the way to bring Rhode Island history alive is to tell it through the personalities who shaped it, and to see it all through the lens and prism of everyday Rhode Islanders—through the stories of their locales, their neighborhoods, their sense of place.

This tactic of Dr. Conley's—to popularize Rhode Island's history while still maintaining a tenacious hold on accuracy and factual documentation—is the hallmark of his career as a historian. It has resulted in truly vivid and compelling work. As he would say, with a characteristic mixture of literal precision and witty irony, "It was the least I could do!" And Conley's least is far better than most.

ALBERT T. KLYBERG
Director of Museum and Program
Heritage Harbor Museum
July 4, 2002

Preface

THE PURPOSE OF THIS VOLUME is to collect and preserve the public addresses and presentations I have made as a Rhode Island historian and attorney. Whether they are worthy of preservation, the reader may judge. They may be memorable only to me, but they contain information that may prove interesting to the student of Rhode Island's history as well.

Supplementing the public speeches are unpublished essays of varying length and format and published articles that have appeared in pamphlets, newspapers, privately printed books of limited circulation, and periodicals not easily accessible to a Rhode Island reader.

It is difficult to traverse tiny Rhode Island's historical terrain without recrossing your own tracks. Therefore, my major concern in selecting these essays is the probability of repetition. I have endeavored, not always successfully, to keep duplication to a minimum. With one exception (the dullest essay), these pieces lack scholarly documentation. My intended audience is the general reader, who may be assured that the statements contained herein are based not only upon authoritative secondary accounts but principally upon in-depth analysis of original documents or personal observation.

I am gratified that the Rhode Island Publications Society affords me the opportunity to see my own speeches in print. From 1966 through 1992 I engaged in speechwriting and position-paper production for a host of Rhode Island political leaders. That litany includes Congressman Robert O. Tiernan, Attorney General Herbert F. DeSimone, Governors Frank Licht, Philip Noel, J. Joseph Garrahy, and Bruce Sundlun, House Speaker Matthew J. Smith, Providence Mayor Vincent A. Cianci, Jr., East Providence City Manager Charles Reynolds, Cranston City Council Presidents Paul J. Pisano and Carlo Spirito, Sr., and a number of lesser luminaries. Except for what I wrote for Tiernan, Cianci, and Reynolds, such oratory was of the campaign variety. Because I labored in relative obscurity as a political ghostwriter, those thousands of words were, for me, written on the wind.

The pieces I have selected are a chrestomathy that spans the entire range of Rhode Island's development from Massasoit and Miantonomi to the millennium, and my career as a historian from a 1962–63 doctoral seminar at the University of Notre Dame to the present.

The opportunity to generate the essays and speeches contained herein stemmed mainly from the volunteer positions I have been fortunate to hold. These have included chairmanships of the Rhode Island Bicentennial [of Independence] Commission (ri76), the Rhode Island Bicentennial Foundation to commemorate the two hundredth anniversary of the Constitution and Bill of Rights, the United States Constitution Council and its Rhode Island trustee, the historians' committee for the centennial observance of the Diocese of Providence, the Rhode Island Historical Society's Dorr Rebellion Sesquicentennial Committee, the Cranston Historic Preservation Commission, the Providence Heritage Commission, the Rhode Island Publications Society, the Bristol Statehouse Foundation, and the Historians' Committee of the Rhode Island Heritage Hall of Fame, and directorships of the Heritage Harbor Museum and the Providence Maritime Heritage Foundation. Such posts have kept me constantly involved in the local historical milieu for a third of a century, and I have learned much from such rewarding experiences.

I have also learned from great teachers, especially Sister Marie Rosaire, R.S.M., at St. Michael's Parochial School in South Providence, Monsignor Philip Hughes, Dr. Aaron I. Abell and Dr. Marshall Smelser of the University of Notre Dame, and the Reverend Cornelius P. Forster, O.P., of Providence College, who advanced my academic career every step of the way, and to whom this volume is dedicated.

PATRICK T. CONLEY

Contents

The Constitution and the Laws

Immigration and Ethnicity

Catholicism

Politics, Rhode Island Style

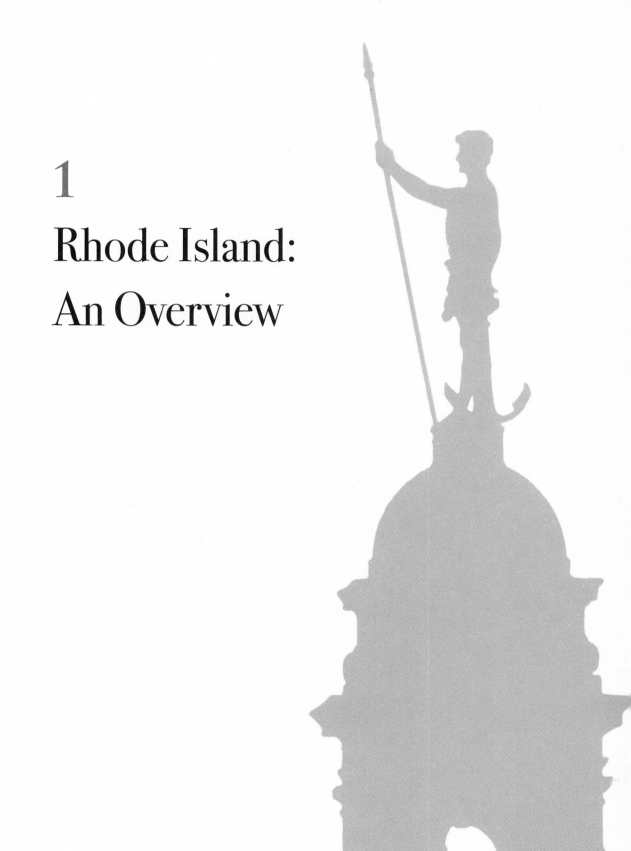

1

Rhode Island:
An Overview

The Independent Man, cast by Gorham, symbolizes the individualism, democratic localism, and religious liberty that characterized
Rhode Island during its formative years.

Rhode Island: Our Microparadise from the Founding to the Millennium

Written in 2001 as an entry in the forthcoming *Encyclopedia of New England Culture*, this essay was downsized to fit the format of the encyclopedia. It is printed here in full.

ONE OF THE SIX NEW ENGLAND STATES and one of the thirteen original colonies, Rhode Island is the smallest state in the nation, with a total area of only 1,214 square miles of land and coastal waters. Despite its diminutive size, it possesses remarkable diversity. Though it is the second most densely populated state (behind New Jersey), about five-eighths of its acreage consists of agricultural, forest, or undeveloped land. Its population is heterogeneous, composed of approximately twenty major ethnocultural groups.

In the census of 2000, Rhode Island had 1,048,319 inhabitants, ranking forty-third in population among the fifty states. Well over 60 percent of that number declare their affiliation with the Catholic Church, making Rhode Island proportionately the most Catholic state in the Union. In the category of race, 891,191 Rhode Islanders described themselves as white, 45,908 as African American, 23,665 as Asian, and 5,121 as Native American.

Traditionally called Little Rhody, Rhode Island is increasingly referred to by its residents as the Ocean State. This more positive nickname suggests such features as the long-standing and growing importance of tourism and recreation to the state's economy, the four hundred miles of shoreline, the state's naval heritage, the development of ocean-related industries, and the significance of beautiful Narragansett Bay, Rhode Island's premier natural resource.

The shores and islands of Narragansett Bay were a haven for Rhode Island's earliest European settlers. In 1636 Englishman Roger Williams established Providence, with the help and acquiescence of the Wampanoag and Narragansett Indians, as a refuge for those persecuted elsewhere because of their religious beliefs. Other dissenters and "seekers" followed Williams to the Narragansett Bay region, and soon a colony developed based on the pioneering principles of religious liberty and complete separation of church and state. Throughout the colonial and Revolutionary eras, individualism, self-reliance, democratic localism, and resistance to external control were characteristic Rhode Island traits, a fact presently symbolized by the statue of The Independent Man atop the state capitol in Providence.

Rhode Island's royal charter of 1663 allowed it the greatest degree of local self-government of any British colony, and when its virtual autonomy was threatened, Rhode Island became a leader in the Revolutionary movement and then a reluctant participant in the new federal Union. "Rogues' Island," as James Madison and other Founding Fathers called it, was the last of the thirteen original states to surrender its self-determination by ratifying the federal Constitution.

In the early period of statehood, Rhode Islanders were chiefly known for their entrepreneurial activity—first in commerce, then in manufacturing. During the course of the nineteenth century, with the mills of Providence, the Blackstone River Valley, and the Pawtuxet River Valley in the vanguard, the state became the most industrialized and urbanized in the Union.

In fact, the principal trends in nineteenth-century Rhode Island were industrialization, immigration, and urbanization. By the 1840s these forces combined to produce an episode known as the Dorr Rebellion—Rhode Island's crisis in constitutional government. The state's royal charter (then still in effect) gave disproportionate representation to the declining rural towns; it conferred almost unlimited power on the legislature; and it contained no procedure for its own amendment. Lawmakers, regardless of party, insisted upon retaining the old real estate requirement for voting and officeholding, even though it had been abandoned in all other states. This freehold qualification became more restrictive as Rhode Island grew more urbanized. By 1840 about 60 percent of the free adult males were disenfranchised.

Because earlier moderate efforts at change had been virtually ignored by the General Assembly, the reformers of 1840–43 decided to bypass the legislature and convene a People's Convention, equitably apportioned and chosen by an enlarged electorate. Thomas Wilson Dorr, a patrician attorney, assumed the leadership of the movement in late 1841. A "Law and Order" coalition of Whigs and rural Democrats used force to prevent the implementation of Dorr's basic law, called the People's Constitution, but they were pressured into making limited changes via a written constitution that became effective in May 1843. That document was designed to disfranchise Irish Catholics, who were then migrating to the state in increasing numbers, by retaining the real estate requirement for the foreign-born.

Dorr's movement effected a realignment of political parties by the 1850s. Native-born Whigs, rural Democrats, and urban workingmen who opposed both slavery and the Irish flirted with Know-Nothingism and then coalesced within the newly formed Republican party, led by arch nativist Henry Bowen Anthony, editor of the *Providence Journal*. A minority of "Yankees" and those Irish who had acquired real estate or were American-born adhered to the wing of the Democratic party formed by Dorr.

The last half of the century was an era of Republican dominance, and when the native-born Irish grew numerous enough to challenge Republican ascendancy, the majority party (led from 1884 by Senator Nelson Aldrich and Charles R. "Boss" Brayton) removed the real estate requirement in order to recruit and enfranchise certain sociocultural foes of the Irish—immigrants from French Canada, England, British Canada, and Sweden. By the end of the century the political battle lines between WASP Republican and Irish Catholic Democrat were sharply drawn, with the newer immigrants holding the balance of power, a balance that temporarily rested with the Republican party. In few states (if any) were ethnoreligious factors so politically influential.

Fashionable Gilded Age Newport, the summer retreat of

America's upper class, stood in sharp contrast to the turbulent urban-industrial milieu or the quiet farm life in South County and the western hill towns. Astors, Vanderbilts, Belmonts, Whitneys, and their peers built spectacular "summer cottages" on Newport's Bellevue Avenue and Ocean Drive, held lavish balls and other galas, and popularized such sports as tennis, golf, polo, and sailing. Though less elegant than Newport, satellite summer colonies in Jamestown, and at Narragansett Pier and Westerly's Watch Hill, enhanced coastal Rhode Island's image as one of America's premier vacation resorts for the well-to-do.

During the early twentieth century Rhode Island experienced important demographic and economic changes. It received a major influx of southern and eastern European immigrants from Italy, Portugal (including the Azores and Cape Verde), Greece, Armenia, Syria, Poland, Lithuania, Ukraine, and Russia (mainly Jews) prior to World War I. In the postwar decade the state's burgeoning population suffered through a precipitous decline in the dominant textile industry.

Politics were also eventful. A conservative Republican party, led by Providence business interests and rural politicians from South County and the farming towns along the Connecticut border, blocked most local reforms usually associated with the Progressive Era. The decades of the 1920s and 1930s, however, witnessed a major transition from Republican to Democratic control.

Economic unrest stemming from such factors as the decline of textiles, the Great Depression, and the local rise of organized labor, coupled with the development of cultural antagonisms between native and foreign stock, combined to weaken the initial allegiance of Franco-Americans and Italian Americans to the Republican party. Vigorous efforts by the Irish-led Democratic party, key constitutional reforms, the 1928 presidential candidacy of Al Smith, and the social programs of the New Deal also combined to bring the newer immigrant groups within the Democratic fold by the mid-1930s.

At that time Democratic leaders such as Theodore Francis Green, Thomas P. McCoy, and Robert Emmet Quinn staged a governmental reorganization known as the Bloodless Revolution of 1935. After a brief electoral rebuke for their excesses (e.g., the "Race Track War" of 1937), the Democrats consolidated their power during the 1940s under Governor J. Howard McGrath and Providence mayor Dennis J. Roberts. From that time until the mid-1980s, Democrats captured most state and congressional elections (with the victories of Republican John H. Chafee a notable exception) and maintained a lopsided edge in both houses of the General Assembly, especially after the reapportionment revolution of the 1960s set in motion by the "one man–one vote" decisions of the United States Supreme Court.

Ethnic diversity, long a hallmark of Rhode Island life, has been enhanced since the late 1960s by a new influx of immigrants. Azorean Portuguese, Irish, Russian Jews, and blacks from the West Indies and Africa (especially Liberia and Nigeria) have augmented older ethnic communities, but the most significant modern migration to Rhode Island has come from Latin America and Southeast Asia. The Hispanic population hails from Puerto Rico and a score of Latin American nations, most notably Colombia and the Dominican Republic. The Asian community consists mainly of arrivals from Vietnam, Cambodia, and Laos, including Laotian hill people known as Hmong. Ethnic and racial clashes have been minimal, and ghettolike neighborhoods are nonexistent in Rhode Island's cities. Providence, the state capital and New England's second largest city, has the highest number in each racial category. Of its total population of 173,618 (down from a peak of 267,918 in 1925), Providence is home to 52,146 Hispanics, 22,103 blacks, 11,303 Asians, and 1,446 Native Americans. (Another set of census figures using multiple ethnicity is higher for each group.)

The major problem revealed by current census figures is that they show an out-migration of well-to-do elderly, a declining middle class, and an exodus of young workers in the 20–to–34 age range. These losses were more than offset numerically by an influx of low-income immigrants, but the economic consequences of these trends are cause for concern.

Although some claim otherwise, there is little in the character of late-twentieth-century Rhode Islanders that derives in unbroken succession from the state's colonial inhabitants, except for some traits and attitudes exhibited by rural, old-stock Rhode Island residents of South County and the western hill towns. But even the distinctiveness and uniqueness of those Rhode Islanders (derisively called Swamp Yankees) has been eroded by modern communication and the stream of ethnic urbanites who have settled in rural subdivisions carved from colonial farms and fields.

While a case may be made for the validity of the Independent Man as a symbol of the leadership role Rhode Islanders have played in the religious revolution of the seventeenth century, the political revolt of the eighteenth century, and the industrial transformation of the nineteenth century, little in modern Rhode Island suggests continued innovation, though there is one salient aspect of Rhode Island life that remains revolting: public corruption.

Organized crime is one aspect of this condition. Rhode Island has been the New England center of such activity for much of the twentieth century. Names of mob figures—Raymond, "Tiger," "Junior," Gerard—have become household words of mythic proportions. And despite a weakening of Mafia power, popular local cartoonist Don Bosquet could still depict (in 1996) the "Loch Ness Mobster" plying the waters of Narragansett Bay.

The good news is that organized crime plays a negligible role in state and local politics and seldom impacts the lives of ordinary, law-abiding citizens. Conversely, political parties, their managers, and their adherents have ravaged Rhode Island's body politic from the 1870s onward. No state, of course, is immune from the virus of public corruption. In Rhode Island, however, this malady is chronic and sometimes virulent.

A long list of bizarre episodes illustrate the state's political perversity. In 1905, at a time when notorious Republican boss Charles R. Brayton was defining an honest voter as "one who stays bought," muckraker Lincoln Steffens labeled Rhode Island a "State for Sale" in an exposé for *McClure's Magazine*.

In June 1924 Republican leaders broke a filibuster of reform Democrats by exploding a bromine gas bomb in the Senate chamber and keeping GOP solons in exile in Massachusetts until after the November elections. In January 1935 Democrats seized control of the General Assembly by parliamentary sleight-of-hand and used their newfound power to depose the entire Supreme Court and pursue the politics of revenge. By 1937 Democratic infighting produced the "Race Track War," in which Governor Robert Quinn put Narragansett Race Track under martial law and dispatched machinegun-toting National Guardsmen to prevent track president Walter O'Hara and his associate, Pawtucket mayor Thomas P. McCoy, from running the fall meet—a resort to force necessitated when McCoy's allies on the new state Supreme Court blocked the governor's peaceful efforts to close the track. In 1958 a partisan Supreme Court stole the gubernatorial election from Republican Christopher DelSesto by disallowing most absentee ballots on a technicality. Coincidently, the beneficiary of this ruling, incumbent Governor Dennis J. Roberts, had a brother on the five-member high court. Thomas Roberts later became the court's chief justice.

Political scientist Duane Lockard, who wrote the first comprehensive scholarly analysis of New England state politics in 1959, labeled his Rhode Island chapter "Politics on the Seamy Side." More recently I have dubbed the state "The Louisiana of the North." The term "Rogues' Island," in use since the eighteenth century, has never become obsolete.

Civic virtue has not improved since the rural-based Republican machine of Charles R. Brayton and Henry Bowen Anthony emerged in the 1870s. Since 1984, for example, mayors in six of the twelve largest municipalities have been formally charged with criminal conduct, and one has been jailed; a governor has been imprisoned on numerous counts of bribery and extortion; and two chief justices of the Supreme Court have been forced from office for misconduct. As this book went to press, Vincent A. "Buddy" Cianci, Jr., Providence's longest-serving mayor, was convicted on federal racketeering charges for running a criminal enterprise out of City Hall, which federal investigators dubbed "Plunder Dome." Judge Ronald R. Lagueux, who presided over earlier city cases, called the Cianci regime the most corrupt administration in Rhode Island history. That assessment, though difficult to quantify, is not without merit. Cianci's 2002 conviction was his second. In 1984 he pleaded no contest to felony assault and was forced from office. A subsequent probe of his first administration yielded thirty indictments, resulting in twenty convictions and sixteen prison sentences. Despite such a record, the charismatic Cianci continues to enjoy widespread, enthusiastic popular support. These recent episodes are only the most visible warts on the body politic. Small wonder that some wags refer to Rhode Island's gleaming and imposing marble State House in biblical terms as "the whitened sepulcher."

Because of its small size and its intense preoccupation with local politics, Rhode Island practices what some knowledgeable observers call "the politics of intimacy," in which nepotism, personal alliances or vendettas, and conflicts of interest abound. Such influences overflow the narrow banks of government and seep into the economic life of the community. Scandals in the state's housing and mortgage corporation (RIHMFC) in the late 1980s and the financial collapse of numerous banks and credit unions in the early 1990s are the most recent economic debacles closely entwined with politics.

Public pension excesses, bogus workers' compensation claims, insurance scams, welfare cheating, kickbacks to public officials, padded bills, no-show jobs, and similar rip-offs are commonplace. In 1905 Steffens proclaimed that Rhode Island had a "government founded upon the corruption of the people themselves." The details have changed since then, but the climate of moral permissiveness that Steffens lamented still endures.

Conversely, Rhode Island's motto is "Hope," and that aspiration has been augmented by action to combat such conditions: A recently created Ethics Commission has aggressively attacked political conflicts of interest; the state's media, especially the *Providence Journal*, have produced zealous investigative reporters to expose white-collar crime; outraged citizens, often goaded by talk radio, have formed a number of militant "good-government" groups such as Common Cause; lone crusaders such as John Hazen White have made expensive and passionate reform appeals to the once-acquiescent electorate; and the state legislature has responded to the public clamor by enacting several significant anticorruption statutes. Through it all, politics, in its larger sense, remains Rhode Island's number-one spectator sport.

Despite its tradition of political turbulence and the trauma caused by the transformation of its economy from manufacturing to service-oriented business, Rhode Island still maintains an ambiance and a vitality that bodes well for its future. Among the service-oriented enterprises, higher education is paramount. The state maintains three public colleges: The University of Rhode Island (established in 1892 as the Rhode Island State College of Agriculture and Mechanic Arts) has a main campus in the village of Kingston, a major extension division in Providence, and satellite programs elsewhere in the state; its Graduate School of Oceanography is one of its most notable academic resources. Rhode Island College (founded in 1854 as a normal school) is located in Providence. The Community College of Rhode Island (established as Rhode Island Junior College in 1964) has campuses in Warwick, Lincoln, and Providence, with a Newport campus on the drawing board.

The major nonstate colleges are Brown University (founded in 1764), an Ivy League institution of international renown with a wide range of excellent programs, including a medical school; Providence College (1919), a liberal arts school with undergraduate and graduate divisions, founded by the Dominican Fathers, which has educated more of the state's professional class than any other college; Rhode Island School of Design (1877), highly acclaimed for excellence in the fine arts, architecture, and design; the U.S. Naval War College (1884), which is the center of a large naval education complex in Newport; Roger Williams University (1919), noted for its school of architecture and the home of the state's only law school; and Bryant College (1863), a top-rated business school. Other colleges and their special areas include Johnson and Wales University (1914), business and culinary arts, and Salve Regina University in Newport (1947), a Catholic liberal arts college. A major scholarly institution, the American Mathematical Society, is based in Providence.

By vigorous and successful programs of historic preservation and environmental protection, by economic diversification, and by cultivating intergroup cooperation, present-day Rhode Islanders are seeking to preserve the best of their heritage while striving to improve the quality of life for Rhode Islanders of coming generations.

2
Colonial
Origins

The Roger Williams Monument stands in
Roger Williams Park, Providence. No portraits
of Williams exist. The face of this statue, un-
veiled in 1877, was modeled on the likeness of
his oldest direct male descendant then living.

Early Rhode Island: A Synopsis | 2

Written in 1990 as an entry in *The Encyclopedia of Colonial and Revolutionary America*, ed. John Mark Faragher (New York, 1990), this concise survey has been revised slightly to include more detailed information on the Native Americans.

THE NATIVE AMERICANS. Before the arrival of the first European settlers, the Narragansett Indians inhabited the area of Rhode Island from Warwick south along Narragansett Bay to the present towns of South Kingstown and Exeter. Their principal rivals, the Wampanoag, dominated the eastern shore region into the Blackstone Valley and contested the Providence-Cranston area and Aquidneck Island with the Narragansetts, while the Nipmuck, a weak tribe by comparison, maintained a tenuous foothold in the inland regions north and west of Providence. To the south the Eastern Niantic populated much of the coastal area of what is now the town of Charlestown, and the Pawcatuck, or Eastern, Pequots maintained a foothold in Westerly from their Connecticut base. These tribes subsisted on farming, fishing, and, to a lesser extent, hunting.

Estimates vary widely, but according to the best anthropological data approximately ten thousand Indians lived within the present boundaries of Rhode Island by 1650, with the Narragansett accounting for six thousand of that number. In 1675–76 the Narragansett and Nipmuck tribes joined forces with the Wampanoag leader Metacom, or Philip, in King Philip's War, a futile effort by some Native Americans to resist the encroachments of the white man. Decimated by battle and famine, remnants of the deposed Narragansett, Wampanoag, and other tribes sought refuge with the Niantic, who had maintained a neutral stance in the war. This aggregate of remnant groups, which also included the Pequots, became the foundation of a new Indian community in Rhode Island that ultimately assumed the name Narragansett.

SETTLEMENT AND COLONIAL PERIOD. In 1524 Florentine navigator Giovanni da Verrazzano, sailing in the employ of France, became the first European to explore Rhode Island and record his activities and impressions. By comparing Block Island with the Mediterranean island of Rhodes, he unwittingly gave the state its name.

The first permanent settlement was established at Providence in 1636 by English clergyman Roger Williams and a small band of followers who had left the repressive atmosphere of the Massachusetts Bay Colony to seek freedom of worship. Williams was granted a sizable tract for his village by Canonicus and Miantonomi, friendly sachems of the Narragansett who had recently wrested control of the area from the disease-weakened Wampanoag. Other Nonconformists followed Williams to the Narragansett Bay region, including Anne and William Hutchinson and William Coddington, who founded Portsmouth in 1638 as a haven for Antinomians. A short-lived dispute sent Coddington to the southern tip of Aquidneck Island (another disputed area purchased from the Narragansett), where he founded Newport in 1639.

The fourth original town, Warwick, was settled in 1642 as "Shawomet" by Samuel Gorton, a dissident from Portsmouth. During this initial decade two other outposts were established — Wickford (1637), by Richard Smith, in the Narragansett Country, and Pawtuxet (1638), by William Harris and the Arnold family on lands occupied by the Pawtuxet subtribe of the Wampanoag Confederation.

Because title to these lands rested only on Indian deeds, neighboring colonies began to covet them, and so Roger Williams journeyed to England and secured a parliamentary patent in 1644 uniting the towns into a single colony and confirming his settlers' claims to their land. This legislative document served as the basic law until the Stuart Restoration in 1660 made it wise to seek a royal charter.

At that time Dr. John Clarke was commissioned to secure a document consistent with the religious principles upon which Rhode Island was founded, and that would also safeguard Rhode Island lands from the encroachment of speculators and neighboring colonies. He succeeded admirably. The royal charter of 1663 guaranteed complete religious liberty, established a self-governing colony with great local autonomy, and strengthened Rhode Island's territorial claims. It was the most liberal charter to be issued by the mother country during the entire colonial era, a fact that enabled it to serve as the basic law until May 1843.

The religious freedom that prevailed in early Rhode Island made it a refuge for several persecuted sects. America's first Baptist church was formed in Providence in 1638/39; Quakers established a meeting on Aquidneck in 1657 and soon became a powerful force in the colony's political and economic life; Sephardic Jewish refugees came to Newport in 1658; French Huguenots settled in East Greenwich in 1686.

Among the more important events of the seventeenth century were King Philip's War (1675–76); the interruption in government caused by the abortive Dominion for New England (1686–89); and the beginning of the intermittent colonial wars between England and France (1689–1763), a long struggle for empire that frequently involved Rhode Island men, money, and

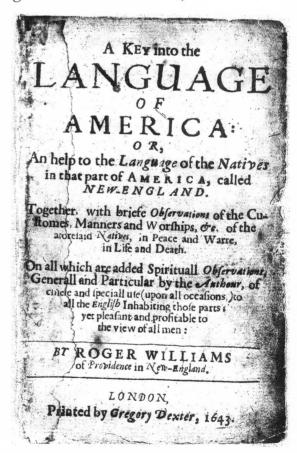

Williams's *Key* was the first English-language dictionary and ethnography of an American Indian people. Sadly, it did not prevent misunderstanding and discord in local Indian–white relations, much to the detriment of the Native Americans.

ships. By the end of the century Newport had emerged as a prosperous port and the dominant community, nine towns had been incorporated, and the colony's population exceeded six thousand inhabitants.

The first quarter of the eighteenth century was marked by the long and able governorship (1698–1727) of Samuel Cranston, who established internal unity and brought his colony into a better working relationship with the imperial government in London. The middle decades of this century were characterized by significant growth. Newport continued to prosper commercially, but Providence began to challenge it for supremacy. This rivalry assumed political dimensions, and a system of two-party politics developed by the 1740s. Opposing groups—one headed by Samuel Ward and the other by Stephen Hopkins—were organized with sectional overtones. Generally speaking (although there were notable exceptions), the merchants and farmers of Newport and South County (Ward's faction) battled with their counterparts from Providence and its environs (led by Hopkins) to secure control of the powerful legislature for the vast patronage at the disposal of that body.

A major boundary dispute with Connecticut was resolved in 1726–27, and a very favorable boundary settlement with Massachusetts in 1746–47 resulted in Rhode Island's annexation of Cumberland and several East Bay towns, including the port of Bristol. During this midcentury period the plantations of South County reached their greatest prominence, and the spread of agriculture on the mainland resulted in the subdivision of Providence and other early towns. By 1774 the colony had 59,707 residents, who lived in twenty-nine municipalities.

THE REVOLUTIONARY ERA. Rhode Island was in the vanguard of the Revolutionary movement. Having the greatest degree of self-rule, it had the most to lose from the efforts of England after 1763 to increase its supervision and control over the colonies. In addition, Rhode Island had a long tradition of evading the poorly enforced Navigation Acts, and smuggling was commonplace.

Beginning with strong opposition to the Sugar Act (1764) and its restrictions on the molasses trade, the colony engaged in repeated measures of open defiance, such as the burning of the British revenue schooner *Gaspee* in 1772. Ward and Hopkins gradually put aside their local differences and united against alleged British injustices. Finally, on May 4, 1776, Rhode Island became the first colony to renounce allegiance to King George III.

During the war itself Rhode Island furnished its share of men, ships, and money to the cause of independence. Volunteers included a significant number of black and Indian slaves, who gained distinction as the "Black Regiment," a detachment of the First Rhode Island Regiment. Esek Hopkins, the brother of Stephen, the signer of the Declaration of Independence, became the first commander in chief of the Continental navy, a force that Rhode Island helped create. The able Nathanael Greene of the Kentish Guards became George Washington's second in command and chief of the Continental army in the South.

The British occupied Newport in December 1776, and a long siege to evict them culminated by August 1778 in the large but inconclusive Battle of Rhode Island, a contest that was the first combined effort of the Americans and their French allies. The British voluntarily evacuated Newport in October 1779, and in July 1780 the French forces under the Comte de Rochambeau landed there and made the port town their base of operations. It was from Newport, Providence, and other Rhode Island encampments that the French march to Yorktown began in 1781.

POSTWAR DEVELOPMENTS. The Revolution did not alter Rhode Island's governmental structure (even the royal charter remained intact), but it had some important effects, including the decline of Newport, the passage of an act providing for the gradual abolition of slavery (1784), and a law prohibiting Rhode Islanders from engaging in the slave trade (1787).

In 1778 the state had quickly ratified the Articles of Confederation, with its weak central government, but when the movement to strengthen that government developed in the mid-1780s, Rhode

Island balked. The state's individualism, its democratic localism, and its tradition of autonomy caused it to resist the centralizing tendencies of the federal Constitution. This opposition was intensified when an agrarian-debtor revolt in support of the issuance of paper money placed the parochial Country party in power from 1786 through 1790. This political faction, led by Charlestown's Jonathan Hazard, was suspicious of the power and the cost of a government too far removed from the grass-roots level, and so it declined to dispatch delegates to the Philadelphia Convention of 1787, which drafted the U.S. Constitution. Then, when that document was presented to the states for ratification, Hazard's faction delayed, and nearly prevented, Rhode Island's approval.

In the period between September 1787 and January 1790, the rural-dominated General Assembly rejected no fewer than eleven attempts by the representatives from the mercantile communities to convene a state ratifying convention. Instead, the Assembly defied the instructions of the Founding Fathers and conducted a popular referendum on the Constitution. That election, which was boycotted by the supporters of a stronger union (the Federalists), rejected the Constitution by a vote of 2,711 to 243.

Finally, in mid-January 1790, more than eight months after George Washington's inauguration as the first president of the United States, the Country party reluctantly called the required convention, but it took two separate sessions—one in South Kingstown (March 1–6) and the second in Newport (May 24–29)—before approval was obtained. The ratification tally, 34 in favor and 32 opposed, was the narrowest of any state.

In the end, a nearly immovable object yielded to an irresistible force; Rhode Island joined the Union that had left it behind and embarked upon a new era of economic and political development.

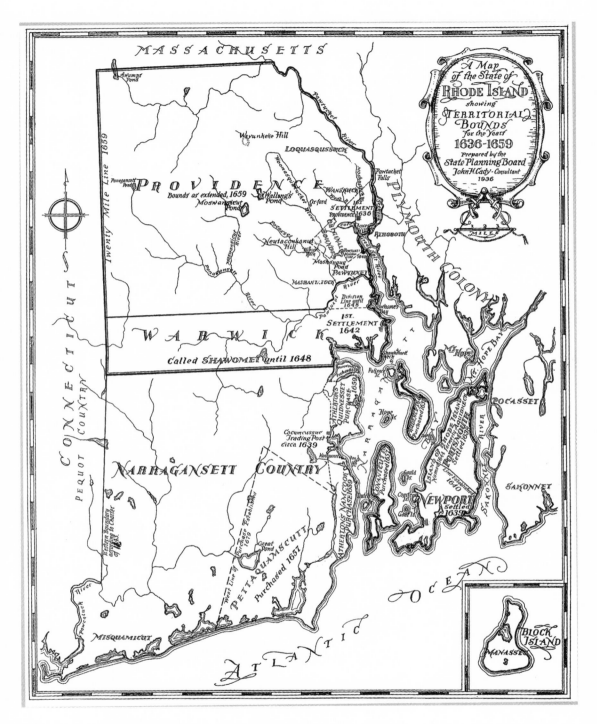

From 1636 to 1659 Roger Williams made several land purchases from the Narragansett Indians which extended his Providence Plantation westward twenty miles from Foxes Hill on present-day Fox Point. At that time the bounds of Providence Plantation comprised all of present-day Providence County west of the Blackstone and Seekonk rivers—an expanse of about 380 square miles. This map by architectural historian John H. Cady shows the boundaries of the four original towns and the early purchases in the Narragansett Country, an area claimed by Rhode Island, Connecticut, and Massachusetts.

Anne Hutchinson was the first significant
white female leader in England's American
colonies. This representation (for no portrait
exists) by sculptor Cyrus Dallin stands before
the Massachusetts Statehouse.

Portsmouth's Founding Mother: Anne Hutchinson

3

Written in 1988, this essay was requested by the
East Bay Newspapers for their commemorative issue celebrating
the 350th anniversary of the founding of Portsmouth.

DURING THE BICENTENNIAL OF THE U.S. CONSTITUTION, we have all heard much about the Founding Fathers. Portsmouth, Rhode Island, however, was the first American community that could boast of a Founding Mother. That female foundress was the irrepressible Anne Hutchinson.

True, William Coddington, a prominent merchant of the Massachusetts Bay Colony, purchased all of Aquidneck Island in 1638 from the Narragansett Indians (who had seized it from the Wampanoags) through the intercession of fellow exile Roger Williams. But Coddington was acting on behalf of a group of religious dissenters known as Antinomians, the most controversial of whom was Mistress Anne Hutchinson

Who was this remarkable Rhode Island pioneer, variously called by historians "a charismatic healer, with the gift of fluent and inspired speech," "another Joan of Arc," a woman whose "stern and masculine mind... triumphed over the tender affections of a wife and mother," and "the troubler of the Puritan Zion"? Her archenemy, Governor John Winthrop of Massachusetts Bay, offered a contemporary estimate: he called her the American Jezebel, an allusion to an Old Testament Phoenician queen legendary for her alleged wickedness.

Anne was born in Lincolnshire, England, in 1591, the daughter of an English clergyman named Francis Marbury, who was censured by the Anglican Church for his Puritan leanings (the Puritans wanted to purify the Church of England from any vestiges of the rejected Roman Catholic religion). In August 1612 the well-bred and educated Anne married William Hutchinson, the son of a prosperous merchant. During the next twenty-two years she dutifully bore her husband fourteen children. Then, in 1634, with the Puritans in disfavor because of the High Church leanings of King Charles I, the Hutchinson family set sail for Boston.

Anne's early religious training, her vigorous intellect, and her restless and inquiring mind led her to take a leading part in the theological life of her intensely religious community. At first she held informal meetings of women at her home, and on these occasions she would discuss the lengthy sermons of the previous Sunday. This activity was unobjectionable. Gradually, however, she began to lecture to mixed audiences of sixty to eighty listeners and to expound her own religious beliefs. This practice caused a furor.

Mrs. Hutchinson and the Reverends John Cotton and John Wheelwright preached a new doctrine that they termed "a covenant of grace." This view, held by a small minority of Puritans, asserted that salvation came principally through the individual's own personal awareness of God's divine grace and love. It challenged the orthodox "covenant of works," which was embraced by established, formal churches whose members gave evidence of their predestined salvation by their works and their status in the community.

Hutchinson and her associates denied that Christian freedom should be restricted by a need to seek evidence of election or salvation in obedience to God's law as interpreted by "hypocritical ministers." Since they placed their own intuitive interpretation of God's law above the civil and religious laws devised by man, those who believed in the covenant of grace were derisively labeled Antinomians, a word that comes from the Greek *anti* (against) and *nomos* (law).

It has been said of seventeenth-century religion that the Anglicans discarded the pope; the Puritans (Congregationalists) then discarded the bishops in favor of a formal, theologically trained clergy; but the Baptists were content with an *ad hoc*, inspirational ministry to spread the word of God.

Hutchinson's view, emphasizing the direct connection between man (or woman) and God, undermined the authority and importance of the established religious and civil leaders of the Massachusetts Bay Colony (who contended that society ought to be governed by Christian magistrates), because she discounted the need for a specially designated and highly educated ministry. In fact, the Antinomians (and their theological successors, the Quakers) dispensed with the clergy altogether and stressed the indwelling of the Holy Spirit and direct relations with God without the need for human intermediaries.

Such dogmas as Antinomianism and Quakerism shook the Bible Commonwealth of Massachusetts to its foundations. When advanced by a female (some labeled Anne a witch), they were even more pernicious. Anne suffered excommunication and banishment for her beliefs, so she, her husband, and numerous followers, including William Coddington, sought refuge in the Narragansett Bay region—an area that Puritans dubbed New England's "moral sewer."

Soon after her arrival at Portsmouth in the spring of 1638, she clashed with her coreligionist William Coddington, who held Indian title to Aquidneck Island in his own name. Joining with the equally rebellious Samuel Gorton, who later founded Warwick, she ousted Coddington from power, so he went to the southern tip of the island and established the town of Newport in 1639.

Although bested temporarily, the very ambitious Coddington was not beaten, for within a year he had cleverly engineered a consolidation of the two island towns under a common administration in which he was "governor." Gorton and at least eleven other Portsmouth settlers responded to Coddington's resumption of power by plotting armed rebellion against him. These Portsmouth dissidents were ultimately banished from the island. Anne soon broke with the Gortonists over the use of violence, and she and her husband joined the Newport settlement.

Shortly thereafter, Anne's fortunes plummeted disastrously. William Hutchinson died, her religious leadership waned, and Massachusetts threatened to absorb the Rhode Island settlements.

Disgruntled and disillusioned, Anne sought refuge in the Dutch colony of New Netherlands in 1642. In the late summer of 1643 her home (near present-day Pelham Bay, New York) was raided by Indians, who killed Anne, two of her sons, and three of her daughters in brutal fashion.

The Massachusetts clergy rejoiced over the grisly murders. The Reverend Peter Bulkeley spoke for most orthodox Puritans when he pronounced this eulogy: "Let her damned heresies... and the just vengeance of God, by which she perished, terrify all her seduced followers from having anymore to do with her heaven." The Bay Colony divines considered Anne Hutchinson's death to be the symbolic death of Antinomianism, but the new religion of the Quakers found many recruits among Anne's followers— William Coddington, her political rival, being the most notable.

Portsmouth's foundress was a remarkable individual. The double oppression of life in a male-dominated society and biological bondage to her own amazing fertility was an impediment to leadership that she successfully overcame. After Anne's arrival in Portsmouth and throughout the remainder of the century, women publicly taught and preached throughout Rhode Island; in part because of her example, the men of the colony protected the liberty of women to teach, preach, and attend religious services of their own choosing. It would not be boosterism or hyperbole to call Mistress Anne America's first great female leader. An indomitable mind, a zeal for equality, and an energy that kept her constantly in motion indicate that this seventeenth-century prophetess was the archetype of the late-twentieth-century woman.

Massachusetts has recanted. Admitting its unjust treatment of Mrs. Hutchinson, it commissioned the famous sculptor Cyrus E. Dallin to fashion a statue of her, enfolding a child within her robes. That artwork now occupies a hallowed niche in the Massachusetts Statehouse for passersby to view and ponder.

If the town that banished Anne Hutchinson can be so lavish in its praise, is it not time for Portsmouth, the town established as a result of the endeavors of this legendary American, to accord its Founding Mother a similar memorial?

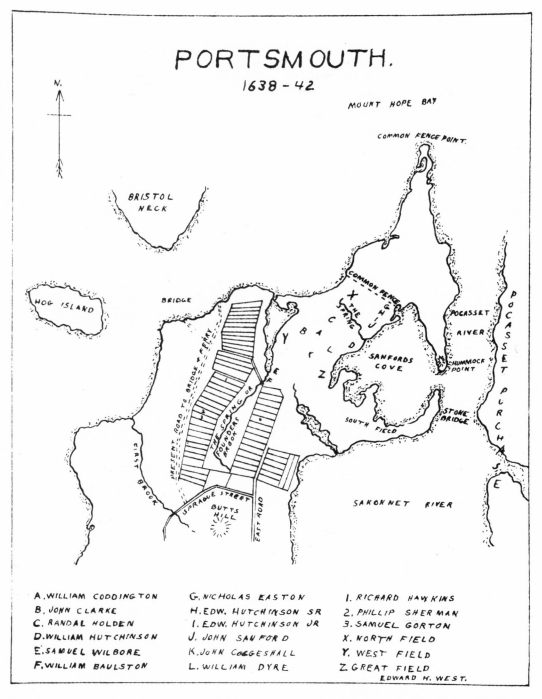

PORTSMOUTH.
1638-42

MOUNT HOPE BAY

COMMON FENCE POINT

BRISTOL NECK

HOG ISLAND

BRIDGE

N.

THE SPRING

COMMON FENCE

POCASSET

POCASSET RIVER

SANFORDS COVE

HUMMOCK POINT

SOUTH FIELD

STONE BRIDGE

SAKONNET RIVER

PRESENT ROAD TO BRIDGE & FERRY

THE SPRING OR FOUNDERS BROOK

CLAY BROOK

SPRAGUE STREET

BUTTS HILL

EAST ROAD

A. WILLIAM CODDINGTON	G. NICHOLAS EASTON	I. RICHARD HAWKINS
B. JOHN CLARKE	H. EDW. HUTCHINSON SR	2. PHILLIP SHERMAN
C. RANDAL HOLDEN	I. EDW. HUTCHINSON JR	3. SAMUEL GORTON
D. WILLIAM HUTCHINSON	J. JOHN SANFORD	X. NORTH FIELD
E. SAMUEL WILBORE	K. JOHN COGGESHALL	Y. WEST FIELD
F. WILLIAM BAULSTON	L. WILLIAM DYRE	Z. GREAT FIELD

EDWARD H. WEST.

Using the early records of the town of Portsmouth, antiquarian Edward H. West prepared this sketch of the original house lots. Besides Anne and William Hutchinson, Portsmouth's first settlers included two founding fathers—William Coddington, who established Newport in 1639, and Samuel Gorton, who settled Shawomet, or Warwick, in 1642.

The royal charter granted to Rhode Island in 1663 endured for 180 years, until superseded by a written state constitution in May 1843. The provisions of the charter shaped colonial Rhode Island.

Colonial Rhode Island: A History, by Sydney V. James, Reviewed

Written in 1977, this essay reviewed Sidney James's colonial survey for *The Journal of American History*.

4

NO PERIOD OF RHODE ISLAND HISTORY has been examined as often as its colonial era. The state's Yankee stock have a lively interest in their forebears, while its new immigrants thus far exhibit nearly no scholarly interest in their Rhode Island antecedents. Samuel Greene Arnold's annalistic two-volume account (1859–60), Irving B. Richman's detailed analysis (2 volumes, 1902) and his subsequent interpretive treatise *A Study in Separatism* (1905), and the multivolume treatments by Edward Field (ed.), Thomas W. Bicknell, and Charles Carroll are mainly or exclusively devoted to pre-1790 Rhode Island. Even recent popularizations by Alderman and Beals demonstrate a preoccupation with the formative years, while biographers studying denizens of this microparadise usually choose such pioneers as Roger Williams, John Clarke, or Anne Hutchinson. Small wonder that a book entitled *Colonial Rhode Island* initially failed to excite this reviewer's interest or arouse an expectation of new disclosures. But the volume by Sydney V. James proved to be a welcome surprise.

Though traveling a well-worn path, James surveys the terrain with greater circumspection and variety than any of his predecessors. The familiar legal and institutional landmarks are properly identified, but economic, social, cultural, and religious vistas are also presented with an understanding and perception that indicate a thorough immersion by the author in all the surviving documents of the period.

The complex religious development of the seventeenth and eighteenth centuries, the interminable and confusing boundary disputes with the surrounding colonies and the Narragansett proprietors, the economic policies of the Newport élite, the long and productive career of hitherto neglected Governor Samuel Cranston (1698–1727), and the role of Rhode Island in the colonial wars (1689–1763) are described more adequately and authoritatively by James than by any other student of early Rhode Island.

This volume, part of the series entitled A History of the American Colonies, seeks "to synthesize the new research, to treat social, economic, and cultural as well as political developments, and to delineate the broad outlines of each colony's history during the years before independence." James has met the stated goals of his editors admirably.

The work has few shortcomings. One is the author's tendency to become immersed in such inscrutable and convoluted detail (e.g., concerning boundaries and the proliferation of churches) that the narrative becomes more suited for reference than for relaxed reading. Conversely, scholars will lament the absence of footnotes which could have precisely identified the many obscure sources from which James gleaned his information. This omission is offset by a splendid, comprehensive annotated bibliography. While the book abounds with newly discovered facts and insights, certain well-known topics are inadequately or imprecisely examined (e.g., the 1719 act denying freemanship to Roman Catholics and Jews, slavery and the slave trade during the Revolutionary era, and the May 4, 1776, renunciation of allegiance to King George III).

Considered in its entirety, however, this study is extremely impressive. James has rendered another survey of colonial Rhode Island superfluous—at least for our generation. Perhaps his success will prompt and inspire others to venture further along the more lightly traveled but equally variegated road of recent Rhode Island history.

Fat Mutton and Liberty of Conscience: Society in Rhode Island, 1636–1690, by Carl Bridenbaugh, Reviewed

5

Written in 1976, this essay reviewed Carl Bridenbaugh's book on Aquidneck Island for *The New England Quarterly*.

CARL BRIDENBAUGH, PROLIFIC COLONIAL HISTORIAN and the first fellow of the Rhode Island Historical Society, has once again turned his facile pen toward colonial Newport, but this time his focus is broader and different. The author of such histories of early urban America as *Cities in the Wilderness*, *Cities in Revolt*, *The Colonial Craftsman*, and studies of eighteenth-century Philadelphia and Williamsburg, Professor Bridenbaugh has surprisingly "faced about like a weathercock" (as he says) and called his colleagues in the historical guild back to the farm. The author justifies his move because "the central theme of early American history is to be found in the nature and achievements (or failures) of an agricultural-commercial society. This society is the matrix in which were formed, and from which issued, the ideas, faiths, ideals, and daily attitudes of the people."

Such a society developed on Aquidneck Island between 1638 and 1690 under the stimulus of "fat mutton and liberty of conscience." That quaint phrase of Sir Henry Moodyes refers to the economic prosperity which sheep raising, exporting, and allied pursuits brought to the island towns of Newport and Portsmouth and to the religious freedom which attracted enterprising Quaker businessmen and merchants to this "heretical Rogues' Island."

Bridenbaugh rebuts the still prevalent seventeenth-century Puritan propaganda that Rhode Island was settled by a "congeries of cantankerous dreamers or ne'er-do-well dissenters." The island settlement, at least, was a "well-planned business venture" by "banished men, yet rich." Another important historical observation is the author's assessment of the primary role played by Quakers in the life of the colony. This persecuted sect, from its arrival in 1657, infused vital energy into the Rhode Island economy.

Dr. John Clarke, a Newport Baptist minister, was a leading advocate of religious liberty and church-state separation. Clarke obtained Rhode Island's charter from King Charles II.

Bridenbaugh tells how shrewd, resourceful "Quaker Grandees," with one foot in the meetinghouse and the other in the countinghouse, established a far-flung trade network characterized by an "extraordinary diversity of cargoes." This commercial empire extended along the coastal trade routes from Boston to New York, the Jerseys, the valley of the Delaware, the Chesapeake Bay region, Virginia, Carolina, the West Indies, Jamaica, Barbados, the Wine Islands, and Europe. The cargoes carried to these distant ports included livestock (especially horses and sheep), meats, and agricultural, forest, and marine produce. These commodities are detailed by Bridenbaugh through citations from shipping records and letter books. "Trade followed the meeting wherever the Friends went in the New World," the author asserts.

Bridenbaugh establishes a close religious and ideological connection between Anne Hutchinson's Antinomians (founders of Portsmouth and Newport) and the Quakers who succeeded them as the leaders of these island communities. In fact, many prominent Antinomians, such as Governor William Coddington, the Brentons, and the Coggeshalls, made an easy conversion or transition to Quakerism.

Rhode Island, Bridenbaugh concludes, enjoyed steady economic growth from 1660 through 1690, except for minor interruptions during the second and third Anglo-Dutch Wars (1664–67, 1672–74) and King Philip's War (1675–76). "It was not, as has always been taught, that the failure of farming drove the men of the Narragansett region down to the sea; rather it was the prospect of marketing a lucrative agricultural surplus...that forced local merchants...to sail to faraway ports." Indeed, the grazing industry was "the prime source of wealth...that built the commercial republic of Rhode Island in the next century."

Professor Bridenbaugh's book excels in style, interpretation, and substance, but some errors and omissions should be noted. Warwick (Shawomet) was founded in 1642, not 1643; the 1647 assembly was not the first held under the parliamentary patent of March 1643/44, but the first session for which records have been preserved; Bridenbaugh's statement that "agriculture in colonial Rhode Island has never had a chronicler" ignores *Plantation in Yankeeland*, a fine study of early South County farming by Professor Carl Woodward. Further, there is no coverage of the portentous plans of William Coddington to erect a separate island colony in 1651; no mention of the slave-trade ban enacted by the mainland settlements in 1652, despite several references to the seventeenth-century Rhode Island slave trade; no citations from the several state agricultural and geological surveys; and no mention of George Fox's colorful controversy with Roger Williams, despite a description of Fox's extended visit to the Rhode Island Quaker community in mid–1672. In accord with the unfortunate custom of the Brown University Press, the bibliography has been omitted.

These defects are minor, however, and they do not diminish the status of this work as the most valuable interpretative analysis of seventeenth-century Aquidneck Island that has ever been written.

Sometime in the 1640s Richard Smith built a large blockhouse, dubbed Smith's Castle, that was destroyed in King Philip's War. The structure shown here, still standing and open to visitors, was erected on the site in 1678.

Plantation in Yankeeland: The Story of Cocumscussoc, Mirror of Colonial Rhode Island, *by Carl Woodward, Reviewed*

6

Written in 1972, this essay reviewed Carl Woodward's book on Cocumscussoc for *The New England Quarterly*.

PLANTATION IN YANKEELAND is the story of Cocumscussoc, or Smith's Castle, the oldest plantation house in the Narragansett Country of southern Rhode Island. At first this historic spot near present-day Wickford was the site of Indian trading posts which sprang up between 1636 and 1639 as a result of attempts by Roger Williams and his friend Richard Smith to establish commercial contact with the Indians. Sometime in the 1640s a large block-house was built, which was dubbed Smith's Castle. Though it was destroyed in King Philip's War, the name was applied to the subsequent structure erected in 1678 and still standing today.

From this frontier enterprise there evolved a prosperous country estate that figured prominently in the affairs of the colony. According to Mr. Woodward, president emeritus of the University of Rhode Island and an accomplished agricultural historian, Cocumscussoc's "broad acres and large herds set the pattern for other plantations which yielded shiploads of produce for the coastal and West Indian trade, and it was a center of social and religious life among the plantation families."

The house and land, which at its greatest extent comprised twenty-seven square miles, passed by marriage from the Smiths to the Updikes, a family of Dutch ancestry, who held it from 1692 through 1812. The plantation reached the pinnacle of its prosperity in the mid-eighteenth century, but the economic and social disruptions that attended the War for Independence sent it into a precipitous decline.

Woodward's account of Cocumscussoc is anecdotal but not merely antiquarian, because the author, in presenting the story of this historic house, has "endeavored to picture the events that transpired in and around it against the background of the times, a wide-angled complex involving conquest of the wilderness, a bloody Indian war, political squabbling, governmental confusion, the building of an agrarian economy, slave labor, mercantile enterprise, missionary endeavors, and a distinctive social life—all climaxed with the crisis of the Revolution and the changes it wrought."

The author is particularly good in his descriptions of Indian agriculture and the plantation system of southern Rhode Island. The proprietors of the great South County estates, Woodward asserts, had much in common with the planters of the southern colonies. Unlike other New England farmers, they composed a landed aristocracy of superior intellectual and social status and lived affluently in spacious country homes in the manner of the English squires. On their estates, which were maintained by slave labor, dairy products and livestock were the chief commodities. Among the latter were the famous Narragansett Pacers, a favorite colonial riding horse, but a breed which is now extinct.

The Narragansett Country, however, produced more than famous livestock; it also furnished a long line of wealthy families—the Perrys, Updikes, Potters, Stantons, Hazards, Robinsons, and Champlins—whose members played an extremely influential role in Rhode Island politics during the eighteenth and nineteenth centuries.

Woodward's account is interspersed with vignettes of famous or colorful personages who graced this rural but cultured society, including Gilbert Stuart, a South County native; the Reverend Dr. James MacSparran and the Reverend Samuel Fayerweather, learned pastors of St. Paul's Episcopal Church in Narragansett, who came from the British Isles; and such illustrious visitors as

Bishop George Berkeley, evangelist Jemima Wilkinson, and painter John Smibert.

The book lacks a wide-ranging bibliography, but most of the essential works are there with a few important exceptions, such as the studies on Connecticut and the Narragansett Country by Robert C. Black III and Richard S. Dunn and a very pertinent primary source, *The Fones Record* (i.e., *The Records of the Proprietors of the Narragansett*, edited by James N. Arnold). Though Woodward utilized the Updike manuscripts at the Rhode Island Historical Society, he failed to consult in that same depository the papers of two important residents and students of the Narragansett Country, Elisha R. Potter, Jr., and William Davis Miller.

The narrative is popularly written, and although episodic, it is presented in an engaging style. The work lacks documentation, but it is factually accurate and contains few dubious statements of judgment or interpretation (the contention that the royal charter of 1663 made Rhode Island a "pure democracy" being a noteworthy exception).

In sum, Professor Woodward has produced a book which is of value to local history buffs, the general reader, and the specialist in agricultural history, and one which merits inclusion in the growing list of South County studies of high quality.

Although denied full citizenship because of his Jewish faith, Aaron Lopez became one of Newport's most prosperous merchants.

Lopez of Newport: Colonial American Merchant Prince, *by Stanley F. Chyet, Reviewed*

7

Written in 1971, this essay reviewed Stanley F. Chyet's biography of Aaron Lopez for *The New England Quarterly*.

AARON LOPEZ WAS A PORTUGUESE JEWISH IMMIGRANT who came to Newport, Rhode Island, in 1752 at the age of twenty-one in search of religious freedom and economic opportunity. He found both. By the eve of the Revolution, Lopez was a distinguished member of a small but thriving Jewish community and a prosperous merchant prince with a fleet of thirty ships. The British occupation of vulnerable Newport, however, and the vagaries of war had a disastrous impact on Lopez's far-flung commercial empire. In 1782, as his thoughts turned toward the reconstruction of his fortune, Lopez drowned in a bizarre accident.

It is the contention of Mr. Chyet that Lopez embodied Newport's golden age of commercial enterprise during his spectacular thirty-year career. The author traces his subject's life with admiration and loving care. Lopez emerges in heroic dimensions—his name was "a synonym for honesty and integrity"; he was "an ornament to society." Chyet accepts Ezra Stiles's eulogy that Lopez was "without a single enemy and the most universally beloved by an extensive acquaintance of any man I ever knew" as an appraisal "not wide of the mark." The author devotes an entire chapter to the recitation of favorable estimates of Lopez's character. In addition to being repetitive, many of these unctuous remarks are unconvincing, especially those directed to Aaron himself by business associates seeking favors.

Chyet's treatment of Lopez the Sephardic Jew and the family man is excellent. The author is only slightly less successful in his analysis of Lopez the merchant-industrialist, but he fails to place his subject firmly in the political and cultural milieu of eighteenth-century Rhode Island. In this latter respect this work falls far short of the standards set by James Blaine Hedges in his business study of the Brown family.

Chyet in the preface of this volume claims that he took "pains to avoid 'presentmindedness'" and that he attempted to judge his characters "by the standards of their own generation." He has generally succeeded, especially in his account of Lopez's smuggling and slave-trading activities, but there is one persistent departure from Chyet's morally relativistic standard, namely, his outraged and impassioned portrait of the Portuguese Inquisition. In fact, the opening chapters of the book read more like a condemnation of Christendom than a biography of a merchant prince.

Lopez's attempt to become naturalized prompted one of Chyet's infrequent ventures into Rhode Island's political thicket. In 1761–62 the state legislature denied Lopez's citizenship petition because he was a Jew. Although Rhode Island never impaired the freedom of worship of any of its inhabitants, the Lopez case is a blemish on the state's famed liberality. However, Chyet is probably correct in assuming that Lopez's political associations with the Stephen Hopkins faction prejudiced the legislature (controlled by Samuel Ward) against him, and that religion was "little more than a pretext in the denial" of his petition. The author's treatment of this important incident, though adequate, could have been rendered more perceptive had he been aware of the excellent article on the civil rights of Rhode Island Jews by David C. Adelman.

The book is generally free from factual errors. The only misstatement that demands correction is Chyet's contention that Rhode Island colony proscribed the slave trade and provided for gradual manumission of blacks in 1652 (p. 67). In that year the colony was divided because of the ambitious schemes of William Coddington, and the act to which Chyet refers was passed only by the northern towns of Providence and Warwick. The island settlements of Newport and Portsmouth were not parties to the measure, nor did it apply to them after Roger Williams secured the reunification of the colony in 1654.

This work's greatest weakness is its prosaic style. Chyet is addicted to the use of long direct quotes which give the text the quality of a sedative. Despite the volume's brevity (only 182 pages of narrative), one must possess uncommon fortitude to read it in one sitting.

These shortcomings aside, *Lopez of Newport* is a solid and useful addition to Rhode Island economic history. It greatly amplifies the only serious study on the subject, a 1931 article by Bruce M. Bigelow published in *The New England Quarterly*, and it enriches our knowledge of Newport's first golden age.

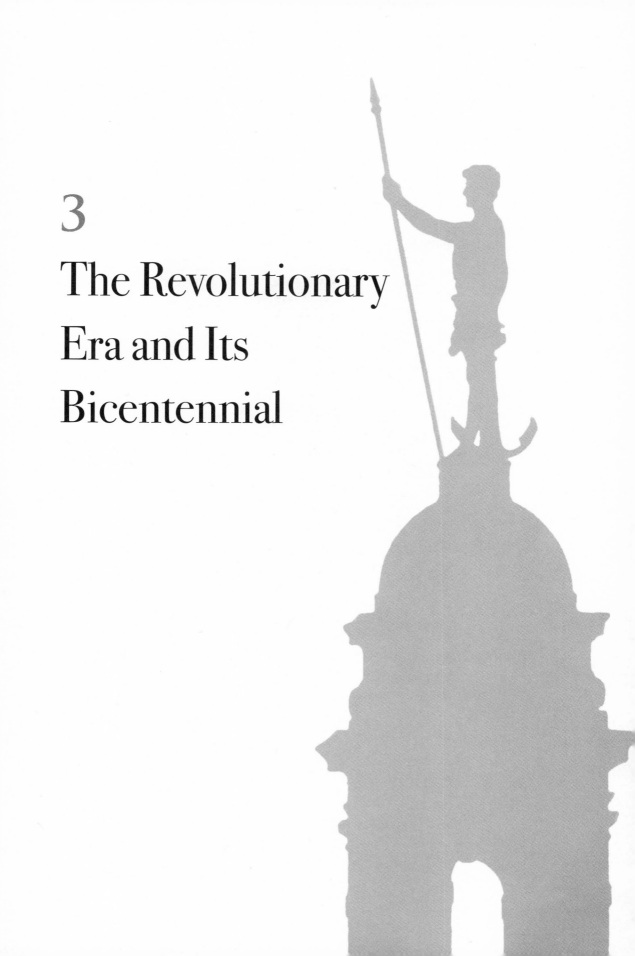

3

The Revolutionary Era and Its Bicentennial

Abraham Whipple, a ship captain in the employ of
John Brown, led the *Gaspee* raiders. Whipple later
gained distinction in the Revolutionary War.

First Blow for Freedom: A Foreword to Richard M. Deasy's Edition of The Documentary History of the Destruction of the Gaspee

8

Written in 1990, this essay introduced Professor Richard M. Deasy's edition of the Gaspee documents, a volume released on Statehood Day, May 29, 1990. My original research on this topic was done for a speech to the Gaspee Days Committee in 1977, when I was grand marshal of the Gaspee Days Parade.

IN THE EARLY 1970S the Rhode Island Bicentennial Commission (ri76) invited historians to find and edit important primary sources pertaining to Rhode Island's role in the American Revolution, with the promise that such sources would be published in the commission's Rhode Island Revolutionary Heritage Series. Eight scholars responded by volunteering to edit materials ranging from manuscript diaries and journals to contemporary political pamphlets to this collection of documentary material about the *Gaspee*.

When the commission's life expired in 1977, three volumes had been published. The others languished on our editor's shelf because the commission lacked money to get them into print. At that juncture the Rhode Island Publications Society (the successor of the Publications Committee of ri76) undertook the task of bringing the project to fruition. This volume, edited by Professor Richard Deasy of Providence College, completes that long effort. Along the way the society sought and received the cooperation and assistance of the Northern Illinois University Press, the Thirteen Colonies Press of Williamsburg, Virginia, the Rhode Island Foundation, the Rhode Island Historical Society, the Rhode Island Supreme Court Historical Society, and the Rhode Island Bicentennial of the Constitution Foundation. The six volumes of the Revolutionary Heritage Series listed at the end of this essay are the legacy of that combined effort. It was a labor of love by editors, foundations, and presses alike, for none gained monetarily from their involvement in this historical enterprise.

46

Professor Deasy's book is the capstone of the series. Of all the volumes, it should generate the greatest local interest, for it deals with an event in Rhode Island's history that is more celebrated than any other—the destruction of the British revenue schooner *Gaspee* on the evening of June 9, 1772. The Gaspee Days observance, initiated in 1966 by David Stackhouse and others, is held annually for a two-week period in late May and early June to commemorate that famous act of defiance. Since the *Gaspee* raiders burned their victim as it lay stranded on Warwick's Namquit (now Gaspee) Point and came ashore in Cranston's Stillhouse Cove, the celebration has centered in the village of Pawtuxet, which straddles the Warwick-Cranston city line. It is run by a dedicated group of volunteers who style themselves the Gaspee Days Committee. Surprisingly, the city of Providence, from where most of the raiders came, has done little to involve itself in these annual festivities, but people from the entire state throng to Pawtuxet each year to celebrate the event and watch a reenactment of the burning.

This book provides a solid and detailed account of the significance of this locally publicized event for those who desire to know the reason for the Gaspee Days observance. Scholars, of course, will profit from the wealth of documentary material contained herein and from Deasy's carefully crafted introduction. Hopefully this book's availability will prompt them to reassess the significance of the *Gaspee* affair in the coming of the American Revolution, for despite the *Gaspee*'s notoriety in Rhode Island, historians have tended to ignore or minimize its importance in the events leading to the war.

Judge William Read Staples (1798–1868) knew well the *Gaspee*'s significance. This learned gentleman served as an associate justice of the state Supreme Court from 1835 to 1854, and as that court's chief justice from 1854 to 1856, but it was history that was Staples's great passion. His compilation of documents pertaining to the destruction of the *Gaspee*, published in 1845, was one of four important historical works that he produced.

Since new source material has come to light during the many years since the *Documentary History* was first published, Professor Deasy has undertaken the useful task of expanding and updating Staples's valuable compilation. In addition, Deasy has drawn upon his graduate research at Brown University to write an introduction to the volume that embraces the latest scholarship and offers new insights concerning the historical significance of the *Gaspee* affair. He places the *Gaspee*'s role in the creation of committees of correspondence in the proper historical context, thus modifying Staples's claim that "the meeting of these commissioners...led to the appointment of committees of correspondence in the several colonies." Such committees, as Deasy shows, first flourished at the time of the Stamp Act crisis in 1765 and exhibited "a variety of structures" from that date onward.

I feel that Staples would have been more accurate had he stated that the *Gaspee* investigation raised colonial apprehensions that the ancient right of trial by jury in the locality where the alleged crime was committed would be violated by a commission that might send those accused of the *Gaspee*'s destruction to England to be tried for high treason. Such fears prompted the Virginia House of Burgesses in March 1773 to appoint a standing committee to correspond with other legislatures or their committees about activities deemed dangerous to the colonials. In a year's time all the remaining colonies, except Pennsylvania, had created agencies modeled on Virginia's. This network of *official legislative* committees of correspondence was novel, and the *Gaspee* investigation was the catalyst for their creation.

Deasy also discusses the English law of high treason as it pertained both to the *Gaspee* incident and to that subsequent act of defiance, in December 1773, known as the Boston Tea Party. Though it was the latter that served as the direct, proximate cause for the Coercive Acts of 1774—measures that led to the call of the First Continental Congress—I have long felt that Rhode Island's defiance in June 1772 and the ensuring cover-up staged by its citizens before the royal investigating commission in 1773 also weighed heavily on the minds of those parliamentary leaders who fashioned the Coercive (or Intolerable) Acts to punish the colonists and force them to submit. In this sense, therefore, the burning of the *Gaspee* ended the period of calm that came with the repeal of the Townshend duties (except the tax on tea) and began the third and decisive phase of colonial opposition, which inexorably led to the War for Independence. Professor Deasy, more cautious than I (and rightly so, in view of the documentary evidence), stops short of such a claim, but he does find that England's reinstatement of the old Treason Act of Henry VIII—a measure to coerce violent protesters by prosecuting them to the limit of the law of constructive treason—"had the effect of dissolving all subsidiary arguments [for dealing with dissent], of elevating tensions to the breaking point, and of insuring one last confrontation. Differences of opinion on both sides of the Atlantic over the nature of the British Empire may have been impressive before [the Crown's response to the *Gaspee*], but now they had become irreconcilable within that empire." Perhaps, suggests Deasy, the epithet "First Blow for Freedom" may fit the *Gaspee* affair after all.

Several prominent historians of the Revolutionary era have failed even to mention the *Gaspee* in their recent general accounts of the coming of the war. Professor Deasy's readily available reissue and update of Judge Staples's long-neglected compilation should prevent future historians from making such an unwarranted and inexcusable omission, and it should thus reinforce Rhode Island's claim to be included with Virginia and Massachusetts in the vanguard of the movement towards independence.

RHODE ISLAND REVOLUTIONARY HERITAGE SERIES

No. 1. *Silas Downer: Forgotten Patriot*, by Carl Bridenbaugh.

No. 2. *The Rights of Colonies Examined*, by Stephen Hopkins. Introduced and edited by Paul Campbell.

No. 3. *Diary of a Common Soldier in the American Revolution, 1775–1783: An Annotated Edition of the Military Journal of Jeremiah Greenman*. Edited by Robert C. Bray and Paul E. Bushnell.

No. 4. *Rhode Islanders Record the Revolution: The Journals of William Humphrey and Zuriel Waterman*. Introduced and edited by Nathaniel N. Shipton and David Swain.

No. 5. *Building Early American Warships: The Journal of the Rhode Island Committee for Constructing the Continental Frigates* Providence and Warren, *1775–1777*. Introduced by John Fitzhugh Millar.

No. 6. *The Documentary History of the Destruction of the Gaspee*, by William R. Staples. Introduced and supplemented by Richard M. Deasy.

William Ellery, Samuel Ward's ally and successor, was one of two Rhode Island signers of the Declaration of Independence.

General Nathanael Greene achieved greater prominence for his Revolutionary War exploits than any other Rhode Islander.

Random Reflections on
The Bicentennial of Independence

Written in late 1976 near the conclusion of my tenure as Rhode Island
Bicentennial Commission (ri 76) chairman, this reflection was distributed
to several local newspapers, which printed it in whole or in part.

ON SEPTEMBER 11, 1974, in the midst of confusion and controversy, I apprehensively assumed the acting chairmanship of the
Rhode Island Bicentennial Commission. Some of my friends felt
it was like accepting the captaincy of the *Titanic*. But after all, I
had studied American history at Notre Dame and taught it for ten
years at Providence College. Now I had the opportunity to teach
it in a much larger classroom, and to share with the people of
Rhode Island my enthusiasm for our heritage.

The chairmanship of the Rhode Island Bicentennial Commission was a once-in-a-lifetime position—a chance not only to teach
history but to make it, and to make the academic world at least a
small part of the daily life of those who would join in commemorating our two hundredth anniversary as an independent nation.

Fortunately, the commission that I inherited contained a nucleus
of honest, dedicated, and energetic civic leaders—people like
Senator Bob McKenna, Professor Joel Cohen, Dean Terrelle
Crum, businessman Dick Belanger, and scholar Al Klyberg, director of the Rhode Island Historical Society. They had been with the
commission since its creation in 1969, and they had laid most of the
plans and groundwork for the big year of 1976.

The commission's greatest asset, however, was its paid staff, led by Ron Tracey, Mary Brennan, Gladys Wyatt, and four newcomers whom I hired shortly after taking office—Glenn LaFantasie, Paul Campbell, Helen Hodde, and "Chas Beau" Healy. The CETA program and the generosity of Governor Noel, who strongly supported the commission, made possible the expansion of this "crack staff" to thirteen full-time members during the hectic months of 1976.

Although these people were the only paid participants in the state's bicentennial effort, they earned every cent they received. The taxpayer often levels criticism against public employees in patronage jobs, but no such criticism could be directed against the ri76 staff—their pay was not great, and their hours were long and irregular. Often they reported to work seven days a week because most of our events were on weekends. Sometimes they started as early at 5:00 A.M., and on other occasions they worked into the early hours of the morning. I took the bows, but they were the unsung heroes of the Bicentennial. Their service was ten times beyond the call of duty; it was a labor of love.

It did not take long to discover that a small core of energetic commissioners and Bicentennial Foundation members (the foundation was the financial arm of ri76) and a willing and able staff were not sufficient to bring the Bicentennial to all the people of Rhode Island; ri76 needed a much broader base and greater diversity. This fact prompted me to direct most of my attention to recruiting volunteers in every conceivable area of Bicentennial concern—to get citizens with enthusiasm and expertise to serve on an ri76 committee in their area of special interest.

The twelve hundred volunteers from around the state who joined the commission were responsible for the impact and scope of ri76. When this expansion and recruitment drive ended, ri76 had nine standing committees and fifty subcommittees, covering everything from parades to sports to women's programs to religious observances to ethnic heritage.

A special category of volunteers who have given of their time in abundance are the members of Rhode Island's militia groups and the state's National Guard under Major General Leonard Holland.

They have consistently provided the pageantry and the manpower essential to the success of our Bicentennial events. Another category was the heritage groups like the Bristol Fourth of July, Gaspee Days, and Tiverton Muster committees, which had already developed traditional historic celebrations that they expanded for the Bicentennial.

These volunteers from established groups were supplemented by recruits from each of the state's thirty-nine cities and towns. The ri76 organization had used its first forty thousand dollars in federal grant money as a catalyst to get the local communities organized for the celebration. Each municipality was given one thousand dollars if it would match that sum, appoint a local Bicentennial committee, and develop projects in the areas of festival, heritage, and horizon. Every community responded, and Rhode Island became the first state in the nation to be fully mobilized for the Bicentennial observance.

On the state level, the commission endorsed or sponsored, and therefore helped implement, more than six hundred projects and events. The combined efforts of the cities and towns at least equaled that number. Such dynamism from the grass roots upward made Rhode Island one of the most active states in the nation in observing the Bicentennial, yet our level of public funding was quite low in comparison to that of other states.

The Rhode Island taxpayer got his money's worth from the Bicentennial. In fact, it could be argued that the regional and national festivals and sporting events staged here for the Bicentennial attracted enough revenue into the public treasury to offset the money allocated to the state and local commissions. Besides our cultural mission, ri76 was concerned with the economy and the promotion of tourism.

The volunteerism generated by the Bicentennial in Rhode Island was one of its most inspiring features. It should not be allowed to wither away. The volunteer committees in each city and town should be transformed into permanent, standing Heritage Committees. They are nonpartisan and represent a cross section of community activists. As such, they could serve as planning boards for historic, cultural, or esthetically oriented community projects. I intend to propose this idea to local officials before the Bicentennial year expires, and before these valuable local resources are disbanded.

I have often been asked to list those Bicentennial events that were the most successful or gave me the greatest degree of personal satisfaction.

The most spectacular event that we cosponsored was undoubtedly Tall Ships—a great adventure in international goodwill. The single biggest in-house festival project was our 1976 Rhode Island Independence Parade, perhaps the largest all-Rhode Island parade in history.

Since I am a history professor and a lawyer, the event that gave me my greatest personal and professional thrill was my Bicentennial Law Day address (May 3, 1976) to the members of the state's judiciary at the Colony House in Newport.

The general program that has been most satisfying and successful is the Ethnic Heritage Program of ri76. This was a pet project related to one of my areas of academic interest. Ethnicity first attracted my serious attention when I was doing research in 1971 for the history of the multiethnic Diocese of Providence. A subsequent grant from the Rhode Island Committee for the Humanities allowed me to continue and broaden my studies. When I became chairman of ri76, I had the chance to transform this academic interest into a working program.

Rhode Island was a natural setting. It is the state most affected by the successive waves of European migration that began with the Irish in the 1820s, and it is a state today with one of the highest percentages of foreign stock. In addition, ethnic heritage was a means of involving more people in the Bicentennial observance, for I have always felt that ri76 was observing not only the events of 1776 but the full two hundred years of American independence.

Not all Rhode Islanders can trace their ancestry back to the *Mayflower* or the American Revolution, but all of us have ancestors who helped our state develop politically, economically, socially, or culturally. Thus the Ethnic Heritage Program of ri76 was designed to commemorate and recall the role of each ethnic group in the history of Rhode Island. Its slogan is "one out of many"; its theme, "knowledge promotes understanding and understanding begets brotherhood."

The response to this program has been most gratifying: we now have a general Ethnic Heritage Committee (chaired by Chester Browning) and eighteen subcommittees, representing every major ethnic component in our state. These groups are working on publications, folk festivals, sporting events, musical projects, art exhibits, and numerous other programs designed to make their culture and contributions better known by their fellow Rhode Islanders. It is my hope that this program will outlive the commission and become a permanent cultural legacy of the Bicentennial.*

Another project that rivals the Ethnic Heritage Program in its long-range significance is the publications program of ri76. Our Publications Committee, staffed by Glenn LaFantasie and Paul Campbell, will produce approximately thirty hardcover books and a dozen historical pamphlets relating to various aspects of Rhode Island's history. This is the largest scholarly publications program ever undertaken by a state agency.

It is these ongoing projects—Ethnic Heritage, Publications, and Historical Preservation—that justify the continued existence of ri76 for the duration of the Bicentennial era (i.e., to 1983). The festival events (which have been directed by the tireless and competent Bob Lynch) will decrease, but there are many Revolutionary occurrences yet to observe in the weeks and months ahead.

Thus far I have written of the pleasures and achievements of the Bicentennial, but I am sure that my readers (knowing of my tendency to be blunt and outspoken) did not wish me to "accentuate the positive and eliminate the negative" (as the song goes). There were indeed frustrations and disappointments.

Although the electronic media (especially WPRO, WJAR-TV, WTEV-TV, AND WPRI-TV) gave the Bicentennial excellent coverage and the smaller newspapers (especially the *Woonsocket Call*)

---

*The Ethnic Heritage Program of ri76 was the seedbed and model for the consortium that constitutes the new Heritage Harbor Museum, a fact alluded to in this book's introduction by Al Klyberg, Heritage Harbor's prime mover.

did likewise, I feel that the *Providence Journal* richly deserved the Benedict Arnold Memorial Bowl as the news medium that did the most to discredit the work of ri76.

This is no reflection on the reporters; Ron Winslow, John Mulligan, Bill Gale, and their associates did a fair and able job of reporting commission activities and Bicentennial events. The problem rested with the board of editors, that smug and self-righteous group of poison penmen who always criticized but never complimented the volunteer efforts of ri76. Whether it was our alleged commercialization of the Independent Man, our effort to coordinate the state government's involvement in Tall Ships, or even such an academic question as our attempt to show that Rhode Island renounced allegiance to the king but did not leave the empire on May 4, 1776, the editors were quick to condemn.

Despite our more than six hundred successful projects, not one favorable editorial appeared in the *Providence Journal* in 1976. Surely there is something unfair and perverse in the *Journal*'s persistent knocking of well-intentioned volunteers. Perhaps such criticism stemmed from the editors' conviction that Rhode Islanders with certain political, religious, or ethnic affiliations were somehow unfit or unworthy to direct the state's Bicentennial observance.

But any event as large and diverse as the Bicentennial must have some frustrations and disappointments. Thankfully, they were few. My many hours of involvement were no sacrifice; in terms of satisfaction, memories, honors, and new friends, the Bicentennial did ten times more for me than I ever did for it!

Thus the positive aspects of the Bicentennial far outweighed the negative. The Bicentennial has been a time for civic and cultural renewal, an opportunity to get involved, a challenge to improve society and enhance the quality of life, a way to transmit our heritage to future generations, and a stimulus to volunteerism and to intelligent patriotism—it was a civic Great Awakening. In Rhode Island, the Bicentennial was no one person or group; it was a mighty outpouring of people and spirit that will not be soon forgotten by those of us who were privileged to have played a part.

Written in 1976 for an address at the Hopkins House in Providence on the occasion of Hopkins's birthday (March 7), this essay was revised for publication as an entry in the new *Dictionary of National Biography*, soon to be published by Oxford University Press.

STEPHEN HOPKINS (1707–85), statesman, pamphleteer, and signer of the Declaration of Independence, was born on March 7, 1707, in Providence, Rhode Island, easterly of a former Indian village called Mashapaug. This site was set off from Providence in 1754, becoming part of the new town of Cranston. It was reannexed in 1868 and is located today in the Elmwood section of Providence.

Hopkins, the second of nine children born to farmers William Hopkins, Jr. (ca. 1681–1738) and Ruth Wilkinson (born 1686), a devout Quaker, moved at an early age with his parents and older brother to a farm at Chopmist, in a part of the "outlands" of Providence that was incorporated as the town of Scituate in 1731. On this agricultural frontier Hopkins grew to manhood, working on his parents' farm and acquiring skill as a surveyor. In 1726 he married Sarah Scott of Providence (1707–53), who bore him seven children in a marriage that endured until her death by suicide after a debilitating illness.

Though he lacked formal education, the man John Adams would later describe as a person of "wit, humour, anecdotes, science, and learning" became the first town moderator of Scituate in 1731 at the age of twenty-four. This post was the initial step in a political career that included election to the office of Speaker of the Rhode Island House of Representatives (seven times), service as governor (nine one-year terms), appointment to the position of chief justice of Rhode Island's highest court (eleven years), and selection as a Rhode Island delegate to the First and Second Continental Congresses (1774–79).

The rise of Hopkins in the world of government was accompanied by a rapid ascent in the business of trade and commerce.

Signer Stephen Hopkins was the most significant Rhode Islander of the eighteenth century. This preliminary sketch by John Trumbull is the only surviving likeness of Hopkins. It was done in Providence by Trumbull in September 1791, six years after Hopkins's death, using Rufus Hopkins to model for his dead father—whom, it was said, he strongly resembled.

Having moved in 1742 from rural Scituate, which he represented in the state legislature, to the port town of Providence, where he immediately secured reelection to the General Assembly and resumed the post of House Speaker that he first held in 1738, Hopkins formed business partnerships with prominent Newport merchant Godfrey Malbone and then with the powerful Brown family, Providence's leading eighteenth-century entrepreneurs. Thereafter, his wealth and financial connections fueled his rise to political prominence.

Hopkins's first significant foray into intercolonial politics came in 1754, when he represented Rhode Island at the Albany Congress. Farsighted enough to see the advantages of colonial cooperation and practical enough to realize the potential usefulness of a strong colonial navy in protecting commerce (one of the plan's prospects), Hopkins favored the plan of union and wrote a pamphlet defending his participation in the locally unpopular conclave.

In 1755 Hopkins was elected to his first term as governor, a post with little constitutional power under Rhode Island's system of legislative ascendancy. Nonetheless he began to exert considerable political strength and influence as the leader of the dominant faction in the colony's emergent two-party system—one of America's first.

In this political milieu, opposing groups, one headed by Samuel

Ward of Westerly and the other by Hopkins, were organized with sectional overtones; generally speaking (though with notable exceptions), the merchants and farmers of southern Rhode Island (Ward) battled with their counterparts from Providence and its environs (Hopkins). The principal goal of these groups was to secure control of the powerful legislature in order to obtain the host of public offices—from chief justice to inspector of tobacco—at the disposal of that body.

The semipermanent nature, relatively stable membership, and explicit sectional rivalry of the warring camps have led historian Mack Thompson to describe Rhode Island's pre-Revolutionary political structure as one of "stable factionalism." Another historian, David S. Lovejoy, has boldly maintained that Rhode Islanders revolted from British rule not only "on the broad grounds of constitutional right to keep Rhode Island safe for liberty and property" but also to preserve "the benefits of party politics"—patronage and spoils.

Rampant factionalism, with Hopkins usually prevailing, endured until 1768, when Ward and Hopkins agreed to retire from future gubernatorial races. In 1770 Hopkins again became chief justice, an office he continued to hold for another six years, even after he and his former rival Ward went to Philadelphia in 1774 to represent Rhode Island's interests in the First Continental Congress.

When England began to reorganize its American empire in 1763 at the conclusion of the Seven Years' War, Hopkins set about developing and articulating economic and political proposals that ran counter to parliamentary enactments. In the radical *Providence Gazette*, which he helped to establish in 1762, Hopkins opposed the renewal of the Molasses Act upon its expiration in 1764. He denounced the measure's six-pence-per-gallon duty on foreign molasses as destructive of Rhode Island's lucrative triangular trade, and a levy that diminished Rhode Island's ability to buy British manufactures or pay British creditors. The Sugar Act of 1764 reduced the duty to three pence, but that toll was far greater than the one-half-of-one-percent duty recommended by Hopkins in his essay, and the new levy was marked by much more vigorous enforcement than the old.

Late in 1764 Hopkins penned a more elaborate analysis of imperial relations, one which shifted from a purely economical defense of colonial rights to a political and constitutional conception of the British Empire. In this pamphlet, *The Rights of Colonies Examined*, Hopkins repeatedly referred not merely to the economic interests of Rhode Islanders, or of the northern colonists (as in his earlier essay), but rather to the broad rights of "Americans." This treatise is notable in that it suggests a federal theory of empire, with Parliament legislating on matters of imperial concern—war, trade, international relations—but with colonial assemblies possessing sovereignty in local affairs, including taxation. In 1766 this bold tract was published in London under the title *The Grievances of the American Colonists Candidly Examined*.

In 1768 another Providence lawyer, Silas Downer, a colleague, friend, and protégé of Hopkins, delivered a path-breaking public discourse at the local "liberty tree" repudiating the recently passed Declaratory Act and denying the authority of Parliament to make any laws of any kind to regulate the colonies. In 1774 Hopkins took attorney Downer to the First Continental Congress to serve as secretary to the Rhode Island delegation, which was headed by Hopkins and his former rival Samuel Ward.

During the Second Continental Congress, which convened in September 1775, Hopkins became chairman of the naval committee and secured for his brother Esek (1718–1802) the position of first commodore and commander in chief of the newly created Continental navy. Then, as chairman of the naval and marine committee, Stephen supervised the civilian administration of the American navy.

In July 1776 Hopkins became one of two Rhode Island signers of the Declaration of Independence (William Ellery was the other). When he affixed his signature to the engrossed copy of this momentous document on August 2, 1776, he guided his palsied right hand with his left, allegedly remarking "my hand trembles, but my heart does not." During this pivotal year Hopkins also served as the Rhode Island member of the thirteen-man committee that drafted the Articles of Confederation, America's first written constitution.

Declining health, including what was then described as "shaking palsy," limited Hopkins's role in the events of the Revolution. Despite his election as delegate, he was unable to attend sessions of the Congress in Philadelphia after 1776, but he did serve from December 1776 to May 1778 on the Rhode Island Council of War, an *ad hoc* body established by the legislature to supervise and direct Rhode Island's war effort. In addition, he was a delegate to the convention of New England states in 1776, 1777, and 1779, serving as convention president in 1777.

In his declining years Hopkins continued his productive relationship with the powerful and versatile Brown family of Providence, with whom he was bound by ties of family, religion, literary and civic projects, and commercial enterprise. In 1781 he had an unexpected visit from George Washington, who had come to Rhode Island to consult with Count Rochambeau, then quartered with his French army in Newport. Houseguest Moses Brown (who, like Hopkins, was a leading Quaker businessman) remarked on the "unaffected friendliness" of the two revolutionaries as they talked about the war and the upcoming Virginia campaign. In January 1782 Ann Smith, his second wife of twenty-seven years, died. By that date five of his seven children (all by his first marriage) had also predeceased him.

On July 13, 1785, Hopkins—governor, jurist, legislator, patriot, pamphleteer, farmer, merchant, educator (he was the first chancellor of Brown University), amateur scientist, and civic leader—died peacefully in his Providence home, a structure now preserved as a national historic site, and was buried in Providence's North Burial Ground.

James Mitchell Varnum's brilliant legal and political career was cut short by his untimely death at the age of forty.

The Constitutional Significance of Trevett v. Weeden (1786)

11

Written in 1976, this speech was my first Law Day address to the
Rhode Island Supreme Court. It was presented at the Colony House
in Newport on May 3, 1976. An expanded version with extensive
documentation appeared later in *Democracy in Decline*, pp. 80–106.

*Honorable Justices of the Supreme Court, Other Distinguished
Members of the Federal and State Judiciary, Your Excellency Governor
Philip Noel, the Honorable Attorney General, Reverend Clergy,
Members of the Bar, Ladies and Gentlemen:*

IN PREVIOUS YEARS THOSE HONORED to deliver the Law Day
address have oriented their talks toward such areas as jurispru-
dence, education, or ethics and morality. But in this Bicentennial
year it is appropriate, as the justices have advised me, that our
theme be one of heritage. Thus my address by design is more infor-
mational than inspirational, more historical than hortatory.

I am neither so presumptuous nor qualified to tell this honorable court what should be, but perhaps I can bring to your attention what has been. This approach, however, is no mere exercise in
antiquarianism, for history is a handmaid of law; so said your
learned colleague Oliver Wendell Holmes, Jr., when he perceptively observed that "the life of the law has not been logic; it has
been experience."

What experience have I elected to recall today? Indeed, the
choice was difficult, for Rhode Island was in the vanguard of the
Revolution that we now commemorate, and its leadership role

lends itself to many topics. Certainly the alleged violations of the civil rights of colonials by the mother country was a principal cause of the War for Independence. Writs of assistance which violated traditional guarantees against unreasonable search and seizure, admiralty courts which failed to incorporate the common-law right of trial by jury, navigation laws which, when overzealously enforced, were confiscatory and violated the right to property were all a source of legitimate colonial grievance here in Rhode Island and elsewhere. And at the heart of the dispute between Americans and the mother country was the constitutional question concerning the nature of the British Empire, because Parliament in its Declaratory Act of 1766 emphatically contended that the empire was unitary, with all power emanating from king and Parliament, whereas the colonials, including Rhode Island's Stephen Hopkins in his *Rights of Colonies Examined*, advanced the countervailing theory of a federal empire in which colonial assemblies were sovereign in the local sphere.

Indeed, the fundamental questions of law and liberty were central to the Revolutionary dispute. Any of these could occupy our attention on this reflective day, but I have chosen to examine an event of our formative years in which the Rhode Island court system was more directly involved.

Let me first observe that the Revolutionary era did not end in 1776 with Rhode Island's renunciation of allegiance, nor in 1781 with the surrender of Cornwallis, nor even in 1783 with the ratification of the Treaty of Paris. As all the leading historians have demonstrated, the Revolutionary movement did not reach fruition until the establishment of a government under the present Constitution of the United States. For most of the original thirteen, that event occurred with the inauguration of George Washington on April 30, 1789.

Rhode Island, which was first in war, was last in peace, and its period of political gestation extended to May 29, 1790, when it reluctantly ratified the handiwork of the Philadelphia Convention (in which it took no part) by the narrowest of margins, and only under political and economic pressure from the new national government. The events leading to Rhode Island's Caesarian birth as

a state in the new federal Union included the case of *Trevett* v.
Weeden, a landmark legal encounter in 1786 involving such essential issues as judicial independence and judicial review.

Trevett v. *Weeden* is among the best-known cases ever tried
before an American state court. Paradoxically, it is a case that has
seldom been properly understood. Legal historians attempting to
trace the origins of the doctrine of judicial review refer to several
state decisions antedating John Marshall's decision in *Marbury* v.
Madison as evidence of the acceptance of that cardinal principle of
American constitutional law by many of our early jurists. *Trevett*
v. *Weeden* is usually cited in such a litany as a major precedent for
judicial review, and most accounts of the case either erroneously
assert that Rhode Island's highest tribunal declared a paper-
money statute unconstitutional in the *Trevett* decision or else are
vague and inexact in this summary of the court's action. Let us
clarify the record.

The controversy emanated from the much-maligned paper-
money law of 1786 (whose history is a story in itself). Rhode
Island's infamous paper-money plan was the offspring of the
state's Revolutionary debt. The plan was originally advanced by
newly ascendant rural politicians from South County and the
western hill towns who were attempting to solve Rhode Island's
financial ills. In May 1786 the pro-paper "Country" or "landholders" party came to power in the General Assembly and passed legislation authorizing the issuance of a hundred thousand pounds
sterling of paper money, or approximately $333,000. Because the
law was opposed by creditors and merchants in the port towns
who set out to discredit the issue and to undermine faith in it
through a palpably false propaganda campaign, the politically
dominant paper-money supporters attempted to defeat, coerce, or
punish their opponents by passing a "force act" in June 1786 that
levied a heavy fine for nonacceptance of the paper or for contributing to its depreciation. To this act was soon added an amendment
providing for trial without jury and without appeal for violators,
and specifying that such trial be held before a *special court* convened for that purpose only.

When John Weeden, a butcher who operated a shop in Newport,

refused to accept a tender of paper money from John Trevett, the latter entered a complaint with the chief justice of the Superior Court of Judicature (the state's highest tribunal) in accordance with the provisions of the force act. This complaint precipitated the case *Trevett* v. *Weeden*, a trial conducted in the very building where we now sit.

Two of the state's ablest lawyers sprang to Weeden's defense—Henry Marchant, a former attorney general and former delegate to the Continental Congress, and James Mitchell Varnum, a Revolutionary War general and member of Congress from Rhode Island. The trial was conducted, despite provisions of the penal law, at a special session of the Superior Court of Judicature, held in Newport on September 22, 1786, with Chief Justice Paul Mumford presiding. The case was highlighted by Varnum's speech for the defense, a brief that Charles G. Haines, the most thorough student of the development of judicial supremacy, has called one "which indicated perhaps better than any other document prior to the Federal Convention, some of the ideas on which reliance was placed in accepting the principle of judicial review of legislative enactments."

At the outset Varnum, a man of eloquence and imposing appearance, prayed that the court would not take cognizance of Trevett's complaint because of three major objections to the act under which the charge was brought. First, defense counsel contended that the act under which Weeden stood accused had expired ten days after the rising of the Assembly. Faulty draftsmanship of the penal statute by the legislature gave this technical allegation much merit.

Varnum informed the judges, however, that "we do not place our principal reliance upon this objection." He then embarked upon a more formidable avenue of attack, namely, that by the statute "special trials are instituted, incontrollable by the Supreme Judiciary Court of the state." This was a gross violation of the long-standing principle that "The highest court of law hath...power to reverse erroneous judgements given by inferior courts and the duty to command, prohibit, and restrain all inferior jurisdictions, whenever they attempt to exceed their authority or refuse to exercise it for the public good."

The final aspect of the penal act to be attacked by Varnum was its failure to provide accused with jury trial. His arguments on this point were most effective. He made several allusions to the charter of Charles II, then the state's basic law, and listed two principal causes of colonial discontent on the eve of the Revolution in the process of developing his position.

"Trial by jury," asserted Varnum, "was ever esteemed a first, a fundamental, and a most essential principle in the English constitution." This "sacred right" was transferred from England to America by numerous royal grants, including Rhode Island's charter of 1663. The charter provision giving colonists the right to "have and enjoy all liberties and immunities of free and natural subjects" of England was then cited in proof of this contention. These privileges and immunities were abridged by the Stamp Act levy and by England's use of admiralty jurisdiction. In fact, attempts of Parliament to deprive colonists of trial by jury "were among the principal causes that united the colonies in a defensive war," contended the learned Revolutionary general.

Now, that long-cherished right of trial by jury was being denied by the Rhode Island General Assembly, claimed Varnum. This was a clear usurpation, for the charter prohibited the legislature from making laws "contrary and repugnant" to the general system of laws that governed the realm of England at the time of the grant. The Revolution, said he, had made "no change" in this limitation on legislative power. Trial by jury, he contended, "is a fundamental right, a part of our legal constitution," and one with which the Assembly cannot tamper. The message was clear: the legislature must not deny to the people the fruits of their successful struggle for liberty!

Then, after references to Coke and other legal authorities, Varnum espoused the doctrine of judicial review in this formidable and forceful summation:

> We have attempted to show, that the act, upon which the information is founded, has expired: That by the act special jurisdictions are erected, incontrollable by

the Supreme Judiciary Court of the State: And that, by the act, this court is not authorized or empowered to impanel a jury to try the facts contained in the information; That the trial by jury is a fundamental, a constitutional right—ever claimed as such—ever ratified as such—ever held most dear and sacred; That the Legislature derives all its authority from the constitution—has no power of making laws but in subordination to it—can not infringe or violate it; That therefore the act is unconstitutional and void. That this Court has power to judge and determine what acts of the General Assembly are agreeable to the constitution; and, on the contrary, that this Court is under the most solemn obligations to execute the laws of the land, and therefore cannot, will not, consider this act as a law of the land.

Contrary to generally accepted belief, Rhode Island's highest court did not, on the basis of Varnum's appeal, declare the penal statue unconstitutional and void. It did, however, accede to his plea by denying jurisdiction over Trevett's complaint, for the court unanimously decided "that the said complaint does not come under the cognizance of the Justices here present, and...it is hereby dismissed." (May I state parenthetically that the original court record has eluded most students of the case and was very difficult to locate. In fact, I found it propping up a radiator in the Newport County Courthouse. Such neglect of historical treasures indicates the crying need for a centralized and professional system of state records management.)

Presumably cognizance was denied because the justices heard the case in special *session* of the regular term and not as a special court as directed by the force act. However, in the commotion that followed the trial, knowledge of the specific decision was somehow distorted, for the infuriated Assembly in special session issued a summons requiring immediate attendance of the judges to render their reasons for adjudging "an act of the supreme legislature of this state to be unconstitutional, and so absolutely void."

This may have been the justices' personal view, but it was not their formal decision. (Unquestionably the Assembly's misstatement is the source of the erroneous notion entertained by numerous historians, a notion this address seeks to correct.)

In early October, after a two-week delay, Judges David Howell, Joseph Hazard, and Thomas Tillinghast appeared to defend their course of action. Chief Justice Paul Mumford and Associate Justice Gilbert Devol were conveniently ill. Both Tillinghast and Hazard, the latter a paper-money supporter, stoutly defended the judgment they had rendered. Howell did likewise in a speech much lengthier and more fully preserved. He asserted that the justices were accountable only to God and their own consciences for their decision. It was beyond the power of the General Assembly to judge the propriety of the court's ruling, the angry Howell continued, for by such an act "the legislature would become the supreme judiciary—a perversion of power totally subversive of civil liberty." Howell then contended for an independent judiciary so that judges would not be answerable for their opinion unless charged with criminality. In support of his position, he made impressive citations from Montesquieu, Blackstone, Serjeant William Hawkins, and Francis Bacon.

Showing little remorse or contrition for his act, Howell boldly informed the lawmakers that the legislature had assumed a fact in their summons to the judges that was not justified or warranted by the records. The plea of Weeden, he pointed out, mentioned the act of the General Assembly as unconstitutional, and so void, but judgment of the court simply was that the information was not cognizable before them. Hence it appeared, chided Howell, that the plea had been mistaken for the judgment. His personal opinion, however, was that the act was indeed unconstitutional, had not the force of law, and could not be executed.

The responses of the judges, especially that of Howell, did little to endear them to the General Assembly. Thus the legislature declared its dissatisfaction with these retorts, and a motion was made to dismiss the judges from office. Before the vote on this imprudent suggestion was taken, a memorial signed by the three judges was introduced and read. They had anticipated the plan to remove them, and they demanded as freemen and officers of the state the right of due process—"A hearing by counsel before some proper and legal tribunal, and an opportunity to answer to certain and specific charges…before any sentence or judgment be passed, injurious to any of their aforesaid rights and privileges." After the memorial was read, General Varnum addressed the legislators in defense of the court.

This determined show of resistance caused the Assembly to waver. A motion was passed directing that the opinion of the attorney general and other learned lawyers be obtained on the question of "whether constitutionally, and agreeably by law, the General Assembly could suspend, or remove from office the judges of the Supreme Judiciary Court, without a previous charge and statement of criminality, due process, trial, and conviction thereon."

Attorney General William Channing (father of the famed Unitarian minister) and others consulted answered in the negative. Thus it was resolved by a large majority of the legislature that "as the judges of said Superior Court are not charged with criminality in giving judgment upon the information, John Trevett against John Weeden, they are therefore discharged from any further attendance upon this Assembly on that account" and allowed to resume their functions.

The forcing statue that sparked the dispute was repealed in December 1786, but the Assembly gained some measure of satisfaction from the independent-minded court when it declined to reelect Howell, Hazard, Tillinghast, and Devol upon the expiration of their terms in May 1787. Chief Justice Mumford, who had failed to testify either because of illness or discretion, was retained. Congressional delegate Varnum and Attorney General Channing were also ousted because of their defiant stand, whereas Henry Goodwin, state's counsel in the proceedings, was elevated by the Country party to the position vacated by Channing.

As the foregoing analysis reveals, the decision of Rhode Island's highest tribunal in *Trevett* v. *Weeden* was a *cause célèbre* that produced great temporary excitement but made little permanent impact upon the operations of Rhode Island's governmental system. After 1786 the legislature continued to exert as much control over the state's courts as before. Judges continued to be elected annually by the dominant party—despite periodic protests of reformers—until establishment of a written state constitution in 1843. The Assembly continued to entertain petitions from individuals adversely affected by legal decisions, and it often honored such petitions by overturning the judgment of the Supreme Court in cases of insolvency and by authorizing new trials in civil suits. These practices were not terminated until 1856, when the state Supreme Court finally asserted its independence of the Assembly in the landmark case of *Taylor* v. *Place.* Until the *Taylor* decision— seventy years after Trevett—no state court dared challenge the Assembly; no Rhode Island justice gave official endorsement to the doctrine of judicial review.

The real significance of the *Trevett* v. *Weeden* episode lies not in the formal action of the court but in the utterances of defense counsel James Mitchell Varnum and, to a lesser degree, in the personal observations of Justice David Howell. General Varnum's statement of the doctrine of judicial review was one of the most forceful and extensive arguments on that subject developed during this formative period. Assuredly his position was known to the framers of the federal Constitution and to such state supporters of that document as James Iredell and John Marshall. Varnum furnished his contemporaries and posterity with a full statement of his views by publishing them in pamphlet form together with an account of the trials of both Weeden and the judges. Varnum's work was widely disseminated and even advertised for sale in the Philadelphia press during April and May 1787, when the delegates were entering that city to participate in the Grand Convention.

To this eloquent attorney and harbinger of judicial review, and also to the courageous Justice David Howell, who defiantly asserted the independence of his court from legislative interference, our courts and our legal historians owe a duty of deference and acknowledgment. It is fitting and just on this Bicentennial Law Day that these legal experiences be recounted, observed, and acclaimed.

STATE of RHODE-ISLAND, &c.

In GENERAL ASSEMBLY, *February Session*, A. D. 1788.

An ACT submitting to the Consideration of the Freemen of this State, the Report of the Convention of Delegates for a Constitution for the United States, as agreed on in Philadelphia, the 17th of September, A. D. 1787.

WHEREAS the Honorable the Continental Congress did heretofore recommend to the Legislatures of the respective States, to appoint Delegates to meet in Convention, at Philadelphia, in May, A. D. 1787, to make such Alterations and Amendments in the present Confederation of the United States as would tend to promote the Happiness, good Government and Welfare of the Federal Union : And whereas the said Delegates, on the 17th Day of September, 1787, did agree upon, and report to the Congress of the United States, a Form of a Constitution for the United States of America : And whereas the said United States in Congress assembled did, by a Resolution passed the 28th Day of September, A. D. 1787, transmit said Report to the Legislature of this State, to be submitted to the Consideration of the People thereof : And whereas this Legislative Body, in General Assembly convened, conceiving themselves Representatives of the great Body of People at large, and that they cannot make any Innovations in a Constitution which has been agreed upon, and the Compact settled between the Governors and Governed, without the express Consent of the Freemen at large, by their own Voices individually taken in Town-Meetings assembled : Wherefore, for the Purpose aforesaid, and for submitting the said Constitution for the United States to the Consideration of the Freemen of this State :

BE it Enacted by this General Assembly, and by the Authority thereof it is hereby Enacted, That the Fourth Monday in March inst. be, and the same is hereby appointed, the Day for all the Freemen and Freeholders within this State, to convene in their respective Towns, in Town-Meetings assembled, and to deliberate upon, and determine each Individual (who hath a Right by Law to vote for the Choice of General Officers) by himself by Poll, whether the said Constitution for the United States shall be adopted or negatived.

AND be it further Enacted by the Authority aforesaid, That the Town-Clerks in the respective Towns shall forthwith issue their Warrants, for the convening of the Freemen and Freeholders to meet, on said Fourth Monday of March inst. at such Place where the Town-Meetings are usually holden : And the same shall be directed to the Town-Serjeants and Constables of the respective Towns, who shall cause Notifications to be set up in the most public Places of Resort within such Towns ; and also shall repair to the usual Place of Abode of the Freemen and Freeholders in such Town, and give them Notice of the Meeting aforesaid, for the Purpose aforesaid. The said Town-Serjeants and Constables to have particular Districts pointed out to them, to warn the Freemen and Freeholders, so as not to interfere with each other's District, that all the Freemen and Freeholders may, if possible, have Notice and attend accordingly. And upon the Convention of said Freemen, they shall appoint a Moderator, who shall regulate such Meeting ; and the Voices of the Freemen and Freeholders shall be taken by Yeas and Nays, and the Town-Clerk of each Town shall register the Name of each and every Freeman and Freeholder, with the Yea or Nay, as he shall respectively give his Voice aloud, in open Town-Meeting, and shall keep the Original in his Office, and shall make out a true and fair certified Copy of the Register aforesaid, with the Yeas and Nays of each and every Person thereon, and carefully seal the same up, and direct it to the General Assembly, to be holden by Adjournment, at East-Greenwich, in the County of Kent, on the last Monday of March inst. and deliver the same to One of the Representatives of such Town, or other careful Person, who will take Charge of the same, to be delivered to the said General Assembly, then and there to be opened, that the Sentiments of the People may be known respecting the same.

AND it is further Enacted by the Authority aforesaid, That in Case it shall so happen that the said Fourth Monday of March inst. shall prove to be stormy or boisterous Weather, so that the Freemen and Freeholders in general cannot conveniently attend, the said Town-Meeting may adjourn, from Day to Day, not exceeding three Days, so that the Voices of the People may be taken.

AND it is further Enacted by the Authority aforesaid, That the Secretary shall forthwith transmit to each Town-Clerk of the respective Towns within this State a Copy of this Act.

A true Copy :

Witness, HENRY WARD, *Secretary.*

[PROVIDENCE : Printed by BENNETT WHEELER.]

This 1788 call for a popular referendum on the ratification of the Constitution made Rhode Island unique among the thirteen original states. In the referendum, those who voted (mostly Antifederalists) rejected the Constitution by a margin of 2,711 to 243.

New Perspectives on the Federal Constitution: A Rhode Islander's View

12

This commentary was written in July 1988.

Literally at the eleventh hour, I accepted an invitation from the Society for Historians of the Early American Republic (SHEAR) to substitute for my colleague and coauthor John Kaminski in critiquing three papers prepared for a panel entitled "The Federal Constitution: New Perspectives." The occasion was the tenth annual meeting of SHEAR, held at Sturbridge and Worcester, Massachusetts, from July 21 through July 23, 1988. One essay, written by J. Edwin Hendricks, dealt with North Carolina's role in the framing and adoption of the federal Constitution; a second, by Ruth Wallis Herndon, suggested an economic interpretation of ratification in Rhode Island by examining the March 1788 popular referendum on the Constitution; a third, by Roger H. Brown, a leading historian of the Early National Period, attempted to show the influence of Scholasticism, or "faculty psychology," on the thought of the Constitution's supporters (i.e., Federalist leaders).

These essays, each about twenty pages in length, came to me on the day before the panel convened. From 10:00 P.M. that night through the early morning hours, I prepared my remarks. When the two-hour session ended at 11:00 A.M., I took a stroll with my wife Gail through Sturbridge Village, where the session was held, sat down on a bench, and, to her embarrassment, immediately fell asleep. What follows is the result of a good night's work.

I have included my panel commentary in this volume because Herndon's essay dealt exclusively with Rhode Island, Hendricks's paper was analyzed in tandem with the Rhode Island story, and Brown's treatise dealt with a philosophical system that is identified more with Providence College and its curriculum than with any other undergraduate program in America.

74

WHEN FIRST INVITED TO COMMENT on these papers, I was somewhat apprehensive, because a commentator's role at these sessions is often like that of the TV analyst who appears after a major political address and tells you what you just saw and heard—such an attempt is usually an exercise in redundancy. I hope I can avoid such a repeat performance. Another problem I face is that these 9:00 A.M. sessions are the first events of this annual meeting that involve commentators, so if I'm too negative and critical in my role, I have to worry about running into the presenters (at dinner, on the bus, or maybe in a dark alley) during two full days of events.

If this were the final session at 3:00 P.M. to 5:00 P.M. on Saturday, I could be really nasty, then slip out the side door and be back in Providence by six o'clock! Given the timing, however, I have no choice but to be complimentary. But the excellence of the papers herein presented also helps me to be effusive in my praise.

Using the historically proper *a posteriori* approach, I will first comment on the individual state essays and then consider the more general and theoretical analysis of Professor Roger H. Brown.

The states of North Carolina and Rhode Island are a natural tandem, especially in any examination of Antifederalism, so a comparison between these two holdouts can shed some light on the most formidable objections posed to the new federal Constitution. Professor J. Edwin Hendricks's essay on the Old North State is well developed, cogent, and persuasively argued. In fact, a historian who prizes the quality of detachment might even complain that it is passionately argued, with the kind of upbeat presentation that I use when I speak to local audiences about Rhode Island and the Union in my capacity as chairman of my state's Bicentennial Foundation. Far be it for me, therefore, to fault a North Carolinian—even if he is a professor—for writing what one might call an *apologia pro patria sua.*

I have just edited a new book on the Constitution's adoption with John Kaminski, the director of the Center for the Study of the American Constitution at the University of Wisconsin and chief editor of the *Documentary History of the Ratification of the Constitution*. (In fact, he was this panel's choice as commentator, but John had to travel a thousand miles, and I was just next door. So at his suggestion I was brought out of the bullpen in the final inning to deliver this pitch.)

Our book is entitled *The Constitution and the States: The Role of the Original Thirteen in the Framing and Adoption of the Federal Constitution* (1988). Each state is analyzed in a chapter-length essay by a specialist in that state's constitutional history. Alan Watson of the University of North Carolina at Wilmington wrote our North Carolina chapter. In 1984 Professor Hendricks wrote an essay entitled "Journey to the Federal Union" in a book coedited by Watson titled *The North Carolina Experience*. Between the two of them they have left little of importance or prominence unsaid concerning their subject.

Professor Hendricks's view, as expressed here, is more striking for its emphasis on North Carolina's prominent role in the development of a federal Union and for convincingly demonstrating (contrary to the assertions of Forrest McDonald and others) that North Carolina was quite willing to join the Union—and even made preparations for such an eventuality by its actions on tariffs and paper money—just as soon as its concerns about states' rights and individual liberties had been addressed.

Conversely, Professor Watson, while agreeing with Hendricks, is more thorough in his treatment of the social, ideological, cultural, economic, and geographic differences between Federalists and Antifederalists in North Carolina. Federalists, asserts Watson, drew their main support from the lawyer-merchant-planter elite; they exhibited a commercial-urban orientation; they had a more cosmopolitan outlook, often fashioned by military service in the Continental army, experience in Congress, or business and educational contacts beyond state bounds; they believed in the right of a natural aristocracy to speak for the people; and they emphasized the importance of an energetic government to provide order and stability.

Antifederalists drew their main support from the small subsistence farmers; they exhibited an agrarian outlook; they were localistic and parochial, scornful of worldly pursuits, suspicious of higher education, and resentful of elitist rule and government too far removed from direct popular control; they were less nationalistic and more jealous of state sovereignty; and they were concerned less for stability than for individual rights.

The commercial-minded-versus-agrarian-minded dichotomy posited by Jackson Turner Main and Lee Benson fits the North Carolina situation. So does the conclusion of Gordon Wood, who contends that the struggle between Federalists and Antifederalists "represented a broad social division between those who believed in the rights of a natural aristocracy to speak for the people and those who did not."

Professor Hendricks is factually sound when dealing with North Carolina—at least to my knowledge—but his references to other states contain some lapses. (1) North Carolina, with 429,442 persons, was not third in population in 1790; it was fourth behind Virginia (821,287), Massachusetts (475,327), and Pennsylvania (434,373). (2) New York was not absent from the first Senate; it was represented in that body by former Massachusetts delegate Rufus King and by Philip Schuyler. (3) Rhode Island ratified on May 29, 1790, not in June.

Further, the paper emphasizes the differences between Rhode Island and North Carolina without noting the similarities. For example, both states had been settled by religious or socioeconomic outcasts: to New England Puritans, Rhode Island became the "moral sewer"; to aristocratic South Carolina and Virginia, the Old North State became "the vale of humility between two mountains of conceit." Both states acquired reputations for individualism and self-reliance; both played leading roles in the movement towards independence (North Carolina's Halifax Resolves of April 12, 1776, were followed shortly by Rhode Island's Renunciation of Allegiance on May 4); both were concerned with state sovereignty; both jealously guarded individual liberty. In both, agrarian control of the state legislature had an adverse effect on ratification; both exhibited a commercial-versus-agrarian division during the ratification contest; both held out until the new government went into operation so it could be observed and tested; both were vilified for their dilatory tactics; both were threatened by the federal government with economic coercion; both proposed amendments to guarantee individual rights; and, when they finally joined the Union, both promptly became its staunch supporters with nary a regret.

Our next paper shifts the focus directly to Rhode Island—or "Rogues' Island," as the Federalists called it. Whereas Dr. Hendricks's essay is macrocosmic, Professor Ruth Wallis Herndon's paper is microcosmic, which is perhaps appropriate when dealing with a microparadise like Rhode Island. In the new book that I edited with John Kaminski, I composed the Rhode Island chapter, a comprehensive account written in the traditional narrative style.

Professor Herndon has chosen to tell a different story. She focuses on a single event—the popular constitutional referendum of March 24, 1788—the only plebiscite conducted on the federal Constitution. The voting lists from the election, states Herndon, "are the only known record of the opinions of common people concerning the federal Constitution." She employs the quantitative approach of social-science history. As I looked at her supplementary tables, equations, and statistical summaries, replete with their "variables," "means," "outliers," and other unfamiliar phrases, I felt Lincolnesque, for it was beyond my power to add or to detract from what she did here!

I finished graduate school at Notre Dame in 1963, the year after my good friend and neighbor Carl Bridenbaugh, professor emeritus of history at Brown University, delivered his presidential address to the American Historical Association. In his oration he lamented that some young, apostate historians had begun to "worship at the shrine of the bitch goddess QUANTIFICATION." Twenty-six years later that goddess is at the center of the historical pantheon, and those traditionalists, like Bridenbaugh and me, have been cast into the exterior darkness. In my other career—as a practicing politician—I also disparage statistics. I often state that politicians and economists use them as the drunk uses the lamppost: more for support than for light.

Despite these professions of ignorance—especially as to method—I can try to offer some suggestions, or at least pose some questions to Professor Herndon.

Essentially, this case study attempts to ascertain the economic status of those Rhode Island freemen who voted in the 1788 referendum. Specific attention is directed towards discovering the real-versus-personal-property holdings of those who cast ballots.

Charles Beard, in his provocative *An Economic Interpretation of the Constitution*, addressed this issue in 1913. One of the basic premises in his hypothesis was that there existed a national division between the holders of real property, who were generally Antifederalist, and the holders of personal property, who generally supported the Constitution because it advanced their economic interests. Robert Brown (in 1956), Forrest McDonald (in 1958), and a host of state monographs convincingly disproved this generalization. Although Beard can be justly praised for inspiring decades of research on the Constitution, his specific premises have met their demise. Is it productive for Herndon to exhume them? Or should we build upon the newer wisdom as expounded by Jackson T. Main, Robert Rutland, Forrest McDonald, and Gordon Wood?

It also seems to me that there are problems with the model—a deficiency certainly beyond the control of Professor Herndon— for craftsmen are only as good as their tools and materials. The 1788 referendum was boycotted by many Federalists. The total turnout was less than 3,000, while 4,170 voted in the previous gubernatorial elections in April 1787. About 850 of these missing electors lived in Providence and Newport; the remainder were scattered throughout such commercial towns as Warren, Westerly, Bristol, and Jamestown. In each of these communities the voter turnout was 21 percent or less, according to Professor Herndon's tables.

Further, only six of the thirty towns were susceptible to analysis, says she, and only four of these show a significant difference of means between "yea" and "nay" voters. Finally, the ten-year span in the tax records she used probably skews the results. Beard was taken to task for using 1791 Treasury records—a four-year discrepancy (I know a person in this room who filed for bankruptcy in 1977 and had a net worth of over $3 million by 1988).

Much attention was paid to the Bay town of Tiverton (which soon thereafter sent Captain Robert Gray to Boston and thence to the Oregon Country in his flagship *Columbia*). Here we are told that "those who favored ratification were, on the whole, large landowners who also possessed significant personal estates as well." Such a finding indicates to me (and to Professor Jackson Turner Main) that well-to-do merchants and commercial farmers supported the Constitution and small subsistence farmers opposed it. That division, rather than real property versus personal property, seems more appropriate.

Professor Herndon concludes that "the Rhode Island data supply hard evidence that bolsters an economic interpretation of the Constitution." I disagree with such monocausationism. In my 1977 book *Democracy in Decline: Rhode Island's Constitutional Development, 1776–1841*, I commented as follows concerning the treatment given to the Rhode Island ratifying convention by Beard on one side and his critics Robert Brown and Forrest McDonald on the other:

> Robert E. Brown's *Charles Beard and the Constitution* (Princeton, N.J., 1956) is a work which casts grave doubts on Beard's general hypothesis but sheds little light on Rhode Island ratification. Forrest McDonald's analysis of the *delegates* to the ratifying convention shows that neither party *in the convention* could reasonably be described as an "agrarian party" or a "debtors' faction." Also, the *delegates*, regardless of their stand, "held approximately the same amounts of the same kinds of securities, and it would appear that there was no line of cleavage between public creditors and non creditors." Finally, nearly equal percentages of both parties *in the convention* borrowed paper in 1786. McDonald, *We the People*, pp. 339–44. I have emphasized that McDonald analyzed the economic interests of the *delegates* only, because I feel that much sharper differences would be apparent if the rank and file of both factions were compared. While a simple class interpretation cannot be sustained, there is no doubt

that most merchants, professional men, mechanics, artisans, and other urban dwellers supported the Constitution, and most of the subsistence farmers in the remote rural towns opposed it. James Varnum's 1787 observation that "the wealth and resources of this state are chiefly in the possession of the well-affected" (the Federalists) was not far from the mark.

On this one basis of division, Professor Herndon and I—though we traveled different roads—ended our journey not far apart. But there were also social, cultural, educational, moral, ideological, and personal influences that affected Rhode Island and the other twelve states. Any satisfactory analysis of the constitutional struggle must embrace them all!

The final essay under review, Professor Roger Brown's "The Framers and the Improvability of Man," in my opinion is imaginative, logical, and very persuasive. His choice of quotations to explicate his thesis greatly strengthens his argument—namely, that a significant number of the Founding Fathers looked to an energetic central government to effect a salutary reformation in human conduct. They held this belief in human improvement, says Brown, because of their exposure to an educational system that stressed "faculty psychology," a variant of a philosophical approach called Scholasticism.

I have no quarrel with any of Brown's contentions. In fact, I have been waiting for twenty-nine years, since I first read Richard Hofstader's iconoclastic essay "The Founding Fathers: An Age of Realism" in *The American Political Tradition and the Men Who Made It*, for someone to come and tell me it isn't so! Hofstader, as you recall, depicted the framers as undemocratic pessimists who had little hope or expectation of reforming or improving the common man.

I herewith offer some observations that may expand or strengthen Brown's impressive theory and suggest a possible influence on the development of what Brown terms "faculty psychology" and its belief in the amelioration of man through learning.

About half of the Philadelphia delegates went to college, an extraordinary proportion when compared to the college attendees among the general populace. The principal universities they attended—for America had only nine—were the College of New Jersey (Princeton), King's College (Columbia), College of Philadelphia (University of Pennsylvania), William and Mary, Harvard, and Yale. Some, like James Wilson and Richard Dobbs Spaight, were schooled abroad, especially in the Scottish universities mentioned by Professor Brown.

As I read this essay, with its emphasis on "reason and conscience" (or, as I was taught, "intellect and will") gaining control over man's passions (or his concupiscible and irascible appetites), and as I read about the role of habit in the formation of virtue, I harkened back to my Dominican training at Providence College in Thomistic psychology, a course that was basically a philosophic analysis of the nature of man. The school of philosophy I studied in depth at Providence College is called Scholasticism. It traces its ancestry from Aristotle through such Christian exponents as Boethius, Erigina, St. Anselm, and the so-called schoolmen of the thirteenth century, the greatest of whom was Thomas Aquinas. The basic goal of these Scholastic philosophers was to unify philosophy and theology in order to discover and demonstrate the harmony of natural and supernatural truth.

It was once thought that the reign of Scholasticism was ended by the Renaissance and Reformation—that it went out of vogue at the end of the so-called Middle Ages. In actuality, however, Scholasticism continued to be the philosophic teaching of some European and all American colleges down to the early nineteenth century. A somewhat obscure and forgotten monograph by James J. Walsh entitled *Education of the Founding Fathers of the Republic: Scholasticism in the Colonial Colleges* (Fordham University Press, 1935) documents this fact beyond reasonable doubt.

Without detailing the colonial American college curriculum, suffice it to say that moral philosophy (ethics) was its capstone and faculty psychology was an integral part of that branch of learning. Moral philosophy, or ethics, was usually reserved for seniors; it dominated the senior curriculum, and it was often taught by the college president or some preeminent professor. Dr. John Witherspoon (mentioned by Professor Brown) taught it from 1768 to 1794 at Princeton, a school that sent nine delegates to the Philadelphia Convention.

82

Samuel Johnson, the father of Connecticut's signer William S. Johnson, was also a Scholastic philosopher. He shaped the teaching of moral philosophy at Columbia, where such founders as Hamilton, Jay, and Gouverneur Morris studied. William Johnson, the chairman of the convention's Committee on Style, became president of Columbia in the 1790s, following in his father's footsteps.

William Smith presided at Pennsylvania, where Benjamin Franklin was chairman of the board. Smith fashioned a curriculum founded on Scholasticism, which emphasized moral philosophy and ethics. Among its products was North Carolina's Hugh Williamson and Thomas Mifflin, a Pennsylvania signer and governor of the Keystone State.

At William and Mary, Professor William Small taught ethics and moral philosophy to Thomas Jefferson, John Marshall, and a generation of other Virginia statesmen. Yale, Brown (then called Rhode Island College), and Harvard, which produced John Adams and Rufus King, had similar course requirements rooted in the Scholastic tradition.

Perhaps it would be fruitful to examine not only the role of faculty psychology but the influence of the entire system of Scholastic philosophy on the founders and on Federalist theory regarding the importance of a strong government to restrain popular excesses and promote civic virtue and the efficacy of education to produce "a reformation of manners." Such an inquiry might reveal that education as well as ideology distinguished Federalist spokesmen from most of their opponents, providing yet another glimpse into the multifaceted minds of the Founding Fathers.

RHODE-ISLAND and PROVIDENCE PLANTATIONS united to the Great *AMERICAN FAMILY.*

* * * * * * * * * * * *

PROVIDENCE, *Monday, May 31, 1790.*

SATURDAY Night, at Eleven o'Clock, an Exprefs arrived in Town from Newport, with the important Intelligence, that the CONVENTION OF THIS STATE had ratified the CONSTITUTION OF THE UNITED STATES.

The Queftion, "*Shall the Conftitution be adopted, or not ?*" was taken on Saturday, about Five o'Clock, P. M.—when the Affirmative was carried by a Majority of *Two*, Thirty-four Members voting for, and Thirty-two againft it.

This pleafing and moft interefting Event was immediately announced here by the Ringing of Bells, and firing two federal Salutes—one from the Artillery on Federal Hill—and another from the Ship Warren, Capt. Sheldon, lately arrived from India.

RATIFICATION *of the* CONSTITUTION *of the* UNITED STATES, *by the* CONVENTION *of the State of Rhode-Ifland and Providence Plantations.*

WE the Delegates of the people of the State of Rhode-Ifland and Providence Plantations, duly elected and met in Convention, having maturely confidered the Conftitution for the United States of America, agreed to on the 17th day of September, in the year 1787, by the Convention then affembled at Philadelphia, in the Commonwealth of Pennfylvania (a copy whereof precedes thefe prefents) and having alfo ferioufly and deliberately confidered the prefent fituation of this State, DO Declare and Make Known——

[*Here is inferted the Bill of Rights, as propofed by the Convention at their Seffion at South-King ftown, and publifhed in the Providence Gazette of March 13.*]

UNDER thefe impreffions, and declaring that the rights aforefaid cannot be abridged or violated, and that the explanations aforefaid are confiftent with the faid Conftitution, and in confidence that the amendments hereafter mentioned will receive an early and mature confideration, and fpeedily become a part thereof: WE, the faid Delegates, in the name and in the behalf of the People of the State of Rhode-Ifland and Providence Plantations, DO, by thefe prefents, ASSENT TO and RATIFY the faid Conftitution. In full confidence, neverthelefs, that until the faid amendments fhall be ratified, purfuant to the fifth article of the aforefaid Conftitution, the militia of this State will not be continued in fervice out of this State for a longer term than fix weeks, without the confent of the Legiflature thereof; that the Congrefs will not make or alter any regulation in this State, refpecting the times, places and manner, of holding elections for Senators or Reprefentatives, unlefs the Legiflature of this State fhall neglect or refufe to make laws or regulations for the purpofe, or from any circumftance be incapable of making the fame; and that in thofe cafes fuch power will only be exercifed until the Legiflature of this State fhall make provifion in the premifes; that the Congrefs will not lay direct taxes within this State, but when the monies arifing from the impoft, tonnage and excife, fhall be infufficient for the public exigences, nor until Congrefs fhall firft have made a requifition upon this State to affefs, levy and pay, the amount of fuch requifition, made agreeably to the cenfus fixed in the faid Conftitution, in fuch way and manner as the Legiflature of this State fhall judge beft; and that Congrefs will not lay any capitation or poll tax.

DONE in Convention, at Newport, in the State of Rhode-Ifland and Providence Plantations, the twenty-ninth day of May, in the year of our Lord one thoufand feven hundred and ninety.

By Order of the Convention,
DANIEL OWEN, *Prefident.*
Atteft. DANIEL UPDIKE, *Secretary.*

AND the Convention do, in the name and on behalf of the people of the State of Rhode-Ifland and Providence Plantations, enjoin it upon the Senators and Representative or Reprefentatives, which may be elected to reprefent this State in Congrefs, to exert all their influence and ufe all reafonable means to obtain a ratification of the following amendments to the faid Conftitution, in the manner prefcribed therein; and that Congrefs, in all laws to be paffed in the mean time, will conform to the fpirit of the faid amendments as far as the Conftitution will admit.

[*Here are inferted the amendments recommended at the former feffion, publifhed in the Providence Gazette of March 13—alfo the following additional amendments, viz.*]

1. That the feveral State Legiflatures fhall have power to recall their federal Senators, and to appoint others in their ftead.

2. That Congrefs fhall not erect any Company of Merchants with exclufive advantages of commerce.

3. That Congrefs fhall have the power of eftablifhing an uniform rule of inhabitancy, or fettlement of the poor, throughout the United States.

4. That whenever two members of either Houfe fhall on any queftion call for the yeas and nays, the fame fhall be entered on the journals of the refpective Houfes.

The Convention likewife paffed the following RESOLVES, *nemine contradicente.*

1. That the amendments to the Conftitution of the United States, agreed to by Congrefs in March, 1789, except the fecond of faid amendments, recommended to the Legiflature of this State for their ratification, purfuant to the fifth article of faid Conftitution.

2. That the thanks of the Convention be prefented to the Prefident, for the candour and impartiality with which he hath difcharged the office of Prefident.

3. That the thanks of the Convention be prefented to the Reverend Clergy who have officiated at this Convention.

DONE in Convention, at Newport, in the State of Rhode-Ifland and Providence Plantations, the twenty-ninth day of May, in the year of our Lord one thoufand feven hundred and ninety.

By Order of the Convention,
DANIEL OWEN, *Prefident.*
Atteft. DANIEL UPDIKE, *Secretary.*

Yefterday Evening the Delegates for this Town arrived from Newport, and on their landing were welcomed by a Difcharge of Thirteen Cannon.—Some further Demonftrations of Joy are expected to take Place.

[Printed by J. CARTER.]

This broadside, printed by Federalist editor John Carter, proclaimed Rhode Island's belated entry into the Union after the state had existed for nearly fifteen months as an independent republic.

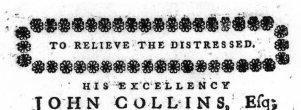

TO RELIEVE THE DISTRESSED.

HIS EXCELLENCY
JOHN COLLINS, Esq;
GOVERNOR.

THE HONORABLE
DANIEL OWEN, Esq;
DEPUTY-GOVERNOR.

1. JOHN MATTHEWSON, Esq; Assistant.
2. JOSEPH STANTON, jun. Esq; Assistant;
3. JOHN WILLIAMS, Esq; Assistant.
4. RICHARD SEARLE, Esq; Assistant.
5. JAMES ARNOLD, Esq; Assistant.
6. WILLIAM HAMMOND, Esq; Assistant.
7. GIDEON CLARKE, Esq; Assistant.
8. THOMAS G. HAZARD, Esq; Assistant;
9. JOHN COOKE, Esq; Assistant.
10. OLIVER DURFEE, Esq; Assistant.

HENRY WARD, Esq; Secretary.
WILLIAM CHANNING, Esq; Attorney-Gen.
JOSEPH CLARKE, Esq; General-Treasurer.

Delegates to represent the State in Congress.

Honorable JAMES M. VARNUM, Esq; 1st.
NATHAN MILLER, Esq; 2d.
GEORGE CHAMPLIN, Esq; 3d.
PELEG ARNOLD, Esq; 4th.

The dominance of the Country party, whose statewide officers are listed on this ballot, or prox, contributed to the strength of Antifederalism in Rhode Island from 1786 to 1790.

Written in 1990 and delivered on May 29 of that year at a formal dinner celebrating the bicentennial of statehood, this address was placed in the *Congressional Record* by Senator Clairborne Pell, who attended the event.

MR. PELL. Mr. President, on May 29, 1990, the State of Rhode Island observed the two hundredth anniversary of its ratification of the Constitution of the United States, marking also its entry into statehood.

The occasion was marked by a full day of colorful events throughout the state, including a reenactment of the debate over ratification of the Constitution at the Colony House in Newport, where the ratifying convention was assembled in May 1790, and concluding with a statehood dinner at Rosecliff on Newport's Bellevue Avenue.

Although the Constitution is today hailed throughout the world as one of the great creative acts of government, there were spirited debates over the provisions of the proposal in a number of the former British colonies before, one by one, they agreed to ratify the Constitution and join the new nation. Nowhere, however, was opposition to the Constitution more spirited, and ratification longer delayed, than in Rhode Island.

At the statehood dinner Dr. Patrick Conley, chairman of the Rhode Island Bicentennial Foundation, delivered a "Bicentennial Reflection" recalling Rhode Island's refusal to participate in the drafting of the Constitution, its strong resistance to ratification, and the critical view taken of Rhode Island by residents of the other new states. Dr. Conley's address, entitled "Were We Really Rogues' Island?" was both entertaining and a vivid reminder of the independent spirit that dominated among Rhode Islanders two hundred years ago. I ask unanimous consent that the text of his address be printed in the *Record* for the benefit of my colleagues and in observance of the Rhode Island bicentennial.

There being no objection, the remarks were ordered to be printed in the Congressional Record, *as follows:*

THE REMARKS OF DR. PATRICK T. CONLEY

May 29, 1990, is the two hundredth anniversary of Rhode Island's entrance into the present American Union. It marks the bicentennial of our ratification of the federal Constitution. Can Rhode Island commemorate this momentous event with head held high, or is our boycott of the Federal Convention and our position as the last of the original thirteen to ratify still cause for embarrassment?

Let us look at the historical record. As I have shown in my booklet *First in War, Last in Peace: Rhode Island and the Constitution, 1786–1790*, the Rhode Island Assembly defeated three attempts by its minority members to send delegates to the Philadelphia Convention, thus making us the only absent state. Then Rhode Island defied the instructions of the Founding Fathers by holding a popular referendum on the Constitution. Adding insult to injury, we voted down that now-hallowed document in March 1788 by a margin of more than 11 to 1. During the ratification period our legislature rejected at least eleven attempts by the Constitution's supporters (called Federalists) to convene a ratifying convention, and when we did finally assemble such a body in March 1790, the new nation had been in operation for nearly a year without us. That convention, held in South Kingstown, proposed thirty-six amendments to the Constitution (to this day all the states have managed only twenty-six alterations), and the defiant conclave adjourned.

In May 1790, bowing to federal political, military, and economic pressure upon our tiny independent maritime republic, the recalcitrant convention reconvened in Newport and grudgingly approved the nation's new basic law, 34 votes to 32 — the narrowest margin of any state. It did so with Providence threatening to secede from Rhode Island if ratification were further delayed.

Small wonder that the Constitution's supporters denounced us. To them we were Rogues' Island, home of the dishonest debtor (a reference to our paper-money issue of 1786). We were also the "Quintessence of Villainy" and an example of "democracy run rampant." For the Federalists the state symbolized the danger to order posed by popularly controlled state legislatures. From the outset, when the *Massachusetts Centinel* described Rhode Island's absence from the Grand Convention as a "joyous rather than a grievous circumstance," to the end of the ratification struggle, when some proposed the state's dismemberment and absorption by the surrounding states, Rhode Island endured repeated insult. Even the temperate James Madison found us exasperating. "Nothing can exceed the wickedness and folly which continue to rule there," he exclaimed. "All sense of character as well as of right have been obliterated." President George Washington agreed, and he snubbed the state when he made his triumphal tour of the Union in 1789.

The most eloquent censure of all came from neighboring Connecticut in the form of a poem called the "Anarchiad, 1786–1787," penned by a group of literati who styled themselves the Connecticut Wits. Striking a derisive note in its opening lines — "Hail! realm of rogues, renown'd for fraud and guile, / All hail; ye knav'vries of yon little isle" — this long satire ended with an admonition: "The wiser race, the snares of law to shun, / Like Lot from Sodom, from Rhode Island run." In those days political critics played hardball!

Was this litany of shame deserved? Were the Federalists correct in their assessment of our microparadise? The answer to these questions, I would argue, is no. Although Rhode Island was physically absent from Philadelphia for the drafting of what the English prime minister William Gladstone once called "the most remarkable work known to me in modern times to have been produced by the human intellect...in its application to political affairs," and although we were notorious in our reluctance to ratify the much-praised Constitution, our state's contribution to the nation's basic law was far from negligible, and our opposition to it was, in some respects, both prophetic and defensible.

The verdict of history often favors the winners. Lost to all but historians is the fact that the Constitution in its infancy met staunch opposition from a group called the Antifederalists. These critics were actually more numerous in 1787–88 than the Constitution's Federalist supporters. In Rhode Island the Antifederalists were the strongest of all. The Constitution is not a perfect document today, and it was much less perfect when it emerged from the Philadelphia Convention in 1787. Antifederalists accentuated the negative.

Rhode Island, a bastion of Antifederalism, took several key positions on the proposed basic law which were meritorious (or at least justifiable), even when considered in retrospect. First, Rhode Island perceived that the new central government would be much more powerful than the one that then existed under our first national constitution, the Articles of Confederation. As a small state with a long tradition of autonomy and self-government, we feared a loss of our state's rights under the new regime. Prior to the Revolution, Rhode Island pamphleteers such as Stephen Hopkins and Silas Downer had helped to develop a theory of federalism in opposition to the attempt by the mother country to centralize power in Parliament and London. They argued that sovereignty was dual and divisible (not unitary and consolidated, as the English claimed), and that the colonial legislatures were sovereign in their local, internal affairs. This federal concept, which divided sovereignty between the central government and the constituent states, was allegedly a basic theory underlying the Constitution.

Most Rhode Islanders, however, noted the absence of effective checks on the growth of national power and feared that the new central government would aggrandize itself at the expense of the states. Rhode Island demanded a guarantee (now called the Tenth Amendment) to protect the states from such encroachment. Despite the enactment of that caveat—"The powers not delegated to the United States by the Constitution, nor prohibited by it to the States, are reserved to the States respectively, or to the people"—

the central government has now realized Rhode Island's worst fears. As we said in 1790, the national government under the Constitution possesses the tendency to swallow up the state and to become extravagant, impersonal, bureaucratic, unresponsive, and a burden to the taxpayers. As a recent successor to George Washington was forced to admit, the federal government is not the solution but the problem. Rhode Island's wary and prophetic Antifederalists have been vindicated. The Constitution has, indeed, been inimical to true, or dual, federalism.

Another concern of Rhode Island in 1790 was that the Constitution created a strong, remote central government without protecting the individual and his rights from abuse by that government. Antifederalists in the ratifying conventions of more than half the states proposed amendments to the Constitution to protect individual liberties or states' rights from the arbitrary exercise of power by the new national establishment. Rhode Island, with its thirty-six suggested safeguards, was the most prolific (though many of her amendments were based upon earlier formulations by states such as Massachusetts, South Carolina, New Hampshire, Virginia, New York, and North Carolina).

The Antifederalist concern for the protection of individual liberty gave rise to the first ten amendments to the Constitution. Ratified in 1791, they became known collectively as the Bill of Rights. Rhode Island, along with North Carolina, had the luxury of debating the merits of the Constitution and the Bill of Rights simultaneously, because both North Carolina and Rhode Island were still outside the Union when the First Congress sent these precepts to the states for approval in September 1789.

The proposal of a Bill of Rights was instrumental in lessening Rhode Island's opposition to the Constitution. When the Founding Fathers addressed our long-standing concern for individual liberty, Rhode Island relented. On June 11, 1790, our General Assembly approved the Bill of Rights (the May ratifying convention was not empowered to do so), and Rhode Island's position was vindicated once again.

Despite its absence from the initial session of the First Congress, Rhode Island in fact exerted an influence on the formulation of the Bill of Rights, especially the First Amendment. Founded by Roger Williams as "a lively experiment" in religious liberty and separation of church and state, Rhode Island was the only New England colony without an established (i.e., tax-supported) church, and true to the wishes of its founder and its charter, it never restricted freedom of worship. In 1789 Rhode Island, the "home of the otherwise-minded," was still a shining example of religious freedom. Although the Virginia Enlightenment tradition, rooted in natural law, was the most direct influence on the Free Exercise and Establishment clauses of the First Amendment, most historians (myself included) believe that the First Amendment's religion clause also emanated from Roger William's biblically based Rhode Island system and from our state's long experience with such freedoms. Here Rhode Island led the way.

Another factor in Rhode Island's rejection of the Constitution was slavery. On this issue we executed the greatest about-face since Saul of Tarsus became the Apostle Paul. During the colonial era Rhode Island merchants led those of all other colonies in their slave-trading activities. In his recent book *The Notorious Triangle*, historian Jay Coughtry shows that Rhode Islanders brought to America more than 70 percent of those Africans who came to these shores in bondage. By the mid-eighteenth century, Rhode Island had an elaborate slave system on the relatively spacious estates of South County—farms run by a group of landed gentry called the Narragansett Planters and based on a slave code resembling that of Virginia.

But the Revolution and the sentiments of the Declaration of Independence brought a change in our attitude towards slavery. So did the conversion of Rhode Island's large and influential Quaker community to abolitionism. The liberation movement began in 1778, when the General Assembly passed a wartime enlistment law stipulating that those slaves (whether "negro," "mulatto," or "Indian") who enlisted in Rhode Island's "colored regiment" would be granted freedom upon completion of their term of duty. A 1779 law forbade the sale of Rhode Island slaves outside the state without their consent.

The Emancipation Act of 1784 was the most significant of the several Revolution-inspired statutes relating to blacks. With a preface invoking the sentiments of English political theorist John Locke—namely, that "all men are entitled to life, liberty and property" (but presumably not property in men)—the measure provided for gradual manumission by giving freedom to all children born to slave mothers after March 1, 1784.

91

Despite this progress in Rhode Island, our local opponents of slavery realized that the Philadelphia Convention (in deference, especially, to South Carolina) had compromised on this issue, and that the Constitution thrice gave implied assent to this evil institution through the clauses on representation, fugitives, and the slave trade. In particular, the twenty-year prohibition on federal legislation banning the foreign slave traffic was a concession too great for many Rhode Islanders to accept, perhaps because they wished to atone for past sins.

Only five weeks after the adjournment of the Philadelphia conclave, the General Assembly passed an act, initiated by the influential and irrepressible Quakers, prohibiting any Rhode Island citizen from engaging in the slave trade. In vigorous language, this statute termed the nefarious traffic "inconsistent with justice, and the principles of humanity, as well as the laws of nature, and that more enlightened and civilized sense of freedom which has of late prevailed." A constitution that gave temporary protection to this trade was not an instrument to be warmly embraced.

Thus the state's antislavery contingent took refuge in Antifederalism, and during the critical year 1790 this connection nearly thwarted ratification. Fortunately, however, there were some abolitionist leaders who began to see the difficulties inherent in Rhode Island's continued rejection of the Constitution. One such man was the influential Quaker Moses Brown of the famous mercantile family. Despite some initial misgivings, he embraced the Federalist cause by 1790. Early in that fateful year Brown toured the state, talking with Friends at the various monthly meetings in an attempt to overcome their opposition. His campaign seems to have met with some success, but the antislavery objections to the Constitution were by no means dispelled when the March session of the ratifying convention assembled.

Slavery engendered much discussion and debate at this South Kingstown meeting. In fact, the slave-trade provision of the Constitution provoked such opposition that an amendment was specifically proposed and approved exhorting Congress to ban the traffic immediately. Rhode Island was the only state to suggest such an amendment to the federal Constitution during the ratification struggle.

As we know, it took the federal statutory ban on the foreign slave trade (effective January 1, 1808) and, ultimately, the Civil War and the Thirteenth, Fourteenth, and Fifteenth Amendments to bring the Constitution in line with the course urged by most Rhode Islanders in the 1780s (slave traders like John Brown and James De Wolf, of course, excepted). Here again, who can deny the merit of Rhode Island's Antifederalism?

Another aspect of Rhode Island's opposition to the Constitution stemmed from the fact that Article III gave the new federal judiciary the power to entertain suits by an individual against a state. An amendment to remove such cases from federal jurisdiction was proposed by the first session of Rhode Island's ratifying convention in March 1790, but the proposal was ignored by the First Congress. However, when the U.S. Supreme Court accepted jurisdiction of a suit against a state by a citizen of another state in the case of *Chisholm* v. *Georgia* in 1793, there was such an angry reaction that the Eleventh Amendment was immediately proposed by an overwhelming vote of both houses at the first session of Congress following the decision, and it was promptly ratified by February 1795. This amendment provided that "the judicial power of the United States shall not be construed to extend to any suit in law or equity, commenced or prosecuted against one of the United States by Citizens of any other state, or by Citizens or subjects of any Foreign State." Although the new amendment did not extend to federal questions or federal suits against a state by its own citizens, it was nonetheless an early concession to Rhode Island's assertive states' rights stand.

Finally, one must note Rhode Island's popular referendum on the Constitution—a referendum that inspired Federalist denunciations because the Constitution's framers had prescribed ratifying conventions as the mode for registering approval or rejection. In March 1788, with most of Rhode Island's Federalists angrily abstaining, the state rejected the now-revered Constitution by a vote of approximately 2,711 to 243 (historians' computations differ slightly because of errors in the original transcriptions). This 11-to-1 trouncing, made worse by the Federalist boycott, would seem to do no credit to Rhode Island. Some towns even shut out the Constitution entirely: the vote was 180 to 0 in Coventry, 177 to 0 in Foster, 156 to 0 in Scituate, and 101 to 0 in Cranston. Yet Rhode Island's insistence on a constitutional referendum now seems no more than reasonable. What new basic law can be enacted today without explicit popular approval at the polls?

In view of Rhode Island's subsequent vindication, we should have no cause for shame today, May 29, 1990. In fact, considering the basis of Rhode Island's opposition to the original Constitution — resistance to an overweening and unrestrained central government; concern for the sovereignty and integrity of the states in the spirit of true federalism; solicitude for individual liberty, especially religious freedom; opposition to slavery and the incidents of servitude; and concern for democratic participation in the constitution-making process — perhaps Americans might ask not why it took Rogues' Island so long to join the Union, but rather why it took the Union so long to join Rhode Island.

Rhode Island observed the bicentennial of ratification and statehood on May 29, 1990. This first-day cover of the Rhode Island statehood stamp marked the event.

Rhode Island's Statehood Stamp | 14

This speech was delivered at
Slater Mill, Pawtucket, on May 29, 1990.

IT IS AN HONOR TO REPRESENT both the Rhode Island Bicentennial Foundation and the United States Constitution Council at this statehood event. During the course of this momentous day, I will speak many times on the theme of Rhode Island's ratification of the Constitution. To avoid repetition, therefore, and to be mercifully brief, I will confine my remarks at this initial ceremony at Pawtucket's Slater Mill to the connection between this stamp, this site, and this ratification date—a relationship that I have already made some effort to establish.

This is the thirteenth stamp in the Ratification Series. Some earlier ones bear an obvious relationship to the Constitution; for example, the image on the Pennsylvania stamp is Independence Hall, site of the Philadelphia Convention. Other stamps, such as New Hampshire's, depicting its Old Man of the Mountain, and South Carolina's and Georgia's, showing their state trees, bear no direct relationship at all.

What about Slater Mill and ratification? Is there a nexus here? Without being too far-fetched historically, I believe there is one. Let's examine the image on Rhode Island's issue.

Our stamp bears the date of Rhode Island ratification—May 29, 1790. That inscription needs no elaboration. It also bears the date 1793, the year the present Slater Mill was constructed. However, December 20, 1790, is an equally appropriate date to associate with Samuel Slater, Moses Brown, and their fellow mechanics and investors. On that day the force of the Blackstone River activated machinery, built from an English model by Slater, David Wilkinson, and Sylvanus Brown, that carded and spun yarn from cotton.

96

This first successful mechanization of textile production in America took place in a now-demolished building that once stood south of this present mill site, just off Quaker Lane, a thoroughfare that Pawtucket residents now call East Avenue. But either date—1790 or 1793—bears an equal relationship to the new American economic climate generated by the adoption of the Constitution and the implementation of that document by our first and most farsighted secretary of the treasury, Alexander Hamilton.

As we all know, the Constitution of 1787 established a stronger Union and a more energetic central government than that which existed under the Articles of Confederation, our country's first basic law. Unlike the Articles, the new Constitution, in Article I, Section 8, gave the central government power to regulate interstate and foreign commerce, power to levy tariffs, and power to tax and spend for projects that promoted the "general welfare." In the hands of ardent economic nationalists like Founding Father Hamilton and his deputy Tench Coxe, these new governmental powers were immediately used to promote the industrialization of America.

In May 1790, the same month in which Rhode Island joined the Union, Coxe, at Hamilton's direction, began research on a project that would become Hamilton's *Report on Manufactures*, a state paper that is still viewed as a classic argument in support of the affirmative exercise of governmental power in the economic realm.

Submitted to Congress at its annual session in December 1791, Hamilton's *Report* was the result of a request from the House of Representatives directing him to "prepare a proper plan...for the encouragement and promotion of such manufactories as will tend to render the United States independent of other nations for essential, particularly for military supplies." Hamilton and Coxe expanded this narrow mandate to prepare and present to Congress a sustained argument in support of the indispensability of manu-facturing to a balanced and prosperous national economy.

The *Report* proposed protective tariffs for such infant American industries as textiles, duty-free status for raw materials needed for domestic manufacture, and the encouragement of foreign invest-ment in American business. Hamilton suggested that American manufactures might be further stimulated by granting those (like Slater and Moses Brown) who contrived to import machinery or industrial secrets from abroad a protection equivalent to that afforded by patent law. Advantage should also be taken of the Old World, said Hamilton, by encouraging immigration to meet America's growing need for an industrial work force.

Time does not permit an enumeration of the many other bold and prophetic recommendations in Hamilton's eloquent plea for national economic planning, a proposal that historian John C. Miller has called "the grand design by which the United States became the greatest industrial power in the world." Suffice it to say that Hamilton's vision was shared by enterprising Rhode Islanders like those of the Providence Association of Mechanics and Manufacturers, who led the fight for Rhode Island ratification immediately upon its formation in 1789; it was shared by entre-preneurs Moses Brown, his cousin Smith Brown, and William Almy, who joined to fund Slater's venture; and it was shared by David Wilkinson, Sylvanus Brown, and other tradesmen whose skill and inventive genius propelled Rhode Island towards an industrial revolution.

Because of such enterprising citizens, Rhode Island made the transformation from a primarily agrarian economy to one with an industrial base, and it made that transformation before any other American state. With that accomplishment came the related de-velopments of urbanization and immigration, both hallmarks of modern American life. Here in Rhode Island Hamilton's vision of a new economic order reached its earliest fulfilment on a statewide basis—and it began with Slater's Mill.

How ironic that the last of the original thirteen to join the new Union should be the first to capitalize upon the economic advan-tages afforded by its new constitutional system! Therein lies the nexus between Rhode Island ratification and Slater Mill. In such a context, this historic structure becomes an appropriate symbol of Rhode Island's extremist character. In linking our ratification with our pioneering thrust toward industrial development, our statehood stamp needs only the biblical inscription "The last shall be first" to be faithful to history.

Rhode Island and the Union, 1774–1795, by Irwin H. Polishook, Reviewed

Written in 1970, this review of Polishook's study of Rhode Island in the Revolutionary era appeared in *The New England Quarterly*.

RHODE ISLAND'S PAST has been seriously neglected by competent professional historians. No more than a handful of historical works relating to Rhode Island would merit inclusion in a select bibliographical compendium such as the *Harvard Guide*. Mr. Polishook's study, a noteworthy exception, is a first-rate local history.

The period covered by Polishook (1774–95) is one of the most significant and controversial eras in Rhode Island history. During this formative age, defiant, individualistic, and nearly autonomous Rhode Island was in the vanguard of the movement toward independence. Then the state was among the first to ratify the Articles of Confederation. During the decade of the 1780s, however, suspicious and separatistic Rhode Island hampered the operation of the Confederation government through its rejection of a national impost, and it then resisted the ratification of the federal Constitution until after the new central government had been in operation for more than a year.

After his thorough examination of this turbulent era, Polishook asserts that he has "found no single interpretation that can connect the different historical factors at work during the period from 1774 through 1795. Rhode Island reacted to the federal Union according to its own state-centered needs, which varied with time and circumstance, and often was influenced by bitter internal divisions." He is to be applauded for his appreciation of the diversity, uniqueness, and atypical nature of the Rhode Island experience, and for avoiding the glib and superficial generalizations that have characterized many accounts of this nation-making epoch.

For example, Polishook's analysis of Rhode Island Antifederalism during the ratification struggle reveals that it drew its strength from a variety of sources, including states' rightism, abhorrence of centrally imposed direct taxes, antislavery, parochialism (or "democratic localism"), a desire to protect the state's paper-money program, and the dominance and determination of the Antifederal Country party. The author's treatment of federalism, a movement that also stemmed from a variety of political, economic, and attitudinal factors, is equally perceptive.

One of the most impressive aspects of this study is the breadth of the sources utilized. The author has drawn upon sixty-nine manuscript collections in eleven depositories and more than fifty contemporary newspapers. In addition, he is the first historian to consult extensively the valuable, unpublished town meeting records of Rhode Island's communities.

This study, which is an outgrowth of the author's doctoral dissertation, will long remain the standard account of the subject that it treats, but it does not completely supplant Frank Green Bates's *Rhode Island and the Formation of the Union* (1898), an old but excellent monograph. Because the existence of these two volumes will discourage future scholars from reworking this same period, perhaps the minor flaws in Polishook's effort should be noted. The author's contention that the Rhode Island Superior Court handed down a declaration of unconstitutionality in the *Trevett* v. *Weeden* case is erroneous; the original court record reveals that it merely refused cognizance. Rhode Island's acceptance of the impost in 1785 was burdened with conditions and qualifications; an approval that was satisfactory to the Confederation government was delayed until 1786. The author blurs this distinction. The secret ballot was not used in eighteenth-century Rhode Island. Polishook, in contending that it was, misinterprets a 1787 statute that merely authorized a written vote rather than a show of hands in town meeting elections. Also, Rhode Island does not have a "modern city of Kingstown." Further, this reviewer would hold with Forrest McDonald and against Polishook that an important factor in the merchants' opposition to the state paper-money issue was that the program made no provision for payment of interest on merchant-held Continental Loan Office certificates. Finally, the author's character descriptions of the era's leading personalities are often skimpy.

It would be a great injustice to Professor Polishook, however, to dwell upon these points or to accentuate the negative in such a brief review. In its totality, *Rhode Island and the Union* is local history at its best. The author has produced a work that ranks along with the studies of David Lovejoy and Peter Coleman as the ablest narratives yet to appear in the field of Rhode Island history.

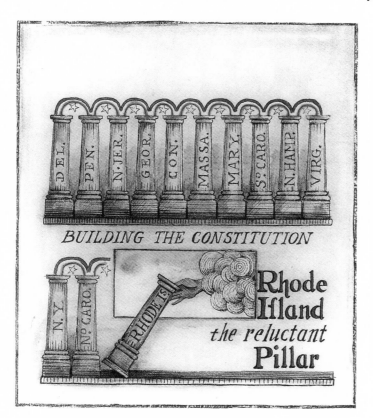

This graphic depicts Rhode Island's grudging ratification of the federal Constitution on May 29, 1790, by a vote of 34–32, the narrowest of any state.

THE
PUBLIC LAWS
OF THE STATE OF
RHODE-ISLAND
AND
PROVIDENCE PLANTATIONS,

As revised by a Committee, and finally enacted by
the Honourable GENERAL ASSEMBLY, at their
Session in *January*, 1798.

TO WHICH ARE PREFIXED,

The CHARTER, DECLARATION OF INDEPENDENCE, ARTICLES
OF CONFEDERATION, CONSTITUTION OF THE UNITED
STATES, and PRESIDENT WASHINGTON'S ADDRESS of *Sep-
tember*, 1796.

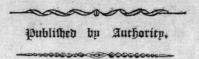

Published by Authority.

IGNORANTIA LEGIS NEMINEM EXCUSAT.
IGNORANCE OF THE LAW IS NO EXCUSE FOR ITS VIOLATION.

The Digest of 1798 was the first codification of Rhode Island law
subsequent to Rhode Island's admission to the Union.

The Digest of 1798:
The State's First Code of Law | 16

This essay was written and delivered as the Law Day
address to the state Supreme Court in May 1998.

*Chief Justice Weisberger, Members of the Supreme Court, Attorney
General Sheldon Whitehouse, Faculty and Students of Roger Williams
University Law School:*

MAY I THANK THE COURT for the privilege of addressing you
here at our state's only law school on yet another Law Day. As
the chief justice may recall, this is my fourth appearance as your
speaker. At the time of my debut in 1976, Chief Justice Bevilacqua
presided. He and associates Doris, Joslin, Paolino, and Kelleher
are all deceased. At that Law Day event in the Bicentennial year,
the presiding justices of the lower courts also attended—Chief
Justice Edward Gallogly of the Family Court, Henry Laliberte of
the District Court, and Joseph Weisberger, presiding justice of the
Superior Court. Only Judge Weisberger, now at the pinnacle of
our state judicial system, survives.

Even Justice Weisberger was not present when the Supreme
Court, acting in its appellate capacity, last met in Bristol on March
10, 1893, or when it last assembled here as a trial court on May 8,
1905. The setting then was the Bristol County Statehouse and
Courthouse, which is now undergoing complete restoration under
the auspices and direction of a foundation that I incorporated and

serve as president. Perhaps on its next visit to Bristol, the court can move from the campus to the courthouse to conduct its session.

I have become accustomed to celebrate historical anniversaries since my tenure as state Bicentennial chairman in 1976. Coincidentally, this year, 1998, is the two hundredth anniversary of a major legal development—the publication of the first comprehensive "digest," or legal code, for the new State of Rhode Island, a volume literally entitled *The Public Laws of the State of Rhode Island and Providence Plantations, As revised by a Committee, and finally enacted by the Honorable General Assembly at their Session in January, 1798*. I have made that event the subject of my talk, not merely because it fits chronologically but because the Digest of 1798 contained two major enactments: a ban on religious qualifications for voting and officeholding and a bill of rights.

What is a digest of laws, and what place does our Bicentennial digest occupy in the continuum of Rhode Island statutory law? Essentially, a digest is a compilation or code of laws assembled periodically (usually every generation) that organizes those general laws of the state currently in effect. In Rhode Island, a digest has often been more than a mere compilation; it can contain new laws that become operative when the publication of the particular digest is approved by the General Assembly. The two rights-related features of the 1798 code that form the basis of my address were enacted not separately but as part of the 1798 revision process.

The Digest of 1798, although the first compilation of state laws, was not the first Rhode Island digest. Under royal prodding, the colonists produced a manuscript code in 1705. This amateurish effort was followed by published digests in 1719 (of which more will be said), 1730, 1745, and 1767. Since statehood, the General Assembly has enacted digests in 1798 (one volume of 652 pages), 1822, 1844, 1857, 1873, 1896 (still one volume, with 1,447 pages), 1909, 1923, and 1938. The last digest, the *General Laws of 1956*, as amended to 1998, contains thirty volumes and approximately 21,000 pages!

The first digest (1705) had its origins in the imperial reorganization that followed the demise of the Catholic King James II and his abortive Dominion for New England. English royalists, styled

Tories, sought to make all colonies subject to royal governors, while the Whigs, the party of parliamentary power, opposed this enlargement of royal prerogative. Rhode Island, one of five non-royal colonies, was caught in the middle of this imperial fray. Her harboring of pirates, her abuse of admiralty court jurisdiction, and her lack of participation in King William's War against French Canada brought the fractious colony under increasing royal scrutiny. In 1699 the Board of Trade authorized Richard Coote, earl of Bellomont and royal governor of Massachusetts, New Hampshire, and New York, to visit Rhode Island, investigate its "irregularities," and get copies of the colony's laws and other public records "relating to the administration of that government." Coote's report, dated November 17, 1699, was generally unflattering, but Rhode Island's legal system inspired words of condemnation. He described Attorney General John Pocock as a "poor illiterate mechanic" and his predecessor John Green as "very corrupt" and "brutish."

Worse than the officials was the system itself. The laws were "kept in loose scripts of paper" in such disarray that the "people are at a loss to know what is law among them." Judicial proceedings were arbitrary and failed to follow "the course and practice of the courts in England"; the judges, who were also members of the General Assembly, knew "very little law" and gave the jury no direction. Bellomont was aghast that the legislature had assumed "a judicial power of hearing, trying, and determining civil cases, removing them out of the ordinary courts of justice, and waiving trial at common law." The Assembly even "alters and reverses verdicts and judgments" and had set up an admiralty court in 1694 nowhere authorized by Rhode Island's charter. (Without doubt, the "old Coote" was the forerunner of the Alan Dershowitz school of Rhode Island legal criticism!).

Rhode Island's response to Bellomont's diatribe was the creation of a county system of court administration in 1703, consisting of the county of Rhode Island (Newport) and the county of Providence Plantations, and the preparation of the manuscript Digest of 1705. Fourteen years later, in 1719, the General Assembly promulgated its first published compilation of its general laws.

The Digest of 1719 figures prominently in any discussion of the implementation of the famed guarantee of religious liberty contained in the charter of 1663. Although the royal charter had specifically stated that no person "'shall be in any wise molested, punished, disquieted, or called in question, for any differences of opinion in matters of religion," the 1719 code contained the following provision:

> All Men *Professing Christianity*, and of Competent
> Estates, and of Civil Conversation, who acknowledge,
> and are Obedient to the Civil Magistrate, though of
> different Judgments in Religious Affairs (*Roman
> Catholicks only excepted*) shall be admitted Free-men,
> And shall have liberty to Chuse and be Chosen Officers
> in the Colony both Military and Civil. [Italics mine]

This act was allegedly passed in the March 1663 session of the General Assembly. Its enactment then or at any time prior to 1719 is possible but highly improbable. No such statute appears in the original proceedings of the General Assembly for 1663, nor is it found in the preserved proceedings of any subsequent session. Further, it is not contained in the manuscript "Laws and Acts" of 1705.

The passage of this restrictive "law" during 1663 is particularly implausible in view of the colonists' statutory enactment in May 1664 of the religious guarantees of the charter. The fact that Roger Williams was a member of the first assemblies renders the act's passage at that time even more doubtful.

It can also be inferred that the controversial "law" was not enacted at any time during the seventeenth century, because Bellomont reported in his journal on September 22, 1699, that the religious Test Act was not enforced in the colony. If Rhode Island had passed the alleged law of 1663 in defiance of her charter, it seems likely that she would have employed such a ready-made excuse as the Test Act to justify this violation.

The discriminatory statute was inserted into the Digest of 1719 by the compilers of that volume to cater to the whims of the recent defenders of their charter, the English Whigs, whose anti-Catholic sentiments had been aroused by the Jacobite efforts in 1715–16 to place the Catholic Pretender on the English throne. In fact, Jacobite uprisings had prompted the passage by Parliament of proscriptive legislation against "Papists" in June 1716.

To Rhode Island's discredit, this statute, enacted as part of the Digest of 1719, was reaffirmed by the Assembly in the Digests of 1730, 1745, and 1767. Not until 1783 was the arbitrary disqualification of Catholics removed. The act that accomplished this, however, not only failed to recognize the true origins of the disabling "statute"; it also neglected to define the civil status of those professing the Jewish faith.

The 1719 digest's civil restriction against those of the Jewish faith bears directly upon our discussion of the Digest of 1798. These volumes are bookends as they pertain to official and legal discrimination against Jews in Rhode Island. Whereas the Catholic restriction had a minimal impact because very few Catholics lived in Rhode Island colony, the effect of the limitation on Jews was commensurate with Newport's sizable and prosperous Jewish community, which dated from 1658.

The key essay on the issue of Jewish political disability was written by David C. Adelman, a Providence attorney and founder of the Rhode Island Jewish Historical Association. In an article entitled "Strangers: Civil Rights of the Jews in Rhode Island Colony" that appeared in *Rhode Island History* magazine in 1954, Adelman detailed the fate of those Jews who sought naturalization and citizenship. Although Jews enjoyed freedom of worship, none, however qualified or competent, was ever made a freeman of the colony of Rhode Island. On the issue of naturalization, both the Superior Court and the General Assembly in 1761–62 denied the citizenship petitions of Aaron Lopez and Isaac Elizer because they were non-Christians. The lower house of the Assembly further admonished them that an adherent of their religion was "not Liable to be chosen into any Office in this Colony Nor allowed to give a Vote as a Freeman in Choosing others."

Adelman asserts that no evidence exists that anyone of the Jewish faith was ever naturalized in the colony of Rhode Island. But the rejection in the Lopez case, it should be noted, stemmed from the petitioner's political as well as religious affiliations. Lopez was closely associated with Nicholas Brown, an ally of Governor Stephen Hopkins. This prompted Hopkins's opponents in the Assembly, led by former governor Samuel Ward, to dismiss the Lopez petition.

The first Jews came to Newport in 1658, encouraged by news concerning the liberality of Roger Williams and his efforts to persuade the Cromwellian regime to admit Jewish refugees from Spain and Portugal into England and her colonies. During the remainder of the colonial era the "Hebrew" population of Rhode Island waxed and waned with changes in trade and commerce. In the 1690s approximately ninety Jewish refugees from Spain and Portugal arrived via the Dutch island of Curaçao, and in the 1740s and 1750s an accelerated Inquisition brought a new influx from Portugal.

In 1763 Newport's Jewish community—organized as Congregation Yeshuat Israel—erected Touro Synagogue, which had two hundred members at its peak on the eve of the American Revolution. British occupation of Newport from late 1776 to 1779 disrupted commerce and dispersed the town's Jewish mercantile community. By 1790 Touro Synagogue was on the verge of closing, when George Washington informed the Hebrew congregation (paraphrasing their own letter to him) that "happily the government of the United States gives to bigotry no sanction; to persecution no assistance."

Ironically, Rhode Island's hands were still unclean. Not until the enactment of the Digest of 1798, at a time when only four Jewish families remained in Newport (Sexias, Levy, Lopez, and Rivera), were adherents of the Jewish faith made first-class citizens by an act "Relative to Religious Freedom and the Maintenance of Ministers." This remarkable statute was as advanced as any drafted or conceived during this era of liberal religious declarations, but it was no more than an explicit rendering of the principles upon which Roger Williams founded his Providence Plantation. The act itself declared that "no man shall be compelled to frequent or support any religious worship, place or ministry whatsoever; nor shall be enforced, restrained, molested, or bothered in his body or goods, nor shall otherwise suffer on account of his religious opinion or belief; but that all men shall be free to profess, and by argument to maintain, their opinions in matters of religion, and that the same shall in no wise diminish, enlarge or affect their civil capacities."

The act's preamble was even more emphatic. It condemned laws compelling a man to contribute money to support opinions in which he disbelieved as "sinful and tyrannical" and called forced contributions to support particular teachers of one's own religion a deprivation of liberty. It also claimed that civil rights had no dependence on religious opinions, and so "the proscribing any citizen as unworthy the public confidence, by laying upon him an incapacity of being called to offices of trust and emolument, unless he profess or renounce this or that religious opinion, is depriving him injuriously of those privileges and advantages to which, in common with his fellow citizens, he has a natural right." Such a proscription, the act concluded, tended "only to corrupt the principles of that religion it is meant to encourage, by bringing, with a monopoly of worldly honours and emoluments, those who will externally profess and conform to it."

This enlightened measure was a vigorous reaffirmation of Rhode Island's long-standing commitment to the principles of religious liberty and church-state separation. Roger Williams would have rejoiced at the enduring nature of his "lively experiment."

Here is an interesting postscript to our saga. On October 5, 1822, Stephen Gould, a prominent Newporter, made this entry in his diary: "Moses Lopez, the last Jew, left Newport for New York." The Jewish community in the City by the Sea was not reestablished until the 1870s. By that date Providence, Pawtucket, and the Woonsocket area had attracted Jewish settlers. The first of these to sit on the bench you now occupy was Justice J. Jerome Hahn, the Louis Brandeis of Rhode Island. He was a Superior Court justice from March 1919 until his elevation to the state Supreme Court on February 27, 1931. His tenure was aborted on January 1, 1935, when his seat was declared vacant as a result of the Bloodless Revolution staged by the Democratic legislature.

In 1931 Hahn conveyed a small plot of land on the westerly side of North Main Street to the city of Providence, a plot containing the original freshwater spring used by Roger Williams and the first settlers of Providence. He dedicated the gift to the memory of his father, Isaac, the first Providence citizen of Jewish faith to be elected to public office, and in honor of Roger Williams, whose principles were vindicated years before by the Digest of 1798. In the 1970s this tiny park became the nucleus for the Roger Williams National Memorial, maintained by the National Park Service, a tribute not only to Williams but to the volume we commemorate today. The Providence park and, indeed, this university that bears his name are continuing reminders of Williams's "lively experiment" in full religious liberty, which has become the American antidote to religious persecution, forced worship, and sectarian strife.

The other major feature of the Digest of 1798 that I have chosen to emphasize today is its statutory bill of rights. These "political axioms or truths" set forth by the legislative compilers were declared "to be of paramount importance in all legislative, executive, and judicial proceedings." These enunciated rights could only be guaranteed by statute, because Rhode Island's basic law, the charter of 1663, contained no such listing nor any procedure for amendment.

The newly enacted guarantees of liberty and property were contained in ten provisions. They included the right of all to a legal remedy for injuries or wrongs to property and character, protection against unreasonable search and seizure, immunity from double jeopardy, protection from excessive bail and from cruel and unusual punishment, the privilege of habeas corpus, a guarantee of procedural due process, the termination of imprisonment for debt once the debtor's estate had been delivered up for the benefit of his creditors, a ban on *ex post facto* laws, freedom from involuntary self-incrimination, and a presumption of innocence until guilt was proven.

In this context, reference should be made to attorney Kevin Leitao's well-researched and imaginative article, "Rhode Island's Forgotten Bill of Rights," published in the *Roger Williams University Law Review* 1 (spring 1996), where the author examines the

"Declaration of Rights" drafted and approved by the 1790 state convention that had been called for the specific and limited purpose of ratifying the Constitution of the United States. This declaration, he claims, was Rhode Island's first bill of rights.

Admitting that his essay "is largely a thought experiment," Leitao believes that by "applying the principles of popular sovereignty, the Declaration of Rights could have been enforced in Rhode Island" as state law. I strongly disagree. This declaration was clearly an expression of concern by the ratifying convention's Antifederal majority to the United States Congress regarding the threat to liberty posed by the new government of the United States. A textual and contextual analysis of the document can yield no other conclusion. No one at that time or since considered it otherwise, and the General Assembly (which never ratified the 1790 declaration) neither included it in the public laws or based its 1798 statutory bill of rights upon it. Finally, the principles of popular sovereignty alluded to by Leitao were repudiated by the Rhode Island Supreme Court and the U.S. federal courts in the aftermath of the Dorr Rebellion. As Leitao asserts, the Declaration of Rights did indeed apply to the "people of the state," but it was intended to protect them not from their local officials but from the novel and distant central government whose potential appetite for power was then unknown.

The 1798 declaration attracted the attention of reformers in the 1830s not because of illiberality but because of its potential impermanency. Critics believed that the mere legislative guarantees of 1798 were a precarious foundation upon which to base civil liberty. The constitution of 1843 effectively addressed this concern by incorporating these rights into Sections 5 through 14 of Article I, the "Declaration of Certain Constitutional Rights and Privileges." They were transferred intact to the constitution of 1986, except for a bail limitation imposed against major drug dealers, and so the Digest of 1798 continues to affect our lives and liberties today.

I would be remiss if I did not allude to another important change effected by the Digest of 1798. The state's high tribunal—this court—was established in 1729 and renamed in 1746 the "Superior Court of Judicature, Court of Assize, and General Gaol

Delivery." In 1798 that archaic appellation was abridged to the "Supreme Judicial Court." The saving in printing costs alone made the Digest of 1798 a revision not to be forgotten in its impact on Rhode Island's political and legal system.

An Act declaratory of certain Rights of the People of this State.

WHEREAS the General Affembly of this State have from time to time paffed fundry acts, declaratory of the rights of the people thereof: And whereas a declaration of certain rights is deemed by this Affembly to be highly proper and neceffary, both for the adminiftration of juftice and the fecurity of faid rights:

Be it therefore enacted by this General Affembly, and by the authority thereof it is enacted, That the people of this State are entitled, among other important and effential rights, to the rights hereafter enumerated, and that the fame are and hereby are declared to be the inherent and unqueftionable rights of the people inhabiting within the limits and jurifdiction of this State: That the political axioms, or truths, herein after mentioned and declared, are, and ought to be, of paramount obligation in all legiflative, judicial and executive proceedings, which fhall be had or done therein, under the authority thereof.

Sec. 1. Every perfon within this State ought to find a certain remedy, by having recourfe to the laws, for all injuries or wrongs which he may receive in his perfon, property or character. He ought to obtain right and juftice freely, and without being obliged to purchafe it; completely, and without any denial; promptly, and without delay; conformably to the laws.

Sec. 2. The right of the people to be fecure in their perfons, houfes, papers and poffeffions, againft unreafonable fearches and feizures, fhall not be violated; and no warrant fhall iffue, but on complaint in writing, upon probable caufe, fupported by oath or affirmation, and defcribing, as nearly as may be, the place to be fearched, and the perfons or things to be feized.

Sec. 3. No perfon fhall be holden to anfwer a capital or other infamous crime, unlefs on prefentment or indictment by a Grand Jury, except in cafes arifing in the land or naval forces, or in the militia when in actual fervice, in time of war, or public danger. No perfon fhall, for the fame offence, be twice put in jeopardy of life or limb.

Sec. 4. Exceffive bail fhall not be required, nor exceffive fines impofed, nor cruel punifhments inflicted; and all punifhments ought to be proportioned to the offence.

Sec. 5. All prifoners fhall be bailable by fufficient fureties, unlefs for capital offences. when the proof is evident, or prefumption great; and the privilege of the writ of *habeas corpus* fhall not be fufpended, unlefs when, in cafes of rebellion or invafion, the public fafety may require it.

Sec. 6. In all criminal profecutions, the accufed fhall enjoy the right to a fpeedy and public trial, by an impartial Jury; to be informed of the nature and caufe of the accufation. to be confronted with the witneffes againft him, to have compulfory procefs for obtaining them in his favour, and to have the affiftance of counfel for his defence; nor can he be deprived of his life, liberty or property, unlefs by the judgment of his peers, or the law of the land.

Sec. 7. The perfon of a debtor, when there is not ftrong prefumption of fraud, ought not to be continued in prifon, after delivering up his eftate for the benefit of his creditors, in fuch manner as fhall be prefcribed by law.

Sec. 8. Retrofpective laws, punifhing offences committed before the exiftence of fuch laws, are oppreffive and unjuft, and ought not to be made.

Sec. 9. No man, in the courts of common law, ought to be compelled to give evidence againft himfelf.

Sec. 10. Every man being prefumed to be innocent, until he has been pronounced guilty by the law, all acts of feverity that are not neceffary to fecure an accufed perfon ought to be repreffed.

The Digest of 1798 continued this "Act Declaratory of Certain Rights of the People of this State." These rights were statutory, because the existing state constitution—the royal charter of 1663—lacked procedures for amendment. During the 1830s political reformers who wanted a popularly written basic law to replace the charter often alluded to the mere legislative guarantees of 1798 as being a precarious foundation upon which to base civil liberty. Article I of the state constitution of 1843—the "Declaration of Certain Constitutional Rights and Principles"—included the 1798 guarantees.

4

Thomas Wilson Dorr
and His Rebellion

The first Providence High School, completed in 1843 on Benefit Street, was a monument to the tenacity of Thomas Dorr. The entering class numbered 245 students—114 boys and 141 girls.

Thomas Dorr: Neglected Educational Reformer

17

This speech, delivered in 1977 at the centennial banquet of the Barnard Club of Rhode Island, was based entirely upon research in the Dorr Manuscripts at Brown University's John Hay Library. It has been my intention to publish this piece as a scholarly essay with full documentation, but this original version must suffice for now. Unfortunately the Barnard Club has since ceased to exist, expiring in the 1990s.

TO THE OFFICERS AND MEMBERS OF THE BARNARD CLUB, may I congratulate you on a century of service to education in Rhode Island, and may I thank you for selecting me as your centennial speaker. When asked to choose a topic, I avoided Henry Barnard himself, for I would feel redundant telling a group of distinguished educators about the exploits of their club's namesake. I also believe that the story of Barnard's accomplishments in Rhode Island and elsewhere have been often recounted, both in biographies of Barnard and in general histories of American education.

Not wishing to be repetitious or to retell a familiar story, I decided to focus my talk on an aspect of the pre-Barnard era in Rhode Island educational development—an aspect that has been overlooked, and thus one that I can relate with originality. My topic concerns the neglected contributions to education of Thomas Wilson Dorr, achievements deliberately obscured by the victorious Rhode Island Establishment because of Dorr's attack on the old political and constitutional order. In fact, however, Dorr was to Barnard what John the Baptist was to Christ. He paved the way.

Thomas Wilson Dorr is known to the student of American history as the leader of the Dorr Rebellion, an ill-fated 1842 uprising which had as its goal the replacement of Rhode Island's royal charter of 1663 with a progressive, written state constitution. During the political revolt that bears his name, Dorr drafted a so-called People's Constitution, served as the "People's governor," and made an abortive attempt to establish his government by force of arms. When Dorr was deserted by many of his less zealous followers, the movement collapsed and the People's governor fled Rhode Island with his "Law and Order" opponents in hot pursuit. After a period of exile he returned, subjected himself to a farcical trial before a packed jury, and was sentenced to life imprisonment for treason against the State of Rhode Island. The harsh treatment accorded Dorr produced a nationwide demand for his liberation. This popular outcry forced the Law and Order party, which had defeated Dorr, to assent to his release in 1845. Dorr's twenty-month stay in prison impaired his already fragile health, and the Rhode Island rebel was forced into semiretirement despite proffers of national office from the Democratic party. In 1854 he died at the age of forty-nine.

Dorr's stormy political career has completely overshadowed his other interests and accomplishments. Further, the sociopolitical Establishment that vanquished the intrepid reformer was only intent on censuring him and depicting him as an ambitious, destructive, radical rabble-rouser. Small wonder, therefore, that Dorr's banking reforms, his antislavery sentiments, his efforts on behalf of the immigrant, and his contributions to the development of public schools have been ignored. A closer look at the career of this many-sided reformer reveals, especially in the area of education, the extent of this neglect.

Dorr was born into one of Rhode Island's most prominent families on November 5, 1805. His grandfather was Ebenezer Dorr, a Boston mechanic who rode with Paul Revere in that fateful April of '75. His father, Sullivan Dorr, was a prominent merchant-industrialist who had amassed a modest fortune in the fledgling China trade. Thomas's mother, the former Lydia Allen, was descended from the William Harris that had accompanied Roger Williams to Providence in the spring of 1636. But even more impressive than the lineage and the social standing of Thomas Dorr were his early achievements and his potential.

Dorr's education was one befitting the eldest son of a merchant prince. It included study at Phillips-Exeter Academy in New Hampshire and Harvard. He entered Harvard College in 1819, at the age of fourteen. In 1823, having been chosen a member of all the college literary societies, he was graduated with high honors, the second-ranking scholar in his class.

From Cambridge Dorr went to New York, where he studied law under the renowned James Kent. After his sojourn with Chancellor Kent, Dorr clerked in the office of John Whipple, Rhode Island's foremost legal craftsman of the Early National Period and a constitutional scholar. After gaining admission to the bar in March 1827, Dorr hung his shingle for a time in Providence. Then, to improve his delicate health, he took an excursion through the West and South. Upon the completion of his travels Dorr practiced briefly in the city of New York. Here he first made contact with a number of distinguished individuals, including John L. O'Sullivan, the Jacksonian exponent of equal rights and manifest destiny, and British inventor William B. Adams, a leading proponent of the famous British Reform Bill of 1832.

It is Dorr's correspondence with Adams, in fact, that first reveals the young lawyer's ardent interest in reform. In his extended letters to the British political pamphleteer, Dorr exulted over France's July Revolution of 1830, deplored Russia's suppression of the Poles, and urged parliamentary reform and suffrage extension in England. His remarks on these momentous events of 1830–32 afford a glimpse into the mind of this young liberal on the eve of his entrance into public life.

Dorr viewed the European upheavals as part of a "universal cause" aimed at asserting "the natural rights of our species" and bringing the "greatest happiness to the greatest number." To him they were symptomatic of a growing demand that "all persons competent to do so may take part in the choice of their rulers, lawmakers and judges, either immediately, or mediately through their chosen representatives; *and that all persons not at present competent may be made so as soon as possible by a general system of public education*" (italics mine). Dorr's letters reveal that liberty and equality were to him, as much as to any reformer of this remarkable age, the indispensable conditions of human activity.

In 1832 Dorr returned permanently to Providence. Once home, he familiarized himself with political and social conditions in his native state. During 1833 he waited in the wings while a number of disfranchised Rhode Islanders waged a campaign for free suffrage. This movement caught his attention and fired his interest. By 1834, at the age of twenty-eight, Dorr was ready to translate his lofty ideals into action. Early in that year he entered public life, and he entered with a flourish.

In February of his coming-out year, the aspiring attorney attended an assemblage called to effect reform in the state's basic law. Later in the year Dorr assumed the leadership of the Constitutional party, an outgrowth of the February meeting, and in September he took his seat as a delegate from Providence to a state constitutional convention. Meanwhile, in April 1834 Dorr was elected as a Whig representative to the state House of Representatives, and in May he was given a position on the Providence School Committee. This appointment began his brief but distinguished career in the field of education.

Dorr's accomplishments as an educational reformer were many and diverse. Perhaps with a premonition that his exploits would interest posterity, Dorr kept careful records of all his public activities. His work on the Providence School Committee was no exception. The hitherto unconsulted Dorr Manuscripts in the John Hay Library of Brown University (volumes 28 and 29) contain detailed information on the activities of school committeeman Dorr.

You educators will be pleased to learn that Dorr's first recorded resolution, presented on November 26, 1834, called for the committee to raise the salaries of the city's teachers. As eventually passed, it gave teachers a pay increase of approximately 15 percent—a lavish $750 per year for male instructors. Salary schedules for this era show that men were paid from 50 percent to 150 percent more than their female counterparts, who outnumbered male teachers by a ratio of 5 to 1.

Dorr was made chairman of the Subcommittee on Teacher Qualification early in his School Committee career. In this capacity he tested and screened the applicants for teaching positions in Providence. Volume 29 of the Dorr Manuscripts is entitled

"Examinations of Applicants for Positions as Teachers in the Public Schools in Providence, 1834–1842." Dorr's evaluations of prospective teachers are quite revealing. His notes show the low caliber of many instructors in this pre-normal-school era, when advanced study and training in educational techniques were neither required nor available.

For example, Samuel P. Dole, the thirty-one-year-old man who prevailed in a competition for appointment as "master" of one of the city's six grammar schools in 1840, was evaluated by Dorr as follows:

Reading — good	Composition — mediocre
Writing — not very good	Geography-History — ditto
Arithmetic — ditto	Ethics — little or none (formal training in ethics, that is)
Bookkeeping — not attended to	The Constitution — little acquaintance with.

Dole, who had taught for seven years, including a two-year stint in Switzerland, was regarded as the best prospect. Dorr judged no fewer than four of the others "poor" readers, while ten applicants were listed as "tolerable" or "mediocre" readers. In 1838 another competitive screening of eighteen candidates for the post of assistant in one of the city's writing schools showed that two applicants were adjudged poor writers themselves.

In August 1835 Dorr began an extremely important educational campaign by introducing a resolution calling for the establishment of a public high school. None existed anywhere in Rhode Island at that time. This proposal, though innovative, was not entirely novel; a high school had been recommended by President Francis Wayland of Brown in 1828, when he headed an educational study commission.

Dorr's first high school resolution languished, and so he introduced another in November 1836. This one brought results. It was approved on December 7 by a vote of 11 to 6. A three-man subcommittee, including Dorr, was appointed to draft a plan and a course of studies for the proposed facility.

Dorr pushed his proposal by contributing several thoughtful

articles to the local press, especially the *Morning Courier*, a paper that Dorr often used to publicize his varied reform ideas. In these essays Dorr cited precedents in nearby Boston, Northampton, Salem, and Lowell, Massachusetts. On December 30, 1836, Dorr set forth his arguments for the proposed high school in another *Morning Courier* essay:

> Establish a thorough system of education like that proposed, and the children of the poor will not longer be sufferers from the want of advantages; those of the more favored in circumstances will be as well taught at less cost than at present; and those of the rich will have an opportunity to partake in instruction provided for all at the public expense.

The lessening of socioeconomic segregation and the softening of class distinctions were clearly goals Dorr sought to achieve by his high school project.

By 1838 Dorr's plan for a high school was completed. Its main features were a three-year program of studies, entrance exams for students, teachers with a college education (or equivalent experience and study), and a master or preceptor, who was to be paid the substantial salary of $1,250 per year. The school hours were set from 8:00 A.M. to 12 noon and from 3:00 P.M. to 6:00 P.M. from April through September and from 9:00 A.M. to 12 noon and 2:00 P.M. to 4:30 P.M. from October through March.

Acting on the completed plan, on March 12, 1838, the Providence City Council passed an ordinance reorganizing the city's public schools. In place of the existing system of five writing-school districts and six primary-school districts, the new educational order consisted of three levels: ten primary schools (students enrolled at age four), six grammar, or writing, schools (age seven), and one high school (age twelve). The enrollment at the high school was limited to two hundred pupils, with up to one hundred girls allowed. Preference was given to residents of Providence. Visitation of schools by committeemen was required by the reorganization ordinance, which also established two schools for "colored children." The School Committee itself was also reorganized. Henceforth it would consist of thirty members appointed by the council from the city's political wards, and women were eligible to serve.

The reorganization act, which Dorr helped to draft, also created the position of superintendent of public schools. On July 23, 1839, Nathan Bishop was appointed the nation's first full-time, full-fledged superintendent of a municipal school system (the claims of Louisville and Buffalo notwithstanding).

Dorr's reform efforts were duly recognized by his peers on September 13, 1838, when he became president *pro tem* of the school board because the incumbent president, former mayor Samuel Bridgham, was in poor health. After Bridgham's death in December 1840, Dorr was elected president in his own right on February 26, 1841.

Dorr's effective, or actual, presidency of the Providence School Committee extended from 1838 to 1842. During this leadership tenure he registered several notable achievements: he was the prime mover in the establishment of Rhode Island's first high school (though sadly, he was in political exile when it opened in 1843); he appointed the first school superintendent; he implemented a thorough system of visitation and inspection of the schools by School Committee members; he completely overhauled school facilities and supervised the building of new, modern schoolhouses in every ward; and he completely revised the bylaws and regulations for the governance of the Providence public schools in 1839.

A request Dorr made of the General Assembly in 1839, however, suggests that some of the problems now confronting the Providence schools are not unique to our time. In December 1839 he asked the General Assembly for an amendment to the state school act which would "provide a remedy against the disturbance of schools by intruders interfering with the same, or by riotous persons from without." Perhaps those days were not so halcyon after all!

Finally, and perhaps most important, during Dorr's tenure on the School Committee the expenditures for the Providence public school system increased by more than 250 percent. The following table indicates the success of his funding efforts:

EXPENDITURES FOR THE FISCAL YEAR

Ending June 1834 (when he came)	Ending June 1842 (when he left)
$6,527	$16,649
$5,000 (city); $1,527 (state)	$11,592 (city); $5,057 (state)

Dorr was instrumental not only in securing the increased contribution from the city; he was primarily responsible for the more than threefold increase in state aid as well. From 1834 to 1837 he was a member of the state House of Representatives, serving on what appears to have been a newly established committee on education, a position that reflected his strong interest in that field.

In 1836 Representative Dorr seized upon the opportunity to strike a major blow for Rhode Island education. President Andrew Jackson's preference for limited government and reduced federal expenditures produced a surplus of revenue in the national treasury. The national debt was liquidated, and Congress, urged by Henry Clay, voted to distribute the treasury surplus to the several states in loans as part of the federal Deposit Act of 1836.

Dorr immediately urged that the state invest this "distribution money" and apply the interest received thereon to the support of public education. He presented this argument in the *Morning Courier* on October 25, 1836, and introduced a resolution at the October session of the General Assembly providing that income from this federal deposit fund be applied exclusively to the support of public schools. His resolution passed.

Rhode Island's share of the federal distribution money was $382,335. The income from the investment of this sum produced an annual revenue ranging from $16,307 to $19,296 in the years from 1837 to 1842. This bonanza allowed an increase in the state appropriation to the towns for education from the $10,000-per-year level established in 1828 to a figure of $25,000 set by statute in 1839. Not only Providence but every town benefited by this 2½-fold increase, the result of an educational-aid formula for which Dorr was the prime sponsor.

Finally, in 1842, Dorr embarked upon an enterprise with which we are all familiar. Because of the refusal of the political Establishment to change the state's antiquated basic law, he and his colleagues bypassed the General Assembly, drafted a People's Constitution, and attempted, eventually by force of arms, to put that constitution into effect.

The People's Constitution, of which Dorr was the principal draftsman, had much more liberal provisions regarding education than the constitution of 1843, which eventually became the basic law of the state. Dorr's document contained a declaration in support of *free* public schools, i.e., schools that were fully supported by public funds, with no assessments for books, ink, fuel, maintenance, or other costs that might burden the poorer student. Such assessments were then common in Rhode Island. In advocating completely free schools, Dorr was in advance of another educational pioneer—a contemporary Connecticut lawyer, a state legislator and educational enthusiast like Dorr himself, whose name was Henry Barnard.

In addition, Dorr's constitution attempted to conserve for the *exclusive* purpose of education not only the permanent school fund established in 1828, a fund that increased as a result of Dorr's efforts in 1839, but also all other moneys appropriated by the authority of the state for public education. This language aimed at the protection of the federal deposit fund that had been raided for noneducational purposes several times since 1836.

Ironically, over $103,000 was withdrawn from the deposit fund in 1842–43 to suppress Dorr's movement for constitutional reform. The money he sought to conserve for education was used against him and his cause. Dorr was vanquished, the People's Constitution was abandoned, and raids on the deposit fund continued, since there was no prohibition against them in the Law and Order constitution that ultimately went into effect in the aftermath of the Dorr Rebellion. Nor did that constitution provide for the establishment of *free* public schools, which were a generation away. The new document did, however, pave the way for the eventual establishment of a state-regulated system of public schools in place of the town system that had been established by the school law of 1828.

The first step in the direction of effective state regulation came in 1843 with the retention of Henry Barnard as state school agent. He immediately began the now famous school survey of 1843–45, which led to the notable Rhode Island School Law of 1845 and to Barnard's appointment as Rhode Island's first commissioner of public schools. At the time of Barnard's selection, Dorr was serving a life sentence in state prison for treason against the state.

Henry Barnard's excellent report noted many educational shortcomings throughout Rhode Island, but the Providence schools elicited his praise: "The city of Providence," said Barnard, "has already gained to itself an extended reputation and made itself a bright example to many other cities." Another learned contemporary writer, Judge William Staples, agreed. In his *Annals of Providence*, published in 1843, Staples observed that the city's schools "will not suffer by comparison with [those of] any other town or city in the Union."

Neither Barnard nor Staples mentioned Dorr by name (after 1843 their writings might have been banned if they had), but it is obvious who was primarily responsible for Providence's achievement. Regrettably, as I mentioned at the outset, Dorr's role as educational reformer has been obliterated. He is not even given a listing in the index of Thomas B. Stockwell's *History of Public Education in Rhode Island* (1876), and Thomas Wentworth Higginson, the chronicler of the state's educational development in Stockwell's volume, does not even mention Dorr in his extended narrative. Only Charles Carroll, in his *Public Education in Rhode Island* (1918), recognized Dorr's efforts, and Carroll's observations are limited to the deposit fund and the People's Constitution.

Even the most recent scholarly account of early-nineteenth-century educational reform in Providence fails to illuminate Dorr's role—or even to mention him. Noted Jacksonian era historian William G. Shade has recently written an article entitled "The 'Working Class' and Educational Reform in Early America: The Case of Providence, Rhode Island" (*The Historian* 39 [1976]: 1–23).

Revealing the prominent role played by the Providence Association of Mechanics and Manufacturers on behalf of free schools and educational improvements, Shade concludes that "in Rhode Island the main thrust for educational reform continued to come from politically active and socially respectable 'middle class' tradesmen worried about an overcrowded, inadequate public school system," who "emphasized establishing literacy and enhancing economic opportunity as well as sustaining the moral fiber of the new nation." All true, except that Shade omits the role played by Dorr. Nowhere in this extensively documented essay is he mentioned, because the early published records upon which Shade relies have been purged of references to Dorr and his contributions to public education in Rhode Island.

The other local educational luminaries of the early nineteenth century, such as John Howland, Francis Wayland, Samuel Bridgham, Nathan Bishop, and, of course, Henry Barnard, have been duly recognized and commemorated. Their names adorn our schools and our educational societies.

It is surely time that Thomas Wilson Dorr received the recognition and acknowledgment that has been denied him, recognition both richly deserved and long overdue. He was not only a constitutional and political reformer, a vigorous foe of slavery, and a champion of the immigrant; the record clearly shows that Dorr was also the principal promoter of free public education in Rhode Island during the pre-Barnard era, and its most effective advocate.

STATE CONSTITUTION.

A CALL
To the People of Rhode-Island
TO ASSEMBLE IN CONVENTION.

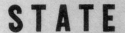

At a Mass Convention of the friends of Equal Rights and of a WRITTEN REPUBLICAN CONSTITUTION for this State, held at Newport, on the 5th day of May, 1841, the following persons were appointed a STATE COMMITTEE for the furtherance of the cause, which the Convention had assembled to promote,—viz:—for

NEWPORT COUNTY,	CHARLES COLLINS, DUTEE J. PEARCE, SILAS SISSON.	BRISTOL COUNTY,	BENJ. M. BOSWORTH, SAMUEL S. ALLEN, ABIJAH LUCE.
PROVIDENCE,	SAMUEL H. WALES, BENJ. ARNOLD, Jr. WELCOME B. SAYLES, HENRY L. WEBSTER, PHILIP B. STINESS, METCALF MARSH.	KENT,	EMANUEL RICE, SILAS WEAVER, JOHN B. SHELDON.
		WASHINGTON,	SYLVESTER HIMES, WAGER WEEDEN, CHARLES ALLEN.

The State Committee were directed "to carry forward the cause of Reform and Equal Rights, and to call a Convention of Delegates to draft a Constitution at as early a day as possible."

At an adjourned meeting of said Mass Convention held at Providence, on the 5th day of July, the instructions before given were reaffirmed; and the committee were directed to call a Convention of the People, on the basis of the Resolutions passed at Newport, "at an early day, for the formation of a CONSTITUTION."

Pursuing these instructions, the Committee held a meeting at Providence, on the 20th of July, and in conformity with the Eleventh Resolution adopted at Newport, which prescribes the call of a Convention of the People at large, to be represented in PROPORTION to POPULATION, passed unanimously the following Resolutions, for the CALL of a POPULAR CONVENTION.

Voted, That we proceed to issue a CALL for the election of DELEGATES, to take place on the LAST SATURDAY in August, (the 28th day,) to attend a CONVENTION to be holden at the STATE HOUSE in PROVIDENCE, on the FIRST MONDAY in OCTOBER, (the 4th day,) for framing a CONSTITUTION to be laid before the People for their adoption.

Voted, That every American male citizen, twenty-one years of age and upwards, who has resided in this State one year, preceding the election of delegates, shall vote for Delegates to the Convention, called by the State Committee to be held at the State House in Providence on the first Monday in October next.

Voted, That every meeting holden for the election of Delegates to the State Convention shall be organized by the election of a Chairman and Secretary, whose certificate shall be the authority required of the Delegates.

Voted, That each Town of *one thousand* inhabitants, or less, shall be entitled to one delegate, and for every additional thousand, one delegate shall be appointed; and the city of Providence shall elect three delegates from each Ward in the city.

Voted, That the Chairman and Secretary be directed to cause one thousand hand-bills to be printed and distributed through the State, containing the call for a Convention of Delegates.

Voted, That the proceedings of this meeting be signed by the Chairman and Secretary, and be published.

On motion, *Voted*, That this meeting stand adjourned to meet at this place on the first day of September, at 11 o'clock A. M.

FELLOW CITIZENS—We have discharged our duty in the call of a CONVENTION of the WHOLE PEOPLE, to provide for the attainment and security of those invaluable rights, which have so long been withheld from them, and without which they are but subjects and slaves in a State only nominally Republican.

Depend upon it that a spirit has been awakened in this State, which cannot be intimidated nor repressed—which has suffered long, until patience has ceased to be a virtue, and which, regarding the Republican institutions every where else enjoyed but here, and prompted by the memory of our venerable and patriotic ancestors, the first to assert the true principles of Religious and Political freedom, will brook no farther delay, and which cannot be more appropriately expressed than when we say, in behalf of the great majority of the PEOPLE,

☞ *GIVE US OUR RIGHTS*, or *WE WILL TAKE THEM.*

We ask for nothing that is not clearly right, and we are determined to submit to nothing so manifestly wrong as the corrupt and anti-republican system of government which has so long subsisted in Rhode Island by the forbearance of the People.

Bear in mind, that there is no CONSTITUTIONAL MODE OF AMENDING our government, except by the People at large, in whom, as the successors to the King of England, the sovereign power resides, and remains unimpaired by any lapse of time, or toleration of past abuses.

That there is no BILL OF RIGHTS in this State, except that *granted* by the Legislature, and which they can at any moment resume and annul.

That the General Assembly is a body irresponsible to the majority of the People, restricted by no constitutional rule of action, virtually omnipotent—making and unmaking the People, doing and undoing what it pleases, according to its "especial grace, certain knowledge and mere motion," in imitation, upon a smaller scale, of the Monarchy of Great Britain.

That the SYSTEM of representation to this Assembly is also the ROTTEN-BOROUGH system of Great Britain now partially reformed; by which system, in this State, a *third of the freemen*, and one *ninth of the People* command the House of Representatives.—

That, by reason of a landed qualification, which it is impossible for the great majority to obtain, *two thirds* of the people are ousted of the birthright acquired for them by their fathers, and are governed, taxed, compelled to do military duty, and subjected in all respects to the will and pleasure of *one third*, with the sole restriction, imposed by the Constitution of the United States.

Instead of enumerating other particulars, we only say—☞ look at the history of Rhode Island legislation.

Fellow Citizens—It is these evils to which the great unenfranchised majority, acting in their *original, sovereign capacity*, propose and intend to apply an effectual remedy. We ask your aid and assistance in this good work. We respectfully urge upon you to assist in the election of delegates to the Popular Convention to be held in October next, not as the friends or opponents of any political party now existing in this State, but as the friends of Justice, of Humanity, of Liberty, of Equal Rights, of well regulated Constitutional Government.

Do not be deceived by the Freeholders Convention called for November next. It is a gross fraud upon the people. The design of its originators was to crystalize in a stronger form the present statute provisions relating to suffrage, and to place them beyond the reach of amendment except by the hand of force.

Once more, we say to the unenfranchised mass of our brethren and fellow-citizens—your rights are in your own hands. Assert and vindicate them like men determined to be free. See to it that a meeting for the choice of delegates is duly held in every town, and that its proportional number is regularly elected. Summon your friends and neighbors to the work—and rely upon it that a CONSTITUTION framed by such a Convention, and SIGNED by a MAJORITY of the people, will be promptly acquiesced in by the MINORITY—will be vigorously sustained, and will become without delay, the undisputed, paramount law of our State.

Providence, July 24th, 1841.

By order and in behalf of the State Committee.

SAMUEL H. WALES, Chairman.

BENJAMIN ARNOLD, Jr., Secretary.

This broadside, issuing the call for a People's Convention, is the quintessential statement of the doctrine of popular constituent sovereignty.

Popular Sovereignty or Public Anarchy? America Debates the Dorr Rebellion

18

This treatise was written as a doctoral research paper in 1962–63 at the University of Notre Dame. Since most of the primary documents relating to the Dorr War were in Rhode Island at Brown University and the Rhode Island Historical Society, I focused my research on available reference sources—the national reaction to the Dorr Rebellion. The result, in slightly different form, was printed in Rhode Island History *60 (Summer 2002), an article that would not have been published save for its retrieval in the process of my compiling this anthology.*

Students of Rhode Island's past are acquainted with the origins and course of the Dorr Rebellion because this controversy is the most important single event in Rhode Island history. In 1841 an organization of landless, and therefore voteless, men organized as the Rhode Island Suffrage Association and called an unauthorized constitutional convention to achieve political change. This group, toward whom the General Assembly turned a deaf ear, recruited patrician reformer Thomas Wilson Dorr to lead them, and when their extralegal convention met in October and November 1841, Dorr became the principal draftsman of the progressive "People's Constitution."

From December 27 to December 29, 1841, the People's Constitution was submitted to a popular referendum. Disregard for the landholding requirement swelled the turnout to nearly 14,000. Of that number, only 52 votes were cast against the document, because the charter adherents boycotted the election. Dorr claimed that the constitution had been ratified by a majority of the people because 13,944 of the state's estimated 23,142 white adult citizens had voted to approve it. The possibility of fraudulent voting was high (as it was for any election in that age), and undoubtedly a number of bogus ballots were cast; but when the results were in, the reformers insisted that the People's Constitution had supplanted the charter as the paramount law of the state.

Nonetheless, Dorr's opposition had every intention of asserting its legal authority, and in the early months of 1842 it made a determined bid to undermine the revolutionaries' position. One weapon was its enactment of the so-called "Algerine Law," which imposed severe penalties upon those attempting to exercise power or hold office under the People's Constitution. Another extremely potent maneuver was the Charterite appeal to Rhode Island's sectional, class, ethnic, and—especially—religious sentiments. The Law and Order party, as the charter adherents were called, alarmed entrepreneurs by alleging that the Dorrites espoused an anticapitalist philosophy, and it aroused farmers by picturing the reformers as voracious urbanites who were determined to usurp all political power unto themselves. In addition, the Law and Order faction played upon the fears of native-born Protestants by informing them that the liberal suffrage clause of the People's Constitution would pave the way for the political ascendancy of the Irish Catholic immigrants who were swarming into the state in ever-increasing numbers.

A third offensive launched by the Law and Order forces consisted of an appeal to President John Tyler for federal protection to preserve the status quo. After some ambivalence, the chief executive promised the Charterites aid if violence erupted.

Despite the resolute efforts of the Law and Order faction to squelch the insurgents, Dorr tenaciously held his ground. On April 18 the revolutionaries staged an election under the People's Constitution, with Thomas Wilson Dorr emerging as the "People's governor." Dorr and those who were elected with him proceeded to establish a skeleton government in violation of the Algerine Law. In the eyes of his opponents, Dorr had now committed treason against the state.

The unprecedented specter of two rival state governments brought this intense but local controversy into the national spotlight. The Rhode Island crisis not only embroiled President John Tyler, both houses of Congress, and the U.S. Supreme Court; it also had a substantial impact on neighboring states, the press nationwide, and the leading politicians and political philosophers of the period. In addition, the Dorr War (as some called it) served as a valuable source of propaganda in the Democratic party's attempt to discredit the incumbent Whigs.*

The national debate over the legitimacy of the Dorr Rebellion — the subject of this essay — has received only scant attention from historians, although discussion of "the Rhode Island question" often transcended mere partisanship and grappled with the basic theories of American constitutional government. The doctrine defended by Dorr can be described as popular constituent sovereignty — the right of the people, without prior authorization from a reactionary legislature, to frame and adopt a new constitution. Opponents of this revolutionary procedure claimed that the American system of government had achieved such stability that constitutional change should and could occur only through the use of approved forms, or with the sanction of the existing government.

During the period from April 1842 through the presidential election of 1844, featuring the Democratic campaign slogan of "Polk, Dallas, and Dorr," the issues involved in the Rhode Island controversy were widely debated and discussed in prominent newspapers and periodicals and reflected upon in the memoirs and private correspondence of the nation's leading citizens.

Prior to the critical April 1842 state elections, the Dorrites had appealed to the Democratic leaders in Congress for support. Dr. J. A. Brown, president of the Rhode Island Suffrage Association, was sent to Washington as agent and lobbyist for the People's government. Following Brown's exhortations, six prominent Democrats wrote letters of encouragement to Dorr.[1]

The earliest recorded response to Dorr's appeal was made on April 12, 1842. The writer (presumably Senator Perry Smith of Connecticut) briefly assured Dorr that he need not fear the use of

---

*The foregoing survey is a synopsis of the material found in my book-length study *Democracy in Decline: Rhode Island's Constitutional Development, 1636–1841* (Providence, 1977). What follows is the hitherto unpublished product of my doctoral seminar at Notre Dame, directed by Dr. Aaron I. Abell.

force by the federal government against the reformers' cause, then closed the missive with a request that the letter be burned.[2]

Senators Levi Woodbury of New Hampshire and William Allen of Ohio corresponded with the People's governor three days later. Woodbury told Dorr that if the people do not have a right to draft a constitution "when and how they please, the whole fabric of our American liberties rests on sand and stubble." The matter was in the people's hands, not in the hands of the adamant legislature, remarked Woodbury. The distinguished New Hampshire solon must not have considered his advice revolutionary, for he concluded the letter with the following admonition: "Shun violence—insubordination—civil war—but move onward…to your just and pure objects *in constitutional methods.*"[3] Seven years later Associate Justice Woodbury would cast the lone dissenting vote in a case arising out of the rebellion, *Luther* v. *Borden,* in which the Supreme Court formulated the political-question doctrine to avoid disturbing the final outcome of the Rhode Island controversy.

That same day Dorr received additional encouragement from the prominent Ohio senator William Allen, who was to lead the fight for the reformers in the upper house during the ensuing months. Allen informed Dorr that he had obtained an interview for Dr. Brown with President Tyler and that he had accompanied the agent of the People's government to the meeting. In the interview, Allen informed the president "that the majority of the people in Rhode Island were in the right on every known principle of public liberty, and that their movement presented not a case authorizing the interposition of the federal government by force or otherwise." Tyler's reaction was not disclosed.[4]

On the next day Senators Silas Wright, Jr., of New York and Thomas Hart Benton of Missouri contacted Dorr. Wright told of the "intense interest" in Washington concerning the Rhode Island situation, and while expressing sympathy for Dorr's cause, he disclaimed any intention to become a partisan in the controversy. The New Yorker concluded philosophically by urging the People's governor to practice caution and forbearance. "You cannot fail to see," concluded Wright, "that your discretion must measure the support which your friends abroad can give you. They can sustain you in doing right. They cannot in doing wrong."[5]

When Dorr finished reading the somewhat noncommittal letter, he opened another bearing the postmark "Washington City" and read the remarks of Thomas Hart Benton. The Missourian assured Dorr "that the Democracy ... fully admit the validity of the constitutional movement of the people in Rhode Island." Benton, however, urged that violence be avoided, because "This is not the age, nor the country, in which to settle political questions by the sword."[6] Time would prove that "Old Bullion" was tragically wrong.

133

The final reply to Dorr's appeal came nearly a month later from the pen of Edmund Burke, the New Hampshire congressman who was to emerge as the reformers' most vigorous supporter. He informed Dorr that Democrats in both Washington and New England were, without exception, "roundly in favor of the suffrage party," and Burke himself gave assurance that he was with the People of Rhode Island "heart and soul."[7]

It should be noted that only the northern wing of the Democratic party was represented in these letters. Dorr discovered later that many southern members approved of his cause but would not endorse general principles of majority rights that could be interpreted to include blacks in their own states.[8] The South's leading Democratic spokesman, John C. Calhoun, was deeply concerned with the progress of the Rhode Island reform movement. A year after the rebellion was thwarted, Calhoun expressed his views in a logical and

By 1842 John C. Calhoun had become the principal defender of the rights of the minority South.

conclusive public letter. He claimed to be in sympathy with the suffrage party in Rhode Island as far as the enlargement of the franchise was involved. Providing that the controversy was confined to discussion and agitation, continued Calhoun, the federal government could not intervene. But after an incisive survey of constitutional precedents, the learned South Carolinian jealously guarded his cherished doctrine of minority rights by declaring that it would be the "death-blow of constitutional democracy to admit the right of the numerical majority to alter or abolish constitutions at pleasure" by resort to extraconstitutional means.[9] Most of his fellow southerners agreed.

The sentiments of elder statesman Andrew Jackson contrasted markedly with those of Calhoun. On May 23, 1842, he wrote to longtime associate Francis P. Blair that the "people of Rhode Island will triumph as they ought in establishing their republican constitution." "Old Hickory" believed that Tyler would never aid the "aristocracy" of Rhode Island by sending a regular force, but if he were weak and foolish enough to perform such a dastardly act, "a hundred thousand of the sovereign people would fly to the rescue to sustain the people's constitution." Jackson's concluding remark would have made Calhoun and his associates shudder: "The people are the sovereign power and agreeable to our system they have the right to alter and amend their system of Government when a majority wills it, as a majority have a right to rule."[10]

In August 1844 Jackson was invited to attend a mass rally in Providence for Dorr (who was then languishing in prison) and for the Democratic presidential candidate, James Knox Polk, and his running mate, George M. Dallas. Over two years after his frustrating defeat, Dorr was still being used by the Democrats as a political martyr and as an example of Whig treachery that must be avenged at the ballot box.

Jackson apologetically informed the Dorr supporters that ill health confined him to the Hermitage, his home, but he made public the sentiments that he had expressed to Francis Blair in the critical days of 1842. Dorr, said Jackson, "committed no offence except that of endeavoring to supersede the royal charter by a constitution emanating directly from the people....Granting even that he erred as to the means adopted, either in reference to time or form, it is difficult to conceive how the severe punishment inflicted upon him can be justified."[11]

Martin Van Buren, George Bancroft, and former governor Henry Hubbard of New Hampshire were also extended invitations by the demonstration committee, but only Hubbard was able to attend.[12] Van Buren's reply indicated strong sympathy for the imprisoned reformer, whose treatment, he believed, was oppressive, "severe, humiliating, and unjust," for it was never Dorr's intention "to prostrate to unworthy, much less criminal objects."[13]

Bancroft—an ardent equalitarian Democrat, a prominent historian, and the Democratic candidate for governor of Massachusetts—gave a stirring reply to the reformers when he indignantly declared that for the first time in history "solitary imprisonment at labor for life has been made the punishment of actions that were but the expressions of political opinions."[14] This ringing condemnation of the Law and Order party no doubt heightened the ardor of the demonstrators, and it gave great personal satisfaction to Bancroft.[15]

Most conclusive evidence that the Rhode Island question was, on the national level, one involving political partisanship as well as principle can be discerned in the sentiments of the Whigs. Even such a vociferous champion of human rights as Horace Greeley condemned the stand taken by Dorr. The editor of the influential *New York Tribune* felt that the franchise in Rhode Island should be broadened, but Dorr's resort to force filled him with apprehension and disgust. In several editorials in the *Tribune* Greeley castigated Dorr and the principles for which he stood. Greeley asserted that the People's Constitution would have transferred political power into the hands of the reformers, and he denounced the resort to violence as a course that could lead only to anarchy. Dorr's attempt to seize the state arsenal on May 18, 1842, inspired Greeley to produce a theory of government remarkable for its spirit of conservatism. The editor stated that those possessing the suffrage should extend it when, in their judgment, it was wise and just to do so. He asserted that it was the American tradition to regard the suffrage not as a natural right, as Dorr had claimed, but as a duty to be assigned by those who already possessed it. The voters would impose this duty when, in their judgment, the time was propitious for its extension to the hitherto unfranchised.[16] Thus, as Glyndon Van Deusen puts it, to the supposedly liberal Greeley "the progress of political democracy rested upon the wisdom and benevolence of those already enfranchised, rather than upon the unalienable rights of man."[17] Van Deusen finds that Greeley manifested gross intolerance by heartily approving Dorr's sentence to life imprisonment, and later for the regret he expressed upon hearing of Dorr's release.[18]

Young Horace undoubtedly received firsthand information concerning the Rhode Island situation from his close associate, the New York Whig potentate Thurlow Weed, who accompanied the Law and Order forces to Acote's Hill in June 1842 for the final encounter of the Dorr War.[19] Weed's presence in Rhode Island was the culmination of a long series of events that had begun in mid-April 1842, when the *New York Evening Post* called attention to a proposed memorial then circulating in New York City calling for the impeachment of Tyler for his threatened interference in the Rhode Island dispute. Although the memorial was never presented, it paved the way for a Democratic sympathy meeting in Tammany Hall on the evening of April 27, at which A. W. Parmenter of Rhode Island pleaded the case for the suffragists. During the next three weeks several other meetings were held, and enthusiasm for the Rhode Island reformers began to mount.[20]

In mid-May, returning from his disillusioning visit with President Tyler, Dorr stopped in New York City, where he was warmly received by several prominent Tammany leaders and invited to attend the Bowery Theater. This cordial act was the first of many showered upon Dorr during his brief stay in the metropolis.[21]

The following morning the People's governor was accorded a reception, and he spent several hours receiving counsel from William Cullen Bryant, Samuel J. Tilden, Eli Moore, and other Tammany leaders. When the time came for the governor to resume his journey homeward, a procession composed of five hundred men, a company of volunteer firemen, and a band formed an escort.[22] Before leaving the city, Dorr was also offered a military escort to Providence by Colonels Alexander Ming, Jr., and Abraham J. Crasto, the leaders of two New York militia regiments. Dorr declined, but he added that "the time may not be far distant when I may be obliged to call upon you for your services."[23]

When he had arrived in New York, it appeared as if Dorr had determined, though quite reluctantly, to use peaceful means to effect a compromise in Rhode Island. It seems quite certain that the encouragement, advice, and promises of support given to Dorr by the New York Democrats greatly influenced his resort to force.

Popular Sovereignty or Public Anarchy? America Debates the Dorr Rebellion

137

Before the month was up, Dorr launched his abortive attack on the state arsenal in Providence.[24]

Dorr's New York friends continued their agitation immediately after his return to Rhode Island. A large demonstration held in the park in front of New York City Hall was attended by such illustrious Democrats as William Cullen Bryant, Samuel J. Tilden, Elijah F. Purdy, Aaron Vanderpoel, C. C. Cambreleng, Eli Moore, and Levi D. Slamm. At this meeting a corresponding committee of twelve was appointed to continue the movement in behalf of the People's party in Rhode Island.[25] Slamm, editor of the New York *New Era*, went so far as to print a call for "Patriot Volunteers" who would march to aid Dorr in the event of armed interference by the federal government.[26]

Slamm's call for volunteers was scarcely off the press when news arrived of Dorr's ludicrous attempt to take the arsenal on May 18, and most New Yorkers saw that further aid was useless. "Judging from their looks," remarked the New York *Commercial Advertiser*, "never did a set of people feel before quite so foolish and forlorn as did the leaders of the Park meeting.... The flag which had been kept flying for several days at Tammany Hall, in honor of Dorr... was struck and all looked as though 'melancholy had marked them for her own.'"[27] Only Levi Slamm continued his vigorous support for Dorr, and the *New Era*'s editor was present when the "war" ended ignominiously on Acote's Hill in late June.[28]

Despite the near collapse of Tammany support, New York continued to be affected by the Rhode Island uprising. Whig governor William H. Seward, as might be expected, collaborated with Rhode Island's Charterite governor Samuel Ward King. On June 13 King informed the New York chief executive that a reward of one thousand dollars had been posted for the capture of Dorr. When King told Seward that the exile was probably in New York City, Seward wrote to inform the Law and Order governor that he would cooperate in apprehending the fugitive.[29]

Seward's concern with the Dorr Rebellion was evidenced by his frequent mention of the disturbance in his letters during mid-1842.[30] He admired Dorr's "coolness and dignity" and remarked that he was "a manifestly superior man,"[31] but when the crisis came to a head in late June, the New York governor sent a two-man delegation—Richard M. Blatchford, his private secretary, and Colonel James Bowen—to tender the support of New York to the charter party. Thurlow Weed, in his usual capacity as unofficial observer, accompanied Blatchford and Bowen at the suggestion of Governor Seward. Weed, later a confidant of Abraham Lincoln, made the sixteen-mile hike from Providence to Acote's Hill with King's forces, aggravating his varicose veins in the process. Of the two hundred stragglers who were apprehended after Dorr's flight, fifteen or twenty were New York "Subterraneans," according to Weed, who gave the following description of the events subsequent to the "daring" capture of Acote's Hill by the Law and Order forces:

> The duties and excitement of the day being over, General McNeill's headquarters were established in a pleasant grove, where hampers of cold meats, poultry, game, etc., etc., with baskets of champagne, soon appeared. The spread was a bountiful one, the repast was animated by patriotic toasts and speeches, and was not concluded until near six o'clock, when the general, with his suite and guests, departed in hilarious spirits for Providence....[32]

This gala ending certainly made the long trek to Chepachet worthwhile.

Other nationally prominent Whigs joined Greeley, Weed, and Seward in condemning Dorr. After the arsenal fiasco John Quincy Adams remarked in his memoirs that "the ignominious flight of the spurious Governor, Thomas W. Dorr, has postponed the heaviest calamity that ever befell this nation." Shortly thereafter, Adams came to Rhode Island to speak before the Franklin Lyceum on the social-contract versus the divine-right theories of government. This November 1842 lecture on the origins of government, later published in pamphlet form, affirmed the popular basis of the state in accordance with the theories of Locke, Sidney, Montesquieu, and Rousseau but repudiated the right of revolution against it, once established, except in cases of extreme tyranny.

Adams departed in emphasis from eighteenth-century social-compact theorists, however, by emphasizing evolving necessity and man's nature as a "social being" rather than will and intent as the basis of government.

Over his long career different practical situations, such as the Dorr Rebellion, produced modifications in Adams's views of the social compact and the conditions that brought it into being. He remained convinced, however, that once government was constituted by the process of social evolution, this agency of the people was confined to action permitted to it by the people through the process of election. Adams, whose political philosophy placed great emphasis on order and stability, favored limited male suffrage which might be extended gradually. He firmly believed that the "protection and security of property" was as important a purpose of the social contract as the protection and security of persons. Tax and property qualifications, asserted Adams, would assure the presence at the polls and in office of those men most likely to fulfill this duty of property protection.

In earlier writings Adams had admitted the primitive right of insurrection, but he believed that it should be used only sparingly and held very much in reserve. Adams told his Rhode Island audience that he endorsed the right to revolt against tyranny, but though he did not say so, he did not consider the charter regime of propertied community leaders a despotic government.

Adams began his address (much of which he prepared prior to the rebellion) by reference to the Massachusetts experience, averring that the people of his commonwealth "have set the example of the gradual enlargement of the right of suffrage quietly, peaceably, without even disturbing the harmony of the community, but by the progress of public opinion ripening into universal assent." The conservative Adams believed that democracy, or universal suffrage, "is but the investment of the multitude with absolute powers." In conclusion, he contended that a constitution is "the work of the people...not of the whole people by the phantom of universal suffrage, but of the whole people by that portion of them capable of contracting for the whole."[33]

Vigorous in his denunciation of Dorr was Adams's fellow Bay

139

Stater Daniel Webster. As Tyler's secretary of state, Webster was on hand when the Rhode Island affair first presented itself to the federal government. He had served as the president's agent in investigating the situation in early June 1842,[34] and seven years later he played a part in the affair's final disposition. It was he who presented the defense of the charter government's agent (Captain Luther Borden) to the U.S. Supreme Court in the case of *Luther* v. *Borden*. The brilliant advocate castigated Dorrism, but he centered his attack on a more technical point: in a series of letters and in his argument before the Court, Webster maintained that the problem of recognizing the legal government in Rhode Island was a political question and therefore not justiciable.[35] The Court expressed its agreement with the indomitable Webster, for Chief Justice Taney's decision declared that the issue of the legitimacy of the rival governments of 1842 was one that was purely political in nature, within the purview of Congress and the president, and therefore it was one upon which the Court must refuse to pass judgment.

It is obvious that the nation's major political figures, especially in the North, were influenced to take a stand on the Dorr Rebellion according to party affiliation. Within the state many leading Democrats, especially those of rural, Protestant, native stock, allied with the Whigs against Dorr, but northern Democrats outside the confines of tiny Rhode Island sought to make political hay by exploiting the alleged tyranny of the Whig-controlled charter government.[36]

This same trend was followed by the newspapers and periodicals that reviewed the Rhode Island drama; they, too, took sides according to their party predilection. The first non-Rhode Island paper to focus its attention on constitutional struggle was the Boston *Post*. This Democratic organ began championing the cause of the suffragists as early as January 1842. Its crosstown rival, the Whig *Atlas*, associated the Democracy with Dorr and heaped obloquy upon the suffrage movement.[37] In New York, as we have seen, Greeley's *Tribune* and the *Commercial Advertiser* condemned Dorr, while the *Evening Post* and Levi Slamm's *New Era* backed him to the hilt. Two other New York newspapers, the *Courier and*

Enquirer and the *American*, gave enthusiastic support to Governor King and bitterly condemned the action of the rebellious Dorrites.[38]

In the nation's capital the revolutionaries found an adamant and implacable foe in the *National Intelligencer*,[39] and in nearby Baltimore Jeremiah Hughes took constant swipes at Dorr in the pages of his *Niles' Register*. Hughes gave considerable coverage to the Rhode Island situation during mid-1842, labeling Dorr's course as one of "violence and blood." The reformer's attack upon the arsenal was described by the *Register* as Governor Dorr's "proclamation of war against the United States."[40] During the next three years, until Dorr's release from prison, Hughes kept the nation informed of the fate of the "usurper" by periodic notices in his weekly chronicle.

Interest in the controversy was also exhibited by several newspapers published south of the national capital. Thomas Ritchie's blatantly Democratic Richmond *Enquirer* admonished the federal government to remain aloof from the disturbance. "Move not a soldier, and send not a musket into Rhode Island," cried the Virginia semiweekly. Dorr's actions created a stir even in distant Louisiana. The New Orleans *Commercial Bulletin*, however, opposed Ritchie's stand and demanded federal interference, claiming that the "posture of affairs in Rhode Island is truly deplorable, and if suffered to proceed much farther will do more to impair American credit and character abroad than any event since the date of our government."[41]

Of all the controversy engendered in the nation's newspapers and periodicals by the Dorr Rebellion, perhaps the most significant was the disputation on political theory between John L. O'Sullivan and Orestes Brownson in the pages of the *United States Magazine and Democratic Review* during 1842–43. O'Sullivan, a devout equalitarian who coined the phrase "Manifest Destiny," was cofounder of the *Review*, a nationally distributed journal oriented toward politics and literature. The magazine was under his sole editorship during the period 1841–46.[42]

Early in 1842 O'Sullivan was moved by the plight of political polemicist Orestes Brownson's financially floundering *Boston Quarterly Review*. Wishing to relieve his fellow Democrat of distress, O'Sullivan suggested that their magazines combine, with Brownson as contributing editor to the *Democratic Review*. The Irishman's gracious offer was accepted, and thus began a stormy relationship.

142

Brownson's contributions during 1842 were not as controversial as they were abstract, metaphysical, and dull. "The *Review*," notes Arthur Schlesinger, Jr., "dealt in the immediacies of action and enjoyment, caring little for the swirling depths of theory."[43]

The erratic Orestes Brownson became the most vocal and persistent national critic of the doctrine of popular constituent sovereignty upon which the Dorr Rebellion was based.

In February 1843 O'Sullivan complained to Brownson that the readers were "much disappointed of the expectation they had entertained of being interested in your articles. Especially now for the coming...numbers...it is necessary to aim at the object of interesting and satisfying the great mass of the subscribers."[44] O'Sullivan would have cause to rue this suggestion, for Brownson abandoned his exposition of synthetic philosophy and turned to the then popular topic of democracy and constitutional government.

The contemporary event that had placed the question of constitutional government in the center of the political stage was the Dorr Rebellion. As early as June 1842, the month of the debacle at Acote's Hill, O'Sullivan had ventured his first opinion on "The Rhode Island Affair." The editor prefaced his remarks by admitting that the present state of his information would cause him to postpone "full examination of the whole question" to a future issue. Nevertheless, he continued, a general outline of the episode could be gathered. The tone of his rather lengthy outline can be perceived from his opening observation:

> One point is so generally conceded as to be beyond
> the necessity for any argument—namely, that the
> Constitutionalists were perfectly right in the main
> object of their enterprise, the establishment of a

constitution containing proper definitions of all the
powers of government, and based on the principles
of universal suffrage.[45]

The liberal Irishman concluded his summary with the statement
that the Dorrites were perfectly entitled to frame a constitution
and to establish a government under it. In sustaining that government, "they were the true party of law and order, occupying a defensive position against disloyal and factious aggression" brought
against their legitimate government by those acting under the
authority of the superseded charter. O'Sullivan also expressed "profound satisfaction" for the pro-Dorr stand taken by the Democratic
governments of Rhode Island's sister states (especially Connecticut and New Hampshire, where Democrats were in control) and
viewed with disgust Tyler's role in the uprising. The *Democratic
Review* further asserted that "nearly the entire body of the Whig
Party have betrayed the true instincts and affinities of their political character, in the course they have taken on this question."[46]

O'Sullivan gave a detailed exposition of the Rhode Island situation in the next issue (July 1842). After another brief summation
of the leading events of the crisis, the *Review* turned to a consideration of the political theory involved in the controversy. Four
questions were posed, and the editor, in the most liberal Democratic tradition, proceeded to resolve them.

To the first problem, "In whom does the sovereignty reside?"
O'Sullivan quite naturally answered, "the people." Then, after
appealing to Locke's social-compact theory, he asserted that the
sovereignty resides in the whole body of adult male permanent
residents of sound mind—i.e., every person in the state who could
be a party to the compact if it were to be formed anew. "If this be
a just conclusion, then the right of a majority of this body to
change the government at pleasure, whatever may be the wishes of
the electors, is beyond dispute." Therefore, since a majority of "the
people" in Rhode Island have ratified the People's Constitution, "it
is the true and real organic law of the state."[47]

O'Sullivan then asked, "What is the right of resistance or of
revolution?" and retorted by claiming that it is a right above all

human law, founded on the natural rights of the individual. It is to be exercised only when governments transcend the limits of just authority. "Resistance to tyranny is a right—nay, a duty—inscribed upon our hearts by Providence." The right of the people to frame and to change their government is unquestionable and unalienable, and if a government steps beyond the limits of its just power, "it may be resisted by virtue of a law higher than human society." This right of resistance, continued O'Sullivan, is also the right of revolution—the right to forcibly overturn tyrannical rule, even though it is supported by a majority of the political society. The right of a *majority* to change their government at will is a legal right; the right of revolution "is a right against law and above law; a right of minorities and individuals."[48]

The next query was less theoretical: "How far does the federal Constitution authorize the interference by the Union with the exercise of sovereignty in a State?" O'Sullivan answered with an interpretation of Article IV, Section 4. This provision conferred upon the federal government the authority to protect the states against domestic violence, and then only upon an application by a state's legislature or executive. The editor interpreted this to mean that the federal government is "to protect *the majority of the social body, on the application of its lawful legislature or executive, against unlawful violence.*" If the majority of the people have the right at all times to change their government, it followed that the new government (Dorr's) was the one to be protected, on the application of the new legislature, against the violence of the old legislature or the old electors.[49]

The fourth and final question was "In a case of domestic violence, within the constitution, in what manner can the United States interfere?" The power to interfere in a case of domestic violence was reserved to the national legislature, claimed the fiery Irishman, and he convincingly cited Madison (*Federalist* no. 43) to substantiate his contentions. This power belongs exclusively to Congress and cannot be constitutionally delegated to the president, for it would "arm him with a more than kingly power." According to O'Sullivan's solutions to the problems he had posed, Dorrism had been vindicated.[50]

In the following month's issue the *Democratic Review* printed an impressive political profile of Thomas Wilson Dorr. The individual conduct of the Rhode Island patriot, said the *Review*, "has in no single respect been wanting in courage, firmness, disinterestedness, or devotion to the cause at the head of which he stood." O'Sullivan did admit, however, that Dorr had been at times mistaken in judgment, and deceived in his estimate of men.[51] Assuredly this was Dorr's fatal weakness.

The Rhode Island controversy disappeared from the columns of the *Review* for several months, but O'Sullivan's suggestion that Brownson contribute articles with a wider appeal brought the issue and its related political and constitutional doctrines once more to the center of the stage. Brownson abandoned his treatment of synthetic philosophy and in April 1843 submitted the first of his controversial political tracts, "Democracy and Liberty." He prepared the way for his series of bombshells by remarking at the outset that his "democratic brethren" would be tried severely, for he intended "to run athwart many of their fondly cherished prejudices, and to controvert not a few of their favorite axioms." To the chagrin of O'Sullivan, in the ensuing issues the unpredictable Orestes would do just that. The liberal Irish editor would receive far more than he anticipated.

With the principles of Dorrism undoubtedly in mind,[52] Brownson began his treatise by contending that we must procure stronger governmental guarantees than those provided by popular suffrage, popular virtue, and popular intelligence. The phrase *Vox populi est vox dei* is "blasphemy," observed Brownson, for if we mean by democracy the form of government that rests for its wisdom and justice on the intelligence and virtue of the people alone, "it is a great humbug."[53] After an elaborate argument to prove the validity of this statement, Brownson turned to a consideration of freedom, or liberty, "the great end with all men in their religious, their political, and their individual actions." Liberty might be misinterpreted and erroneous measures adopted to establish or guarantee it, he said; many of the younger members of the Democratic party were guilty of the former abuse, because they did not see that anything other than the establishment of a perfectly democratic government was necessary to render every man practically free. But this notion was impossible, concluded Brownson, because the virtue and intelligence of the people are imperfect, and therefore the people "are *not* competent to govern themselves."[54]

146

Brownson continued by remarking that the very term "self-government" implies a contradiction, for it makes the governor and the governed the same and is, therefore, "no government." Likewise, if the instrument of government, a constitution, emanates from the people and rests for its support on their will, it is absolutely indistinguishable from no constitution at all. If the people are to be governed, there must be a power distinct from them and above them. This power, whatever it be, wherever lodged, must be separate from the people and sovereign over them.[55]

It must not be overlooked, said Brownson, that government is needed for the people as the state, as well as for the people as individuals. To assume that the people, as the body politic, need no governing is wrong. Brownson objected to the definition of democracy which asserts that it consists in the sovereignty of the people. If the doctrine of popular sovereignty were to be recognized as valid, nothing would prevent even an individual from applying it to himself, thereby disowning all authority external to him. The people as an aggregate of individuals are not sovereign; the only sense in which they are sovereign at all is when organized into a body politic and *acting through its forms*. All action done in opposition to the state or accomplished outside its prescribed forms "is the action of the mob, disorderly, illegal, and to a greater or less degree criminal, treasonable in fact, and as such legitimately punishable." The justice and desirability of the end must not make men blind to the illegality of the means by which they wish to attain it. "Without an efficient Constitution, which is not only an instrument through which the people govern, but which is a power which governs them, by effectually confining their action to certain specific subjects, there is and can be no good government, no individual liberty."[56]

Democracy, declared Brownson, has been wrongly defined to be a form of government. It is, in fact, a principle, the end rather than the means. The proper goal of human society is the freedom and progress of all men, but the means by which this happy circumstance is to be obtained is not necessarily by instituting the purely democratic form of government. We have been too ready to conclude that if democracy—universal suffrage without constitutional restraints on the power of the people—is established as a form of government, the end will follow necessarily. But the desired end "will not be secured by this loose radicalism with regard to popular sovereignty," nor by "these demagogical boasts of the virtue and intelligence of the people, which have become so fashionable." The only true way of securing freedom and progress is through society's existing institutions. In expressing a view not unlike that of contemporary German philosopher Georg Hegel, Brownson contended that liberty comes only in and through order—not by rejecting authority, but by and in obedience to authority. "Liberty without the guarantee of Authority, would be the worst of tyrannies," concluded the outspoken Orestes.[57]

This rebuke of Dorrism was somewhat surprising: in 1841, at Dorr's invitation, Brownson had addressed a suffrage association in Providence, and upon Dorr's installation as governor in the spring of 1842, Brownson had written him a letter of encouragement.[58] This about-face caused the horrified O'Sullivan to remark that the young liberal, after passing the grand climacteric of life, was becoming the old conservative.[59] The irate editor appended a note to Brownson's article attempting to refute this "daring heresy" respecting the sovereignty of the people. O'Sullivan, an ardent Jacksonian Democrat, admitted that the people err, but he added an eloquent plea: "Give us...Self-Government—Self-Reliance—Self-Development—Freedom—yes, freedom to make mistakes... rather than the external and superincumbent pressure" of an extraneous government.[60]

In the May issue Brownson accelerated the tempo of the controversy in an article entitled "Popular Government." He reasserted his belief that the constitution of a state was not merely a written instrument drawn up by the people and alterable at their pleasure and, as some of his Democratic friends had "contended in the case of Rhode Island, alterable at the pleasure of a bare majority...coming together informally, and acting without any regard to its provisions." If a constitution was such an instrument, what restraint could it impose on the will of the majority? Brownson asked. A constitution that cannot govern the people as well as the individual or the minority is obviously no restraint on the sovereign power; it leaves the sovereign power absolute and therefore is as good as no constitution at all. If the validity of Dorr's action were to be admitted, said Brownson, it would mean that the will of the people, even though unorganized and independent of the constitution, was the true sovereign and might at any time rightfully override the constitution itself.[61]

Brownson's concept of a constitution would not admit of this possibility, however, for he believed that "the *Constitution is itself ultimate*"; it is not a mere written instrument but the actual organization of the state. "It is the sovereign, and, when wisely adapted to the real character of the country, the genius and pursuits of the people, it is always self-sufficing." The inscrutable author did admit that the whole governing power is, and should be, vested in the people, but in the people *organized*—organized not in one consolidated body but in such a way that "the action of the whole is always through the parts, or at least can never transcend what all the parts will tolerate." What Brownson was proposing was the minoritarian doctrine of concurrent majorities, a theory, he said, that is "much more *popular*, and secures a much larger share of individual freedom . . . than the consolidated democracy" against which he was protesting.[62] Here the unpredictable Brownson had become the theoretical ally of Calhoun, and even enlarged upon the South Carolinian's doctrines.

Once again O'Sullivan's feathers were ruffled. Another note was appended to the remarks of the irrepressible Orestes. To protect minorities against the oppression or improvidence of majorities was one thing, exclaimed the editor, but to abandon all confidence in the intelligence and competency of the people for self-government, and to denounce them as "cattle," was a different thing, a thing to be scorned. O'Sullivan said that he had long regarded Mr. Calhoun's "favorite doctrine of concurrent majorities . . . as a political truth of the highest value," but, he added, Brownson's attacks on the capacity of the people for self-government and his repudiation of popular sovereignty extended far beyond the doctrines of Calhoun.[63]

Brownson concluded his study of political theory in a series of three articles on the "Origin and Ground of Government," which appeared in the August, September, and October 1843 issues of the *Review*. In the process he terminated his tenuous association with the exasperated O'Sullivan. The philosopher began his valedictory discourse by lamenting that politics as a science had been neglected shamefully by Americans. He proposed to do his share to remedy this lack of philosophical inquiry of a political nature by examining the essence, origin, and end of government.[64]

The essence of government is to govern, said Brownson, and that force which governs is the sovereign, or that which constitutes the state. This concept necessarily demands two correlative terms, the *governor* and the *governed*. Brownson's earlier assertions about the inadmissibility of "self-government," where the ruler and the ruled are identical, were repeated.

Government is also that which has the right to govern. The governed, then, are not only forced but morally bound to obey. Obedience is a duty; allegiance is owed to government, and this is the foundation of loyalty. The very conception of self-government, however, excludes that of loyalty, Brownson asserted.[65]

With these principles established, the theorist proceeded to define political or civil liberty as "freedom from all obligation to obey any commands but those of the legitimate sovereign." To have no obligation to obey the rightful sovereign was not liberty but license. Liberty was freedom from all restraints but those imposed by the legitimate ruler. These restraints, Brownson continued, "are never to be regarded as tyrannical or oppressive, however stringent they may be." The true sovereign must be obeyed unto the loss of property, personal freedom, and even life itself. He may command all; the individual may withhold nothing, for his right "is simply the right to obey."[66]

How may we discover who or what is the legitimate sovereign? This question, said Brownson, leads directly to the "Origin and Ground of Government." Addressing that topic, Brownson proceeded to examine the four main theories of governmental genesis: that government originated (1) in the express appointment of God, (2) in the spontaneous development of human nature, (3) in the authority of the father of the family, or (4) in the social compact formed by the people in convention assembled.

Considering these theories in inverse order, Brownson first demolished the social-compact concept of government—the basis of Dorrist philosophy—by "several weighty objections." He proclaimed the state of nature to be a falsehood and denied that civilization and civil society were unnatural to man. The origin of government in a social compact is not susceptible to historical verification, he continued; moreover, if we accept the theory that government originated in a compact, we would be obliged to assume that the people could act before they existed, for their action in forming the compact presupposes their existence as civil society. Even if all these objections are waived, Brownson asserted, the compact theory affords no sufficient ground for the authority of government. Several allusions to the Rhode Island constitutional controversy appear in this convincing refutation of the social-compact theory.[67]

In concluding the first of his three articles, Brownson rejected also the concept that the state was of patriarchal origins. The family could not be the germ of the state because both are "primary institutions." The other two theories concerning the origin of government—the spontaneous development of nature and divine ordination—are "both in the main true and worthy to be accepted," said Brownson. But the state did not originate in human spontaneity alone, nor only in the direct ordinance of God. The right to command must be an expression of the will of God, and it must respond to an inherent and essential want of human nature or there would be no reason for its existence.[68]

In the remaining two articles the master theorist showed an irresistible inclination toward the view that the origin of government must be ascribed to the sovereign authority of God operating through the natural freedom of man. The sovereignty of God must be practically represented among men, Brownson claimed, or it would have no efficacious existence. In the purely human relations of men, this divine sovereignty is represented by the state, but the constitution of the state is established neither by divine or human appointment exclusively. While the legitimate power and authority of the sovereign state must come from God, he normally acts in accordance with human nature. Finally, Brownson concluded that the creation of that authoritative institution, the state, an exigency of human nature, occurred in such a way as to preserve human freedom.[69]

Occasionally citing the Dorr Rebellion as a hideous example of the excesses of democracy,[70] Brownson also reiterated his beliefs in the inviolability of the constitution (i.e., the state) by extraconstitutional means. He stridently proclaimed that the true watchword and battle cry for us is not "*The majority have the right to govern, but THE CONSTITUTION must govern.*"[71]

Brownson also attempted to demolish the other basic premise of Dorrism—the right of revolution. The master of abstraction vehemently remarked again and again that "the right of rebellion and revolution, *on the part of the people*, is no right at all." The people have not, and never can have, the right to rebel; they do not have even the right to act, save through the forms prescribed by the supreme authority.

The basic question posed by the Dorrites was then considered: If such is the character of the existing political order, that it is impossible for the people to modify the practical organization of the state by the authority of the state itself, must one submit and endure this circumstance? In reply, Brownson admitted the right to resist and even to subvert the civil government (those charged with putting the constitution into effect) when necessary for human freedom, because civil government is only the subordinate department of government. Showing his strong religious bent, Brownson asserted that the people are subject to a higher sovereign than that of civil government. When this higher sovereign, the Will of God, commands, the people have a duty to resist the civil ruler and, if need be, to overthrow the civil government. Since the Will of God is represented by "THE CHURCH," it belongs to the church (which may be either a formal institution, "the public conscience," or the "moral authority organized") to determine when resistance is proper and to prescribe its form and its extent.

But if the church has been, "as in some Protestant countries," perverted to a function of the state, or if it has itself become corrupt and oppressive, or if there is no moral element of reform in the state that one can seize to sanction his movement, then "NOTH-ING" can be done to get rid of bad government.[72]

In December a very disturbed O'Sullivan printed a retort to Brownson's bold doctrines and restated the theory of democracy that he had expounded a year and a half earlier, when the constitutional controversy in Rhode Island was at its zenith. The disgruntled editor's remarks reveal that the Dorr Rebellion was the catalyst that had prompted Brownson to embark into the realm of political theory. According to O'Sullivan,

> Rhode Island was the only one of our States which
> accident had left in a position affording occasion for
> any important practical application of the leading
> doctrines of these articles.... In Rhode Island a com-
> bination of unfortunate circumstances has caused the
> failure of Mr. Dorr's attempt to reorganize the State
> in the mode and on the principle which we have
> sustained, and which it is the general drift of
> Mr. Brownson's articles to attack...."[73]

In October 1844 Brownson himself stated that his arguments in the essays on the "Origin and Ground of Government" discussed "the whole doctrine involved" in the Rhode Island controversy.[74]

By late 1843 Brownson's controversial pronouncements had ruptured his relationship with the *Democratic Review*, and he had departed, much to the relief of O'Sullivan, to edit *Brownson's Quarterly Review*. In the fourth issue of his new vehicle of expression, he once more attacked the democracy endorsed by the *Democratic Review*, a government that made the people the primary and fundamental sovereignty and the source and foundation of all legitimate authority. That was tantamount to no government at all, maintained Brownson.[75]

As late as October 1844, the month the unpredictable Orestes entered the Catholic Church, he devoted an article to "The

Suffrage Party in Rhode Island." This essay was a review of the pamphlet *Might and Right*, in which Frances Harriet Whipple, one of the women among Dorr's large contingent of female supporters, attempted to justify the actions of the Dorrites. At the outset of his review Brownson explained his change of sentiment regarding the Rhode Island controversy (it will be recalled that he spoke at a suffrage meeting in Providence in 1841). The change had come about, he said, when he learned that the limitation of suffrage by a freehold qualification was not a provision of the charter but an act of the legislature. The discovery of this fact demonstrated that there was a legal authority in the state competent to grant the elective franchise to all, if such an extension was advisable. Thus the proceedings of the suffrage party could no longer be countenanced.

In his explanation, however, Brownson sidestepped his own constitutional scruples. Before his "new information" caused him to turn against the Dorrites, he admitted, he regarded the whole proceedings of the suffrage party as illegal and revolutionary, but he was

> not disposed to condemn them with much severity, because we could not perceive how any amendment could be legally introduced, or the evils complained of legally redressed. We supposed the restriction on suffrage was a provision of the charter, and, if so, it could not be altered by any legal authority in the state, as the charter did not provide for its own amendment.
>
> Taking this view of the question, we argued, that, let the measures for the extension of suffrage, or the formation of a new constitution emanate from what source they might, from the suffrage association or from the general assembly. Since not authorized by the charter from which existing authorities derive their existence and power, they must needs be, in fact, illegal and revolutionary. The people's constitution is, we said, confessedly illegal in its origin; but so also must be a constitution framed by a convention called by the gen-

eral assembly, for the general assembly has no authority from the charter to call a convention. Since, then, the suffrage association have called a convention, since that convention has framed a constitution, and since a majority of the people of Rhode Island, as it is alleged, have voted for it, it is decidedly best to let it go peaceably into operation. Presuming... that an immense majority of the people were satisfied with it, we concluded that nothing was wanted but a little firmness on the part of Mr. Dorr and his friends in its defense to induce the charter party to yield, and suffer the new government to go quietly into operation...."[76]

This was hardly an adequate explanation for a man who, earlier in his consideration of the subject, remarked that a constitution is itself ultimate, not a mere written instrument but the actual organization of the state; a man who had also stated that if the validity of Dorr's action were to be admitted, it would mean that the will of the people, even though unorganized and independent of the constitution (or the charter), was the true sovereign and might at any time rightfully override the constitution itself. Brownson's account of his altered position on the controversy was a most unsatisfactory rationalization. In his final swing at Dorrism, the polemical Orestes ignominiously descended from the exalted theoretical pedestal erected in the pages of the *Democratic Review* to defend a more pragmatic position.

To say that the Dorr Rebellion was the only factor that encouraged Brownson to compose his profound (and confusing) treatises on political theory would be erroneous. The "mistake of the masses" in the election of 1840, his growing affinity with the doctrines of John C. Calhoun, and his emerging Catholicism inspired these outpourings.[77] The Dorr Rebellion and O'Sullivan's reaction to it, however, appear to have been the catalysts.

It is obvious from this examination that the effect of the Rhode Island rebellion upon national sentiment was substantial. The Dorr War was no tempest in a teapot. While its national impact was largely the result of Democratic propaganda aimed at discrediting the Whigs, the rebellion also inspired notable contributions by men of the stature of Horace Greeley, John C. Calhoun, John L. O' Sullivan, Orestes Brownson, George Bancroft, John Quincy Adams, and Daniel Webster to the theories of suffrage, majority rule, minority rights, and constitutional government. Herein lies its greatest significance.

NOTES

1. John B. Rae, ed., "Democrats and the Dorr Rebellion," *The New England Quarterly* 9 (September 1936): 476.

2. [Perry Smith?] to Thomas W. Dorr, Apr. 12, 1842, Rae, 481. Perhaps for purposes of secrecy the letter was sent not to Dorr himself but to Dorr's lieutenant, Burrington Anthony. After the uprising the letter was seized, but the signature had been cut out. It was given to Whig U. S. representative R. B. Cranston of Rhode Island for identification, and though Cranston did not name the writer openly, he implied that the author was Senator Perry Smith. Rae, 481–82.

3. Levi Woodbury to Thomas W. Dorr, Apr. 15, 1842, Rae, 476–77.

4. William Allen to Thomas W. Dorr, Apr. 15, 1842, Rae, 477–79.

5. Silas Wright, Jr., to Thomas W. Dorr, Apr.16, 1842, Rae, 479–80.

6. Thomas H. Benton to Thomas W. Dorr, Apr. 16, 1842, Rae, 480–81.

7. Edmund Burke to Thomas W. Dorr, May 8, 1842, Rae, 481–83.

8. Thomas W. Dorr to Walter S. Burges, May 12, 1842, summarized in Rae, 476.

9. John C. Calhoun to William Smith ("A Public Letter on the Subject of Rhode Island Controversy"), July 3, 1843, *The Works of John C. Calhoun*, ed. Richard K. Crallé (New York, 1854–57), 6:229–34.

10. Andrew Jackson to Francis P. Blair, May 23, 1842, *The Correspondence of Andrew Jackson*, ed. John Spencer Bassett (Washington, 1926–35), 6:153.

11. Andrew Jackson to the Committee of Dorr Supporters in Rhode Island, Aug. 22, 1844, in *Niles' Register* 67 (Sept. 14, 1844): 23.

12. Ibid., 22–23.

13. Martin Van Buren to the Committee of Dorr Supporters in Rhode Island, 1844, partially printed in ibid., 23.

14. George Bancroft to the Committee of Dorr Supporters, 1844, partially printed in ibid., 23.

15. George Bancroft to Mrs. E. D. Bancroft, September, 1844, *The Life and Letters of George Bancroft*, ed. M. A. DeWolfe Howe (New York, 1908), 1:257. Bancroft said that "Van Buren liked my view [on Dorr] better than his own."

16. *New York Tribune*, May 24, 1842, editorial entitled "The Law of Organic Changes in Popular Government"; summarized in Glyndon G. Van Deusen, *Horace Greeley* (Philadelphia, 1953), 74–75, 81. "In 1855 Greeley recognized the 'right' to vote, but said that it could be held in abeyance, due either to presumed choice (women) or to public necessity." Ibid., 81.

17. Van Deusen, 75.

18. *New York Tribune*, June 27 and 28, 1844, June 30, 1845, in Van Deusen, 75, 82.

19. *Autobiography of Thurlow Weed*, ed. Harriet A. Weed (Boston, 1883), 530–31.

20. Arthur M. Mowry, "Tammany Hall and the Dorr Rebellion," *American Historical Review* 3 (January 1898): 294–95.

21. Ibid., 295.

22. Ibid., 296.

23. Alexander Ming, Jr., and Abraham J. Crasto to Thomas W. Dorr, May 13, 1842, and Dorr to Cols. Ming and Crasto, May 14, 1842, in *Niles' Register* 67 (May 21, 1842): 179. Mowry incorrectly lists Ming as "Wing." Mowry, 296.

24. Mowry, 295–302.

25. Ibid., 299–300.

26. New York *New Era*, May 20, 1842, ibid., 300.

27. New York *Commercial Advertiser*, in Mowry, 301.

28. Mowry, 301.

29. William H. Seward to Samuel Ward King, June 16, 1842, *The Works of William H. Seward*, ed. George E. Baker (New York, 1853), 2:612. On May 22 Seward had told King that he had issued a warrant for Dorr's arrest. Seward to King, May 22, 1842, James D. Richardson, ed., *Messages and Papers of the Presidents* (New York: National Institute of Literature, 1917), 5:2151–52.

30. William H. Seward, *An Autobiography from 1801 to 1834 with a Memoir of His Life, and Selections from His Letters, 1831–1846*, ed. Frederick W. Seward (New York, 1891), 605–7, 613.

31. William H. Seward to his wife, May 31, 1842, ibid., 606.

32. Weed, 530–33. Weed mentions that the term "Barnburner," later applied to the reform wing of the New York Democratic party, was coined during the Dorr Rebellion to describe Dorr's more radical followers. Weed to [George W. Curtis], Dec. 16, 1873, ibid., 534.

33. *Memoirs of John Quincy Adams*, ed. Charles Francis Adams (Philadelphia, 1874–77), 11:152, 160, 514, 527–28, 12:10, 54, 137; John Quincy Adams, *The Social Compact*...(Providence, 1842). A useful analysis of Adams's political thought (though it fails to mention the former president's reaction to the Dorr Rebellion) is George A. Lipsky, *John Quincy Adams: His Theory and Ideas* (New York, 1950), esp. 87–103 and 128–36.

34. Daniel Webster to John Tyler, June 3, 1842, Richardson, 5:2153.

35. Daniel Webster, *The Rhode Island Question* (Washington, D.C., 1884), 3–26; *The Writings and Speeches of Daniel Webster*, National Edition (Boston and New York, 1903), 11:217–42.

36. Local Democratic leaders in opposition to Dorr included James Fenner, Elisha R. Potter, Jr., and John Brown Francis.

37. Mowry, 293–94.

38. Ibid., 294. The *Evening Post* was the leading Democratic paper in New York City; its editor was William Cullen Bryant. The *Tribune*, edited by Greeley, and James Watson Webb's *Courier and Enquirer* were the city's leading Whig organs. Frank Luther Mott, *American Journalism* (New York, 1941), 257–58, 260–61. Excerpts from the *American* are reprinted in *Niles' Register* 62 (May 28, July 2, 1842): 195, 276; Mott makes no mention of this paper in his study.

39. Mowry, 294. The *National Intelligencer* was a Whig organ at this time. Mott, *American Journalism*, 255–56, 260.

40. *Niles' Register* 62 (May 7, 1842): 147–48, (May 14): 165–66, (May 21): 178–80, (May 28): 194–95, (June 11): 225, (June 25): 259, (July 2): 276–78, 288, (Aug. 2): 368, (Aug. 27): 403. An account of the rebellion and, particularly, Dorr's subsequent imprisonment is reprinted from the *United States Gazette* in the *Register* 67 (Feb. 8, 1845): 361–63. The *Gazette* was a Whig paper. Mott, *American Journalism*, 260.

41. Quotes are from Mowry, 294. On the affiliation of the Richmond *Enquirer*, see Mott, *American Journalism*, 188–89, 256–67.

42. Frank Luther Mott, *A History of American Magazines* (New York, 1930), 1:677–80. The newly established *Cincinnati Enquirer* supported Dorr enthusiastically and gave extended coverage to the rebellion during the turbulent months in mid-1842, publishing extended commentary and reproducing important documents relating to the struggle.

43. Arthur M. Schlesinger, Jr., *Orestes Brownson: A Pilgrim's Progress* (Boston, 1939), 155–56.

44. John L. O'Sullivan to Orestes Brownson, Feb. 12, 1843, in H. F. Brownson, *Brownson's Early Life, 1803–1844* (Detroit, 1898), 347.

45. [John L. O'Sullivan], "The Rhode Island Affair," *United States Magazine and Democratic Review* 10 (June 1842): 602–7, esp. 602 (hereafter cited as *Democratic Review*).

46. Ibid., 606–7.

47. [John L. O'Sullivan], The Rhode Island Question," *Democratic Review* 11 (July 1842): 70–80.

48. Ibid., 71, 81.

49. Ibid., 71, 81–82.

50. Ibid., 82–83.

51. [John L. O'Sullivan], "Thomas Wilson Dorr, of Rhode Island," *Democratic Review* 11 (August 1842): 201–5. It was the *Review*'s policy to print a political profile in each issue, but the sketch of Dorr was not due to be printed for several months. It was published in August because of interest in the Rhode Island controversy. Ibid., 201.

52. Orestes A. Brownson, "Democracy and Liberty," *Democratic Review* 12 (April 1843): 384–85.

53. Ibid., 374–80.

54. Ibid., 380–82.

55. Ibid., 382–83.

56. Ibid., 382–85.

57. Ibid., 386–87.

58. H. F. Brownson, 342–43. For Brownson's explanation of his change in sentiment regarding Dorr, see the discussion of his "Suffrage Party in Rhode Island" below.

59. [John L. O'Sullivan], "Note," *Democratic Review* 12 (April 1843): 387, 391.

60. Ibid., 390–91.

61. Orestes A. Brownson, "Popular Government," *Democratic Review* 12 (May 1843): 534–35.

62. Ibid., 534–36.

63. [John L. O'Sullivan], "Note," *Democratic Review* 12 (May 1843): 537–38, 542.

64. Orestes A. Brownson, "Origin and Ground of Government," *Democratic Review* 13 (August, September, October 1843): 129–32.

65. Ibid., 133–36.

66. Ibid., 136.

67. Ibid., 136–45.

68. Ibid., 145–46.

69. Ibid., 241–62, 353–77, esp. 258–62.

70. Ibid., 246, 247, 251, 373.

71. Ibid., 252.

72. Ibid., 373–75. Brownson's three articles on the "origin and ground" of government were rewritten and, with some additions, published after the Civil War under the title *The American Republic*. H. F. Brownson 148.

73. [John L. O'Sullivan], "Mr. Brownson's Recent Articles in the *Democratic Review*," *Democratic Review* 13 (December 1843), 654–55. O'Sullivan published a poem dedicated to Dorr in the June 1844 issue of the *Review*.

74. [Orestes A. Brownson], "The Suffrage Party in Rhode Island," *The Works of Orestes A. Brownson*, ed. H. F. Brownson (Detroit, 1882–87), 15:510.

75. Ibid., 508–10. This article appeared in *Brownson's Quarterly Review* 1 (October 1844).

76. Ibid.

77. Chilton Williamson, in *American Suffrage from Property to Democracy* (Princeton, N.J., 1960), 292–93, has pointed out that Brownson was convinced that Protestantism was by nature too individualistic and democratic to provide immutable standards for human behavior. The religion that was the most effective political and social stabilizer, Brownson believed, was Catholicism, because it was "a religion which is above the people and controls them." For an elaboration of this statement, see *Brownson's Quarterly Review* 2 (October 1845): 514–30.

The Dorr Rebellion: A Study in American Radicalism, 1833–1849, by Marvin E. Gettleman, Reviewed

19

This review of Marvin Gettleman's history of the Dorr War appeared in *The New England Quarterly* in March 1974.

IN 1901 ARTHUR MAY MOWRY PUBLISHED the standard study of the Dorr War, a view from the right which was critical of the Dorrites and sympathetic to the moderate members of the Law and Order faction who vanquished Dorr. In the seven decades since Mowry's effort, many historians have examined the rebellion either in brief interpretative articles, in unpublished theses, or as part of longer general works. The most notable of these efforts were made by Clarence Brigham, Charles Carroll, Joseph Brennan, Anne Newton, Chilton Williamson, Peter Coleman, George Dennison, Patrick Conley, and William Wiecek. Not until the appearance of the present volume by Marvin Gettleman, however, has a book-length study been published on this famous Rhode Island episode. This new analysis contrasts with Mowry in many ways—first, because Gettleman is a New Left historian who views the rebellion as "a study in American radicalism." Such a perspective might tempt some traditional historians to suspect that Gettleman's effort is infused with the presentism, self-justification, and special pleading characteristic of much New Left literature, and to dismiss it summarily. To thus prejudge the work would be a grave error, for Gettleman has produced a first-rate piece of local history.

Despite the fact that Professor Gettleman uses the word "radical" or its variants *ad nauseam* in his effort to place the Dorr Rebellion in the radical tradition, he admits at the outset that "along any spectrum, Dorrism would be a weak, compromised and ambiguous radical movement." Basically Gettleman claims that the Dorr Rebellion was radical because of its controlling ideology of "popular constituent sovereignty"—an eighteenth-century revolutionary doctrine according to which the "People" at large possess a preeminent right to draft and adopt a constitution regardless of the wishes of the legislature. This was and is a theory well to the left on the American political spectrum, as Gettleman contends. Insofar as the Dorrites attempted to defend and implement this ideology, therefore, their movement could be termed a "radical" one.

TO THE CITIZENS
OF PROVIDENCE!!!
You are reqested FORTHWITH to repair to the

State Arsenal
and TAKE ARMS.

SAMUEL W. KING.

Governor of the State of Rhode Island.

Providence, **May 17, 1842, 6 o'clock P. M.**

The radicalism of Dorr's effort and the hysteria it generated among his opponents are graphically depicted in this call to arms by Law and Order governor Samuel Ward King.

While few traditional historians would argue with Gettleman's use of the adjective "radical" to describe the rebels' constitutional theory, some might balk when the author faults the Dorrites for neglecting "to prepare for the eventuality of intensified struggle," and for their inability "to distill from their principles any realistic strategy that squarely faced the probability of armed conflict."

In its technical aspects, Gettleman's study is competent and professional. His book is heavily documented, and the footnotes are crammed with such interesting data as to create (for good and for ill) a parallel narrative. He has heavily utilized the voluminous Rider Collection of Dorr manuscripts at the John Hay Library, an advantage denied to Mowry by the eccentric and cantankerous Sidney Rider, a Providence bibliophile who wrote an extensive but never-published constitutional history of the state. In addition, Gettleman has plowed through a mountain of archival material, including the Simmons Papers at the Library of Congress and the Potter and Francis Collections at the Rhode Island Historical Society. There appears to be no pertinent manuscripts or contemporary pamphlets which have eluded the author, who illuminates these raw materials with fresh insights drawn from sociology, psychology, and the literature of contemporary radicalism.

Gettleman's handiwork, though most impressive, does have some deficiencies. In one important area he has failed to progress beyond Mowry. W. E. B. DuBois in his revisionist study of Reconstruction indicted traditional historians of that era for ignoring the Negro, "leaving the reader wondering why an element apparently so insignificant filled the whole Southern picture at the time." The same charge could be levied against Mowry and Gettleman for their failure to acknowledge the significance of political nativism and the issue of Irish Catholicism as prominent ingredients in the constitutional imbroglio of 1841–43. The xenophobic editorials of Henry Bowen Anthony and William Goddard, the broadsides and pamphlets of the Dorr War, the correspondence of Law and Order men, the ties between the Dorrites and the local Irish community, and, especially, the retention of the freehold suffrage requirement for the foreign-born in the state constitution of 1843 all bear witness to the great significance of the Irish Catholic problem in the

Dorr Rebellion. Yet Mowry suppressed it, and Gettleman, intent on proving another thesis, dismisses it in two paragraphs. On this point, therefore, the volume fails to profit from the insights and researches of the shorter analyses of the rebellion by Brennan, Williamson, Coleman, and Conley, all of whom saw nativism as a primary source of conflict.

The second weakness in Gettleman's account is his treatment of postrebellion political shifts and alignments. The author's contention that the Dorr liberation campaign of 1845 "initiated the fragmentation of the Rhode Island Whig Party, which in conjunction with national political developments led to the emergence of a new state Republican Party in the next decade," is a superficial judgment. The modern party system in Rhode Island developed in large part out of the issues of the Dorr War, but the campaign of 1845 was certainly not the matrix for party realignment. If one must pick certain elections as pivotal, this reviewer would opt for those of 1854, 1855, and 1856. If any issue was decisive throughout the postrebellion era as a party index, it was suffrage extension and not the transitory cause of liberation.

In sum, Gettleman has written a very good book, one far superior to Mowry's long-standard work. It is the best study of the Dorr Rebellion; but its perspective and its omissions ensure that it will not be the last.

Thomas Wilson Dorr: The Man and the Monument | 20

Written in 2002, this fresh appraisal of Dorr was presented to the board of directors of the Heritage Harbor Museum to explain my rationale for commissioning and donating (with my wife, Gail) a sculpture of Dorr by Joseph Avarista for display in the museum's entrance rotunda.

THOMAS WILSON DORR is the pivotal figure in Rhode Island history. He drew his heritage, training, and moral values from the old order and applied them towards the betterment of the new. He exemplified the best traits attributed to old-stock Rhode Islanders—individualism, daring, defiance of unjust authority, and a passion for democracy and self-determination. Simultaneously, he inaugurated the role of patrician reformer typified in the modern era by such Rhode Island statesmen as Theodore Francis Green (who admittedly drew inspiration from Dorr), Claiborne Pell, and John Hubbard Chafee.

Dorr thus serves as the bridge between early and modern Rhode Island, between old stock and new, and between the charter government that served Rhode Island for 180 years and the present constitutional order.

More than any other person, Thomas Dorr influenced the governmental transition from the old royal-charter regime to a new political system based upon a written constitution. And although his preferred basic law—the People's Constitution—was denied implementation, its provisions and principles were gradually incorporated into the Rhode Island Constitution throughout the century and a half since Dorr's defeat.

164

But Dorr was not merely a force for constitutional change; he was the quintessential reformer of America's first great age of reformist activity. In the economic realm, he drafted and secured the enactment of the first statute in any state providing for governmental regulation of state-chartered banks, and he worked diligently for the abolition of imprisonment for debt. He might well be described as Rhode Island's first consumer advocate. Dorr also attacked neomercantilism, whereby the state granted special privileges and monopolies to private business corporations; such a practice, he declared, was a violation of equal rights. Dorr was a pioneer in his advocacy of an economic system regulated in the public interest—the modern regulated economy.

Dorr's reformist zeal also extended to the social order. He was an early member of the American Anti-Slavery Society, led by William Lloyd Garrison and Rhode Islander Arnold Buffum, and he fought, albeit unsuccessfully, to enfranchise blacks via the People's Constitution. His efforts were extolled, in the aftermath of his defeat, by the abolitionist poet John Greenleaf Whittier.

Governor Dorr also encouraged the involvement of women in the public sphere. His leadership of the People's party in 1842 inspired the first large-scale involvement of Rhode Island women in the political process. Support of Dorr's cause and sympathy for him because of the harsh treatment accorded the deposed People's governor led women to undertake such unprecedented political activities as forming free-suffrage associations, raising funds for the relief of those imprisoned for supporting the People's government, staging rallies and clambakes in support of reform, organizing a campaign for Dorr's liberation, and writing political and legal defenses of the People's movement, most notably *Might and Right* (1844), by Frances Harriet Whipple.

In addition, Dorr made a major contribution towards the development of free public education in Rhode Island both as a state legislator, where he earmarked the famous federal deposit and distribution of 1836 for the permanent school fund, and as a member and then president of the Providence School Committee, where he played the leading role in implementing such modern improvements as the appointment of Providence's first superintendent of schools, the establishment of teacher certification and training programs, the creation of Rhode Island's first public high school, and the construction of modern school facilities.

On the burning issue of foreign immigration, Dorr attacked the nativism of his day. As early as 1833, when nativist violence first erupted, he made a public appeal for toleration toward Roman Catholics. Dorr's exhortation to his fellow Rhode Islanders revealed his humanity:

> It is quite time that a better state of feeling should prevail, and that narrow illiberal prejudices should be discarded. Whatever good the division into sects may have done, it is time that they should overlook the party lines behind which they have entrenched themselves, and extend to each other the hand of fellowship. If men cannot agree in religious opinions—and, from the constitution of the human mind, such an agreement can never exist—they certainly can agree to differ peaceably. There is a common ground of good will and charity on which they can and ought to meet as brethren.

Consistent with his principles and pronouncements, Dorr befriended and defended the Irish Catholic immigrants of the 1840s, structuring the People's Constitution to give naturalized Irishmen equal rights with native-born citizens. He helped to organize the defense for John Gordon in the famous Amasa Sprague murder trail, and then spoke against the death penalty meted out to this hapless Irish Catholic merchant of Spragueville.

Optimism, articulateness, concern for the oppressed—these were among the qualities of Thomas Dorr. Belief in fundamental human goodness, the brotherhood of men, and majoritarian rule were basic articles in his political creed. Liberty and equality were to him, as much as to any reformer of this remarkable age, the indispensable conditions of human activity.

Dorr's 1843 lament—"All is lost save honor"—may well have been the story of his rebellion and his life, but it is not his legacy nor the ultimate verdict of history. At the conclusion of his trial for treason, Dorr made an impassioned plea: "From the sentence of the court I appeal to the People of our State and of our Country. They shall decide between us. I commit myself without distrust to their final award." To his credit—and to ours—the confidence of this optimistic, if somewhat naive, democrat continues to experience an inexorable though painfully gradual vindication. In the many decades since his defeat and death, the judgment against him from a biased court has been properly overruled by time and experience.

In December 2001 my wife, Gail Cahalan-Conley, and I commissioned noted Rhode Island sculptor Joseph A. Avarista to produce a life-size statue of Thomas Wilson Dorr to stand as a focal point in the rotunda of the new Heritage Harbor Museum on the Providence waterfront. Avarista is sculpting Dorr from a block of basswood that he will paint, seal with lacquer, and mount on a five-foot granite base. The project's total cost will be $120,000, and the dedication of the statue will occur shortly after the museum's formal opening. Shown here is the artist's model, based on an original daguerreotype.

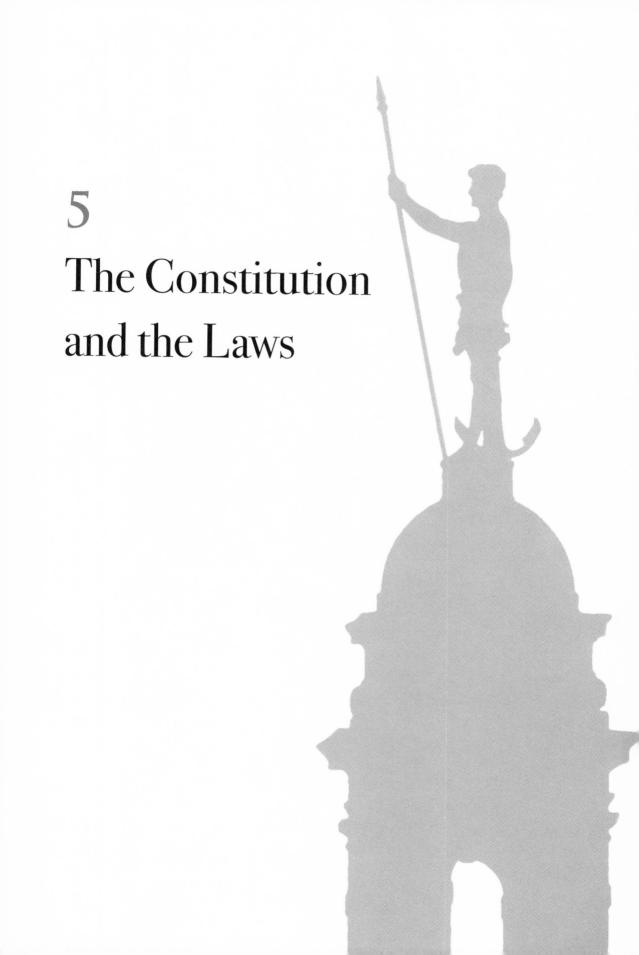

5

The Constitution
and the Laws

Governor James Fenner, conservative Democrat and Dorr's arch rival, served as president of the Whig-dominated Law and Order convention that framed the constitution of 1843.

The Constitution of 1843: A Sesquicentennial Obituary

21

This essay was written and delivered as the Law Day address to the state Supreme Court in May 1993. The setting was the same as for my first Law Day address—the Chamber of Deputies in the Newport Colony House.

TODAY IS A SPECIAL OCCASION FOR ME: it marks my third appearance before you as a speaker. When I rendered my first Law Day oration in May 1976 as state Bicentennial chairman, I gazed up at a wholly different Supreme Court, consisting of Chief Justice Bevilaqua and associates Doris, Joslin, Paolino, and Kelleher. They have departed, and all of you have ascended to the high court since then. Yet I am still standing down here! Perhaps success is passing me by.

The special nature of this event is also due to the judicial debut of Justice Victoria Lederberg, the newest (and perhaps the last) Supreme Court member to be appointed (or, should I say, anointed) by the Rhode Island General Assembly. Justice Lederberg, today you make your first public appearance as a Supreme Court justice, and I am honored to be the first Rhode Island attorney to address you in your new role.

This Law Day has been chosen as a time for observing the sesquicentennial of the Rhode Island constitution that became effective on May 2, 1843—150 years ago, almost to the day. The choice creates a quandry. Is this a birthday observance for a living document or the commemoration of a now defunct relic? Many lawyers, historians, and politicians continue to refer to our existing basic law as the constitution of 1843. They view the work of the recent 1986 constitutional convention as merely a cleanup operation. The secretary of state who published the annotated edition of the 1986 revision says that "as a result of the 1986 constitutional convention the Rhode Island Constitution of 1843 was modernized and amended." Later in that volume, convention president Keven McKenna (for whom I served briefly as general counsel) calls the 1986 product "a new constitution."

As a historian I would ordinarily opt for longevity and contend that the constitution of 1843 lives on—albeit with a facelift. In support of that proposition I would need to look no further than Massachusetts, whose convention of 1820, despite performing substantial revisions, allowed the historic 1780 basic law to continue in effect. For this reason Massachusetts can boast that it possesses the oldest functioning, popularly written constitution in the world.

Despite this precedent and others thereafter, I would prefer to remove the life support on the constitution of 1843 and consider today's event a memorial observance. Our program should read "Constitution of 1843, died 1986, age 143; Rest in Peace." I advocate constitutional euthanasia because I have a low regard for that so-called Law and Order constitution. Its provisions sowed the seeds of political discord and ethnoreligious strife in Rhode Island for the better part of its long life.

What do most Rhode Islanders know about the origins of the document whose 150th anniversary we commemorate today? Very little, I would suggest. Most with an interest in Rhode Island history know that it replaced the royal charter of 1663, the state's archaic basic law; that it was produced by the political and social upheaval known as the Dorr Rebellion; and that it came to be regarded as Rhode Island's first popularly written state constitution.

In 1901, when historian Arthur May Mowry wrote *The Dorr War*, the first scholarly, book-length analysis of the constitutional crisis, he concluded that "the constitution that went into effect in May, 1843 was liberal and well-adapted to the needs of the state." Until 1935 a majority of the Supreme Court had always agreed with that bland assessment. So did virtually all legal historians. In addition, popular wisdom regarded the state constitution as the culmination and fruition of the reform effort led by Thomas Wilson Dorr.

This view is misleading and false. The constitution of 1843 was the frustration rather than the fulfillment of the reform movement. Dorr knew this better than anyone else. In May 1843, as the conservative Law and Order government of James Fenner took office under this new constitution, Dorr wrote to a friend: "All is lost, save honor!" Such an utterance is a curious remark for one whose principles had allegedly triumphed!

To understand my contention and Dorr's disappointment, we must review (very briefly) the causes and course of the Dorr Rebellion. It erupted in 1841 after two decades of reform effort had been repeatedly frustrated by the freemen who controlled the omnipotent General Assembly. The principal reform demands, in probable order of urgency, were suffrage extension, equitable reapportionment, an independent judiciary, a more equal distribution of the powers of government, and a constitutional bill of rights. When the legislature persisted in its obstructionism, reformers took matters into their own hands, bypassed the General Assembly, and convened a "People's Convention" to frame a progressive basic law for Rhode Island. This course of action, which Dorr, Joseph K. Angell, and seven other distinguished attorneys defended as a valid exercise of "popular constituent sovereignty," produced the very liberal People's Constitution in November 1841. A popular referendum on its ratification, with conservatives abstaining, resulted in overwhelming approval. Had the supporters of the old system voted in this December 1841 plebiscite, it would not have altered the result, because a careful tabulation of votes indicated that a clear majority of Rhode Island's adult males had expressed support for the People's Constitution.

Time does not permit a recitation of the events that followed. I have covered them in some detail in *Democracy in Decline*. Suffice it to say that the opponents of sweeping reform, bolstered by their control of the existing charter government, beat back the People's movement and forced Dorr, who had been elected governor under the reform document, into exile. Then, to appease most of those who were dissatisfied with the limitations imposed by the charter of 1663, this victorious Law and Order faction drafted the constitution of 1843—a slightly revised version of their Landholders' Constitution that the voters had rejected in March 1842—and secured its ratification. Reformers boycotted this November 1842 referendum. The vote for the Law and Order constitution (7,024) was approximately half of the number (14,059) who had cast a vote for the People's Constitution the previous December.

The two major changes made by conservatives that differentiated their constitution of 1843 from their Landholders' Constitution of March 1842 related to black suffrage and Senate apportionment. Over Dorr's strenuous objection, the People's Convention refused to extend the vote to blacks. This flaw was exploited by opponents, and Providence blacks took up arms against the so-called Dorrites when military confrontations occurred in May and June 1842. To reward their support, the Law and Order party drafted its new constitution without a "white" voting restriction, but allowed for the insertion of the qualifier "white" if the person casting his ballot chose to exclude blacks from the franchise. Insertion of the word "white" was favored by 1,798 men, but 4,031 voted against it. That outcome was no surprise to the knowledgeable. Congressman Elisha R. Potter, Jr., observed that "Our blacks are conservative and go with the wealthy part of the community . . . by whom most are employed." Such an observation, of course, suggests a socioeconomic division between Dorrites and the supporters of Law and Order.

The second significant alteration from the Landholders' Constitution came when the Law and Order convention scrapped regional districts for state Senate apportionment in favor of the more reactionary principle of one town, one vote.

Unfortunately, the lopsided November 1842 vote in favor of the Law and Order constitution—7,024 to 51—has served to delude some historians into thinking it must have been a popular compromise, worthy of praise. Today, however, I come here not to praise it but to bury it!

One of Dorr's sympathizers was Massachusetts poet John Greenleaf Whittier, an abolitionist known as "the bard of freedom." In a beautiful, nostalgic poem entitled "Maud Muller,"

Whittier wrote these lines: "Of all sad words of tongue or pen, / The saddest are these: 'It might have been!'" Such was the lament of Dorr over the demise of the People's Constitution, so let us today examine what might have been, had it prevailed over the constitution of 1843.

The two documents were as different as night and day—the Law and Order constitution seeking to salvage the old system, the People's basic law reaching towards the new. They differed dramatically on such issues as education, separation of powers, the role of the governor, the independence of the judiciary, and the relationship between the government and the economy, but in three areas their profound differences were productive of more than a century of intense political and ethnocultural strife. Those points of greatest friction concerned suffrage, reapportionment, and procedures for constitutional change, precisely the three issues that had produced the Dorr Rebellion!

The People's Constitution guaranteed free suffrage for all white adult male citizens with one year's residence in Rhode Island, regardless of their country of birth. The blemish here is the qualifier "white." Dorr led the fight against its insertion during the People's Convention, and though he failed by a vote of 46 to 18, he and those associates fully committed to equal rights gained approval for a referendum on removing the white qualification at the first annual election following the initial session of the People's legislature (i.e., in April 1843). Dorr's document safeguarded the voter from economic pressure and intimidation by mandating a secret ballot in all elections.

In contrast, the constitution of 1843 ignored the secrecy of the voting process and set up distinctions between native-born and foreign-born and between the well-to-do and poorer native citizens. Its complicated suffrage clause was an exercise in ethnocultural and socioeconomic discrimination. The Law and Order men established three classes of voters: absolute, those who were native-born with one year's residence and owned real estate, or had two years' residence and paid taxes on real or personal property valued at $134 or more; registry, those who had two years' residence and paid a $1 annual registry tax, except that this class of poorer citizens could not vote on financial questions or in elections for the city council in Providence or any other city that might thereafter be created; and those foreign-born naturalized citizens who qualified to vote or hold office by owing real estate. The real estate qualification for this category remained the same as it was before the Dorr Rebellion, and its clear intent was to disfranchise those Irish Catholic immigrants who were arriving in Rhode Island in ever-increasing numbers. At the time of its enactment it was the most nativistic suffrage clause in the nation.

The Irish knew they had been targeted. As early as 1846 Irish leader Henry Duff, an ally of Dorr, presented a free-suffrage petition to the General Assembly, a petition that the Law and Order-dominated body ignored. In the turbulent 1850s the remnant of Rhode Island's Democratic party pushed for a constitutional amendment removing the real estate requirement for naturalized citizens, while the newly emergent and instantaneously dominant Republican party, led by *Providence Journal* editor Henry Bowen Anthony, resolutely opposed that removal. At the height of the struggle on this divisive issue, the *Journal* made the comment on the danger of eliminating the suffrage restriction: "Rhode Island will no longer be Rhode Island when that is done. It will become a province of Ireland: St. Patrick will take the place of Roger Williams, and the shamrock will supersede the anchor and Hope!"

Agitation over the real estate requirement continued to convulse the state throughout most of the nineteenth century. In 1880 a U.S. Senate investigation, instigated via petition by Charles E. Gorman, Rhode Island's first Irish Catholic attorney, gave the following evaluation of voting in Rhode Island under the provisions of the constitution of 1843:

> Restricted suffrage, registry taxes upon poor men alone, statutory closing of the polls at sunset, instead of eight o'clock, as formerly, by which the operatives in the mill are prevented from voting, and the compulsory payment of the registry tax ten months prior to the general election in a Presidential year, cause great complaints upon the part of the poor men and foreign-born

citizens in Rhode Island; and to these feature of her laws many intelligent witnesses ascribe the small percentage of voters among her people and the large amount of corrupt practices in the elections of the State....

Your committee believes that there are good grounds for the complaints made that the government of Rhode Island, under its present constitution, is nearer an oligarchy than a democracy.

This Senate condemnation of the Rhode Island system (which was stoutly defended on the floor of that chamber by Republican senator Henry B. Anthony) gave impetus to another reform effort in the 1880s known as the Equal Rights Movement. This agitation led to the ratification in 1886 of Amendment VI to the state constitution, removing the real estate qualification for those naturalized citizens who had served honorably defending the Union in the Civil War (that gesture had been thrice defeated previously, in 1863, 1864, and 1876). Of much greater impact was Article of Amendment VII, the so-called Bourn Amendment, sponsored by Senator (and former governor) Augustus O. Bourn of Bristol, a staunch ally of Republican party boss General Charles R. Brayton.

Why did the Republicans have a change of heart? Were Brayton and Bourn sincerely moved by the arguments and campaign of the friends of equal rights? Hardly! They simply looked at the results of the most recent Rhode Island state decennial census of 1885. It revealed that Rhode Island then had a population of 304,000, of which 125,000, or 41 percent, were of Irish stock. The real estate requirement for naturalized citizens was then much less effective as a weapon against the rising political influence of the state's Irish citizens. But it was effective against newly arriving French Canadians, Germans, Swedes, and English from both Canada and the British Isles. The Republicans felt, quite correctly, that these ethnocultural groups could become political allies if they were given the vote immediately upon naturalization, without the necessity of owning real estate. Herein lies the reason for Republican acquiescence in the Bourn Amendment of 1888. It was not only a reform but also a political master stroke by Brayton that preserved Republican ascendancy for nearly a half century.

Bourn's "reform," which sapped the vitality from the Equal Rights Movement, had another catch: it contained a property-tax paying requirement in city council elections. At the time the amendment was proposed, Rhode Island had three incorporated cities—Providence (1832), Newport (1853), and Pawtucket (1885). It soon added Woonsocket (1888) and Central Falls (1895), then Cranston (1910). In those municipalities, which all had strong-council, weak- mayor charters, the poorer class could vote for the ceremonial mayor, but nearly 60 percent of those voters were barred from voting for the dominant council and on fiscal questions. The Bourn Amendment left the control of cities and municipal patronage in the hands of the upper class. That two-tier system produced great discord in the early twentieth century until another reform surge effected its removal in 1928 via Article of Amendment XX to the 1843 constitution. Not until 1973, however, did Rhode Island, under U.S. Supreme Court mandate, remove the last vestige of its property requirement for suffrage. The constitutional convention of 1973 proposed, and the electorate ratified, Amendment XXXVIII, which eliminated the property requirement for voting in financial town meetings.

The battle over apportionment of the powerful General Assembly was a contest equally as long and turbulent as the one involving the right to vote. Again discord and inequity were hallmarks of the regime established by the constitution of 1843. Whereas the People's Constitution apportioned the House of Representatives fairly (as did the constitution of 1843) and created a Senate of twelve districts with regional, demographic, and socioeconomic balance, the Law and Order party created a rotten-borough Senate that completely disregarded population (i.e., people) as a factor in its composition. Every town, regardless of size, was given an equal vote. This system—similar to John Calhoun's doctrine of the concurrent majority—provided a rural veto on all legislation and constitutional change. As Rhode Island became ever more urban and industrial (largely through immigration) and the rural towns declined in population, the legislative imbalance became more glaring. By 1925 Providence, with a population of 267,914, was checked in the upper house by West Greenwich, population 407. With Rhode Island's population then at 604,000, the smallest twenty-three towns, possessing 23 of the 39 Senate votes, had a combined population of 60,000. Throughout the entire period 1843–1966, strife over the apportionment issue vexed Rhode Island politics, especially when the Senate thwarted progressive legislation.

The 1843 system was modified slightly in 1928 because of the incessant pressure exerted by urban political leaders. Article of Amendment XIX gave each municipality with 25,000 electors (not people) one additional senator for each additional 25,000 electors (or more than one-half of that number) who resided therein. The reform gave Providence a total of five senators, and Pawtucket became entitled to two. Not until the 1960 census did Warwick and Cranston gain an additional member in the upper house.

The rotten-borough system created by the constitution of 1843 was not displaced until Rhode Island responded to the impetus provided by the U.S. Supreme Court in the early 1960s. That tribunal generated a reapportionment revolution throughout America by its "one man, one vote" rulings in the cases of *Baker* v. *Carr* (1962) and *Reynolds* v. *Sims* (1964). In 1965 the General Assembly enacted a reapportionment plan which embodied that democratic principle and ended more than a century of strife over the composition of the General Assembly.

The third major defect in the constitution of 1843 was the obstacle it posed to constitutional change. The People's Constitution encouraged the call of constitutional conventions to keep the state's basic law in tune with the times. It embraced the doctrine of popular constituent sovereignty, whereby the people in their primary capacity could convene a convention "even without prior legislative authorization." The People's document allowed amendments to be made by a mere majority vote of two successive General Assemblies (with annual elections, a new one sat each year) and a majority vote of the people voting thereon.

In contrast, the amendment procedures of the constitution of

1843 were inflexible and cumbersome. That basic law repudiated the doctrine of popular constituent sovereignty upon which the Dorr Rebellion rested by asserting that "The constitution which at any time exists, until changed by an explicit and authentic act of the whole people [i.e., by act of the General Assembly], is sacredly obligatory upon all." The Law and Order faction was so wedded to the status quo that its basic law contained no provision setting forth procedures for the call of future constitutional conventions! The only avenue for change was a winding and narrow one indeed: the constitution could be amended only by a majority vote of the full membership of each house of two consecutive General Assemblies, a general election intervening, and then approval by three-fifths of the electors voting thereon.

In the 1880s, when the Equal Rights Movement demanded that a convention be convened to implement its reform agenda, the conservatives in control of the legislature blunted the reform effort when the Senate obtained an advisory opinion from the Rhode Island Supreme Court declaring that the General Assembly was not empowered by the constitution of 1843 to call a constitutional convention. Because of this peculiar ruling, reformers had to content themselves with legislatively appointed constitutional commissions to recommend change. Three such commissions were created—more to appease than to ameliorate—but these efforts in 1898, 1899, and 1912–15 came to naught.

One goal of Rhode Island's bizarre "Bloodless Revolution" of 1935 was to install a new Supreme Court that would reverse the reactionary advisory opinion of 1883 barring the call of constitutional conventions. The new Democratic-appointed high court did just that in a landmark advisory opinion to the General Assembly in April 1935.

Divisions among party leaders sent mixed signals to the electorate, who ironically rejected a convention referendum, but at least a mechanism for change had been recognized. Since the amendment procedure was rendered more difficult in 1912 when the General Assembly went from one-year to two-year sessions (Amendment XVI), those seeking constitutional change repeatedly resorted to the device of limited constitutional conventions to place their reforms before the people. Five such limited conclaves were summoned between 1944 and 1973.

The limited convention of 1973, wherein I served as delegate and secretary, went beyond its strict mandate. With Dorr as my inspiration, I introduced, and the convention approved, what became Article of Amendment XLII. This addition to the constitution of 1843 accomplished a twofold purpose: it provided a mechanism for a periodic popular referendum on the need to call a constitutional convention, and it streamlined the procedure for amending the constitution by requiring only a majority vote of each house of the legislature followed by a simple majority of the electors voting thereon. This amendment led directly to the call of the unlimited 1986 constitutional convention and the consequent demise of the constitution of 1843.

In sum, the constitution of 1843—the focus of today's observance—was a reactionary document productive of much political and social turmoil in Rhode Island. It encouraged ethnocultural clashes; it pitted class against class and urbanites against rural dwellers; its discriminatory provisions harmed Rhode Island's image among its sister states; it facilitated political corruption; and its formidable obstacles to change led reformers and their opponents to resort to drastic and bizarre actions, such as the gassing of the Senate in 1924 and the Bloodless Revolution of 1935—actions that further tarnished Rhode Island's reputation.

Today I would like to hark back 151 years—to May 3, 1842—when Governor Thomas Dorr attempted to put the People's Constitution into effect, for the present basic law of Rhode Island is now much closer in form, content, and spirit to that document. Save for separation of powers, the constitution of 1843 is largely a relic. It is the People's Constitution that has prevailed!

Elmer E. Cornwell, Jr., a professor of political science at
Brown University, served as a consultant in every major
constitutional episode from 1962 through the present.

The Constitutional Cavalcade, 1960–2000 |

22

This essay was written in 1998 for my book Liberty and Justice: Law and Lawyers in Rhode Island, 1636–1998, and updated for publication here.

DURING THE FINAL FOUR DECADES of the twentieth century, Rhode Island experienced significant constitutional ferment, as it has in most decades since the 1820s. My training in history and law, coupled with my involvement in state politics, allowed me to participate actively during this period in events relating to the amendment and interpretation of our state's basic law. This account of my involvement will attempt to avoid any conflict between the objective historian and the subjective participant.

In December 1964 Rhode Island's first open, unlimited constitutional convention since 1842 convened. Its call had been approved and its delegates selected (81 Democrats and 19 Republicans) in the November 1964 general election. Early in 1965, as a young history professor at Providence College, fresh from the graduate school of the University of Notre Dame, I applied for a position on the convention's research staff, which was directed by Dr. Elmer E. Cornwell Jr., professor of political science at Brown University, and his assistant, Dr. Jay S. Goodman (now both a professor of political science and a Providence attorney). This talented duo would eventually write a detailed analysis of the gathering, appropriately titled *The Politics of the Rhode Island Constitutional Convention* (1969), under the auspices of the National Municipal League.

Although tarnished by the Long Count of 1956, former governor Dennis J. Roberts secured election as convention chairman. As the convention began its work, however, a Democratic legislative faction under the lead of Family Court judge John F. Doris, a former Woonsocket state representative, took political control of the gathering.

The convention's blueprint for action was the well-crafted *Report of the Commission on Revision of the Rhode Island Constitution*, prepared in 1962 by a thirteen-member blue-ribbon legislative panel chaired by prominent Providence attorney and legal scholar William H. Edwards. Chairman Roberts diminished his influence with the Doris faction by championing a unicameral legislature, a radical innovation that the Edwards Commission had considered and rejected and that the General Assembly strongly opposed.

For more than three years the convention dragged on, hampered by factionalism and extremely cumbersome rules that made delay the order of the day. Since the Democrats controlled the convention by a lopsided majority, both the *Providence Journal* and incumbent Republican governor John H. Chafee repeatedly criticized the gathering and made political hay from its controversies and its conservatism. Ironically, such prodding encouraged some significant reforms, and the document that was eventually submitted to the voters in April 1968 was a vast improvement on the existing state constitution.

The proposed constitution, however, had a fatal image problem. The public began to judge it by its parentage—a squabbling, dilatory convention—rather than on its substance and its merit. Because I firmly believed then (as I do now) that every article in the 1968 constitution represented an improvement over the existing basic law, I wrote "A Statement in Defense of the Proposed Constitution" for publication in the January 1968 issue of the *Bar Journal*, and I resigned my research-staff position to organize a statewide ratification campaign. William Edwards came aboard as my cochairman, and Roman Catholic bishop Russell J. McVinney, in a rare and unusual move, became our ratification group's honorary chairman; but neither faith nor reason would prevail. Behind the scenes, Judge

Doris (who would later move to the Supreme Court) and Providence Democratic chairman Larry McGarry gave us various kinds of assistance. Even the *Providence Journal* eventually bestowed its grudging editorial endorsement upon the new document, but three years of negative news stories about the convention and its delegates had a much greater impact on public opinion.

Arrayed against ratification were a resentful and disappointed chairman Roberts and the enormously popular Governor John Chafee, whom the advertising firm of Fitzgerald-Toole had sold to the voters as "The Man You Can Trust." Bill Edwards and I "debated" Roberts and Chafee on prime-time TV, but the format insisted upon by the opponents of ratification did not produce a true debate—each side had a half hour in isolation to present its position.

The ratification referendum was held on April 16, 1968, the Tuesday after Easter. Although the convention's Public Information Committee was blocked by a Superior Court ruling from spending money to explain and promote the document, Governor Chafee gave a substantial sum to his public relations agency to run an incessant media blitz against the proposed constitution over the Easter weekend. To say that the anticonstitution ads were inaccurate and distorted would be a charitable understatement, but the negative campaign was a stunning success. The proposed basic law succumbed to the popular will by a 4-to-1 margin, 68,940 to 17,464.

Though constitutional change was stymied in 1968, such persistent issues as legislative pay, lotteries, four-year terms for state officials, suffrage, and grand jury reform prompted a call for a limited constitutional convention in 1973 to consider these specific items. By that date I had completed my doctoral dissertation on Rhode Island's constitutional development. Being politically ambitious and tired of the dull and subservient role of researcher, I secured the Democratic nomination for convention delegate from Cranston's Fifteenth Senatorial District. To prevent a partisan imbalance such as that which had afflicted the 1964 convention, the enabling statute called for each party to nominate one candidate in each of the fifty senatorial districts. Since nomination was almost tantamount to election, I achieved victory at the polls for the only time in my checkered political career, and even then I ran behind the Republican candidate with whom I was paired. With Alexander Hamilton, I can state emphatically that "this American political world was not made for me!"

186   Away from the scrutiny of the general public, I fared better. Despite the attempt at parity, some Democrats cheated the system and gave their party a 56-to-41 delegate margin, with 3 independents, in the 100-member convention. Because of my long-standing interest in Rhode Island constitutional issues, I had persuaded several of my political associates and fellow teachers, as well as a few former students, to run as delegates. Thus I had a strong nucleus of votes for convention chairman. Party leaders, however, wished to confer that distinction on William E. Powers of Central Falls, a former attorney general and retired Supreme Court justice.

Though I had the votes to win, I withdrew in favor of Judge Powers for several reasons—some altruistic, some not. Powers was brilliant and eminent, and the chairmanship would be a nice capstone on his distinguished career, whereas I had time for such honors (or so I thought). In addition, by placating Larry McGarry and Charles Reilly, the Democratic state chairman, I hoped for their favor in my eventual quest for state office. Also, I extracted concessions for my withdrawal—the post of convention secretary, control of the limited patronage, and decisive influence in the selection of committee chairpersons.

Accordingly, my law associate Fernando S. Cunha became the convention's executive director, my former supervisor Elmer Cornwell became director of research, and Matthew J. Smith, my former student and boyhood chum, was appointed assistant director of a research staff that included such other former students as Paul Campbell, attorney Edward Newman, and Marjorie Tarmey, who had also been my research assistant when I chaired the Cranston Charter Review Commission in 1972.

In sharp contrast to its immediate predecessor, this convention ran smoothly, efficiently, and rapidly. It removed the last vestige of the ancient property qualification by eliminating the property-tax paying requirement for participation in financial town meetings, and it enacted (with me as principal sponsor) a campaign finance disclosure amendment (now Article IV, Section 9, of the state constitution). In addition, the convention expanded the role of grand juries, gave eighteen-year-olds the vote, and removed the ban on state lotteries. Its proposals for a legislative pay increase and four-year terms for general officers were narrowly rejected by the voters.

However, the product of this convention that gave me the greatest personal satisfaction was the proposal that became Article of Amendment XLII (Article XIV of the present basic law). It streamlined the amendment process and set up a mechanism for the regular call of state constitutional conventions. I based the new amendment procedure upon a similar majoritarian provision in the People's Constitution of 1841, while the convention section stemmed from my belief that the failure of the constitution of 1843 to provide for the calling of constitutional conventions had been productive of political turmoil for nearly a century.

This reform, described editorially by the *Providence Journal* as "the most significant substantive alteration ever made in the state constitution," involved some sleight of hand by Judge Powers (who favored it) and me. The 1973 convention was a conclave limited to the consideration of certain definite topics. Amendment procedures and constitutional convention calls were not specified in our mandate, but we were charged with "revision of the election laws." Accordingly, I developed the far-fetched theory (with Justice Powers concurring) that amendments and conventions were within our purview because each procedure was submitted to the electors for approval. Hence I titled my proposed amendment "Election Requirements for Constitutional Revision" and sent it to the Elections Committee, which was headed by my academic colleagues Professor William T. Murphy, Jr., of Brown (chairman) and Professor Robert J. McKenna of Salve Regina (vice chairman). The amendment passed the convention on October 4, 1973, by a margin of 93 to 1. The lone dissenting vote was cast by Pawtucket Republican Ronald R. Gagnon (who would later attain a Superior Court judgeship and become my friendly nemesis on the Formal and Special Cause Calendar in a host of tax title cases).

The Rhode Island Supreme Court later ruled in *Malinou* v.

Powers, 114 R.I. 399, 333 A.2d 420 (1975), that the legislature's authority to limit the power of the 1973 convention to propose amendments that were outside the call legislation governing our agenda became moot, since there was no indication that any proposals were ruled out of order, and since the convention finally adopted a resolution (mine), and entertained others, that exceeded the restriction set forth in the enabling legislation.

As the convention prepared to adjourn without mishap on October 4, Judge Powers laughingly recalled the admonition of state Democratic chairman Charles Reilly at the outset of our deliberations one month before. "Keep an eye on this convention" Reilly had urged; "don't let the Republicans get out of hand." Ironically *an* eye was all we had between us. Powers, of course, was rendered sightless by a boyhood accident, and I am blind in my right eye. To take a cue from Hollywood, a movie of the proceedings of the 1973 convention might well be titled "My Left Eye."

Article of Amendment XLII was the proximate cause (to use a tort analogy) of the highly productive 1986 open convention, ably presided over by attorney Keven McKenna. I had difficulty establishing a permanent residence that year, so I did not run for delegate. I did, however, pen a detailed blueprint for constitutional change, which appeared as an article in the *Bar Journal* in May 1985 and is printed elsewhere in this volume.

Sensing my desire to be included and aware of my role in providing for the convention's call, President McKenna retained me as his paid general counsel. That post was short-lived, for many things had changed since my glory days in '73. For one, I had defected from the Democratic party in 1977 after Governor J. Joseph Garrahy turned a deaf ear to my requests for a state position, despite my chairmanship of his 1976 campaign advisory council. Mayor Buddy Cianci, sensing the rift, picked up my option in September 1977 and named me director of the Providence Crime Commission. I took the post in the belief that Cianci would challenge Garrahy for governor in 1978. When the polls said no, the mayor ran for reelection, pitting me, as Cianci's campaign advisor, against Frank Darigan (now Judge Darigan), a South Providence friend and a candidate of high integrity. Cianci's change of heart left me on the horns of a dilemma, but my plight evoked little sympathy from Matt Smith, Darigan's most powerful Providence ally. Things were never the same between us after that campaign.

After defeating both Darigan and attorney Fred Lippitt in 1982, Cianci was forced to resign as mayor when he pleaded nolo to a charge of assault in an incident with his former wife's lover. Citizen Cianci eventually took a job as a radio talk show host. In 1986, as the General Assembly debated the impeachment of Chief Justice Joseph Bevilaqua, Cianci conducted a media blitz against House Speaker Matt Smith in an attempt to discredit the legislative leaders who were contemplating Bevilaqua's removal. When the attacks got quite detailed and personal, Smith assumed that I had supplied the former mayor with his "inside" intelligence. Actually the gossipy Cianci, in J. Edgar Hoover-like fashion, had acquired the information on his own. Nonetheless, an understandably irate Speaker Smith called President McKenna with an ultimatum: either general counsel Conley goes or your convention funding goes. Thus ended, at least for now, my paid career as a constitutional reformer. Even my appointment as volunteer chairman of the Rhode Island Bicentennial of the Constitution observance was jeopardized by Cianci's tirades. For months, until he was assured that I was innocent of smearing him, Smith held my appointment in abeyance, although the other eight members of the foundation had long been selected.

The 1986 convention did a fine job. Among its reforms was a provision banning convicted felons from public office (Article III, Section 2). Ironically, that provision was used in an attempt to block Cianci's return to the Providence mayor's chair after his 1990 election victory. Attorney Ronald W. DelSesto (son of Christopher, the Long Count victim), William J. McGair, and I successfully persuaded the Supreme Court that the disqualification provision was prospective only and did not bar Cianci from taking office (see *State of Rhode Island ex rel. Floyd Edmund Webb III* v. *Vincent A. Cianci, Jr.*, 591 A.2d 1193).

In another notable reform, the 1986 constitution directed the General Assembly to establish an Ethics Commission (Article III, Section 8). This commission has since turned on its creator by invoking both conflict-of-interest and separation-of-powers arguments to deter legislators from serving on state administrative boards and commissions. In November 1997 Governor Lincoln Almond rhetorically requested an advisory opinion from the Supreme Court regarding the constitutionality of this long-standing General Assembly practice. Entering the fray, I presented an *amicus* brief, a legal and historical justification upholding the constitutionality (at least in Rhode Island) of this legislative function. My brief (if one could give such a name to a 190-page treatise) was entitled "Neither Separate nor Equal." After the case was decided, it was published in book form, with illustrations, as *Neither Separate nor Equal: Legislature and Executive in Rhode Island Constitutional History* (Providence: Rhode Island Publications Society, 1999).

This attempt by the Ethics Commission to bar members of the General Assembly from making appointments to, or serving on, state administrative boards and commissions, styled Regulation 5014, posed a major constitutional question. In this century only the 1935 Supreme Court advisory opinion relative to the power of the Assembly to call a constitutional convention rivals this issue in significance.

After tracing the appointive power of the Rhode Island legislature from its origins in the royal charter of 1663 through two constitutions to the present, I made the following findings and conclusions: (1) the General Assembly has always possessed and exercised the power to create state boards and commissions of an administrative nature, to make appointments thereto, and to sit thereon; (2) contrary to the assertions of the governor and the Ethics Commission, Rhode Island never adopted the federal model of separated powers, nor is that model binding upon the states; (3) Chief Justice Samuel Ames, in the landmark decision of *Taylor* v. *Place* (1856), established the independence of the judiciary without enhancing the power of the governor; (4) the Rhode Island Constitution of 1843 (which the 1986 convention left relatively intact) was a Whiggish document that exalted the legislative branch of government and reserved for the General Assembly nearly all of the power it had exercised under the charter of 1663;

and (5) the Ethics Commission's Regulation 5014, which prompted the governor's request for an advisory opinion, is an unconstitutional infringement upon the power of the legislature.

Happily, the Rhode Island Supreme Court agreed! In a 4-to-1 opinion, the Weisberger court (with Justice Robert Flanders dissenting) told the governor that "the ethics commission lacks the power to enact Regulation 5014, which fundamentally alters the constitutional structure of this state." (*In re Advisory Opinion to the Governor* [*Rhode Island Ethics Commission – Separation of Powers*], 732 A.2d.55 [R.I. 1999]).

Principal counsel for the General Assembly in this classic struggle for political ascendancy was Lauren E. Jones, prominent appellate attorney and then incumbent president of the Rhode Island Bar Association. Among my other colleagues in this defense of the Assembly's power was Professor Elmer E. Cornwell, former parliamentarian of the House and aide to Speaker John Harwood. Another was political science professor Jay S. Goodman, who followed my route from doctorate to law school and is now a practicing attorney in Providence. In thirty-three years of constitution making, I have come to see the wisdom of the old French maxim "The more things change, the more they remain the same"!

In the Ethics Commission case, the Supreme Court declined to rule on two other questions posed by Governor Almond: whether or not Rhode Island's system of separated power conforms to the federal model, and whether or not the Rhode Island system imposes "any limits whatsoever on legislative appointments to a public board or body." In order to answer these questions, said the court majority, "we would be required to make factual determinations," and therefore "we defer our response until a litigated case is presented to us with a factual record upon which we more properly can address concrete questions rather than abstractions or hypotheses."

The concrete case and controversy was not long in coming, but the governor was so eager to pressure the court that he foolishly chose to fight the five-hundred-pound gorilla—the Rhode Island Lottery Commission. In this high-visibility case, in which the governor challenged the power of the legislatively dominated commission to extend video gambling, I was called upon as an expert witness at the Superior Court hearing before Judge Michael Silverstein. In that forum I testified first as a historian documenting absolute legislative control over state lotteries from their inception in 1744 for financing public improvement projects and private endeavors to their ban in the constitution of 1843. Then I testified as secretary of the 1973 constitutional convention concerning the intent of that body in removing the constitutional ban on state-run lotteries. Clearly that convention intended that the legislature create and control an agency to run a state lottery.

Again the Supreme Court agreed. In *Almond* v. *Rhode Island Lottery Commission, Newport Grand Jai Alai, LLC, and Burrillville Racing Association d.b.a. Lincoln Greyhound Park*, 756 A.2d 186 (R.I. 2000), Justice Joseph Weisberger for the majority (with Justice Maureen McKenna Goldberg abstaining and Flanders dissenting) upheld the power of the legislatively dominated Lottery Commission to authorize an expansion of video gambling at Lincoln and Newport (the action that gave rise to the case). "The Rhode Island Constitution," said Weisberger, "does not prohibit the appointment of legislators to administrative boards and commissions." The Rhode Island General Assembly, he concluded, "unlike the federal Congress, need not look to the state Constitution as a source of authority by virtue of its historical plenary power (preserved in both the 1843 and 1986 Constitutions). It may exercise any power unless prohibited in this Constitution," and its delegation of power to the Lottery Commission was proper.

In the four decades since 1960, when I first began my research into Rhode Island constitutional development via a term paper at Notre Dame on the Dorr Rebellion, this subject has consumed much of my academic, political, and legal attention. For me, Rhode Island's constitutional system has been forever controversial and forever fascinating, and our next constitutional convention will surely make it more so.

Speech in Support of the Amendment Reforming the Process of Constitutional Change at the 1973 Constitutional Convention

23

This speech was delivered on October 2, 1973. For a full account of this convention, consult Patrick T. Conley, comp., *The Proceedings of the Rhode Island Constitutional Convention of 1973* (Providence, 1973).

THE CHAIRMAN [WILLIAM E. POWERS]: The chair will point out to the delegates that there remains on General Orders for today [October 2, 1973] Proposal 48, which was reported from the Committee on Elections. It purports to amend Article 13 of the constitution, so as to reduce the time in which amendments may be proposed by the legislators from the two-year provision presently in force to one session, the reason of course being that at the time the constitution was adopted, the General Assembly met annually in April and these proposals could be considered expeditiously. That is no longer so. Now it seems important to the chair that we consider Proposal 48. If you favor, it can be referred to the Committee on Style and Drafting. Otherwise, it is going to lie here.

Before the convention at this moment is the question on Proposal 48. The chair recognizes delegate Conley, the author of the proposal.

DR. CONLEY: Mr. Chairman and fellow delegates, this Proposal 48, entitled "Election Requirements for Constitutional Revision," was proposed by me. There are similar proposals introduced subsequently by delegates Godin and Murphy of Tiverton. Basically, this particular proposal is similar to the article on amendments that was recommended by the previous constitutional convention [in 1968]. It was submitted primarily because I felt that it would be a major reform of the constitution. It has attracted very little notice thus far, but I think if it is passed by this convention, it might rank in significance to the Bourn Amendment of 1888, the Twentieth Amendment of 1928, and the Home Rule Amendment of 1951. It is a far-reaching provision that would profoundly affect the future course of the state's constitutional development. The present constitution can only be amended by a cumbersome procedure, namely, passage by two consecutive General Assemblies, a general election intervening, and a three-fifths vote of the people.

Patrick T. Conley, secretary of the 1973 constitutional convention, presides over that convention when chairman William E. Powers took the floor. Vice chairperson Helen Migliaccio of Cranston is shown seated next to Conley.

As the chairman pointed out, that initial process was easier than it is today because the General Assembly in 1843, when the amendment procedure was enacted, was elected on a yearly basis, and now it is elected for two-year terms, and a general election must intervene before the General Assembly can act again.

That amendment procedure is one of the most difficult in the entire nation, and it is one that has caused the state and the General Assembly to resort on several occasions to the device of a limited constitutional convention to gain approval for necessary changes in our basic law. This had to be done in 1944, 1951, 1955, and again in 1958. The calling of a limited convention is also somewhat of a cumbersome procedure which is a considerable expense to the electorate. The present provision on amendments was inserted into the 1843 constitution for a reason which most of us would not approve of today.

In 1843 the conservatives who drafted the present constitution disenfranchised the Irish Catholic immigrants to Rhode Island, and these nativists felt that the best way to make that discrimination stick was to make the amendment process extremely difficult so that election revision could not take place easily and this downtrodden group would be kept in an inferior position.

Judging from the composition of this convention, the prime motive for the insertion of that cumbersome amendment provision in the original constitution no longer applies. Therefore, I would suggest that this procedure should be removed from the constitution. I would like to commend the Elections Committee who approved my proposal unanimously, and I would urge its passage by this assembly.

Basically, the proposal as it is drafted would facilitate the General Assembly's power to amend the constitution by simply requiring a roll call vote of a majority of the members elected to each house, but only one such vote. Then the particular question would be submitted to the people, who would vote on it. The electorate would be able to amend the constitution, not by a three-fifths vote, but by a simple majority.

This particular amendment adheres to two basic characteristics of American government. This is a democratic republic based upon the principle of majority rule. The notion of republicanism is satisfied by the General Assembly's acting in its representative capacity in approving amendments by majority vote, and the democratic principle is satisfied by requiring a majority of the people to approve any proposed constitutional change.

Finally, I think the amendment procedure would strengthen the governmental role of the General Assembly and prevent it from resorting to the subterfuge of a limited convention to gain needed changes. Most important, perhaps, the question of a general constitutional convention will be referred to the people every ten years for their consideration, and if the General Assembly fails to act, then this proposal authorizes the secretary of state to submit the question [to the voters in the twelfth year], so that we will have periodic general constitutional revision to keep the basic law of this state up to date. I think this is a very progressive feature of the proposed amendment, and therefore, fellow delegates, I urge its passage.

POSTSCRIPT

Proposal 48 passed the convention by a vote of 93 to 1. On November 6, 1973, the electorate approved it by a vote of 56,072 to 34,953, making this provision Article of Amendment XLII of the constitution of 1843. In 1986 the first constitutional convention called pursuant to the procedures established by my amendment incorporated the provision into the new constitution intact. Presently it is Article XIV of Rhode Island's basic law. Its text is as follows:

ARTICLE XIV
Constitutional Amendments and Revisions

SECTION 1. The general assembly may propose amendments to the Constitution of the state by a roll call vote of a majority of the members elected to each house. Any amendment thus proposed shall be published in such manner as the general assembly shall direct, and submitted to the electors at the next general election as provided in the resolution of approval; and, if then approved by a majority of the electors voting thereon, it shall become a part of the Constitution.

SECTION 2. The general assembly, by a vote of a majority of the members elected to each house, may at any general election submit the question, "Shall there be a convention to amend or revise the Constitution?" to the qualified electors of the state. If the question be not submitted to the people at some time during any period of ten years, the secretary of state shall submit it at the next general election following said period. Prior to a vote by qualified electors on the holding of a convention, the general assembly, or the governor if the general assembly fails to act, shall provide for a bipartisan preparatory commission to assemble information on constitutional questions for the electors. If a majority of the electors voting at such election on said question shall vote to hold a convention, the general assembly at its next session shall provide by law for the election of delegates to such convention. The number of delegates shall be equal to the number of members of the house of representatives and shall be apportioned in the same manner as the members of the house of representatives. No revision or amendment of this Constitution agreed upon by such convention shall take effect until the same has been submitted to the electors and approved by a majority of those voting thereon.

The 1986 State Constitutional Convention: The Salient Issues

24

Written in 1985, this proposal was released to the media and published in the *Rhode Island Bar Journal* in May 1985. In 1986 I served briefly as general counsel to Keven McKenna, president of the constitutional convention.

IN NOVEMBER 1984 the voters of Rhode Island gave decisive approval to a referendum authorizing the call of a constitutional convention during calendar year 1985. As the secretary and record keeper to the 1973 limited constitutional convention and the sponsor of Article of Amendment XLII, which mandated the 1984 referendum, I have a long-standing interest in Rhode Island constitutional development, an interest that prompts the following expression of opinion.

Our last (and only) open constitutional convention of this century produced a notable and reasonably progressive proposed constitution that should serve as a guide to those delegates who will be charged with reform of our state's basic law in the forthcoming convention. Though the 1968 document was rejected by the voters, its defeat could be ascribed more to the partisan political opportunism of the Republican governor, the terrible image of a convention that sat more than four years (probably the longest such conclave in the history of constitution making), and the reluctance of Democratic conservatives in that body to make innovations that might upset the status quo until forced to yield by public and, especially, media pressure.

The voters, in effect, judged that constitution not by its content but by its parentage. The influential *Providence Journal* tried to prevent this voters' bill of attainder at the eleventh hour. After numerous (and justifiable) stories sharply critical of the convention, it undertook a lengthy article-by-article editorial analysis of the proposed document in the months prior to the April 1968 vote and concluded by endorsing the ratification of the proposed constitution. This about-face was too little, too late.

In addition to the many specific reforms that it embodied, the 1968 document represented a vast improvement over the present tangled, sometimes inconsistent, and much-amended basic law. The 1968 constitution was simple, logically arranged, succinct, and economically worded. It achieved these qualities because it properly dealt only with the organization and form of government and left the details for statutory determination.

In 1973 Rhode Island held what will probably become its last *limited* constitutional convention. Of the fourteen or so basic articles that a streamlined constitution should contain, the efficient and successful 1973 gathering was authorized to deal only with two — suffrage and the amendment process. Concerning the former topic, however, more specific constitutional provisions relative to residency and absentee voting procedures might be considered anew in 1985 because of recent abuses in those areas.

Among the major parts of any constitution, of course, are the articles defining the powers and structure of the three branches of government — legislative, executive, and judicial. I favor a new legislative article that would combine and integrate Articles IV (Legislative Power), V (House), and VI (Senate) of the present document and the many amendments relating to legislative affairs, such as borrowing in anticipation of taxes (XXXI), the veto process (XV), urban redevelopment (XXXIII), and the creation of corporations (IX), into one comprehensive and coherent provision.

The substantive changes that should be made in a modern legislative article, however, are much more important. For example, we do not at present have a constitutional system for apportioning our General Assembly. Every basic law, at least in its inception, contains such a clause. Ours was invalidated by the U.S. Supreme Court in the reapportionment revolution of the 1960s (*Baker* v. *Carr* and *Reynolds* v. *Sims*), and since that time apportionment has rested only on statute. We should have a constitutional apportionment plan that meets the requirements of the federal Fourteenth Amendment as interpreted by the Supreme Court—one that requires mandatory redistricting of the state after each federal census, with such redistricting to be performed by our Supreme Court if the General Assembly itself fails to act. Such a reapportionment plan could consider whether or not the present 100 representatives, 50 senators formula ought to be revised downward in the interest of efficiency, but I personally would not alter the present allocations, nor do I favor unicameralism.

Legislative pay is an old and thorny topic that needs to be addressed, despite the emotions it will engender. The present rate is archaic and demeaning. A specific pay should not be spelled out in the basic law in view of the constantly rising cost of living and the increasing demands on legislators' time, both in and out of session. Any unreasonable "salary grab" can be checked by executive veto and ultimately punished by the voters.

Also archaic in the area of legislative finance is the presence in the constitution of a referendum requirement for any state borrowing in an amount exceeding fifty thousand dollars (Article of Amendment XXXI). This incredibly low ceiling impedes needed spending and causes the state to resort to subterfuges to finance routine yet essential projects. That 1951 ceiling should be raised to a more realistic level, perhaps one million dollars.

I do not favor the initiative as part of the legislative process; not only is it cumbersome and complex, but any voter can get a bill introduced by request. I do favor, however, a constitutional provision that would facilitate the release of a bill from legislative committee by requiring only a one-third vote of the whole membership, as opposed to the majority vote or the vote of the entire minority party required under present rules. Such a provision would give more influence to the Assembly's minority party.

Finally, the legislative article should extend the veto power of the governor by allowing him more time to veto, and thus more time to consider and evaluate legislation. The governor should be allowed ten days (like the president), instead of the present six, to consider legislation while the Assembly is sitting, and thirty days, instead of the present ten, to review the flood of bills that comes before him at the end of a legislative session. I would also favor an item veto for the governor.

The veto process leads us to the executive article. Here certain statutory reforms enacted during the Bloodless Revolution of 1935 should be solidified by placing them in the state's basic law. This includes the governor's power to appoint department heads. As constitutional reforms, these measures now seem inconsequential in view of the fact that the governor possesses such powers by statute, but statutes can and have been changed far more easily than constitutional provisions. A study of the role of the governor in this state from the Brayton Act of 1901 until the Reorganization Act of 1935 demonstrates the need to protect his executive prerogatives from erosion or encroachment.

Discussion of executive appointments and departments focuses attention on the offices of secretary of state and general treasurer. These are primarily ministerial rather than policy-making positions. Custodianship of state records and funds should be performed by department heads appointed by the governor. I favor gubernatorial appointment of the secretary of state and the general treasurer. If any appointed state official might be added to the roster of elected general officers, I would consider an independent general auditor for that designation.

The prolongation of political campaigns, especially since the introduction of the primary in 1947, and the escalating cost of campaigning because of the recent enlargement of the role of image-makers and the media make four-year terms for general officers a desirable and overdue change.

Finally, the new executive article should establish a clear line of succession to the governorship, extending through the lieutenant governor, attorney general, and Speaker of the House (presuming that the secretary of state and general treasurer are made appointive; otherwise they would precede the Speaker in line of succession). Such a provision is *necessary* to supersede the confusing provisions of the present constitution, wherein Article VII, Section 10, places the presiding officer of the Senate after the lieutenant governor in the line of succession and Article XI, Section 4, directs the General Assembly in Grand Committee to fill the offices of governor and lieutenant governor if both should become vacant. The Twenty-fifth Amendment to the federal Constitution and Sections 9 through 11 of the executive article of the proposed 1968 constitution offer good guidelines in dealing not only with succession but also with the more difficult issue of executive disability.

The present constitutional provisions relating to the judiciary have several defects resulting from the historical fact that here in Rhode Island the courts were long subservient to the General Assembly. Even after nearly three and a half centuries, that struggle for judicial independence is incomplete. Our Supreme Court justices do not have life tenure; they serve at the pleasure of the General Assembly, the body that elected them in Grand Committee. I feel that those justices should be given tenure during good behavior until a mandatory retirement age of seventy. The same protection should apply to judges of the lower courts as well. Tenure for judges is in accord with federal practice, and it contributes to a more autonomous judiciary. If a judge abuses his or her power of discretion, the remedy of impeachment is always available.

I also feel that General Assembly appointment of Supreme Court justices is fraught with the risk of partisan political maneuvering. It ought to be discontinued and replaced by a system resembling the federal model—appointment by the chief executive with the advice and consent of the Senate, perhaps by two-thirds vote. If a life-tenure provision is enacted, a new judiciary article also should include a procedure for determining the disability of judges.

Another key part of the constitution that should receive delegate scrutiny is the Declaration of Certain Constitutional Rights and Principles—the present Article I. The need for change here has been rendered less compelling by the U.S. Supreme Court's practice of "selective incorporation," whereby in recent years it has made most areas of the federal Bill of Rights applicable to the states. We were left local latitude in the area of grand jury action, so the 1973 constitutional convention drafted an amendment (XL) detailing our indictment procedures. Perhaps thought should be given to the need for state provisions on electronic surveillance and search and seizure that do not violate federal standards.

The last, and in some ways the most complex, basic area pertains to local government. Our Article of Amendment XXVIII (1951) set forth a procedure for the enactment of home rule charters that was designed to strengthen local autonomy and to rebut the so-called "creature doctrine," embraced by our state Supreme Court in the *Horton* (1900) and *Moulton* (1932) decisions, which asserted that Rhode Island's cities and towns were mere "creatures" of the legislature, with no inherent rights of self-government. These decisions, though questionable from a historical viewpoint, stood until 1951, when they were apparently superseded by the Home Rule Amendment. But our court has not abandoned the creature doctrine, despite the enactment of the present home rule article. In 1952 it advised the House of Representatives that cities or towns without a home rule charter remained "creatures" of the legislature. In the years since, the court's decisions have even whittled away the autonomy that was to have been enjoyed by those municipalities that had adopted a home rule charter.

According to those experts on local government with whom I have discussed these judicial constrictions, the unfavorable determinations stem from the vulnerability of the "property, affairs, and government" phraseology of most home rule articles, Rhode Island's included. These experts suggested a bolder and more positive method of achieving local governmental autonomy and self-sufficiency. That approach consists in embracing the so-called "residual powers" principle, whereby the constitution confers upon cities and towns all powers not specifically denied them by the constitution, their charters, or general law.

As the foregoing observations indicate, there is a real need for continuing constitutional scrutiny and reform. Hopefully the delegates to the upcoming constitutional convention will respond to that need by drafting—without partisan rancor—an updated, improved, and streamlined basic law to govern a changing Rhode Island in the challenging years that lie ahead.

RHODE ISLAND CONSTITUTIONAL CONVENTION

19 86

GET THE FACTS KNOW THE ISSUES

Shall the action of the Constitutional Convention in amending the Constitution in the following manner be ratified and approved?

1   **REWRITE OF THE PRESENT CONSTITUTION**
☐ YES   Shall the Constitution of 1843 and the 44 amendments ratified since
☐ NO   then be adopted as rewritten, in proper order, with annulled sections removed? Shall the Constitutional Convention publish the Constitution in proper form, including new amendments, if they are approved by the voters? (Resolution 86-00042 B)

2   **JUDICIAL SELECTION AND DISCIPLINE**
☐ YES   Shall a non-partisan, independent commission be established to
☐ NO   nominate judges for appointment by the general assembly in the case of supreme court vacancies and for appointment by the governor in the case of vacancies in other courts? Shall the commission have authority to discipline or remove all judges? Shall judges appointed hereafter be required to retire at 72 years of age? Shall the duty of the supreme court to give advisory opinions be abolished? (Resolution 86-00080 A)

3   **LEGISLATIVE PAY AND MILEAGE**
☐ YES   Shall the daily pay of general assembly members be established at a
☐ NO   sum equal to the average weekly wage of Rhode Island manufacturing workers, divided by a four-day legislative week (about $76), the speaker receiving twice that amount; and shall mileage compensation be equal to the rate paid U.S. government employees, such pay and mileage to be limited to 60 days per year? (Resolution 86-00094 B)

4   **FOUR-YEAR TERMS AND RECALL**
☐ YES   Beginning in 1988, shall the governor, lieutenant governor, secretary
☐ NO   of state, attorney general, general treasurer and members of the general assembly be elected to four-year terms and be subject to recall by voters? (Resolution 86-00028 A)

5   **VOTER INITIATIVE**
☐ YES   Shall voters be empowered to petition certain laws and/or constitu-
☐ NO   tional amendments onto the ballot for voter approval or rejection? Shall future constitutional convention candidates be elected on a non-partisan basis? (Resolutions 86-00001 B, 86-00136)

6   **ETHICS IN GOVERNMENT**
☐ YES   Shall more specific impeachment standards be established? Shall an
☐ NO   ethics commission be established with authority to adopt a code of ethics and to discipline or remove public officials and employees found in violation of that code? Shall the general assembly adopt limits on campaign contributions and shall the general assembly enact a voluntary system of public campaign financing, coupled with limitations on total campaign spending by participating candidates? (Resolutions 86-00047 A, 86-00060 A, 86-00145 A)

7   **BUDGET POWERS AND EXECUTIVE SUCCESSION**
☐ YES   Shall the governor be constitutionally empowered to present an
☐ NO   annual budget? Shall the speaker of the house become governor if both the governor and lieutenant governor die or are unable to serve? (Resolutions 86-00222, 86-00246)

8   **RIGHTS OF THE PEOPLE**
☐ YES   Shall free speech, due process and equal protection clauses be added
☐ NO   to the Constitution? Shall the state or those doing business with the state be prohibited from discriminating against persons solely on the basis of race, gender or handicap? Shall victims of crime have constitutionally endowed rights, including the right to compensation from perpetrators? Shall individual rights protected by the state constitution stand independent of the U.S. Constitution? (Resolutions 86-00033, 86-00032, 86-00140, 86-00002 B, 86-00171)

9   **SHORE USE AND ENVIRONMENTAL PROTECTION**
☐ YES   Shall rights of fishery and privileges of the shore be described and
☐ NO   shall the powers of the state and local government to protect those rights and the environment be enlarged? Shall the regulation of land and waters for these purposes not be deemed a public use of private property? (Resolutions 86-00003, 86-00004A)

10   **FELON OFFICE HOLDING AND VOTING**
☐ YES   Shall felons' voting rights, removed upon conviction, be restored
☐ NO   upon completion of sentence and probation or parole? Shall felons and certain misdemeanants be banned from holding office for three years after completion of sentence and probation or parole? (Resolutions 86-00149 A, 86-00025 B)

11   **LIBRARIES**
☐ YES   Shall it be a duty of the general assembly to promote public libraries
☐ NO   and library services? (Resolution 86-00098)

12   **BAIL**
☐ YES   Shall the courts be authorized to deny bail to persons accused of the
☐ NO   unlawful sale or distribution of controlled substances punishable by a sentence of ten years or more? (Resolution 86-00153 B)

13   **HOME RULE**
☐ YES   Shall cities and towns with charters have more authority over local
☐ NO   affairs, within the limits of the General Laws, including the power to tax and borrow with local voter approval (unless overridden by a three-fifths vote in the general assembly); to protect public health, safety, morals and the environment; to regulate local businesses and local planning and development? Shall new or increased tax exemptions pertaining to cities and towns be subject to local voter approval? Shall cities and towns be reimbursed for certain state-mandated programs? Shall charter adoption and amendment procedures be simplified? (Resolution 86-00196 B)

14   **PARAMOUNT RIGHT TO LIFE/ABORTION**
☐ YES   To the extent permitted by the U.S. Constitution, shall all persons,
☐ NO   including their unborn offspring, without regard to age, health, function, or condition of dependency, be endowed with an inalienable and paramount right to life; and to the extent permitted by the U.S. Constitution, shall abortion be prohibited, except that justified medical procedures to prevent the death of a pregnant woman shall be permitted? Shall the use of government monies to fund abortions be prohibited by the Constitution? (Resolution 86-00212 A)

VOTE
ON THE CONSTITUTIONAL QUESTIONS
TUESDAY, NOVEMBER 4th

This broadside set forth the issues confronting the voters in the November 1986 referendum on the changes proposed by the constitutional convention of 1986. Items numbered 1 (the neutral rewrite), 6, 7, 8, 9, 10, 11, and 12 were ratified.

Attorney John Whipple, a staunch defender of legislative supremacy, was Rhode Island's foremost constitutional lawyer of the early nineteenth century.

The Separation of Powers in Rhode Island: A Defense of the Supreme Court

25

This review essay was written in 1999 in the aftermath of the Supreme Court's decision *In re Advisory Opinion to the Governor (Rhode Island Ethics Commission – Separation of Powers)*, 732 A.2d 55 (R.I. 1999).

In June 1999 the Rhode Island Supreme Court issued a 4–to–1 advisory opinion relating to separation of powers in Rhode Island, with Justice Robert Flanders the lone dissenter. Specifically, it ruled that the federal model of strict separation had not been embraced by Rhode Island; that the General Assembly retained vast powers rooted in the royal charter of 1663; and that the practice whereby legislators served on state boards and commissions and made appointments thereto was therefore a permissible and constitutional exercise of the General Assembly's residual power.

Though firmly based upon history and law, the opinion caused disappointment and even disgust among those who regarded a diminution of the legislature's power as an urgent reform. The high court's ruling also drew criticism from lawyers and theorists who regarded the federal system of separated powers a desirable model that Rhode Island should emulate.

Two law professors and a prominent attorney who had unsuccessfully argued the case for strict separation boldly challenged the advisory opinion in articles in the November 1999 issue of the Rhode Island Bar Journal. *Having argued successfully before the Supreme Court in support of legislative power, I was asked by the* Bar Journal's *editors to defend the advisory opinion against the three critics — Matthew Harrington, associate dean at the Roger Williams University School of*

Law; Carl T. Bogus, an associate professor at the law school; and James Marusak, Esq., a practicing attorney. Their arguments are presented in full in the Bar Journal's *November 1999 issue. My commentary, which follows, restates each disputed position sufficiently to be intelligible without the necessity of reproducing the critics' entire arguments in this format.*

AT THE INVITATION of the *Bar Journal*, I have penned this impressionistic commentary on the three critiques of the Supreme Court's recent advisory opinion relating to the separation of powers. My observations may be supplemented by the 188–page brief I submitted to the high court, a brief that has now evolved into a 218–page, copiously footnoted hardcover book. That volume, entitled *Neither Separate nor Equal: Legislature and Executive in Rhode Island Constitutional History*, emphatically affirms the appointive powers of the General Assembly.

Now that our Supreme Court has upheld the historic right of the Rhode Island legislature to make appointments and serve on the various state boards and commissions, I have been asked to move from the position of *amicus* to that of *defensor* in responding to criticisms of the majority's opinion—a task I assume more with a feeling of weariness than with trepidation.

Since I have the gall to joust with three fine scholars, I have (in Caesarian fashion) divided my commentary into three parts, moving from an analysis of the essay with which I have the least objection to that which troubles me the most. As *defensor curiae*, I hope to take the middle ground between professorial pedantry and lawyerly combativeness.

Dean Harrington's article is measured, well-crafted, and temperate. It is based on impressive original research and the work of the greatest historical authority on American colonial government, Charles McLean Andrews. But Harrington essentially documents the truism that sovereignty resides in the people and not in their instruments of government. And he is not the first observer of early Rhode Island's political landscape to advance that view. For example, the Reverend Andrew Burnaby perceptively observed in his travels through the colony in 1760 that the "men in power, from the highest to the lowest, are dependent upon the people, and frequently act without that strict regard to probity and honour, which ever ought invariably to influence and direct mankind." Chief Justice Daniel Horsmanden of New York, in a 1773 report to the earl of Dartmouth during the *Gaspee* investigation, disdainfully described Rhode Island as a "downright democracy" whose governmental officials were "entirely controlled by the populace," and conservative Massachusetts governor Thomas Hutchinson lamented to George III that Rhode Island was "the nearest to a democracy of any of your colonies."

Harrington's solicitude for the locus of sovereignty is rooted in certain pronouncements by earlier justices that are quoted with apparent approval by the present court. In *Payne & Butler* v. *Providence Gas Company*, 31 R.I. 295 (1910), and *Nugent* v. *City of East Providence*, 103 R.I. 518 (1968), the court employed the term "powers of sovereignty" in reference to the legislature when it most likely meant "powers of government." Noted political theorist T. E. Holland defined sovereignty as "that supreme authority which is externally independent and internally paramount." Even Rhode Island's General Assembly would not fit that definition!

Like Dean Harrington, the Weisberger court knows the important distinction between sovereignty and the powers of government. That court's repeated references to the charter of 1663 and our popularly written constitutions as the sources of legislative power indicate its awareness of this distinction and its acknowledgment that sovereignty resides ultimately in the people of Rhode Island and not in their legislature. Dean Harrington is justified in correcting the imprecise language of earlier courts, but his fear that this or any American court will dislodge the people from their seat of sovereignty is unfounded.

The essay by James Marusak poses more problems for me. Marusak is a skilled attorney, an avid history buff, and a person of broad cultural interests. In short, he is a lawyer of the old school, and when I need an articulate, skilled attorney, I become his client. Yet his essay often departs dramatically from the generally accepted interpretation of Rhode Island history. This divergence is, perhaps, explained by Marusak's introductory statement: "History is an interpretive art." Such a subjective definition (to which few, if any, professional historians would subscribe) explains his heavy reliance on observations by writer Washington Irving and geographer Jedidiah Morse to buttress his novel assertions.

In his *American Universal Geography* (1796), Morse observed of Rhode Island that "the supreme executive power is vested in a governor." Although Marusak hails this misstatement as a "clinical examination," contemporaries took Morse's book to task. Secretary of the Treasury Oliver Wolcott claimed that certain sources used by Morse were unreliable, and botanist Manasseh Cutler wrote that Morse's "accounts of both animals and vegetables ... I conceive to be very erroneous and defective." A Morse biographer, Elizabeth Noble Shor, described his research technique as follows: "Morse's sources of information for his geography book were primarily written ones, not his own excursions. In 1787 he began circulating a questionnaire asking for knowledge of their places of residence from 'such Gentlemen as are able and likely to furnish answers.'" Perhaps his Rhode Island correspondent was Caleb Almond! Using Morse as an authority is today's equivalent of citing Frommer, Baedeker, or the Triple-A Guide.

Marusak's essay contains a few factual lapses, e.g., the patent of 1643/44 emanated not from the Crown but from Parliament, the same entity that revoked the Coddington grant of 1651 (the king was beheaded in 1649); but it is the author's imaginative interpretation of facts that jars the orthodox historian. The governor, a mere member and executive agent of the General Assembly until 1909, is dubbed a "super executive." The period from Rhode Island's renunciation of allegiance to the Crown in May 1776 until the effective date of a popularly written constitution in May 1843 is labeled an "interregnum" during which Rhode Island had no valid basic law. Whatever theoretical merit this assertion may possess, in fact the people acquiesced in the retention of their royal charter as a constitution, and Rhode Island was admitted to the Union with that frame of government, despite its royal roots and its lack of separated powers. The interregnum theory is analogous to such idle constitutional speculations as those about the unconstitutionality of judicial review, the invalidity of the Reconstruction amendments because their ratification was coerced, or the illegality of a federal tax on incomes because of the imprecision of the Sixteenth Amendment. Federal prison camps are full of those who indulge in that latter bogus theory. The historian must separate fact from fancy and reality from imagination.

The essay by Professor Bogus is, to me, the most objectionable. Perhaps its harsh tone and its didactic manner produce that effect, or maybe its straw men and sinister scenarios detract from its scholarly merit. I even grimaced at its title—"A Radical Decision by the R.I. Supreme Court." Given the accepted definition of the word "radical" (pertaining to fundamental change), how can a judicial decision that reaffirms a 336-year-old tradition be labeled "radical"?

Bogus makes his strongest point (in agreement with the other essayists) when he disputes the majority's dicta that Rhode Island exemplifies "a quintessential system of parliamentary supremacy." Metaphors, like absolutes, invite qualifications and exceptions, and the court's parliamentary analogy is a case in point. Sometimes rhetoric gets the best of reality. Both the majority and minority opinions were written (at least in part) in the expansive prose of the Romantic era when the constitution of 1843 came into being. That style lends itself to occasional hyperbole and dramatic assertions. Like Bogus and the other essayists, I do not equate legislative dominance in a three-branch system with parliamentary government, nor do I subscribe to the minority opinion's equally Romantic soliloquy that concludes with the maxim *Vox populi, vox Dei*. Justice Flanders and I are listening to different people!

My fundamental disagreement with Professor Bogus, however, is his substitution of wishful thinking for legal thinking in urging our court to ignore the Whig influences upon the executive article of the document he calls "the Algerine Constitution" of 1843 (on this crucial point, please consult *Neither Separate nor Equal*, pp. 61–82) and in suggesting that our high tribunal venture into the terra incognita of the federal Guarantee Clause relative to the need for a "republican form of government" to check the power of our General Assembly.

Professor and attorney Jay S. Goodman, in the role of *amicus curiae*, presented to the Supreme Court a concise and convincing analysis of the Guarantee Clause and its relationship to the separation of powers. Goodman persuasively maintains that the U.S. Supreme Court's "Dreyer Doctrine" explicitly holds that "there is no federal mandate for state separation of powers" and that the Guarantee Clause of the federal Constitution is not justiciable in the Rhode Island Supreme Court. The rationale for nonjusticiability, concludes Goodman, is "federal uniformity."

James Madison defined a republic as a state wherein there is "a delegation of the Government... to a small number of citizens *elected by the rest*" (italics mine). It follows that a pure republic is one in which all of the power of government is delegated by the people to their elected officials. As historian Samuel G. Arnold observed in the first scholarly history of the state, Rhode Island was a pure republic at the time of its creation: its general officers and both houses of its legislature were elected by the freemen. Even its highest court embodied the republican principle, for it consisted of the popularly elected governor and assistants (i.e., senators).

Ironically, Rhode Island lost its pure republican character in 1746/47 when the governor and General Assembly opted for an appointive high court. But just as gold is often more functional as an alloy, republicanism can work well when it is less than pure. The existence of an appointive judiciary certainly did not rob us of our republican character, for there are degrees of republicanism just as there are gradations of separationism.

The phrase "republican form of government" is most associated with the federal Constitution. Although Rhode Island failed to attend the Grand Convention of 1787, the state figured prominently in the debate over that constitutional provision. James Madison felt that "an article ought to be inserted expressly guaranteeing the tranquility of the states against internal as well as external danger [because] unless the Union be organized efficiently on republican principles, innovations of a much more objectionable form may be obtruded." The matter was first debated at the convention on June 11, and the language of Madison's proposal was changed to "Resolved that a republican constitution and its existing laws ought to be guaranteed to each state by the United States."

When the clause came before the convention again on July 18, the aristocratic Gouverneur Morris, one of the convention's most conservative delegates, remarked, perhaps facetiously, that he found the proposed language objectionable because he "should be very unwilling that such laws as exist in R[hode Island] ought to be guaranteed to each State of the Union." Undoubtedly he had in mind the paper-money issue of 1786 and the laws enforcing its acceptance, laws that had led to the famous case of *Trevett* v. *Weeden* (1786). At Morris's whim, Madison suggested alternative language: "The Constitutional authority of the States shall be guaranteed to them respectively against domestic as well as foreign violence."

Whereas Edmund Randolph was concerned with the existence of republicanism as well as its protection, Madison's fellow Virginian proposed to add the words "and that no state be at liberty to form any other than a Republican government." With this proviso, James Wilson moved "as a better expression of the idea" almost the present language of the Guarantee Clause, which was adopted and sent to the Committee on Style.

Professor William Wiecek, the author of the only scholarly monograph on the Guarantee Clause—and, incidentally, an authority on the Dorr Rebellion—says that the clause "was not meant to solidify republican government in the mold of existing political institutions. It obviously could not, if only because the state governmental structures in 1787 were too varied and too changing to share any but the broadest common characteristics. In the clause's negative thrust it was designed to prohibit monarchical or aristocratic institutions in the states."

From the foregoing, it is apparent that the Founding Fathers knew and considered the Rhode Island system of government and yet welcomed (actually forced) that state into the Union in 1790. That test of acceptance, whereby Congress seats our congressional delegation and the executive interacts with our state government, has never been seriously called into question, except for the challenge on behalf of the People's government in the U.S. Senate in April and May of 1842 and Charles E. Gorman's suffrage-based appeals to the Congress in the 1870s under the Equal Protection Clause. Both efforts were decisively rejected.

The broad power of the Rhode Island legislature and the issue of whether such power was consistent with a republican form of government were twice again in the national spotlight during the early nineteenth century, once under the charter and then under the new constitutional system. In both instances, legal assertions concerning the Rhode Island legislature's violation of the republican guarantee were brushed aside by the U.S. Supreme Court.

In *Wilkinson* v. *Leland* (1829), John Whipple defiantly defended the Rhode Island legislature's vast power. He argued to the Marshall Court—that architect of judicial nationalism—the inapplicability of the republican guarantee to the issue of separated powers:

> [Opponents claim] that legislative, executive and judicial powers must be in different hands to constitute a republican form of government. That this should be so is a great and important principle, but it is not a test of republican government. There is nothing which prohibits the exercise of all the powers of government by a legislature. If the guarantee of a republican form of government by the United States was violated by the government of Rhode Island, why had not the United States interfered?
>
> The charter of the government of Rhode Island is a skeleton; it does not form the government. It is the usages of Rhode Island that compose the constitution. The people say their legislature shall have certain powers, and be unlimited; this is therefore the form of government with which they are satisfied. Politicians may protest, and orators may declaim; but this does not affect the case. This Court will not take away from them what they have said they will have.

With the issue squarely and boldly before it, the Supreme Court, with Justice Joseph Story writing the opinion, upheld the power of the General Assembly and the constitutionality of its challenged statute.

The next, final, and precedent-setting look at Rhode Island's system of government from the perspective of the republican guarantee was, of course, *Luther* v. *Borden* (1849). In that *cause célèbre*, John Whipple joined with Daniel Webster in defense of the regularly constituted governments of Rhode Island under both the charter and the new constitution. Intense scrutiny and long arguments, by Whipple and Webster on one side and Benjamin Hallett and future U.S. Supreme Court justice Nathan Clifford on the other, attended this landmark decision. The Court developed the doctrine of the "political question" in avoiding a ruling on the claim of the People's government to legitimacy. The justices properly declined to define the meaning of the phrase "republican form of government," leaving that determination to the "political branches"—Congress and the president.

One can be quite sure, however, that a partisan Jacksonian jurist like Chief Justice Roger B. Taney, who wrote the Court's majority opinion, would have proffered dicta to discredit the Law and Order regime and its Whig defenders if he had the slightest inkling that Rhode Island's government violated republican principles.

Since the United States Supreme Court has never attempted to define or delineate what constitutes a "republican form of government," it would be folly for a state court to rush into this semantic void. The United States—specifically its Congress and the president—are to enforce this nonjusticiable guarantee as the need arises. There is no similar provision in the Rhode Island Constitution, and if there were, the political-question doctrine should preclude the court from applying it.

The line of cases from *Dreyer* v. *Illinois*, 187 U.S. 71 (1902), is controlling, and the assertion in *Whalen* v. *United States*, 445 U.S. 684, 689 n.4 (1979), is clear—"The doctrine of separation of powers embodied in the federal Constitution is not mandatory on the states."

One can only imagine the problems that could arise if state courts assumed the practice of interpreting the federal Constitution in the absence of federal standards. This is the reckless course that some strict constructionists would urge upon the Rhode Island Supreme Court. Ironically, the "antirepublican" abuse they

214

seek to eradicate would carry us further away from the pure republicanism of our original charter. State legislators are directly elected by the people in true republican fashion; appointive members of powerful boards are not. If republican government, as Madison tells us, is a government of *elected* representatives, how can banning these officials from public boards make our state government more republican in form? The establishment in Rhode Island of a solely appointive regulatory bureaucracy from which elected representatives of the people are excluded is the antithesis of republican government.

If one were to argue that the now-prevailing system under question is a denial of a republican form of government, he would be correct, but only if he spelled Republican with a capital *R*. A cynic might observe that both the Rhode Island House and Senate have been dominated by Democratic legislators since the U.S. Supreme Court imposed its "one man, one vote" ruling upon the states in the mid-1960s. At present, Democratic legislators constitute more than 80 percent of the membership of each chamber.

For some, this issue is a partisan attempt to make political capital out of the Assembly's exercise of its constitutional appointive power. These partisans and their nobly intentioned allies who raise the republican-form-of-government objection seem to know as little about republican theory as they know about Montesquieu, Madison, or Rhode Island constitutional history.

State of Rhode Island *v.* Reverend Ephraim K. Avery (*1833*): *The Legal and Geographical Setting*

26

This essay review of a volume published in 1986 was prepared for a reenactment of the Avery trial in the newly restored Bristol County Courthouse, where the proceedings began. The November 1998 reenactment marked my last event as founding president of the Bristol Statehouse Foundation. The essay was published in the *Rhode Island Bar Journal* 47 (May 1999).

Fall River Outrage: Life, Murder, and Justice in Early Industrial New England, a detailed study of the Avery murder trial of 1833 by Professor David R. Kasserman, was published by University of Pennsylvania Press in 1986. Because the book had a limited printing owing to its distribution by a scholarly press, and because the volume's title suggested a Massachusetts *cause célèbre*, Rhode Islanders gave little attention to Kasserman's effort. This review seeks to place the famous episode in its proper Rhode Island framework, especially since plans are under way to recreate the trial on a regular basis where the case began—in the Bristol County Courthouse.

Built in 1816, the Bristol Statehouse and Courthouse is now undergoing extensive restoration and renovation under the direction of the nonprofit Bristol Statehouse Foundation with generous funding from the Champlin Foundation. The restored structure will be used for historical exhibits, particularly those pertaining to Rhode Island legal and constitutional history, and for a variety of civic, educational, and cultural purposes. One such event will be the recreation of the trial of the Reverend Ephraim K. Avery for the murder of Sarah Cornell. The initial dramatization on November 22, 1998, included such practicing attorneys as William P.

Dennis, Sanford Gorodetsky, and John C. Corrigan. Supreme Court chief justice Samuel Eddy, who presided over the trial, was played by a newcomer to Bristol — Oscar-winning Hollywood actor Anthony Quinn.

216

* * *

On the morning of December 21, 1832, the body of Sarah Cornell, a young textile worker, was found in the Fall River section of the town of Tiverton, Rhode Island. John Durfee, a farmer visiting his stockyard where the winter's supply of hay was stored, discovered Sarah's lifeless and bruised body hanging from a pole.

The title of *Fall River Outrage*, Professor David Kasserman's fine book describing this gruesome incident and the ensuing murder trial of Bristol's newly installed Methodist minister Ephraim Avery, is deceptive. Kasserman, a social anthropologist, is less than precise about the geographical and jurisdictional details of Cornell's death and Avery's indictment. My essay seeks to clarify these issues.

At the root of the confusion is the fact that in 1832 much of the area of present-day Fall River south of Interstate 195, including the Durfee farm, which was on the present site of Kennedy Park, was part of the Rhode Island town of Tiverton, in Newport County. A Massachusetts town of Fall River had been carved from the southwesterly portion of old Freetown in 1803, but when Sarah died, that municipality (then called Troy) and the state line were several hundred yards north of where Durfee discovered her lifeless body.

In 1856 the Rhode Island General Assembly set off the industrialized northern portion of the town of Tiverton, including Globe Village, to form the separate municipality of Fall River, Rhode Island. It did so in the midst of litigation between Massachusetts and Rhode Island concerning the proper boundary between

Samuel Eddy, a former congressman, served as chief justice of the Rhode Island Supreme Court from 1827 to 1835.

Tiverton and the Massachusetts town of Fall River. That dispute, stemming from a faulty survey done when the East Bay region was ceded to Rhode Island in 1746, was resolved by the U.S. Supreme Court in favor of Massachusetts. Thus on March 1, 1862, Fall River, Rhode Island (measuring about two miles north to south), with well over three thousand inhabitants, was ceded to Massachusetts and merged with its namesake to form modern-day Fall River. Elsewhere, Rhode Island was compensated by annexing the town of Pawtucket, Massachusetts (present-day Pawtucket east of the Blackstone River) and western Seekonk, which was promptly incorporated as the town of East Providence.

These boundary shifts three decades after the Avery trial have caused such confusion that Kasserman's generally excellent study identifies the Bristol County Courthouse where Avery's first probable cause hearing was begun on Christmas Day, 1832 (so much for the myth of the old-time New England Christmas!) as being located in Massachusetts, which also has a Bristol County. Another source of confusion concerning the episode was the interaction among industrialists on both sides of the state line (i.e., in both Fall Rivers) who formed an *ad hoc* Fall River Committee to bring the Reverend Mr. Avery to justice. Ironically, the leader of this group was Nathaniel B. Borden, then a Massachusetts state legislator and later a Whig congressman and mayor of Fall River, whose relative Lizzie would figure in another famous murder case in the 1890s.

The great strength of Kasserman's history of this controversial episode lies in his depiction of the trial as a contest between the Fall River Committee of textile magnates and the leaders of the New England Conference of the Methodist Episcopal Church who defended Avery by expending huge sums of money to pay both witnesses and a battery of prominent defense attorneys. According to Kasserman, the case had significance beyond the actual incident because of the symbolic and institutional associations of the victim and the accused:

> Sarah Cornell was one of the first generation of
> American women to attain the social and economic

218

independence offered by employment in the cotton mills rising beside New England's streams. The very fact of her death contradicted the assertion of industrial capitalists that the women on whom they depended for labor were as safe in mill towns as they were at home under their parents' care, and the assault on the dead woman's character that figured prominently in Avery's legal defense was an open challenge to the industrialists' claim that factory life did not impede their worker's moral development. The defense of Sarah Cornell, then, easily became a defense of an industrial lifestyle. Although she had lived in Fall River less than three months when she died, that community's capitalists and mill operatives had good reason to adopt her cause as their own and work zealously to avenge her death. In trying to clear her name, they protected their own.

Ephraim Avery, on the other hand, belonged to a church that was in the vanguard of New England's Second Great Awakening. The Methodists preached a novel form of Christianity, based on feeling and free salvation, that had great appeal to the developing working class but posed an ideological threat to the dominant Calvinist Congregational church. The Methodists' emphasis on emotional conversion made their ministry suspect in a society that had always required years of rigorous intellectual training for those who held spiritual authority, while their episcopal government, which centralized power and made them a highly efficient evangelical organization, was at odds with the philosophy of local autonomy that had pervaded New England life for two centuries. Like the Masons, they were castigated as an antidemocratic society, and, worse than the Masons, they were believed to be enthusiasts whose intellects could not always be depended on to control the excesses of their passions. Already viewed with suspicion and engaged in an intense missionary effort, the church could hardly afford the scandal associated

with the Reverend Ephraim Avery's possible conviction
for murder.

Avery's trial thus became a contest between two
emergent institutions, both of which believed that the
opportunity for future growth depended on a favorable
verdict from the jury.... Everyone who followed the
progress of Avery's case was aware that the issue had
grown beyond a single death. The decision that was
reached would not only free or hang an accused man, it
would also go far to condemn a way of life.

On a more mundane level, the case's sexual overtones of course
titillated the scandal-mongering general public. Thirty-year-old
Sarah, though unmarried, was pregnant at the time of her death,
and many assumed that her religious confidant had seduced her
and then killed her to prevent harm to his reputation and career.
Physical evidence strongly suggested murder rather than suicide,
and circumstantial evidence showed that the thirty-six-year-old
Avery had the motive and the opportunity to kill.

That this trial began in the Bristol County (Rhode Island)
Courthouse gave rise to certain jurisdictional problems. Although
Avery resided in Bristol, the alleged crime occurred in Newport
County. Acting precipitously, prior to a ruling by a Tiverton
coroner's jury, John Durfee, who found the body, went with local
postmaster Seth Darling to Bristol to swear out a private complaint against Avery with Judge John Howe. This justice of the
peace issued a warrant for Avery's arrest and then refused to relin-
quish control over the hearing or transfer it to the site of the
alleged crime.

The state therefore convened its probable cause hearing in
Avery's place of ministry, where he had some popular support, and
Justices of the Peace Howe of Bristol and Levi Haile of Warren
presided at the hearing. William R. Staples, a noted lawyer and
historian who would eventually become chief justice of the state
Supreme Court, served as prosecutor. Nathaniel Bullock, Bristol's
collector of customs and later (1842) lieutenant governor of Rhode
Island, was the first of what became a large defense team. He was

soon joined by Richard K. Randolph, a prominent Newport Whig who would later become the Speaker of the Rhode Island House of Representatives.

By January 7, after many days of testimony, Howe and Haile, a future state Supreme Court justice, denied that they had heard sufficient probable cause to bind Avery over for trial on the charge of murder. Judge Howe's opinion was shocking not only for its complete exoneration of Avery but for its scathing denunciation of Sarah Cornell as a woman "addicted to every vice," an "undoubted prostitute" who had profaned the Sabbath by dedicating it to the "sensual gratification of a young man" (not Avery), and a woman who had been "notoriously afflicted" with a venereal disease. In view of Howe's performance, it is not surprising that his descendants, George Howe and Mark A. DeWolfe Howe, omit all references to the Avery inquest in their histories of Bristol.

People in the towns of Fall River, Massachusetts, and Tiverton denounced this ruling and demanded a rehearing in Newport County. When the apprehensive Avery left Bristol for a New Hampshire refuge, Massachusetts deputy sheriff Harvey Harden supported the bistate Fall River Committee's demand for a new probable cause hearing in the proper county. Harden secured a new warrant from Tiverton justice of the peace Charles Durfee and tracked Avery from Boston to Rindge, New Hampshire. With the help of authorities in those jurisdictions, Harden returned Avery to Tiverton for a rehearing before Justices Durfee (who had issued the warrant) and Asa Gray. This court of inquiry promptly declared the evidence sufficient to warrant a trial at the county seat in Newport before the Rhode Island Supreme Judicial Court, which (until 1905) was a trial court as well as an appellate tribunal.

Committed to the Newport jail, with no opportunity to post bail, Avery awaited the presentation of his case to a Newport County grand jury in early March. On March 8 that body confirmed the findings of Durfee and Gray and indicted the Methodist minister for murder in the first degree.

The Avery murder trial began on May 6, 1833, in the Newport's Colony House before a three-man Supreme Court presided over by Chief Justice Samuel Eddy, a former U.S. congressman, and including Charles Brayton and future chief justice Job Durfee of Tiverton. The trial took nearly a month to complete, making it one of the longest murder trials in American history up to that time. It not only drew great local attention but captivated the national press as well. The Methodist conference paid a total of over six thousand dollars to a parade of witnesses drawn from every community in which Avery and the much-traveled Sarah Cornell had lived. These recruits upheld the character of Avery and degraded the reputation of Cornell. In addition, the conference engaged Jeremiah Mason of New Hampshire (whom Daniel Webster regarded as his greatest legal rival) and such prominent Rhode Island attorneys as Richard Randolph, future attorney general Joseph Blake, George Turner (who later defended Thomas Dorr in the latter's treason trial), and future Rhode Island House Speaker and U.S. congressman Henry Y. Cranston. For the prosecution, Staples was joined by Attorney General Albert C. Greene and former state attorney general and U.S. congressman Dutee J. Pearce.

The well-financed defense used the now common strategy of "proving" that the female victim of a sexually related crime was of such bad character or engaged in such inviting conduct that her male assailant could not be guilty. According to Kasserman's detailed analysis, "the court was regaled with an overwhelming volume of unsubstantiated stories depicting the dead woman's dishonesty, promiscuity, deviousness, and incipient insanity. Crowds that attended the trial hoping to witness a memorable show were not disappointed when the defense was allowed to introduce as evidence small-town gossip that was otherwise heard only over backyard fences."

After hearing 239 witnesses over twenty-one court days, during which Mason and his associates had kept the idea of a conspiracy against Avery and the Methodist Church constantly before the jury, that body was charged by Justice Eddy with returning a verdict. Shortly after noon on Sunday, June 2, 1833, the jury's foreman Eleazer Trevett (whose ancestor John Trevett had been involved in another famous Newport trial) announced the finding of not guilty.

Although the result was somewhat of a surprise, since rumors had indicated that ten of the twelve jurors were convinced of Avery's guilt, it produced no indignant public outburst, and Avery made his way home to Bristol by boat late that afternoon unmolested.

Shortly thereafter, the New England Conference of the Methodist Episcopal Church also exonerated Avery, but he had become an embarrassment to his sect. By the mid-1830s he had left the ministry and was living in Richmond, Massachusetts, employed as a carpenter. In the 1850s he took up residence in Lorain County, Ohio, on Lake Erie west of Cleveland, where he worked as a farmer until his death on October 23, 1869. He was survived by his wife, Sophia, who had remained with him through the years since Bristol, for better and for worse.

Brotherly Love: Murder and the Politics of Prejudice in Nineteenth–Century Rhode Island, *by Charles Hoffman and Tess Hoffman, Reviewed*

Written in 1995, this review appeared in *The New England Quarterly* 68 (September 1995). For my version of the episode, consult "Death Knell for the Death Penalty: The Gordon Murder Trial and Rhode Island's Abolition of Capital Punishment," *Rhode Island Bar Journal* 34 (May 1986), which won the first annual writing contest of the Rhode Island Bar Association.

27

EIGHTY YEARS BEFORE the infamous Massachusetts saga of Sacco and Vanzetti, neighboring Rhode Island experienced its own inglorious version of blind justice—the Gordon murder trial. Similarities between the two *causes célèbres* abound. In both, the defendants were recent immigrant arrivals, Catholic in religion (at least nominally), members of the working class, and supporters of unpopular political views. In both, nativism, prejudice, and a repressive legal system elevated circumstantial evidence beyond the realm of reasonable doubt. In both, the alleged perpetrators were denied postconviction relief or governmental clemency and were executed. In both, sober reflection produced widespread skepticism about actual guilt and led many to question the wisdom of capital punishment

Charles and Tess Hoffman, professors of English by trade and training, go far beyond mere doubt in their detailed analysis of the murder of Cranston industrialist Amasa Sprague. With poetic license and subjectivism forbidden to historians, they not only exonerate the Gordons; they also implicate U.S. senator William Sprague in the murder of his brother and business partner, Amasa.

Who were the protagonists in this important but neglected episode in American legal history? Amasa Sprague, the unlikely victim, was a powerful, wealthy, and influential man. He was the administrator of the A & W Sprague textile empire, a portion of which was based in Cranston, Rhode Island. Amasa personally supervised the Cranston complex at Sprague's Village in the manner of a feudal baron, with several hundred Irish men, women, and children in his employ. William Sprague, his younger and more venturesome brother, served first as governor of Rhode Island and then as U.S. senator, an office he held at the time of Amasa's death.

Amasa Sprague (1798–1843) ran the Sprague textile empire.

The alleged murderers, Nicholas, John, and William Gordon, were Irish immigrants who lived in Sprague's mill village. Nicholas, the first of his family to arrive in America, emigrated from Ireland in the mid-1830s. He opened a small store, which eventually included a pub, near Sprague's mills. His commodities were in such demand in this dreary industrial village that in 1843 Nicholas was able to finance the migration of his family—his aged mother; three brothers, John, William, and Robert; and a niece.

But Gordon's liquor sales also produced a confrontation with Amasa, who felt the intoxicating brews were severely affecting the productive capacity of his factory hands. Thus Sprague used his considerable political weight in June 1843 to block a renewal of Nicholas Gordon's liquor license. Tempers flared, harsh words and threats were exchanged, and six months later, on December 31, 1843, Sprague's body was found on a well-used path between his mansion and a large farm he owned in the neighboring town of Johnston. Amasa had been shot in the right forearm and then brutally beaten to death. The sixty dollars found in the victim's pocket seemed to eliminate robbery as a motive, making the crime appear to be one of hatred or revenge.

Suspicion immediately centered on the Gordon family. Nicholas, John, and William were promptly indicted on circumstantial evidence—John and William for murder, Nicholas for being an accessory before the fact, the implication being that

Nicholas had instigated his brothers to commit the murder in revenge and had even imported them for that purpose. Nicholas received the lesser charge because a preliminary investigation proved he was in Providence on the day of the murder, first at Mass and later at a christening.

225

The Irish communities in Providence and Cranston rallied to the support of the Gordons, as did several leading lawyers associated with the jailed constitutional reformer Thomas Wilson Dorr. In the recently concluded Dorr Rebellion, the Irish had been Dorrites, while the Spragues had joined the antireform Law and Order coalition that vanquished Dorr.

U.S. senator William Sprague (1799–1856), younger brother of Amasa, represented the family's interests in the public sector until Amasa's murder.

In the ensuing trials the prosecution zeroed in on the hapless twenty-one-year-old John, who alone could not prove his whereabouts on that fateful December afternoon. In his summation, Attorney General Joseph Blake told the jury that the Gordons came to America "with the idea which is so common to many of their countrymen, that the laws here, in this free country, are less severe, and may be more easily evaded, than the laws of their own country—that they would be less restrained in their indulgences, and less liable to punishment here, than under the strict police of their own country." In his charge to the jury, Judge Job Durfee, who would soon preside with great partiality in the treason trial of Thomas Dorr, drew a distinction between the testimony of native-born witnesses and that of the Gordons' "countrymen," implying that the latter was less credible.

That jury, devoid of Irish or Catholic membership, promptly returned a verdict of guilty against John, and the Draconian Durfee sentenced him to death. Dorr's arch rival, Governor James Fenner, and his legislative allies refused a pardon, so on February 14, 1845, John Gordon became the last Rhode Islander to be executed for a crime.

The Hoffmans make full use of the secondary literature pertaining to their subject but neglect unpublished court records and manuscript accounts that may have yielded more detail. They have accepted this reviewer's conclusions regarding the strong nexus between anti-Irish Catholic nativism and the Dorr Rebellion and noted the interaction between Dorrite leaders and the Gordons. They are probably correct in exonerating John Gordon, but their indictment of ambitious and grasping Senator William Sprague for conspiracy to commit fratricide is based on even flimsier circumstantial evidence. The defense, with similar resourcefulness, charged "Big Peter," a shadowy mill worker who had strong resentments against Amasa and permanently disappeared from the village immediately after the murder.

We will never know who killed Amasa Sprague. We do know that as soon as the Dorrites gained brief control over state government in 1852, they joined with members of the antigallows movement to abolish capital punishment—undoubtedly with John Gordon in mind. Like Big Peter, the death penalty has not returned to Rhode Island as yet.

At its December 2000 meeting, the board of editors of the *Rhode Island
Bar Journal* decided to publish a biographical profile of Chief Justice Joseph R.
Weisberger on the occasion of his retirement on February 24, 2001, and
requested that I write it. I accepted and conducted a three-hour
interview with the chief justice on December 18, 2000, to obtain the
background material for this essay, which appeared in the
Rhode Island Bar Journal 49 (February 2001).

NON SUB HOMINE SED SUB DEO ET LEGE — Not under man but
under God and law—is the inscription some obscure craftsman
carved above the Rhode Island Supreme Court bench in 1933 as
the Providence County Courthouse neared completion. Fortui-
tously, this Latin maxim would epitomize the private and public
life of the man who emerged as the intellectual and moral leader
of that Supreme Court during the final two decades of the
century—Joseph R. Weisberger.

Joe Weisberger was born on August 3, 1920, as President Woodrow Wilson and Senate Republicans led by Henry Cabot Lodge
battled over the Treaty of Versailles and its League of Nations
Covenant, and as the Republican presidential ticket of Warren G.
Harding and Calvin Coolidge squared off against James M. Cox
and his charismatic running mate, Franklin Delano Roosevelt. In
that same August the Nineteenth Amendment was finally ratified,
ending a seventy-two-year struggle by American woman to gain
the right to vote.

Ann Meighan Weisberger's great achievement that August was
not in a political ward but rather in the maternity ward of a small
hospital on Parade Street in Providence. Here, at age twenty-four,
she gave birth to her only child. He was baptized Joseph Robert at

St. Edward's Church on Branch Avenue, near the Veazie Street home where the Weisbergers resided.

St. Edward's Parish was also home to Ann's maternal family, the Rattigans, who migrated from County Roscommon, Ireland, in the late nineteenth century. Ann Elizabeth Meighan was a working mother whose job was "textile mender" at the huge Wanskuck Mills, where the Metcalf family had produced woolen goods since the Civil War. These same Metcalfs also ran another Providence business—a propaganda mill that was called the *Providence Journal*.

Samuel J. Weisberger, the father of the future chief justice, was a Catholic of Austrian ancestry who was born in New York in 1890 and enlisted in the U.S. Navy in 1906. Sam became a career Navy man who began his long period of service with the "Great White Fleet" of U.S. battleships that circled the globe at the behest of President Teddy Roosevelt to show the American flag and show off U.S. naval prowess. One of the ships in that imposing armada was the battleship *Rhode Island*, on which seaman Weisberger served. Prior to World War I he saw duty in Nicaragua and Haiti, and he then participated in convoy duty during the war itself.

Chief Justice Joseph R. Weisberger

By the time that Joe Weisberger was born, his father had risen through the ranks to the position of chief boatswain's mate, the master sergeant of the sea. Like most chiefs, he was a strict disciplinarian. "My father," recalls the judge, "expected me to toe the mark, and I did just that." Although duty caused Sam Weisberger to be away from home occasionally, the judge feels absence made the heart grow fonder. "My mother and father were very devoted, and they both worked to give me all the advantages that they themselves did not enjoy."

When Joe was two, the family moved to 279 New York Avenue in the Washington Park neighborhood. There young Joe Weisberger attended the California Avenue and Broad Street Schools and worshiped at St. Michael's Church in South Providence, where he made his First Communion. When Joe was eleven, the Weisbergers moved to Philmont Avenue in the predominantly Swedish Eden Park section of Cranston, then within the parish of Saint Matthew.

In September 1935, after attending three different Cranston public schools, Joe Weisberger enrolled in Cranston High (now Cranston East) and chose the classical course of studies, which included four years of Latin. Under the tutelage of Miss Hattie Holt ("a great inspiration"), the future chief became conversant with Caesar, Cicero, Tacitus, Livy, and Virgil; and like Caesar's wife, he began to live a life without reproach. As a graduating senior, Weisberger received the Virgilian Medal for Excellence in Latin.

In addition to Latin (which still can be detected in his speeches and opinions), Weisberger studied German, the language of his paternal grandfather, Petrus, who had migrated from Austria in the early 1880s to work as a tailor in New York's garment industry very near the time that another Austrian native, Felix Frankfurter, made a similar trek from Vienna to New York.

While at Cranston High, Weisberger displayed an attraction for speech in all its forms. He served as president of the school's dramatic society (the Thyrsis Club) and as coeditor of the student newspaper, and he was a member of the debating society. To deter those less cultured students who might harass an "egghead," Weisberger fought in the intramural boxing club as a middleweight. Although the judge did not admit it to me, a fellow pugilist, he probably could have been a contender.

In 1938 Weisberger graduated near the top of his class among a group that included Douglas E. Leach, one of America's premier historians of early Indian-white relations, and several others who would earn distinction in business and the professions. Despite stiff academic competition, Weisberger earned membership in the Rhode Island Honor Society and was voted by his classmates "The Boy Most Likely to Succeed."

After high school graduation in the "Thunderbolt" class of '38,

Weisberger enrolled at Brown, the only university to which he applied. I asked if he considered Providence College, to which he carefully responded that "PC was then a good local college, later attended by all three of my children, but Brown had great prestige as an Ivy League college and possessed a national reputation."

Majoring in history at Brown, Weisberger came under the tutelage of James Blaine Hedges, a noted economic historian. At one point, recalls Weisberger, "I was his only student in an honors course, where I analyzed Albert K. Beveridge's monumental four-volume *Life of John Marshall*. I always had to come to class prepared, because I could not rely on someone else being called upon for commentary."

In addition to the "very inspirational" Hedges, Weisberger fondly remembers Professor Ben Brown, the head of the Theater Department, a Shakespearean scholar, and the director of Sock and Buskin, Brown's famous dramatic society. "The Shakespearean roles I played not only gave me a great grasp of Shakespeare; they were the best education I could obtain in the use of the English language." Especially memorable to Weisberger was his portrayal of Shylock in *The Merchant of Venice*.

It was at Brown that the young Weisberger developed his first career goal—the Foreign Service. His inspiration was Sir Anthony Eden, the British secretary of state for foreign affairs (1940–45), who was then attempting to defuse the European crisis. To prepare for this occupation, Weisberger augmented his history courses with offerings from political science and diplomacy. His academic performance earned him a Brown scholarship, but as he recalls, tuition was only four hundred dollars per year. His academic work at Brown also earned him membership in Phi Beta Kappa.

As we know, neither Anthony Eden nor anyone else could stem the tide of aggression that inundated much of the world by early 1940, so when France fell in May of that year, Weisberger responded to the crisis by enlisting in the U.S. Naval Reserve. "It was time to get involved!" His willingness to interrupt his stimulating academic experience at Brown to embark upon an uncertain and probably perilous military mission speaks volumes for Weisberger's character, patriotism, and sense of duty. He was truly a contributing member to what Tom Brokaw has termed "the Greatest Generation." For Weisberger, "World War II was a time of national unity that has never been duplicated since."

At the end of his junior year in mid-1941, Weisberger left Brown, enrolled in naval officers' school, and became an ensign. He now outranked his father, who saluted him with the reminder that "the Navy is run by chiefs," after the elder Weisberger was recalled to active duty in 1942 for service aboard a minesweeper. This assignment cost fifty-three-year-old Sam four fingers from his right hand in a depth-charge accident.

Joe Weisberger trained on Narragansett Bay at Melville for underwater defusing work. Later, in 1942, he was dispatched to the southwest Pacific, first to Australia and then to New Guinea. "My task was to try to make anchorages at advance bases safe for American ships," he explains. "I became a specialist in placing net and boom defenses in harbors where U.S. ships might anchor." Rising to the rank of lieutenant and, by war's end, to that of lieutenant commander, Weisberger accomplished his most heroic exploits as officer in charge of what he fondly calls his "Splinter Fleet," a motley flotilla of ocean-clearing vessels. Among them was a British "mine exploder" called the HMS *Springdale*, which served as his flagship, and which had a giant magnet (later removed) to explode floating mines. Equally magnetic were the squadron's group of Welsh seamen, who regaled their American comrades with a vast repertoire of songs from Celtic to current. As flotilla commander, Weisberger might have coined some memorable naval slogans, such as "a mine isn't a terrible thing to waste," but he confined his oratorical skills to barking commands. After his successful mine-clearing stint, he returned to the United States in September 1944.

Once the Pacific was swept not only of mines but also of the emperor's ships, Weisberger, after a ten-month tour of duty in Norfolk, Virginia, headed for the Japanese home islands as part of the U.S. occupying force. At this point he began to reassess his career objective. After two years in the Pacific, says Weisberger, "I thought it would be nice to stay home." Thereafter, Weisberger's only nautical command was his twenty-seven-foot sloop-rigged sailboat, on which he cruised Narragansett Bay. Too busy to sail regularly, he eventually donated the boat to Brown because "it was not cost effective as a form of amusement."

Returning to Rhode Island in 1946, Weisberger joined his father and mother in the home to which they had moved on Waterman Avenue in the central section of East Providence, in Sacred Heart Parish. Thereafter he never left town. In 1951 the elder Weisbergers moved to Edgewood. Sam passed away in 1963; Ann died in 1985 at the age of eighty-eight.

Upon his delayed graduation from Brown, where he completed his studies *magna cum laude* in early 1947 as a member of the class of '42, Weisberger matriculated at the prestigious Harvard Law School in February 1947 and graduated in June 1949. His motivation for enrolling was pragmatic: "I felt a law degree would be of value, even if I didn't enter into the practice of law."

As a student at Harvard, Weisberger found that his interest in law as a profession was stimulated by a galaxy of legal scholars of national renown. With great admiration, Weisberger remembers such luminaries as Austin Wakefield Scott, a "great teacher who made the dry subject of trusts come alive"; A. James Casner, the "brilliant" authority on future interests; property expert Barton Leach; and the illustrious Dean Erwin Griswold, who taught taxation and "had us all terrorized."

Rhode Island's Zechariah Chafee was Weisberger's professor in equity. "He had a booming voice and wore a raccoon coat from the twenties that made him look like a great bear." Chafee was not only brilliant, says Weisberger, but a "delightful person." Closer in age to his students was Archibald Cox, then a fledgling professor of labor law (and, much later, Watergate prosecutor). Cox was a good teacher and a "real person," with "lots of personal charm." As students, remembers Weisberger, "we could relate to Cox, whereas the others were sort of demigods."

After graduation Weisberger returned to Rhode Island and clerked for six months with attorney Walter Adler. Following the completion of this requirement for aspiring lawyers, he stayed with Adler for about one year and then associated with the two-man firm of Quinn and Quinn, whose principals were the flam-

232

boyant Patrick Henry Quinn and his son Thomas. The elder Quinn was an extremely prominent Democratic politician who in 1913 had carved for himself a political fiefdom composed of mill villages in Warwick's western sector, which the General Assembly incorporated as the town of West Warwick.

Weisberger recalls that Colonel Patrick Quinn was an "excellent raconteur" who spun tales of Rhode Island politics in the turbulent twenties and thirties, when the state experienced a transition from Republican to Democratic ascendancy. "I loved to listen to his stories of political intrigue and the development of the labor movement." Weisberger also got an insider's view of the famous Bloodless Revolution of 1935 from its principal architect, Judge Robert Emmet Quinn, the colonel's nephew, a former Democratic governor and a frequent visitor to the law office.

Surprisingly, for all their political experience and (except for the Race Track War) their political wisdom, the Quinns failed to recruit their captive audience, Weisberger, into the ranks of the Democratic party, despite his Irish Catholic working-class background. Had they been more insightful, a Governor Weisberger would have been a distinct possibility a decade hence.

Conjecture aside, however, young Joe Weisberger took the road less traveled: he became a Republican. Like Saul on the road to Tarsus, Weisberger was converted by a chance occurrence—a visit to his neighborhood gas station. That facility was owned by East Providence Republican activist Daniel E. Marso, who fueled Weisberger's interest in Republican politics. In 1952 Marso (who eventually became mayor when East Providence achieved city status) convinced the ambitious Weisberger to run for town moderator against the enormously popular incumbent Raymond Hawksley, who simultaneously served as the general treasurer of Rhode Island. When the energetic young lawyer said "Why not?" Marso persuaded him to run simultaneously against Senator John Coffey for the East Providence seat in the General Assembly. Although the brash young Republican lost to Hawksley, he rode the coattails of Dwight Eisenhower (at the top of the state column) to victory over Coffey by a 522-vote margin (10,462 to 9,940).

Weisberger entered the Senate in January 1953 as a member of the majority party; in that last bastion of Republican political strength, the GOP held a 26-to-18 edge over the Democrats. On the minority side across the aisle were Frank Licht of Providence and Newport's Florence Kerins Murray. By then a polished orator, Weisberger spoke frequently on the floor, his freshman status notwithstanding. Pitted against him on several issues was Licht, himself a forceful speaker. "We had more oratory in the Senate than most, but we never changed a vote!" Governor Licht confided to Justice Weisberger much later in their careers.

Weisberger again posed a double threat to East Providence Democrats in the midterm elections of 1954. Without Eisenhower, the state column was a liability. In a turnout approximately 3,000 votes less than in the 1952 presidential year, Weisberger edged Democratic challenger David B. Lovell, Jr., by 447 votes (8,925 to 8,478). And on the town level, Weisberger triumphed as well, beating Ray Hawksley in a much-publicized upset. "These twin victories shook up the Democratic hierarchy," Weisberger recalls with great pleasure.

When he returned to the Senate in January 1955, the upper chamber was equally divided—22 Democrats and 22 Republicans—and so the deciding vote on key issues would be cast by the presiding officer, Democratic lieutenant governor John S. McKiernan. As a consolation, however, the rising young Republican star was selected as minority leader by his peers, the most influential of whom was George D. Greenhalgh of Glocester, a former Republican chairman and a twenty-year Senate veteran. That the wily and influential Greenhalgh favored Weisberger was obvious from the fact that the new Glocester town solicitor was none other than Joseph R. Weisberger.

Although the Republican party's political front-runner in the mid-1950s was former Democrat Christopher DelSesto, Governor Dennis J. Roberts and his advisers knew that Joe Weisberger, with his impressive double victory in Rhode Island's seventh most populous community, was a contender to soon be reckoned with at the state level. In 1956 Roberts called Senator Weisberger and offered him a Superior Court judgeship just after the governor had elevated Thomas Roberts, his brother, from the Superior to the

Supreme Court. Weisberger met with Roberts but initially declined the appointment, because the Republican caucus had already settled upon former Cranston mayor Hoyt W. Lark to take that position. The GOP had been generous to Senator Weisberger, and so he was content to defer to party leaders in filling this seat on the Superior Court.

But Roberts was persistent. He called Weisberger to his office a second time. I know you are loyal to your leadership, said the governor, but "I will not appoint Hoyt Lark, so it's you or someone else." With that information, recalls Weisberger, "I then rethought my position. At age thirty-five, becoming a Superior Court judge was a magnificent opportunity. Never for one moment have I regretted that decision or my service on the Superior Court bench." "I never really knew why Denny Roberts appointed me," Justice Weisberger told me with a mixture of modesty and political naiveté.

In the 1950s Joe Weisberger made two public choices that shaped his life: he became a Republican and he accepted a judgeship. He also made a personal choice that affected his life even more. On June 9, 1951, he married vivacious and personable Sylvia Pigeon, who was then assistant director of nursing services at Rhode Island Hospital. The holder of a bachelor's degree from Albertus Magus College in New Haven and an RN from Rhode Island Hospital's School of Nursing, Sylvia was just what the doctor ordered for the success of Joe Weisberger. Over the years she bore him three children, Joseph Jr., now an attorney with Wistow and Barylick, Paula A. Wroblewski, now the manager of the East Providence branch of Sovereign Bank, and Judith M. Greene, MSW, presently a social worker and licensed therapist for Northern Rhode Island Mental Health. This trio, all PC-educated, have thus far presented the Weisbergers with four grandchildren. Justice Weisberger and Sylvia will celebrate their fiftieth wedding anniversary in June 2001, and the bond between them is stronger than ever. "Sylvia has been my life's companion," says Weisberger with considerable emotion; "she has supported me fully in everything I have ever tried to do!"

My first encounter with Judge Weisberger came in 1957, shortly after he became a judge and shortly after my uncle Tom Conley had coaxed me into joining the Knights of Columbus at St. Paul's Council in Edgewood, where he was Grand Knight. Weisberger was not only a Knight but also a speaker on the Catholic communion breakfast circuit. My uncle thought that the new judge would be an ideal motivator—even if he was a Republican—and so he got the honorable Mr. Weisberger to speak to St. Paul's Council, and he prevailed upon me to abandon my South Providence buddies to attend the quasi-religious function. Part of the enticement was Uncle Tom's assurance that "this guy will impress you. He's so sharp that Denny Roberts made him a judge to short-circuit a promising political career." Tom was right on at least one count; I was duly impressed. I remember that the judge's general topic concerned the role of the Catholic layman, but the specifics have been buried in the sands of time. Unforgettable, however, was Judge Weisberger's presence and his aura of intellectuality. It is said that one never gets a second chance to make a first impression, and Weisberger's impression on an eighteen-year-old South Providence street-kid was indelible.

The judge spoke with eloquent and elegant precision; all eyes and ears were riveted upon him as his theatrical gestures and intonations mesmerized the blue-collar audience. During my adult life Rhode Island has produced four great orators—the bombastic and inspirational John O. Pastore, the logical and didactic Father Joseph Lennon, the flamboyant Leo Patrick McGowan, and Joseph R. Weisberger, whose combination of style and substance is unequaled. On that morning at St. Paul's, the judge looked as good as he sounded. Erect and magisterial, he appeared much taller than his actual height, and there seemed to be no limit to his stature. He had the aspect of a senator, not from Rhode Island but from republican Rome. I, too, had studied Latin, and I saw Judge Weisberger as nothing less than Ciceronian. My Aunt Julia, who was volunteering in the kitchen of St. Paul's, put it more simply when she rhetorically asked, "Isn't he so handsome?"

As a Superior Court judge, Weisberger not only rode the lecture circuit; he also traveled among the counties dispensing justice. He welcomed this duty. "I loved being in the counties where every day was a new challenge." He preferred this routine to his initial assignment on the old Domestic Relations calendar. As a devout Catholic, he found the trauma of divorce "stressful." Weisberger recalls that he "made great effort to reconcile the parties and mediate their differences. Any success buoyed me up."

Not only have domestic relations cases left the Superior Court; so too has common-law pleading. Weisberger relished the latter for nine years before the Rules of Civil Procedure were adopted. During his entire tenure, however, his precise and orderly mind made him a master of procedure and a legal craftsman in every sense of the word. For Weisberger, order in the court meant formality, a reverence for decorum, and a profound respect for the integrity of the judicial process. As the fictional Yale-educated Judge Chamberlain Haller of Beecham County, Alabama, told neophyte New York attorney Cousin Vinny Gambini, "Rise, speak in a clear, intelligent voice," and above all "look lawyerly," because "when it comes to procedure, I am an impatient man."

Weisberger took G. Frederick Frost, his first presiding justice, as his role model for the practice of judicial dignity and decorum. Frost, like Weisberger, was a Brown graduate who had taken up residence in East Providence, and he had twenty-five years of service on that tribunal by the time Weisberger came to the bench. Weisberger describes Frost as "a paragon of gentlemanliness and civility and a model of how a judge should operate."

Among his peers on the Superior Court, Weisberger had high praise for Fred B. Perkins ("brilliant"), Frank Licht ("his intellect on a scale of 10 was 10"), James C. Bulman, Ronald Lagueux (later chief judge of the U.S. District Court), and Florence K. Murray. Several trial attorneys also made highly favorable impressions, most notably James O. Watts, Edward Bottelle, Leo Patrick McGowan, and Lawrence Hogan, whose cross-examination in the case of *DeCotis* v. *Providence Journal* was "wonderful to behold."

One of Weisberger's most memorable trials was the Newport County case of *State* v. *Sellers*, involving the novel *Peyton Place*. Raymond Pettine, the assistant attorney general, served as prosecutor, and the very experienced New York lawyer Horace Manges defended for the Dell Publishing Company. Since the prevailing U.S. Supreme Court standard on obscenity required the "dominant theme" of the challenged work "to be taken as a whole" (*Roth v. U.S.*, 1957), Pettine was instructed to bring in a bridge lamp and a comfortable chair to read the book to the jury and into the record. Says Weisberger: "Ray did such a wonderful job of reading from the text that I credit his dramatic rendition with convincing the jury that *Peyton Place* was, in fact, obscene."

Weisberger's longest and most arduous trial was labeled *Rhode Island Turnpike and Bridge Authority* v. *Bethlehem Steel Company*. It involved the quality of the protective coating on the Newport Bridge. After a nonjury trial lasting 115 days and a remarkable presentation by attorney Edward Hogan, Weisberger issued a three-hundred-page decision awarding the state an eight million dollar judgment against Bethlehem Steel. An even more memorable aspect of this case was the site inspection performed by the trial judge. Weisberger actually climbed over the rail to examine "the underportions of the bridge to determine if the paint was holding or peeling." Had this courageous act been generally known to the General Assembly when it renamed the Newport Bridge, the majestic span might also have a hyphenated name like the one connecting Jamestown to the West Bay. Who could possibly object to the Pell-Weisberger Bridge?

During the late 1960s and early 1970s, Weisberger presided over the difficult Miscellaneous Calendar, which consisted of three days of nonjury trials, one day of motions, and one day for formal and special-cause matters and administrative appeals. His effort and versatility were rewarded in 1972 when Governor Frank Licht appointed Weisberger, his old Senate and court colleague, to the post of presiding justice of the Superior Court. Weisberger embarked upon his new administrative duties with great enthusiasm. He held monthly meetings with his judges "to keep the cases flowing," and he also continued to do "a varied menu of criminal and civil trials." His six-year tenure as presiding justice afforded him "great pleasure" and "no negative memories," and his total experience as a trial judge convinced him that this post was "one of the most interesting and challenging jobs a person can have."

In 1978 an opening occurred on the state Supreme Court when Justice Thomas R. Paolino announced his retirement. Since the

Bloodless Revolution of 1935 rearranged the high tribunal, it had been the unwritten political custom to staff the court with three Democratic and two Republican justices. Paolino had occupied a Republican seat, so it was generally expected that the heavily Democratic General Assembly's Grand Committee would appoint a member of the GOP. Louis Jackvony, a Republican, expressed interest, and so did Superior Court judge Florence Murray, a strong Democrat who had frequently defied convention. Republican Weisberger, as presiding justice and senior judge on the Superior Court, quickly emerged as the favorite, but he felt constrained by his position from campaigning vigorously. "Many people worked on my behalf," said Weisberger, "and ultimately Mr. Jackvony and Florence withdrew, so I was elected unanimously."

The usually self-assured Weisberger admits to being "a little worried" when he assumed his new post because of observations by respected colleagues like Judge Fred Perkins that "as a trial judge you only have to satisfy yourself, whereas on the Supreme Court you have to convince four other people that you are right. There is a need for collegiality."

Because the partisan allocation of Supreme Court justices often produced ideological divergence, the court was not always as unanimous as the legislature had been in elevating Weisberger to the position of associate justice. Not only were there spirited dissents to several of Weisberger's "significant opinions," but the court itself soon entered a time of trial. Weisberger's chief was Joe Bevilacqua, a former House Speaker and noted criminal defense lawyer. By the mid-1980s Bevilacqua's continuing association with former criminal clients had undermined his position and led to impeachment hearings in the very House that he once led—a body now directed by Matthew J. Smith. The media had a feeding frenzy on Bevilacqua's reputation because of his "mob connections" and other personal indiscretions. With political and popular pressure demanding his removal, Bevilacqua stepped down. His eventual replacement was not the unblemished and enormously able Weisberger, as many reformers had hoped, but rather Thomas F. Fay, a Family Court judge and a former legislative ally of Democrat Matt Smith. After all, Bevilacqua had held a Democratic seat.

Chief Justice Fay was an honest man, but he was an old-style politician who believed (as I do) that political loyalty should be rewarded by patronage and favors. Eventually Fay appointed another honest, old-style politico as state court administrator— retiring Speaker Matthew J. Smith. This selection of a nonlawyer and political associate caused a groundswell of indignation from the reform elements that had been unleashed by the 1986 state constitutional convention. The duo of Fay and Smith needed to be beyond reproach; they had to avoid not only actual wrongdoing but even the appearance of impropriety. For honest but patronage-oriented politicians, the former was easy, but the latter proved impossible.

Just as climatic change destroyed the dinosaurs, the hothouse growth of governmental reform undid Rhode Island's old-style political practitioners like Matthew Smith and Thomas Fay. They were among the last of a dying breed. In the early 1990s, for indiscretions that would have been business-as-usual in the 1950s, both Smith and Fay—men of basic decency—were subjected to an intense media barrage that inspired legal sanctions against them, and these, in turn, drove both from the high-court offices they held. Both were victims of moralism run rampant.

Although Associate Justice Weisberger was the unintended beneficiary of these recurring crises, he feels "deeply sorry" for his two ill-fated predecessors and freely acknowledges Bevilacqua's "superb administrative ability." While not condoning their actions, he feels the media assault on them was out of proportion to their offenses.

In August 1993 Weisberger became "acting" chief justice, a tenuous position he held until March 1995, when a newly established Judicial Nominating Commission was able to implement a process of judicial selection that diminished the appointive power of the General Assembly. Weisberger became the first chief justice in Rhode Island history not elected by the legislature's Grand Committee, as well as the second presiding justice of the Superior Court to become chief justice (the first was William H. Sweetland, who became Rhode Island's top judge in the year that Weisberger was born).

During his twenty–three–year tenure on the state's high court, Weisberger has written approximately eight hundred opinions and orders. All of these rulings cannot be summarized in this brief format, but a few are worthy of note as indications of his style and his judicial philosophy.

State v. *Burbine* (1982) is a Weisberger decision that was vindicated on appeal to the U.S. Supreme Court. In that case a divided Rhode Island court upheld the finding of Justice John Orton that convicted murderer Brian Burbine's custodial confession was voluntary and made following an intelligent waiver of his right to counsel and his right to remain silent. Burbine had attempted to suppress his incriminating statements on the ground that interrogating officers had received a call from the public defender informing them that Burbine was represented by another attorney in the public defender's office, who, though unavailable then, would act as Burbine's legal counsel in the event police intended to question him.

Weisberger's learned opinion outlined the historical development of the modern doctrines of custodial interrogation as the U.S. Supreme Court "groped towards a means of striking a balance between the societal need for police interrogation and the protection of the accused from undue coercive pressures." In concluding, he observed with concern that "as the crime rate increases and as organized society seems ever more impotent to deal with crime on our streets, in our neighborhoods, and in our homes," Burbine's attempted "addition to the *Miranda* requirements seems as unwise on policy grounds as it is unnecessary on constitutional grounds."

Weisberger ruled that the *Miranda* warning regarding the right to remain silent and the right to counsel resided with the accused (who had waived those rights) and not with benign third parties. Chief Justice Bevilacqua and Justice Thomas Kelleher, both of whom were often defendant-oriented, registered vigorous dissents and Burbine appealed.

In the hearing before the U.S. Supreme Court on Weisberger's ruling (*Moran* v. *Burbine*, 475 U.S. 412), twenty-eight state attorneys general filed *amicus* briefs supporting Weisberger, while the American Bar Association and the National Association of Criminal Defense Lawyers weighed in against him. Sandra Day O'Connor, for a six-judge majority, upheld the Rhode Island Supreme Court and the principle of federalism by ruling that "the challenged conduct [of the police interrogators] falls short of the kind of misbehavior that so shocks the sensibilities of civilized society as to warrant a federal intrusion into the criminal processes of the states."

In *State* v. *DiPrete* (1998), Weisberger's concern for "societal need" was among the factors that prompted his lengthy and meticulously crafted opinion remanding the criminal case against former Republican governor Edward DiPrete and his son Dennis to Superior Court for trial on its merits. The case presented many incongruities. It was prosecuted by the office of Republican attorney general Jeffrey Pine, whose staff delayed the production of impeaching material that could have been used by the defense to discredit state witnesses who had been granted immunity. Trial judge Dominic Cresto, former counsel to Democratic governor J. Joseph Garrahy, believed that the delay was so flagrant as to constitute prosecutorial misconduct and dismissed twenty-two criminal counts of an indictment returned by Pine's duly constituted grand jury. Weisberger, despite his Republican roots, rejected Cresto's bold ruling in the face of a vigorous dissent by Justice John Bourcier, formerly a prominent Johnston Democrat. Partisan politics were clearly not a factor, despite the high-profile political figures involved.

Weisberger's careful scrutiny of Cresto's action led him to conclude that federal guidelines, the so-called *Brady* principles, regarding the effect of nondisclosure of exculpatory or impeaching evidence created a posttrial remedy that had no relevance to pretrial discovery. He ruled further that the use of the Superior Court's "inherent supervisory power," if considered analagous to the discretion exercised by federal courts, "would not permit a state court to create exclusionary rules not otherwise constitutionally authorized or to dismiss indictments in the absence of both outrageous conduct and demonstrable and otherwise incurable prejudice." The court, said Weisberger in a tone of restraint, holds the supervisory power within "narrow limits." "We must bear in mind," he concluded, "that when a grand jury returns an indictment, the people of the State of Rhode Island are entitled to have the issues of fact and the issues of guilt or innocence tried on their merits. The punishment of an errant prosecutor by dismissal of the charges is in effect a punishment imposed upon the people of this state," and thus unjustified unless there has been "flagrant prosecutorial misconduct accompanied by severe and incurable prejudice."

The most momentous case to come before the Weisberger court was *In re: Advisory Opinion to the Governor (Rhode Island Ethics Commission — Separation of Powers)*. This controversy, generated by Ethics Commission Regulation 36–14–5014, revolved around the historic appointive power of the General Assembly and the constitutional right of legislators to sit on state boards and commissions of an administrative nature. Governor Lincoln Almond allied with the Ethics Commission (a creature of the 1986 constitutional convention) to raise one of the two most significant Rhode Island constitutional questions of the twentieth century, equaled only by the 1935 debate and opinion relative to the power of the General Assembly or the people to convene a constitutional convention (55 R.I. 56). The earlier case dealt with the ultimate source of governmental power; the recent dispute dealt with the distribution of that power. Here the first branch of government, the legislature, resisted the challenge of the executive to its appointive power, while the third branch sat in judgment to decide who would control the fourth branch—the administrative bureaucracy.

The media, members of the bar, academia, and special-interest groups also joined the fray and took sides. In the actual argument before the court on November 10, 1998, seven attorneys, including those representing the House, the Senate, the attorney general, and the American Civil Liberties Union, spoke on behalf of legislative power, while five advocates, including attorneys representing the governor, the Ethics Commission, Common Cause, the State Council of Churches, and the Environmental Council, urged the high court to uphold Regulation 36–14–5014. Nearly four hours of argument were presented as a packed gallery listened with deep interest and great attentiveness.

On June 29, 1999, after a long delay occasioned by the preparation of a lengthy dissenting opinion by Justice Robert Flanders, the Supreme Court vindicated the appointive power of the General Assembly. The majority opinion was collaborative, with the chief justice composing much of the historical argument on both the American and British systems of government, including an observation that disheartened would-be reformers: "Rhode Island's history is that of a quintessential system of parliamentary supremacy." Then, deferring to the principles of federalism, Weisberger correctly declared that "the framers of our Constitution in 1842 and in 1986 have treated the executive power quite differently than did the framers of the federal Constitution." Those who attempted to use the federal Guarantee Clause to force Rhode Island into a uniform federal mold were only guaranteeing their defeat.

Since the advisory opinion on the separation of powers left some specifics unresolved, because the issue did not come before the court as a "case or controversy," the governor made another effort to persuade the Supreme Court to rewrite the state constitution by challenging the power and composition of the legislatively controlled state Lottery Commission. Weisberger, writing for the four-justice majority, again used the lessons of history to convincingly rebut arguments offered by the executive and the lower court based upon the federal theories of improper delegation, bicameralism, and presentment. "We must also be reminded," he boldly stated, "that the Rhode Island Legislature (unlike the Federal Congress) need not look to the state Constitution as a source of authority by virtue of its historical plenary power (preserved in both the 1843 and 1986 Constitutions)."

Those who attempted to impose federal models upon Justice Weisberger were perhaps unaware that his "hero" was Justice John Marshall Harlan (1955–71), whom Weisberger described as "a magnificent judicial craftsman and also an advocate of judicial restraint." Harlan often allied with Felix Frankfurter to resist the activism of the Warren Court. According to his biographer, "Harlan frequently voted to sustain the objections to the Supreme Court's power to decide" because of "his concern lest the Congress, the legal profession, and the general public lose confidence in the judiciousness and self-restraint of members of the Court."

Harlan's caveat in his *Reynolds* v. *Sims* dissent in 1964 has been echoed by Weisberger's rulings in the local controversy over the separation of powers: "The vitality of our political system . . . is weakened by reliance on the judiciary for political reform."

Coupled with his restraint was Harlan's federalism, so evident in several of Weisberger's rulings. In the *Reynolds* dissent, Harlan declared that his philosophy of federalism relied upon "the people, that is, upon political solutions devised and implemented by the people's representatives, rather than federal judicial formulas that have the effect of placing basic aspects of state political systems under the pervasive overlordship of the federal judiciary."

Weisberger's interest in history, constitutionalism, and theater coalesced in 1987 when he became the executive producer of *That Summer in Philadelphia*, a sixty-two-minute film about the Philadelphia Convention of 1787. Written and produced by Judge John A. Mutter and Edward L. Gnys, Jr., the historical piece used a news-reporter format to dramatize the work of the Grand Convention and Rhode Island's reaction to that conclave. The actors were prominent members of the Rhode Island Bar, including the judge's son and namesake, who played Richard Dobbs Spaight, a delegate from North Carolina. As chairman of the state's Bicentennial of the Constitution Commission, I worked with Judge Weisberger in publicizing and promoting this very well made documentary, a project in which he took justifiable pride, and Weisberger, in turn, invited me to give the Constitution Day address to the Supreme Court on September 17, 1987.

When questioned about the personalities that he encountered as a Supreme Court justice, Weisberger avoided, with characteristic discretion, any discussion of living Supreme Court judges, but among his deceased peers he singled out Justices Alfred H. Joslin and Thomas F. Kelleher for their legal intelligence and proficiency. Weisberger also noted his debt to the administrative ability of Robert C. Harrall and the present quartet of chief judges presiding over the lower courts—Joseph F. Rodgers, Jr., Jeremiah S. Jeremiah, Jr., Albert E. DeRobbio, and Robert F. Arrigan.

Regarding the appellate attorneys, Weisberger was more forthcoming. "There are so many fine lawyers today, it is most difficult to assess their respective abilities. Rhode Island has an excellent bar, and at least thirty-five to forty attorneys appear before me who have impressed me with their high intelligence, thorough preparation, and legal expertise." When asked if any of these stand out, Weisberger noted that some have a special style or flair that sets them apart. In this group he cited Lauren Jones (a "most versatile" appellate attorney), Peter McGinn (who does a "wonderful job on complex cases involving public utilities, which he presents in a most competent manner"), and Patrick Conley ("who is without peer in his knowledge of Rhode Island constitutional history" and possesses "the gift of eloquence" that makes him "a pleasure to listen to"). Other appellate attorneys praised by the chief justice included the late Raoul Lovett (the "master" of worker's compensation), Edward M. Fogarty, James P. Marusak, Joseph S. Larisa, Jr., the governor's counsel, and the "extremely able" Joseph V. Cavanaghs, Sr. and Jr. When one considers that six of these ten lawyers argued to the court in the Separation of Powers case (Jones, Fogarty, and Conley for the legislature and Larisa, Marusak, and Cavanagh Jr. for the governor), the momentous nature of that case becomes even more apparent.

Chief Justice Samuel Ames (1856–66) has been dubbed "the Great Chief Justice" by Rhode Island legal historians. The principal basis for this superlative is Ames's forceful and courageous decision in *Taylor* v. *Place* (1856) repudiating the General Assembly's long-standing practice of reviewing and overruling decisions of Rhode Island's highest court. This power, clearly constitutional under the charter of 1663, was undermined by the written state constitution that became effective in May 1843. It took thirteen years, however, for Ames to declare it an infringement upon the independence of the judiciary.

If Ames earned the appellation "Great" for rendering the Rhode Island judiciary free of direct legislative control or influence, perhaps Justice Weisberger can lay claim to greatness because of his successful twelve-year crusade to free the judges of all states from the threat of civil damages arising from their rulings.

The battle began in 1984, when the United States Supreme Court decided the case of *Pulliam* v. *Allen*, 104 S.Ct. 1970, a

5–to–4 opinion penned by Justice Harry Blackmun of *Roe* v. *Wade* fame. In *Pulliam*, the majority held that a Virginia magistrate could be enjoined by a federal district court for setting bail with surety on a nonincarcerable offense. In addition, however, the federal court awarded costs of $7,691.09 to the plaintiffs, who had been incarcerated for failure to make bail. Of this sum, $7,038.00 was awarded as a counsel fee pursuant to 42 U.S.C. 1988. In opposition, Justice Lewis Powell, citing an unbroken line of nearly four hundred years of consistent judicial decisions to the contrary, vigorously dissented from Blackmun's opinion. *Pulliam* opened the floodgates to cases against state judges for alleged violations of the Civil Rights Act of 1971.

When *Pulliam* was decided, Weisberger was the chairperson-elect of the Appellate Judges Conference of the American Bar Association. From this pulpit he began the fight "to restore judicial immunity" and to reverse this challenge to independent judicial decision making. He promptly penned a forceful essay ominously entitled "The Twilight of Judicial Independence—*Pulliam* v. *Allen*," which appeared in the fall 1985 issue of the *Suffolk University Law Review*. He also worked with Irene R. Emsellum and others to draft a resolution, passed by the American Bar Association, that urged Congress to amend 42 U.S.C. 1983 and 1988 so as to prohibit the award of injunctive relief and counsel fees against any judicial officer "for an act committed in his or her capacity as a judicial officer, and not clearly in excess of his or her jurisdiction."

When the ABA's House of Delegates passed the resolution, Weisberger became the principal draftsman of amendatory legislation designed to nullify *Pulliam*. This amendment was introduced by Senator Howell Heflin of Alabama, who became its leading congressional supporter. Unfortunately, progress was slow, despite the testimony of Weisberger and other prominent jurists before successive Congresses, and notwithstanding the urgings of the American Bar Association, the Conference of Chief Justices, and the American Judges Association. But fortunately persistence prevailed.

In 1995, with the help of Chief Judge Frank Q. Nebeker of the Court of Veterans' Appeals, Weisberger secured Senator Strom

Thurmond to sponsor "A Bill to Prohibit an Award of Costs Including Attorney's Fees, or Injunctive Relief against a Judicial Officer for Action Taken in a Judicial Capacity." Senators Heflin, Orrin Hatch, Charles Grassley, and Alfonse D'Amato signed on. The bill eventually became an amendment to the Federal Courts Improvement Act of 1996 and rode its way into law. Weisberger's 1996 report to the ABA as chairman of its Judicial Immunity Committee took satisfaction "that a significant service has been provided to the judges of America in restoring their ability to make independent and unbiased decisions without looking over their collective shoulders in fear of actions (often frivolous) being brought by disappointed litigants." Shades of Samuel Ames!

In reflecting upon his tenure as chief justice, Weisberger expressed satisfaction with the progress made by his court in several areas. "We have computerized all the courts of our system and have implemented one integrated criminal-justice information system for Rhode Island," he said. Moreover, he has endeavored to "foster good relationships with the General Assembly and the governor," and he believes he has succeeded, despite the battle over the appointment power, because both branches "have been very supportive of our needs."

Weisberger has attempted, with considerable success, to make the judicial system more open and more respected. To these ends he has formed committees to deal with such issues as minorities and women, public trust and confidence, and "user friendly" courts. He has also appointed a Committee on Judicial Evaluation, informed by lawyers, litigants, and witnesses as "a means of self-improvement." And in the spirit of Judge Frost and U.S. Chief Justice Warren Burger, he has made a priority of bringing "civility and professionalism" to the court system and has even created a committee that developed a civility code. Weisberger has subscribed completely to the exhortation made by Chief Justice Burger in a 1971 address to the American Law Institute: "Lawyers who know how to think but have not learned how to behave are a menace and a liability, not an asset, to the administration of justice.... I suggest the necessity for civility is relevant to lawyers because they are the living exemplars—and thus teachers—every day in every case and in every court; and their worst conduct will be emulated... more readily than their best."

Justice Weisberger always appears to be at his best, and our court system is far better for his leadership and the image of integrity that he has always projected. His abilities have been repeatedly recognized in the diverse positions of leadership and honor he has held, including (but hardly limited to) the chairmanship of the Appellate Judges Conference of the American Bar Association, the chairmanship of the National Conference of State Trial Judges, the chairmanship of the Governor's Council on Mental Health, and the vice chairmanship of the board of trustees of Rhode Island Hospital. His church has honored him by making him a Eucharistic minister at St. Brendan's Church, and Pope John Paul II bestowed upon him the office of Knight Commander with Star, Order of St. Gregory. In addition, thirteen honorary degrees have been conferred upon Justice Weisberger, including awards from Brown University and Providence College, and in 1980 he was inducted into the Rhode Island Heritage Hall of Fame. He is not only an Honorable Justice; he is a much-honored one as well.

Retirement from the bench, effective on February 24, 2001, will not bring retirement from law. Weisberger is an experienced educator. Since 1966 he has taught courses on the Fourth Amendment (search and seizure) and the Fifth Amendment (custodial interrogation, double jeopardy, and the privilege against self-incrimination) at the National Judicial College in Reno, Nevada. During these sessions (originally lasting four weeks, now shortened to three), Weisberger claims to have encountered "close to four thousand judges with whom I have had the privilege of sharing thoughts on the constitutional aspects of criminal law." Preparation for teaching these courses led Weisberger to write several law-review articles. For his efforts at the Judicial College, Weisberger received the Erwin Griswold Award for Excellence in Teaching in 1989.

Ever the educator, Weisberger has signed up to teach Professor Robert Kent's course in Rhode Island practice one day a week at Roger Williams University Law School, and he may update his own standard text on Supreme Court procedure, *Rhode Island Appellate Practice*, first published in 1985. He is also available "to fill in as needed" on the Supreme Court, following the example of his retired colleagues Donald Shea and Florence Murray. "If they want me," he stated, "I'm available."

When asked for a concluding thought, Weisberger confessed that he is retiring "with mixed feelings" and is "overwhelmed by nostalgia." But "reaching eighty, I feel it is time for me to pass the torch to a younger person." As a parting thought, as his voice quivered, he exclaimed: "I have been uniquely blessed!" So have we who have known him; and so have the people of Rhode Island who have benefited from his wisdom and integrity during his half century of public service. In truth, his life's work has implemented the great exhortation of Cicero: "*Salus populi suprema lex esto*" — "Let the welfare of the people be the final law!"

6
Immigration and Ethnicity

The Rhode Island Irish Famine Memorial, executed by sculptor Robert Shure of Woburn, Massachusetts (who also executed the Korean War Memorial in front of the Licht Judicial Complex in Providence), will grace the entrance to the Heritage Harbor Museum on the Providence waterfront. According to its sponsors, "it will illustrate and tell the story of the Famine, the immigrant experience, and the contributions Irish men and women have made to all walks of life in Rhode Island."

Written in 1999 as an entry in *The Encyclopedia of the Irish in America*, ed. Michael Glazier (Notre Dame, 1999), 803–8, this essay is an abridgement and update of my 1986 booklet in the Rhode Island Ethnic Heritage Pamphlet Series.

THE PROTESTANT PIONEERS

THE IRISH PRESENCE IN RHODE ISLAND dates from the mid-seventeenth century. Our knowledge of this Irish vanguard stems from the researches of several Irish American genealogists and apologists, such as Rhode Island's Thomas Hamilton Murray, who scoured the records of the American colonies to establish a long Irish American lineage and thus overcome the charge of "foreignness" hurled at the nineteenth-century Irish and their Catholic Church. Ironically, most of these early Irish Rhode Islanders were Protestants—mainly Baptists, Quakers, Presbyterians, or Anglicans—and those few with Catholic antecedents soon lost their religious affiliation for lack of Catholic clergy within the colony. Among the handful of seventeenth-century Irish Rhode Islanders were Charles McCarthy, an original proprietor of (East) Greenwich in 1677, and Edward Larkin of Newport and Westerly, who served briefly in the colonial legislature.

In the early eighteenth century the colony's most notable Irishmen were clergymen or schoolmasters. Among the former was Derry-born Reverend James MacSparran (1680–1757), for thirty-seven years the distinguished rector of St. Paul's Church (Wickford), which served the spiritual needs of South County Anglicans. MacSparran, who tutored President Thomas Clap of Yale, gained renown by publishing *America Dissected* (Dublin, 1753), a collection of his letters to friends in Ireland, which proved for its British audience a valuable source of information on the American colonies. Another even more illustrious Irish scholar and clergyman was George Berkeley, the Anglican essayist and philosopher, who stayed at Whitehall Farm in present-day Middletown during his eventful sojourn in America from 1729 to 1731. After the failure of his cherished but impractical project of establishing an Anglican college in Bermuda, Berkeley returned to Ireland, where he was rewarded with the bishopric of Cloyne.

Notable Irish tutors (of whom there were a good number in relation to the small Irish population) included Stephen Jackson (1700–1765), who left Kilkenny and settled in Providence. This teacher and prosperous farmer had a son, Richard, who became president of the Providence-Washington Insurance Company (1800–1838) and a four-term congressman, and a grandson, Charles, a prominent industrialist who served as governor in 1845–46 after campaigning on a platform calling for the liberation of imprisoned reformer Thomas Wilson Dorr.

Other Irish schoolmasters were John Dorrance (1747–1813), a Providence civic leader, and the Reverend James "Paddy" Wilson of Limerick, first a teacher and then the colorful pastor of Providence's Beneficent ("Roundtop") Congregational Church. James Manning, first president of the College of Rhode Island (now Brown University) and the son of a New Jersey farmer, was probably of Irish descent. Though a Baptist in religion, Manning graduated from the College of New Jersey (Princeton), then a citadel of Irish Presbyterianism. Despite the fact that Manning's Celtic origins are in doubt, it is certain that Protestants in Ireland financed much of the initial endowment for his College of Rhode Island.

Colonial Rhode Island's most famous Irish craftsman was Kingston silversmith Samuel Casey, and its most renowned business family (Irish or otherwise) were the Brown brothers of Providence—James, Nicholas, Joseph, John, and Moses. The Browns' mother, Hope Power, was the daughter of Nicholas Power (1673–1734), a native of Ireland who served in the Rhode Island

General Assembly and as a colonel in the state militia. Colonel Power's oldest daughter, Mary, was the mother of Nicholas Cooke, the state's Revolutionary War governor (1775–78). In view of the sparseness of their numbers (one genealogist counted only 166 Irish surnames in the pre–1776 colonial records), the impact of the Irish on the English colony of Rhode Island was considerable.

During the American Revolution nearly three hundred Irish names appeared on Rhode Island's military and naval rolls, and the American commander in New England's largest military engagement, the inconclusive Battle of Rhode Island, was General John Sullivan of New Hampshire, whose parents had migrated from Ireland in the 1720s. When Rochambeau's French army came to Newport as allies of the American cause in 1780, many of its soldiers were Irish nationals, particularly those men from Colonel Arthur Dillon's regiment who served in Lauzun's Legion.

A strong journalistic supporter of the Revolutionary cause was John Carter (1745–1814), the son of an Irish naval officer killed in the service of the Crown. Carter came to Providence as a journeyman printer from Philadelphia, where he had been apprenticed to Benjamin Franklin. From 1767 until 1814 he molded public opinion in Providence as the editor of the *Providence Gazette*. A major supporter of the ratification of the federal Constitution, Carter also served as Providence postmaster from 1772 to 1792. His daughter Ann (1769–98) married Nicholas Brown, Jr. (son of the famous Providence merchant), the great benefactor of Brown University. The present-day Brown family is descended from their only child, John Carter Brown.

Whereas John Carter was the child of an Irish naval officer, two notable Rhode Island commodores of the early national period were sons of an Irish immigrant mother. Newport's Oliver Hazard Perry (1785–1819), hero of the decisive Battle of Lake Erie (1813), and Matthew Calbraith Perry (1794–1858), who opened Japan to Western trade and influence, were the children of Sarah Wallace (Alexander) Perry, a native of Newry in County Down, and mariner Christopher Perry of South Kingstown, who met Sarah when he was confined to a British internment camp in Kinsale, Ireland, as a Revolutionary War prisoner. After the conflict, Perry sailed back to Ireland to bring Sarah to America.

THE CATHOLIC EXODUS, 1815–1922

The first significant migration of Catholic Irish to North America began in the aftermath of the War of 1812, and Rhode Island partook of this influx. During the three decades between 1815 and 1845, a million Irishmen, most of whom were Roman Catholics, came to North America. Perhaps five thousand of these settled in Rhode Island.

The overwhelming majority of Irish migrants to Rhode Island became urban dwellers despite their rural background. They entered this unfamiliar milieu because they needed immediate employment, which Rhode Island's burgeoning economy provided, and because they lacked the funds to continue onward to frontier areas. The federal census of 1850, the first national survey to record the nativity of the population, revealed that Rhode Island had 23,111 foreign-born out of a total population of 147,545. At this point the natives of Ireland totaled 15,944, or 69 percent of the foreign-born. By the time of the first state census in 1865, the foreign-born population had climbed to 39,703; of this figure the Irish-born accounted for 27,030, or 68 percent. By the federal count of 1870, there were 31,534 of Irish birth, and Providence ranked sixth among the cities of the nation in its number of Irish-born residents.

By 1875—sixty years after the onset of their immigration—the Catholic Irish had established settlements and churches in all the urban and industrial areas of the state, including Newport (especially the lower Thames Street neighborhood), Providence (mainly in Fox Point, the North End, Smith Hill, Olneyville, Manton, Wanskuck, and South Providence), Pawtucket, Woonsocket, the mill villages of Lincoln and Cumberland (including Central Falls, Valley Falls, Lonsdale, and Ashton), Harrisville, Pascoag, Greenville, Georgiaville, Cranston (especially Arlington and the Print Works district), the Pawtuxet Valley (particularly the villages of Crompton, Riverpoint, and Phenix), East Greenwich, Wakefield, Westerly, Warren, and Bristol. Aside from the English, no other Rhode Island ethnic group dispersed so widely.

Of the thousands of Irish who flocked to the state in the middle decades of the nineteenth century, many found their circumstances bleak. Depressed to the status of paupers by the conditions of their flight from Ireland, driven into debilitating slums or drab mill villages by their position as unskilled laborers, and isolated intellectually by their cultural background and physical segregation, these Irish saw insuperable social, economic, and religious barriers between themselves and the so-called "Yankees."

On the eve of the Civil War, the Irish were the substratum of Rhode Island society. Spurned as lower-class menials, politically impotent, and discriminated against as Catholics ("No Irish Need Apply"), they were caught in a web of poverty and social alienation from which they would not escape until new immigrants came to take their place. Even politics, the traditional road of the Irish to power and prestige, was blocked by formidable constitutional obstacles such as the real estate requirement for voting, imposed by Rhode Island's basic law upon those of foreign birth.

*   *   *

During the nineteenth century, Irish immigration and the growth of the Catholic Church were closely intertwined. The first tiny Irish Catholic communities were at the Portsmouth coal mines and in the Fox Point section of Providence near that town's bustling harbor. French priests from Boston began to visit both areas during the second decade of the century. The Providence Irish secured the use of a building on Sheldon Street as the state's first Catholic church in 1813, but the structure was destroyed by the Great Gale of 1815.

A more significant influx of Irish occurred in the mid-1820s, prompting Bishop Benedict Fenwick of Boston to dispatch Father Robert Woodley to Newport in 1828 as Rhode Island's first resident priest. There, in April 1828, the young cleric founded St. Mary's, the state's oldest parish. In 1829 the busy Woodley—whose mission territory included the states of Rhode Island and Connecticut in their entirety, plus southeastern Massachusetts—built the state's first Catholic church specifically constructed for that purpose at St. Mary's, Pawtucket.

When Woodley came to Rhode Island to establish a Catholic presence, Rhode Island's Roman Catholics numbered about 600 out of a total state population of 97,000, a mere six-tenths of 1 percent. The 600 faithful served by Woodley in 1828 were concentrated in Newport, where they worked as laborers on Fort Adams; in Portsmouth, where they were employed as miners at the coal pits; and in Providence, Cranston, Pawtucket, and Woonsocket, where they served the needs of the growing factory system or were employed in such public works projects as the construction of the Blackstone Canal. Nearly all of them were Irish. In the 1830s, as the railroad came to Rhode Island, this Irish migration continued, and in the 1840s and 1850s, in the wake of Ireland's disastrous famine, it reached impressive proportions. By 1865 three out of every eight Rhode Islanders were of Irish stock, the state's Irish Catholic community numbered nearly 50,000, and pioneer missionary priests like the Reverend James Fitton had established twenty widely scattered parishes. The energetic and seemingly ubiquitous Fitton, a founder of Holy Cross College (1843), was a driving force in the development of Rhode Island Catholicism, serving in every major area of Irish settlement.

To accommodate the Catholic Irish influx of the mid-nineteenth century, the Diocese of Boston was subdivided and the Diocese of Hartford created in 1844. This new administrative entity included the states of Connecticut and Rhode Island. Its first bishop, William Tyler, was a Yankee convert from Protestantism. Although the see city of his new diocese was Hartford, Tyler decided to govern from Providence, which was a more prosperous community with a larger Catholic population.

The decade of the 1840s saw several important developments affecting the Irish Catholic community. One was the famous Dorr Rebellion, which occurred between 1841 and 1843 over an attempt to broaden democracy in Rhode Island and replace the antiquated royal charter of 1663 with a written state constitution. The opponents of political reformer Thomas Dorr were partly motivated by anti-Catholic prejudice and political nativism, themes that have often been ignored in discussions of this colorful episode. Over the objections of Dorr, Rhode Island's state constitution of 1843 established a real estate requirement for foreign-born voters that was designed to discriminate against Irish Catholic immigrants.

Another event of importance was the John Gordon murder trial—the Sacco–Vanzetti case of the nineteenth century. This 1844 travesty of justice, which on the basis of circumstantial evidence resulted in the hanging of a young Irish Catholic immigrant for the killing of prominent industrialist Amasa Sprague, caused such misgiving that it contributed to the abolition of the death penalty in Rhode Island eight years later.

In 1850 William Tyler was succeeded as bishop of Hartford by Irish-born Bernard O'Reilly, called "Paddy the Priest" by some native Rhode Islanders. In 1851 this bold and strong-willed bishop brought Mother Mary Frances Xavier Warde and the predominantly Irish Sisters of Mercy to Providence, where they immediately founded a school for girls, St. Xavier's Academy, the first Catholic secondary school in the state. Four years later, during the height of the Know-Nothing movement, O'Reilly personally defended the Mercy nuns from an anti-Catholic mob that had congregated at St. Xavier's Convent to "free" a young girl who had allegedly been confined therein. Returning from a clerical recruiting trip to Europe in 1856, O'Reilly perished at sea when his ship was lost in a North Atlantic storm.

The last bishop of Hartford to preside over Rhode Island Catholicism was Francis Patrick McFarland, whose episcopacy coincided with the Civil War and Reconstruction years. This gentle and scholarly prelate's tenure was marked by the emergence of a Catholic presence in the social and political affairs of Rhode Island. McFarland's energy and learning built the first bridges to the non-Catholic community of the state, resulting in a lessening of the ethnocultural antagonisms that had dominated the 1840s and 1850s.

The Civil War was a testing ground that also helped to mollify native fears of Irish Catholics. Animated by a desire to preserve the Union and thereby prove their Americanism, Irish immigrants and their sons fought side by side with Yankee boys. Two members of the local Irish community—John Corcoran and James Welsh— were recipients of the newly created Congressional Medal of Honor for their wartime heroism.

The other salient fact of this period was the role of the lowly

Irish immigrants in building the Diocese of Providence. During the years prior to 1872, almost the only influences upon Rhode Island Catholicism were those distinctive Irish traits that gave the local Catholic community a unified religious outlook and produced what was in reality an Irish national church. The creation of the Diocese of Providence (with Irish-born Thomas F. Hendricken its first bishop) was the Irish immigrants' first notable achievement in Rhode Island.

*   *   *

During the last third of the nineteenth century, the era of America's Industrial Revolution, the Irish of Rhode Island made a slow yet significant climb up the socioeconomic ladder as new immigrants from French Canada, eastern Europe, and the Mediterranean took their place on the bottom rungs. Political advancement also became less difficult as more native-born Irish reached voting age. Whereas the 1865 state census revealed that "only one in twelve or thirteen of the foreign-born of adult age was a voter," economic advancement for the Irish immigrant and native birth for his male children combined by the 1880s to make the real estate requirement for voting and officeholding much less restrictive.

According to the census of 1885, the state had 92,700 citizens with at least one parent of Irish birth, but for the first time more than half of these (50,313) were native-born. When these foreign-stock Irish (immigrants or their children) were added to second- and third-generation Irish Americans and Irish migrants from England, Scotland, and Canada, the total number must have approximated 125,000 in a general Rhode Island population of 304,000. This ratio was the relative high point of the Irish numerical presence in the state.

Numbers plus native birth equaled political clout. Leading the Irish political advance was Charles E. Gorman (1844–1917), Boston-born of an Irish father and a Yankee mother. An outspoken advocate of equal rights and suffrage reform, Democrat Gorman successively became the first Irish Catholic member of the Rhode Island bar (1865), state legislator (1870), Providence city councilman (1875), Speaker of the House (1887), and U.S. attorney

(1893). His younger colleague, attorney Edwin Daniel McGuinness (1856–1901), became the first Irish Catholic general officer, winning election as secretary of state in 1887. In 1896 Democrat McGuinness also became Providence's first Irish Catholic mayor, but the city's most notable chief executive of this or any era was Thomas Doyle, of Irish Protestant stock, whose eighteen years of service between 1864 and 1886 constituted an unparalleled era for Providence's growth and development. A contemporary of Doyle's, Dublin-born Thomas Davis, was a prominent businessman who served one term (1853–55) in the Congress of the United States. Although Davis was a Protestant, he was an outspoken foe of nativism.

In the state's other cities, where the urban-dwelling Irish had also congregated, similar political breakthroughs occurred. In Pawtucket, Irish Catholic Hugh J. Carroll gained the mayoralty in 1890, followed by coreligionists Patrick J. Boyle in Newport (1895), Thomas McNally in Central Falls (1905), and Edward Sullivan in Cranston (1910), the first mayor of that city.

Attorney James H. Higgins, who had succeeded the colorful and dynamic John J. Fitzgerald as mayor of Pawtucket in 1903, won election in 1906 and again in 1907 as Rhode Island's first Irish Catholic governor. Galway-born Democrat George O'Shaunessy (1868–1934) became another local Irish Catholic pathbreaker, securing election four times to the U.S. House of Representatives (1911–19). He was followed to Washington two years later by Irish Republican Ambrose Kennedy of Woonsocket, who served five terms in the House. In 1913, with the victory of Joseph Gainer, the Irish began their unbroken sixty-two-year grip on the Providence mayoralty, and by that time they were firmly in control of the organizational structure of the Democratic party.

The Irish economic rise, though less spectacular, had some rags-to-riches scenarios. The most notable climb was made by Joseph Banigan (1839–98), Rhode Island's first Irish Catholic millionaire. The Irish-born son of parents who migrated to Rhode Island from Scotland in 1849, Banigan got in on the ground floor of the emerging rubber-goods industry and improved Charles Goodyear's process for the vulcanization of rubber. By 1889 he opened the Alice Mill in Woonsocket, then the largest rubber-shoe factory in the world. Three years later Banigan helped form the massive U.S. Rubber Company and became its president (1893–96). In 1898 he financed the construction of Providence's first "skyscraper," the ten-story Banigan Building.

264

By the end of the century Irish-born William and Thomas Gilbane had directed their firm (established in 1873) to the forefront among local building contractors, and James Hanley (1841–1912), another Irish immigrant, had become the region's most prominent brewer. Though such Horatio Alger stories were not common, Irish American small businessmen, lawyers, and physicians were becoming increasingly so in the early years of this century. Especially notable was Dr. John William Keefe, a founder of St. Joseph Hospital, a World War I surgeon, president of the Rhode Island Medical Society (1913–14), president of the American Association of Obstetricians, Gynecologists, and Abdominal Surgeons (1916–17), and founder of a surgical center in Providence.

In the blue-collar field, Irish Americans made great strides in the building trades, acquiring skills as masons, carpenters, plumbers, steamfitters, painters, plasterers, electricians, and ironworkers. Railroad, streetcar, and public-utility employment, professional police work, and firefighting also had strong appeal.

As Irish American labor leaders affiliated with the Knights of Labor or the AF of L led the fight for the eight-hour day, Americans used their newly acquired leisure to partake of such popular spectator sports as professional baseball. The new national pastime produced a number of local Irish American luminaries, including "Orator Jim" O'Rourke, batting star of the national champion Providence Grays, and Hugh Duffy of Cranston, whose 1894 batting average of .438 with Boston of the National League is still the unapproachable major league record. Both O'Rourke and Duffy are enshrined in the Baseball Hall of Fame.

A more genteel spectator activity of great popularity was vaudeville. Here also the Rhode Island Irish community produced performers of national stature, the most magnetic of whom was George M. Cohan. Born in the Fox Point section of Providence on July 3, 1878, to variety performers Jerry and Nellie (Costigan)

Cohan, George joined his sister Josie and their parents on stage well before he reached his teens. The four Cohans left the local circuit for Broadway during the 1890s. Cohan eventually became America's most successful theatrical producer, and during his fifty-five years in show business he composed more than five hundred songs, including such patriotic airs as "Over There," "You're a Grand Old Flag," and "Yankee Doodle Boy."

In 1917 Bishop Matthew J. Harkins, the fourth and most productive in a line of seven Irish Catholic bishops of Providence spanning the years from 1850 to 1971, joined with a group of Irish professionals and businessmen and the Dominican Fathers of the Province of St. Joseph to found Providence College. The original purpose of the college—to provide higher education with a Christian perspective to aspiring young men from the local Catholic community—was proclaimed at the dedication mass offered at the doors of Harkins Hall in May 1919. A major participant in these exercises was Dr. Charles Carroll, Rhode Island's most prominent public educator. The scholarly Carroll would eventually write the most authoritative multivolume history of the state, the first such work to give prominence to Rhode Island's more recent immigrants.

By the time Providence College was founded, Rhode Island Irishmen had already achieved distinction for their cultural and literary attainments. In 1884 Alfred Thayer Mahan, descendant of an eighteenth-century Irish immigrant, began a productive tour of duty at Newport's newly created Naval War College, where he served both as professor and president. In 1890 Mahan (1840–1914) published *The Influence of Seapower upon History*, the most famous and influential of his numerous historical volumes advocating American expansion on strategic grounds.

In the late 1880s and early 1890s, the local Irish were given an advance look at the literary efforts of several promising young Irish authors by a most unlikely source—the *Providence Journal*. For forty-five years (1839–84), while the paper had been under the malign influence of nativist and machine Republican Henry B. Anthony, Irish Catholics and Democratic politicians had been its twin enemies. This changed (at least temporarily) when Alfred

M. Williams (1840–96) began his seven-year tenure as *Journal* editor in 1884. The most notable aspect of Williams's career became his study and promotion of Irish literature. He wrote several works on the topic and published in the newly created *Providence Sunday Journal* the early efforts of several then-obscure Irish authors, including William Butler Yeats, Douglas Hyde, Katherine Tynan, and Mary Banim. Professor Horace Reynolds, in his booklet *A Providence Episode in the Irish Literary Renaissance*, calls these works "a record in miniature of the beginnings of a movement that is today recognized as one of the most distinctive in the stream of English letters."

In January 1897 the American-Irish Historical Society was formed, largely through the efforts of Thomas Hamilton Murray, editor of the Woonsocket *Evening Call*, who became this national organization's first secretary-general and the editor of its widely circulated historical journal. Murray wrote a number of well-researched articles on the early Rhode Island Irish for his journal and hosted several of the society's national conventions. Many prominent Rhode Islanders of Irish ancestry (regardless of their religious affiliation) joined the organization, including Thomas Z. Lee of Providence, who succeeded Murray as secretary-general, and Father Austin Dowling of Providence, who wrote the first scholarly history of the Diocese of Providence in 1899 and later became archbishop of St. Paul, Minnesota.

By 1922, the year the Irish Free State was created, Rhode Island's Irish had made major advances in all walks of life. No major political office, except for U.S. senator, had eluded their grasp, and they dominated the hierarchy of the state's Democratic party, though that party was still the minority.

THE IRISH ARRIVE, 1922–1999

In the three generations from the early 1920s to the present, Rhode Island's Irish Americans achieved distinction and success commensurate with their rapidly increasing numbers. With two of every nine Rhode Islanders claiming Irish ancestry by the 1990 federal census, an essay of this limited scope can scarcely do justice to its subject.

During the two decades between world wars, the state experienced a turbulent political transformation from traditional Republican party dominance to rule by the Democrats. The Irish were the architects of that upheaval. By finally mastering the game of ethnic politics (much later than their counterparts elsewhere) and taking advantage of economic shifts, social changes, and cultural trends on both the state and national levels, Irish Democratic politicians weaned Franco-Americans, Italians, Jews, Poles, and blacks from their traditional Republican allegiance and ushered them into an Irish-led Democratic fold that dominated state government from 1940 through 1984.

The spearheads of this Irish political advance were a handful of youthful legislators who entered the General Assembly in the years following the outbreak of World War I. Foremost among them were William S. Flynn of South Providence, Holy Cross, and Georgetown Law School; Robert Emmet Quinn, a Brown- and Harvard-educated attorney from West Warwick and the nephew of Colonel Patrick Henry Quinn, who had carved the mill town of West Warwick from Warwick's western sector in 1913; Francis B. Condon, a Georgetown Law School graduate from Central Falls; and Thomas Patrick McCoy, a Pawtucket streetcar conductor.

Of this bright, ambitious group, Flynn was the first to rise and the first to fall. Having won an upset victory in the 1922 gubernatorial race, he saw his administration made turbulent by zealous Democratic attempts to enact constitutional reforms, attempts that were countered by equally determined Republican moves to maintain the status quo. In 1924, after the adjournment of the infamous "stink-bomb legislature," Flynn lost his bid to become Rhode Island's first Irish American United States senator.

Tom McCoy moved from the legislature to the city chairmanship and then to the mayoralty of Pawtucket (1936–45). Though his plans for statewide office were thwarted, he was a major strategist in the Bloodless Revolution of January 1935—that "first hurrah" whereby the Democratic party seized control of state government in a bold coup. McCoy also exerted a great impact on state policies and elections from his Pawtucket command post. There, with the aid of House Speaker Harry Curvin, he constructed Rhode Island's best example of a genuine, smooth-functioning political machine.

Francis B. Condon, McCoy's Blackstone Valley neighbor from Central Falls, operated on a more elevated plane. He moved in succession from the Rhode Island House (1921–26) to the Congress (1930–35) to the state Supreme Court (1935–65). For his last seven years on the bench, Condon served as chief justice, succeeding Edmund W. Flynn (William's brother), who had assumed direction of the high court on January 1, 1935, as a result of the Bloodless Revolution. Flynn's twenty-two-year tenure has been the longest in Rhode Island's history.

Of all those Irish political leaders of the post–World War I era, Robert Emmet Quinn was the most durable. Quinn rose from the state Senate (1923–25 and 1929–33), where he led the famous 1924 filibuster, to the lieutenant governorship (1933–37), where he presided over the Bloodless Revolution, to the governorship (1937–39), where he battled with Narragansett Park director Walter O'Hara in the ludicrous and nationally scandalous "Race Track War" of 1937, called by *Life* magazine "the War of the Wild Irish Roses." Although that episode and a national recession cost "Battling Bob" reelection, he was later appointed to the Rhode Island Superior Court (1941–51) and then to the newly established U.S. Court of Military Appeals (1951–75), where he served as chief judge.

One Rhode Island Celt who sought from the start to carve out his political career on the national level was Thomas Gardiner ("Tommy the Cork") Corcoran (1900–81), a leading draftsman and lobbyist for much of the legislation now labeled Franklin D. Roosevelt's New Deal. Recommended by his Harvard Law School professor Felix Frankfurter, Corcoran joined the New Deal "Brain Trust" and drafted such landmark laws as those creating the Securities and Exchange Commission, the Federal Housing Administration, the Tennessee Valley Authority, and the Fair Labor Standards Board. Corcoran, a Pawtucket-born son of an Irish immigrant, often entertained Roosevelt with Irish ballads as well as drafting some of the president's political speeches. Another local Irishman lured to the Potomac was John Fanning, a twenty-five-year member of the National Labor Relations Board, which he chaired from 1977 to 1981.

During the decades following 1935, when the Irish-led Democratic party solidified its hold on state government, a new wave of home-grown Irish American political leaders emerged. Most notable of these Roosevelt-era luminaries were J. Howard McGrath, John E. Fogarty, Dennis J. Roberts, William E. Powers, and Harry F. Curvin.

Curvin was the protégé and ally of McCoy. He represented Pawtucket in the House from 1931 to 1964. During the last twenty-three years and 223 days of that long tenure, he presided (some say dictatorially) as Speaker. No one has ever approached Curvin's longevity record as House leader.

William E. Powers of Central Falls overcame the handicap of blindness, the result of a childhood accident, to rank at the top of his Boston University Law School class. After five terms in the House (1939–49), Powers served nine years as attorney general before his elevation in January 1958 to the state Supreme Court. In 1973, having stepped down after fifteen distinguished years on the high-court bench, he reemerged to chair that year's highly successful state constitutional convention.

Dennis J. Roberts, a noted high school athlete at LaSalle Academy, was perhaps the most powerful figure in state government during the decade following World War II. From 1941 to 1951 he served as mayor of Providence under that city's first strong-mayor charter, and he presided as governor from 1951 to 1959.

John E. Fogarty was even more durable. This bricklayer-turned-politician went to Washington as congressman from Rhode Island's Second District in January 1941. There he remained until his sudden death twenty-six years later. Fogarty's many achievements in the area of health care legislation won him the national title of "Mr. Public Health," but the man with the green bow tie was equally renowned as an unrelenting supporter of Irish unification.

Woonsocket-born J. Howard McGrath was undoubtedly the state's most versatile politician. After spending the war years as Rhode Island's governor, he was appointed U.S. solicitor general by his close political ally Harry S. Truman. In 1946 McGrath was elected to the U.S. Senate, the first Rhode Island Irish Catholic ever elected to that office. The following year Truman named him Democratic national chairman, and McGrath quickly proved his worth in the 1948 elections by overseeing Truman's surprising upset of presidential hopeful Thomas E. Dewey. In the following year the ambitious Rhode Islander gave up his Senate seat to become U.S. attorney general. After resigning this post in 1952, he returned to private business and the successful practice of law.

In addition to this political "big five" of the past half century, passing mention, at least, should be accorded also to United States senator Jack Reed; U.S. congressmen Jeremiah O'Connell, James M. Connell, Robert O. Tiernan, Eddie Beard, and Patrick Kennedy (of the famous Kennedy clan); Supreme Court chief justices Thomas Roberts (brother of Governor Roberts), Thomas Fay, and Joseph R. Weisberger (whose mother was a Meighan); Lieutenant Governor, Acting Governor, and Superior Court justice John S. McKiernan; interim U.S. senator and federal District Court judge Edward L. Leahy; and four-term governor J. Joseph Garrahy. An impressive roster, certainly, even without all of those mayors, general officers, legislators, federal and state jurists, legislative leaders, and long-tenured civil servants who are simply too numerous to be included here.

In the annals of Irish achievement, the past two decades have been notable for the rise of women to the top of the political ladder. One such achiever worthy of special mention is Florence Kerins Murray of Newport, who became, successively, the first woman associate justice of the Superior Court (1956), that court's first female presiding justice (1978), and the first woman to sit on the Rhode Island Supreme Court (1979).

From the 1920s until 1971, Irish Americans continued their dominance in the local hierarchy of the Catholic Church. William Hickey became coadjutor bishop of Providence in 1919, when Matthew Harkins was in declining health, and having ascended to the See of Providence in his own right on Harkins's death in 1921, he presided until 1933. Hickey's successor, Francis P. Keough (1934–47), was a popular bishop who made some important innovations, most notably the creation of the Catholic Youth Organi-

zation (1935), the establishment of Our Lady of Providence Seminary for the education of young men preparing for the priesthood
(1941), and the founding of Salve Regina University (1947). A cru-
sader against obscenity in movies and in print, Keough served as
national chairman of the Bishops' Committee of the National
Organization for Decent Literature (Legion of Decency). After
the departure of Keough to the archbishopric of the primal See of
Baltimore in 1947, Russell J. McVinney (1948–71) assumed spiritual direction of the diocese—the only Rhode Island native to
hold that post. The impressive material gains that the Church
made during his episcopacy attested to McVinney's administrative
expertise. His tenure was a period in which Rhode Island Catholicism expanded its social role.

Many other able Irish clerics served as administrators in the
Providence diocese or were raised here and then departed to
assume positions of church leadership elsewhere. John Cardinal
Dearden, archbishop of Detroit, was born and spent his boyhood
in the Blackstone Valley, and Daniel P. Reilly of South Providence, a former diocesan chancellor, became bishop of Norwich,
Connecticut, and then of Worcester, Massachusetts.

The Rhode Island Irish have been less conspicuously successful
in the world of business and corporate finance. With the exception of the nationally ranked Gilbane Building Company
(founded in 1873), which has spearheaded the revitalization of
downtown Providence and is currently the state's largest private
firm with over $2.6 billion in 2001 revenue, there are no spectacu-
lar success stories, no Browns or Banigans, no Fortune 500 companies to the credit of Rhode Island's modern Irish community.
However, former pharmacist Thomas M. Ryan now serves as
chairman, president, and CEO of Woonsocket-based CVS, Rhode
Island's largest Fortune 500 firm.

The Catholic Irish have not been well represented at the top
echelon in the major white-collar businesses of insurance and
banking, but there have been two notable exceptions: John J.
Cummings, Jr., and his protégé J. Terrence Murray, who have held
in succession the top position at Fleet National Bank (now Fleet
Boston), Rhode Island's major financial institution and, under

Murray's leadership, one of America's ten largest banks. A more local and more typically Irish business, the distribution of beer and liquor, gained wealth and prominence for Cumberland's John McLaughlin and John E. Moran. In turn, they became civic leaders, philanthropists, and prominent Catholic laymen—pillars of their community and their Church.

In the field of letters, Rhode Island's Irish American community produced two noteworthy novelists of Irish American life as well as a noted poet. In 1946 Edward McSorley, who lived for a time on Providence's South Side, published *Our Own Kind*. This widely circulated Book-of- the-Month Club selection poignantly depicts the travails of the McDermotts, an Irish working-class family in St. Malachi's (St. Michael's) Parish. Its sequel, *Young McDermott*, appeared three years later. Even more famous and widely read than McSorley was Woonsocket's Edwin O'Connor (1918–68). This product of LaSalle Academy had among his credits such Irish American literary classics as *The Last Hurrah* (1956), the Pulitzer Prize-winning *The Edge of Sadness* (1961), and *All in the Family* (1966). Galway Kinnell, a major American poet, has Rhode Island roots in Pawtucket. Among his many honors are a Pulitzer Prize and the National Book Award.

In Irish American nonfiction, George W. Potter, an editor at the *Providence Journal*, penned one of the best general histories of the early-nineteenth-century Irish migration—his popularly written and posthumously published *To the Golden Door: The Story of the Irish in Ireland and America* (1960). Following the example of *Journal* editor Alfred Williams, Potter also bequeathed his Irish books to the collections of the Providence Public Library. Another *Providence Journal* editor, John C. Quinn, went on to become one of America's leading newspapermen and a founder of *USA Today*.

Thomas N. Brown, who taught for six years at Portsmouth Priory, was the author of *Irish-American Nationalism, 1870–1890* (1966), the standard account of Irish American reaction to the home rule movement led by Charles Stewart Parnell. More recently, Professors Robert W. Hayman, Matthew J. Smith, and Patrick T. Conley of Providence College have published books on nineteenth-century Rhode Island Catholicism emphasizing the impact of the Irish on Church growth, while Professor William G. McLoughlin of Brown University established himself as one of the foremost authorities on the history of American Protestantism. Another Brown historian, David Herlihy, was a leading scholar in the field of medieval history, and the immediate past president of the American Historical Association at the time of his death in 1991.

In the modern period, the Rhode Island Irish community produced several nationally prominent entertainers, most notably Eddie Dowling of Woonsocket (1889–1976), a Pulitzer Prize-winning playwright, Broadway composer, and producer; jazz trumpeter Robert L. "Bobby" Hackett (1915–76) from Providence; Woonsocket's famed soprano Eileen Farrell; Warwick's James Woods, a noted Hollywood actor; and Cumberland's Farrelly brothers, Peter and Bobby, who write and produce popular comedy films.

Irish competitiveness and pugnacity have brought prominence to many in the annals of Rhode Island sports. In boxing, Leo Flynn achieved national prominence, serving as Jack Dempsey's manager in the years following the Manassa Mauler's loss of his heavyweight crown to fellow Irish American Gene Tunney. In football, another hard-hitting sport, the local Irish rooted for D. O. "Tuss" McLaughry, Brown's most successful football coach and the mentor of the famed "Iron Men" of 1926, and for U.S. Navy ace pilot John A McIntyre, an All-American lineman at Notre Dame and a highly decorated war hero, who earned the Silver Star, two Distinguished Flying Crosses, and four Air Medals for his exploits in World War II and Korea.

But it was in baseball that Rhode Island's Irish Americans made their greatest impact. O'Rourke and Duffy of an earlier era were succeeded in the Hall of Fame by Woonsocket-born Charles "Gabby" Hartnett. The oldest of fourteen children, Hartnett made his major league debut with the Chicago Cubs in 1922 and played with them for a nineteen-year span that included four World Series. Joe McCarthy, the great Yankee manager, labeled Hartnett "the best catcher of all time."

Also making their mark in the big leagues were the Cooney

family of Cranston. James John Cooney, born in Cranston in 1865, was the patriarch of the clan. He had four ballplaying sons, and they in turn produced six grandsons in the same mold. Jimmy Cooney, Sr., played for three years as a shortstop with Cap Anson's Cubs in the early 1890s. He then passed on the fundamentals of the game to his sons, two of whom—Jimmy Jr., known as "Scoops," and John—also went on to the major leagues. Scoops Cooney won acclaim as one of the classiest-fielding shortstops of his era. In May 1927 he accomplished that extreme rarity in baseball, an unassisted triple play. Johnny Cooney played for twenty seasons in the major leagues with Boston and the Brooklyn Dodgers. An excellent outfielder, he led the National League twice in fielding and made only thirty-four errors during a career consisting of 1,172 games. On the distaff side, Elizabeth "Lizzie" Murphy of Warren was a nationally prominent pioneer in women's baseball.

In recent years basketball has held center stage among those sports played in Rhode Island. Providence College teams under Joseph P. McGee (also of Providence Steam Roller fame) and "General" Al McClellan won national recognition in the late 1920s and early 1930s, as did Frank W. Keaney's fine squads at the University of Rhode Island in the 1940s. Keaney (who also coached four other sports at URI from 1920 to 1955) helped revolutionize basketball with his racehorse style of play and his "point-a-minute" teams that starred such renowned players as Ernie Calverley.

From the late 1950s through the 1970s, Providence College basketball again held the limelight. The Friars, under the successive tutelage of Joe Mullaney and Dave Gavitt, became a national basketball power featuring such luminaries as John Egan, Mike Reardon, Kevin Stacom, Fran Costello, Billy Donovan, and Providence's own Joe Hassett, all of whom made it to the pros, and Ray Flynn, who became mayor of Boston and U.S. ambassador to the Vatican. A lesser-known but even more successful (and more Irish) athletic program at Providence College has been cross-country. For a decade in the 1970s and early 1980s, Friar runners dominated New England long-distance events and were consistently among the best in the nation. This dominance was due primarily to a steady stream of Irish imports, some of whom took up permanent residence in Rhode Island. The most notable performer among this wave of talented Irish harriers was John Treacy, who won the 1984 Olympic silver medal for Ireland in the marathon.

Despite the effects of acculturation and assimilation in the several generations following the onset of the great Irish exodus, and notwithstanding the impact of intermarriage, suburbanization, upward social mobility, and the dwindling of immigration, Irish heritage and culture remain vibrant in Rhode Island. Nearly every major college in the state has Irish scholars in residence. The best known is L. Perry Curtis, Jr., of Brown University, a prominent authority on Irish history.

Traditional Irish fraternal groups continue to be active. These organizations, though primarily for socializing, also engage in constructive social and cultural efforts. Meanwhile, the strong Newport Irish community and their Pawtuxet Valley counterparts faithfully continue their impressive St. Patrick's Day parades in Newport and West Warwick each year, and Providence has revived its parade as well.

Although it is now more than three centuries since the first Irish pioneers settled in Rhode Island, the Irish community remains a distinct and vigorous presence in Rhode Island: local Irish traditions are much in evidence, interest in the ancestral homeland continues strong, and the tendency of Irish Americans to identify themselves as such is pronounced and decisive. The newly commissioned and massive Irish Famine Memorial, which will stand at the entrance to Heritage Harbor, Rhode Island's new state museum in Providence, will give permanent and prominent testimony to the historical fact that the Irish have exerted a significant impact on Rhode Island in every walk of life. In few other American states, if any, has the Irish community been so prominent in relative numbers and achievements.

Precious Blood Parish, Woonsocket, dating from 1872, is Rhode Island's oldest French national parish. Its church (shown here) was completed in 1881 under the direction of Father Charles Dauray.

La Langue, La Foi, et La Patrie:
The Arrival of the Franco-Americans

30

This essay, written in 1976, is excerpted from *Catholicism in Rhode Island: The Formative Era*, which I coauthored with Matthew J. Smith. I have elected to reprint it herein with some additions, so that Rhode Island's three major ethnic groups—Irish, French, and Italian—will receive equal coverage in the present volume.

Where is the thatch-roofed village, the home of
  Acadian farmers,—
Men whose lives glided on like rivers that water
  the woodlands,
Darkened by shadows of earth, but reflecting an
  image of heaven?
Waste are those pleasant farms, and the farmers
  forever departed!
Scattered like dust and leaves, when the mighty
  blasts of October
Seize them, and whirl them aloft, and sprinkle
  them far o'er the ocean.
Naught but tradition remains of the beautiful
  village of Grand-Pré.

THOSE POIGNANT WORDS of Longfellow describing the forced French Canadian evacuation of Acadia in the mid-eighteenth century were equally applicable to the nineteenth-century province of Quebec. The emigration of French Canadians to the United States, particularly New England, during the period from 1860 to 1924 caused a depletion of the Quebec countryside. By 1900 more than 700,000 French Canadians resided within the borders of the United States, and of this number approximately 500,000 had settled in New England. This large exodus served to enrich American culture and invigorate Catholicism in the northeastern regions of the United States.

Less than a year after the British came to Jamestown, Samuel Champlain chose Quebec in 1608 as the first settlement of New France. The French Jesuits who accompanied this intrepid explorer made Catholicism an integral part of the colony. This tiny settlement was slowly and sporadically nourished by immigrants from the mother country as the French presence in the New World took shape. The French government, in an effort to encourage settlement, offered to its lesser nobility grants of land in Canada called *seigneuries*. The landlords, or *seigneurs*, parceled out their holdings to colonists, but their attempt to establish the feudal system in the New World met with only limited success.

Other efforts to stimulate settlement in New France were also unproductive. By 1673 the colonial population of Canada was still less than 10,000. It is perhaps this failure of the mother country to supply her American colony with an adequate number of immigrants that resulted in the Canadian predilection towards early marriages and large families.

There was, however, one notable instance of significant French migration to Canada: the emigration of the *Filles du Roi*—in English, the King's Daughters—to Quebec during the decade from 1663 to 1673. This migration consisted of approximately 700 women who left their lives in France behind to marry men in Quebec whom they had never met and to spend the remainder of their lives on the frontier of New France building homes and raising families. Although their impact on population growth was slow in relation to the vastness of France's North American empire, the courageous King's Daughters were the progenitors of millions of modern-day Franco-Americans, both in Canada and the United States.

The French were very adventuresome. Their *coureurs de bois*, or frontier explorers, established a series of trading posts and commercial towns along the great interior waterways of North Amer-

278

ica. Starting with Quebec and Montreal on the St. Lawrence, the French influence eventually spread through the entire Great Lakes region, penetrated the Ohio River Valley at Fort Duquesne (Pittsburgh), and extended to the Mississippi Valley, where the outpost of St. Louis anchored the northern settlements and Mobile and New Orleans became French windows on the Gulf of Mexico. This far-flung empire of the Bourbon monarchy not only supplied raw materials to the mother country but also served to check the territorial encroachments of Protestant England.

The friction between England and France over the European balance of power and colonial ascendancy resulted in a series of wars that continued sporadically during the three-quarters of a century following England's Glorious Revolution of 1688, an event that marked the ouster of England's Catholic king, James II. The last conflict, popularly known as the French and Indian War (1754–63), resulted in a sound defeat for the forces of Louis XV. The Treaty of Paris (1763) that concluded this "Great War for Empire" stripped France of her North American empire (except for two small islands in the Gulf of St. Lawrence) and placed the French colonists under English rule.

French Canadian culture certainly did not die with General Montcalm on the Plains of Abraham in 1759, but the collapse of the French Empire caused many French officials to return to their homeland. This exodus of civil authorities created a leadership vacuum. Faced with the prospect of English rule and the attempted imposition of the Protestant religion upon them, the rural French *habitants* looked to the clergy to preserve their religion, language, and culture. *La foi et la langue* became the twin pillars supporting French Canadian cultural persistence. The bond between language and faith became inseparable. To adopt the English tongue became synonymous with a surrender to Protestantism. Consequently, all those who learned English or assumed English surnames were not only considered defectors; they were thought to be lost souls as well.

In 1774, as a result of British fears that the brewing revolution in the American colonies might spread to her newly acquired French subjects in Canada, Parliament passed the Quebec Act. This act granted religious toleration to the Catholics of that colony, extended the boundaries of Quebec province southward to the Ohio River, eliminated the antipapal oath of allegiance to the British Crown, and permitted a small degree of self-government. While slightly mollifying anti-British feeling, this opportunistic legislation did not win the loyalty of the French. In religious spirit, language, and culture, the *habitants* refused to be assimilated.

The French of Canada are a proud people. Their history is filled with a strong allegiance to Catholicism that has its roots with Champlain and his initial settlement. Like the Irish, the French Canadians have a national identity forged by a severe test for survival in their British-dominated homeland. The comparison extends further, for the *habitant* and the cottier shared a common socioeconomic lifestyle. They both came from an agricultural background that sometimes bordered on the subsistence level; they raised large families; they migrated to escape economic deprivation; and they were clannish by nature. The Church of France had been the defender and tutor of Irish Catholicism after Henry VIII's separation from Rome. The same strains of mysticism, moral rigor, and authoritarianism flowed through both churches to varying degrees. For both ethnic groups, religion and nationalism became a single entity from which they received the spiritual subsistence needed to lighten the hardships of a subjugated life.

Ironically, these two groups failed to coexist in harmony. The French-Irish friction was one of the most serious internal problems that the Diocese of Providence faced during the first sixty years of its existence. This strife can be best understood when viewed from an economic and cultural perspective.

Life among the *habitants* of Quebec became one of increasing hardship. The farmlands, exhausted by overuse, produced smaller crop yields. The problem of inheritance and land tenure accelerated the economic decline. When a father died, his farmland was subdivided among his surviving children. Because of this fragmentation of agricultural land and the bare subsistence farming it produced, many began to look beyond the Canadian borders for relief.

The trickle of what would become a flood of French Canadian immigrants to Rhode Island began in 1815. During that year Francis Proulx and his family settled in Woonsocket. Six years later the families of Prudent and Joseph Mayer chose northern Rhode Island as their new home. By 1846 a "statistical survey of Woonsocket" conducted by S. C. Newman revealed that 250 inhabitants in the Woonsocket area were of French Canadian ancestry in a total population of 4,856.

Most of the new arrivals were responding to what some have called "the lure of the loom." As early as 1810 Woonsocket textile entrepreneurs had opened the Social Manufacturing Company. Within a short period the clatter of textile shuttles could be heard along the banks of the Blackstone River. The continued expansion of the textile industry in Rhode Island prompted the mill owners to recruit the eager *habitants* of French Canada who were already experienced in the domestic production of textiles. With the coming of the Civil War, the need for manpower to replace those serving the Union cause became so acute that many New England manufacturers set up employment agencies in Quebec province.

For those seeking an escape from the privations of farm life, the promise of a steady job and good pay was too tempting to refuse. And for those with large families, children now became an asset as potential wage earners. Many left Quebec, never to return. Possessions and land were often auctioned off to provide train fare. Some *habitants*, however, envisioned their stay in America as a temporary one that would provide the means of insuring financial security when they returned to their homeland.

The reception of Franco-Americans in a strange land was often less than cordial. Willing to work a fifteen-hour day, six days a week, for a meager wage, the French Canadians represented a clear threat to the economic security of both Yankee and Irish mill hands. These economic fears partially explain the failure of the Irish to welcome the newcomers from French Canada. And since cotton and woolen manufacturing dominated the state's economic scene well into the twentieth century, the basis for this ethnic tension was slow to be eliminated. In the late 1880s politics became another point of Franco-Irish friction when most *habitants* reacted to Irish antagonism by allying with their employers—the Yankee Republican industrialists.

French Canadian immigrants to Rhode Island retained that strong adherence to their faith, language, and customs that had sustained their cultural identity in English-dominated Canada, but even their mode of Catholicism clashed with that of their Irish coreligionists. In Quebec the parish church was the center of religious activity, and the higher echelons of Catholic authority exerted little, if any, control over their *curés*. Virtually all power was vested in the parish council, which usually consisted of three laymen and the parish *curé*, or pastor, who served as president. Canadian immigrants to America found a centralized Catholic church—a church whose power base lay not in the parish but rather with the bishop. After 1866 legal authority to transact the business of the parish in Rhode Island was vested in a parish corporation, but it was the bishop, not the pastor, who served as president. To a people accustomed to local control by French-speaking *curés*, this centralized church organization, dominated as it was by Irish prelates, represented a threat to religious traditions. The Franco-Americans not only belonged to a church; in a sense, they felt that it also belonged to them.

There were other novelties that caused the French Canadians to be uncomfortable in their new religious surroundings. Seat money and other offerings were levies to which they were unaccustomed because of the well-endowed status of their church in Canada. English-language sermons and confessions hampered them in the practice of their faith. The demand by the Franco-Americans for the preservation of their native tongue did not strike a responsive chord with many Irish priests who felt that rapid Americanization of foreign-born Catholics would dispel the Church's foreign or alien image. Finally, the *habitant* missed the colorful and elaborate religious rituals that Irish priests, sensitive to Yankee criticisms of "popish pageantry," often simplified or eliminated.

The anxieties that these differences created could best be relieved, and the spiritual needs of the migrants from French Canada could best be served, by the ministrations of French Canadian priests working within the framework of French Canadian national parishes. This became not only the desire but the demand of the transplanted *habitants*. *Survivance*, the maintenance of their culture, was threatened by *les églises irlandaises* (the Irish churches).

By 1865 there were 3,384 foreign-born Rhode Islanders from "British America," and a substantial majority of this number were people of French descent from Quebec. Five years later the federal census recorded 10,242 immigrants from this source. Woonsocket continued to be the population and cultural center for the state's Franco-Americans, but the Blackstone Valley mill villages of Manville, Ashton, Albion, Slatersville, Central Falls, Pawtucket, and Marieville also attracted large numbers of *habitants*. Further to the south, the Olneyville section of Providence, the town of Warren, and the Pawtuxet Valley textile centers of Arctic, Natick, and Lippittsville were affected by the influx of Franco-American migrants. Clearly the time had arrived to recognize the special religious and cultural requirements of this rapidly growing Catholic community.

Finally, in 1872, Bishop Francis McFarland gave the French their long-awaited national parish by incorporating l'église du Precieux Sang (Precious Blood). Although the church building itself was not completed until 1881, Precious Blood, Woonsocket, is regarded as the Franco-American mother church. It was followed by Notre Dame du Sacré Coeur of Central Falls in 1873. The parishioners there, led by young, dynamic Father Charles Dauray, were the first to complete and occupy their church, dedicating that structure on October 2, 1875.

By 1880 the French Canadian community was also served by St. Jean Baptiste in West Warwick, St. James in Manville, and St. Charles in Providence. Fifteen more French national parishes would be established in the years that followed, for a total of twenty. Through the medium of the national church and its cultural ally, the French national society, the heritage of Rhode Island's transplanted *habitants* was now secure.

Republican Aram Pothier, Franco-American political leader, served longer as governor of Rhode Island—nine years and two months—than any other chief executive of the twentieth century. He died in office on February 28, 1928.

Ethnic Politics in Rhode Island: The Case of the Franco-Americans

31

This lecture was delivered in Woonsocket in 1981 as part of a series of public sessions, sponsored by the Rhode Island Committee for the Humanities, entitled "Woonsocket, R.I.: The Americanization of a Foreign City."

RHODE ISLAND POLITICAL HISTORY has been characterized by passion and turbulence. One reason for this volatility is the importance of ethnic and religious factors as determinants of voting behavior.

Until the fourth decade of the nineteenth century, Rhode Island was a homogeneous state whose population was overwhelmingly of English stock. In the 1830s, however, the situation changed. The influx of Irish Catholics produced a reaction known as political nativism, a systematic attempt by native Americans to exclude naturalized citizens from participation in the political process.

One of the principal issues of the famous Dorr Rebellion—an upheaval that produced our present state constitution—was the issue of whether or not to confer the vote on naturalized citizens, most of whom were Irish Catholics. It was decided by the conservative leaders who defeated the Dorrites to impose a real estate requirement for voting and officeholding upon the foreign born, while allowing native-born citizens without property to vote merely by paying a one-dollar registry tax. This discriminatory double standard endured until the ratification of the Bourn Amendment in 1888.

From the time of the Dorr Rebellion until the decade of the 1880s, the real estate requirement imposed upon the foreign-born was a source of great political agitation. First the Whig party during the 1840s, and then the Republican party (established in 1854), fought to maintain the real estate requirement. Led by such reformers as Thomas Wilson Dorr, Henry J. Duff, Philip Allen, and Charles E. Gorman, the urban wing of the Democratic party campaigned unsuccessfully for its abolition.

By the decade of the 1880s, the real estate requirement was becoming increasingly less effective as a measure to disfranchise Rhode Islanders of Irish stock. The state census of 1885 revealed that two out of every three Rhode Island Irishmen were native-born and therefore exempt from the real estate requirement. These native-born Irish were swelling the ranks of the Democratic party, a political organization that had been the minority faction since 1854.

Republican political leaders under the direction of Charles R. (Boss) Brayton analyzed Rhode Island's political status in the wake of that revealing 1885 census—a compilation that also showed the increasing numerical presence of recent immigrants from French Canada, British Canada, England, and Sweden. Of these newer arrivals, the French Canadians were by far the most significant numerically.

Brayton and his associates knew that Protestant immigrants from England, British Canada, and Sweden could be counted upon to join their Yankee cousins in the ranks of the Republican party once they were granted the vote. Brayton also felt that the Catholic French could be won over to the GOP as a result of their economic community of interest with the Yankee Republican mill owners who employed them. Further, the perceptive Brayton had detected an increasing antagonism between Rhode Island's Irish and their coreligionists from Quebec. The Irish resented the French Canadians as economic rivals who were willing to work for lower pay and derisively dubbed them "the Chinese of the East." They also resented French encroachment into their traditional neighborhoods in the Blackstone and Pawtuxet Valleys. The French Canadians, in turn, chafed at Irish control of the local

Catholic Church and the lack of Irish sympathy for the preservation of Franco-American cultural traditions, language, and religious observances.

The Republicans, showing much more sagacity than the Democratic Irish, exploited these economic and ethnocultural rivalries, and they courted and won the political allegiance of the Franco-American community. Before accomplishing this feat, however, they had to deal with a major stumbling block—the real estate requirement imposed by the state constitution upon naturalized citizens. The Bourn Amendment (Article of Amendment VII to the Rhode Island Constitution) was drafted and supported by Republican leaders. When it became law in 1888, it allowed thousands of formerly voteless Franco-American citizens to participate in the political process. It also immediately enfranchised naturalized immigrants from England, British Canada, and Sweden, all of whom opposed Irish Catholic Democrats primarily on religious grounds.

Rather than a genuine reform, the Bourn Amendment was a political masterstroke that blunted the rising threat of the Irish-led Democratic party and preserved Republican political ascendancy in Rhode Island for another half century. Under the lead of the astute Boss Brayton, the GOP had won the initial game of ethnic politics: they had forged a dominant Republican coalition by successfully appealing to the religious, ethnic, economic, and cultural interests of Rhode Island's newer immigrant groups.

As some historians have noted, Irish Catholic Democrats and Yankee Protestant Republicans battled during the late nineteenth and early twentieth centuries for the allegiance of the state's remaining ethnic groups. Political dominance went to that party which successfully wooed the newer ethnics. In this political courtship the most desired ethnic group was the Franco-Americans, both because of its numerical size and because of its tendency to support en masse one political party or the other. It was French allegiance to the Republican party in the period from the Bourn Amendment to the Great Depression that, more than any other factor, accounted for GOP ascendancy during that era. As Father Austin Dowling, first historian of the Diocese of Providence, observed in 1899, "The French Canadian...votes the Republican ticket. It is his vote which keeps Rhode Island Republican."

Yankees were well aware of the importance to the GOP of the Franco-American vote. The Republicans therefore gave very early sponsorship to French politicians and elevated two of them, Aram Pothier and Emery San Souci, to the governorship and another, Felix Hebert, to the prestigious office of United States senator. The rise of the French Canadian in Rhode Island politics was in fact more rapid than that of the Irish, thanks to the French connection with the dominant Republicans. Although substantial Irish migration began in the mid-1820s, the first Irish (and the first Catholic) state legislator, Representative Charles E. Gorman of North Providence, a lawyer and constitutional reformer, was not elected to the General Assembly until 1870; the first Irish (and the first Catholic) general officer, Secretary of State Edwin D. McGuiness, was not chosen until 1887; the first Irish (and first Catholic) governor, James H. Higgins, was not elected until 1906, and only then because of a defection from Republican ranks produced by the formation of the reform-oriented Lincoln party.

Although they arrived here in substantial numbers four decades after the Irish, the French claimed their first seat in the General Assembly in 1887, their first mayorality (Woonsocket) in 1894, their first general state office in 1897, and their first governorship in 1909. One man — the able, articulate, and popular Aram J. Pothier — accounted for all these firsts. That the Republican Pothier immediately succeeded Governor James Higgins did little to improve relations between the Irish and the Franco-American communities.

As historian John D. Buenker has shown, during the early part of the twentieth century the Irish Democratic minority in the General Assembly championed social reforms, consumer protection bills, prolabor legislation, and culturally pluralistic programs that appealed to Franco-Americans, Italian Americans, and other new immigrant groups. These legislative efforts made the Democratic party attractive to certain Franco-American leaders. Further, Irish Democratic politicians, taking a cue from the departed

288

Boss Brayton and his Republican successors, began to advance French Canadians to elective office and high positions within their party's hierarchy.

The most important of these early Franco-American Democrats was the articulate author and businessman Alberic A. Archambault of West Warwick, the political protégé of the Pawtuxet Valley Democratic boss Patrick Henry Quinn. In 1918 Archambeault made an impressive bid for governor, becoming the first Franco-American Democrat to vie for that lofty office. As a reward for his respectable effort, he was elevated by the Irish chieftains to the chairmanship of the state Democratic party in 1919.

Another pioneer responsible for the transformation of the Franco-American vote from the Republican to the Democratic party was the intense and volatile Felix Toupin of Woonsocket. Toupin's rapid rise in Democratic circles coincided with several Republican blunders in 1922, blunders that dramatically weakened the GOP's hold on the French vote.

In 1920 the Republicans successfully ran a Franco-American (Emery San Souci) for governor. Widespread disillusionment with the administration of President Woodrow Wilson gave the Republicans landslide victories at every level. In the immediate wake of the 1920 state elections, the position of the GOP seemed impregnable. During San Souci's term, however, textile mill owners dramatically cut the wages of their workers to combat the effects of a severe postwar recession. A 22.5 percent cut was accepted in 1921, but the workers rebelled when the owners attempted another cut of 20 percent in 1922 and raised the work week for women and children in their factories from forty-eight to fifty-four hours.

When a major strike erupted in January 1922, Governor San Souci, at the urging of Republican leaders (many of whom had financial interests in the textile industry), called out the National Guard. The nine-month strike was marked by sporadic violence, which included several injuries and a death. Because the mill owners used labor injunctions, evictions, and other devices in their unsuccessful attempt to break the strike, this episode severely strained the Franco-Americans' economic bond with their Yankee employers.

In the midst of this controversy, Irish Democratic leaders sponsored legislation to reduce the maximum hours of work for women and children in industry from fifty-four to forty-eight hours per week. This reform measure, which had the support of the Franco-American work force, was killed by the Republican-dominated Senate.

In 1922 it seemed that the Republicans were manifesting a political death wish, for in addition to their economic insensitivity to the plight of the Franco-American worker, they showed a cultural insensitivity to the preservation of the Franco-American's language. Caught up in the spirit of 100 percent Americanism that swept the country during the intolerant decade of the 1920s, Republican National Committeeman Frederick Peck sponsored an education act that stirred French resentment. In its most controversial provision, the Peck Act of 1922 required all instruction in private schools (except for classes in religion and language) to be conducted in English. The act's novelty was that it provided for *state* supervision and enforcement. A similar English requirement had been on the statute books since 1893, but it placed control of instruction in the hands of local politicians who, in places like Central Falls and Woonsocket, ignored it. French Canadian reaction to the Peck Act was vehement, prompting one national periodical to call the outcry "the Gallic War in Rhode Island."

The French got their revenge in the 1922 state elections, when the minority Democrats made the greatest comeback since Lazarus. Democrats nominated South Providence Irishman William S. Flynn for governor and Felix Toupin as his running mate. By exploiting the Republican use of the National Guard in the textile strike, GOP opposition to the forty-eight-hour bill, and Republican sponsorship of the Peck Act, the Democrats gained a sufficient percentage of the Franco-American vote to win the governorship, the lieutenant governorship, and control of the House of Representatives. The Republicans narrowly retained control of the rural-based and malapportioned Senate, but Felix Toupin, as lieutenant governor, would preside over the upper chamber.

The Democrats used their newfound power to push for political reform, especially the call of a constitutional convention, the reapportionment of the Senate, and the removal of the real estate requirement for voting in council elections, a device that prevented the new immigrants from vying for control of the cities in which they resided. Although Democratic reform efforts failed with the collapse of the infamous 1924 filibuster, they had made significant inroads upon the Franco-American vote.

The Republicans, sensing the erosion of French Canadian support, recalled the popular Aram Pothier from retirement to run against Toupin in the gubernatorial battle of 1924. Partly because of Toupin's tumultuous conduct during the legislative filibuster, Pothier was victorious. He was reelected in 1926 and died in office in 1928, having served longer in the position of governor than any other Rhode Island chief executive of the twentieth century.

During the late 1920s, after the death of Pothier, the Franco-American vote gradually yet emphatically continued its move into the Democratic column. Many factors influenced this important trend: (1) the textile industry experienced a drastic decline from 1923 onward, creating high unemployment in the Franco-American community and dissolving the economic bond between the French and their Yankee Republican employers; (2) Irish Democrats continued to woo the Franco-Americans by sponsoring working-class legislation and advancing Franco-Americans to prominent positions in the Democratic party; (3) the shift in national Democratic leadership from William Jennings Bryan's agrarian wing to an urban ethnic base made the party more attractive to blue-collar workers; (4) the presidential candidacy of Catholic Democrat Al Smith brought Catholic ethnics into the Democratic fold; (5) the failure of the Republicans to deal effectively with the Great Depression caused disillusionment with the GOP, especially among the unemployed; and (6) the social programs, labor legislation, and proethnic attitude of the federal government under the New Deal cemented the allegiance of French Canadians and other new ethnics to the Democratic party.

One obstacle to the transition of the Franco-American vote from the Republican to the Democratic column was the eruption of the long-simmering Sentinellist controversy, a clash between the Irish-led Roman Catholic hierarchy under Bishop William

Hickey and Franco-American dissidents led by Elphege Daigneault of Woonsocket and the Reverend Hormidas Beland of Central Falls. At issue was local versus centralized control within the Catholic Church. After much passion and rancor, cooler heads and Bishop Hickey (they were not one and the same) prevailed. This dispute, which might be called the darkness just before the dawn in French-Irish cultural relations, began to subside in 1928 with the excommunication of Daigneault and evaporated by 1933 with the death of the autocratic bishop and the appointment of a conciliatory successor, Francis P. Keough.

In the fateful 1932 state election, the Franco-American vote lined up behind Democrat Theodore Francis Green and insured his gubernatorial victory. In that year the Democratic slate of general officers indicated that the party had finally mastered the game of ethnic politics. In addition to Green, a Yankee patrician, it included Irish Lieutenant Governor Robert E. Quinn; Secretary of State Louis W. Cappelli, the first Italian American to hold general office in Rhode Island; Irish Attorney General John P. Hartigan; and Franco-American cultural leader Antonio Prince as general treasurer.

The 1934 U.S. senatorial election showed the extent of Franco-American conversion to the Democratic party. Incumbent senator Felix Hebert, a distinguished Franco-American from the Pawtuxet Valley, ran for reelection. His opponent was Yankee Democrat Peter Gerry. The Woonsocket vote tells the story. Gerry beat the incumbent Franco-American senator in that city by a vote of 10,056 to 4,870—a more than 2–to–1 margin. As this election dramatically revealed, the Franco-Americans had formed a political coalition with the Irish and Italians, one that generally endured and continues to dominate the politics of Rhode Island to the present day.

The New Immigration and Rhode Island Catholicism | 32

This essay, written in 1977, was intended to introduce the section of a projected second volume on Rhode Island Catholicism dealing with the arrival of Catholic ethnics in Rhode Island from the 1880s to the 1920s.

MARCUS LEE HANSEN, the scholar who established immigrant history as a valid field for historical study, has contended that three distinct stages of European migration to America marked the nineteenth and early twentieth centuries. The first began in the mid–1820s and continued until 1860, reaching its crest in the years from 1847 to 1854. It was spearheaded by the Catholic Irish. "To this exodus," states Hansen, "the adjective 'Celtic' may properly be applied." The next great wave of migration spanned the decades between 1860 and 1890. In this era English, Scandinavians, and north Germans from Prussia and Saxony predominated. "This exodus was Teutonic in blood, in institutions, and in the basis of its language," Hansen contends. Its peak occurred in the decade of the 1880s.

In the third wave, extending from 1890 to 1914, two new and distinct geographic regions sent a flood of migrants to America. One was Mediterranean and southern European in origin and was composed primarily of Italians, Greeks, Portuguese, and minorities from the Turkish Empire, including Armenians, Syrians, and Lebanese. The other was predominantly Slavic and eastern European in origin. This segment was composed mainly of minority or subject peoples within the Austro-Hungarian and Russian

Empires, such as Poles, Lithuanians, Ukrainians, Serbs, Czechs, Slovaks, Slovenes, Ruthenians, and such non-Slavic groups as Hungarians, Austrians, Romanians, and Jews from Poland and Russia. This mass migration crested in the decade prior to 1914 and was temporarily and abruptly curtailed by the outbreak of World War I.

This third exodus, known as the "new immigration," primarily because it flowed from southern and eastern Europe rather than from the traditional northern and western sectors of the continent, represented only 8 percent of the total immigration to the United States in 1882, but by 1896 it surpassed the old migration in magnitude. In 1907, the year in which immigration to the United States reached an all-time high of 1,285,349, about 80 percent of the arrivals came from southern and eastern sectors of the European continent.

These newcomers, like those in the earlier waves of migration, were uprooted by a combination of forces. A few fled from political or religious oppression, but mainly this outpouring was prompted by the widening impact of economic change. In northern and

The *Venezia*, a ship of the Fabre Line, brings Italian and Portuguese immigrants to the Port of Providence in 1913.

western Europe the collapse of the old agrarian order and the rise of industrialization had transformed social and economic life earlier in the nineteenth century, and in conjunction with the pressure of mounting population, it had provided the impetus for emigration. In the later decades of the nineteenth century, this condition spread eastward and southward and produced a similar effect.

As increasing numbers of these "new" immigrants, with their unfamiliar languages, customs, and religious practices, congregated in the ethnic districts of crowded cities in the Northeast and Midwest, native Americans became alarmed and blamed the new immigration for lowering living standards, depressing wages, creating slums, generating unemployment, producing crime, and spreading disease. Intellectuals, Progressive Era social reformers, organized labor, rural Americans, and even the "old" immigrants and their native-born offspring began to press for restrictions upon these allegedly inferior new ethnic strains.

From the 1880s through 1924 the exclusionists campaigned for a selective immigration program. Their arguments revealed a variety of beliefs and fears: Anglo-Saxon supremacy, suspicion of urban values, anti-Semitism, xenophobia, and anti-Catholicism were the most pronounced. These exclusionists saw themselves as the true defenders of traditional American ideals, and they felt they were upholding cherished patterns of life against the invasion of foreign ideologies imported by men with sharply different social, cultural, and religious standards. The unfounded fears of the restrictionists were buttressed by a biased and logically deficient forty-one-volume government report on immigration prepared between 1907 and 1911 by the Dillingham Commission.

From the 1890s onward, the adoption of a literacy test for immigrants became the principal goal of exclusionists. They finally secured the enactment of such a device over President Wilson's veto in 1917. When the flood of immigration resumed in the aftermath of World War I, the opponents of the new immigration demanded harsher standards, and their wishes prevailed. In 1921 and 1924 a policy of severe restriction through a highly discriminatory national-origins system was implemented, and the new immigration was effectively curtailed.

The overall effect of the new influx on Rhode Island growth was dramatic: between 1880 and 1910 the state's population nearly doubled, increasing from 276,531 to 542,610. By 1900 over 31 percent of Rhode Island's population was foreign-born, a proportion higher than that of the neighboring states of Massachusetts (30 percent) and Connecticut (26 percent) and all other states of the Union as well.

The third exodus gave Rhode Island its distinctive ethnic diversity, further stimulated industrialization and urbanization, and swelled the ranks of the Roman Catholic Church in the Diocese of Providence. The unprecedented influx of Italians, Portuguese, Poles, and, to a lesser extent, Lithuanians, Syrians, and Austrians—all of whom were predominantly Catholic—catapulted the Church into a position of numerical dominance within Rhode Island by 1905. In answer to a direct question concerning religious preference asked in the Rhode Island state census of 1905, 50.8 percent of the total population declared themselves to be Roman Catholics. This figure established Rhode Island as proportionally the most Catholic state in the Union. This position has never been relinquished; in fact, it has been greatly enhanced by continued Catholic immigration, a high birth rate, and, to a much lesser degree, conversions. These factors have easily offset losses through death and apostasy.

It is difficult and dangerous to generalize regarding the impact of the new immigration on Rhode Island Catholicism. Perhaps the best approach is to analyze the various Catholic ethnic groups separately to discover the motives for their migration, their areas of settlement within the state, their numerical significance, their national parishes, and the nature of their Catholicism.

Historians and sociologists are finally coming to recognize, in the words of Andrew Greeley, "that religion and ethnicity are intertwined, that religion plays an ethnic function in American society and ethnicity has powerful religious overtones." Thus an exploration into the relationship between religion and ethnicity within Catholicism will be much more revealing than a simple litany of ethnic "contributions." As Rudolph J. Vecoli, the leading student of Italian Catholicism, has observed: "The impact of the immigrants upon the Church, as well as the influence of the Church upon the immigrants, has clearly been a central feature of American Catholic history. The clash and accommodation of variant Catholic traditions, the conflicts between the American and foreign clergy, the controversy over the Americanizing role of the Church, the institutional responses of the Church to the needs of the poor and exploited, and the struggles between Catholics and Protestants for the fealty of the children of the immigrants—such phenomena expressed the ethnic diversity which has been fundamental to the shaping of American Catholicism." Another social historian, Father John O'Grady, has observed that the new immigration imposed a severe strain on the leadership and resources of the Church, "which had only caught up with the religious needs of older immigrants when it was called upon to solve even greater socio-religious problems."

It has been estimated by the most careful student of Catholic population trends, the Reverend Gerald Shaughnessy, that immigration between 1881 and 1910 increased the Catholic population of the United States by 4,791,000. While these new arrivals shared a common faith with the older Catholic immigrants, the two groups were widely separated by ethnicity, nationality, and culture. Differences of language created a social chasm that could not be bridged in the first generation. Often the historic and contemporary conflicts in Europe influenced the groups within the Church in the United States. Old ethnic antagonisms were imported. National differences were accentuated by economic conflict and competition in America. The new immigrants were feared, resented, or scorned by the old, who felt their job security and living standards were jeopardized by the recent flood of new arrivals. Even the nature of the Catholicism of the older and newer immigrants often differed, so that the one ostensible common bond was ironically another divisive factor.

Nowhere in the United States was there more pronounced ethnic diversity, a higher percentage of foreign-stock Catholics among the population, or a greater potential for ethnic conflict than in the Diocese of Providence during the tenure of Bishop Matthew Harkins (1887–1921). The peaceful accommodation of these groups, their spiritual welfare, and their educational and social needs became the central problems of Harkins's episcopacy. To his enduring credit, he met these enormous challenges with a minimum of tension and great success. Rhode Island Catholicism was stronger because of his accomplishment.

Originally prepared in 1976 as a speech before the Rhode Island
Italo-American Club, this survey was committed to print in 1982
as the introductory chapter in a book I wrote with Paul R. Campbell,
The Aurora Club of Rhode Island: A Fifty-Year History (1982).

THE ITALIAN IMPACT UPON RHODE ISLAND dates back to
the Age of Discovery. The first recorded European visitation to
the lands that became Rhode Island occurred in April 1524, when
Giovanni da Verrazzano, a navigator from Florence, Italy, sailing
in the employ of France, anchored in the harbor of present-day
Newport and spent fifteen days exploring the entire Narragansett
Bay region.

Verrazzano reported to his royal sponsor that he observed fertile, open fields; forests of oak and cypress; "many kinds of fruit";
an "enormous number of animals—stags, deer, lynx, and other
species"; and friendly natives. The Italian described the Indians
(probably Wampanoags) in glowing terms. He also likened Block
Island to the Mediterranean isle of Rhodes, thus indirectly providing the state with its present name.

On another voyage four years later, Verrazzano was cannibalized
in the West Indies by the ferocious Carib Indians. A municipal park
in front of the Providence County Courthouse on South Main
Street is dedicated to the memory of this intrepid Italian explorer.

Aside from an occasional Italian visitor during the colonial era
and the early nineteenth century—usually an intellectual, a
mariner, or a craftsman from the north of Italy—Rhode Island

waited for more than 360 years after Verrazzano before experiencing an Italian impact again in a major way. As late as 1883, according to the *Providence Board of Trade Journal*, the Italians in Providence numbered only "twelve families and a few single men who were boarding out." Except for a dozen or so from southern Italy, nearly all came from Tuscany. The 1880 census listed only 313 residents of Italian stock in Rhode Island as a whole.

In the decade of the 1880s, however, a number of factors began to cause discontent or to upset the traditional way of life in the rural villages and farms of southern Italy. These factors combined to produce a massive migration of Italian peasant farmers (*contadini*) and their families from this area to the United States. Rhode Island received a generous share of that outpouring.

One cause of migration from southern Italy was the social disorganization caused by the Italian unification movement, a struggle that altered traditional patterns of political and economic activity. Centralization of the government also rendered many provincial laws restricting out-migration ineffective.

Overpopulation was another influence prompting the exodus to America. Census figures revealed a 25 percent population increase in southern Italy in the period from 1871 to 1905. While the density of population was still not great in absolute terms, the ratio of persons to useable farmland became too high.

The most significant factor inducing Italians to seek opportunities elsewhere was the depressed condition of agriculture in the southern provinces. The *contadini* were exploited by absentee landlords who charged exorbitant rents but made scant effort to improve the land or to introduce modern agricultural techniques. The breakup of feudalism led to the abandonment of the practice of primogeniture, whereby the eldest son inherited all the family land intact. The consequent dividing of agricultural plots among children for two or three successive generations created a condition that Italians called *frazionamento*—the excessive subdivision of land to the point where lots were too small to be farmed profitably. Italian agriculture was also depressed by foreign market conditions, especially the rise of the American citrus industry in Florida and California (a competition that hurt growers in Calabria and Sicily) and the erection by France of high tariff walls against Italian wines.

To these economic setbacks was added an even more devastating factor—the incidence of malaria. After the secularization of church lands following unification, such land was redistributed to peasant farmers. Much of the former church property was forested, and the new owners cleared it for cultivation. This deforestation in the hilly terrain of the South led to erosion, and when the topsoil was washed away during the rainy season, the valleys became swamps where disease-bearing mosquitoes bred and flourished. Malaria killed tens of thousands of *contadini* and left many more physically debilitated.

Small wonder that these conditions encouraged Italians to look elsewhere for economic opportunity and *la dolce vita*. The annual immigration to the United States from Italy increased dramatically: 2,891 in 1870, 12,354 in 1880, 52,003 in 1890, and 285,731 in 1907, the peak year. During the period from 1900 to 1914, before World War I interrupted the flow, over 100,000 Italians came to these shores every year.

From 1898 to 1932 the United States commissioner of immigration compiled statistics detailing the volume for each ethnic group. During that thirty-four-year period a total of 54,973 Italian arrivals landed at the Port of Providence, a facility that had become one of the nation's major immigrant-landing stations after the Fabre steamship line located there in 1911. Of that total, 3,054 were designated "northerners"; the remaining 51,919 came from the south of Italy.

Over 80 percent of the Italian newcomers migrated prior to World War I. Following a sharp drop during the war years, a revival began in 1920. It was this postwar upswing that panicked nativist congressmen into passing the Emergency Quota Act of 1921 and the National Origins Quota Act of 1924. These discriminatory measures—especially the latter—were designed to restrict the volume of newer immigrants (particularly Italians, Jews, and Slavs) to the United States. With the help of a global economic depression and a second world war, these laws accomplished the intent of their xenophobic sponsors. The brief age of the great Italian migration was over.

One final statistic relating to the Italian presence in Rhode Island is worthy of note, namely, the number of "emigrant aliens departing" from the Port of Providence. From 1908 to 1932 (the entire period for which those statistics have been compiled), over 13,000 Italians were listed as returnees to Italy via the Fabre Line. Many of these departures were permanent, a fact that has lessened the numerical presence of Italian Americans in the Rhode Island population. Despite these departures, however, the 1930 federal census listed 32,493 Rhode Islanders born in Italy. Together with those born in America of Italian parents, the Italian-stock population totaled 92,036, making it the third largest ethnic group in the state after the Irish and the Franco-Americans. Providence had 19,181 foreign-born Italians and 34,454 first-generation Italian Americans in 1930, for a total of 53,635, or 21.2 percent of the city's population of 252,981.

One of the quaint and curious characteristics of Italian migration was the partial transplantation of villages to the New World. For example, residents of the Italian village of Fornelli settled in Natick, many from Frosolone settled on Federal Hill, those from Itri established a new home in Knightsville, and those from the province of Benevento migrated to West Barrington. This process is detailed in an anecdotal study by Ubaldo Pesaturo, *The Italo-Americans of Rhode Island* (1926; revised edition, 1940).

Most Italians who migrated to Rhode Island settled in the Greater Providence area. Their earliest and most important settlement was on Federal Hill, but they also came to dominate the North End (Charles Street, Eagle Park, and Wanskuck) and Silver Lake. Later, large numbers moved to the Elmhurst and Mount Pleasant sections of the city. Other significant areas of settlement in Greater Providence were in Johnston (Thornton, Hughesdale, and Simmonsville), Cranston (Knightsville, Arlington, and, in recent years, such newly developed residential areas of western Cranston as Stony Acres, Dean Estates, and Garden Hills), and North Providence (Lymansville, Marieville, and Centredale).

Further areas of significant settlement include the western sectors of Warwick (Ward 8), the Natick section of West Warwick, and the East Bay communities of Barrington, Warren, and Bristol. Italian American settlements also exist in Pawtucket, Woonsocket, and Westerly.

Generally, the early Italian immigrants worked in the textile industry, in the metals trades, or as laborers for government or private contracting firms. Only a small percentage engaged in agriculture, despite the rural roots of most southerners. But Rhode Island's Italians have evidenced a strong entrepreneurial spirit, prompting many to abandon the status of wage earner and to enter business for themselves. They have enjoyed considerable success in the construction trades, the jewelry and cutlery industries, and retail merchandising. For such entrepreneurs, Horatio Alger is more than a myth. There are so many rags-to-riches stories in the local Italian American experience that it would be no exaggeration to claim that the sons and daughters of Italy have achieved the highest level of upward socioeconomic mobility of any Rhode Island Catholic ethnic group.

Mention of Catholicism leads us to another dimension of Italian American life. These countrymen of the pope are, of course, overwhelmingly Roman Catholic in religion. Since their arrival in Rhode Island, they have created sixteen national parishes. The oldest, or "mother church," is Holy Ghost on Federal Hill, established in 1889. The Italian missionary order responsible for many of these early national parishes was the Pious Society of the Missionaries of St. Charles, called Scalabrinian Fathers after their founder, Giovanni Scalabrini (1839–1905), bishop of Piacenza. This bishop, called "Father to the Immigrants" by his biographer, Icilio Felici, came from Italy to Providence in 1901 to dedicate the cornerstone of the present church of the Holy Ghost.

In the establishment of the early Italian parishes, the Scalabrinian Fathers (who were principally from northern Italy) received the strong and enlightened assistance of Matthew Harkins, the Irish Catholic bishop of Providence (1887–1921), a prelate who was very responsive to the needs of Rhode Island's ethnic Catholics. Others among the dominant Irish clergy were not as enlightened, and friction sometimes occurred in the diocese between Irish and Italian Americans and between northern priests and their southern parishioners. Despite these antagonisms, efforts by various Protestant groups to convert Italian Americans were largely unsuccessful.

The religious friction between the Irish and Italians stemmed from a number of factors, including diverging attitudes towards the clergy, contrasting views concerning the papacy, differing levels of devotional attachment, liturgical dissimilarities, and disagreements over the role of the laity in providing financial support for the Church. As Peter Bardaglio has shown in his article "Italian Immigrants and the Catholic Church: Providence, 1890–1930" (*Rhode Island History*, May 1975), these conflicts have gradually diminished. One strong force for accommodation with the Irish American hierarchy was Monsignor Anthony Bove of St. Ann's Parish in Providence, the leading Italian American churchman in Rhode Island during the early twentieth century.

As strong as the religious sentiments of the early Italian Americans was their passion for politics. Surprisingly, the political affiliation of most first-generation Italians was Republican. This preference for the GOP stemmed from several conditions: Republicans courted the Italian vote and gave patronage to the Italians, especially in Providence, by providing them with lower-level municipal jobs; Republicans pursued national policies like the high protective tariff, making their party appear to be the party of jobs, prosperity, and the "full dinner pail"; and the Yankee-led Republican party exploited the economic and cultural antagonism between the Italians and the Democratic Irish.

In the 1920s a dramatic transformation occurred in the political allegiance of Rhode Island's Italian Americans. This transformation was prompted by many factors. For example, the Democrats backed much social and economic legislation for the benefit of workers and consumers, and they championed the elimination of Sunday blue laws and the repeal of other culturally restrictive measures, like Prohibition, that were also opposed by the Italians. Conversely, local Yankee Republicans were prohibitionists, immigration restrictionists, and opponents of working-class and pro-union legislation. Further, the decline of the textile industry and the onset of the Great Depression discredited the Republican image as the party of economic prosperity.

Most importantly, however, the Republicans advanced too few Italian Americans to high public office, whereas the Italians were vigorously wooed by the Irish-led Democratic party from the late 1920s onward. Putting aside their prejudice, the Democrats advanced such Italian Americans as Luigi DePasquale, running him for Congress in 1920 and making him Democratic state party chairman in 1924. In 1932 they nominated Louis W. Cappelli for secretary of state. With his victory Cappelli became Rhode Island's first Italian American general officer. Later he became lieutenant governor, then a distinguished jurist, and eventually the presiding justice of the Rhode Island Superior Court.

On the national level, the candidacy in 1928 of Al Smith (whose paternal grandfather was an Italian immigrant) accelerated the trend of Italian Americans towards the Democratic party, and the social programs of the Democrat Roosevelt and his New Deal won the support of most Italian Americans and other working-class ethics. By 1934–35 all these factors had brought the Italians (and the Franco-Americans) into a political coalition with the Irish. This coalition has resulted in Democratic party dominance on the state level ever since, and it has paved the way for the success and political longevity of such Italian American statesmen as John O. Pastore.

Louis W. Cappelli, educated at LaSalle Academy, Brown University, and Yale Law School, became Rhode Island's first Italian American general officer in January 1933. He capped his distinguished public career as presiding justice of the Rhode Island Superior Court from 1959 to 1966.

Thus by the early 1930s a firm foundation had been laid by the labor and the sacrifice of the immigrant generation in business, religion, government, the arts, and the professions, a foundation upon which their children and grandchildren could and would build. In many ways the Aurora Club in Providence — created in 1931 by the most successful members of the founding generation and, especially, their aspiring sons—indicated the arrival of the Italian American to a position of dignity and respectability, offering proof that ability, honesty, dedication, and hard work, rather than accidental circumstances like noble birth, were the measures of a man's worth in this nation of immigrants. The aurora—the light of dawn—was indeed a fitting symbol for this second, youthful generation of Italian Americans to adopt as it began its climb to even greater heights of local influence, power, and success.

34

The Ukrainians of Rhode Island: The Founding and the Fragmentation of an Ethnic Community, 1903–1938

This essay, written in 1978 for my projected second volume on Rhode Island Catholicism, has been modified slightly to reflect the sovereignty of Ukraine and to provide more legal detail regarding the church schism. For a comprehensive survey of both Uniats and Orthodox Ukrainians, consult Rt. Rev. John J. Mowatt, The Ukrainians in Rhode Island (1988), in the Rhode Island Ethnic Heritage Pamphlet Series.

THE HISTORY OF UKRAINIAN RELIGIOUS GROUPS in Rhode Island is a complex one, as is the history of Ukraine. This region is an agricultural area in east central Europe north of Romania and the Black Sea and east of Poland, Austria, and Slovakia. Until the breakup of the Soviet Union, Ukraine was the constituent Ukrainian Soviet Socialist Republic. Now independent, it embraces a number of subregions, including Ruthenia and Galicia in the western sector around the Carpathian Mountains. During the nineteenth century and down to World War I, the region was controlled by czarist Russia in the east and Austria in the west.

Greek Christianity affected this area as it spread north from Byzantium through Romania, Galicia, Ruthenia, and Ukraine, and thence to Russia proper. Two religious rites developed in Ukraine as offshots of the Greek Rite of Byzantium, the Carpatho–Ruthenian Rite of the western sector and the Ukrainian Rite of the eastern sector, the Balkans, and Russia.

Both rites separated from Rome in the Great Schism of 1054 but were reunited, the Ruthenians about 1595, largely through the efforts of the Jesuits, and the adherents of the Ukrainian Rite in 1652. There are several similarities between the two groups. Both are dependent upon the Sacred Oriental Congregation in Rome, and thus are known as Uniats, and because the adherents of both are Slavic, Old Slavonic is used as their basic liturgical language. One group, however, supplements the Slavic with the Ruthenian language, the other with Ukrainian. Most of the Catholics who migrated to America were of the Ruthenian Rite of western Ukraine.

The Ukrainians are religiously heterogeneous. In addition to these two Uniat rites in communion with Rome, there are two groups of Ukrainians affiliated with the Greek Orthodox Church, another with the Russian Orthodox, and still another adhering to Protestantism.

Most students of the subject cite 1870 as the starting date of substantial migration to the United States from Ukraine. This migration came principally from the western provinces. During the 1870s it was sporadic, but from the 1880s to World War I the influx was continuous. Estimates of the number of Ukrainians in the United States in 1899 ranged from 200,000 to 500,000, with the lower figure being more plausible. Since then, immigration authorities have developed greater precision in recording the races and nationalities of foreign arrivals. According to the annual immigration reports for the years from 1899 to 1930, a total of 268,311 Ukrainian immigrants entered the ports of this country. They are listed under the obsolete and less than generic terms "Ruthenians" or "Russniaks."

St. Michael's Ukrainian Catholic (Uniat) Church on Blackstone Street, Woonsocket

Rhode Island received 2,041 of this total. Undoubtedly others came prior to 1899, when nationality rather than ethnic group was the means of designation, and these were listed as Russians or Austrians. The state's peak year for Ukrainian immigration was 1913, when 337 migrants entered Rhode Island. The principal source of this influx was Galicia. Those Uniat Catholics who came from that region were attached to the Ruthenian Rite, in which priests were allowed to marry by virtue of an agreement with the pope at the time of reunion in 1595.

The causes for Galician migration to the United States in the pre-World War I era were many. The leading student of American Ukrainians, Wasyl Halich, contends that Russian political and cultural oppression was the primary factor, but even those Ukrainians from East Galicia and Ruthenia who were under Austrian rule prior to 1918 were quite discontented with their lack of national identity. Other motives for migration were economic: the promise of high wages and steady employment, the prospect of free homestead land, and the existence of poor conditions at home, including farms that were too small, taxes that were too high, and industry that was too limited. Social and cultural discrimination by Russians or Polish and Hungarian officials within the Austrian Empire were also sources of discontent.

It appears that a good number of those labeled "Austrian" or "Russian" immigrants in the Rhode Island state census were from Ukraine. This observation is especially true for the city of Woonsocket, where the 1920 census found that 6.1 percent of the population was of "Austrian" stock. It was in Woonsocket that a Ukrainian Catholic church dedicated to St. Michael the Archangel was founded and continues to function.

As early as 1903, Ukrainians in that city and its environs formed a voluntary "religious society" and rented an unused Protestant church at Cumberland Hill for their services. Because some of the Ukrainians were affiliated with the Russian Orthodox Church and others were Uniats, tensions developed and the society divided, with the Uniats relocating to Cloutier's Hall, Woonsocket. In 1909 the Uniats purchased a parcel of land and two buildings on West School Street and incorporated under the name of St. Michael's Greek Catholic Ruthenian Church. In 1919 they acquired another site in Woonsocket on Blackstone Street, and here they completed a church in 1924 to serve a congregation of approximately 250 adults.

Meanwhile, a national controversy had arisen over the status of Ukrainian Catholics (also referred to as Greek Catholics or Uniats) in the United States. The problem was partially resolved in 1912 when the Uniats received their own bishop, Stephen S. Ortynsky, and the Ruthenian Greek Catholic Diocese of America was created.

In March 1916 the forceful and efficient Ortynsky died, and his seat remained unfilled until March 1924. In that year Bishop Wasyl Takach was appointed to preside over the churches built by the people from the region of Ruthenia, and Bishop Konstantin Bohachewsky was given charge of the parishes formed by Ukrainians from Galicia. At this point the policies of Bohachewsky collided with the interests of the parishioners at St. Michael's Uniat Church in Woonsocket, and a dispute erupted that was even more intense and acrimonious than the famous Franco-American Sentinellist controversy that also shook Woonsocket Catholicism in the 1920s.

The Woonsocket Uniat imbroglio began in June 1923, when the Galacian church amended its original charter to change the name of the corporation by inserting the word "Ukrainian" in place of the word "Ruthenian." This alteration was validly approved, but other unauthorized alterations in the corporate charter were then made at the direction of pastor Onufri Kovalsky. These alterations, which the courts found to be invalid and fraudulent, purported to amend the charter by declaring that the church was in formal affiliation with Rome, by affirming the right of the bishop to appoint the pastor, and by placing the parish property under the control of the Greek Catholic bishop of North America. These unapproved changes were filed with the Rhode Island secretary of state on February 16, 1924.

The affiliation and appointment declarations were in accord with actual practices, but the provision relating to church property became the root of the crisis, especially in view of the completion of the new Blackstone Street church, which Bishop Bohachewsky blessed on September 24, 1924. The irregular change established a five-man board consisting of four members selected from the congregation and a fifth, the chairman, the Ukrainian Catholic bishop or his designee. The board was to have full power in financial concerns. Armed with this ostensible authority, Bohachewksy appointed Father Chlib Werchowsky, a Russian, as pastor of St. Michael's in 1925. The choice was singularly unfortunate. Russians and native Ukrainians were antagonists because of Russian mis-rule in the old country. Although the Woonsocket parishioners from Galicia had been under Austrian rather than Russian control, Werchowsky could speak only Russian.

Father Werchowsky attempted to implement the disputed bylaw revisions soon after his arrival in Woonsocket. Perhaps realizing their bogus nature, he secured the introduction of a bill into the January 1926 session of the General Assembly that authorized a majority of the trustees of the church to transfer its property to a corporation consisting of the bishop, the diocesan chancellor, and the pastor (all *ex officio*) and two lay trustees selected by the three *ex officio* members. The measure, which became law in April, galvanized opposition to Bohachewsky and Werchowsky. According to the state Supreme Court, the "litigation [that followed] can be traced to the introduction of the above-mentioned bill [H 1040] in the General Assembly, more than to anything else."

A large contingent of the parishioners insisted with some persuasiveness that changes in the corporation's charter in 1923 had been made illegally. A majority of their corporation, they contended, was 126, not 5, because under the original charter every person who contributed to the maintenance of the church was a corporation member. In defiance of actual practice since 1909, they further asserted that it was the corporation, and not the bishop, who was entitled to appoint the pastor.

At this juncture Roman Catholic bishop William Hickey of the Providence diocese, a staunch centralizer himself, entered the fray on behalf of his fellow prelate Bohachewsky. A number of embarrassing incidents followed, and a complex and protracted court battle began that extended from 1926 to 1938. The most bizarre episode occurred in mid-1926, when a majority of the church corporation demanded that Bohachewsky remove Werchowsky as pastor. When this request was defiantly rejected, the majority refused to attend services, picketed the church, and finally drove the pastor from St. Michael's after pelting him with eggs.

Bishop Bohachewsky sought a Superior Court injunction to restrain the corporation majority from interfering with Werchowsky's religious services, and the dissidents responded by filing a counterclaim against the bishop and his pastor. After an extended hearing the bishop's prayer for temporary relief was denied, and a decree was entered enjoining the bishop and the pastor from interfering with church assets and property (including the parish house and church edifice), giving the majority the right to choose a new pastor, and requiring Werchowsky to vacate the parish house or rectory in thirty days, even though he had remained in possession of that property.

In 1927 the Rhode Island Supreme Court voted 4 to 1 to allow the temporary restraining order to stand pending a hearing on the merits (*St. Michael's Church* v. *Bohachewsky*, 48 R.I. 234). That hearing was long delayed; since the protester-petitioners were now in control of the church property, they were in no hurry to move the case forward. But the dissidents were not idle. In 1928 they allowed the disputed 1909 corporate charter of St. Michael's Ukrainian Greek Catholic Church to lapse along with its legislative amendment, organized a new corporation, St. Michael's Ukrainian Orthodox Church (a.k.a. the Autokafalic Church), and transferred all the property of the old St. Michael's to the new entity.

Eventually the tenacious Bohachewsky resumed the initiative. He was now represented by Ambrose Kennedy, a former U. S. congressman, a prominent Woonsocket Catholic layman with close ties to the Providence diocese, and the biographer of Monsignor Charles Dauray. The bishop had the matter set down for trial early in 1935. When the Superior Court hearing on the merits went against Bohachewsky, attorney Kennedy appealed to the state Supreme Court. In 1938 Associate Justice Francis B. Condon, also a former congressman, penned a unanimous decision that reversed the Superior Court ruling and sustained the bishop's appeal.

After reviewing fourteen hundred pages of testimony and "an immense quantity of documentary evidence," the Supreme Court restored the church to the Uniat minority, ruling that "no majority of the congregation, however large, could alter the uses to which its property was first dedicated"—namely, to the use of the Uniat Greek Catholic Church. It was clear, found the court, "that St. Michael's Church, as a corporation, continued to acknowledge, as it did while a voluntary society, that it was part of a general church body of the Greek Catholic Church in the Ruthenian Rite in union with Rome and that its property was dedicated to the teaching and practice of the doctrines, rites, and discipline of that church" (see *St. Michael's Church* v. *Bohachewsky*, 60 R.I. 1, 1938).

When the high court awarded the Blackstone Street premises to the persistent Bishop Bohachewsky and his supporters, it also held out an olive branch to the schismatics by ordering that "all persons who were members on July 14, 1926, but who thereafter joined the Autokafalic Church, will be given the privilege, if they so desire, to profess in writing their adherence to the Greek Catholic Church in the Ruthenian Rite in union with Rome and thereupon be listed as members of the corporation." This ruling finally ended the stormy twelve-year controversy that is among the least flattering episodes in the history of Rhode Island Catholicism.

Once the air had cleared, the tiny Uniat parish returned to relative tranquility under the pastorate of Father Vasyl Tremba, though it and its rival were saddled with sizable debts for legal fees. On February 6, 1938, the Uniat parishioners reconsecrated their newly regained Blackstone Street church, which soon served as the setting for the first liturgy and Mass of a native son, Father Nestor Romanovych. Since its time of troubles the parish has flourished, and today it serves as a center of Ukrainian culture within the state.

Postscript

The Ukrainian Orthodox congregation of St. Michael's, established in 1926 when its founders broke with Bishop Bohachewsky, also continues to prosper. After relinquishing the Blackstone Street church under court order, the parish built an imposing house of worship at 74 Harris Avenue, Woonsocket.

Another dissenting Ukrainian group, first formed in the Lincoln village of Manville in 1917 as a Uniat church, also broke with Rome during the Bohachewsky controversy. Their parish, St. Stephen's, became Orthodox in 1927 and maintained its separate identity until it merged with St. Michael's Orthodox Church in the 1970s.

Rhode Island's fourth Ukrainian parish, St. John's, was Orthodox from the outset. It was formed in South Providence in 1921, gathered for a time on Pilgrim Street, and moved to a new house of worship at 628 Public Street in the Elmwood section of the city in August 1955. The massive out-migration to suburbia from Providence's South Side soon depleted the congregation and led to the 1982 sale of its relatively new Eastern-style church building to a Hispanic Pentecostal group.

In 1976, as chairman of the Rhode Island Bicentennial Commission, I formed a Ukrainian-American Heritage Subcommittee of ri76, including both Uniats and Orthodox. The subcommittee was active and creative, and everyone got along famously! Eventually they collaborated in the production of an ethnic heritage pamphlet entitled *The Ukrainians in Rhode Island: Faith and Determination*, written by Rt. Rev. John M. Mowatt and edited by me, that described their shared and colorful history and cultural traditions.

St. Michael's Ukrainian Orthodox Church on Harris Avenue, Woonsocket

Rhode Island's Christian Arabs: The Origins of the Syrian–Lebanese Community

35

This essay was written in 1978 for my projected second volume on the history of Rhode Island Catholicism.

IN THE LAST QUARTER OF the nineteenth century a movement to America from the troubled Middle East began. Its source was Lebanon and Syria, at the eastern end of the Mediterranean. The factors that produced migration from these areas included over-population, primitive methods of agriculture, high taxation, lack of industrial development, and the oppressive actions of the Turkish Empire. In addition, the completion of the Suez Canal in 1869 dealt a severe blow to the region's commerce by altering the old routes of trade, and it inflicted an equal setback on the area's chief export, silk, by opening the door to Japanese competition.

Although the area from which these immigrants came is predominantly Muslim in religion, nearly all those who made the trek to America were Christians, and a good number of these were affiliated with the Church of Rome.

These Catholic immigrants fell into two main groups, the Maronites and the Melkites, both of whom could be classified as Syrians. The Maronites, who are based in present-day Lebanon, adhere to a form of liturgical worship known as the Maronite Rite. The name is derived from the noted Syrian hermit St. Maron (died 433) and his monastery shrine, Bait-Marun. The Maronite Rite was instituted in the seventh century, but this religious group split off from the Imperial or Greek Church about a century later. The Maronites came into communion with Rome in 1182 as a result of the twelfth-century Crusades, and they have retained that affiliation since. Their worship is a modified Antiochian liturgy in the Syriac tongue (the Syrian Rite of Antioch), but the Gospel and some other parts of their service are read in the vernacular Arabic (Aramaic), the language spoken by Christ himself.

These peasant herders and farmers from the mountains of Lebanon experienced two brutal massacres at the hands of a neighboring Muslim group, the Druses, in 1841 and 1860. The latter outrage prompted the European powers, especially France, to press for an end to direct Turkish rule in the area and the creation of a political unit known as Great Lebanon. This autonomous entity, established in 1861 under a Christian governor, evolved into the independent nation of Lebanon in 1944.

The continued political and religious strife that attended the decline of the Ottoman Empire produced a substantial migration from Lebanon around the turn of the twentieth century. More than 400 of these exiles found their way to Providence and settled in the Federal Hill area. The men sought work as peddlers, laborers, and, eventually, shopkeepers. Because of the language barrier and because of a strong attachment to their ancient liturgical traditions, before long these Lebanese petitioned Roman Catholic bishop Matthew Harkins for their own church and a priest who could communicate with them in their native tongue. At that time they were worshiping in the basement of St. John's Church on Atwells Avenue.

Responding with characteristic sympathy, Bishop Harkins established St. George's Maronite Parish in a remodeled tenement house on America Street in May 1911, with the Reverend Joseph Ganen as its pastor. Ganen would continue to serve the Providence Lebanese community until his departure for Alabama in 1922. Despite the difference in rite, St. George's was under the jurisdiction of the bishop of Providence and remained so until the creation of a national Maronite Exarchate in 1966, with the headquarters of the new Maronite sect in Detroit.

The adherents of the Melkite Rite migrated from Syria (Iraq) around the turn of the century to escape the harsh rule of the Ottoman Turks and to improve their economic condition. They came principally from the areas around Damascus and Aleppo (Halab), where many had worked as weavers. According to one source, they first came to Providence in 1902 during the Olneyville textile strike. Because of their unfamiliarity with the local labor situation and because of their need for income to provide the necessities of life, they worked during the strike and slept in the mills. After the dispute they moved to the Blackstone Valley cities of Pawtucket, Central Falls, and Woonsocket. Two factors probably prompted this population shift. First, there were many French Canadians in these communities, and some of the Syrians were familiar with the French language because of France's strong presence in the Middle East. Further, there were silk mills in the Blackstone Valley, and a number of Syrians were familiar with this type of manufacturing.

The Melkite Rite of these immigrants differed from the Maronite Rite in several respects. The Melkites represent a segment of Syrian Christianity that separated from Rome in 1054 and adhered to the Imperial or Byzantine Church (hence their name, from *malok*, the Syrian word for "king") for 670 years. Although they have been in union with Rome since 1724, they have retained their original Byzantine Rite with Greek and Arabic liturgical language.

It was to preserve this Melkite religious and cultural tradition that the 400 Syrians of Pawtucket and Central Falls requested their own national church in 1908, when they learned that the Reverend Ananias Boury was willing to take up residence among them and serve their needs. Bishop Harkins obliged, and Father Boury began his Melkite services in the basement of St. Joseph's Polish Church in Central Falls. The Melkites began a fund-raising drive for their own national parish, and by October 1910 Harkins was able to preside over the dedication of St. Basil's Melkite Church, also in Central Falls. Father Boury was replaced in 1919 by the Reverend Timothy Jock, who established the first parochial school of any Melkite parish in America. At the height of its growth the school's enrollment numbered 156 students. Here the Arabic language was studied daily, but this pioneering effort to preserve the Melkite culture received a setback when the Great Depression forced the school's closing. Undaunted, Father Jock turned his efforts to the Woonsocket Syrian community and established a mission church, St. Elias's, in 1931 to serve its needs.

Father Jock's successor at St. Basil's and St. Elias's, the Reverend Archimandrite Najmy, ministered to the Syrians of the Blackstone Valley from 1947 to 1966. In the latter year he became the country's first Melkite bishop and the head of the newly created Melkite Exarchate of the United States. Najmy's elevation was a singular honor for Rhode Island's small but loyal and devout Melkite community of 1,400 souls.

The religious rites of the Syriac people of St. George's, St. Basil's, and St. Elias's offer an interesting contrast to the Roman Rite in art, music, the celebration of the Mass, and the reception of the sacraments, a contrast that serves as a witness to the universality of the Church. The Eastern liturgy emphasizes the divine, theological, invisible, and sacrificial aspects of the faith.

Many Syriac Catholics, who partake of both Eastern and Western culture, believe they can act as an ecumenic instrument in promoting unity between the Church of Rome and those members of the Orthodox Church with whom the Maronites and Melkites share a common language and tradition. This long-awaited rapprochement is one of their major religious and cultural concerns.

In this photo from the mid–1940s, parishioners of St. George's Maronite Catholic Church on America Street in Providence's Federal Hill neighborhood pose with pastor Ne'matallah Gideon, who served the parish for twenty-five years.

Father Timothy Jock, who established the first Melkite parochial school in the United States at St. Basil's, Central Falls, in 1920, presides here over the 1934 First Communion class of St. Basil's Parish.

Dr. Ramon Guiteras of Bristol was Rhode Island's most prominent
Hispanic American of the early twentieth century.

Rhode Island's Earliest Latin Americans: Their Church and Their Culture

36

This essay was written in 1974 as a project of the Rhode Island Ethnic Heritage Program, a scholarly enterprise that I directed at Providence College. John Carpenter, then my graduate student and now chairman of the history department at LaSalle Academy, conducted all of the interviews. The essay appeared serially in the *Providence Visitor*, the official Catholic diocesan newspaper, in August 1974.

MIGRATION TO RHODE ISLAND FROM LATIN AMERICA is a modern development. Prior to the 1950s, arrivals were very few in number. In the colonial era some Sephardic Jews, fleeing oppression in Spain and Portugal, came to Newport via South America (usually Brazil) or the Caribbean islands. The last of this tiny but influential community left Newport in 1822.

During the 1790s, slave revolts on the islands of Santo Domingo and Guadeloupe brought a small number of French and Spanish refugees to Newport and Bristol, towns that had close commercial ties with these areas because of the slave trade. It appears that most of these West Indian exiles resided only briefly in Rhode Island before returning to their European homelands.

The first census conducted by the state in 1865 counted only 12 inhabitants born in South America and 20 from the West Indies in Providence's total population of 54,595. Newport, Rhode Island's other city, had 1 Mexican-born resident and 2 from the West Indies. Forty years later the state census of 1905 enumerated 86 natives of South America, 6 Puerto Ricans, 18 Cubans, and 237 from other West Indian islands. There is no evidence, however, that these Latinos formed an identifiable or cohesive community, although 228 of the 347 listed above resided in Providence (total 1905 population, 198,635).

Certainly the most prominent person of Latin American heritage during these years was Ramon Guiteras, a native of Bristol. He was the son of a prominent Cuban banker with financial ties to Bristol's De Wolf family. Because the De Wolfs maintained substantial investments in Cuba, family connections followed those of a financial nature. Ramon Guiteras, Sr., married Elizabeth Wardwell of Bristol, and the couple became the parents of Ramon, who was raised in that bayside town. After completing his studies at Harvard University and its medical school, Ramon moved to New York, where he became a prominent surgeon, president of the Spanish-American and Latin American Medical Association, and secretary for many years of the Pan-American Medical Congress. Upon his death in 1917 his will provided a $350,000 bequest to the town of Bristol for the construction of a large school building to honor his mother. That beautiful colonnaded brick and limestone structure, Guiteras Memorial School, was modeled after the De Wolf mansion on Poppasquash Neck. Completed in 1925, the school overlooks Bristol harbor and serves as one of the town's most visible and significant landmarks.

Though it would be interesting to trace and identify the scattered arrivals from Hispanic America who came to Rhode Island prior to the early 1950s, our intent is different. The focus of this essay is the origin and formation of the *modern* Latin American *community* and the role of the Catholic Church in that development.

* * *

The church of Providence has always been the church of the immigrant. The diocese was founded by peasant stock from Ireland who descended upon Rhode Island from the 1820s onward. The Irish were followed by a wave of migrants from French Canada, who began to appear in large numbers during and after the Civil War. At this time a small contingent of German Catholics also ventured to our state. Then came the great influx of "new" immigrants from southern and eastern Europe in the period from the 1880s until the discriminatory National Origins Quota System was established in 1924. The largest group of "new" immigrants were the Italians, followed by the Portuguese and the Poles; but smaller numbers of Catholic Lithuanians, Ukrainians, Syrians, and Lebanese gave our diocese a remarkable ethnic diversity.

The church of Providence responded to the challenge of the immigrant in many ways. It established national parishes, recruited ethnic clergy, founded schools, and created social agencies to deal with the spiritual and physical needs of the new arrivals.

The quota system, economic depression, and global war put a damper on immigration from the decade of the 1920s to the decade of the 1960s. Then an upturn in the economy and the ending of the National Origins Quota System by the Immigration and Nationality Act of 1965 brought an upturn in non-Western Hemisphere migration to Rhode Island, especially from Portugal and her island possessions. The recent Portuguese migrants have at least one advantage: they can join a community of fellow ethnics who are well established in Rhode Island and whose roots extend back for approximately a century.

There is another major contingent of recent immigrants, however, who can partake of no such tradition; they are new in every sense of the word. This group consists of Spanish-speaking people from the various nations of Latin America. These newest immigrants are the subject of this essay.

By far the biggest organizational problem in writing an analysis of the Latin American community in Rhode Island is that this "community" is really composed of several different Hispanic nationalities that are often quite different from one another. We have worked on the assumption that Latins come by and large from the same cultural and religious milieu. Since most of these new immigrants have arrived here in Rhode Island in the relatively recent past and have faced similar problems, there are enough similarities in their experience to justify discussing them within the same topical framework. We will endeavor, however, to emphasize the differences between various Latin groups where appropriate.

The history of the Latin American community in Rhode Island is indeed a brief one, for the great majority of Latin people have come to Rhode Island since 1960. This is ironic, since the Immigration Act of 1965 imposed for the first time a limit of 120,000 persons a year who could immigrate to the United States from the independent and self-governing nations of the Western Hemisphere.

The first evidence of increasing Latin migration occurred in the late fifties. At that time a substantial number of Puerto Ricans arrived in the state as migrant farmhands. They worked at nurseries in South County, Barrington, and in the Newport area. Most stayed only temporarily, laboring from April to September before returning to Puerto Rico, but some remained, brought their families, and settled down to work in local factories. Unlike other Latins, the Puerto Ricans are United States citizens and therefore are not subject to numerical immigration restrictions.

The number and impact of these early migrants upon Rhode Island was quite small. In 1957 the director of Spanish Catholic Action for the Archdiocese of New York sent a letter to the chancery of the Diocese of Providence stating that a conference would be held in New York concerning the Puerto Rican migrants. He invited the Providence diocese to send a representative to this conclave, but the invitation was declined; "there do not seem to be enough of them here to merit our sending a representative" was the local chancery's response. In the 1960 federal census for Rhode Island, Puerto Ricans did not receive special listing, presumably because their numbers still did not warrant such notice. The decade of the sixties, however, was marked by a significant migration of Puerto Ricans to our state. The census of 1970 revealed that 1,435 were residing here, of whom 877 were born on the island.

An upswing in immigration from other areas of Latin America also occurred in the period from 1960 to 1970, as table 1 shows. Statistics from the 1970 census for Brazil and Argentina have not been included in this tabulation. Many of the 791 Brazilians in Rhode Island are of Portuguese extraction, while a number of those persons of Argentinean stock resident here are neither recent arrivals nor of Spanish ancestry.

TABLE I

Foreign Stock from Latin America Resident in Rhode Island

Country	Census of 1960	Census of 1970
Mexico	115	407
Central America	109	214
Cuba	157	516
Jamaica	53	89
Dominican Republic	4	92
Other West Indies	247	394
Colombia	23	448
Venezuela	11	21
Ecuador	0	55
Peru	8	55
Bolivia	0	42
Chile	28	92
Uruguay	0	114

This cold and impersonal data does not really give an accurate picture of the size of the Spanish population in 1974. First of all, with such a rapid increase in that population between 1960 and 1970, it is obvious that figures can become quickly dated. Furthermore, the official statistics seem to be inaccurate. The Census Bureau itself has admitted that it probably undercounted those here, and there are some inconsistencies in the census data. For example, the 1970 tabulation lists 6,961 "persons of Spanish language" in Rhode Island, but this figure is nearly double the combined Puerto Rican population of 1,435 and the 2,539 foreign-stock Latins from the countries listed in the table.

There are several reasons why these statistical discrepancies might have occurred. One factor is the language differential. People interviewed who did not understand English could have become confused and given inaccurate information. A second factor is the great mobility of these Latin groups; many, particularly Puerto Ricans, return periodically to their homeland. A third and crucial reason why the census figures are inaccurate is that many Spanish-speaking people are here without the proper immigration papers. This is a problem of national concern (as many as four million such people are estimated to be in the country now), and its effect has been felt in Rhode Island. Apparently many Latin Americans come to the state with a visitor's permit and then settle and secure employment without getting the necessary labor-certification papers from the Department of Immigration.

Thus it is almost impossible to get a precise fix on the size of the Latin American population of Rhode Island. Perhaps the only way to obtain a reasonably accurate description of this heterogeneous group is to rely on the observations of those associated with the Latin community. Such informal sources as the Reverend Raymond Tetreault, director of the Latin American Apostolate for the Diocese of Providence, Mrs. Mercedes Messier, executive director of the Latin American Community Center, and Dr. Alfredo Incera, president of the Cuban Club of Rhode Island, believe that it ranges between 8,000 and 10,000 people.

The most noteworthy characteristic of our Latin American population is its diversity, both in nationality and in area of settlement. There is no one place that houses a majority of Latin Americans; every major city of the state contains some Hispanics. The largest groups, however, are from Puerto Rico, Cuba, Colombia, and Mexico. The Colombians are principally located in the Blackstone Valley communities of Pawtucket, Central Falls, and Cumberland, but some also live in West Warwick. Those from the Dominican Republic live primarily in the South Providence, West End, and Smith Hill areas of Providence. The Puerto Ricans are scattered throughout Providence, Pawtucket, and West Warwick, and the Mexicans also seem to be widely dispersed. The Cubans are located predominately in Providence; a few live on the East Side, but most live either on Smith Hill or in the West Elmwood section.

The specific reasons why these people have come to Rhode Island over the last decade are almost as diverse as the number of people here, but there are many similarities in the reasons for their migration. The exception is the Cuban community. Unlike most Latin Americans who have been drawn to the United States by hopes of economic betterment, Cubans are more like refugees, driven from their homeland by what they regarded as intolerable living conditions after the establishment of the Fidel Castro regime. Virtually all Cubans coming to Rhode Island since 1960 who were interviewed for this study emphasized their negative reaction to Communist rule as the principal reason for their departure from Cuba; seldom did they mention any specific attractions for this state.

One major reason for their exodus seems to have been an inability to "integrate into the revolution"; that is, a failure to make the necessary changes in life-style that would have required accepting a whole new order of social, political, and religious values. Once the Castro regime took power, it was very difficult to stand aside and not participate; one was for the revolution or against it. The citizenry were required to work the cane fields periodically or join the militia. For several, such requirements were simply intolerable violations of individual rights, and they left. For others, the Communist character of the new regime was enough to cause their departure. One Cuban exile who arrived in Rhode Island in 1961 stated that he left Cuba because of "militarism, Communist leanings of the government, and an oppressive atmosphere." More particularly, he objected to compulsory militia service.

Economic deprivation was another important motive for emigration from Cuba. Some successful businessmen left after Castro confiscated their property. One fled after his upholstery business was seized. Others left not because of any direct loss of property but because they were suffering from a declining standard of living under Castro. The Garcia family, who arrived in Rhode Island in 1966, complained that Castro had set quotas on foodstuffs; citizens were allowed to buy only four ounces of meat per person per week, and only two ounces of coffee per person per week. Reluctantly, they left in order to "earn a living without wondering where the next meal is coming from."

Of the tens of thousands of Cuban refugees, only about five to six hundred have come to this state. Probably the basic reason for their presence in Rhode Island is that they knew someone who was already a resident. The Garcias, for example, came because a sister had lived here since 1958. Another early arrival, Joe Egozi, who came in 1963, chose Rhode Island because "family friends from Cuba, the Barrocas family, lived here."

The conditions of migration for other Hispanic peoples have not been political, but rather economic. Puerto Rico has had a sizable migration to the United States since the 1940s. Between 1946 and 1960 an average of 41,500 more people left the island than returned each year. This figure dipped in the early sixties, but it increased again in the latter part of the decade, with net emigration to the mainland reaching 34,500 in 1967. The development of this migration has much to do with the program established by Luis Marin's Popular Democratic party after it gained power in 1940. Until then, Puerto Rico had been a miserably poor area; in 1940 per capita income was $121 a year, 17 percent of the labor force was unemployed, and an even greater percentage was underemployed.

Marin gained power on the strength of a platform whose primary focus was modernization of the economy to overcome the abject poverty on the island. In 1940 he began "Operation Bootstrap," a program that was intended to help industrialize the economy of Puerto Rico. His government encouraged industrial growth by building roads and electrical plants, and through a system of long-term tax exemptions for certain businesses. This program was generally successful in modernizing Puerto Rico. Per capita income increased to $1,047 by 1967, and health care had improved to the point that the life expectancy was seventy years, the same as in the United States.

However, such an economic plan was not without its costs. The emphasis on industrialization led to large-scale increases in the urban population, and the improved health services meant a further population increase. As a result, there simply were not enough jobs for the people, and many found it necessary to leave the island to find work. Migration was facilitated by Puerto Rico's improved communication and transportation facilities. San Juan Airport became one of the largest in the Western Hemisphere, and it was possible to travel by plane to New York in 1950 for less than one hundred dollars.

By 1953 the island had twenty-five radio stations and two television stations. Word from the United States was easier to get than ever before. More and more people were becoming aware of the post-World War II boom in the American economy and the need for labor here. Emigration provided its own momentum. Once some settled successfully on the mainland, it was far easier for others to follow. Moreover, there was no sense of finality about coming to the mainland; since Puerto Rico was an American possession, its people could come here free from immigration restrictions, and if things did not work out, the trip back to Puerto Rico was quick and uncomplicated. Finally, it should be emphasized that those who came to the mainland were not just those who could not find work in Puerto Rico. On the contrary, most who left had skills and industrial jobs in their homeland. They migrated because of increased expectations; they had improved their lot, but not enough to be satisfied, and they came to the mainland hoping to progress more rapidly here.

The experience in the Dominican Republic is a sadder story. The country is still only beginning a modernization program like Marin's, and it is one of the poorest nations in the Western Hemisphere. Nearly 50 percent of the rural population of the country is unemployed. Many Dominicans have migrated to the United States because the situation seems so hopeless in their homeland.

Most of those who leave Puerto Rico or the Dominican Republic travel to major cities along the East Coast. New York is the principal magnet, but Newark, Philadelphia, and Boston attract their share. Overall, the extent of direct migration to Rhode Island from the Caribbean has been fairly small.

Since Puerto Ricans are United States citizens and not technically immigrants, there are no official records kept on their migration. However, an organization called Catholic Aid to Puerto Rican Emigrants asked Puerto Ricans leaving San Juan Airport to fill out a questionnaire which, among other things, asked for the individual's destination. This group believed that its form reached about one-third of those leaving every year. The statistics are shown in table 2. Unfortunately the organization ceased functioning in 1970, and no further statistics are available. It would be interesting to see if the trend developing in the late sixties has continued. The reason for the increased migration to Rhode Island in recent years is hard to pinpoint. Word of mouth undoubtedly was a factor; once some newcomers arrived and successfully found employment, they were likely to tell friends and relatives at home to join them.

TABLE 2

Puerto Ricans Leaving San Juan Airport for Providence

Year	Number Interviewed	Those Bound for Providence
1958	19,555	23
1959	15,887	11
1963	12,710	2
1964	18,622	3
1965	16,404	2
1966	20,588	3
1967	25,376	14
1968	26,782	30
1969	27,982	35
1970	27,092	66
Total	210,998	189

This pattern seems applicable to the Dominican migration as well. Most members of this group come from the Santo Domingo area. They were out of work or wanted a better job, and they either heard rumors of job opportunities here or knew someone who was working in Providence.

Active recruitment of labor by local factories has also accounted for some Hispanic migration to Rhode Island. Arturo Gonsalves, a Puerto Rican who is presently living in the West Broadway section of Providence, explained that this is what brought him to the state. He had lived in New York for nine years beginning in 1960, but conditions became so bad that he returned to Puerto Rico. He could not find employment there, but he was told at the employment office that there was a job opening to work in a spinning mill in West Warwick, Rhode Island. When he accepted, the mill loaned him money to finance his trip and lodged him and his wife in a hotel for three days until he could find his own residence.

Recruitment by industry also accounts for the large Colombian population in the state. Although Colombia has not sent nearly as many people to the United States overall as Puerto Rico has, many who have come have settled in Rhode Island because they were actively sought by Rhode Island businessmen, particularly for work in the textile industry. Jay Guittari, personnel manager of the Lyon Fabrics Company of Central Falls, observes that several hundred Colombian weavers and loom fixers have been brought into the country since 1966. Most of them come from Medellin and Baranquilla, two coastal towns that have many large weaving factories. The people who left hoped for economic advancement; the jobs offered here pay better than the ones in their native Colombia. Again, once the migration begins and word gets around, others seeking new opportunity are likely to follow.

It is probable that immigration prompted by job recruitment will decrease in the future. In order for aliens to come to the United States to work, the secretary of labor must certify that there are no adequate workers available in the United States. Local mill owners claim that there is indeed a shortage of workers, but a local official of the Division of Immigration Certification in the Department of Labor disagrees. He believes that "things can be done to make the [textile] jobs more attractive to the mass of unemployed [natives], such as improving working conditions and giving higher wages." To promote jobs for those unemployed already here, he is discouraging the hiring of immigrant labor by reducing the number of work-certification permits granted. This will not stop legal immigration from Latin American countries, since immigrants here are entitled to bring in close relatives without work certification, but immigration for employment purposes may be reduced.

Besides direct migration from abroad, much of the state's Hispanic population, particularly among Puerto Ricans and Dominicans, has come from large cities in the Northeast where living conditions have become increasingly unbearable. Both Arturo Gonsalves and Artuso Liz, former president of the Latin American Community Center and a Dominican who had first settled in New York for eight years before coming here in 1970, cited over-crowding and crime as reasons for their departure from New York City. Providence was attractive to them because it seemed rela-tively small, uncrowded, and quiet.

Most Hispanics who have come to Rhode Island regard living here as a step up the socioeconomic ladder. Compared to what they left, Rhode Island is a "paradise," as Mrs. Peter Nazario called it. Nevertheless, most Latin Americans have faced severe prob-lems in trying to adjust to their new home, for they have found themselves in a world that is alien in language and culture.

Often their unfamiliarity with American customs, coupled with the language barrier, resulted in their exploitation by unscrupulous natives. One documented case described the experience of a His-panic living in Providence who could not read English. He went to a furniture store to buy a parlor set, and upon choosing one to his liking, he was given a contract to sign indicating purchase of the set. But the contract contained the serial number of an inferior set, and this was the one he received. Very often also, as with immi-grants of earlier times, Hispanics have been victimized by mem-bers of their own group who have been here awhile and "know the ropes."

Ignorance of the language has often led Latins to accept infe-rior housing without complaint. They did not know that they should not be paying $130 a month for a run-down four-room apartment on Constitution Street in Providence. They did not know that housing codes existed that required landlords to do something if mice kept scurrying through the house or if the plumbing would not work.

There are many other rights and privileges the average American takes for granted that newer arrivals have not asserted. Most of these recent immigrants were unaware of when and how they were entitled to unemployment or disability compensation. Though few were on welfare, many who were eligible did not apply because the language barrier made it impossible for them to communicate with the proper officials.

One of the most common and difficult problems confronting

many new immigrants has been that of obtaining a driver's license. Applicants have had to identify traffic signs and explain their meaning in English. Unable to pass that requirement, several purchased bootleg licenses at costs of up to two hundred dollars.

The language barrier has also limited the types of jobs available to the newcomers. The great majority found themselves working in textile mills or jewelry plants, making between $1.60 and $3.00 per hour. Although for most this was an improvement over the situation they faced in their home country, a great many have still been compelled to work two jobs and toil fifteen hours a day to make ends meet.

Discrimination has often complicated problems created by the language barrier. As a result, Hispanics have found apartments "already rented" upon inspection. Artuso Liz claimed he was discriminated against in trying to find a job in the construction field. He could not gain admittance to a union and was unable to get a job without being a union member.

Before 1970, Hispanic immigrants were in a cultural and religious wilderness. Although they came from overwhelmingly Catholic countries, there were no Spanish priests in Rhode Island to satisfy their spiritual needs prior to 1970. Moreover, since there was no organized place for Latins to meet, there was little opportunity for these transplanted people to express themselves culturally.

The family is also undergoing strain in this new environment. In Latin America the family had always been a close-knit unit. Parents were usually obeyed, respected, and cared for in their old age. Families were also patriarchal; the father was dominant. Here, with both parents working long hours, problems arose. Working women now have a degree of independence not enjoyed in Latin America, and many husbands are deprived of their traditional role when this newfound independence is asserted. With parents working, children naturally have had less direction, and after being exposed to the freedom enjoyed by American children, especially adolescents, they too have assumed a degree of independence that Hispanic parents do not appreciate.

Compounding these varied and difficult problems of adjustment was the fact that Hispanics had few places to turn for help. Before

1970 the only institution available with personnel that could speak Spanish was the International Institute in Providence. This organization had been founded in 1921 as a social agency designed to aid all immigrants regardless of nationality. It helps to find jobs and homes, assists in filling out immigration papers, and provides information on citizenship requirements.

The institute was particularly helpful to Cuban refugees who came in the early sixties. It worked with the leadership in the Cuban community to sponsor meetings and helped the Cubans organize a celebration of Cuban Independence Day (May 20, 1898) beginning in 1963. Today the International Institute continues to provide its services to Hispanics of all nationalities who wish to take advantage of them. Presently, in 1974, 160 cases are being handled by this organization.

But although the institute provides such help, it alone can not meet the pressing need of the Hispanic people. After all, it has other immigrant groups to deal with, some of which, like the Portuguese, are much larger in number than the Hispanics. Moreover, according to Raymond O'Dowd, its director, the institute does not wish to intrude itself into Latin American affairs. According to O'Dowd, "Our purpose is service, not advocacy. We want to help Latins as well as other immigrants to help themselves. We will gladly cooperate with them, but we want them to come to us first." Except for the Cubans, however, who have several lawyers, teachers, doctors, and other professionals willing to exert leadership, and who quickly took advantage of the International Institute's services, other Hispanic groups have not turned to the institute as readily.

Thus one of the basic problems facing Hispanics during the decade of the sixties had been that the "community" had no center, no focus, where interested Hispanics could get or give help. The Diocese of Providence became increasingly aware of this situation as it witnessed the predominantly Catholic Spanish-speaking "community" growing rapidly, and it had certain advantages in trying to deal with the new Latin American immigrants to Rhode Island.

This lack of a service agency had been a concern of the Catholic Church in New York since the heavy influx of Puerto Ricans in the fifties, and much had been discussed and written about their situation. In 1955 the New York archdiocese had made an intensive study of Puerto Rican migration and had formulated some solutions to meet the needs of these arrivals. Many observations made in that study were now applicable to the situation developing in Rhode Island. As Father Joseph Fitzpatrick, a leading sociologist, has noted, "In Catholic life, the immigrant community was centered on the national parish. It seems doubtful that the immigrant would have kept the faith, had he not had the constant support of his own people in this type of community which more or less reproduced in the United States the little village from which he and his people had come." But, Fitzpatrick went on to add, "One of the great difficulties that faces the Puerto Ricans in their adjustment to the culture of the mainland is the fact that for various reasons, they may not have an opportunity to develop as a community.... Thus, a much greater effort must be made to accept the Puerto Rican into parish life."

On a more practical level, the Church was aware that it must respond actively to the social as well as the religious needs of these immigrants or lose them to Protestant denominations. Protestant sects had made inroads into the Hispanic population of New York because they stressed social and cultural action and provided the Latin American immigrants with hospitals, clinics, and schools. Catholic leaders also felt that unless vigorous steps were taken, it was likely that the materialism of American society would have a corrupting influence on the new Hispanic migrants, especially the young.

In response to all of these factors, the Providence diocese undertook a program of special assistance to Spanish-speaking people. On June 10, 1970, Bishop Russell McVinney appointed the Reverend Raymond Tetreault the director of the newly created Latin American Apostolate in the Diocese of Providence.

Father Tetreault's job, as the bishop described it, was to serve "Spanish-speaking people who for reasons of language or cultural identity are not able to be served through existing parishes of the Diocese." The apostolate became a member agency of the Catholic Charity Fund Appeal and received $17,500 to operate in 1971. In addition, the diocese brought a dwelling at 3 Harvard Avenue, Providence, for $8,200 in September 1970 for use as a Latin American community center. However, the diocese did not see itself as having any long-term involvement in this project; the center was to be a secular organization funded by the Urban Emergency Fund.

Both the apostolate and the community center set about the task of integrating the Latin people into the community at large. The center's goal was to give "this ethnic group a sense of purpose and community organization it presently lacks." On a more practical level, it attempted to be an immediate source of help to those many Hispanics suffering from the problems of transplantation by providing information and counseling and by furnishing a place that would allow Hispanics to maintain contact with their own culture.

To achieve these ends, the Latin American Community Center established a whole series of programs. It tackled the most immediate problem facing the Hispanic immigrant by conducting language classes. To help overcome difficulties in housing and employment, the center provided information in Spanish about rights and obligations under the Social Security system, about how to obtain small business loans, FHA loans, or low-interest loans for repairing housing in Model Cities areas, and about housing codes and regulations. In an attempt to reach the widest possible audience with such information, Mercedes Messier, executive director of the center, arranged to have a weekly program broadcast in Spanish over WLKW in Providence beginning in June 1972. A televised version was later begun over Providence's WSBE-TV, Channel 36.

To promote cultural unity, and hopefully to bring all Hispanics in the community together, the diocese has sponsored shows periodically at Bishop McVinney Auditorium. Occasionally these take the form of talent contests, with Dominicans, Puerto Ricans, Colombians, and other Latin American groups competing against each other. Last year the Latin American Community Center helped sponsor a large party at the Biltmore Hotel, which was well attended by various segments of the Hispanic community.

The center has also worked to improve the educational opportunities for Spanish–speaking children. As late as 1970, Rhode

Island schools were not prepared to deal with these children. Most often Latin American youngsters were simply given a crash course in English and then placed in regular classrooms with English-speaking pupils. Most fell behind, became discouraged, and left school as soon as they reached sixteen. In 1970 Artuso Liz, the first president of the Latin American Community Center, asked superintendent of Providence schools Richard Briggs to use his influence to remedy this situation. Dr. Briggs agreed, and a bilingual program was set up for Spanish-speaking children in the Providence schools. Other municipalities followed this example, and by mid–1972 ten Rhode Island communities had bilingual programs for Spanish- and Portuguese-speaking children.

Other secular agencies have developed in the last few years to render assistance to the Hispanics, especially with their language and citizenship problems. By 1972 eleven communities were conducting Americanization classes, teaching immigrants English, and preparing them for citizenship with courses in civics. Numerous other organizations have also provided language courses for Spanish-speaking people to learn English. One of these is Project Persona, which holds classes two evenings a week at the Elmwood branch of the Providence Public Library. This project also makes tapes of lessons so that people who work and cannot attend classes will be able to study at home.

Another very useful development has been the opening of the Latin American Medical Clinic on Broad Street in Providence. At its inception the clinic was operated by three doctors, one Cuban and two Colombians, each of whom devoted twenty hours a week to patient care at this agency. Now many Hispanics with medical problems, who had suffered because of their inability to communicate in English, can be helped by someone who can speak their own language and understand their needs.

Finally, the Latin American Apostolate of the diocese has worked diligently to maintain a strong religious sense among Hispanics. However, Father Tetreault believes that the apostolate has more than a purely religious function; he has stated that it should also help in the "social adjustment of Spanish-speaking immigrants to their new environment." In accord with this philosophy,

337

the Catholic Charities Office has given the apostolate money to carry on the following religious and social programs:

(1) Mass is said in Spanish every week at St. Michael's Church in Providence, St. Edward's in Pawtucket, and Holy Trinity in Central Falls. Special religious celebrations, using films, songs, scripture, and catechesis, are held during Christmas and Holy Week.

(2) Marriage counseling is given to Spanish-speaking young couples.

(3) Teenage Formation Groups have been established to "help teenagers grow in their faith, considering difficulties of sudden exposure to American youth culture."

(4) Catechetical programs are conducted by Sister Veronica Huerta, a Carmelite nun, who visits Hispanic families to instruct children and adults in their religion.

One can see that much has been done in the last few years to help the newly arrived Latin Americans adjust to living in Rhode Island. But how successful have these programs been? Do Hispanics take advantage of them? Is real progress being made toward an integrated society in which Hispanics understand and respect their new adopted culture while maintaining their identity as Latin Americans? Of course, the subjective nature of these questions makes it impossible to answer them with certitude; and how one answers them depends largely on one's frame of reference.

For very many Hispanics, Rhode Island is better than anything they have ever experienced. Moreover, there is considerable objective evidence suggesting that advances toward adjustment are being made. No doubt the efforts of the groups described above have made the plight of the Hispanic less difficult. Many concrete improvements have been implemented. Any Hispanic who wants to learn English can do so. The development of bilingualism in the schools should prove especially fruitful. The newest educational programs properly emphasize both the importance of integration into

American society and the maintenance of cherished Latin American cultural traditions.

In Providence, for example, Spanish students are placed in classrooms with an equal number of English-speaking students. The Spanish-speaking children are taught their subjects in Spanish; the others in English. Then, for one period a day, the children switch languages and study the other group's language and culture. The idea, says Grace Glynn, chief of academic services in the state Department of Education, is to give the Hispanic students "a sense that their language is a good language and their culture is a good culture, and it teaches the American students to understand their new neighbors."

Perhaps another indicator that Hispanics are beginning to integrate into American society is their willingness to adopt American entrepreneurial techniques. Small businesses are developing quite rapidly in areas where Hispanics live. Despite the relatively small population of Hispanics and the newness of their arrival, there are now several Latin American businesses located on Broad Street in Providence, including two grocery stores, two restaurants, and one record shop. Douglas Avenue, also in Providence, has two Hispanic businesses, and several more are located on Providence's Daboll Street and Cranston Street, and in Central Falls as well. These new immigrants are displaying an extremely strong entrepreneurial drive that bodes well for their upward socioeconomic mobility.

Another factor that has facilitated the adjustment of Latin Americans into the Rhode Island community is that more and more Hispanics are migrating here from other parts of the United States rather than directly from abroad. Considering the present policies of the Immigration Bureau, this trend is likely to continue. Many of those coming from elsewhere in America have already completed the most difficult part of the adjustment to life in the United States, and they know enough English to take care of themselves. There is also evidence that more Hispanics are buying their own homes, and that respect and care for property generally has a high priority among them.

Among the Hispanics, the most successful adjustment to life in the United States has been achieved by Cubans. A majority of the Cuban residents in Rhode Island come from the upper and middle classes, and they had such American goods as refrigerators, televisions, and dishwashers in their home country. Indeed, some Cuban refugees, especially young people, were deeply resentful when Americans asked them questions like "How does it feel to own a pair of shoes now?" Reacting to that, one young Cuban noted that "one of the things we miss most is that we had a much better life in Cuba than we have here. We were not rich, but we had three maids in our house."

Moreover, most of these Cubans were strongly attached to the traditional American values of capitalism and individualism; in fact, this is why most left Cuba. They also have the middle-class American's reverence for education, and few drop out of school.

Cubans have shown a deep affection for their traditional culture and a strong community spirit. There has been an active Cuban Club in Rhode Island since 1967. The club does not have a fixed meeting place, but members take turns holding meetings in their homes. Parties and picnics, with Cuban food and music, are held five or six times a year. A typical Christmas party, for instance, might have a traditional Cuban meal of roast pig, black beans, and rice.

Despite these encouraging signs of adjustment, especially within the Cuban community, Rhode Island's newest wave of immigrants is faced with some serious problems. For example, despite development of the English as a Second Language program, Spanish children still drop out of school at a much higher rate than native American children. In Central Falls, with its sizable Colombian population, there were three hundred immigrants in school last year (1973), but only one was in the tenth grade and none were in the eleventh or twelfth.

In addition, probably less than 50 percent of the Hispanics in the state are taking citizenship courses or courses to learn English. There are a variety of reasons for this neglect. For those who work long hours each week, the prospect of nighttime study is obviously not very inviting. Further, many Hispanics do not feel the need for such instruction, for they see themselves as temporary residents who will return home and live prosperously with the money they earn in the United States. In this respect they are similar to some earlier Italian and Portuguese visitors to our shores. Even many of those who intend to stay see no urgent need to learn much about American ways. They spend all day in factories working with other Hispanics, talk Spanish at home, and can even do some of their shopping in Spanish stores.

Finally, many Hispanics are wary of structured organizations, or they are distrustful of asking institutions for help because of bad experiences in their former homeland. For example, Dominicans who lived through the Trujillo era often suffer from a "psychology of conspiracy" and are very hesitant to trust impersonal authority. This attitude is similar to that held by many nineteenth-century Irish immigrants to Rhode Island because of their experiences with British misrule.

Another distressing point is that the effort of the Roman Catholic Latin American Apostolate does not appear strikingly productive, at least in quantitative terms. Attendance at Spanish Masses at St. Michael's Church varies between thirty and seventy-five, and at St. Edward's from twenty to one hundred. If there are eight to ten thousand Hispanics in the state, as community leaders claim, then only 2 percent are attending these Masses. Again, bad experiences in the homeland may account for such limited participation. In most Latin countries, where there might be one priest for eight thousand people, many Catholics were obviously too remote from a parish to attend regularly. Moreover, in places like the Dominican Republic and Colombia, anticlericalism is strong. People often associate the Church with the rich and powerful elements of the country. In the Dominican Republic the hierarchy supported Trujillo but denounced Juan Bosch, who was regarded as a savior to many poorer Dominicans. Indeed, clerical opposition contributed to Bosch's overthrow, an event that for many discredited the Church. In Colombia the Church has suspended many activist priests who had sought to improve the lot of the downtrodden, and this action obviously lost Catholicism some adherents among the poorer elements in the population.

To offset this lack of devotional attachment to Catholicism and better provide for the social needs of this new immigrant group, the Latin American Apostolate has been gradually expanded. Father Xavier Rogo has served the Hispanics of St. Michael's Parish for two years, and Father Larry Olszewski, C.S.C., began his ministry to the Hispanics in September 1973 at Holy Trinity in Central Falls, a parish in which the natives have shown an encouraging degree of cooperation with the local Colombians. Sisters Veronica Huerta and Delphine Napolatonio are also actively involved in the new apostolate. Other clergy who have contributed time and effort to caring for the spiritual and social needs of the Latins include Father Antonio Saez, who worked with the new Hispanic arrivals part-time from 1970 to 1973, and the Reverend John Rubba, O.P., a popular professor of Spanish at Providence College, whose varied social projects have brought credit to him and to the Dominican Order.

When queried, Father Tetreault did not seem discouraged by the small number of Latin Americans attending Mass. He felt that the most pressing function of his apostolate was not to fill churches but to get people working together "to create a community alive in the spirit of Christ."

So again we come back to the theme of community. Unfortunately, however, it seems quite clear that no such sense of community presently exists among Spanish-speaking Americans. Indeed, evidence is substantial that factionalism and nationalistic feeling are seriously undermining community effort. Many have stated that the Latin American Community Center is unsuccessful; in the words of Judy Murphy of Project Persona, "It is not working at all." Presently the center is dominated by Dominicans, and other nationalities seldom use its facilities. Even Mercedes Messier, who, as noted above, was cheerfully optimistic about the successful community attendance at dances, admits that animosity exists between Dominicans and Puerto Ricans. Arturo Gonsalves also mentioned this rivalry. In referring to the Spanish-language radio program aired over radio station WRIB, he mentioned that several of his Puerto Rican countrymen would not listen to the program because they felt it was "being taken over by Dominicans."

Thus there seems to be a trend, for better or worse, for Hispanics to act and think not as one group but rather as members of separate and competing nationalities. The Dominicans have emulated the Cubans in founding a social club, and the Colombians and Puerto Ricans are forming their own organizations as well. In some important respects, therefore, the Latin American community that we set out to describe is not really a single community at all.

The one recent development that may work to alter this situation was the creation of the Congresso de Accion Hispaña, an umbrella organization that has been formed to coordinate the efforts of Rhode Island's various Latin American groups and societies. In some respects Accion Hispaña resembles other recently formed ethnic cultural federations like the Polonia Coordinating Committee of Rhode Island and the Rhode Island Federation of Italian-Americans, but it appears from the resolutions adopted at its June 1974 convention that its emphasis will be more on social reform than on cultural projects. This is a proper focus, however, in view of the newness and the socioeconomic status of the community that it represents. Perhaps by adhering to the maxim that "in unity there is strength," Rhode Island's Latin Americans, through the agency of Accion Hispaña, can hasten their inevitable upward socioeconomic mobility, exert political influence, and preserve their rich cultural and religious traditions.

In concluding, we want to stress that it is not our purpose, nor is it within our competence, to judge or evaluate the success of Latin Americans in adjusting to life in their adopted land. Our essay is merely a descriptive attempt to acquaint Rhode Islanders, and especially the Catholic community, with a new, important, and sizable immigrant group. Such acquaintance will hopefully produce a degree of understanding and respect for our Latin American neighbors that will prevent them from becoming "strangers in our midst." History shows that their experiences are similar to those encountered by earlier ethnic migrants to Rhode Island, and we are confident that they will respond as successfully to the challenges of adjustment as those immigrants who preceded them to our multiethnic state.

7

Catholicism

Local artist Robert Pailthorpe painted this watercolor of the Cathedral of SS. Peter and Paul in 1972 for the centennial observance of the founding of the Diocese of Providence.

This essay was written in 1984 as part of a historical guidebook
that I prepared in hopes that the Diocese of Providence
would make wide use of it. The pamphlet also contained a listing of
historic sites of Catholic interest. The diocese showed
little enthusiasm for the project.

THE DIOCESE OF PROVIDENCE (which is coterminous with the
state of Rhode Island) was created in 1872, but Catholics were a
factor in Rhode Island history long before that date. In 1524 Giovanni da Verrazzano, an Italian sailing in the employ of the king of
France, became the first European and the first Catholic to visit
Rhode Island, which he both explored and named. Rhode Island
was not colonized until 1636, however, and the original settlements
were made not by French Catholics but by English Baptists and
Antinomians seeking a haven where they could worship freely
under a system that separated church and state.

Catholics in English-dominated colonial Rhode Island were
rare, but a few have come to light, including Irish exile Charles
McCarthy, an incorporator of the town of East Greenwich, and
several prominent mid-eighteenth-century Portuguese merchants,
most notably James Lucena of Newport.

The state's first significant exposure to Catholicism came during
the American Revolution, when France came to aid America in its
struggle for political independence. The French presence was especially strong in Newport, the point of debarkation for the troops of
Count Rochambeau. When the war was over, a few Frenchmen
decided to remain and make Rhode Island their permanent resi-

dence. In the 1790s they were joined by a small band of French refugees from the wars of black liberation that were then convulsing the French West Indian islands. At this time also some discontented Irish migrated to Rhode Island to escape British religious, political, and economic oppression. These groups were the Catholic vanguard of Rhode Island. The baptismal register in Holy Cross Cathedral, Boston, reveals that they were visited periodically by priests from that city during the period from 1789 to 1828, most notably by Father Francis Matignon and Bishop Jean Cheverus. These dedicated and zealous French clerics baptized, preached, and said Mass in Newport, Portsmouth, Bristol, and Providence, each of which contained a tiny community of Catholics. In Providence the faithful secured the use of a building in the Fox Point section as the state's first Catholic church in 1813. The structure was destroyed by the Great Gale of 1815.

During the formative period 1789–1808, Rhode Island was under the jurisdiction of Bishop John Carroll of Baltimore. Carroll, the first American prelate, visited Rhode Island on at least one occasion. In 1808 several new dioceses were created, including one at Boston which had jurisdiction over all New England. Jean Cheverus became its first bishop, and Rhode Island was under his care.

Cheverus was succeeded in 1825 by Benedict J. Fenwick. It was Fenwick who dispatched Father Robert Woodley to Newport in 1828, where the young priest founded St. Mary's, the oldest permanent parish in Rhode Island. In 1829 the busy Woodley—whose mission territory included the states of Rhode Island and Connecticut in their entirety, plus southeastern Massachusetts—built the state's first Catholic church specifically constructed for that purpose at St. Mary's, Pawtucket.

When Woodley came to Rhode Island to establish a Catholic presence, Rhode Island's Roman Catholics numbered about six hundred out of a total state population of ninety-seven thousand, a mere six-tenths of 1 percent. The faithful served by Woodley in 1828 were concentrated in Newport, where they worked as laborers on Fort Adams; in Portsmouth, where they were employed as miners at the coal pits; and in Providence, Cranston, Pawtucket, and Woonsocket, where they served the needs of the growing factory system or were employed in such public works projects as the construction of the Blackstone Canal. Nearly all of them were Irish. In the 1830s, as the railroad came to Rhode Island, this Irish migration continued, and in the 1840s and 1850s, in the wake of Ireland's disastrous famine, it reached impressive proportions. By 1865 three out of every eight Rhode Islanders were of Irish stock, the state's Irish Catholic community numbered nearly fifty thousand, and pioneer missionary priests like the Reverend James Fitton had established twenty widely scattered parishes.

It was to accommodate this influx that the Diocese of Boston was subdivided and the Diocese of Hartford created in 1844. This new administrative entity included the states of Connecticut and Rhode Island. Its first bishop, the frail, devout William Tyler, was a Yankee convert from Protestantism. Although the see city of his new diocese was Hartford, Tyler decided to govern from Providence, which was a more prosperous community with a larger Catholic population. Thus in 1844 Rhode Island got its first resident Roman Catholic bishop. Tyler's successors adhered to the precedent that he established and made their cathedral at Providence's original church of SS. Peter and Paul.

During the decade of the 1840s, there were several notable developments that affected the Catholic community. One was the famous Dorr Rebellion, which occurred between 1841 and 1843 over an attempt to broaden democracy in Rhode Island and replace the antiquated royal charter of 1663 with a written state constitution. The opponents of political reformer Thomas Dorr were partly motivated by anti-Catholic prejudice and political nativism, themes that have often been ignored in discussing this colorful episode. Over the objections of Dorr, Rhode Island's state constitution of 1843 established a real estate requirement for foreign-born voters that was designed to discriminate against Irish Catholic immigrants.

Another event of importance was the John Gordon murder trial—the Sacco-Vanzetti case of the nineteenth century. This travesty of justice, which resulted in the hanging of a young Irish Catholic immigrant on the basis of circumstantial evidence, caused such misgiving that it contributed to the abolition of the death penalty in Rhode Island several years later. Another development in the 1840s was the beginning of the parochial school system of the diocese at crude and cramped facilities at St. Patrick's, Providence (1843), and the cathedral parish (1845).

Bishop Tyler was succeeded by Bernard O'Reilly (1850–56), called "Paddy the Priest" by some native Rhode Islanders. In 1851 this bold and strong-willed bishop brought the Sisters of Mercy to Providence, where they immediately founded St. Xavier's Academy for girls, the first Catholic secondary school in the state. Four years later, during the height of the Know-Nothing movement, O'Reilly personally defended the Mercy nuns from an anti-Catholic mob that had congregated at St. Xavier's Convent to "free" a young girl who had allegedly been confined therein. Returning from a clerical recruiting trip to Europe in 1856, O'Reilly perished at sea when his ship was lost in a North Atlantic storm. This pugnacious prelate was a man for the times who courageously resisted nativistic attacks upon his Church.

The last bishop of Hartford to preside over Rhode Island Catholicism was Francis Patrick McFarland, whose episcopacy coincided with the Civil War and Reconstruction years. This gentle and scholarly prelate's tenure was marked by the emergence of a Catholic presence in the social and political affairs of Rhode Island. McFarland's energy and learning built the first bridges to the non-Catholic community of the state, and his gestures mollified the virulent nativism that had dominated the 1840s and 1850s. In retrospect, his most significant single achievement was the establishment of LaSalle Academy (1871), later to become a diocesan boys' high school, with his choice of the Brothers of the Christian Schools to staff it.

By 1872 the Catholic population had grown so dramatically that the Diocese of Hartford was itself divided and the Diocese of Providence created. This new entity originally included not only Rhode Island but also southeastern Massachusetts. (In 1904 the Massachusetts portion was set off as the Diocese of Fall River under the leadership of Providence's Reverend William Stang.)

The prehistory of the Diocese of Providence in these formative years before 1872 contains a number of noteworthy themes. The

Church was a poor and struggling enterprise often dependent on aid from foreign mission societies. It was attempting to grow in a hostile environment of bigotry and nativism; it took genuine courage to be a practicing Catholic. These were lean, tough years, and they took their toll on the pioneer bishops: Tyler died at age forty-three, O'Reilly at fifty-two, and McFarland at fifty-five.

The other salient fact was the role of the lowly Irish immigrants in building the church of Providence. During the years prior to 1872, almost the only influences upon Rhode Island Catholicism had been those distinctive Irish traits that had given the local Catholic community a unity of religious outlook. The vast majority of clergy were either trained in Ireland or educated in American facsimiles of the Irish seminaries. The laity of Providence was also overwhelmingly Irish in origin and perspective. Irishness and Catholicism had fused and produced what was in reality an Irish national church.

A basic problem besetting the diocese during much of its first century was that of harmonizing and reconciling the intense Irish brand of Catholicism with the needs and attitudes of successive groups of Catholic immigrants, who found the Irish church significantly if not essentially different from their own. When social, cultural, linguistic, economic, and even political conflicts were added to the religious factor, the task confronting the multi-ethnic Diocese of Providence assumed formidable and challenging dimensions, as the course of its history would amply reveal.

The impact and contributions of other Catholic ethnic groups who migrated to Rhode Island in the late nineteenth and early twentieth centuries have made a rich mosaic of Rhode Island Catholicism. The larger communities included the devout French Canadians, who began their large-scale immigration during the Civil War years and came to form the backbone of the work force in what was then Rhode Island's major industry, textiles; the Portuguese, who came first as whalers and then in much larger numbers as factory hands, farmers, and maritime workers; the Italians, who came to dominate the state's jewelry and construction industries and brought the colorful religious pageantry of their homeland; and the Poles, who migrated from the turn of the century onward to work in the base-metal industries of Providence and the Blackstone Valley, where their staunch Catholicism, steady habits, and unique traditions made them an asset both to their Church and their adopted state.

Catholic ethnics who came to the diocese in much smaller yet culturally significant numbers during this era included Germans, Cape Verdeans, Lithuanians, Ukrainians, Syrians (Melkite Rite), and Lebanese (Maronite Rite). For each group the Old World background, the motives for migration, the areas of local settlement, and the nature of its Catholicism (customs, ritual, religious attitudes) were different, and this diversity occasionally generated controversy and tension within the Rhode Island Catholic community. But such conflict has now generally been resolved through such agencies as the national parish and such trends as ethnic intermarriage and the passing of the Old World generation.

Since the Church is not a democracy, and the bishop has considerable power and influence over the spiritual and ecclesiastical affairs of his diocese, some mention should be made of the thoughts, the policies, and the goals of the bishops of Providence. The first prelate of the diocese, Thomas F. Hendricken (1872–86), recruited in Ireland by Bishop O'Reilly, was a "brick and mortar" bishop, one concerned with establishing the physical presence of the Church. His principal project was the construction of the magnificent Cathedral of SS. Peter and Paul, to which he devoted many years of his administration. Ironically, he died on the eve of the cathedral's completion, and his funeral was the first event held in that elegant structure. Hendricken's "cathedral dream" was a manifestation of the spirit of devotion and self-sacrifice that characterized the faithful of his diocese.

Matthew Harkins (1887–1921) presided over the church of Providence for more than one-third of its first century. This dignified prelate was renowned for his administrative ability, for his tact in handling immigrant assimilation, for his efforts in the field of education (especially the founding of Providence College), and, perhaps above all, for the manner in which he extended the social and charitable apostolate of the Church. This "Bishop of the Poor," as he was sometimes called, found two diocesan social agencies when he came to Providence from the Boston archdiocese in 1887. When he died, there were about twenty such agencies, including St. Joseph's Hospital, St. Vincent de Paul Infant Asylum, Carter Day Nursery, Hospice St. Antoine, St. Francis Home, St. Margaret's and St. Maria's Homes for Working Girls, and the House of the Good Shepherd. They were his legacy to the poor and the socially deprived. Thanks to Harkins, the Diocese of Providence provided more social services than the state itself in the years prior to the New Deal. Harkins in fact performed so well that a visiting European priest in 1921 informed his superiors that "Providence is the pearl among the dioceses of the United States."

William Hickey became coadjutor bishop of Providence in 1919, when Harkins was in declining health, and ascended to the See of Providence in his own right when Harkins died in 1921. Of all the bishops of Providence, Hickey (1921–33) had the most complex character to analyze. A man of impulse who was quick to anger but also quick to forgive, he had authoritarian tendencies that were mingled with a simple love for children and a genuine concern for the educational and social needs of those entrusted to his care. One of his major efforts was to bring order and centralization to the affairs of the diocese. An example of such centralized coordination was Hickey's inauguration of the Catholic Charity Fund Appeal in 1927. Another such effort was his High School Fund Drive, which provided a tremendous boost to diocesan secondary education and resulted in the founding of Mount St. Charles Academy (Woonsocket), St. Raphael's Academy (Pawtucket), and the now defunct De La Salle Academy (Newport). Unfortunately, Hickey's centralization plans and his high-handed manner led to clashes with certain segments of the Franco-American community and furnished the background for the Sentinellist controversy of the 1920s, one of the most fascinating, turbulent, and difficult episodes in the history of Rhode Island Catholicism. The 1920s were also marked by schisms in the Polish and Ukrainian Catholic communities of the Blackstone Valley.

Hickey's successor, Francis P. Keough (1934–47), was a warm, kindly, and popular bishop who set about the tasks of healing the ill feelings engendered by the Sentinellist agitation and adjusting to the administrative changes wrought by his predecessors, Harkins and Hickey. For this reason Keough's episcopacy has been called "The Era of Conciliation and Consolidation." Keough, however, made some important innovations of his own, most notably the creation of the Catholic Youth Organization (1935), the establishment of Our Lady of Providence Seminary (1941) for the education of young men preparing for the priesthood, and the founding of Salve Regina College (1947). Keough also crusaded against obscenity in movies and in print. He served as national chairman of the Bishops' Committee of the National Organization for Decent Literature (Legion of Decency). His efforts in Rhode Island and nationally were evidently viewed with favor by his ecclesiastical superiors, for Keough was elevated to the archbishopric of the primal See of Baltimore in 1947.

After the departure of Keough, Russell J. McVinney (1948–71) assumed spiritual direction of the diocese—the only Rhode Island native to hold that post. During his episcopacy the Church made impressive material gains that attest to McVinney's administrative expertise. His tenure was a period in which Rhode Island Catholicism expanded its social role. As the immigrants began their slow but inexorable move up the socioeconomic ladder, the Church turned a sympathetic hand to the plight of the black community. These efforts, beginning with the establishment of the Catholic Interracial Council (1951) and the opening of the Martin de Porres Center (1954), were intensified by the civil rights revolution. By the mid-sixties the bishop, in conjunction with several zealous urban priests, had embarked upon a program of quiet social activism that extended beyond the confines of the Catholic community.

In the field of education, the Catholic school system achieved a new high in the number of schools and pupils by 1960, only to experience a precipitous decline during the next two decades owing to the convergence of many factors, including the exodus to suburbia, the decline in vocations, the advantage given to public education by government funding, and constitutional obstructions against public aid to Catholic education. Presently the condition of the elementary school system has stabilized, with the first enrollment increase in seventeen years recorded in 1980.

Bishop McVinney was confronted with the enormous challenge of presiding over the Church in an age of social, educational, liturgical, and attitudinal flux. Despite his basically traditional posture, he met this challenge extraordinarily well, and next to Matthew Harkins, McVinney ranks as the man who exerted the most significant and beneficial impact on Rhode Island Catholicism.

In 1972 Louis Gelineau assumed spiritual direction of the diocese. His motto, "Rejoice in Hope," appropriately reflected the feelings of the state's large Franco-American community. After 122 years of Irish American prelates, that community now had "one of its own." But Bishop Gelineau has been a bishop to all the faithful. In concert with popular Auxiliary Bishop Kenneth Angell, this episcopacy has been characterized by visibility and the personal touch, as well as by growth and sound administration.

Though it is proper to concentrate upon the bishops in this brief narrative because of the particular nature of hierarchical authority and influence, one should note that many other able clerics served as administrators in this diocese. Perhaps a dozen of these left Rhode Island to become bishops in their own right, such as Austin Dowling, archbishop of St. Paul; German-born William Stang, first bishop of Fall River; John Cardinal Dearden of Detroit, who was born and spent his boyhood in the Blackstone Valley; and Daniel P. Reilly, bishop first of Norwich, Connecticut, and then of the Diocese of Worcester. Monsignor Peter E. Blessing served with dignity and distinction as vicar general for a third of the present century while holding the pastorate of St. Michael's Church in South Providence when it was Rhode Island's largest Catholic parish.

The diocese produced or served as the workshop for other notable Catholic figures — nationally renowned scholars and writers like the Reverend Bernard O'Reilly, the Reverend John LaFarge, Monsignor John Sullivan, the Reverend Edward Flannery, the Reverend Thomas Cullen, and the Reverend John McLaughlin, S.J.; social reformers like the Reverend Charles Curran, the Reverend Anthony Robinson, and the Reverend Monsignor Edmund Brock; ethnic leaders such as Melkite Archimandrite Justin Najmy, Monsignors Anthony Bove, Camille

Villard, and Charles Dauray, and Fathers Anthony Serpa and Flaminio Parenti; and distinguished college-level educators such as Dominicans Joseph Robert Slavin, Lorenzo C. McCarthy, Vincent C. Dore, Raymond T. A. Collins, Joseph L. Lennon, Cornelius P. Forster, John P. Kenny, Thomas R. Peterson, and John Cunningham.

Women of Catholic religious orders have worked effectively in the fields of education, health care, and social service since the arrival of Mother Mary Frances Xavier Warde and her Mercy Order in 1851. During the nineteenth and early twentieth centuries, members of Catholic religious communities were directing hospitals, schools, and various social service agencies. This social apostolate has continued despite the recent decline in religious vocations, although it sometimes assumed new forms in the years since Vatican II.

The laity has also played a significant role in the development of Rhode Island Catholicism. Lay organizations, particularly the St. Vincent de Paul Society, the Knights of Columbus, and the Daughters of Isabella, have been important. So also have prominent Catholic laymen such as inventor, industrialist, and philanthropist Joseph Banigan (1840–99), the diocese's greatest benefactor, and those pioneer political leaders who paved the way for the advancement of their coreligionists in public life. Notable among these Catholic statesmen were Charles E. Gorman (first Catholic legislator, 1870, and Speaker of the House, 1887); Edwin D. McGuinness (first Catholic general officer as secretary of state, 1887, and first Catholic mayor of Providence, 1896–98); James H. Higgins (first Irish Catholic governor, 1907–8); Aram J. Pothier (first Franco-American governor, 1909–15, 1925–28); George F. O'Shaunessy (U.S. congressman, 1911–19); Felix Hebert (U.S. senator, 1929–35); and John O. Pastore (the nation's first elected Italian American governor, 1945–50, and its first U.S. senator, 1950–76, of Italian American stock).

Of the twelve Rhode Island governors who have served in the period from 1937 to the publication of this guide in 1984, nine have been Roman Catholics with close ties to their Church and diocese. Of the thirteen lieutenant governors since that date, twelve have been Catholic, as have five of the six secretaries of state, seven of the nine attorneys general, eight of the nine U.S. congressmen, all four chief justices—and the list goes on.

Today, with Catholics constituting nearly 65 percent of Rhode Island's population, the highest such percentage of any of the fifty states, the Church and its adherents are very influential in all areas of Rhode Island life. But despite the growth and strength of this diocese, challenges abound. In 1983 its oldest secondary school, St. Xavier's, was compelled by financial and other pressures to close its Providence facility and relocate on a smaller scale in Coventry. In 1984 two other girls' schools, St. Mary's Academy of the Visitation (Providence) and St. Patrick's High (North Providence), were merged with LaSalle Academy as an economy move after much public debate.

Other problems of considerable magnitude have also been addressed. The rapid expansion of the Hispanic population and the recent influx of Southeast Asians (many of whom are Catholic because of French missionary work in the former French Indochina) have necessitated the renewal of the Church's apostolate to the immigrant, while the abortion controversy has evoked a vigorous effort from Catholics for Life and other pro-life organizations. A decline in vocations to the priesthood and religious life has been alleviated by the rise of a dedicated diaconate.

Though the challenges are many, the responses of the diocese have generally been prompt and effective. What was said in 1921 by that observant European cleric appears no less true today: Providence remains a pearl among the dioceses of the United States.

Matthew Harkins presided over the Catholic Church in Rhode Island from 1887 to 1921, longer than any other bishop.

Bishop Matthew Harkins: A Study in Character

This essay, on the character of Bishop Harkins and his career as an administrator, and the following essay, on the bishop's social apostolate, were written in 1978 for the projected second volume of my history of Rhode Island Catholicism. A third essay, detailing Harkins's educational achievements, including the founding of Providence College, has already been published as "Matthew Harkins: Catholic Bishop and Educator" in *Rhode Island History* 53 (August 1995).

THE DEATH OF PROVIDENCE'S BISHOP Thomas F. Hendricken on June 11, 1886, created a void in the Archdiocese of Boston that Archbishop John Williams moved to fill. On July 8 he convened a meeting of the suffragens of the province to nominate a successor to the vacancy, which was under the temporary administration of the vicar general, the Very Reverend Michael McCabe of St. Charles, Woonsocket. When the bishops assembled, several clerics were discussed, but the first three candidates suggested were rejected for being "too old," "in poor health," and "unfit."

Bishop James A. Healy of the Diocese of Portland, Maine, then made his presence felt. Healy, the first black prelate in the United States, was the son of Michael Healy, an Irishman who emigrated to Georgia in 1823, and Michael's black slave Eliza. The marriage of this couple produced ten children, three of whom became priests, while two daughters entered the sisterhood. James came north with his family, graduated from Holy Cross with honors, received ordination in 1854, and eventually became the pastor of the important parish of St. James in Boston. From this post he was elevated to the bishopric of Portland in 1875.

It was Bishop Healy's decision to sponsor Matthew Harkins, the pastor of St. James's Church, whose seventeen thousand members made it the largest parish in New England. A general discussion followed this proposal, after which young Harkins was nominated as Hendricken's successor by a majority vote. When Archbishop Williams forwarded the names of three candidates to Rome after the selection session was concluded, he underscored Harkins as his personal choice. "I know the Rev. Matthew Harkins," he wrote, "and can nominate him without reservation. He has all the qualities for the place."

Rome honored the wishes of Williams and Healy, and five months later Father Harkins received word that he had been chosen to become the second bishop of Providence. His reaction, recorded in his diary, was characteristically humble but uncharacteristically apprehensive: "This news causes me a great sorrow. I feel utterly unworthy of such a dignity and incapable of properly discharging its duties. What shall I do? God only knows."

On April 14, 1887, before an enormous throng including some five hundred priests from New England and beyond, Father Harkins was consecrated at the new Cathedral of SS. Peter and Paul. Archbishop Williams, who officiated, admonished the audience to "take good care of him; he's the best we've got." Bishop Healy, who preached the sermon, agreed. Harkins would vindicate the confidence of his sponsors during his thirty-four-year administration, so much so that his close friend Healy would one day attempt to secure for Harkins the prestigious post of archbishop of Boston.

Despite his own reservations and self-doubts, Harkins had been prepared in superb fashion for his duties in Rhode Island. Born in Boston on November 17, 1845, to Patrick and Mary Margaret (Kranich) Harkins, the future bishop received a public education and graduated from the Quincy School with a Franklin Medal for the highest academic achievement. After completing studies at Boston Latin, Harkins attended Holy Cross for a year and then, in 1863, went abroad to study under the Benedictine Fathers at the English College at Douai, France. Like so many other American clerics, he was ordained at the Seminary of St. Sulpice, Paris.

After his ordination on May 22, 1869, Harkins spent over a year at the Gregorian University in Rome, where he engaged in further theological study, witnessed the Vatican Council, and became conversant in Italian. In 1870 he returned to his native diocese of Boston and was soon assigned to the Church of the Immaculate Conception at Salem. Here he gained valuable experience in ethnic relations, which he would apply with consummate skill in later years.

His first parish contained a growing number of French Canadians, lured south by the prospect of employment in the growing North Shore textile industry. Their inability to speak English led Father Harkins, who could read, write, and speak the French language fluently, to conduct the first Mass in the French vernacular at Salem on June 30, 1872. Witnesses commented that "he spoke with a great facility." After this auspicious beginning, Harkins was entrusted with the spiritual welfare of the French parishioners and began the practice of celebrating the nine o'clock Mass every Sunday in French. He also began a Sunday school for the French Canadian youth of the parish. In May 1873 Harkins turned these functions over to a new French Canadian curate, but whenever the new cleric was absent, Father Harkins "watched over the interest of the French people."

It was at Salem, too, that this zealous young priest began working with the impoverished people of the parish. He mobilized the ladies to conduct an extremely successful clothing campaign during the harsh winter of 1873–74. Harkins would retain this concern for the downtrodden throughout his life, eventually earning the title "Bishop of the Poor."

Williams recognized Harkins's exceptional abilities in April 1876 by elevating him to the pastorate at St. Malachi's Church in Arlington, Massachusetts. When the young priest relinquished his Salem assignment, his pastor enthusiastically noted Harkins's special qualities: "I have lived for years among priests, old and young, and never have I seen one more faithful to all his duties than Father Harkins."

Success in Arlington earned the future bishop another promotion by 1884, this time to the prestigious church of St. James in Boston. During that same year he accompanied Archbishop Williams to the Third Plenary Council at Baltimore as the archbishop's theologian. Two years later Williams appointed him to the important posts of consultor and synodal examiner.

In 1887 Matthew Harkins was ready to assume the duties of the episcopacy in his own right. Those who knew this second bishop of Providence when he commenced his term described him as five feet six inches tall and "strong and compact in build." He was dark-complexioned with "thinning dark hair" and aquiline features, a man who "scarcely looks his forty years." His piercing eyes "beam with intelligence," said another observer, and "he speaks with ease and fluency; and one would never tire of him."

Harkins came to his new post with an enormous capacity for work and exceptional organizational ability—traits that the *Providence Visitor* called "his strongest executive qualifications." The new bishop, who would guide the Providence diocese for more than thirty-four years, was also described as "a man of acute mind, extremely well-informed, by nature rather retiring and simple, and full of disdain for show and vain pretensions." He was ambitious and assertive but self-effacing. Harkins disliked fanfare intensely, and as bishop of Providence he felt that he should "avoid publicity." This characteristic would remain constant throughout his lifetime. Thirty years later he became upset over the suggestion that the Catholic college he proposed for his diocese should be named in his honor.

Harkins was a man of proven intelligence, but his letters reveal that he was very unsure of his rhetorical abilities. Although the press praised his oratorical efforts, his feelings of inadequacy in this area led him to avoid whenever possible the task of preaching before a large audience. "The few times that I have spoken outside of my own church," he confided to Archbishop Williams, "have convinced me that I am totally unfit for a sermon or an important or more solemn celebration." To an old friend, Bishop Charles E. McDonnell of Brooklyn, Harkins also confessed his "very little facility in composition" and his "almost complete lack of imagination."

But if Harkins was not eloquent, he was certainly persuasive, for he rarely failed to strike a responsive chord in his various charitable appeals. Among his more successful special campaigns were those to aid victims of the San Francisco disaster of 1906, the eruption of Italy's Mt. Vesuvius in the same year, and the Italian earthquake of 1908. He was also vitally concerned with the support of the foreign missions. After the fund drive of 1895, Harkins could reflect with satisfaction that more money for foreign missions had been raised in his Diocese of Providence than in any other American diocese of comparable size.

Harkins was a compassionate man, but he was also businesslike and somewhat authoritarian, especially to the religious under his supervision. He was acutely sensitive to the leadership position of parish priests and would neither condone nor permit any relaxation of his exacting standards. Financial irresponsibility resulted in suspension or in a request for the resignation of the erring cleric. Effective management and organizational ability, Harkins's strong points, were expected of his priests as well. Inefficiency was intolerable to the bishop; he removed one priest for "notorious and injurious incapacity" and suspended another for failing to submit required reports. If a cleric displayed a lethargic approach towards his work, he was promptly transferred to another post where his new pastor could call "to his attention anything in his conduct that should be corrected—and likewise to quicken his zeal from time to time."

Disobedience was dealt with harshly by Harkins. He threatened one nun with expulsion for failing to walk in the appointed manner from the school where she taught to her convent. "I prefer to have no further relation with you," he crisply wrote to a religious student who had left college without his permission.

Harkins was no ecumenist; but then neither were most of his non-Catholic contemporaries. Toward other religious groups, and toward organizations without Catholic membership or representation, Harkins remained cool and aloof. He withdrew official Catholic support and involvement from the Pawtucket Cotton Centenary in 1890 because Protestant ministers were scheduled to address the audience, which would include Catholic schoolchildren. Characteristically, he refused press interviews concerning the issue. He declined to participate at the cornerstone laying at the new State House in 1896 because "the ceremonies had been entrusted to the Masonic Fraternity." In the following year he expressed his disapproval to Providence politician Patrick J. McCarthy over the Protestant makeup of the Providence Public Library's board of trustees, and in 1899 he chastised a priest for participating in a Methodist funeral, calling services of this kind "heretical forms of worship." Harkins also refused to join the interdenominational Federation of Churches and was sharply criticized for that refusal. Since this was the era of the anti–Catholic American Protective Association and continuing political nativism on the state and local level, Harkins's hypersensitivity to the inferior status of Catholics in Rhode Island is not surprising. In sum, Harkins manifested an attitude that some sociologists have described as "fortress Catholicism."

While the bishop could sometimes become embroiled in local issues, he generally avoided comment on national affairs. He preferred, it seems, to allow the *Visitor*, under the successive direction of such learned individuals as Fathers John Tennian, Henry F. Kinnerney, Austin Dowling, and George Parsons Lathrop, to expound upon national and international concerns. Neither Harkins's diary nor his letters reflect much opinion on the broader issues of the day, but this localism was somewhat typical of the American hierarchy in that period of internal growth and development.

Two notable departures from his relative silence on national affairs occurred with his political support for the nation's involvement in the Spanish-American War and World War I. In the midst of the first conflict, facetiously referred to by one diplomatic historian as "America's Coming-Out-Party," Harkins correctly predicted the emerging role of the United States in world affairs. In a Fourth of July 1898 address, delivered at the dedication of a school in St. Charles's Parish, Woonsocket, he observed that the United States was "approaching a crisis in its history, when she emerges from the retirement she has so long occupied as a colony and an independent nation on this side of the Atlantic to a prominent place in the field of international politics." He concluded that this country, by virtue of her new position in international affairs, would become "a known and recognized power among all the nations of the earth."

The perspective of time has proven that this era was indeed a watershed in American history wherein we abandoned our traditional nineteenth-century policies of neutrality, isolationism, and hemispheric exclusiveness and assumed an active and directing role in world affairs. Harkins was most perceptive in identifying this transition, and his remarks on this occasion seem to indicate that his silence on national issues was the result of choice rather than ignorance.

With the involvement of America in World War I, Bishop Harkins again took a public stance when he urged the whole-hearted support of the diocese "in our battle to rid the world of the power of a nation that knows no law but that of might." He also considered the war a significant test of Catholic patriotism—an opportunity for an enduring testament of Catholic support for American national aims. We are living in an age of fact, he stated, and "evidence must be on hand to prove to succeeding generations ... the extent of Catholic response to the call to arms." Harkins feared that the so-called "hyphenated Americans" of German and Irish descent would resist this country's participation as an ally of England in a war against Germany. Such reluctance by these groups did, in fact, bring a nativistic response during the postwar era in the form of "100 percent Americanism," and it was just such a situation that Harkins was attempting to avoid by his stirring pastoral letter of 1918.

The Catholic group that responded most vigorously to the war effort both in Rhode Island and the nation was the Knights of Columbus, but the Ancient Order of Hibernians was less than enthusiastic. That Irish fraternal order became totally disenchanted with President Wilson when he refused to back self-determination for Ireland in the postwar settlement.

These very infrequent forays into the national arena did not deter Harkins from his major role—the building of the Diocese of Providence. The influx of the so-called "new immigration," the social needs of his working-class flock, and the educational mandates of the Third Plenary Council of Baltimore preoccupied him and challenged his enormous administrative ability. In the first two endeavors—accommodation of the immigrant and social work—

he was aided especially by the Society of St. Vincent de Paul. For all three tasks he called upon numerous religious orders for assistance. Over two dozen such groups were established in the diocese by Harkins and enlisted in his social and educational crusade. Half of the present orders now operative in Rhode Island trace their local origins to Bishop Matthew Harkins. It would be neither an exaggeration nor a slight to other able Catholic leaders to assert that Harkins made a greater and more enduring impact upon Catholicism in Rhode Island than anyone before or since.

This essay was written in 1978. Since that time many of the social agencies described herein have closed. They were victims of changing times and techniques, but their value to their own generation was substantial.

SINCE HIS EARLY DAYS at the Immaculate Conception Church in Salem, Massachusetts, Matthew Harkins had demonstrated a deep commitment to social action. As bishop of Providence, he translated this social consciousness into positive programs and permanent institutions to serve the needs of his people from their infancy through old age.

Perhaps his largest and most flourishing project was St. Joseph's Hospital (Providence, 1892), but Harkins left many other social monuments as well, some of which survive and continue to function in a beneficial way. For infants, he sponsored the St. Vincent de Paul Asylum (Providence, 1891); for young children, l'Orphelinat St. François (Woonsocket, 1904), the St. Vincent de Paul Home (Woonsocket, 1905), and the Mercy Home and School (Newport, 1915); for young working males, the Rhode Island Home for Working Boys (Providence, 1899); for their female counterparts, St. Maria's Home for Working Girls (Providence, 1890) and its affiliate, St. Margaret's Home (Providence, 1905); for wayward and delinquent girls, the House of the Good Shepherd (Providence, 1905); and as a summer vacation spot for needy children, Tower Hill House (South Kingstown, 1907).

Nor did Harkins neglect the poor, the sick, the elderly, the working mother, or the immigrant. St. Joseph's Convent (Pawtucket, 1905), the Nazareth Home (Providence, 1907), and St. Clare's Home (Newport, 1908) provided visiting-nurse service to the poor, and the latter two also served as day-care centers for the children of working mothers. L'Hospice St. Antoine (Woonsocket, 1913) ministered to the aged poor. There were, in addition, three day nurseries established for the benefit of the Providence Italian community, St. Ann's (1914), Scalabrini (1916), and St. Raphael's (1916). The St. Raphael's facility had also operated an industrial school for girls and a visiting nurse service since its initial incorporation in 1909 under the guidance of the Franciscan Missionaries of Mary.

Harkins's most ambitious undertaking was St. Joseph's Hospital. On August 1, 1891, he purchased the old Harris Estate on Broad Street in what was then a fashionable section of Providence as the site for his proposed hospital. The Harris mansion, facing on Broad Street between Plenty and Peace Streets, was renovated and converted into wards and private rooms. On March 19, 1892, the feast of St. Joseph, the facility was dedicated, and three weeks later, on April 6, the first patient was admitted.

St. Joseph's Hospital on Broad Street in Providence as it appeared in 1894, shortly after its opening

Care of the hospital was entrusted to the sisters of the Third Order of St. Francis from the motherhouse at Glen Riddle, Pennsylvania. This community of nuns, dedicated to the service of the poor and operating under the Rule of St. Francis, was founded in 1855 by the Venerable John N. Neumann, C.SS.R. (1811–60), bishop of Philadelphia. This group has subsequently merged with the sisters of the Third Order of St. Francis of Allegany, but they have continued their apostolate at St. Joseph's.

The first contingent of sisters from Glen Riddle, under the superiorship of Sister Mary Johanna, arrived in Providence on January 22, 1892, in response to a request from Harkins and the Reverend William Stang, the bishop's assistant in the founding of St. Joseph's. Their hospital, established "for the purpose of providing medical aid and surgical treatment for the sick of all denominations," was immediately deluged with patients. In fact, so many people applied for care that only half could be accommodated in the Harris mansion. The bishop moved rapidly to relieve this inadequacy by constructing an additional building. On July 1, 1893, the cornerstone for the "new" St. Joseph's Hospital, or the east wing, as it is now called, was laid and blessed by the renowned James Cardinal Gibbons, archbishop of Baltimore. The new section was opened on the feast of St. Joseph, 1895. Built by the Gilbane Company, it was a handsome five-story structure that increased the hospital's capacity to 175 patients.

The hospital complex continued to grow during the remaining years of the Harkins episcopacy. Soon an outpatient department was added, and in 1899 a training school for nurses was established. By 1913 a large nurses' residence had been constructed, and two years later the state Board of Registration granted its approval to the nursing school. The medical staff of the hospital soon gained a reputation for proficiency. Its most distinguished member was Dr. John W. Keefe, a founder of St. Joseph's and a nationally known surgeon.

In 1904 the Franciscan Sisters enlarged their apostolate to the sick by establishing St. Joseph's Hospital Annex on farmlands at Hillsgrove in Warwick. This facility was devoted to victims of consumption, or tuberculosis, then a very prevalent disease. At first tents and a cottage were used, but when these proved inadequate, a building was erected in 1908. The annex continued to be utilized until its patients were transferred to the new Our Lady of Fatima Hospital in 1954.

To defray the considerable cost of this operation, a ladies' sewing circle was formed to provide linens and sheets. Harkins, of course, gave both the Providence and Hillsgrove installations generous support. That aid was well deserved. The first inventory of diocesan social services, conducted in September 1910, revealed that 15,667 patients had been received in the Providence facility since its founding, and another 38,523 had been treated in the outpatient department. Further, 955 consumptives had been treated in Providence prior to the opening of the Hillsgrove annex, which had then cared for an additional 607 tubercular patients.

In view of the impoverished clientele to which the hospital and annex ministered, this impressive performance was obviously costly. Thus Harkins overcame his reservations concerning public aid and sought government funds for his medical enterprise. He based his request upon the fact that St. Joseph's accepted patients without regard to race, creed, or color, and that it also cared for "incurable patients who were not received in any other hospital of the city."

When Monsignor William Stang, treasurer of the hospital, petitioned the city government in Providence for a subsidy in 1902, the Yankee Republican-controlled Common Council (the lower chamber) indefinitely postponed the request. Stang, justly indignant, called the action "a clear case of bigotry." In the following year the council created a committee to consider appropriations to local hospitals for their charitable work. Relying in part on this group's study, an ordinance allocating $25,000 to Rhode Island Hospital, $4,000 to Lying-In Hospital, and $2,000 to St. Joseph's was introduced in the Common Council in April 1904.

A protest was then immediately registered in the upper chamber by Alderman Dennis F. McCarthy of Ward 3, who complained that the amount assigned to St. Joseph's was too small. In support of McCarthy's contention, Harkins and Stang prepared a concise

"Statement of Case," which was sent to the alderman. The brief contained the free-treatment figures developed by the 1903 hospital committee: Rhode Island Hospital, 59,474 days; St. Joseph's, 25,088 days; Lying-In, 3,646 days. It was clear that the Catholic hospital was discriminated against, for while it accounted for 29 percent of all free treatment, it was apportioned only 6 percent of the hospital allotment.

Bishop Harkins's statement suggested that a system be developed "by which those in need of hospital care and unable to provide it for themselves may be sent to a proper hospital and paid for by the city." This specific proposal for per capita reimbursement was not adopted, but the council did alter its original schedule of funding. On September 12, 1904, a revised appropriation bill was presented to the Common Council which gave $40,000 to heavily endowed Rhode Island Hospital and $5,000 each to St. Joseph's and Lying-In. It passed without discussion. Four days later, when the measure came before the aldermen, another objection was raised by Dennis McCarthy, apparently with the urging of Harkins. McCarthy contended that the hospital "that is doing twenty-nine percent of the work should get more than the hospital that is doing four percent." He then moved for an increase in the St. Joseph's appropriation to $10,000. The amendment passed, the Common Council concurred, and St. Joseph's was $8,000 richer than it would have been if not for the outspoken efforts of Harkins and McCarthy.

The bishop's determination and foresight in preparing persuasive supporting documentation in his brief to McCarthy proved to be a decisive factor in this political joust, which ended in victory for the recipients of free hospital treatment—the poor. Harkins was quite pleased at the outcome. "Can a better basis be found for the use of public money" than for care of the sick poor? he asked rhetorically.

In Matthew Harkins, both St. Joseph's and its impoverished patrons had a warm and vigorous ally. But Harkins was not alone in supporting this expensive enterprise. Philanthropist Joseph Banigan, who died in 1898, left the hospital a bequest of $25,000 in his will, and the St. Vincent de Paul volunteers (the Vincentians) gave generously of their time and energy. With such support, St. Joseph's was destined to succeed.

Another group of prime concern to Bishop Harkins was the youth of his diocese. Here especially, the Vincentians were his strong right arm. When Harkins became bishop in 1887, St. Aloysius's Home was the only orphanage in Rhode Island, though St. Vincent's Asylum of Fall River, founded by Bishop Thomas Hendricken in 1885, gave the Providence diocese (which then included southeastern Massachusetts) a total of two. In 1889 a third such institution was added when the French of Fall River opened St. Joseph's. This institution, staffed by the Sisters of Charity (Grey Nuns), attracted a very sizable enrollment from the outset. The Grey Nuns who came to St. Joseph's in 1890 were the first of the order to establish themselves in the United States. Another Massachusetts facility, St. Mary's Home in New Bedford, was cosponsored by the English and Portuguese parishes of that city in 1892. This institution, which was under the care of the Sisters of St. Francis, curiously combined an orphanage with a home for the aged.

But Harkins's Rhode Island efforts and establishments were more impressive. In 1889 he built two large wings on the Prairie Avenue facility housing St. Aloysius Orphanage and later strengthened its sources of financial aid. The home was originally supported by the Orphans' Fair and an occasional special collection in the churches. It was Harkins's decision to underwrite the expenses incurred by St. Aloysius and the newer orphanages by an annual assessment on the parishes.

The most important of the new orphanages was St. Vincent de Paul Infant Asylum, founded in Providence in 1892. The name of this new establishment was an explicit recognition by the bishop of the work done for the youth of the diocese by the local members of the St. Vincent de Paul Society. Since becoming a bishop, Harkins had witnessed a number of youth projects conducted by the Vincentians, such as their aid to the Sisters of Mercy in running the Orphan's Fair, their annual boat excursion down Narragansett Bay for the children at St. Aloysius, and their work with the Catholics at Sockanosset, the state school for wayward boys, where the society gave regular catechetical classes and presented awards to the inmates for excellence in various competitions.

The Providence council of the society, which had incorporated "for the purposes of charity," raised the substantial sum of $1,500 in 1888 and presented it to Harkins two years later as the nucleus of a fund for the erection of a home for infants under four years of age who could not get adequate care at St. Aloysius. The bishop, in turn, honored the society with the promise that the institution, when established, would bear its name.

The Vincentians did not have long to wait, for Harkins moved swiftly. On May 1, 1891, the General Assembly granted the bishop a charter empowering him to establish the St. Vincent de Paul Orphan Asylum "for the aid and support of poor, friendless children," regardless of race, color, or creed. Next a funding drive was launched, with "memberships" ranging from $5 per year to a life membership for a $500 donation. It was estimated that the monthly expense for each child would be $9, and that the annual budget of the institution would be from $4,000 to $5,000.

On July 5, 1891, John W. Kiley, vice president of the corporation, concluded his search for an appropriate site by recommending the acquisition of the Furlong estate at 42 Park Street in Providence. The purchase was consummated, and the Sisters of Divine Providence were chosen to staff the orphanage. This religious order, founded in Lorraine, France, in 1762, had made American establishments in Austin, Texas (1866), and Covington, Kentucky (1889). It was from the Kentucky provincial house that two sisters came in 1891—Mother Maria, the first superior of the asylum, and Sister Mary of the Sacred Heart, superior of the home from 1898 to 1915. By the time the home was blessed and formally opened by Harkins in February 1892, the number of sisters had increased to five.

Certain bylaws for the operation of St. Vincent's were adopted in January 1892. The facility was to admit children up to three and one-half years of age (soon amended to six years) as a temporary home "of four weeks or so until a suitable permanent home shall be obtained" for the child; it "will be in no sense a foundling asylum, and any such abandoned children placed in the premises will be at once transferred to the civil authorities." In September 1892 Harkins established the Association of St. Vincent de Paul to supervise and provide for the maintenance of the asylum and appointed Monsignor Dennis M. Lowney to serve as director of the association and president of the home.

During 1892, the asylum's first full year of operation, the sisters cared for 109 infants. By 1895 the number had risen to 137, and the facilities were becoming very inadequate. At that juncture Joseph Banigan came to the rescue. He provided $22,000 for the purchase of a seven-acre parcel near Davis Park, which had been the old Cornell estate. A large modern structure was built on this site and opened in the spring of 1898. This new facility was costly to operate, so the help of the laity was sought. The Vincentians, of course, were most active in supporting the institution that they had helped found, and the munificent Mr. Banigan left the asylum $25,000 in his will. But even broader-based support was needed and obtained. To this end the St. Vincent de Paul Sewing Circle and St. Anthony's Guild were formed in the 1890s. Later, in 1925, St. Vincent's Assembly, a confederation of charitable, civic, and fraternal societies, came into existence to further the work that the Vincentians and the Sisters of Divine Providence were doing for the orphaned infants of the diocese.

But the Providence Vincentians did not rest on their laurels. As the decade of the 1890s advanced, they undertook new projects for the needy youth of the diocese. In 1897 they employed full-time a man who acted as an agent of the various Catholic institutions before the juvenile session of the Sixth District Court. This service was part of the society's nationwide effort to provide special attention to the problems and plight of the youthful offender. In the same year the Vincentians began systematically placing children from St. Aloysius's and St. Vincent's in foster homes—one of the earliest efforts of its kind in the entire country. Then, in 1906, they cooperated in the establishment of a vacation summer home for the infants of St. Vincent's at Nayatt Point in Barrington, a facility that was maintained until 1920. The Vincentians also assisted Harkins in opening Tower Hill House in South County as a vacation resort for deprived children. No other lay group approached the Vincentians in the quality and scope of their social endeavors.

With St. Vincent's on firm footing and the orphans of Providence well cared for, Harkins extended his efforts to other sections of the state, specifically to Woonsocket and Newport. In the former city the St. Vincent de Paul Home was established on Pond Street, in St. Charles's Parish, largely through the efforts of Father George Mahoney. According to its charter of January 1905, this agency was founded "for the purpose of aiding and supporting poor, friendless children, and also for the purpose of aiding and supporting the aged poor." During its early years the institution concerned itself exclusively with the young.

The 1910 diocesan census of social agencies revealed that the Pond Street home sheltered 41 residents and had received 101 children during the first five years of its existence. It also conducted a small day nursery in 1910 that cared for another 9 Woonsocket children. The home was operated by the sisters of the Third Order of St. Francis of Allegany, New York, with the assistance of Father Mahoney and his St. Charles parishioners, especially the young ladies of the Immaculate Conception Sodality. After nearly three decades of operation the orphanage was gradually phased out, but the home's charter, which granted authorization to care for the "aged poor," was implemented with the opening of St. Francis House in 1933 as a boarding home for retired persons.

A third orphanage established in Rhode Island under the aegis of Bishop Harkins was the Mercy Home and School in Newport. This agency was incorporated in April 1915 to provide "a home for the support and education of poor, neglected, or indigent children." It was situated on Malbone Avenue in a former Newport estate known as Eagle Crest. The Sisters of Mercy who ran the orphanage also conducted a school for the orphaned children. Most of the inmates were from the Newport area; some had been transferred back from St. Aloysius to relieve the crowded conditions there. At the end of its first full year of operation, the home housed approximately 34 parentless boys and girls. After operating for twenty-six years, the Mercy Home closed in 1941 when the land upon which it was situated was taken by the federal government by eminent domain for the purposes of national defense.

The final effort made during the Harkins era on behalf of orphans was launched by the Franco-Americans of Woonsocket, particularly by Father Charles Dauray and his parishioners at Precious Blood Parish. On January 14, 1904, five sisters of the Institute of the Franciscan Missionaries of Mary came to Rhode Island and took possession of a house on Hamlet Avenue diagonally across from Precious Blood Church. This new order of missionary sisters, founded in France in 1877, were invited to Rhode Island by Dauray primarily to operate a home for the aged, but since plans for such an institution had not matured, they were employed to solve another pressing problem — the needs of the young.

Under Dauray's direction the sisters began their service by caring for children whose parents worked long hours in the mills. The Hamlet Avenue operation, legally known as l'Institut des Franciscaines Missionaires de Marie but popularly called "the French Orphanage," was basically a day-care center rather than an orphanage for the first two years of its existence. Then, because of the generosity of Dr. Joseph Hils, a prominent physician and a parishioner of Precious Blood, it developed a complete program for housing and caring for parentless children. By 1910 it had ministered to 400 orphans.

At his death in February 1906 Dr. Hils bequeathed the sisters the sum of $50,000 for the purpose of building an orphanage in Woonsocket. Hils's wishes were implemented when a tract of land on Bernon Heights was purchased in 1910. It consisted of one-third of an acre within the parish and had a commanding panoramic view of Woonsocket and the Blackstone Valley. In November 1912 a brick and stone structure, known as St. Francis Orphanage (l'Orphelinat St. François), was dedicated on this site. Bishop Harkins, speaking entirely in French, praised Father Dauray and the Franciscan Missionaries of Mary for their efforts. In September 1913 the orphanage was completed and opened for occupancy. Shortly thereafter the Hamlet Avenue Institut was dissolved and its property transferred to St. Francis. This asylum, which can accommodate nearly 200 children at one time, continues in existence and has recently opened a day-care center on the premises. It stands as one of the major social agencies sponsored by the French community, and as a lasting monument to the social concern of Father Dauray and the munificence of Dr. Hils.

The great efforts made by the Catholics of the Providence diocese to care for orphaned children might appear in retrospect to be a product of misplaced zeal, but such a view would reveal an ignorance of the motives and apprehensions that brought these agencies into being. In the nineteenth and early twentieth centuries, Catholics believed that Protestants were using public child-caring institutions as devices to deprive Catholic children of the faith of their parents. This religious conquest was accomplished by placing Catholic children in Protestant foster homes. The Reverend Dr. John O'Grady, in a pioneering monograph on Catholic charities in the United States, cites numerous instances of such Protestant proselytism. One method employed, according to O'Grady, was to remove the children to areas where Catholics were few in number —for example, from eastern cities to the homes of Methodist, Baptist, and Lutheran families in the Middle West.

In the files of the Catholic press of the late nineteenth century are innumerable references to such a practice. For example, in January 1876 posters in Peru, Illinois, heralded the arrival of a number of orphans from a New York institution for distribution to interested local families. On the appointed day a great crowd gathered to witness this peculiar spectacle. A few German and Irish Catholic families endeavored to make the necessary arrangements for receiving the children, but they were informed by the agent of the public institution that all the wards were to be placed in Methodist families and brought up in that religion. Upon inquiry, a local priest found that nine of the fifteen children offered for placement were Catholics.

A letter to James McMaster's *New York Freeman's Journal* of May 26, 1866, called attention to the "sale" of forty or fifty children, principally of Irish Catholic parentage, at Piqua, Missouri, two months previously. Because bidders were scarce at this auction, a local Catholic priest secured five of the children.

Closer to home was a prolonged dispute in Connecticut during

1892–93. A typical incident involving a Catholic ward who was placed in a Methodist family by the county Children's Home of New Haven in 1892 brought a challenge to this long-standing practice. Catholic officials sought judicial relief and claimed that a public institution was not free to disregard the religion of its ward when assigning him to a foster home. The *Connecticut Catholic* had earlier charged that public agencies had been "diverted from their original purpose to well-directed channels of religious prose-lytism." The state's supreme court disagreed, contending that since the institution was the child's legal guardian, it should not be governed by the parents' religious affiliations.

Connecticut's Catholics wielded their newfound political power in 1893 to secure the passage of a law providing that children should be placed in homes of the same religious faith as that of their parents. When public agencies tried to evade the law, Bishop John Nilan of Hartford established a diocesan commission to supervise the adoption process. This nearby controversy undoubtedly reenforced the views of Bishop Harkins. Harkins's concern for the protection of youth in fact extended from the infants at St. Vincent de Paul's, through the intermediate-age orphans at St. Aloysius's in Providence, St. Vincent's and St. Francis's Woonsocket, and the Mercy Home in Newport, to teenaged boys and girls and young adults, for whom he built St. Maria's and St. Margaret's Homes for Working Girls, the Rhode Island Home for Working Boys, the House of the Good Shepherd, and several day nurseries and industrial schools. His efforts on behalf of the youth of his diocese have never been equaled.

St. Maria's Home for Working Girls, incorporated in February 1890, was the first diocesan social agency designed to offer protective religious care to adolescents and young adults, although any working woman was eligible for admission. Harkins secured the Sisters of the Third Order of St. Francis of Allegany, New York, to conduct the operation. This order, which made its American foundation in 1859, was charged with aiding "all women who are endeavoring to obtain honorable support, by providing them with a comfortable home and surrounding them with such moral and religious influence as will best promote their temporal and eternal welfare." As usual, Joseph Banigan was there to render assistance to this social project. In fact, this benevolent industrialist paid for the entire construction of St. Maria's Home on Governor Street in Providence.

The building's four floors contained simply furnished single rooms that accommodated 130 women. It was originally designed to house those immigrant girls, most of whom were Irish, who worked in the mills or as housekeepers in the mansions of wealthy East Side residents. Banigan financed construction of St. Maria's when he was informed that the girls "were forced to live in places of questionable repute because they could afford nothing better." As time passed, however, widows and retired businesswomen constituted an increasing percentage of the St. Maria's residents.

A smaller companion agency, St. Margaret's Home for Working Girls, was founded on Friendship Street, Providence, in 1905. Staffed by the same sisters and dedicated to the same purpose, it was designed to handle the overflow from St. Maria's. This facility endured until the 1950s, when its obsolescence and the demands of highway construction caused its demolition. A new St. Margaret's Home, which came closer to fulfilling its original purpose than did St. Maria's, was opened on Dean Street, Providence, in the 1950s under the auspices of the Sisters of Mercy, but it too has now ceased operation.

The Sisters of the Third Order of St. Francis of Allegany maintained St. Maria's until its closing, as well as the St. Francis Home in Woonsocket. In addition, this congregation has absorbed the Franciscan Sisters from Glen Riddle, and in so doing it has assumed the direction of St. Joseph's Hospital as well as Our Lady of Fatima. Few orders can match its record of social service in this diocese.

Another agency was established by Harkins for girls who had fallen prey to those "sinister influences" against which St. Maria's and St. Margaret's were designed to defend. This foundation was the House of the Good Shepherd. To maintain it, the bishop recruited the Sisters of Our Lady of Charity of the Good Shepherd in 1904. Founded in France by St. John Eudes in 1641, this order was brought to the United States in 1842 and made its principal task the rehabilitation of wayward girls. Harkins called these sisters to his diocese "for establishing and maintaining in the City of Providence, a refuge and home for unfortunate women and for educating and reforming children (girls) exposed to dangerous influences as regards morality."

Six sisters took up residence in November 1904 on Eaton Street in the former Bailey estate, which the bishop had purchased for $15,000. Renovations were promptly begun, a charter was issued by the General Assembly in January 1905, and the house was formally opened the following June. As the years passed, the facilities were expanded to include a laundry, a power plant, a barn and stable, a poultry house, and a four-story brick building known as the "training school," which was completed in 1929. The house accommodated more than 175 girls.

The training methods employed by the Sisters of the Good Shepherd were interesting, though perhaps quaint by today's standards. Harkins explained the general organization of the house in a letter to the pastors of the diocese in 1904: "Under its roof will be sheltered two classes. In the first class will be erring women who have become a bane to themselves and to society by sin," and who enter as "voluntary penitents." The other group would consist of "involuntary penitents because they are brought by the superior authority of parents or of the State where such provisions have been made by law." Those "involuntary" inmates referred to the house by probation officers were subsidized by the state on a per capita basis for a period of up to six months. Almost immediately after the house's foundation, a group of dedicated laywomen formed the Shepherdess Association to help the sisters operate and finance their operation.

The sisters had an interesting program for the inmates of their facility. The basic elements in their system of rehabilitation were religion, work, and education. Every girl who was admitted received the advantages of religious instruction and practice and was encouraged to receive the sacraments frequently. A second very important element in the Good Shepherd program was careful and systematic work: it was the aim of the nuns to keep their charges busy throughout the entire day with manual labor, schoolwork, and recreation. The products of the girls' labor helped to finance the operations of the house. The final ingredient was education. The Eaton Street house operated a high school called Mary Immaculate, which in the 1940s had an enrollment of over 150 girls per year. At that time the house was staffed by about thirty Sisters of the Good Shepherd.

Another feature of the sisters' rehabilitation program was to divide the inmate community into various groups. One such division was between delinquent and predelinquent girls. The latter would include those who were not offenders but merely "exposed to the temptations of wrongdoing." Among the delinquents were further divisions, such as that between "Magdalen" and "penitent." The former designation, from the model of Mary Magdalen, was applied to those penitents who maintained good behavior for a period of three years and who desired to take religious vows and remain in the house to aid the sisters in caring for new inmates.

This large-scale enterprise gradually fell victim to financial pressures, changing mores, and new standards of care for delinquents. In the early 1950s the Eaton Street operation was phased out. The property of the House of the Good Shepherd was acquired by an adjacent and expanding Providence College in 1955, and the sisters, after a half century of devoted service, left the Diocese of Providence.

Another important youth-oriented social endeavor was the establishment in 1899 of the Rhode Island Home for Working Boys. This agency, first located at 42 Park Street, Providence, in the house vacated by the original St. Vincent de Paul Asylum, was opened for the "aid of poor friendless children," and especially "for the purpose of caring for, educating, and assisting poor boys, desirous of becoming self-reliant and self-supporting."

The concept of a working boys' home for teenagers was first implemented in 1846 by the Brothers of St. Joseph of South Bend, Indiana, in conjunction with the University of Notre Dame. During the 1860s and 1870s this project was spearheaded by Dr. Levi Silliman Ives of New York City, organizer of the Society for the Protection of Destitute Catholic Children, and Archbishop Martin J. Spalding of Baltimore. The working boys' home (or "protectory" or "industrial school," as it was variously called) was designed to guard young boys newly entering the workaday world from "sinful influences" and to attempt the rehabilitation of those tending towards delinquency. Its other basic function was to prevent boys from losing their faith because of a lack of religious guidance during the critical period of adolescence. According to Archbishop Spalding, "the only practical remedy" against this threat was "the establishment, on a large scale, of protectories or industrial schools, in which poor boys, exposed to the danger of losing their faith, may be religiously educated and trained up to pursuits which will fit them to become useful members of society and ornaments of the Church."

The financial patron and sponsor of the Rhode Island Home was St. Aloysius's Asylum. The directors of the orphanage were eager to make provisions for the boys who left the asylum to join the work force. The project was directed by the Reverend James T. Ward, and it received the strong financial and moral support of the St. Vincent de Paul Society. After one year of operation 40 boys were in residence, 35 of whom were employed. The home also provided the boys with the opportunity to continue their education at night.

The 1910 survey of diocesan social service agencies showed that 1,200 boys had been cared for by the institution during its first ten years of operation. The Home for Working Boys continued to function for more than a half century, but changing economic and social conditions brought about its demise. There were also two industrial schools for girls established in the diocese during this productive era: St. Raphael's (1909), on Federal Hill, and St. Ann's (1914), in the North End of Providence. These two facilities operated in primarily Italian neighborhoods.

While youth received top priority and emphasis was placed upon the spiritual, cultural, and physical welfare of those in their formative years, the social apostolate of the church of Providence was not confined to the young. The Daughters of the Holy Ghost afford a good illustration of this diversity. They are another of the many orders founded in France, having been established there in 1706. When this mother country of so many religious communities saw fit to suppress them by restrictive legislation in 1902, the sisters departed to Belgium, England, and America. As early as 1903 they entered Fall River, in the Massachusetts sector of the Diocese of Providence. Then, in 1905, they established an American provincial house in Hartford and moved into Rhode Island as well. These nuns, known as the White Sisters because of the striking habit they once wore, are devoted to the Christian education of young children, but their special work is the care and visitation of the sick.

Their first Rhode Island establishment, St. Joseph's Covent, Pawtucket, was founded in 1905 with the aid of Monsignor Dennis Lowney, the pastor of St. Joseph's Parish and a close associate of Bishop Harkins. From this base the sisters began their visitations to the infirm of the Pawtucket-Central Falls area and their deliveries of medicine, food, and other necessities to the "sick poor." This initial establishment at St. Joseph's was soon assisted by local laywomen, the Society of the Ladies of Charity, who raised money for the maintenance of the convent and made clothing and other articles for distribution by the nuns.

Encouraged by this initial success, the White Sisters opened a second convent in 1907, the Nazareth Home on Pine Street in Providence. The Reverend Austin Dowling, a protégé of Harkins and future bishop of St. Paul, Minnesota, was made treasurer of the Nazareth Home Corporation. To keep his treasury well stocked, Dowling called upon the Queen's Daughters, the women's affiliate of the Vincentians, for support. The group, numbering over four hundred, attracted national attention by their warm and enthusiastic response. They assumed responsibility for financing the work of the White Sisters in Providence.

Within two years the Providence sisters opened the Edward A. Carter Memorial Day Nursery at the Nazarene Home. This facility, one of the five day-care centers established under Harkins, accommodated about 125 children nine years old and younger, and it admitted children regardless of race or religion. It had a large playground, and its facilities were described by a contemporary social worker as excellent. The nursery continued at the Pine Street location until the 1950s, when a new building was constructed for it on Public Street in Providence. Its operation was then entrusted to the Sisters of Mercy.

The third foundation by the White Sisters was St. Clare's Home, Newport, incorporated in 1908 and opened the following year. In the City by the Sea, as in Providence, the Queen's Daughters assumed the task of supporting the sisters' efforts. In 1910 St. Clare's Nursery was begun on Thames Street to care for children between the ages of six months and nine years. Six years later Mrs. Brockholst Cutting, another of the many Newport benefactors of Catholicism, bequeathed funds to St. Clare's Corporation for the construction of a modern building. The Cutting Memorial was accordingly built, dedicated by Bishop Harkins, and occupied by the sisters. Later ventures of the Newport Daughters of the Holy Ghost included the establishment in 1926 of Stella Maris, a home for convalescents, and the opening of St. Clare's Home for Aged Women in 1927.

Certain changes have been made in the Newport ministry of the White Sisters over the years. The day-care center, now serving children from three to five, operates on Spring Street as the Garrettson Memorial, while the Home for Aged Women occupies the site of the original nursery on Thames Street. Stella Maris Home for Convalescents was taken over in the 1950s by the Sisters of St. Joseph of Cluny, but it still serves the needs of women who desire limited nursing care and a place in which to recuperate or rest. It has also developed into a permanent home for retired women.

The Daughters of the Holy Spirit, as the order is now called, have compiled a notable record in the area of charitable work since 1905. They have cared for hundreds of aged women, thousands of young children, and tens of thousands of those who needed home medical treatment. Their visitation work in fact prompted one sociologist to comment that the White Sisters and similar orders "make themselves a part of the home, and they give more attention to the details of family life than any other agency." Unfortunately their Pawtucket convent closed in the 1960s, but the sisters continue to operate from their new Providence base on Parkis Avenue and their Newport convent on Spring Street with the same dedication that they brought to the diocese when Matthew Harkins called them here nearly seven decades ago.

The final major social agency established during the era of Bishop Harkins was l'Hospice St. Antoine, opened in Woonsocket in 1913. This was another of the many enterprises of the remarkable Charles Dauray. This home for aged poor had its origins in the testamentary gift of Dr. L. Gedeon Archambault of Precious Blood Parish. Dr. Archambault died on April 8, 1903, leaving a will in which he bequeathed the substantial sum of $40,000 for the establishment and maintenance of a home for the aged people of his parish.

With the intention of immediately implementing the late physician's desires, Dauray journeyed to Quebec to enlist the services of the Franciscan Missionaries of Mary to supervise the proposed institution. The sisters came, but priorities were altered and the French orphanage and day care center on Hamlet Avenue was opened instead. Then, in 1906, another parish physician, Dr. Joseph Hils, died and bequeathed both $50,000 to the Franciscan Missionary sisters for the recently opened orphanage and another $25,000 to Father Dauray to be applied to the establishment of a home for the elderly. The latter project was delayed for several years because of the greater urgency of other parish activity, such as education and the orphanage, but in 1913, when the children's asylum moved to new quarters on Bernon Heights, l'Hospice St. Antoine was established in the vacated Hamlet Avenue structure.

With the approval of the bishop, Dauray again went to Canada on a recruiting mission and appealed to the superior of the Grey Nuns at St. Hyacinthe to send members of that order to assume the administration of the home for the aged. This community was admirably trained for such work. Since their foundation in Montreal in 1738, they had been constantly engaged in corporal works of mercy. In 1747, as one of their earliest assignments, they were placed in charge of the main hospital in Montreal under the title of the Sisters of Charity of the General Hospital. This became their formal name, although the color of their habit provided them with their popular appellation, the Grey Nuns. They were not strangers to the Diocese of Providence. Twenty-three years before coming to Woonsocket, members of this sisterhood had been entrusted by Harkins with the administration of St. Joseph's French Orphanage in Fall River.

The coming of the Grey Nuns to Woonsocket further accentuated the dominant role that French and French Canadian sisters played in the diocese. A survey by Alexander Belisle in 1910 had revealed that they accounted for 222 of the 551 nuns serving the social and educational needs of Rhode Island's Catholic population. The work of the Grey Nuns with the aged of Woonsocket was remarkably successful. Hospice St. Antoine operated at full capacity from the outset, and eventually, in 1941, a new and larger facility was opened in Fairmount, just beyond the Woonsocket city line in the town of North Smithfield. L'Hospice St. Antoine is no longer a parish unit of Precious Blood, but rather a large diocesan institution admitting aged and infirm persons from all parts of the state.

Toward the end of Harkins's episcopacy another type of social agency began to develop at the parish level, the so-called community house. The social survey of 1920 listed two such facilities, one at St. Edward's Parish on Branch Avenue in Providence and the other at St. Margaret's Parish in Rumford. The former was opened in April 1917 "to provide proper recreation and social opportunities" for the men and women of the parish; the latter was begun in January 1920 "to promote mental, moral, religious, and physical welfare" by conducting such activities as "lectures, concerts, evening school classes, gymnastics, millinery, sewing, and athletics." These socioeducational "community houses" increased in number during the twenties and thirties and added a new and important dimension to parish life.

As the foregoing narrative indicates, social action had become a major feature of Rhode Island Catholicism during the episcopacy of Bishop Harkins. The advance of the diocese in maturity and resources had made this emphasis possible, but also important was Harkins's own commitment to social reform—a commitment emphasized by such acts as applying the thousands of dollars in gifts he received in 1912 on the occasion of his silver jubilee as a bishop to the charitable works that he had begun. It was largely the leadership of Bishop Harkins that transformed the church of Providence from one almost exclusively preoccupied with pastoral goals to one that stressed social action as well. When Harkins came to Providence in 1887, there were only two Catholic institutions of social welfare in Rhode Island (St. Aloysius's Asylum and the Home for the Aged of the Little Sisters of the Poor in Pawtucket); when he died in 1921, there were, excluding the parish community houses, nineteen such agencies, some of which performed multiple functions. Matthew Harkins had well earned the soubriquet "Bishop of the Poor."

8
Politics, Rhode Island Style

An Act for Declaring the Rights and Priviledges of His Majesties Subjects within this Colony.

BE IT ENACTED By the General Assembly of this Colony, And by the Authority of the same it is hereby Enacted, That no Free-man shall be Taken or Imprisoned, or be deprived of his Free-hold, or Liberty, or Free Customs, or Out-Lawed, or Exiled or otherways Destroyed, nor shall be passed upon, Judged or Condemned, but by the Lawful Judgement of his Peers, or by the Law of this Colony; And that no Aid, Tax, Tailage, or Custom, Loan, Benevolence, Gift, Excise, Duty or Imposition whatsoever, shall be Laid, Assessed, Imposed, Levied or Required of or on any of His Majesties Subjects within this Colony, or upon their Estates, upon any manner of Pretence or Colour whatsoever, but by the Act and Assent of the General Assembly of this Colony. *No Free-men to be Imprisoned, or deprived of his Liberty, &c. But by his Peers, &c. No Tax or Duty to be raised, but by the General Assembly.*

AND that no Man, of what Estate and Condition soever, shall be put out of his Lands and Tenements, nor Taken, nor Imprisoned, nor Disinheretd, nor Banished, nor any ways Destroyed, nor Molested, without being for it brought to Answer by due course of Law; And that all Rights and Priviledges Granted to this Colony by His Majesties Charter, be entirely kept and preserved to all His Majesties Subjects residing, in or belonging to the same; And that all Men Professing Christianity, and of Competent Estates, and of Civil Conversation, who acknowledge, and are Obedient to the Civil Magistrate, though of different Judgmnts in Religious Affairs (Roman Catholicks only excepted) shall be admited Free-men, And shall have Liberty to Chuse and be Chosen Officers in the Colony both Millitary and Civil. *No Person to be Deseised of his Lands, or otherwise molested, but by due Course of Law. All Persons of Estates, and Obedient to the Magistrate, to have liberty to Elect, and be Elected to Officers.*

This 1719 statute denied civil rights to Roman Catholics and persons of the Jewish faith.

Civil Rights and Civil Wrongs in Rhode Island: Church, State, and the Constitution, 1636–1986

This was the keynote address delivered to the annual spring meeting of the American Catholic Historical Association, hosted by Providence College on April 10, 1987.

OUR STORY BEGINS IN 1636, when the Puritan magistrates of Massachusetts Bay banished Calvinist clergyman Roger Williams into the winter wilderness. An avowed Separatist from the Church of England, the Cambridge-educated Williams was ousted for attacking the cornerstones upon which the Puritans' Bible commonwealth was built—the theology of the covenant and the use of civil magistrates to enforce that theology.

A vital area of disagreement between Williams and the builders of the Bay Colony was that Williams considered some religious doctrines propounded by the Puritans to be a prostitution of theology. His alternative to the orthodox Puritan approach was a cause for his exile. This alternative was a major element in Williams's notions of religious freedom and the separation of church and state, principles that found their expression in Rhode Island's basic law.

Roger Williams's challenge to covenant theology revolved around a method of interpreting the Bible, specifically the relation of Old Testament to New, which is called typology. His version of the typological method was based upon a belief that everything in the Old Testament is merely a prefiguration of the New Testament, that each event in the history of Israel could be understood only when it came to fruition in the life of Christ, and that the Old Testament lacked literal and historical content.

In its practical application to the life of Massachusetts Bay, this complex method of Biblical exegesis had important consequences. Among other things, Williams's method of interpreting the Scriptures was at variance with the historical mode of typological interpretation upon which covenant theology rested. Orthodox typology held that the Old Testament was simultaneously a literal and a spiritual work. On the literal level, Israel's scriptural theocracy provided the eternal pattern of civil justice, while on the spiritual level, Israel, as the Promised Land, prefigured Christ. Orthodox typology thus intermingled the church and the civil state, and it supported the Puritan contention that the Christian magistrates of Massachusetts Bay could enforce religious conformity by basing their actions on similar powers exercised by the Biblical Israelites.

Williams's brand of typology, being of a purely spiritual nature, disputed the Massachusetts Puritan belief that any political or social arrangement could be legitimized by reference to a similar arrangement described in the Old Testament. Specifically, Williams denied the right of the Massachusetts magistrates to use the civil power to enforce religious conformity, a right claimed on the basis of Israelite precedent. It was Williams's contention that the events and the laws of Israel, having found completion in the New Testament, were without exception purely moral and ceremonial, and not to be emulated by seventeenth-century New Englanders.

Another crucial theological disagreement between Williams and the Massachusetts Puritans stemmed from their divergent views of the Ten Commandments. These divinely revealed injunctions were divided into two "tables": the first table—commandments one through four—was concerned with God and the worship of God, and was called "ceremonial"; the second—commandments five through ten—was directed towards governing human relations, and was called "moral."

Pointing out that judges and kings in the Old Testament state of Israel enforced both tables, Puritan divine John Cotton and his associates contended that this function continued to be valid.

According to their interpretation, the task of enforcing the first table (worship of God) resided with civil magistrates and ministers acting in concert.

Williams believed that Jesus had abrogated this Hebraic system. He contended that Christ had set forth new laws of worship that had stripped judges, kings, and civil magistrates of their right to enforce ceremonial provisions of the first table. These matters now belonged purely to the spiritual realm. "Soul liberty," to use Williams's phrase, pertained to the first table; it was exclusively an affair of private of conscience, and the magistrate had no jurisdiction whatsoever in this area.

As a result of these exegetical efforts, Williams concluded that the temporal power exercised over the religious sphere in the Old Testament was merely the archetype of spiritual power in the New, and thus, whenever the modern state attempted to enforce conformity of religious belief, it was acting in an unjustifiable manner. That false assumption of power, asserted Williams, had led and would lead to persecution and religious wars. Williams's obsession with religious persecution and its baneful effects upon both spiritual and civil life occupied a prominent place in his thought.

The fiery minister's topological approach had as its logical corollary liberty of conscience, and it contributed substantially to Williams's dogma of separation of church and state. It is important to note that the theologically obsessed Williams sought this separation not to protect the state from the dominance of the church but to free the church and the individual conscience from the interference and coercions of the state. Williams's religious creed thus led him into the political sphere, where he was essentially a traditionalist who believed in stability and deference. "So far as the political order was concerned," historian Edmund Morgan has observed, "Williams had really only one revolutionary statement to make. He denied that the state had any responsibility for the only form of life which has absolute importance—the life of the soul." Indicative of how strongly Williams felt about state domination of the church, in one burst of vituperation the polemical theologian asserted that such a condition would render the church, "the garden and spouse of Christ, a filthy dunghill and whore-house of rotten and stinking whores and hypocrites." Obviously Williams did not take the issue of separation lightly.

Among the conclusions that historians have drawn from Williams's earthy and passionate theological writings, the following seem to be the most significant: (1) any attempt by the state to enforce religious orthodoxy "stinks in God's nostrils," because it perverts God's plan for the regeneration of souls, and it is productive of persecution and religious wars; (2) God had not favored any particular form of government, and it is therefore to be inferred that forms of government will vary according to the nature and disposition of the people governed; (3) political and, especially, religious diversity was inevitable; and (4) the human conscience must be completely emancipated through the establishment of religious freedom and the separation of church and state.

Perry Miller, a noted historian of early American religious thought, has said of Williams that "he exerted little or no direct influence on theorists of the Revolution and the Constitution, who drew on quite different intellectual sources, yet as a figure and a reputation he was always there to remind Americans that no other conclusion than absolute religious freedom was feasible in this society."

Professor Sydney Ahlstrom agrees with this view in his *Religious History of the American People* (1975). Calling Rhode Island "the first commonwealth in modern history to make religious liberty (not simply a degree of toleration) a cardinal principle of its corporate existence and to maintain the separation of church and state on these grounds," Ahlstrom then observes that "Rhode Island seems to illustrate in an almost tragic way the ... dictum, often voiced by historians of science, that premature discoveries are uninfluential." In the view of Miller and Ahlstrom, Williams was to Madison, Jefferson, and the Enlightenment–era framers of the First Amendment as Leif Eriksson was to Columbus—prior in time but lacking in influence.

Other recent historians of American religion and constitutionalism—including LeRoy Moore, Edwin Gaustad, Richard Perry, Martin Marty, and Glenn LaFantasie (editor of an edition of

Williams's unpublished works)—hold a contrary view. According to these scholars, the Founding Fathers were well aware of the Rhode Island system of disestablishment and soul liberty. It was still intact under the same frame of government when the Bill of Rights was drafted and ratified. The guarantees in Rhode Island's famed charter of 1663 influenced similar grants of religious liberty in the proprietary charters of East New Jersey, West New Jersey, and Carolina issued shortly thereafter; and Williams's views on religion and the state were distilled and reiterated by Algernon Sydney and other English writers of the Whig libertarian tradition with whom our founders were quite familiar. Professor Marty has said it best: The American church-state outlook has issued "chiefly from two parallel, often congenial, sometimes conflicting, and occasionally contradictory positions"—the Rhode Island dissenting tradition, with its Biblical base, and the eighteenth-century Virginia Enlightenment tradition, rooted in natural law and natural rights.

While one may debate the question of Williams's impact on the First Amendment, his influence on Rhode Island's basic law is indisputable. All of the state's founding documents bear the indelible impress of his fundamental beliefs. The Providence town compact of 1637, that settlement's first frame of government, gave political power to the original "householders" but contained the all-important proviso that such control was to be exercised "only in civil things." A more detailed "plantation agreement" of 1640 (which has merited inclusion in Henry Steele Commager's *Documents of American History*) reiterated this limitation; and the colonial patent that Williams obtained for the original towns in 1644 from the Long Parliament gave implicit sanction to the separation of church and state.

The culmination of this pioneering process, however, was Rhode Island's royal charter of 1663, obtained from King Charles II by tenacious Newport Baptist John Clarke, an important religious leader whose views closely paralleled those of Roger Williams. This document allowed the establishment of a self-governing colony wherein all local officials, from the governor and assemblymen to the viewers of fences and corders of wood, were either chosen directly in town meeting by the freemen or appointed on an annual basis by the elected representatives of the people.

The charter's most liberal, generous, and unusual provision, however, bestowed upon the inhabitants of the tiny colony "full liberty in religious concernments." The document commanded that

> noe person within the sayd colony, at any time hereafter, shall bee any wise molested, punished, disquieted, or called in question for any differences in opinione in matters of religion.

This guarantee of religious liberty was a vindication of Williams's beliefs and royal recognition of the fundamental principles upon which the Providence Plantation was founded—absolute freedom of conscience and complete separation of church and state. As Williams observed, this liberality stemmed from the king's willingness to "experiment" in order to ascertain "whether civil government could consist with such liberty of conscience." This was the "lively experiment" upon which the government of Rhode Island was based.

With good reason, the charter of 1663 won the overwhelming approbation of the colonists. Later it prompted nineteenth-century historian (and Rhode Island summer colonist) George Bancroft to remark, with only a modicum of hyperbole, that "no where in the world were life, liberty and property safer than in Rhode Island."

Because such a system prevailed in seventeenth-century Rhode Island, this "moral sewer" (as the Puritans dubbed it) became a haven for Baptists, Separatists, Antinomian followers of Anne Hutchinson, Gortonians, Quakers, Sephardic Jews, and Huguenots. In 1702 disgruntled Puritan leader Cotton Mather wrote that Rhode Island was "a motley collection of all sects except Roman Catholics and true Christians" (i.e., Congregationalists).

But has Rhode Island continued to practice what its founder preached? That is the other half of our story. To a great extent, it has: never has freedom of worship been impaired within Rhode Island's borders. Such a record is truly commendable.

And yet for nearly two centuries this spirit of Rhode Island's famed guarantee was violated, for both colony and state imposed various civil disabilities and discriminatory policies upon religious minorities, especially Roman Catholics. Rhode Island, after Williams passed from the scene, too often exemplified the condition lamented by the Irish satirist Jonathan Swift: "We have just enough religion to make us hate," said Swift, "but not enough to make us love one another."

Rhode Island's religiously inspired litany of civil wrongs began in 1719, when the General Assembly enacted a code of laws containing a statute denying freemanship—the right to vote and hold office—to Catholics and non-Christians. Enacted during the frenzy over the possible return of the Catholic Pretender James III to the English throne, this statute was reaffirmed by the General Assembly in the legal codifications of 1730, 1745, and 1767. Not until 1783, after the benevolent occupation of Rhode Island by Count Rochambeau and his French forces, was the arbitrary disqualification of Catholics removed.

The act that accomplished this, however, neglected to define the civil status of those professing the Jewish faith. The Rhode Island colony's refusal to naturalize Jews was another blemish on the charter's guarantee of religious equality. Although Jews enjoyed freedom of worship, none, however qualified or competent, was ever made a freeman of the colony. On the issue of naturalization, both the Superior Court and the General Assembly, in 1761 and 1762 respectively, rejected the citizenship petitions of merchants Aaron Lopez and Isaac Elizer because they were non-Christians.

The colonial statute denying freemanship to Catholics was directed against a nearly nonexistent danger. In the middle decades of the nineteenth century, however, Catholicism became, for some native Rhode Islanders, a clear and present menace. This occurred when the onset of large-scale Irish Catholic immigration coincided with an originally unrelated movement to replace the royal charter (which Rhode Islanders had retained through the Revolutionary upheaval) with a written state constitution. The principal reform demands were reapportionment and the removal of the real estate requirement for voting—an eighteenth-century relic that all states except Rhode Island had abandoned by 1830.

When the constitutional reformers, led by Thomas Wilson Dorr, proposed "free suffrage" for all citizens, native-born and naturalized alike, opponents of sweeping change resorted to the device of political nativism to discredit and defeat Dorr and his campaign for equal rights. As part of their efforts, conservatives devised a dual system of suffrage that retained the real estate requirement for naturalized citizens, the bulk of whom were Irish Catholics. The mouthpiece of the anti-Dorrites, the *Providence Journal*, utilized the acid pen of editor Henry Bowen Anthony to succinctly state the nativist case. In Rhode Island, wrote Anthony,

> the balance of power rests in the hands of the Senators from the agricultural areas of the state. Where will the balance be under Dorr, [Dr. John A.] Brown and Company?... Where but among 2,500 foreigners and the hundreds more who will be imported. They will league and band together, and usurp our native political power.... Their priests and leaders will say to a political party as they say in New York City, give us by law every opportunity to perpetuate our spiritual despotism. At the feet of these men will you lay down your freedom.... Foreigners still remain foreign and are still embraced by mother church. He [*sic*] still bows down to her rituals, worships the host, and obeys and craves absolution from the priest. He cannot be assimilated.... Now is the time to choose between the two systems, the conservative checks [of the Freemen's Constitution] or foreigners responsible only to priests.

Unfortunately, such emotional harangues prevailed: Dorr was defeated and the present state constitution included in its original form a discriminatory double standard for voting and officeholding. Rhode Island had adopted, for religious motives, the most nativistic suffrage provision of any American state. This discriminatory system endured for the next forty-five years despite persistent local efforts at reform and harsh, though belated, criticism from the Congress of the United States.

In the early 1850s, when Dorr Democrats sought again to extend suffrage to naturalized immigrants, the *Journal* warned that if this were done, "Rhode Island ... will become a province of Ireland: St. Patrick will take the place of Roger Williams, and the shamrock will supercede the anchor and Hope."

In 1869 Henry Anthony, by then a Republican United States senator, fought against a proposal to broaden the Fifteenth Amendment to the U.S. Constitution. The proposed enlargement of the amendment's coverage would have abolished not only those qualifications for voting or holding office based on race, color, and previous condition of servitude but also those relating to nativity, property, education, and religious belief. Fearing that such an expansion would strike down Rhode Island's discriminatory suffrage system, Anthony admonished the Senate that his state's voting laws "were made for us, and whether right or wrong, they suit us and we intend to hold them; and we shall not ratify any amendment to the Constitution of the United States that contravenes them."

Because of southern opposition to enfranchisement of blacks, Rhode Island's support for the Fifteenth Amendment was critical, so the effort to expand it was dropped in the face of Anthony's threat. The Fifteenth Amendment, in its final form, was limited to blacks, and such ethnic minorities as the Irish of Rhode Island were left unprotected.

In the mid-1850s an anti-Catholic political faction—not unique to Rhode Island—captured control of state government. This American (or Know-Nothing) party was fortunately short-lived. During its brief ascendancy, however, it passed a ludicrous measure empowering school committees to inspect tax-free institutions (the so-called nunnery bill) and made vain attempts to extend the residency period for naturalization from two to twenty-one years and to declare attendees of parochial schools truants from the public schools.

Unfortunately, most Know-Nothings were absorbed by the

local Republican party, a development that helped to produce that partisan polarization of white Anglo-Saxon Protestant Republican versus Irish Catholic Democrat that marked Rhode Island politics for the next century. In few other American states, if any, have ethnic and religious factors shaped the political culture so dramatically.

It was also in the turbulent 1850s that the Rhode Island body politic was first convulsed by the divisive issues of state aid to sectarian education and Bible reading in the public schools (not whether the Bible should be read, but whether it should be the King James Version only or the Douay-Rheims Bible as well). The former issue still retains much of its volatility in the land of Roger Williams.

In the late nineteenth century the local Catholic minority continued to struggle against officially imposed discrimination that was often more subtle than overt. The suffrage restriction was eliminated in 1888, not because of enlightened ecumenism but because so many Irish American adults were now native-born that the qualification no longer served its intended purpose.

Still the Catholic community was compelled to contend for other civil rights. The state revenue code of 1876 removed tax-exempt status from parochial schools. Catholic services at state correctional and charitable institutions were not allowed for years, and when they were finally permitted in 1887, the state government refused to give any compensation to the Catholic chaplain, although his Protestant counterpart received a stipend of eighteen hundred dollars per year and other benefits. Then, in the 1890s, the American Protective Association formed locally to protest the rise of Catholic political power and influence.

By the early years of the twentieth century, that influence was sufficient to halt official acts of discrimination. Since the 1860s a large influx of new Catholic immigrants—French Canadians, then Portuguese, Italians, Polish, Lithuanians, Ukrainians, and Syrians—had swelled the ranks of the local Catholic community. The Rhode Island census of 1905 revealed that 50.8 percent of the Rhode Islanders who stated their religious preference declared themselves to be Roman Catholics. At least numerically, Catholics had become a majority.

Since the long-dominant Republican party then depended on the support of French Canadian and Italian votes to check the rising threat of the Irish-led Democratic party, overt anti-Catholicism by the GOP became a politically dangerous practice. The era of religiously inspired civil wrongs expired in view of this demographic reality, except for a brief and futile foray into local politics by the Ku Klux Klan in the mid-1920s.

During the Depression decade, for a myriad of economic and ethnocultural reasons, the local Irish Democrats wooed the French Canadians, the Italians, the Jews, the blacks, and other ethnic minorities away from their traditional Republican allegiance. This Irish-led and largely Catholic ethnic coalition seized control of state government in the aftermath of the 1934 election by a political coup known locally as the Bloodless Revolution. With few interruptions that coalition has dominated state politics ever since.

The ethnocultural homogenization produced by economic depression and war (bo·ʰ hot and cold), and by the first wave of suburbanization in ·ʾ   put a lid on religious rivalries during the first three ḏ   Democratic ascendancy. In most of the United ʳ   de Island, the new cult of consensus gaˑ   t historians of modern America·   ” This condition, articulated ·   ᴵerberg in his book *Protes-*   ·ion of religious accom-   ·spects this “American   was the calm before

          ·ed in one recent   ·d a tidal wave   ·ᴵ consensus; o·   ·ose who were pasᴸ   part o·   ·allenge to authority and ᴸ   ·uantly Catholic ethnic coalition still held the reins of government, its power augmented in 1966 by a U.S. Supreme Court decision that decreed a reapportionment of the General Assembly diminishing the influence of rural Protestants in the legislative process.

During the tumultuous 1960s the liberal Warren Court rendered several decisions on the relationship between religion and education that ran counter to the American Catholic tradition. In Rhode Island most legislative efforts to aid the state's financially troubled Catholic schools were thwarted by this Court's new and expansive view of the First Amendment's Establishment Clause. In 1969 the state legislature, with Protestant lawmakers largely in opposition, passed an act to supplement the salaries of teachers in parochial elementary schools. After an ACLU challenge, the U. S. Supreme Court, in the 1971 case of *Di Censo* v. *Robinson* (403 U.S. 602), struck down the measure because it provided "substantial support for a religious enterprise" and caused "an excessive governmental entanglement with religion." Shortly thereafter the federal District Court for Rhode Island invalidated a state school-bus law requiring towns to bus private school pupils beyond town boundaries if necessary. This decision prompted the legislature to create regional bus districts to circumvent the court's ruling. Today the legal tension between the Establishment Clause and the proponents of state aid to sectarian education still persists.

In 1973 the high court made its controversial decision on abortion in *Roe* v. *Wade*. Since that time the state legislature has displayed much more opposition to abortion than the general Catholic population, as evidenced by the decisive defeat of a pro-life amendment proposed by the 1986 state constitutional convention. Although abortion is basically a moral rather than a religious issue, in Rhode Island the battle has assumed sectarian overtones and church-state implications. Militant support for abortion and militant anti-Catholicism often go hand in hand.

Numerous laws to blunt the effect of *Roe* have passed the General Assembly, including one declaring that life begins at conception, another requiring spousal or parental permission for abortion, and another requiring the informed consent of the prospective patient, followed by a forty-eight-hour waiting period. Most of these laws have failed to pass constitutional muster in our federal District Court.

The latest church-state issue to pierce the thin veil of local ecumenism involves the use of public funds for religious displays. Here Rhode Island produced another nationally significant case in *Lynch* v. *Donnelly*, 465 U.S. 688 (1984). In this confrontation the ACLU challenged the city of Pawtucket's inclusion of a nativity scene in its Christmas display. In a 5-to-4 decision, Chief Justice Burger, speaking for the majority, dismissed the complaint in part because "it has never been thought either possible or desirable to enforce a regime of total separation" of church and state. Despite this 1984 ruling, however, the local ACLU has recently challenged the long-standing existence of a wayside cross on property owned by the town of East Greenwich; and so the battle continues.

As this sketchy survey reveals, even in the land of Roger Williams, where religious liberty has always existed and where no established church has ever reigned, history seems to support Montesquieu's cynical observation that "there has never been a kingdom given to so many civil wars as that of Christ." Yet if one must choose between a society in which those who are unified and dominant *may* grant rights to dissent and one in which those who are diverse and discordant must struggle towards accommodation and justice, I think that I must surely prefer the latter. One thing is certain: After 350 years, Rhode Island's "lively experiment" continues to be just that!

Postscript

Since my 1987 address to the American Catholic Historical Association, Rhode Island has generated another high-profile Establishment Clause case for the U.S. Supreme Court. *Lee* v. *Weisman*, 505 U.S. 577 (1992), developed from a graduation ceremony at Nathan Bishop Middle School in Providence at which a student, Deborah Weisman, objected to an invitation by Robert E. Lee, the principal, to clergymen to give the invocation and benediction. The Supreme Court ruled, in a 5–to–4 decision, that a school requirement that a student stand and remain silent during a "non-sectarian" prayer at the graduation exercise in a public school violated the Establishment Clause, even though attendance at the ceremony was completely voluntary. The student, said the Court, should not be required to give up her attendance at the graduation, "an important event in her life, in order to avoid unwanted exposure to religion."

404

This profile was written in 1990 for *Political Parties and Elections in the United States: An Encyclopedia*, ed. Louis Maisel (New York, 1991).

HENRY BOWEN ANTHONY (April 1, 1815–September 2, 1884), United States senator from 1859 until his death in 1884, was the principal organizer, publicist, and nurturer of Rhode Island's Republican party during its formative years.

Of old-line Rhode Island stock, Anthony was born in the rural town of Coventry in a mill village named for his father, a prominent textile manufacturer. At the age of twenty-three, five years after concluding his formal education at Brown University, he became the editor of the *Providence Journal*, then a small newspaper with Whig party affiliations. A skillful and trenchant writer, Anthony held this post until entering the Senate in 1859. Thereafter he presided as the newspaper's publisher, making the increasingly influential *Journal* the organ of Rhode Island's Republican party.

Political nativism was one persistent and undistinguished feature of Anthony's long journalistic and governmental career. From the year he assumed the editorship of the *Journal* in 1838, he made war upon "the foreign vagabond" (read "Irish Catholic"), who, he said, "came here uninvited and upon whose departure there is no restraint." Wielding his acid pen during the Dorr Rebellion in 1842, Anthony led the Law and Order party and zealously supported a real estate voting requirement for naturalized citizens. He successfully defended that discriminatory restriction against all challenges (both in Rhode Island and in the U.S. Congress) until his death in 1884, compiling a record of persistence nearly unmatched in the annals of American nativism.

While serving in Washington, Anthony groomed General Charles R. "Boss" Brayton to direct the organizational efforts of Rhode Island's Republican party. The most notable product of this political coalition (other than its pervasive corruption) was five-term United States senator Nelson W. Aldrich (1881–1911).

In Congress, Anthony supported protective tariffs, sound money, and congressional reconstruction of the South. Though he served as president *pro tempore* of the Senate in 1869, 1870, and 1871,

he was not a dominant or legislatively productive member of the upper house. Within Rhode Island, however, his political power was unsurpassed. Even Anthony's arch foe, Irish Democratic leader Charles E. Gorman, grudgingly acknowledged in eulogy that Anthony had "possessed in a preeminent degree that peculiar and necessary power in American politics to understand men and to direct their action; to discern the political forces, active and dormant, and to control and bring them into play, so that the political ideas and principles one maintains may be carried to success."

Henry Bowen Anthony

Charles R. Brayton | 42

This profile was written in 1999 for *American National Biography*, ed. John A. Garraty and Mark C. Carnes (New York, 1999).

CHARLES RAY BRAYTON (August 16, 1840-September 23, 1910), soldier and politician, was born in Warwick, Rhode Island, the son of William Daniel Brayton, a Republican congressman (1857 to 1861), and Anna Ward (Clarke) Brayton. He traced his Rhode Island roots back to 1643 and the founding of his native town of Warwick.

During four decades, between 1870 and his death in 1910, Charles Ray Brayton manipulated the politics of Rhode Island as the prototypical boss of a highly successful rural-based political machine. Brayton, a Brown University attendee (1859–61), compiled a distinguished Civil War career, capped by his brevetting as brigadier general of volunteers.

Shortly after the Civil War, General Brayton became the chief political lieutenant of U.S. senator Henry Bowen Anthony, the principal organizer of Rhode Island's Republican party. Anthony secured for his protégé such politically sensitive positions as those of the United States pension agent for Rhode Island (1870–74) and U.S. postmaster for Providence (1874–80). In 1876 Brayton began his long tenure as chairman of the Republican state party, whose members he addressed as "fellow machinists."

The controversial Brayton resigned from the post office under fire in 1880 for allegedly using the mails to distribute fixed ballots and for converting postal funds to party purposes. When he was stoutly defended by most of the state's elected Republicans and allowed to maintain his party position, the situation gave credence to the lament of a contemporary reformer who had observed that "if a man is an expert in all the deviltry known to politics, in Rhode Island he is made chairman of the Republican State Committee instead of being sent to jail."

General Charles Ray Brayton

For the next three decades Brayton survived repeated political scandals, incurring some dents but no disabling damage to his political machine. After Senator Anthony's death in 1884, Brayton directed his considerable talents towards ensuring the longevity, and hence the seniority, of U.S. senator Nelson W. Aldrich. Both men weathered a 1905 exposé of their political methodology in an article by Lincoln Steffens entitled "Rhode Island: A State for Sale."

The key to Brayton's success, in addition to his qualities of leadership and his deserved reputation as a stern disciplinarian, was his ability to control the General Assembly through old-stock rural legislators from the country towns, because each of the state's municipalities, regardless of size, had one vote in the Senate. Cynically remarking that "an honest voter is one that stays bought," Brayton used the contributions of Providence businessmen to buy up the vote in these small towns. This practice prompted Steffens to allege that "the political system in Rhode Island ... is grounded on the lowest layer of corruption that I have found thus far—the bribery of voters with cash at the polls."

When growing Democratic strength rendered the office of governor politically insecure, "the Boss" sponsored a law—the so-called Brayton Act of 1901—which placed the appointive and budgetary powers of the state in the hands of the rotten-borough Republican

Senate. Though never a member of the legislature, Brayton maintained an office in the new State House. In a highly publicized confrontation, the general was ousted from this command post in 1907 by James H. Higgins, the first Irish Catholic Democrat to win Rhode Island's governorship.

A loss of sight in 1903 diminished Brayton's effectiveness, but only his sudden death in 1910 broke his grip on the reins of power. Brayton's forty-year ascendancy, unparalleled in Rhode Island history, ranks him as the most successful and enduring machine politician in a state long renowned for organizational politics.

Nelson Aldrich, "General Manager of the United States"

This profile was written in 1990 for *Political Parties and Elections in the United States: An Encyclopedia*, ed. Louis Maisel (New York, 1991).

NELSON WILMARTH ALDRICH (November 6, 1841–April 16, 1915), Republican senator from Rhode Island for three decades (1881–1911), became the acknowledged leader of the conservative, business-oriented wing of the national Republican party during the administrations of William McKinley, Theodore Roosevelt, and William Howard Taft.

A protégé of Henry Bowen Anthony and a partner of Rhode Island Republican boss Charles R. Brayton, Aldrich owed his political longevity to a rural-based Republican machine that relied upon malapportionment and purchased votes to maintain dominance. In 1905 muckraker Lincoln Steffens examined the grass roots of Aldrich's power in an exposé entitled "Rhode Island: A State for Sale."

Had Aldrich been content merely to hold national office (like his sponsor, Senator Anthony) rather than wield national power, his association with Brayton would have been sufficient. However, Aldrich was ambitious, relentless, and resourceful in his pursuit of success, both political and financial. He cultivated friendships and business relationships with the great captains of industry and supported their demands for sound money (i.e., the gold standard), high protective tariffs, and minimal governmental interference with private enterprise. They, in turn, provided Aldrich with stock participations, loans, and other business opportunities that enabled the man many called "the General Manager of the United States" to achieve great personal wealth despite his humble beginnings as a grocery clerk in Providence.

Aldrich's most notable alliance was the one forged with the Rockefellers when his daughter Abby married John D. Rockefeller, Jr. That union produced several prominent children, the foremost of whom, Nelson Aldrich Rockefeller, became governor of New York and vice president of the United States (1974–77).

The respect which Aldrich commanded from contemporaries is epitomized by a frank admission of Theodore Roosevelt, leader of the Progressive Republicans: "Aldrich is a great man to me," Roosevelt once confided to Lincoln Steffens, "not personally, but as the leader of the Senate. He is the kingpin in my game. Sure, I bow to Aldrich; I talk to Aldrich; I respect him, as he does not respect me. I'm just a president, and he has seen lots of presidents."

Unfortunately for Aldrich, the tide of Progressive reform eroded his influence during his last term. As chairman of the Senate Finance Committee, he failed in his efforts to create a central bank controlled by private banking interests, and his emasculation of the revisionary Payne Tariff in 1909 helped to set off a wave of insurgent protest that eventually split the Republican party.

Jim Kiernan: Rhode Island's "Mr. Democrat" | 44

This tribute was written in December 1965
for publication in a Democratic party newsletter.

ON A CRISP JANUARY MORNING IN 1915, when the country
and its Democratic president, Woodrow Wilson, were grappling
with the problems of neutrality, when Jack Johnson held the
heavyweight crown, when Frank "Home Run" Baker had just
notched another American League title with eight circuit clouts,
and when Lillian Gish and Mary Pickford were the stars of the
silent screen, a young and vigorous freshman representative from
Mount Pleasant strode into the Rhode Island state capitol. This
novice legislator of that bygone day was none other than James
Henry Kiernan. For the next fifty-one years Jim Kiernan would
serve with distinction in the Rhode Island House, and for thirty-
five years, until the opening day of the 1950 session, he would
never miss a meeting.

Back in 1915 Jim Kiernan was a member of a dynamic but out-
numbered Democratic party in the General Assembly. In the half
century that followed, Jim not only witnessed the rise of the
Democrats to a position of dominance in the General Assembly
but was among those most responsible for that ascendancy.

When the Democratic party made its determined bid for political supremacy in 1932, Kiernan was there to assist, to advise, and to
guide Theodore Francis Green into the governor's chair. In the

elections of 1934 Green was reelected and the Democrats finally gained control of the General Assembly. In the session of January 1935 which followed, Kiernan was in the thick of the bitter fight that removed the Republicans' infamous Brayton Law from the books and reorganized state government, including the state Supreme Court.

414

Jim Kiernan's prominent role in the "Bloodless Revolution" of '35 was soon acknowledged when his colleagues chose him Speaker of the House for the 1937–38 session. It was during these turbulent thirties that "Mr. Democrat" first became chairman of the powerful House Judiciary Committee, floor leader of the Democratic majority, and a member of the Democratic State Committee. He held the judiciary committee post continuously from 1939, and the position of majority leader continuously from 1940, until his death in 1965. In these offices he displayed the leadership and skill that earned him the respect of political colleagues and adversaries alike. As the party's floor leader, he sponsored hundreds of bills that benefited Rhode Islanders in all walks of life.

James Kiernan, "Mr. Democrat," is shown here in 1937 during his one term as Speaker of the House of Representatives.

Jim Kiernan was a fighter for humane legislation throughout his career. When the historic Fair Housing Bill passed the Assembly in April 1965, the frail but militant Mr. Kiernan was reported by the *Journal* not only as voting in its behalf but as being the only representative to rise to his feet from his venerable desk no. 26 to give his "aye" for all to see.

Many honors came to "Mr. Democrat" during his long and illustrious career. On January 15, 1963, the General Assembly devoted its entire proceedings to praising the esteemed Democratic leader. In the following month the University of Rhode Island conferred an honorary doctor of laws degree upon a beaming Kiernan, who called the presentation the "most singular event of my life."

A gloomy and overcast December 9, 1965, was indeed a sad day for the Democratic party and for all Rhode Islanders, for it was on that day that the venerable eighty-one-year-old Jim Kiernan died. An appreciative public was allowed to pay him a final tribute when his body was placed in the rotunda of his beloved state capitol, the first time a public official had been so honored since Governor Aram J. Pothier lay in state in February 1928.

Fellow Democrats heaped praise upon Kiernan as expected, but even Republican governor John Chafee joined the chorus. "He displayed unfailing courtesy to even the humblest members of the House," said Chafee, a former legislator. "I have a deep affection for Jim. We loved him for his flair and dash, his quick wit, and his colorful ability to recall the old days."

"The Democratic party made me; else I would have been an ordinary practitioner," Jim Kiernan once said. "If I have been successful, and I have been fairly so, the Democratic party has been responsible for it, and I owe the party a debt I will never be able to repay if I live for 150 years." Of course, Jim Kiernan did not live 150 years, but as any Rhode Island Democrat will tell you, his debt to our party has indeed been paid in full.

Mary Brennan and I at a Bicentennial function in 1976

Mary Brennan: A Reminiscence 45

This tribute, written in January 1996, appeared in the *Pawtucket Times*.

ON JANUARY 10, 1996, Mary Partington Brennan of Cumberland died after a long contest with cancer. Her published obituary —given its subject—was relatively modest and brief; thus I have penned this addendum.

I first met Mary in 1973, when she left her travel business and entered state employ as staff coordinator of the Rhode Island Bicentennial Commission (ri76), an agency that I chaired. In the several years that followed, Mary worked sixty- and seventy-hour weeks, with no adjustment in salary, to make Rhode Island's independence celebration one of the most comprehensive and successful of any state.

Governor Joe Garrahy was one of thousands of Rhode Islanders who marveled at her energy and efficiency, so when the Bicentennial commemoration ended, he recruited her as a top aide and de facto chief of State House protocol. After eight years of dedicated, round-the-clock service for the governor, Mary moved on to become director of marketing at Green State Airport, there combining her travel experience with her social skills in the service of the state and its business community. Despite her terminal illness, she worked at Green until a few weeks before her all-too-early death.

Mary Brennan was a woman of scrupulous honesty, sincere humility, and boundless energy who loved people and lived to help and motivate them. When I hear the usual bad rap that Rhode Islanders affix upon state workers, I am reminded that Mary Brennan was a state employee for twenty-three years. During that public career she worked more hours, helped more people, and directed more special projects than anyone I know in any walk of life.

Mary Brennan was a social genius. She never wrote a book, painted a picture, founded a lucrative business, made a million, secured election to high public office, starred as an athlete, or enthralled us with her musical talent. She even lacked a college degree, and she was not mechanically skilled. Yet she was one of a handful of women to be inducted into the Rhode Island Heritage Hall of Fame; and she filled the Cathedral of SS. Peter and Paul on two-day notice with friends, admirers, and mourners who came to say farewell at her funeral Mass.

How did Mary earn such love and respect? She did it by giving love and respect to everyone she encountered. She did it by making all her many friends and patrons feel special, because to her they *were* special. She did it by letting her bosses and associates reap the praise for work she had dutifully performed. She did it by unswerving fidelity to her family and her church. Mary's life was testimony to the inspiration of a kind word, the exhilaration of a smile, and the transforming power of a helping hand.

Mary Brennan has come to the end of her earthly travel. Those who knew her are confident of her ultimate destination.

This essay appeared as commentary in
the *Providence Journal* in December 1999.

LLOYD GRIFFIN died on November 24, 1999, at the age of fifty-
nine. His memorial Mass on December 1 at Holy Rosary Church
in his native Fox Point was well attended for an ordinary man; but
Lloyd was not an ordinary man, and the church was far from over-
flowing. A few black community leaders were present—notably
Cliff Montiero, Mike Van Leesten, and John Rollins—but white
politicians were few. The only politico of stature was Fred Lippitt,
of whom it may be said that had his eloquence matched his integrity, sense of decency, and loyalty, Fred would have been the mayor
of Providence in 1990, with Lloyd's help.

The real mayor was absent. His failure to appear was ironic. Had
it not been for Lloyd Griffin in 1978, His Honor might have been
a one-term mayor. But Lloyd delivered Democratic South Providence and a suitcase full of absentee ballots in the 1978 election to
seal a Cianci victory over South Side challenger Frank Darigan.
For his brilliant performance in that election, I dubbed Lloyd
"Satchel" Griffin. He loved the metaphor. Of course, we can forgive
Buddy his absence, just as we forgave him for missing the funeral
mass of Dr. Vito Russo, the other major architect of the mayor's
1978 victory. Cianci, it seems, is a true Jeffersonian; like the great
Virginian, he believes that "government belongs to the living."

But what about Lloyd Griffin; what did he believe? I feel that he believed that politics was more than a popularity contest. To Lloyd, it was a means of doing good and wielding power, especially economic clout. As the legendary councilman from South Providence, Lloyd not only displayed legislative and governmental skills; he excelled at entrepreneurial endeavors. He combined self-interest with the public interest in a commendable way. He built more housing for his constituents, provided them with more jobs, and empowered them politically to a far greater degree than any local politician of his era.

420

Lloyd T. Griffin, Jr.

Lloyd was charismatic, he was blunt, he was strong, he was abrasive, he possessed a commanding presence; and he was successful. It is a rule of human nature that a person with these qualities is not widely liked. Lloyd was envied, resented, feared, and, above all, respected, but he was not widely loved. He willingly sacrificed affection for accomplishment.

As the first black councilman from South Providence, Lloyd was heir to a long line of politically adroit, popular, and talented Irish American politicians. In ability and achievement, he far exceeded them all! His style was reminiscent of "Battling Bob" Quinn, Felix Toupin, and Thomas P. McCoy—Rhode Island political mavericks of an earlier era. Like them, he was investigated, castigated, denigrated, and vilified by resentful opponents.

The detractors of these earlier politicians have long been forgotten, while their targets are enshrined in Rhode Island's political pantheon. So it will be with Lloyd T. Griffin, Jr.—the dominant ward leader of his era and the greatest Afro-American politician in Rhode Island's history.

This speech was delivered to a joint session of the
General Assembly at the Colony House, Newport, on May 4, 2000.

MILLENNIUM ADDRESS TO THE
RHODE ISLAND GENERAL ASSEMBLY

AT THE OUTSET, I thank Speaker John Harwood for according
me the great honor of addressing the General Assembly at this
millennium session. Since this gathering is not only symbolic but
also a regular session of the legislature, I will heed his advice and
that of Majority Leader Gerard Martineau, who introduced me,
and deliver *brief* remarks.

Rhode Island celebrates today—May 4—as Independence Day
primarily because of the zeal and persistence of James S. Slater,
who prevailed upon the General Assembly to declare it so in 1908.
In fact, Rhode Island's House of Deputies passed a resolution on
May 4, 1776, renouncing allegiance to King George III. The vote
was 60 to 6, with the six deputies from Newport in opposition.
But Rhode Island's ratification of the Declaration of Indepen-
dence did not occur until July 18, 1776—our real Independence
Day. Further, your predecessors passed their momentous resolve of
May 4, 1776, not in Newport but in the Providence statehouse on
Benefit Street.

So are we gathered in the wrong city on the wrong day? Not really, because the main reason for your presence in the Colony House today is to commemorate Newport's primacy as a capital of Rhode Island from 1644, when the three earliest towns convened under the new parliamentary patent, to May 1900, after which Providence became sole capital.

In the book *The Statehouses of Rhode Island*, I have described the era of the rotating legislature, during which the people's representatives literally traveled in political circles. In the seventeenth and early eighteenth centuries, these meetings were usually held in the four original towns. With the establishment of the county system—Newport, or Rhode Island, County and Providence County in 1703 and King's (later Washington) County in 1729—those original towns that were not county seats were eliminated from the rotation. Portsmouth was eliminated in 1739 and Warwick in 1741.

The Colony House in Newport, begun in 1739, is Rhode Island's oldest surviving statehouse/courthouse.

In 1746 Rhode Island annexed present-day Bristol County from Massachusetts, with Bristol the shire town, and in 1750 the General Assembly created Kent, the fifth and final county, with East Greenwich as its seat. The legislature held its first East Greenwich session in 1759, and it first came to Bristol to sit in 1785.

Because the General Assembly rotated its sessions among the five county seats, tiny Rhode Island could boast five simultaneous capitals—a striking example of the democratic localism that prevailed here. To accommodate its growth, which increased by two deputies with the creation of each new town, the legislature authorized the construction of buildings in each of the five county seats. These buildings were to serve the dual purpose of both statehouse and courthouse. Prior to their erection, the Assembly had usually met in taverns, church buildings, or spacious private homes.

Each of the final county structures built to accommodate the

422

General Assembly has survived and been restored—a tribute to the vitality of Rhode Island's preservation efforts. These citadels of government are Newport's Colony House (1739–43), Providence's Old State House (1760–62), the Kingston Courthouse (1775–76), the East Greenwich Statehouse (1804–5), and the Bristol County Statehouse and Courthouse (1816–17).

The oldest, most architecturally significant, and most prestigious of Rhode Island's surviving statehouses is the one we occupy today. Newport's Colony House, designed by Richard Munday, hosted its first Assembly session in 1742. In addition to its legislative functions, including the ratifications of the Declaration of Independence on July 18, 1776, and the U.S. Constitution on May 29, 1790, it has hosted such momentous legal proceedings as the investigation into the sinking of the *Gaspee* (1773), the case of *Trevett* v. *Weeden* (1786), the sensational Avery murder trial (1833), and the treason trial of Thomas Wilson Dorr (1844).

Until 1912 the legislators and general officers were elected for one-year terms and took office in May. The primary session of the General Assembly, where all appointments were made or renewed, was held in Newport's Colony House, attesting to Newport's position of first among equals. In May 1776, with Newport threatened by a British fleet, the renunciation session was held in Providence, as were the May sessions from 1777 through 1779, when the English troops actually occupied Newport.

Although the forces of the mother country evacuated the City by the Sea in October 1779, the building was soon preempted by the friendly French army of Rochambeau for use as a hospital. Using it also to minister to the soul, the French celebrated Rhode Island's first public Roman Catholic Mass in this structure during their stay in 1780–81. Thus displaced by the French, the legislature held a May session in Touro Synagogue. Ironically, although both Catholics and Jews were tolerated at this point in Rhode Island history, both were denied the status of freemen and its attendant right to vote.

Rhode Island implemented a popularly written state constitution in 1843 without disturbing the five-capital system, but in 1854 Amendment III to that document limited the legislative sessions to Newport (the last Thursday in May) and to an "adjourned session" in Providence. The General Assembly held its last session in South Kingstown in 1851, in Bristol in 1852, and in East Greenwich in 1854.

As Providence grew rapidly in population, territory, and economic significance during the late nineteenth century, Newport's days were numbered. With a large and beautiful new statehouse already under construction on Providence's Smith Hill, in 1900 the legislature proposed, and the people passed, Article of Amendment XI, decreeing that the Assembly would meet on the first Tuesday in January 1901 in Providence, and only there from that date forward.

Newport's last primary session was held in May 1900, and until today the Assembly sat in this Colony House only once thereafter—a historic and commemorative session, such as this, held in 1976. As state Bicentennial chairman, I had the honor of addressing the legislators on that memorable occasion also.

Having traced Newport's history as a seat of government, let us focus on the last primary session held in Newport, the event whose centennial we observe today. Since the town of Narragansett was not established until 1901 and West Warwick not until 1913, the May 1900 state Senate consisted of thirty-seven members —one from each city or town. It also included Republican governor William Gregory as presiding officer and Republican lieutenant governor Charles Dean Kimball as a voting member. The party lineup was lopsided: thirty-four Republicans and three Democrats. The one-town, one-senator rule that prevailed in Rhode Island through the 1928 elections gave the rural-based Republican party complete dominance in the upper chamber. "The senate," exclaimed future Democratic congressman George F. O'Shaunessey, "was a malign influence exercised over state government by the abandoned farms of Rhode Island."

The House on that final Thursday in May 1900 had seventy-two members, sixty of whom were Republicans. There were no women and no blacks in that assemblage, although four blacks had recently served in the House from Newport: Mahlon Van Horne, 1885–87;

Joseph Banks, 1888; John Jenkins, 1888–89; and Joseph H. Monroe, 1894–96. Only Banks was a Democrat.

In 1900 most of the ancestors of today's legislators were found among the landless peasantry of Poland, Italy, Portugal, Russia, or Greece, or they worked as sharecroppers or tenant farmers in the South, or locally in mills, or on public works projects, or as domestic servants.

In May 2000 gender is no longer a legal barrier to political office, and the unwritten and subtle religious, ethnic, and racial barriers to legislative service have evaporated. Today's General Assembly is more open, diverse, pluralistic, democratic (both small and big *D*), and representative than it ever has been. Race, religion, ethnicity, gender, and sexual preference are not the impediments they were when the General Assembly last sat in primary session at Newport.

Today's General Assembly is also far less prone to the scandals that made Rhode Island at the turn of the last century "A State for Sale" (to quote muckraker Lincoln Steffens). In 1900 there were no investigative reporters with their suspicious and ever-watchful eyes on the proceedings of this body (perhaps because the dominant newspaper, the *Providence Journal*, was then allied with the dominant party). There was no Ethics Commission or legal code of conduct for public officials, and there was little public scrutiny of the General Assembly's work. In 1900, legislators swam in a secluded country fishing hole. Today you swim in a fishbowl.

Can one imagine such a political dinosaur as General Charles R. "Boss" Brayton roaming the halls of the State House today? Though never an elected member of this body, Brayton dominated its deliberations to such a degree that the legislature was often called "the General's Assembly." Through his mastery over the Republican party organization, he controlled state government. The Boss addressed the members of his state Republican committee as "fellow machinists," and he subscribed to the motto, in an era of blatant vote buying, that "an honest voter is one who stays bought." Today's political climate has rendered bosses like Brayton extinct and impossible.

Although the physical setting in which the General Assembly

meets has shifted and the composition and conduct of this body have changed dramatically, one thing has been constant—the plenary power of the General Assembly, as derived from the charter of 1663, from subsequent constitutions, and ultimately from the people. For all its good work and noble intentions, the Ethics Commission lost the recent separation-of-powers case because it did not know Rhode Island's history.

As our Supreme Court has advised, perhaps with some deference to my historical brief (now published in book form), the General Assembly is the dominant branch of state government in Rhode Island, a state that has chosen not to adopt the federal model of separation of powers. The colonial charter's broad grant of power to the legislature has been carried forward by Article IV, Section 10, of the 1843 constitution, which is now Article VI, Section 10, of the present basic law: "The General Assembly shall continue to exercise the powers they have heretofore exercised unless prohibited in this constitution."

Both the Bible and the electorate, however, tell us that from those to whom much is given, much is expected. The people of Rhode Island have conferred great power on their legislature—first by acquiescence, but since 1843 by constitutional mandate. They have the absolute right to expect that such broad power be wielded with prudence, restraint, and justice for all.

I sincerely believe that the historian who delivers this address a century hence will tell your successors that the Rhode Island General Assembly of the millennium year 2000 both defended its prerogatives tenaciously and used its vast power wisely and well!

Tradition and Turmoil: Government and Politics in Rhode Island, 1636–1986

48

I delivered this narrative in the autumn of 1986 in a series of three lectures sponsored by the Rhode Island Historical Society, which was celebrating Rhode Island's 350th anniversary. Since a comprehensive survey such as this must inevitably repeat material found in other essays in this volume, I wrestled with the decision to delete it (as I have deleted several other pieces for that reason). However, because the narrative is a cohesive, thematic, and integrated rendering of a particular aspect of Rhode Island history, I decided to include it with instructions to the reader to skip the familiar parts.

IF WE DISREGARD THE TRIBAL ORGANIZATIONS of Narragansetts, Wampanoags, Niantics, Nipmucks, and Pequots (as most American historians do, to their discredit), government in Rhode Island began when religious exile Roger Williams and about a dozen disciples founded Providence in the spring of 1636. During the town's early months, civic affairs were conducted by a fortnightly meeting of "masters of families," or "householders," who considered matters relating to the "common peace, watch, and planting." As the number of settlers increased, a formal government became necessary, so Williams and the initial settlers drafted articles of self-incorporation in 1637. Then these "masters of families" entered into a mutual compact creating a "town fellowship," and thirteen other inhabitants who were either unmarried or minors signed a submission agreement to obey the householders and all whom "they shall admit into the same fellowship and privilege."

These documents were the fundamental papers of Providence town government. The major features of these first governmental agreements were the vesting of administrative control in a majority of the householders and the all-important proviso that such control was to be exercised "only in civil things." This latter clause reflected the desire of Roger Williams to establish a colony based on the then revolutionary principles of religious liberty and the separation of church and state.

Other dissenters soon followed Williams to the Narragansett Bay region, and two additional towns took root: Portsmouth (1638), founded by William Coddington in concert with Antinomian preacher Anne Hutchinson, and Newport (1639), established by Coddington after a squabble with the fiery woman the Puritans called "the American Jezebel." By the end of 1639 the ambitious Coddington succeeded in engineering a consolidation of the two island towns under a common administration, of which he was governor. This new political entity proclaimed itself a democracy in 1641 and guaranteed religious liberty to all. Because title to the entire island of Aquidneck (or Rhode Island) was in his name, Coddington began to entertain thoughts of creating a political domain of his own, distinct from Williams's Providence Plantation. This ambitious plan constituted the most serious internal obstacle to the creation of a united colony during Rhode Island's formative years.

Legal title to the lands on which the early towns were planted rested only upon deeds from the Narragansett chiefs, or sachems, because Williams had been so bold as to declare that the king of England's authority to grant these New World lands to English colonists rested upon "a solemn public lie." This view, though just, was unacceptable to the neighboring colonies of Plymouth, Massachusetts Bay, Connecticut, and New Haven. The more orthodox Puritans who resided therein, angered by the defiance of Rhode Island's religious outcasts, began to cast covetous eyes upon the beautiful Narragansett Bay region, which, they said, had been transformed by Williams, Hutchinson, Samuel Gorton, and their kind into "a moral sewer."

To unite the towns against this threat, to thwart Coddington's political designs, and to secure parliamentary protection for his holy experiment, Williams journeyed in 1643 to an England on the verge of civil war to secure a patent that would unite the settlements of Portsmouth, Newport, and Providence into a single colony and officially confirm the settlers' claims to the lands they held by Indian purchase, even though some of the deeded territory was claimed by the Wampanoags. Williams obtained the desired patent from Robert Rich, earl of Warwick, and his parliamentary Committee on Foreign Plantations. Significantly the patent lacked the royal seal, for King Charles I had already begun to lose power and control to the parliamentary opposition.

The patent of March 14, 1644, was the first legal recognition of the Rhode Island towns by the mother country. It authorized the union of Providence, Portsmouth, and Newport under the name of "the Incorporation of Providence Plantations in Narragansett Bay in New England," and it granted these towns "full power and authority to govern and rule themselves" and future inhabitants by majority decision, provided that all regulations that were enacted were "conformable to the laws of England" so far as the nature of the place would permit. This initial patent specifically conferred political power upon the inhabitants of the towns. The repeated emphasis of the document upon "civil government" gave implicit sanction to the separation of church and state, whereas the use of the words "approved and confirmed" rather than "grant" in conjunction with the right to the land was a vindication of Williams's questionable contention that the Indian deeds were valid. Williams's adroitness and diplomacy had won the day, and he was greeted with great enthusiasm when he returned to Providence, patent in hand, in September 1644.

In 1642, while Williams was in England, volatile Samuel Gorton—another freethinking and quarrelsome religious leader—had succeeded in establishing Shawomet, a mainland settlement to the south of Providence that Gorton eventually called Warwick in honor of his English benefactor. Here, as in Providence, liberty of conscience prevailed. Although his new town was not mentioned in the patent, Gorton sought and eventually secured its inclusion under the patent's protective provisions, despite the vigorous attempts of Massachusetts to annex the Warwick settlement.

The two island towns of Portsmouth and Newport also embraced the legislative patent, and representatives of the four communities met initially on Aquidneck Island in November 1644. After this and three subsequent sessions, they held the momentous Portsmouth Assembly of May 1647 to organize a government and to draft and adopt a body of laws. According to Charles McLean Andrews, the leading historian of colonial America, "the acts and orders of 1647 constitute one of the earliest programmes for a government and one of the earliest codes of law made by any body of men in America and the first to embody in all its parts the precedents set by the laws and statutes of England."

The assembly that drafted this code was attended by a majority of the freemen of the four towns. Upon convening, the delegates agreed that they were "willing to receive and to be governed by the laws of England ... so far as the nature and constitution of this plantation will admit." However, they further declared that the form of government for the colony was "democratical," in that it rested on "the free and voluntary consent of all, or the greater part of the free inhabitants." This claim was vindicated by the first list of colonial freemen, published in 1655. When compared with the population figures of the towns, it reveals that one-half the adult male residents in Providence, two-thirds in Portsmouth and Newport, and nearly 90 percent in Warwick had the right to vote and hold office.

The 1647 assembly elected officers, established a system of representation, and devised a legislative process containing provisions both for local initiative (repealed in 1650) and popular referendum. Then it enacted the remarkable code, an elaborate body of criminal and civil law prefaced by a bill of rights. Finally, for the administration of justice, the productive assembly established a General Court of Trials with jurisdiction over all important legal questions. The president, who was the chief officer of the colony, and the assistants, who represented their respective towns, were to constitute this high tribunal. By inference, the existing town courts were to possess the jurisdiction they heretofore exercised in matters of minor and local importance.

The code and the court system of 1647 would serve as the cornerstones of the judicial establishment of both the colony and the state of Rhode Island. Thus did the four original towns and their inhabitants combine to create a fairly systematized federal commonwealth and deal a temporary blow to the forces of de-centralization.

This promising union was immediately threatened, however, by the ambitious William Coddington. In 1651 the Newport leader secured from the English Council of State a commission that contravened the patent of 1644 by granting him exclusive ownership and proprietary rights to the islands of Aquidneck (Rhode Island) and Conanicut (Jamestown). A determined group of Newporters opposed this power grab, and they dispatched Dr. John Clarke to England to obtain a recision of this extraordinary commission. Clarke sought the aid of the influential Roger Williams, and the two men made the tedious journey to the mother country. As a result of the intercession on Williams's behalf by Sir Henry Vane and Oliver Cromwell, the Council of State responded by annulling the Coddington commission and reaffirming the patent. After a brief immersion in English domestic affairs, Williams returned to Rhode Island in 1654 and immediately began to counteract the divisive forces within the settlement. He was determined to reunite and consolidate the four towns, and by mid-1657 his efforts produced an encouraging degree of cohesion.

There were still stormy seas ahead for the Rhode Island ship of state, for no sooner had a semblance of internal unity and stability been created than there arose two external dangers, one of which menaced the colony's landed possessions and the other its very existence. The first danger resulted from the claims of the Connecticut-based Atherton land company to much of present-day Washington County; the second and greater threat arose from the restoration of the Stuart dynasty to the throne of England in 1660. The Restoration rendered doubtful the legal validity of the parliamentary patent of 1644 and placed Rhode Island in a precarious position because of her close ties with the antimonarchical Commonwealth and Protectorate of Oliver Cromwell.

Fearful for its legal life, the colony commissioned the diligent Dr. John Clarke (who had remained in England upon completing his successful mission of 1651–52) to obtain royal confirmation of its right to exist. After an exasperating delay stemming from

Rhode Island's and Connecticut's conflicting claims to the Narragansett Country, Clarke, with the assistance of Connecticut agent John Winthrop, Jr., secured from Charles II the royal charter of 1663. This coveted document was immediately transported to Rhode Island, where it was received by the grateful colonists in November 1663.

The 6,500-word instrument had the legal form of a corporate or trading company charter. It devoted relatively brief space to the organization of government, but it did provide for the offices of governor, deputy governor, and ten assistants. The original holders of these positions were named in the charter itself, but their successors, called magistrates, were "to be from time to time, constituted, elected, and chosen at-large out of the freemen" of the colony (or "company").

The charter also provided that certain of the freemen should be "elected or deputed" by a majority vote of fellow freemen in their respective towns to "consult," to "advise," and to "determine" the affairs of the colony together with the governor, deputy governor, and assistants. It specified that Newport was entitled to six of these "elected or deputed" representatives; Providence, Portsmouth, and Warwick received four each, and two were to be granted to any town that might be established in the future. This was an equitable apportionment in 1663, but in the early nineteenth century it would become a source of grave discontent.

The governor, deputy governor, assistants, and representatives (or deputies) were collectively called the General Assembly. Each member of this body had one vote. The Assembly, with the governor presiding, was to meet at least twice annually, in May and October. The only charter-imposed qualification for members was that they be freemen of the colony.

Rhode Island's legislature was endowed by the charter with extraordinary power. It could make or repeal any law, if such action was not "repugnant" to the laws of England; it could set or alter the time and place of its meeting; and it could grant commissions. It could exercise extensive powers over the judicial affairs of the colony, prescribe punishments for legal offenses, grant pardons, regulate elections, create and incorporate additional towns, and "choose, nominate and appoint such … persons as they shall think fit" to hold the status of freemen.

The royal charter also mandated annual elections for all at-large officers of the colony, provided for the raising and governing of a militia, and established acceptable boundaries (which included the Pawcatuck River as the western line of demarcation). Further, the document asserted, with language not unknown in other colonial charters, that inhabitants of the colony "shall have and enjoy all liberties and immunities of free and natural subjects … as if they … were born within the realm of England." This clause and its alleged violation would cause the mother country serious difficulties a century hence.

Finally, the charter's most liberal and generous provision bestowed upon the inhabitants of the tiny colony "full liberty in religious concernments." The document commanded that no person shall be "molested, punished, disquieted, or called in question for any differences in opinion in matters of religion" that "do not actually disturb the civil peace of our said colony."

This guarantee of absolute religious liberty was a vindication of Williams's beliefs and royal recognition of the fundamental principles upon which the Providence Plantation was founded— absolute freedom of conscience and complete separation of church and state. As Williams observed, this liberality stemmed from the king's willingness to "experiment" in order to ascertain "whether civil government could consist with such liberty of conscience." This was the "lively experiment" upon which the government of Rhode Island was based—an experiment that prompted some to observe that Massachusetts had law without liberty, but Rhode Island now had liberty without law.

The charter of 1663 won the overwhelming approval of the colonists, and with good reason: as the nineteenth-century American historian George Bancroft remarked, with only slight exaggeration, "No where in the world were life, liberty and property safer than in Rhode Island."

During the last three decades of the seventeenth century, Rhode Island's governmental progress was halting and uneven. In 1675 and 1676 King Philip's War—a fierce struggle with the

Wampanoag, Nipmuk, and Narragansett Indians—caused racial embitterment, drained the colonial treasury, disrupted civil government, caused widespread property damage, and took a high toll of human lives. From 1686 to 1689 Rhode Island's charter was suspended as King James II and his colonial agent, Sir Edmund Andros, attempted to consolidate the coastal colonies from New Jersey to Maine under one regional government called the Dominion of New England. Then King William's War erupted between the English colonies and those of New France.

That the seventeenth century ended with Rhode Island intact was a minor miracle. Despite freewheeling dissenters, jealous neighbors, internal secessionists, hostile Indians, avaricious land speculators, and imperial reorganizers, Rhode Island survived. The manner of its survival, however, failed to impress investigators sent by the Crown. One report at century's end by Richard Coote, earl of Bellomont, observed that Rhode Islanders had a disdain for learning and were "shamefully ignorant." His report also disclosed an unjustified exercise of the judicial function by the General Assembly, violations of the Acts of Trade, usurpation of admiralty jurisdiction (which belonged only to the mother country), and the harboring of pirates. Bellomont concluded his twenty-five-point indictment, which listed many deviations from the directives of the charter, by asserting that "his Majesty is neither honored nor served by that government, as at present it is managed."

From 1696 onward, however, the colony began to achieve a measure of stability. In that year the General Assembly developed more systematic and workable procedures and formally became bicameral, dividing into the House of Magistrates, or Senate, and the House of Deputies, or Representatives. In imitation of the English Parliament, the deputies assumed the task of preparing the tax bill and choosing their own Speaker and clerk.

In 1698 Samuel Cranston was elected governor. During his tenure of twenty-nine years, by far the longest of any of Rhode Island's governors (he died in office on April 26, 1727), Cranston established internal unity and brought his colony into a better working relationship with the imperial government in London.

One valid criticism of the colony leveled by Bellomont had concerned the absence of a code of general statutes, in consequence of which "the people are at a loss to know what is law among them." This deplorable condition was remedied in 1705, when a satisfactory manuscript digest was prepared. Then, in 1719, the Assembly issued its first printed compilation of Rhode Island's general laws. On the debit side, this digest contained a statute banning Catholics and Jews from voting or holding office—a violation of the spirit, if not the letter, of the charter of 1663.

During the Cranston regime the colony's western boundary dispute with Connecticut was resolved in Rhode Island's favor. A second important territorial development, with a direct impact on Rhode Island's network of statehouses, was the creation of the county system in 1703. By that date the Assembly had incorporated five towns in addition to the original four: Westerly (1669), New Shoreham (1672), Kingstown (1674), East Greenwich (1677), and Jamestown (1678). The five mainland communities were assigned to the County of Providence Plantations, while the four island settlements were included in Rhode Island County. From the outset, however, these counties were merely militia districts and units of judicial administration, not separate layers of government as they are in nearly all other states.

In 1729, six years after Kingstown was divided into North and South, King's (later Washington) County was created, with Little Rest (Kingston) its seat, and Providence County assumed its present name. In 1746 the readjustment of the colony's eastern boundary with Massachusetts brought Tiverton and Little Compton into Newport County (formerly Rhode Island County) and Cumberland into Providence County, and it prompted the creation of Bristol County from the former Massachusetts communities of Bristol—which became the county seat—and Warren, which then included present-day Barrington. This new judicial unit of less than twenty-five square miles became and remains America's second smallest county.

Finally, in 1750, Kent County was set off from the southern tier of Providence County, with East Greenwich its shire town. At this juncture Rhode Island boasted a population (according to a 1748 census) of 34,128 residing in twenty-four towns, of which Newport was easily the largest and most prominent. The vast majority of the people, however, lived in a rural, agrarian setting.

The five counties created between 1703 and 1750 influenced the operations of Rhode Island's government for more than a century. Each of these governmental units prompted the construction of a county house in which the General Assembly could meet and the courts could deliberate. Because the legislature rotated its sessions from county seat to county seat, each of these buildings became, in effect, a colony house and each county seat became a capital. The largest, oldest, and most imposing of these citadels of colonial government presently standing was erected in Newport in 1739, and each newly elected legislature convened and organized there annually on the first Wednesday in May from 1742 until 1900.

The county system served mainly to systematize judicial proceedings. By the charter's general charge to the legislature "to appoint, order and direct, erect and settle, such places and courts of jurisdiction, for the hearing and determining of all actions, cases, matters and things ... as they shall think fit," the basic law of 1663 did not fundamentally alter the judicial structure of 1647. The General Court of Trial was retained, and in 1664 the Assembly ordered that its sessions be held semiannually, with the governor or deputy governor and at least six assistants presiding. From time to time several inferior courts were also created.

Because legislative and judicial functions were for a time combined in the same body of men (namely, the governor, deputy governor, and assistants), the General Assembly often exercised functions new considered the exclusive domain of the judicial branch. Almost any part of the judicial process was open to its inspection and possible correction. The nature of its involvement in judicial affairs appeared to Lord Bellomont (and many observers since) to have been a usurpation of power not justified by the charter.

The rearrangement of the court system in 1729, through the use of three counties (Newport, Providence, and King's) as units of judicial administration, was a change of primary importance. The lowest tribunal in this county-based structure was the local court of the justice of the peace. This agency, which was in continuous session, had original jurisdiction in minor matters and bound over more serious offenders to the higher court having jurisdiction. On the next level were the Courts of General Sessions of the Peace and the Courts of Common Pleas. The former, established in each county, were conducted by all the local justices of the peace or any five of them, and they were empowered to try all criminal cases, capital crimes excepted. Their sessions were semiannual and their decisions could be appealed to the highest court. They in turn exercised appellate jurisdiction over all petty offenses originally triable by a justice of the peace.

The Courts of Common Pleas were civil courts conducted by "judicious" persons chosen by the Assembly from their respective counties. These appointees, upon their selection, were elevated to a justiceship of the peace. The jurisdiction of these courts, which was both original and appellate, extended to the trial of nearly all civil actions arising in the county. Their business was conducted semiannually together with that of the Courts of General Sessions. Although the Courts of Common Pleas and the Courts of General Sessions were nominally distinct from one another, both were usually conducted by the same personnel.

At the apex of the county system was the Superior Court of Judicature, Court of Assize, and General Gaol Delivery, as the General Court of Trial was renamed in 1746. Held at Newport, it consisted of the governor, deputy governor, and assistants. The Superior Court possessed original jurisdiction in certain major cases, but its primary function consisted in reviewing appeals from decisions of the Courts of General Sessions and the Courts of Common Pleas. Petitions from decisions of the Superior Court, however, were often entertained and acted upon by the General Assembly, and occasionally appeals from the court's verdict were accepted by the king in council.

In February 1746 the governor and assistants were removed from the bench of the Superior Court and replaced by one chief justice and four associates, but legislative influence was not significantly diminished by this change. Judges could still be members of the Assembly, so those deputies or assistants appointed to the bench usually retained their legislative posts. Furthermore, all judges were subject to annual appointment by the Assembly. During the session preceding the 1746 Superior Court Act, the legislature established a formal procedure for receiving, "hearing and determining" petitions praying relief from court decisions, thus strengthening and reaffirming its appellate powers, which were similar to those possessed by the English House of Lords. These practices endured for the remainder of the colonial period. In fact, the petition process and the system of annual appointment persisted until the establishment of the state constitution in 1843.

The development of executive power under the charter of 1663 was comparable to the growth of judicial autonomy: both were repressed by the powerful legislature. Apart from making the governor the presiding officer of the General Assembly and granting him the right to convene special sessions of that body, the charter bestowed upon him few exclusive powers of significance. As little more than the executive agent of the Assembly, he had no appointive power, for that important prerogative resided in the legislature. Even the governor's charter-conferred position of commander in chief was carefully circumscribed by the Assembly.

A final significant implementation of the charter concerned the creation of freemen and their consequent power to vote. Contrary to widely held opinion, the basic law of 1663 did not establish a specific suffrage requirement; it simply empowered the Assembly to "choose, nominate and appoint" freemen of the colony. However, both the framers and recipients of the charter apparently considered the franchise a privilege to be exercised only by those who had been elevated to the status of freemen, and indeed such was the practice in both the towns and in the colony prior to 1663. Thus, under the royal charter freemanship remained a prerequisite for voting, and the colonial legislature in 1664 declared "that none presume to vote . . . but such whom this General Assembly expressly by their writing shall admit as freemen."

According to the voting-rights statute of 1664, any person of "competent estate" could become a freeman of the colony either by direct application to the Assembly or through being proposed by the chief officer of the town in which he lived. In the normal course of events Rhode Islanders secured dual freemanship. First they gained the right of inhabitancy and acquired a "competent estate" in the town where they had chosen to reside, and then they applied and were admitted to town freemanship by their fellow townsmen of that status. Finally their names were proposed, or "propounded," to the General Assembly for admittance as freemen of the colony by the town's chief officer or the town clerk. When a town freeman was proposed to the Assembly in this manner, his acceptance as a freeman of the colony was practically assured. Once he was approved, his name was entered in the records of the colony.

In 1723 a statute was passed by the Assembly that set the first specific landed requirement for town freemanship, and since that status was the usual and nearly automatic prelude to colonial freemanship, the act is worthy of citation. This law stipulated that a person must be a "freeholder of lands, tenements, or hereditaments in such town where he shall be admitted free, of the value of one hundred pounds, or the [rental] value of forty shillings per annum, or the eldest son of such a freeholder." In 1729 the real estate requirement was increased to £200, and in 1746 to £400, but by 1760 it had been reduced to £40 (about $134). These drastic and erratic changes were more the result of inflationary and deflationary trends than of stringency or fickleness of the General Assembly.

The freehold requirements and suffrage stipulations enacted by the legislature might cause the uncritical reader to assume that the franchise was a privilege enjoyed by a select minority. Such an inference would be erroneous. The real estate requirement for freemanship was not a measure of oppression or restriction in a rural, agrarian society where land tenure was widely dispersed. The suffrage statute of 1746 declared that the manner of admitting freemen was "lax" and the real estate qualification was "very low." Authoritative students of Rhode Island's colonial history estimate that 75 percent of the colony's white adult male population were able to meet the specific freehold requirements from the time of their imposition in 1723 to the outbreak of the War for Independence.

This fact, however, needs some qualification. Being allowed to vote and hold office was not synonymous with exercising those privileges. Normally less than half the freemen bothered to vote, and those that did often elected to office men from the upper socio-economic strata. Rhode Island democracy was one of indifference and deference, though it was a democracy nonetheless.

Although the incentive to participate politically was not widespread, it was strong in some quarters, as evidenced by the development of a system of two-party politics in the generation preceding the American Revolution. Opposing groups, one headed by Samuel Ward and the other by Stephen Hopkins, were organized with sectional overtones; generally speaking (though there were notable exceptions), the merchants and farmers of southern Rhode Island, led by Ward, battled with their counterparts from Providence and its environs, the faction led by Hopkins. The principal goal of these groups was to secure control of the powerful legislature in order to obtain the host of public offices — from chief justice to inspector of tobacco — at the disposal of that body. In these circumstances the governor, as party leader, acquired an informal influence far beyond his meager official power.

The semipermanent nature, relatively stable membership, and explicit sectional rivalry of the warring camps have led one historian to describe the state's pre-Revolutionary political structure as one of "stable factionalism." Jackson Turner Main, the leading authority on the early formation of American political parties, has unequivocally stated that "Rhode Island produced the first two-party or, more accurately, two-factional, system in America." Another historian, David Lovejoy, has maintained that Rhode Islanders revolted from British rule not only "on the broad grounds of constitutional right to keep Rhode Island safe for liberty and property" but also to preserve "the benefits of party politics" — patronage and spoils.

As noteworthy as the development of the party system in mid-eighteenth-century Rhode Island were the rules by which the political game was played. The charter provided the broad framework within which elections were conducted, but a succession of resourceful, imaginative politicians supplied the unique details through an intricate combination of custom and statute.

The salient and most significant feature of Rhode Island government under the charter was that the crucial electoral arena was the colony—and later the state—as a unit. The governor and deputy governor, together with a secretary, an attorney general, and a treasurer, were elected annually in April on a colonywide or at-large basis, as were ten "assistants" who constituted the upper house. Only the deputies, elected semiannually in April and August, were chosen on a local basis. Thus there existed an obvious inducement to form colonywide parties in order to elect a full slate of general officers.

For these at-large contests, Rhode Islanders devised a peculiar system known as "proxing." A "prox" was a ballot upon which a party placed the names of its at-large candidates. On the third Wednesday in April, the elector in his town meeting took the prox of his choice, made any deletions or substitutions on it that he deemed desirable, and signed it on the reverse side in the presence of the town moderator. The voter then submitted the prox to the moderator, who forwarded it to the town clerk to be recorded. When this ritual was concluded, the proxes were sealed in a packet and taken to Newport by one of the town's state legislators for the start of the May session of the Assembly. On "election day," the first Wednesday in May, ballots were opened and counted by the incumbent governor in the presence of the incumbent assistants and newly elected deputies sitting jointly in Grand Committee. The candidate having a majority of the total vote cast for his respective office was declared elected.

Under this system a party's success was dependent upon many procedural factors: how widely its printed prox could be distributed, how many new voters could be qualified by fraudulent transfers of land, how many electors of the opposite persuasion could be induced by bribes to abstain from voting. Rhode Island was also a democracy of corruption and chicanery. An English visitor, the Reverend Andrew Burnaby, perceptively observed in his travels through the colony in 1760 that the "men in power, from the highest to the lowest, are dependent upon the people, and frequently act without that strict regard to probity and honor, which ever ought invariably to influence and direct mankind."

Rhode Island's political antics, not to mention its autonomy, scandalized many a squeamish observer. In the eyes of the colony's conservative critics, the land of Roger Williams, even on the eve of revolt, was "dangerously democratic." Chief Justice Daniel Horsmanden of New York, in a 1773 report to the earl of Dartmouth during the *Gaspee* investigation, disdainfully described Rhode Island as a "downright democracy" whose governmental officials were "entirely controlled by the populace," and conservative Massachusetts governor Thomas Hutchinson lamented to George III that Rhode Island was "the nearest to a democracy of any of your colonies."

Because of such "democratic" conditions, the years prior to the War for Independence saw no protests or attempts at reform directed against the suffrage requirements or the charter-imposed system of legislative apportionment. Rhode Islanders of the Revolutionary generation and their individualistic forebears knew well that they enjoyed near-autonomy within the empire and broad powers of self-government within their colony, and they were also keenly aware that their self-determination flowed in large measure from the munificent charter of Charles II. Thus they harbored a passionate attachment to that document and defended it against all challenges. Allowed to weather the Revolutionary upheaval, the charter would remain the basic law of the state until 1843—a point far beyond its useful life.

Because of its history and its circumstances, Rhode Island played a leading role in the American Revolutionary movement. Having the greatest degree of self-rule, it had the most to lose from the efforts of England to increase her supervision and control over her American colonies after 1763. In addition, Rhode Island had a long tradition of evading the poorly enforced Navigation Acts, and smuggling was commonplace.

Beginning with strong opposition in Newport to the Sugar Act of 1764, with its restrictions on the molasses trade, the colony engaged in repeated measures of open defiance, such as the scuttling and torching of the British customs sloop *Liberty* in Newport harbor in July 1769, the burning of the British revenue schooner *Gaspee* on Warwick's Namquit Point in 1772, and Providence's own "tea party" on March 2, 1775, when the English leaf was burned in

Market Square. Gradually the factions of Ward and Hopkins put aside their local differences and united by endorsing a series of political responses to alleged British injustices. On May 17, 1774, after parliamentary passage of the Coercive Acts (Americans called them "Intolerable"), the Providence Town Meeting became the first governmental assemblage to issue a call for a general congress of colonies to resist British policy. On June 15 the General Assembly made the colony the first to appoint delegates (Ward and Hopkins) to the anticipated Continental Congress.

In April 1775, a week after the skirmishes at Lexington and Concord, the legislature authorized a 1,500-man "army of observation," with Nathanael Greene as its commander. At its organizational session on May 4, 1776, the Rhode Island General Assembly, sitting in Providence's colony house because of the presence of a British fleet hovering off Newport, became the first colonial legislature to renounce allegiance to King George III. Meeting again in Newport's colony house, the English threat having temporarily subsided, the Assembly voted on July 18, 1776, to approve the Declaration of Independence and to substitute the word *state* for *colony* in the royal charter. Contrary to popular opinion, it was these votes, and not the renunciation of allegiance on May 4, 1776, that constituted Rhode Island's acts of independence.

In December 1776 the British occupied Newport. A long siege to evict them culminated in August 1778 in the large but inconclusive Battle of Rhode Island, a contest that saw the first combined effort of the Americans and their French allies. The British voluntarily evacuated Newport in October 1779, and in July 1780 the French army under Rochambeau landed there and made the port town its base of operations. During their stay the Catholic French conducted the first public Masses ever celebrated in Rhode Island, with Newport's colony house the setting for the most formal of these religious observances.

The Revolution did not alter Rhode Island's governmental structure (even the royal charter remained intact), but it did prompt some legal and political changes. For example, the Revolution and the reform sentiments it generated influenced legislation affecting Catholics and black slaves.

444

Whatever anti-Catholicism existed in Rhode Island was mollified by assistance rendered to the struggling colonials by Catholic France and by the benevolent presence of large numbers of French troops in Newport under General Rochambeau, some of whom remained when the struggle was over. Thus the General Assembly in February 1783 removed the disability against Roman Catholics, imposed in 1719, by giving members of that religion "all the rights and privileges of the Protestant citizens of this state."

The most significant of several statutes relating to blacks was the emancipation act of 1784. With a preface invoking sentiments of Locke, that "all men are entitled to life, liberty, and property," the manumission measure gave freedom to all children born to slave mothers after March 1, 1784. Since the Providence statehouse was the site of such momentous revolutionary measures as the renunciation of allegiance, the Catholic equality law, and the emancipation statute, it well deserves (but has not been accorded) the designation as Rhode Island's "Liberty Hall."

The emancipation act was followed by a concerted effort of Rhode Island reformers—particularly the influential Quaker community—to ban the slave trade. This agitation had a salutary result when the General Assembly, sitting in Little Rest (Kingston), seat of the recently renamed Washington County, enacted a measure in October 1787 that prohibited any Rhode Island citizen from engaging in this barbarous traffic. The legislature termed the trade inconsistent with "that more enlightened and civilized state of freedom which has of late prevailed."

A side effect of the Revolution that had important consequences for Rhode Island's political and constitutional development was the decline of Newport. Its exposed location, the incidence of Toryism among its townspeople, and its temporary occupation by the British combined to produce both a voluntary and at times a forced exodus of its inhabitants. In 1774 Newport's population was 9,209; by 1782 that figure had dwindled to 5,532. The population of Providence—more sheltered at the head of the bay and a center of Revolutionary activity—actually increased during these turbulent times from 4,321 in 1774 to 6,380 in 1790.

The Revolution was a blow from which Newport never fully recovered. British occupation adversely affected both its population and its prosperity. From this period onward, numerical and economic ascendancy inexorably moved northward to Providence and the surrounding mainland communities.

In 1778 the state had quickly ratified the Articles of Confederation, with its weak central government, but when the movement to strengthen that government developed in the mid-1780s, Rhode Island balked. The state's individualism, its democratic localism, and its tradition of autonomy caused it to resist the centralizing tendencies of the federal Constitution. This opposition was intensified when an agrarian-debtor revolt in support of the issuance of paper money gave rise to Rhode Island's second party system and placed the parochial Country party in power from 1786 through 1790. This political faction, led by South Kingstown's Jonathan Hazard and Joseph Stanton, was suspicious of the power and the cost of a government too far removed from the grass-roots level, and so it declined to dispatch delegates to the Philadelphia Convention of 1787, which drafted the United States Constitution. Then, when that document was presented to the states for ratification, Hazard's faction delayed (and nearly prevented) Rhode Island's approval.

In the period between September 1787 and January 1790, the rural-dominated General Assembly rejected no fewer than eleven attempts by the representatives from the mercantile communities to convene a state ratifying convention. Instead, the Assembly defied the instructions of the Founding Fathers and conducted a popular referendum on the Constitution. That election, which was boycotted by the supporters of stronger union (called Federalists), rejected the Constitution by a vote of 2,708 to 243.

Finally, in mid-January 1790, more than eight months after George Washington's inauguration as first president of the United States, the Country party reluctantly called the required convention, but it took two separate sessions, one in South Kingstown (March 1–6) and the second in Newport (May 24–29), before approval was obtained. The ratification tally—34 in favor and 32 opposed—was the narrowest of any state, and a favorable result was obtained only because four Antifederalists either absented themselves or abstained from voting.

Rhode Island's course during this turbulent era—first in war, last in peace—is attributable in part to its tradition of individualism, self-reliance, and dissent. Most of its residents feared the encroachment on local autonomy by any central government, whether located in London, Philadelphia, or the soon-to-be-created District of Columbia. This ideology, coupled with the economic concerns of the agrarian community, explain Rhode Island's wariness toward the work of the "Grand Convention." Those economic worries consisted principally of a fear that the new central government would be financed by exorbitant taxes on land and that the new Constitution's ban on state emissions of paper money would terminate the inflationary financial scheme formulated by Hazard and the Country party to discharge public and private debts.

Because the Constitution three times gave implied assent to slavery, the influential Quaker community also denounced it. These factors explain the strength of Antifederalism. Small wonder that "Rogues' Island," as Federalists called it, withheld ratification until May 29, 1790, making it the last of the original thirteen states to join the new federal Union.

During the decade and a half following the adoption of the federal Constitution, political rivalries subsided. Though a bitterly divisive national party system emerged in the mid-1790s, pitting incumbent Federalists led by John Adams and Alexander Hamilton against Democratic-Republicans organized by James Madison and led by Thomas Jefferson, Rhode Island's political waters were relatively placid. Governor Arthur Fenner of Providence, a 1790 nominee of the Country party, was usually unopposed by local Federalists. His string of election victories extended from 1790 to 1805, when he died in office. Presumably his Providence connections and his support for ratification of the federal Constitution led to his acceptance by the commerce-oriented Federalists, who carried the state for their presidential candidate in four of the five national elections from 1796 to 1812.

With Fenner's death and the adoption of embargoes and other commercial restrictions as instruments of diplomacy by Presidents Jefferson and Madison, two-party rivalry intensified. When Madison and Democratic-Republicans in Congress took a hard line toward England, our leading trading partner, during that nation's war with Napoleon, the resentful Federalists seized control of Rhode Island's government. In power from 1811 to 1817, Governor William Jones and the Federalist legislature were especially vocal in their opposition to the commerce-crippling War of 1812 with England, which they denounced as "Mr. Madison's War."

In the aftermath of that inconclusive struggle, the national Federalist party, hurt by charges of elitism and disloyalty, experienced a rapid decline. Though it survived as a force in Rhode Island politics for a short time after its national disintegration, by the early 1820s Rhode Island's two-party system had temporarily evaporated. From 1824 through 1830 Democratic-Republican James Fenner, son and political protégé of Arthur, won the governorship, usually without opposition.

By 1830, however, national political trends again exerted an impact on Rhode Island. The second American party system had formed, with the Democrats, led by Andrew Jackson, arrayed against the Whigs. In Rhode Island the rural, agrarian towns in South County and along the state's western border lined up in the Democratic column, while Providence, the industrial areas in the Blackstone Valley, and commercial centers like Newport, Warren, and Bristol supported the Whigs. Except for the gubernatorial successes of Democrats John Brown Francis (1833–37) and Philip Allen (1851–53), the commerce- and industry-oriented Whigs generally controlled state government until that party divided and disbanded nationally in the mid-1850s over the issue of slavery. Locally, the Whig cause was aided by the inexorable transformation of the state's economy from an agrarian to an industrial base.

During the fifty years (1790–1840) that these political realignments and partisan battles were occurring, the structure of Rhode Island's government remained virtually unchanged owing to the inflexibility of the colonial charter, which was still the state's basic law. Sustained agitation for reapportionment of the General

Assembly and for a diminution of its powers, beginning in 1817, led the reluctant legislature to authorize Rhode Island's first constitutional convention, which convened in Newport's county house in June 1824. This body—whose delegates were apportioned in the same manner as those in the state legislature—suggested modest reforms, but these were decisively rejected in the subsequent referendum. With overwhelming opposition from voters in those towns destined to lose political influence if the proposed reapportionment was implemented, the constitution of 1824 was defeated by a 2-to-1 margin. Ten years later another convention, also a replica of the General Assembly, met inconclusively and adjourned without even drafting a basic law for the state's voters to consider.

The economic transformation of Rhode Island during the five decades following Samuel Slater's cotton textile venture of 1790 had a profound effect on the state's politics and intensified the demand for constitutional reform. During this era the production of cottons, woolens, and base and precious metals steadily expanded and came to dominate the state's economic life. As this transformation occurred, agriculture declined, many farms reverted to forest, and many rural towns experienced a substantial out-migration.

Industrialization and its corollary, urbanization, combined by the 1840s to produce an episode known as the Dorr Rebellion, Rhode Island's crisis in constitutional government. The state's royal charter, nearing its 180th anniversary without a change or a blemish, gave disproportionate influence to the declining rural towns, conferred almost unlimited power on the General Assembly, and contained no procedure for its own amendment. State legislators, regardless of party, insisted upon retaining the old real estate requirement for voting and officeholding, even though it had been abandoned in all other states. As Rhode Island grew more urbanized, this freehold qualification became more restrictive. By 1840 about 60 percent of the state's free adult males were disfranchised.

Because earlier moderate efforts at change had been virtually ignored by the General Assembly, the reformers of 1840–43 decided to bypass the legislature and convene a People's Convention, equitably apportioned and chosen by an enlarged electorate.

Thomas Wilson Dorr, a patrician attorney, assumed the leadership of the movement in late 1841 and became the principal draftsman of the progressive People's Constitution, which was ratified in a popular referendum in December 1841. Dorr was elected governor under this document in April 1842, while the charter adherents reelected Whig incumbent Samuel Ward King of Johnston in separate balloting.

With the two rival governments preparing to assume power on May 3–4 under their respective basic laws, a clash appeared imminent. On Tuesday, May 3, the suffragists prefaced their accession to office by staging a colorful parade in Providence from the Hoyle Tavern in the West End to the Providence statehouse on North Main Street. The entourage featured the Providence Brass Band, members of the People's government, and a strong military contingent including the sixty-member Dorr Troop of Horse—the insurgent governor's personal guard. Only the eventual setting of the People's legislature diminished the luster and triumph of the occasion. Since the Charterites had locked the statehouse—which contained the state's seal, its archives, and other symbols of sovereignty—the suffragists were forced to retreat to a preselected alternative site, an unfinished foundry building on Eddy Street near Dorrance, to conduct their legislative deliberations.

Dorr unsuccessfully opposed such timid acquiescence. Later he ruefully observed "that it was here that the cause was defeated, if not lost." In chiding his more moderate associates, Dorr contended that "the period for decided action had now arrived." A valid government, he said, "was entitled to sit in the usual places of legislation, to possess and control the public property, and to exercise all the functions with which it was constitutionally invested. A government without power, appealing to voluntary support, destitute of the ability or disposition to enforce its lawful requisitions, was no government at all and was destined to extinction." Had the Providence statehouse been seized, lamented Dorr, "right would have been confirmed by possession, the law and the fact would have been conjoined, and the new order of things would have been acquiesced in by all but a minority" of powerless reactionaries. In Dorr's view, therefore, the failure to possess the statehouse as a symbol of legitimacy loomed large in deciding the unhappy fate of the People's party.

The reformers were resisted by a "Law and Order" coalition of Whigs and rural Democrats led by Governor King and a "council of war," consisting of Democratic former governor James Fenner and six prominent Whigs. Operating from the Newport statehouse, they authorized the use of force and intimidation to prevent the implementation of the People's Constitution. When Dorr responded in kind by unsuccessfully attempting to seize the state arsenal in Providence on May 18, 1842, most of his followers deserted the cause, and Dorr fled into exile. When he returned in late June to reconvene his People's legislature in Chepachet (but not to wage war, as his enemies claimed), a Law and Order army of twenty-five hundred marched to Glocester and sent Dorr into exile a second time.

Although the Dorr Rebellion had been effectually ended, the turmoil and popular agitation against the charter forced the victors to consent to the drafting of a written state constitution. Their Law and Order coalition held its officially sanctioned convention in Newport's statehouse during September 1842. This conservative gathering, presided over by James Fenner and Henry Y. Cranston, produced a draft constitution and adjourned to November to allow delegates to discuss the document with their constituents. In early November the convention reconvened in East Greenwich at the United Methodist Church and quickly sent its handiwork to the General Assembly, then sitting in the nearby Kent County statehouse.

Arthur May Mowry, the first major historian of the Dorr War, calls this instrument "liberal and well-adapted to the needs of the state" because it improved House apportionment, contained a comprehensive bill of rights, and removed the real estate requirement for native-born citizens. Mowry's appraisal, however, neglects one important item: the 1842 constitution established a $134 freehold suffrage qualification for naturalized citizens, and this anti-Irish Catholic restriction—not removed until 1888, and then only as a political maneuver—was the most blatant instance of political nativism found in any state constitution in the land. Other defects included the stranglehold on the Senate that the document gave to the rural towns (there was to be one senator from each town, regardless of its population), cumbersome amendment procedures that made reform of the document a very difficult task, and the absence of a secret ballot.

This constitution, overwhelmingly ratified in November 1842 by a margin of 7,024 to 51, became effective in May 1843. Despite the margin of victory, the turnout was meager, for there were more than 23,000 adult male citizens in the state. That the opposition, in mute protest, refrained from voting explains in part the constitution's apathetic reception and the lopsided vote.

The reformers failed in their vigorous last-ditch effort to win the April 1843 elections, held under the provisions of the Law and Order constitution, when James Fenner defeated Dorr's ally and Democratic leader Thomas F. Carpenter by a vote of 9,707 to 7,392. In a prophetic realignment, the Dorr Democrats made a strong showing in northern industrial towns once solidly Whig, and Fenner rolled up impressive pluralities in previously Democratic South County. Informed of the result, a distraught Dorr wrote a letter from New Hampshire to supporter Aaron White in which he exclaimed, "If our party will not fight or vote, in God's name what will they do!"

A disillusioned Dorr returned from his New Hampshire refuge in October 1843 to surrender to local authorities. Immediately arrested and jailed until February 1844, Dorr was prosecuted for treason against the state. In a trial of less than two weeks, he was found guilty by a jury composed entirely of political opponents and sentenced to hard labor in solitary confinement for life. He served one year before Governor Charles Jackson—elected on a "liberation" platform—authorized his release. A Democratic General Assembly restored Dorr's civil and political rights in 1851, and in 1854 it reversed the treason conviction. But these gestures did little to cheer the vanquished reformer, whose spirit and health were broken. Disillusioned, he died in December 1854 in the midst of a local Know-Nothing campaign directed against immigrant Irish attempts to secure the vote.

The Know-Nothing, or American, party was a political aberration formed during the early 1850s in many northeastern states to curb the recent heavy influx of Catholic immigrants (mainly Irish) and to delay the citizenship applications of those already here. This secret organization swept town, city, and state elections in Rhode Island in the mid-fifties. Its candidate, William W. Hoppin, captured the governorship in 1855, and another standard-bearer, James Y. Smith, won the Providence mayoralty. Some of the party's more zealous adherents even planned a raid on St. Xavier's Convent, home of the "female Jesuits" (the Sisters of Mercy), but the angry mob dispersed when confronted by Bishop Bernard O'Reilly and an equally militant crowd of armed Irishmen.

The rise of the American party was a by-product of the disintegration of the second national party system (Democrats vs. Whigs) and the emergence of a third. By 1854 the Whig party—split nationally over the issue of slavery into "Cotton" and "Conscience" Whigs—fragmented locally. Those who considered the spread of slavery the country's greatest evil embraced the newly formed Republican party, while those who saw Catholic immigration as the main menace joined the American (Know-Nothing) party, at least temporarily.

Rhode Island Democrats also divided. Reform-oriented followers of Thomas Dorr maintained their party allegiance to Governor Philip Allen (1851–54), Dorr's uncle, former foe, and then sometime ally, but many rural Democrats who had supported the cause of Law and Order during the Dorr Rebellion affiliated with the Know-Nothings. When that one-issue party also declined after 1856, both these rural Democrats and nativist Whigs gravitated toward the rapidly growing Republican party, bringing with them their anti-Irish Catholic attitudes. Know-Nothing governor William Hoppin became the state's first Republican chief executive in 1856, and American party mayor James Y. Smith served as GOP governor from 1863 to 1866. From the birth of the Republican party until the 1930s, the Democrats were consigned to the position of Rhode Island's minority party.

During the turbulent 1850s two notable governmental changes occurred. In November 1854 the quaint but cumbersome custom of rotating General Assembly sessions among the five county seats was abolished by Article of Amendment III to the state constitution. This revision stated that "there shall be one session of the

General Assembly holden annually on the last Tuesday in May at Newport and an adjournment from the same shall be holden annually at Providence." The smallest state thus progressed from five capitals to only two.

In 1856, the new constitution's nebulous language pertaining to the independence of the judiciary was clarified. In the landmark case of *Taylor* v. *Place*, Chief Justice Samuel Ames once and for all rejected the power of the General Assembly to review or reverse decisions of the highest state court.

453

Rhode Island, like every state in America, keenly felt the impact of the Civil War—a conflict many Rhode Islanders had hoped to avoid. Yankee businessmen, especially those producing cotton textiles, had forged economic ties with the South, ties that war would (and did) disrupt. As some critics remarked, there seemed to be an unholy alliance between "the lords of the loom" (the cotton textile manufacturers) and "the lords of the lash" (the slaveholders). In addition, many foreign-born Irishmen, resentful that they needed land to vote while local blacks were subjected to no such discrimination, had little sympathy for freeing those who might journey northward and become their rivals for jobs on the lower rungs of the economic ladder.

Consequently, when in 1860 the Rhode Island Republican party nominated Seth Padelford for governor—a man whose antislavery views were extreme—a split occurred in the party ranks. Supporters of other Republican aspirants and Republican moderates of the Lincoln variety joined with Democrats (who were softer on slavery) to nominate and elect a fusion candidate on the "Conservative" ticket. Their choice was twenty-nine-year-old William Sprague of Cranston, the heir to a vast cotton textile empire and a martial man who had attained the rank of colonel in the Providence Marine Corps of Artillery. Sprague outpolled Padelford 12,278 to 10,740—a victory celebrated as a rebuke to abolitionism by the citizens of faraway Savannah, Georgia, who fired a hundred-gun salute in Sprague's honor. Once the Civil War began, however, the Republicans were reunited by their common desire to preserve the Union.

During the last third of the nineteenth century and the first third of the twentieth, the GOP skillfully maintained its political dominance. Such party stalwarts as U.S. senator and *Providence Journal* publisher Henry Bowen Anthony (1815–84) and his protégés Charles Ray Brayton (1840–1910) and U.S. senator Nelson W. Aldrich (1841–1915) consistently deflected attempts by Yankee reformers and Irish Catholic Democrats to dislodge the GOP.

For a quarter century after the arch nativist Anthony's death in 1884, Aldrich and Brayton ran the Rhode Island GOP. Of this dynamic duo, Aldrich was "Mr. Outside," operating for thirty years on the national stage in concert with John D. Rockefeller, Sr., J. P. Morgan, and other giants of business and finance. Officially, he was majority leader of the United States Senate; unofficially, he was by common estimation "the general manager of the United States." Brayton, on the other hand, stayed home. As "Mr. Inside," he took charge of the nuts and bolts of GOP organization and discipline. His boldness was legendary. From 1901 until he was ousted by Democratic governor James Higgins in 1907, Brayton directed the actions of the legislature from the sheriff's office in the newly constructed (and present) statehouse. With the completion of that structure in 1900, Article of Amendment IX mandated that an annual session of the General Assembly convene at Providence beginning on the first Tuesday of January 1901—an enactment that left Providence the state's sole capital from that date onward.

The Republican organization of the Brayton-Aldrich era owed its ascendancy to many factors, not least of which was the political system established by the state constitution of 1843. That document, carefully drafted by the Law and Order coalition of upperclass Whigs and rural Democrats that vanquished Thomas Dorr, was designed to prevent the old-stock industrialists and Yankee farmers from succumbing to the numerically superior urban proletariat, especially those of foreign birth and Catholic faith. When the Republican party formed during the 1850s in response to the slavery issue, it revived the Law and Order coalition of the preceding decade, and by adopting that group's nativistic posture, it determined to use and preserve the Law and Order party's constitutional checks upon the power of the urban working class.

Included in those checks were (1) a malapportioned Senate that gave a legislative veto to the small rural towns; (2) a cumbersome amendment process to frustrate reform; (3) the absence of procedures for the calling of a constitutional convention; (4) the absence (until 1889) of a secret ballot; (5) a General Assembly that dominated both the legislatively elected Supreme Court and the weak, vetoless (until 1909) governorship; and (6) a real estate voting requirement for the naturalized citizen. This last-mentioned check was eliminated by the Bourn Amendment (Article VII) in 1888, but it was replaced by a $134 property-tax paying qualification for voting in city council elections. This requirement had the practical effect of preventing those at the lower socioeconomic levels, usually Catholic immigrants, from exercising control over the affairs of the cities in which they resided. This was true because the mayors, for whom all electors could vote, had very limited powers, while the councils, for whom only property owners could vote, were dominant, controlling both the purse and the patronage.

The State House in Providence hosted its first General Assembly session in 1901.

As if constitutional checks were not sufficient, in 1901 "Boss" Brayton for good measure engineered the enactment of a statute designed to weaken the power of any Democrat who might back into the governor's chair by virtue of a split in Republican ranks. With a few limited exceptions, this "Brayton Act" placed the ultimate appointive power of state government in the hands of the Senate. In the aftermath of its passage, a governor could effectively appoint only his private secretary and a handful of insignificant state officials.

By 1920 the Senate—the possessor of state appointive and budgetary power—was more malapportioned than ever. For example, West Greenwich, population 367, had the same voice as Providence, population 237,595! And the twenty smallest towns, with an aggregate population of 41,660, outvoted Providence 20 to 1, although the capital city had over 39 percent of Rhode Island's total population. As Democratic congressman George F. O'Shaunessy (1911–19) observed, the Senate was "a strong power exercised by the abandoned farms of Rhode Island."

The Progressive Era (ca. 1898–1917) was an age of national reform—political, economic, and social—but Rhode Island's reactionary political system survived the period relatively intact. Boss Brayton, Nelson Aldrich, and their successors proved more than a match for Lucius Garvin, James Higgins, Charles E. Gorman, Robert H. I. Goddard, Theodore Francis Green, Amasa Eaton, and other supporters of governmental reform. The Brayton-Aldrich combine even survived a national exposé by noted muckraker Lincoln Steffens, who described Rhode Island as "A State for Sale" in a 1905 article for *McClure's Magazine*.

The Progressive movement was eclipsed by American involvement in World War I. Pro-Allied sentiment ran high in Rhode Island, conditioned in part by the Anglophilic *Providence Journal*, whose editorials, generated by editor John R. Rathom, repeatedly urged intervention to halt alleged German aggression.

With the return of peace in Europe, Rhode Island's political wars resumed. The stormy decades of the 1920s and 1930s witnessed a major transition from Republican to Democratic control in state government. Economic unrest—stemming from such factors as the decline of the textile industry, the stock market crash of 1929, the ensuing Great Depression, and the local rise of organized labor—coupled with the development of cultural antagonisms between native and foreign stock to weaken the normal allegiance of local Franco-Americans and Italian Americans to the Republican party. Simultaneously, vigorous efforts by the Irish-led Democratic party to woo ethnics, key constitutional reforms such as the removal of the property-tax requirement for voting in council elections (by Amendment XX in 1928), a shift in control of the national Democratic party from rural to urban leadership, the 1928 presidential candidacy of Irish Catholic Democrat Al Smith, and the social programs of Franklin D. Roosevelt's New Deal all combined by the early 1930s to pull the newer immigrant groups towards the Democratic fold.

A highlight of the turbulent twenties, and one of the most bizarre episodes in the history of any state, was the stinkbombing of the Senate in June 1924. At that stormy session the Democratic minority, led by Robert E. Quinn and Lieutenant Governor Felix Toupin, the presiding officer, staged a marathon filibuster to force weary Republicans to pass a bill to convene a constitutional convention that had already cleared the Democratic House. Toupin's strategy was to wear some of the elderly Republicans down, then call for a vote on the question when they snoozed or strayed.

In the forty-second hour of the filibuster, as the vigilant Democrats awaited the success of this scheme, Republican party managers authorized some thugs imported from Boston to detonate a bromine gas bomb under Toupin's rostrum. As the fiery Woonsocket politician keeled over unconscious, senators scrambled for the doors. Within hours most of the Republican majority was transported across the state line, where Toupin's summons could not reach them. There they stayed (Sundays excepted) until a new Republican administration assumed office in January 1925. Ironically, the defeat of the Democrats in the 1924 state elections was due in part to the fact that the *Providence Journal* wrongly accused them of the bombing. In that year the newspaper had its own reasons for discrediting the Democrats, inasmuch as Jesse H. Metcalf, brother of the *Journal*'s president, was the GOP candidate for U.S. Senate in the fall election against incumbent Democratic governor William S. Flynn.

The Democratic setback in 1924 was only a temporary reversal in a seemingly inexorable political trend. By the General Assembly session of January 1935, Democratic leaders—especially Governor Theodore Francis Green, political boss Thomas P. McCoy of Pawtucket, state senator William Moss, and Lieutenant Governor Robert Emmet Quinn—were on the verge of achieving political ascendancy and were ready to stage a governmental reorganization now known as "the Bloodless Revolution." This bizarre coup, made possible by a controversial scheme that gave the Democrats narrow control of the state Senate in defiance of election-day returns, resulted in the repeal of the Brayton Act, the reorganization of the state government through the replacement of the commission system with the present departmental structure, the seizure of state patronage by the Democrats, and the dismissal of the entire five-member Republican Supreme Court. With vivid memories of the 1924 bombing, Quinn ringed the Senate chamber with state policemen and sheriffs to prevent the startled Republicans from escaping and preventing a quorum prior to the execution of the Democratic plan.

Soon after this takeover, Democratic factionalism became intense; promised reforms such as the calling of an open constitutional convention went unfulfilled; and in 1937 a scandalous "Race Track War" erupted between Governor Quinn (1937–39) and Narragansett Park owner Walter O'Hara, with whom Pawtucket mayor Tom McCoy was allied. These local embarrassments were compounded by a national recession that brought temporary disillusionment with the Democratic New Deal. In consequence, the state elections of 1938 returned the Republicans briefly to power.

Although the GOP enacted a state merit-system law in 1939, its well-intentioned governor, William Vanderbilt, became ensnared in a wiretap controversy during his overzealous attempt to implicate Mayor McCoy in vote fraud, and in 1940 the Democratic tide rolled in once more—this time for a long stay. United States district attorney J. Howard McGrath, who had made political hay with Vanderbilt's federally illegal wiretap, won the governorship and took a giant step upward in a political career that would include several high national offices. Congressmen Aime J. Forand and John E. Fogarty also launched long and successful tenures in that 1940 campaign, as did Dennis J. Roberts, who became mayor of Providence under a new charter that strengthened the powers of that city's chief executive. For the Democrats, happy days were here for the first time since the early 1850s!

In the four decades from 1940 to 1980, the Democratic party enjoyed its era of ascendancy. Of the nine governors elected during that span, seven were Democrats. So too were all the members of the state's congressional delegation until 1976. In addition, Republican control of Rhode Island's smaller towns was weakened by the large-scale influx of urban ethnics and the application of the "one man, one vote" principle to state legislatures by a 1964 decision of the U.S. Supreme Court (*Reynolds* v. *Sims*). Prior to that time Senate apportionment gave small rural Republican towns an undue influence in state affairs. After a 1965 redistricting statute was enacted, however, the fifty-member state Senate, like the one-hundred-member House, became overwhelmingly Democratic.

More Rhode Island politicians attained national prominence during the post-World War II era than in any comparable period. Theodore Francis Green, who had gone to the U.S. Senate in 1937, became chairman of the Senate Foreign Relations Committee in 1957 at the age of eighty-nine. John O. Pastore also rose to political heights. Becoming governor in 1945 and U.S. senator five years later, Pastore earned the distinction of being the first person of Italian ancestry to be elected governor of any state and the first Italian American to serve in the U.S. Senate. After more than a quarter century of congressional service, including the chairmanship of the Joint Committee on Atomic Energy, Pastore retired in December 1976.

Claiborne Pell, Green's successor in the Senate, has also served with distinction for a quarter century, during which time he has become nationally known for his sponsorship of higher education grants to low-income students, his support of the humanities and oceanography, and his role as ranking Democrat on the Senate Foreign Relations Committee. In the House, John E. Fogarty (1941–67) became recognized as "Mr. Public Health," and Aime J. Forand (1937–39, 1941–61) has been acclaimed as "the Father of Medicare." Forand's successor in the First Congressional District, Fernand St Germain, has established both an expertise and a national reputation in the area of commercial banking legislation since beginning his tenure in 1961.

The most successful and durable Republican of the era has been John H. Chafee. After a stint in the legislature, part of it as minority leader, and three terms as governor (1963–69), Chafee served as secretary of the navy (1969–72) in the Nixon administration. Despite an unsuccessful U.S. Senate campaign against Pell, Chafee made a second senatorial bid and won. In 1982 he was reelected by a narrow margin, and he now (1986) plays an influential role in the Republican-controlled Senate.

The highest-ranking federal appointee in recent years has been

G. William Miller, former board chairman of Textron, Inc., the state's leading conglomerate. Miller served the Carter administration first as chairman of the Federal Reserve Board (1978) and then as secretary of the treasury (1979–81).

J. Howard McGrath was undoubtedly the state's most versatile politician. After spending the war years as Rhode Island's governor, he was appointed U.S. solicitor general by his close political ally Harry S. Truman. In 1946 McGrath was elected to the U.S. Senate. The following year Truman named him Democratic national chairman, and McGrath quickly proved his worth by overseeing Truman's surprising upset of presidential hopeful Thomas E. Dewey in 1948. In the following year the ambitious Rhode Islander gave up his Senate seat to become U.S. attorney general. After resigning this post in 1952 amidst controversy, he returned to private business and the successful practice of law.

State legislative luminaries during these years were numerous, but the most notable in terms of influence and tenure were Harry F. Curvin of Pawtucket and James H. Kiernan of Providence. As House speaker, Curvin firmly held the reins of power from 1941 to 1964 (twenty-three years, 223 days), capping off more than thirty-three years of continuous legislative service. Kiernan represented Providence's Mount Pleasant section in the House for a record-setting fifty-one years, from January 1915 to December 1965, serving as House Speaker in 1937–38 and as majority leader from 1940 until his death in office at the age of eighty-one. North Providence's Frank Sgambato has been the longest-tenured majority leader in the Senate (1963–1972), a body that in recent years has produced a succession of forceful and energetic leaders.

By the three-and-a-half-century mark, Rhode Island's three branches of government were closer to parity, but the General Assembly remained dominant. Though the office of governor was little strengthened by the constitution of 1843, several subsequent amendments have enhanced the power of the chief executive. In 1909 Article of Amendment XV endowed him with veto power, subject to a three-fifths override by the General Assembly. Two years later his term (together with that of the other four general officers) was lengthened from one to two years by Amendment

XVI. The reorganization act of 1935 greatly enlarged the governor's appointment powers and his control over the state budget, both advances being made at the expense of the Senate. Thus far, however, a four-year term and a line-item veto have been denied him.

Though the constitution of 1843 mandated a Supreme Court, the framers retained a close legislative check on the judiciary. In its *Taylor* v. *Place* ruling (1856), the not-so-high court asserted a measure of independence by terminating the Assembly's long-standing habit of reviewing and remanding its decisions. In 1903 Amendment XII ratified the *Taylor* rule and paved the way for the Court Reorganization Act of 1905. This statute, the root of our present system, established the county-based Superior Court and relieved the Supreme Court of its trial duties. Curiously, the new Superior Court judges (who were elected by the legislature until 1930) were given office for life ("during good behavior"), while a Supreme Court justice remained removable by a mere resolution of the General Assembly—a fate that confronted the five judicial victims of the Bloodless Revolution. Conversely, Edmund W. Flynn, the chief justice appointed by the Democrats in their 1935 coup, presided over the Supreme Court for more than twenty-two years, the longest such tenure in the state's history.

461

In 1961 another substantial adjustment in the judicial system included the creation of a Family Court, a tribunal at the same level as the Superior Court, to hear cases dealing with divorce, support, custody, paternity, adoption, juvenile crime, and related issues.

The District Court system, established in May 1886, constitutes the third and basic level of the state's judicial structure. The District Courts do not hold jury trials, although they may hear lesser cases when the right to jury trial has been waived. Presently, civil matters that involve five thousand dollars or less, a small-claims procedure, and criminal cases including felony arraignments and misdemeanors are handled by the gubernatorially appointed judges of this court, who also hold life tenure.

From four original towns, Rhode Island's municipal system has cell-divided and expanded into eight cities and thirty-one towns, the last, West Warwick, created in 1913. The county system has scarcely changed in purpose, composition, or function since 1750, except for some East Bay boundary shifts in 1862 (when Rhode Island acquired eastern Pawtucket and East Providence in exchange for Fall River) and the transfer of New Shoreham (Block Island) from Newport to Washington County in 1963 because of the ferry link.

As of 1986, the 143-year-old constitution had been amended forty-four times, with suffrage requirements the most altered area. Although the amendment procedure was once very cumbersome, a change in the basic law can now be ratified by a majority of the whole membership of each house of the legislature, together with a majority of those electors voting thereon at a general election. This simpler process was accomplished in 1973 by Article of Amendment XLII, one of five changes successfully proposed by the limited constitutional convention of that year. In addition, that amendment provided a mechanism for allowing the voters to convene constitutional conventions on a regular basis at twelve-year intervals, a change described editorially by the oracle of Fountain Street, the *Providence Journal*, as "the most significant substantive alteration every made in the state constitution."

The unlimited convention of 1986, which exercised its power to restructure Rhode Island's government, is Amendment XLII's direct legacy. That convention integrated the forty-four amendments of the existing constitution into a concise, streamlined "neutral rewrite." Of the 1986 convention's fourteen proposals, the people have ratified not only the neutral rewrite but such political provisions as those creating an ethics commission, conferring budgetary power upon the governor, and banning felons from officeholding for three years after their sentence has been completed. Proposals for increasing legislators' pay from the present five dollars per day and for giving the governor and general officers four-year terms were defeated by the electors. In effect, we now have a new basic law—the constitution of 1986.

In politics, the decade of the 1980s has been as turbulent and eventful as most. Scandal and corruption, though probably no more severe than in previous eras, are now more visible and notorious because of the hyperbolic media's relentless exploitation. The long period of Democratic dominance and one-party rule has

462

reached an end; in the aftermath of the 1984 elections, half of the four-member congressional delegation and three of the five general officers were Republican. Only the legislature remained a bastion of Democratic strength.

Though Rhode Island women received the vote in 1920, it has been only in the last decade that they have exerted a powerful influence in local and state politics. Most notable in this respect is Claudine Schneider, who in 1980 became the first woman ever elected to Congress from Rhode Island. Two years later Susan Farmer was elected secretary of state, thus becoming the Ocean State's first female general officer. Meanwhile, from 1975 to 1984 Lila M. Sapinsley efficiently presided as minority leader of the state Senate. The most spectacular breakthrough of all, however, occurred in 1984, when former Sister of Mercy Arlene Violet, on her second try, became Rhode Island's (and America's) first female attorney general, attracting nationwide recognition in the process. Significantly, all four of this political vanguard are members of the GOP, a party that also selected a woman, Leila Mahoney, as its state chairman in 1986. On the Democratic side, the most notable lady achiever has been a judge—Florence Murray. She has served successively as state senator from Newport, associate justice and presiding justice of the Superior Court, and associate justice of the Rhode Island Supreme Court.

Looking back on 350 years of government, one is impressed with both the durability of Rhode Island's basic law and the volatility of its political system. If one regards the patent of 1644 as merely a license to survive, the colony and state have had but two fundamental laws: the corporate charter of 1663, which endured for 180 years, and the constitution of 1843, which enjoyed 143 years of life until its replacement in November 1986. These documents have been like the granite walls of a Grand Canyon, through which has rushed the agitated and turbulent stream of Rhode Island parities and politicians—and the view has often been spectacular.

Both tradition and turmoil have been hallmarks of Rhode Island's political culture. And most Rhode Islanders seem to relish, or at least to accept, this fascinating dichotomy.

Charles E. Gorman was Rhode Island's first prominent Irish Catholic political leader and a champion of equal rights for all citizens.

The Persistence of Political Nativism in Rhode Island, 1893–1915: The A.P.A. and Beyond

49

Written in 1986, this lecture was delivered in Hibernian Hall, Newport, to commemorate the 150th anniversary of the establishment of the Ancient Order of Hibernians in America.

DURING THE LATE 1880S a new wave of anti-Catholicism, as virulent as the Know-Nothing movement of the 1850s, swept the country. Nationalistic and ethnic rivalries among workmen, the rise of the Irish to positions of power in urban politics, the renewed agitation of the Catholic school question following the Third Plenary Council of Baltimore's call for a school in every parish, the growth of militant Catholic fraternal groups such as the Ancient Order of Hibernians and the Knights of Columbus (established 1882), the great increase in the numerical strength of Catholicism as a result of mounting immigration—all these combined to arouse traditional apprehensions and to provoke a growing fear that this country was destined to fall into "Catholic alien" hands.

The new movement first assumed importance in Chicago, and from that city spread to other communities in the Middle West, expressing itself in the form of small local societies. Of these proscriptive organizations, by far the most important were the United Order of Deputies and the American Protective Association (A.P.A). In the Northeast, the British-American Association was also quite influential. The old, long dormant Know-Nothing orders also grew rapidly in numbers, and in some places they dominated this new wave of bigotry.

466

In the early 1890s a national organization was considered desirable, and the A.P.A., as the strongest society, gradually assumed the leadership of the so-called "patriotic" bodies. Founded in 1887 by Henry Francis Bowers of Clinton, Iowa, the A.P.A. was dedicated to preserving the Republic from what it regarded as the insidious threat of a foreign power with international ambitions — the Roman Catholic Church. The organization's members were accustomed to sign their letters "Yours in F. P. and P." ("Yours in Friendship, Purity, and Protection"), to which they sometimes added the old Orange slogan "T.H.W.T.P." ("To Hell with the Pope"). This was a succinct reflection of the double nature of the group: To the public it was intended to appear as a society with a positive and fairly respectable set of goals to be attained by political action; to its members it was anti-Catholic not only in politics but in personal relationships.

Perhaps the primary purpose of the A.P.A. can be best discerned from a reading of the solemn oath its members took upon initiation:

> I hereby denounce Roman Catholicism. I hereby
> denounce the Pope now sitting in Rome or elsewhere.
> I denounce all his priests and emissaries all over the
> world, and the diabolical intrigues of the Roman
> Catholic Church. I will not knowingly vote for, recom-
> mend nor appoint, nor assist in electing or appointing
> a Roman Catholic nor anyone sympathizing with
> Roman Catholicism to any political position whatever,
> and in all my public and political actions will be
> governed by the principles of this order.

The A.P.A.'s members were pledged not to reveal the nature of the order's activities or the names of its adherents. Only by secrecy, its founders believed, could the members escape the injurious effects of Catholic retaliation, and the society avoid the disintegrating influence of public criticism.

The techniques used by the A.P.A. against the "wily Jesuits" were varied, and some, in a more enlightened age, seem amusing.

Before elections, the society circulated lists of candidates marked "C" (Catholic), "c" (Catholic sympathizer), or "P" (Protestant). They used forged papal encyclicals and pastoral letters, sensational "confessions" by "ex-priests" and "escaped nuns," and bombastic allegations to the effect that the political life of the nation was dominated by the "modern Holy Alliance: Rum, Rome, the saloon, and the priest." Stories of a murderous nationwide Catholic plot were circulated; it was claimed that the pope would establish himself in Washington; and a strong attempt was made to link the Church with the assassination of President Abraham Lincoln.

This anti-Catholic movement under the umbrella of the A.P.A. was about 2.5 million strong and centered in the Midwest. It was also powerful in neighboring Massachusetts, where 75,000 members were reported. Fortunately Rhode Island was spared its wrath, for this state had a listed enrollment of only 2,700 as of 1897. However, by that year the movement had crested and was on the wane as a result of public condemnation following the disastrous Boston riot of July 4, 1895.

Rhode Island's first notable evidence of the new nativism came in 1893, when Irish Catholic Democrat Edwin D. McGuinness made his initial bid for mayor of Providence. On the eve of this election, the A.P.A-affiliated United Order of Deputies reared its head and attempted to exert an influence on the ward caucuses of the Republican party. The Republicans resisted this tactic and were duly praised by the *Providence Visitor*, but after several public rallies, attended largely by British American immigrants, the Order of Deputies endorsed the Republican candidate, who emerged victorious.

Roman Catholic bishop Matthew Harkins usually remained silent during the A.P.A. controversy, but his official diocesan voice, the *Providence Visitor*, spoke out on all important Catholic issues: the school question, the A.P.A., bigotry, political elections, and state constitutional reform. When the A.P.A-supported Republican candidate for the office of overseer of the poor in Providence was defeated by three thousand votes in the 1894 municipal elections, the *Visitor* termed the victory "the answer which the voters ... have made to the vile electioneering circulators of the party of bigots." The A.P.A-sponsored attempt in the fall of 1894 to repeal the Rhode Island law exempting parochial schools from taxation also met with failure. Generally speaking, the A.P.A. movement in Rhode Island was small and relatively impotent.

But there were more subtle and more effective ways of blunting Catholic political and economic influence in late-nineteenth-century Rhode Island than the blatant and often ludicrous approach of the A.P.A. Discrimination by the local press was one method. The *Providence Journal*, for example, ran help-wanted notices which, though acceptable then, would be considered racist, sexist, and anti-Catholic by today's standards. Advertisements called for "a Protestant girl," "a Swede, German, or Nova Scotia girl," or "a colored man," or to accentuate the negative, they might specify that "no Irish need apply." When Irish Catholic Democrat James McNally ran for mayor in 1887, however, the *Providence Journal* reversed itself, claiming that the motto of the Democratic party was "'No American need apply.'"

This subtle discrimination was also present in the public schools and other government agencies. One spelling test conducted in a Providence elementary school during our war with Spain contained this sentence: "The Spanish priests tried to persuade Commodore Dewey to enter a mined bay." The word being emphasized was "persuade," but the real message to the students was obvious.

A situation that arose at the state institutions at Howard in 1898 also revealed religious discrimination. Serving the spiritual needs of the inmates were a Protestant minister and a Catholic priest, both preforming comparable functions. The minister held the title of "Religious Instructor" and received an $1,800 annual salary from the State Board of Charities, plus free housing and the use of a carriage for Sunday transportation. During the ten previous years of Catholic service to state inmates, on the other hand, the Catholic priest received no stipend or other compensation, but instead relied on diocesan-supported parish contributions for the maintenance of his efforts. Although the *Visitor* would not "indulge in any animadversion upon the equity of the situation" at Howard, Bishop Harkins's personal appeal in 1898 for continued funds to support this ministry left no doubts concerning his disgust with the situation. The Catholic protest had a salutary result, for in 1899 the State Board of Charities allocated a salary to the Catholic chaplain. A similar controversy arose in 1902–4 over a grossly inadequate and discriminatory municipal subsidy to St. Joseph's Hospital. Such incidents, it seems, were commonplace in Rhode Island as the state entered the twentieth century.

Equally discriminatory and much more widespread in its impact was the political structure of the state in the two generations following the passage of the Bourn Amendment in 1888. One might persuasively venture the opinion that the A.P.A. was not as active in Rhode Island as in many other states because the bugbear of the A.P.A.—Irish Catholic political power—was effectively circumscribed in Rhode Island by the prevailing constitutional system.

The Bourn Amendment of 1888 was not a genuine reform but rather an ingenious device to blunt the rising political power of the Irish Democrats. As the increasing number of native-born Irish threatened to render the 1843 discrimination against naturalized citizens from Ireland ineffective, the Republicans, led by General Charles R. "Boss" Brayton, moved to enfranchise their newfound allies, the Franco-Americans. This group had been repelled by Irish intolerance towards them and had forged an economic bond with their employers, the Republican mill owners and industrialists, on such issues as jobs and the protective tariff. In the bitter political feud between Yankee and Celt, the French Canadians came to hold the balance of power after their enfranchisement by the Bourn Amendment. In September 1895 the Providence *Evening Telegram* stated Brayton's technique precisely: the policy of Boss Brayton was to "play off the French against the Irish" and win or divide the other national groups.

Two other foreign-born contingents who were natural Republicans, and therefore uppermost in Brayton's mind when he backed their immediate enfranchisement by the Bourn Amendment, were natives of England and those immigrants designated "non-French Canadians," or British Americans. In the census of 1890 these groups ranked third and fourth respectively on the list of Rhode Islanders of foreign birth. Many of their members were in sympathy with the aims of the recently created British-American Association, a national, A.P.A-affiliated group formed in part to counteract the growing Irish influence in American political life.

Later immigrants, notably the Italians, were also alienated by the Irish and espoused the cause of Republicanism. Even the party's name had a familiar and welcome ring: Garibaldi, Mazzini, and other champions of Italian nationalism had been "republicans" also. But the Italians did not embrace the Republican party in Rhode Island as avidly as did the French, in part because the party was not as receptive to the Italo-Americans. During the Republican era of ascendancy, which lasted until the 1930s, the GOP never ran an Italian for state office.

Three abortive attempts to remedy defects in the political system were made by constitutional commissions in 1898, 1899, and 1915 in response to repeated reform pleas by the Democratic party, the *Providence Visitor*, and several "good government" organizations. The commission device was utilized because of the Supreme Court's dubious contention in 1883 that the General Assembly had no power to convene a constitutional convention (*Opinion to the Senate: In re The Constitutional Convention*, 14 R.I. 649). The proposed state constitution drafted by the 1898 commission was approved by a vote of 17,360 to 13,510; but the document, put forth as an amendment to the original constitution, lacked the three-fifths margin necessary for ratification. Some 9,632 ballots were declared unmarked or defective and invalidated in this referendum.

When presented again in substantially the same form in 1899, the proposed basic law was voted down by a 3–to–1 margin, 12,742 to 4,097. The reasons for this puzzling turnabout are not altogether clear. It appears that conservatives became increasingly displeased by the document's progressive alterations: a gubernatorial veto, biennial state elections (which would deprive many of their annual bribe), a provision for only one state capital (Providence), a slightly more equitable system of apportionment in the House, a one-year state residency requirement, and a provision for a referendum every twenty years for voting on the calling of a constitutional convention.

On the other hand, Democrats and reformers became increasingly disenchanted with its illiberal features, especially its failure to alter the composition of the Senate and to remove the property qualification in council elections. The fact that both commissions were Republican-appointed and Republican-dominated also discouraged Democratic support, as did the provision to create representative districts within those cities or towns entitled to more than one state representative and the provision to have state contests coincide with national elections.

Both the constitution of 1898 and that of 1899 contained a provision which would have denied the vote to anyone who could not "read this constitution in the English language and write his name," but which would not have affected those who already had the franchise. This literacy test may have satisfied the nativistic inclinations of some commission members, but it was self-defeating. The French, Italians, and other new immigrants were vigorously opposed to it, as were a few of the more politically oriented Republican bosses who cultivated the French and Italian vote. In view of such multiple and varied objections, it is not surprising that these proposed constitutions failed of ratification. The sharp reversal in 1899 could also be explained, as the *Providence Journal* observed, because "'oil and elbow grease' were not applied to the Republican machine." In short, Brayton became indifferent to the fate of his commission's offspring and let it wither at the polls. Also, the opposition was more informed about the contents of the proposed basic law on its second time around, and it had more time to mobilize.

When another attempt at constitutional reform was made by the so-called Jennings Commission (1912–15), the proposed document was so liberal (among other reforms, it abandoned the property qualification, reapportioned the Senate, and repealed the Brayton Act) that the Republican-controlled Assembly refused to submit it to the people. This remarkably progressive instrument died in the House Committee on Special Legislation.

In view of the state's political climate in the late nineteenth and early twentieth centuries, it becomes obvious why the A.P.A. generated such little enthusiasm in Rhode Island. The negligible impact of the A.P.A. stemmed in part from the fact that the Catholic immigrant vote was either manipulated, blunted, purchased, or effectively controlled by Boss Brayton's rural- and native-dominated Republican machine operating under the ingenious but reactionary framework of the state constitution.

472

* * *

The influx of Catholic immigrants to the urban areas of the state continued to arouse nativist resentment through the early decades of the twentieth century. In the 1920s that hostility found expression through the agency of the Ku Klux Klan. The first Klan had been a purely southern, antiblack phenomenon of the Reconstruction era. The second Klan, dating from 1915, was not only anti-Negro but also hostile to foreigners, Catholics, and Jews, and it was national in scope. Klan activity occurred in Rhode Island during 1923, peaked in the following year, and then gradually died away in the early thirties.

In Rhode Island the Klan was mainly a rural phenomenon demonstrating the resentment and antagonism that agrarian, Republican, Protestant, old-stock Rhode Islanders felt toward the increasingly numerous and influential urban ethnics. Cross burnings and camp meetings—such as the 1927 Georgiaville gathering shown right—occurred in many small outlying towns. But Providence did not escape the contagion; Klan rallies were held also in Washington Park, and in January 1925 a thousand people attended a public dinner-dance held by the Providence County Klanton at Rhodes-on-the-Pawtuxet.

The most spectacular incident involving the local Klan was its infiltration of the Providence First Light Infantry Regiment. According to a *Providence Journal* exposé and a subsequent legislative investigation, nearly two hundred officers and men of this state militia group were Klan members, and recruiting for both organizations was carried on simultaneously.

Not Georgia but Georgiaville!

9
The
Sporting Scene

Pasquale "Pat" Abbruzzi

When I was editing the Rhode Island Ethnic Heritage Pamphlet Series, I sometimes provided the authors with research data from my personal files, which were particularly stocked with information on demographics, immigration, religion, and politics. Dr. Carmela E. Santoro did a fine job on the Italian pamphlet, especially on the social and cultural aspects of the Italo-American experience, but when she requested editorial assistance in the area of sports, I wrote this small portion of *The Italians in Rhode Island* in 1990.

NO LITANY OF LOCAL ITALIAN AMERICAN ACHIEVERS would be complete without reference to athletic competition. To list those who have earned distinction in schoolboy, sandlot, collegiate, and even professional sports would fill a volume. Some Italian American athletes, however, stand out above the rest.

Vincent "Poosha" Maddona was the first local Italian sports hero. He engaged in an unlikely field of athletic endeavor—cycling. Crowds flocked to the old Providence Cycledrome during the 1920s to cheer this record-setting performer as he rose to national prominence as a bike racer. Another Italian American with a penchant for speed was Carl Lisa. Now a successful Providence attorney, Lisa earned All-Yankee Conference honors in 1960 as a sprinter. His most memorable achievement that year was a 9.5 clocking in the 100-yard dash, a time that remains the fastest ever run by a Rhode Islander.

Boxing is another sport in which local Italo-Americans have excelled. Romeo "Johnny" Curcio had an undefeated reign as New England welterweight and middleweight champion between 1934 and 1937. Less than a decade later, the tough and popular Ralph Zannelli of Federal Hill won his New England middleweight title while compiling a pugilistic record that recently earned him election to the Rhode Island Heritage Hall of Fame. During his long career Zannelli fought nine world champions while winning 185 of his 200 professional bouts. Currently the local boxing hero is Vinny Pazienza, a flashy, glib, and skillful fighter who briefly held the world International Boxing Federation lightweight title in 1986.

Rocky Marciano, the greatest Italian American fighter of all time, had strong local connections. Although he was a native and resident of nearby Brockton, Massachusetts, Rocky also belonged to Providence. He fought in that city twenty-eight times from 1948 to 1952 en route to compiling a career record of 49 wins and no defeats, before retiring undefeated as the undisputed heavyweight champion of the world.

In football, Rhode Island's premier Italian American performer has been Pasquale Abbruzzi, the longtime coach at Warren High School. An All-Yankee Conference fullback at URI, Pat is one of the all-time greats of the Canadian Football League, where he starred during the 1950s. Canada's Player of the Year in 1955 as a member of the Montreal Alouettes, Abbruzzi was a first-team All-Pro during the four years he played in the CFL, and he was named to the All-CFL silver anniversary team as well. Don Panciera of Westerly was another notable gridiron star. After quarterbacking the famed 1945 LaSalle Academy team—a squad that played to a tie in the Sugar Bowl for the mythical national high school championship—Panciera starred at Boston College and the University of San Francisco and then played with several teams in the National Football League. He then became a Wakefield businessman.

In basketball, Ernie DiGregorio of North Providence was preeminent. After winning All-State honors at North Providence High, "Ernie D" became an All-American guard for Providence College and led the Friars to the final four of the 1973 NCAA championship tournament. Following his brilliant career at PC, DiGregorio turned professional and promptly became the National Basketball Association's Rookie of the Year. A phenomenal passer and playmaker, Ernie D is regarded by most fans as Rhode Island's premier basketball player of all time.

In ice hockey, Chris Terreri of Warwick was another Providence College standout. An All-Stater at Pilgrim High and twice a first-team All-American at PC, in 1985 he led the Friars to the finals of the NCAA hockey championships. Terreri subsequently played for the U.S. Olympic and national teams and in 1989 began a professional career as goaltender for the New Jersey Devils of the National Hockey League. Cranston's Capuano brothers, Jack and Dave, both former All-State performers, earned All-American hockey honors at the University of Maine, and both have recently launched professional careers in the National Hockey League. Yet another local hockey luminary is Clark Donatelli of North Providence. Donatelli went from Moses Brown to Boston University, where he was an All-American wingman; then, after a stint on the 1988 U.S. national and Olympic teams, in 1989 he joined the Minnesota North Stars of the NHL.

To this day Rhode Island's brightest rink star has been Zellio "Topper" Toppazzini, Rhode Island Reds standout in the 1950s. His pro career, which began in 1947, also included stints with Boston, New York, and Chicago of the National Hockey League and Hershey and Cincinnati of the American Hockey League. Although Topper is a native of Ontario, Canada, he settled in Rhode Island when his career with the Reds ended and later became the PC hockey coach (1964–68).

Not to be forgotten in the local sports arena are the numerous promoters, owners, and coaches of Italian extraction. Among the most prominent and successful of these figures have been Peter A. Laudati, owner of the old Cycledrome on North Main Street and sponsor and secretary of the Providence Steam Roller football team, NFL champions in 1928; Louis A. R. Pieri, owner of the Rhode Island Reds of the American Hockey League from 1938 to 1967; Robert Amato, a former PC track star, who developed a series of nationally ranked Providence College cross-country teams in the 1970s and early 1980s, including two second-place finishes in the NCAA tournament, by recruiting runners from Ireland; John Toppa, for more than three decades the highly successful coach of the perennially powerful Rogers High School football team; and Lou Lamoriello, a Providence College hockey standout, the Friars' winningest hockey coach, the school's athletic director, and, since 1987, the general manager of the New Jersey Devils of the National Hockey League.

In addition to these native Italian Americans and those who settled in Rhode Island, there have also been notable birds of passage. Famed football coach Joe Paterno played at Brown University and coached there briefly before beginning his illustrious career at Penn State University, and Rick Pitino was basketball mentor at Providence College just long enough to guide the Friars to their second final-four appearance in the 1987 NCAA tourney before accepting successive coaching positions with the New York Knicks of the NBA and the University of Kentucky.

The triumphs of these superstars and the achievements of many lesser but very talented Italian American athletes have been chronicled or recalled by Bill Parrillo, chief sportswriter for the *Providence Journal*, and his colleague Gene Buonaccorsi; and for many years local athletes of all backgrounds were repaired and refitted for competition by the late Dr. Americo A. Savastano, a nationally renowned orthopedic surgeon and authority on sports medicine. Clearly, in every phase of sport, Rhode Island's Italian Americans have gained their full measure of distinction.

My proposal to save PC baseball was written in August 1999 and fell on deaf ears. The introductory, impressionistic historical survey of PC baseball was written for this book, and it should be expanded by someone into a book of its own. I relied upon my own recollections and four major sources: John Farrell's typescript history of PC athletics from 1921 through 1938, scrapbooks of newspaper clippings through 1966 compiled by Farrell, the college yearbooks, and the brochures and media guides produced by the Department of Athletics from 1973 through 1999. All can be found in the college's archives, under the expert management of Miss Jane Jackson.

ON APRIL 15, 1920, newly opened Providence College optimistically launched its athletic program, just as it had inaugurated its academic curriculum seven months earlier. The academic side, presented by nine Dominican priests to seventy-five incoming freshmen on September 18, 1919, featured Thomism, the philosophical and theological approach to knowledge based on the writings of St. Thomas Aquinas, the greatest Dominican friar and the most learned Scholastic philosopher.

The athletic component featured baseball, America's National Pastime, enhanced locally by the exploits of a galaxy of diamond greats. Most old-timers remembered John Montgomery Ward, the dazzling pitcher for the Providence Grays, who led his 1879 team to the National League championship with ample assistance from "Orator Jim" O'Rourke and George Wright—all three future members of the Baseball Hall of Fame. And no Rhode Islander could forget Charles "Old Hoss" Radbourne, the sixty-game winner who led the 1884 Grays to the championship of the first-ever World Series, or his talented teammate, outfielder Paul Hines, the team's top hitter, who may still (and should) join Radbourne, Ward, O'Rourke, and Wright in the Hall of Fame.

A decade later, Rhode Island's local baseball lore was further embellished by Hugh Duffy of Cranston, whose 1894 single-season batting average of .438 is still baseball's all-time record. Then Woonsocket's Nap Lajoie, baseball's greatest second baseman, took center stage. The "Big Frenchman" compiled a career batting average of .339 over twenty seasons with three major league teams. He led his league in batting three times, his .422 average in 1901 being the second highest in modern major league history. Providence even had a piece of baseball's new home run king, a converted pitcher called Babe Ruth, who had played for the reorganized minor league Grays in 1914. Clearly, the Friar nine from its inception was heir to a local baseball tradition of impressive dimensions.

The first PC squad, coached by Patrick Duff, consisted only of freshmen. It played its first game against Dean Academy in Franklin, Massachusetts, and lost, 10 to 6.[1] A star performer on that inaugural team, Joseph Vincent Dore, displayed such staying power that he became a Dominican priest after his graduation in 1923. Taking the religious name Vincent Cyril, he eventually rose to the position of seventh president and first chancellor of Providence College. Father Dore once confided to me that playing baseball at PC on that pioneer team was one of his most cherished lifetime memories.

The 1923 Friar nine, the school's first senior squad, was led by pitcher John McCaffrey, who had become the Friars' first team captain as a sophomore in 1921. The college indicated the seriousness of its intention to be competitive in baseball by hiring Joey Connolly, a native of North Smithfield, as coach. Connolly had played four seasons as a Red Sox outfielder (1913–16), generating a respectable lifetime batting average of .288. His 1923 team compiled a 9 and 11 won/lost record. After that single season as coach, Connolly departed in favor of another major leaguer, Jack Flynn.

Charlie Reynolds (1904–1972)

The Friars started slowly, developing

rivalries with such long-established Catholic college powers as Holy Cross, Boston College, Georgetown, Fordham, Seton Hall, Villanova, and St. John's University of Brooklyn. They also began to schedule the Ivies—Harvard, Yale, and Dartmouth—at a time when these schools were prominent on the national sports scene. Their major foe was crosstown Ivy League power Brown University.

This baseball schedule put the fledgling college on the map by the late 1920s and gained it instant recognition and more respect than did any other sport or academic program. Imagine a new local college fielding its first football team in 2002 and playing Notre Dame, Michigan, Alabama, Oklahoma, Nebraska, Florida State, and the New England Patriots in its first several seasons. The Providence College baseball team accomplished just this kind of feat. During its first decade of existence, baseball did for Providence College what football did for Notre Dame.

On June 7, 1924, the fledgling Friars made their first contribution to national baseball lore by registering a 1–to–0 victory over Brown at Andrews Field in a twenty-inning pitchers' battle—still the longest college game ever played. To add to the drama, Providence College sophomore hurler Charlie Reynolds went the distance to earn the victory, the same Charles Reynolds who later became a Providence Gray, then mayor of Pawtucket, and finally East Providence city manager. The winning run in that memorable contest came when right fielder Bill Beck, a defensive standout, drove home Ray Doyle on a bloop single to center. Later Beck became baseball coach at URI and the father of Olympic skier Bill Beck, Jr.

The loss was truly a heartbreaker for Brown's great hurler Elmer Duggan, who struck out twenty-nine Friars in this four-hour-and-seven-minute struggle. Doyle was the only Friar to get past second base. Duggan earned a measure of revenge a week later when he beat the Friars, 2–1, with a one-hitter. After the season he signed to play in the Yankee farm system, but arm trouble kept him from rising to the parent club.

Eddie Doherty, a reserve pitcher for the 1924 Friars, would also make a great contribution to baseball. Though he lacked the sheer talent of Reynolds, Doherty was second to none in his commitment to the sport. Eddie got his start in baseball in 1914 as a fourteen-year-old batboy for the Providence Grays, where he first met a twenty-year-old pitcher named Babe Ruth. After a hitch in the Navy during World War I, Doherty entered PC, where he played baseball and served as manager of the football team. He continued his baseball career after graduation as a minor league player, public relations agent for the Boston Red Sox, manager of two Sox farm teams, sportswriter for the *Providence Journal*, president of the American Association (an AAA minor league circuit), and general manager of the Washington Senators. He was inducted into PC's Athletic Hall of Fame in March 1971, four months before his death.

The 1924 Friar team was coached by John Anthony Flynn, a native of South Providence, who had played three seasons of major league ball, from 1910 through 1912, as first baseman with the Pittsburgh Pirates and the Washington Senators. Flynn, whose .725 winning percentage over his ten seasons as coach (1924–25 and 1927–34) has never been equaled, was to PC baseball what his contemporary Knute Rockne was to Notre Dame football.

Though distinguished in his own right, Flynn was raised amid talent. When the forty-one-year-old Jack Flynn began his first season as coach, his brother William was Democratic governor of Rhode Island; when a heart attack took Jack's life in March 1935, before the start of that season, another brother, Edmund, had just begun a record-setting twenty-two-year reign as chief justice of the Rhode Island Supreme Court.

Jack Flynn's tenure, from 1924 to 1935, was interrupted in 1926 by his one-year stint as coach of New Haven in the Class A Eastern League. Under his guidance PC won three Eastern Regional baseball championships—1928, 1931, and 1932—with Flynn compiling a coaching record of 147–55–2 against collegiate competition.

In 1926 John White filled in for Flynn and led the Friars to a record of 17 and 8. The game of the year was again with Brown, and senior Charlie Reynolds was again the star. On May 22, playing at Aldrich Field before six thousand spectators, the crosstown foes battled eighteen innings before PC prevailed by a score of 6 to 5. Iron man Reynolds pitched the entire game, as did his Brown counterpart, Bill Quill.[2] This game, like all the others in every PC sport from 1921 through 1938, has been painstakingly chronicled by baseball manager and sports correspondent John Farrell ('26) in a voluminous typescript preserved in the college's archives. So many people in so many ways have built the baseball tradition at Providence College!

485

During the 1926 season the Friars played their first professional team, the Eastern League champion Providence Grays, whose player-manager Rube Marquard had just completed eighteen seasons as a major league pitcher en route to the Hall of Fame. The Friars lost, 5 to 2. The following year they split a two-game series with the Grays at Kinsley Field, winning the second contest on April 16 by the score of 4 to 2.

The Friars' greatest professional competition came in 1932, the year they won their third Eastern crown with a record of 15 and 2 against college rivals. On May 24 the Boston Red Sox came to Hendricken Field. Going into the last half of the ninth inning, Boston led the tenacious Friars, 8 to 4. Aided by Red Sox errors, PC rallied for five runs and a 9 to 8 victory—the kind of amazing comeback of which legends are made.

Coach Jack Flynn (1883–1935)

On June 1, 1936, the Sox returned to Providence, largely through the influence of Eddie Doherty, to play a memorial game in honor of the late Jack Flynn. The contest began at 4:00 P.M. before a crowd of thirty-one hundred spectators, with Chief Justice Edmund Flynn throwing out the first ball. Two Friar Hall of Fame athletes, right-hander Karl Sherry and Fred "Lefty" Collins, shared the pitching duties. The crowd came to its feet in the third inning when Sherry struck out the great slugger Jimmy Foxx, a former Providence Gray, with runners in scoring position. Entering the last of the ninth, Boston led, 7 to 5, when Fred Collins doubled to right with one out. Anticipating another comeback like the miracle of 1932, nearly five hundred excited fans encroached upon the field of play. Suddenly, with the tying run at bat, major league umpire Red Ormsby called the game, thus preserving a Sox victory. The closeness of this hard-fought contest brought credit to the Friars, as did their uncomplaining acceptance of Ormsby's ruling.

Providence's greatest collegiate victory during these formative, yet golden, years came at the conclusion of the 1928 season, during which Providence and Holy Cross shared the Eastern college championship with identical 19-and-3 records. The Friars' nineteenth victory came on June 14, at season's end. The victim was charismatic Notre Dame, already a twenty-one-game winner, and one of the dominant teams in the Midwest. The Irish were concluding a six-game eastern trip to end their season. Only five days before their game with Providence, they had drubbed a strong (18-and-9) Harvard squad by a score of 20 to 1.

Approximately four thousand fans, the largest number ever to watch a Friar game at Hendricken Field, saw PC hurler Ed "Lefty" Wineapple duel undefeated Ed Walsh, son of the great Hall of Fame pitcher "Big Ed" Walsh. It was no contest; Walsh was wild, while Wineapple was wonderful. The PC ace struck out nine and allowed only six hits en route to a 6-to-1 victory. Before the 1928 baseball season was over, Walsh, having turned professional, had pitched in fourteen games for the Chicago White Sox, his father's former team.

In 1929 Ed Wineapple, who was also PC's first basketball star, pitched four innings for the Washington Senators, thereby beginning and ending his abbreviated major league career. He returned to PC to graduate with the class of '31. Despite his failure to achieve major league stardom, Wineapple became a sports legend at PC and was an early inductee into the college's Athletic Hall of Fame.

The 1928 team won PC's first baseball championship because of a great corps of pitchers. In addition to Wineapple, who posted a 5-2 record that included the program's first no-hit game, a 9-0 victory over Lowell, the pitching staff boasted Leo Smith, a football star, baseball captain, and future member of the Friar Hall of Fame, and Tom McElroy, the team's winningest pitcher, with a record of 6 and 1. Patient, mild-mannered, and the quintessential gentleman, McElroy later became a teacher and coach.[3]

During the 1930s PC added more luminaries to its instant baseball tradition—George "Birdie" Tebbetts ('34), of Nashua, New Hampshire, was a Friar catcher before he became a star receiver for the Detroit Tigers, the Boston Red Sox, and the Cleveland Indians, as well as a major league manager. In fourteen seasons Birdie compiled a lifetime batting average of .270 and was regarded as one of the finest catchers of his era. He never ceased to appreciate or to acknowledge his debt to his alma mater. Henry "Hank" Soar ('37), of Pawtucket, starred in both football and baseball for Providence College. In the former sport he went to the NFL, where he played for nine seasons with the New York Giants (1937–46) as an all-purpose back. In baseball he became a legendary major league umpire whose career spanned twenty-four years. Besides his place in the PC Hall of Fame, in 1967 Soar was inducted into the Rhode Island Heritage Hall of Fame as well.

In addition to the dynamic pitching duo of Sherry and team captain Collins, two other versatile senior athletes played with Soar on the 1937 squad, the last of three coached by Jack Egan (1935–37)—catcher Alfred Hagstrom and second baseman Ray Beliveau. Each lettered in football, basketball, and baseball, and each earned induction into PC's Hall of Fame.

In his three seasons at the helm, Egan compiled a winning record of 40–28–1. He had coached the Providence Grays from 1915 through 1917 and then directed several other minor league teams before coming to PC on short notice in 1935 to replace Jack Flynn. Egan's baseball career also included time as a minor league player and a major league umpire. In the latter capacity he served as a role model for Soar. When the Red Sox offered a full-time scouting position to Egan in March 1938, he left PC as abruptly as he had arrived, prompting the college to fill the vacancy with Dr. Arthur Quirk.

Quirk ('30), a former PC player and a professor of physics at the college, coached from 1938 through 1942, compiling an impressive 50–30 won/lost record during his five seasons at the helm. Quirk's son and namesake did not attend PC, but he did become a major league pitcher for Baltimore and Washington under his father's tutelage (and he was the best hurler I ever faced).

Among Dr. Quirk's star players was catcher Robert Reilly, who in 1942 won the Mal Brown Award, PC's oldest athletic prize. The award, honoring an early Afro-American athletic trainer, is presented annually to the person who best emulates the attributes of loyalty, leadership, and sportsmanship that characterized Mal Brown.

In addition to his baseball exploits, Reilly captained the basketball team. In 1942 he was voted PC's athlete of the year. Reilly was also a class officer and sports editor of *The Cowl*, the student newspaper. He later became a prominent business executive, a member of the college corporation, one of PC's major benefactors, and an inductee into the college's Athletic Hall of Fame.

Other standouts of the Quirk regime were center fielder Ed Bobinski ('38); Joseph Elton "Big Els" Deuse, of Fall River, a six-foot four-inch catcher who captained the 1939 team; pitcher Joe Kwasniewski ('40); shortstop Johnny Ayvazian ('40); and second baseman Carl Toti ('42), who became the long-tenured baseball coach at LaSalle Academy. From that post Toti sent dozens of his high school standouts to play for his alma mater.

During the 1942 season, the first year following American entrance into World War II, the PC nine did its part to create a wholesome diversion and outlet for America's servicemen. Added to the Friar schedule that year were such teams as Quonset Naval Air Base, Newport Naval Training Center, Fort Devens, and the Tenth Coast Artillery at Fort Adams.

From 1943 through 1945 the Friars did not field a team, since school enrollment was depleted by the demands of war. When the Friars returned to the diamond in 1946 for an abbreviated eight-game schedule under coach Dona Maynard, they compiled five wins, including victories over archrivals Holy Cross and Brown (who had fielded teams throughout the war).

Whereas baseball had shared the spotlight with Friar football in the 1930s, the demise of the gridiron sport after the 1941 season gave baseball the undisputed athletic ascendancy in the postwar decade. True, there was basketball, but PC played its home games in the Mount Pleasant High School gym against such basketball behemoths as Gorham State Teacher's College, M.I.T., Colby, American International, and Upsala.

Unfortunately, from 1947 through 1960 the Friar nine managed only four winning seasons, a performance that dampened the zeal for baseball on campus. Although it sometimes appeared that PC had deemphasized athletics during this time, the baseball program continued to produce a significant number of first-rate players.

Coached by Harold Martin for nine seasons, 1947 through 1955, the Friars compiled a record of 59–74–1. Rifle-armed right-hander Tom "Red" O'Halloran ('48), later a prominent attorney and co-owner of the Rhode Island Reds, was Martin's star hurler in the late 1940s. Principal members of O'Halloran's supporting cast were team captain Oliver "Bill" Angelone ('48) at first base, outfielder John McBurney ('48), who was later a prominent Pawtucket politician, and hurler Tom Keenan ('49). Red O'Halloran pitched the first game Martin coached, and the "Springfield Rifle" threw a no-hitter against the Quonset Flyers on April 17, 1947, striking out twelve Navy men in the process.

Friar standouts in the early fifties included Art Weinstock (catcher and captain of the 1950 squad), shortstop Walt Lozoski ('50), shortstop Howie McGuiness (captain of the 1952 team and a former *Providence Journal* Honor Roll Boy from LaSalle), catcher Ed Ryder (captain of the 1954 squad), Gerry Romberg (team captain in 1955), and pitcher Tom Army ('55). The most impressive feat in the Martin era occurred on May 21, 1955, when Martin coached his last game. On that day sophomore Jim Coates ('57) pitched a no–hit, no–run game against hapless Brandeis, the first such feat against collegiate competition for PC since Eddie Wineapple's whitewashing of Lowell in 1928.

My vote for the most impressive player during Martin's tenure goes to Bob Grenier of West Warwick, cocaptain of the 1953 Friar nine. A power-hitting left hander, Grenier played the outfield with poise and savvy and was every inch the complete ballplayer, in batting, fielding, throwing, and speed. During my playing days

I competed in the sandlot leagues or at PC with or against nearly all the Friar stars from Grenier ('53) to Bellemore ('66), and none impressed me more than Grenier.

When Bob Murray assumed the coaching position in 1956, he was only four months shy of his sixty-second birthday. Like coaches Connolly and Flynn, he had made the majors, playing briefly in 1923 as an infielder for the Washington Senators.

A native and resident of northern New England, Murray had a gentle and amicable temperament; one might say he was grand-fatherly. Unfortunately, opponents were not as kind towards him. In his four seasons—1956 to 1959—only his 1956 team, led by infielder Art Aloisio (later a prominent state legislator), registered a winning record. Besides Aloisio ('56), the most impressive individual performers for Murray were pitchers Herbie Hearne ('57) and Bob Ritacco ('58), third basemen Rollie "Red" Rabitor ('58), a hockey star from Burrillville, and Jim "Red" Maloney, PC's outstanding student-athlete of 1959, catchers Tom Cahill ('57) and Dan Mulvey ('59), and shortstop Herb Nicholas ('58). A slick fielder and a fine hitter, Nicholas captained the 1958 Friars. The highlight of his career was a 6–for–6 game against Assumption on May 5, 1957, a feat unsurpassed in Friar baseball history.

The other great individual accomplishment during the Murray years was Bob Ritacco's performance against Boston College on May 19, 1956. The fireballing right-hander pitched, à la Charlie Reynolds, complete games at both ends of a doubleheader, shutting out the Eagles 4 to 0 in the opener and shutting them down 12 to 2 in the finale. The double victory on the last day of the schedule ensured a winning season for the Friar nine and a tiny slice of immortality for Bob Ritacco.

Lost in the litany of head coaches and their regimes are the unsung heros of PC baseball—the junior varsity and freshman coaches. The identities of some are not even revealed in the college records. Their inglorious job has been to assemble a team of twenty-five young varsity hopefuls, play a limited schedule as a sideshow, and then perform the unenviable task of recommending a handful of prospects for varsity competition. Vin Cuddy served as my freshman coach, and he directed our squad to the intrastate championship over Brown and URI in 1956. Though his freshman coaching chores were mundane, he relished them. And unlike many freshman mentors, Cuddy's name is not lost to history; in fact, his service to PC was longer and more varied than any head baseball coach.

A native of Naugatuck, Connecticut, Cuddy came to PC as head basketball coach in 1949 after starring in baseball, football, and basketball at the University of Connecticut. After relinquishing his basketball position to Joe Mullaney in 1955, Cuddy coached the freshman baseball team for more than a decade, serving simultaneously as sports information director and coordinator for the Department of Athletics. He concluded his career as associate athletic director and entered the Friar Hall of Fame in 1977. As much as any other player or coach mentioned herein, J. Vincent Cuddy embodied the athletic tradition of PC.

At this point in our narrative it is well to remember that PC's baseball universe is not composed of stars alone. Without trainers like Mal Brown and Pete Louthis, team managers and scribes like Jim Farrell, promoters and publicists like Eddie Doherty, and auxiliary coaches such as Vin Cuddy, Friar baseball stars would not shine nearly as bright.

In July 1955 the college dedicated Alumni Hall, with its spacious basketball facility. Seven months later, on February 14, 1956, PC beat a visiting Notre Dame five in overtime on a last-second shot by Gordie Holmes. From that point onward, Our Lady of the Hoop became PC's patron saint, with Johnny Egan and Lenny Wilkens her first acolytes. In the decades that followed, basketball was king of Bradley Hill; and when the Friars also achieved top-three national ranking in both hockey and cross-country, indicating the ongoing strength of those programs, baseball was consigned to the bleachers.

The Friar nine fielded many good teams during its final four decades. In 1960 Alex Nahigian replaced the kindly, patient, but unsuccessful Bob Murray. Over the next nineteen seasons Alex compiled a record of 221–173–2 (.561) and saw the PC program progress from a thirteen-game schedule in 1960 to a thirty-game campaign in 1975. At the conclusion of the 1963, 1968, 1970, 1972,

1973, and 1974 seasons, Nahigian's teams competed in the NCAA District 1 playoffs.

During the 1960s the interest of many college students was diverted from sports to social issues and war, but the disruption to baseball was far less significant than that which occurred during World War II. Among the diamond stars of that decade were shortstops Don Mezzanotte ('60) and his brother Nick ('62); catcher-outfielder Jim Healey ('61), All-State in the 300-yard dash when a student at LaSalle; pitchers Jim Hodgkins ('62), Bill Canning ('64), Noel Kinski ('66), and Bill Pettingill ('68); catchers Ray Choinere ('63) and Frank Canning (cocaptain of the 1964 squad); utility man Lou Lamoriello ('63); catcher-third baseman Bob Bellemore ('66); third baseman Don Pastine ('65); shortstop Leo McNamara (cocaptain of the 1966 team); second baseman Steve Saradneck ('68); and outfielders Al Bodington ('64) and Jack Connolly (cocaptain of the 1965 Friars). Bodington, a slugger from Hope High in Providence, later achieved local fame for hitting amazing tape-measure home runs in the sport of slow-pitch softball.[4]

In addition to the hitting heroics of Don Mezzanotte, the highlight of the 1960s, Nahigian's first decade, was the hurling of Noel Kinski. Better known to Friar fans as the diminutive cocaptain of the 1965–66 PC basketball team, Kinski was equally impressive in baseball. He suffered only one defeat in three seasons of varsity pitching and fired the fourth no-hitter in Friar annals in a PC rout of Assumption College on April 25, 1965.

For both their immediate and long-range impact on Providence College, none of Nahigian's charges equaled Don Mezzanotte, Lou Lamoriello, and Bob Bellemore—all of whom have been inducted into the Friar Athletic Hall of Fame.

Mezzanotte, who played his first three seasons at shortstop under coach Murray, a big-league infielder, set the PC single-season batting record in 1960 with an unbelievable average of .477. Mezzanotte also shares the PC record for highest career batting average with his protégé, Ed Walsh ('88). Both batted .375.[5] In 1979 Mezzanotte succeeded Nahigian as coach of the Friars, about which more will be said.

Lou Lamoriello played both hockey and baseball at PC, and he played them well. In baseball he was an infielder, an outfielder, and a catcher while compiling a career batting average just above .300. What he accomplished after graduation was even more impressive. He became a player-manager in the prestigious Cape Cod collegiate league, served as assistant baseball coach to Alex Nahigian for six seasons, and presided as head coach of varsity hockey at PC for fourteen years. Then he made a move to the professional ranks, eventually becoming president and general manager of the New Jersey Devils of the National Hockey League.

Since his days as an All-ECAC goalie and the captain of the 1966 Friar baseball team, Bob Bellemore has maintained a longtime affiliation with PC athletics. He served as an assistant hockey coach to Lou Lamoriello and as assistant coach of the women's hockey team. Having been a defensive standout in baseball, both as a catcher and as a third baseman, after graduation Bellemore turned his attention and his "great hands" to fast-pitch softball, a game that emphasizes defensive play. In short order he was chosen an All-World third baseman for the famed Raybestos Cardinals. Like so many other Friar baseball greats during the program's first half century, Bellemore, Mezzanotte, and Lamoriello all came to PC from LaSalle Academy, where they had been coached by Carl Toti.

Nahigian's second decade of coaching began auspiciously. In 1970 Rhode Island Words Unlimited, an organization of the state's sportswriters and broadcasters, named Nahigian Rhode Island Coach of the Year. Since the 1970 Friars were only 11 and 9, it appears that the award was cumulative, but it was nonetheless deserved.

By 1973 the scope of the baseball program began to change. In the early 1960s fifteen–game seasons were the norm; in the late 1960s twenty–game seasons were common; but from 1973 until Nahigian's retirement in 1979 the shortest schedule consisted of twenty-six games, a number that would increase still further when PC joined the Big East at the conclusion of Nahigian's tour of duty.

Like every decade, the 1970s produced its share of standouts, and most of these luminaries were pitchers: Ed Szado ('70); Gary

McKenna ('70); John Scanlon ('72), who over his career gave up fewer earned runs per game than any other Friar pitcher (1.11); Kevin Sheehan ('73), a strikeout artist from Warwick; Tom Amanti ('74); Phil Welch (cocaptain of the 1975 squad); Rich McGeough ('76), who later joined the effort to save the PC baseball program; Mike O'Connell ('76); and Mike Cuddy ('77), youngest son of Vin Cuddy. Mike began his career as a sophomore by posting a school-record 7–0 mark, only to be plagued by injuries in his junior and senior seasons.

The outstanding batsmen during the final years of the Nahigian era were shortstop Dick Kane (captain of the 1970 team); second basemen Mike Gabarra ('70); George Mello (cocaptain of the 1973 team); first baseman Ted Barrette ('75), from Pilgrim High in Warwick; infielder Joe Marcoccio ('77), also from Pilgrim; slugger Steve Rose ('75), who became a Friar assistant coach under Nahigian; Barry Sullivan ('76); and third baseman Ed Bassinger ('78), whose career batting average of .365 ranks third on PC's all-time list.

Of all these stellar performers, Barry Sullivan, from nearby Somerset, Massachusetts, was the most impressive. His .422 average in 1975, the second highest in Friar history, earned him the New England collegiate batting crown. He was also a defensive whiz; in one hundred games he registered 170 putouts in center field, and he committed only two errors in his entire four-year college career.

Don Mezzanotte ('60) began his eleven-year tenure as head baseball coach in 1979. During the Mezzanotte era PC's schedule increased to forty games by 1982 and fifty by 1986. The enlarged schedule enabled Mezzanotte to became the Friar's all-time winningest coach, with a record of 228–222–4 (.507). His teams were led by such All-Big East players as third baseman Ed Cahir ('80); outfielder George Susce ('81); catcher-left fielder John Caianiello ('83), who batted .398 in his senior year; Ernie Pacheco ('84), a heavy-hitting pitcher-first baseman from Hope High; shortstop Paul Rizzo ('86); All-American third baseman Roger Haggerty ('86); Jim Navilliat ('86), Big East pitcher of the year as a senior, with a record of 7–0; utility man Ed Statkiewicz ('88), who led the Friars in hitting in 1988 with a .370 average and also led PC's pitchers with a 1.71 earned run average; first-baseman Ed Walsh ('89), who equaled Mezzanotte's career batting average record of .375; versatile outfielder Steve Castro ('89), of Bristol; and utility man Bill Butler, an academic All-American in 1989. Injuries prevented catcher Steve DellaPosta ('81), of Cumberland, from realizing his potential as a player (a fate I also shared), but not from winning the Mal Brown Award in his senior year.

Paul Kostacopoulos ('87), my former student and a fine second baseman, became the next Friar mentor. In his seven seasons from 1990 through 1996, Paul amassed a won/lost record of 220–137–2 (.615). Perhaps the finest squads, man-for-man, in PC history, his teams were led by Lou Merloni ('93) and John McDonald ('96), both future major league infielders; third baseman T. J. Delvecchio ('95); pitcher Mike Macone ('96), Big East pitcher of the year in 1995; catchers Jim Foster ('93) and Bob O'Toole ('96), Big East player of the year in 1996; outfielders Don Martone ('92), Mike Lyons ('94), and Pete Tucci ('96); and utility man Tom Mezzanotte ('90). Dr. Tom Mezzanotte, son of coach Don, was an academic All-American and graduated *summa cum laude* in pre-med.

In 1992, when the Friar baseball team (29–23) won its first Big East championship, it went to the NCAA South 1 Regional Playoffs and was designated Rhode Island's Team of the Year by the sportswriters of Rhode Island Words Unlimited. Kostacopoulos received Coach of the Year honors as well. Unfortunately the Friars were quickly eliminated. Paul's highly regarded 1995 team (44–15) was selected to play in the NCAA Midwest 1 Regional but also fared poorly.

Pitching coach Ray Jarvis was one of Paul's top assistants. A Providence native who had pitched two seasons (1969–70) with the Boston Red Sox, Jarvis was the fourth Friar coach with major league experience to share with his players.

Coach Charles Hickey came to PC in 1997 to continue the Friars' winning baseball tradition. Instead, the thirty-one-year-old Hickey became, in effect, the captain of the *Titanic*. During his first two seasons he made good use of some great talent inherited from Paul Kostacopoulos, most notably Pat Carey ('98), whose career batting average of .360 is the fourth highest in PC history, center fielder Brian Tamul ('98), second baseman Scott Palmieri ('97), outfielder Mike Harrington ('97), and ace hurlers Todd Incantalupo ('98) and Andy Byron ('97). Incantalupo is PC's all-time leader both in career wins, with 27 victories, and in complete games, with 22.

Catcher Scott Friedholm, PC's athlete of the year in 1998, was Hickey's mainstay during his first two seasons. Despite Friedholm's graduation in 1998 and the departure of Carey, Incantalupo, and Tamul, PC was poised for its greatest postwar season in the spring of 1999.

The talent-laden 1999 baseball team won the Big East championship (the second such crown for the Friars), compiling an overall record of 49–16 and earning a berth in the NCAA tournament. Three members of that ultimate team won All-American honors — senior pitcher Marc DesRoches, sophomore left fielder Mike Scott, and junior right fielder Keith Reed. DesRoches, with 14 wins and 2 losses, and Scott, with a .420 batting average and 13 triples to lead the nation, made the third team. Reed, a first-round selection of the Baltimore Orioles, was the second Providence College player ever named a First Team All-American by the American Baseball Coaches Association, joining third baseman Roger Haggerty, who earned that high honor in 1986. Another Friar, senior third baseman Angelo Ciminiello, made the All-American academic team. Tragically, PC's decision to drop baseball disrupted the promising careers of Reed, Scott, freshman Neal McCarthy, and other standouts who had enrolled at PC primarily because of its baseball program and tradition.

The blow to Neal McCarthy—whose father, Bob, was my former student, a Harvard Ph.D., a professor of history at PC, and a fine ballplayer in his own right—was especially disheartening. The younger McCarthy had hit a gaudy .603 in his senior year at Bishop Hendricken High and was named USA Today's Rhode Island Player of the Year in 1997. Seemingly destined to perform as well on Hendricken Field as he had at Hendricken High, he set several PC freshman records in a starring role on the great 1999 team. But when the spring of 2000 came, the dugouts and stands at the Hendricken diamond had been demolished; all traces of baseball had been obliterated, just as Rome had erased Carthage by plowing it under; and McCarthy was attempting to resume his athletic career at Boston College.

The incredible 1999 season, the program's grand finale, was played despite the death sentence imposed upon PC baseball by an administration disdainful of tradition and destitute of imagination. After completing one of its greatest years in eight decades of baseball, the Friar nine did not earn a reprieve. Providence College president Father Philip A. Smith, O.P., acting in concert with myopic bean-counter Michael Frazier, the college's CFO, did something opposing teams could not do: they silenced the Friars' bats. Faced with the options of downscaling the baseball program or destroying it, they chose the latter course. And by adding the value of baseball scholarships to the cost of the program, they convinced a supine college corporation that the sport was a luxury beyond the ability of PC to afford.

The abrupt decision to terminate prompted a lawsuit (still pending) by several younger players who claimed that the college was guilty of deception in encouraging them to bypass other schools to play baseball at PC. In effect, the college's precipitous action disrupted their collegiate careers.

* * *

From its modest inception on April 15, 1920, in Franklin, Massachusetts, to its tragic end on May 30, 1999, in Tallahassee, Florida, Providence College baseball embodied the finest aspects of college sport. In its seventy-seven seasons the program produced only four major league players—Washington pitcher Eddie Wineapple ('31), Detroit, Boston, and Cleveland catcher George "Birdie" Tebbetts ('34), Red Sox infielder Lou Merloni ('93), and Cleveland infielder John McDonald ('96)—and a major league umpire, Hank Soar ('37), plus a relative handful of minor league stars. However, if we count, as we should, the freshman and junior varsity squads of earlier years, PC baseball helped well over a thousand student-athletes on their road to manhood. Most of us who played at Providence College ended our baseball competition at that level and then embarked upon professional or business careers in which we applied the lessons of teamwork, tenacity, dedication, and discipline, learned on Hendricken Field, to the game of life.

My favorite sportswriter, Bill Reynolds of the *Providence Journal*, penned a column in May 1999 to lament the passing of the Friar program, a column in which he contrasted baseball with the money-tarnished, professional minor league sports that PC chose over it:

> …This is college baseball we're talking about. College baseball in New England, where the springs are cold, the stands are empty, and the glamour is usually somewhere else. College baseball in New England, where the players often line the fields themselves. College baseball in New England, where many of the players are playing for the old-fashioned love of the game. Seemingly an arcane notion in this age of big-time college sports where the sports page is full of teenage basketball players leaving college for the kind of wealth that used to be reserved for kings and robber barons.
>
> College baseball, which next year will be about memories.
>
> And the really unfortunate part is that this is what college sports are supposed to be about, but so rarely are anymore.
>
> Which is why this story is so special.

Although I read of the decision by the PC administration to drop baseball when it was first announced in October 1998, it seemed too astounding to be taken seriously. How, I asked, could such a tradition–laden, low–budget sport be scheduled for extermination?

In May 1999, when the Friars won the Big East title and headed towards the College World Series, reality set in. The death sentence was reiterated by Father Smith, the college president, even in the afterglow of victory. At this point, I joined the Committee to Save PC Baseball, uniting with Rich McGeough, Bob Bellemore, Tim Cavanaugh, John and Jim Navilliat, Jim Bedford,

Barry Sullivan, Bob Hargraves, P. J. O'Toole, Dr. Roland Landry, David Meyer, my old teammate George Brown, and other naively optimistic PC baseballers. We received a great boost from local sportscaster Mike Lyons, a former catcher for Southern Illinois University. Our goal, in retrospect, was impossible, because our dealings with Father Smith proved that there are none so blind as those who will not see. And the financial justification for this decision, generated undoubtedly by Michael Frazier, only proved that figures don't lie, but liars figure.

A host of top-flight professional athletes, male and female, from many sports lent their support to our efforts. Many of these stars, including former Rhode Island major leaguers and former Friar foes Mike Roarke (Boston College), Dave Stenhouse (URI), and Bill Almon (Brown), attended a save-the-team rally and sports auction held on July 29, 1999, at the Roger Williams Park Casino. The event was hosted by Mayor Vincent Cianci and Speaker of the House John Harwood, a hockey and baseball star at the University of Pennsylvania. We were foolish enough to believe that something—reason, tradition, sentiment, money, public opinion, common sense, student outcry, alumni pressure, whatever—could reverse the decision to discard baseball at Providence College.

We were wrong. Our efforts got us one meeting with a pompous, intractable Father Smith and his smug, effete vice president, Father Terence Keegan. Both are classic examples of all that is currently wrong with the Catholic clergy. They promised to answer our appeal, but no answer came. PC baseball died, and the committee to save it faded away.

In retrospect, I regard PC's action to eliminate baseball as a stupid decision, caused by a lack of imagination, perpetuated by obtuseness, and defended with arrogance and deceit. Someday a replay of the decision will reverse that lousy call, and the baseball Friars will become the Lazarines.

I wrote the following memo to Father Smith after our fund-raising effort, auction, and rally, and although I still harbored the vain hope that he could be a reasonable man. I apologize for attempting to confuse him with the facts!

A Modest Proposal To Save
Providence College Baseball

MEMORANDUM

TO: Reverend Philip A. Smith, O.P., President
FROM: Dr. Pat Conley, Professor of History (Retired)
DATE: August 2, 1999

In the immediate aftermath of our July 30th meeting concerning the preservation of the PC baseball program, at which we apprised you of our significant financial efforts thus far (over $40,000 raised in 45 days), I am offering these random thoughts and suggestions to assist you in your final decision.

Our discussions revealed to me two basic administration concerns—finances and Title IX requirements.

A. The financial problem can be addressed as follows:

    1. REDUCING EXPENDITURES:
    (a) Eliminate costly southern trips and extended swings.
    (b) Eliminate scholarships.
    (c) Curtail the schedule to 35 games.
    (d) Employ a coach who will serve part-time without benefits.

    2. RAISING EARMARKED REVENUE:
Establish a booster organization from the existing *ad hoc* committee to SAVE PC BASEBALL ("The Dugout Club"). This volunteer group could:
    (a) Solicit annual donations on behalf of the team.
    (b) Obtain corporate sponsors.
    (c) Hold an annual sports auction to benefit PC baseball.
    (d) Sponsor an annual fund-raising team banquet.
    (e) Devise other community-based fund-raising projects (e.g., Friar Day at McCoy Stadium).
    (f) Establish an endowment to help fund the PC baseball program.

A deemphasized program could still compete at the Division 1, Big East level, albeit not as successfully as in the past. Was it not a former baseballer, Grantland Rice, who observed, "It's not if you won or lost, but how you play the game!" A thirty-five game schedule featuring play against nearby colleges—e.g., Brown, URI, RIC, Roger Williams, Bryant, Salve Regina, Holy Cross, Stonehill, St. Anslem's, Tufts, Brandeis, Coast Guard, Assumption, U Mass–Dartmouth, Southern Connecticut, AIC, Springfield, or Dean, where it all began—would be economical for the college and challenging to our walk-on athletes. If the specter of Big East competition is too formidable for a nonscholarship program, PC could play an independent schedule with the teams above in the same manner that Big East member Notre Dame opts to play a nonconference schedule in football.

B. The Title IX problem is more daunting and less subject to our control. In my view, however, it poses more of a challenge than an obstacle. The administration feels that inane and irrational federal formulas and regulations leave PC no recourse but to eliminate baseball. I feel that creative and bold moves can bring PC into compliance without subjecting baseball to the death sentence.

As I understand the administration's logic, a gender imbalance in the student body—59% females to 41% males—has necessitated a corresponding imbalance in sports programs. The obvious long-term solution is to restore parity to the student body (50–50 sounds about equal).

I, for one, am bewildered by how the all-male student body of 1971 was transformed into one with a sizable preponderance of females by 1999. How did this sex change take place? What standards of selection and admission produced it? I admit that women are biologically superior to men, but are they intellectually dominant also—and, if so, by a ratio of 59 to 41?

The journal *Mensa* recently rated the 100 greatest intellects in human history, and only two selectees were female. Presumably a similar list prepared by the Title IX Office of Civil Rights would raise that number to 50, and the crack staff in PC's admissions office would boost female representation to 59. Which men would get the axe? Everyone knows that philosophers, especially those long dead, generate few fans and little money. By those criteria we can cut Aristotle, Augustine, and Aquinas in deference to writers Jackie Collins, Judith Krantz, and Danielle Steel. Sound ridiculous? Yes, but only in degree, not in kind, from the reverse sexism that has been allowed to afflict PC under the guise of economics and gender equity.

If PC admission policy is tuition-driven, why not accelerate the present trend and convert the college into an exclusive finishing school for rich young ladies? This course of action will surely banish the specter of Title IX and render the baseball issue irrelevant—unless the ladies wish to play in a league of their own.

Does Providence College just get applications from bright gals and dumb guys? If not, select enough male applicants for admission to restore student body parity. This step alone could save baseball, even under present federal regulations.

That process takes time, say you. The cumbersome federal bureaucracy takes longer, say I. At our meeting the administration expressed the fear that present noncompliance would bring loss of federal aid, and that the office of civil rights would move swiftly against a noncompliant PC. The verbal threat of a low-echelon federal enforcement officer was cited as a cause for alarm.

We stated that the federal bureaucracy only moves at glacial speed, that picky peons have superiors, often more flexible and disposed to reasonable solutions, and that PC is not without alumni who might intercede while the college is restructuring its population and its athletic programs. Two of my former students, U.S. senator Chris Dodd and Congressman Patrick Kennedy, are among many influential PC alumni who would certainly secure a fair hearing for PC and prevent an inane summary judgment against their alma mater.

When challenged by the civil rights compliance officer, we can respond like sheep or like the fox. PC can give its future student body an injection of testosterone, and it can hold the line until the present federal administration and its fanatical application of the Equal Protection Clause is superseded by a more rational regime.

In the short term, the administration can play the Title IX numbers game by making the following adjustments in its athletic program:

502

1. Eliminate men's golf (a game of Dutch and
   Scottish origin).
2. Eliminate men's tennis (a game of French origin).
3. Eliminate men's track and field (a game of Greek origin).

Although my son Patrick Jr. ('84) and I had some success in the
javelin throw when competing for PC, I believe that indoor and
outdoor track are expendable. PC has always shamefully neglected
this sport. The college never built facilities for outdoor track,
always ignored the field events, and never developed a dual meet
schedule. To put men's track and field out of its misery is the one
form of euthanasia I could support.

4. Reinstitute women's lacrosse (a game of Native American
origin). It existed a few years back, only to be discontinued. You
would be lax not to restore women's lacrosse to help save baseball.

5. If these adjustments fail to achieve "equity," eliminate
men's soccer (a game of English origin evolving from a ninth-
century Anglo-Saxon practice of kicking the severed heads of
slain enemies around an open field). Compared to baseball, it is a
johnny-come-lately to PC, and it lacks the tradition of PC baseball. Far fewer alumni and friends of the college would complain
if you gave soccer the boot to head off the demise of baseball.

C. Final queries concerning PC's Title IX dilemma:

1. How do colleges with 100-member football squads
manage to retain baseball as part of their athletic program? My
other Catholic alma mater, Notre Dame, does it. So do those
quasi-Catholic Jesuit schools, Boston College and Holy Cross.

2. Brown University (one mile distant) spent six million
dollars and many years dealing with the intricacies of Title IX.
Did PC ever consult with those involved in the Brown case or
seek guidance from them to deal with our dilemma?

D. Some concluding rhetoric:

In the United States, baseball is the National Pastime. It has
become a sport of mythic proportions. It is part of the national
psyche. The feeling towards baseball transcends logic and defies
explanation. For an American college with the vaunted athletic

history of PC to eliminate baseball defies reason and demands explanation.

Such action is equivalent to Canadian colleges dropping hockey, German universities discarding gymnastics, Finland banning the javelin, or Prince Edward Islanders (like yourself) outlawing all water-related sports. Such decisions would evoke emotional responses far out of proportion to the intrinsic importance of the action. Why this fact is not evident to the college administration mystifies me.

When you cut golf, tennis, track, soccer, or even football at an American college, you amputate an arm or a foot, you remove a kidney or even a lung; when you cut baseball, you remove the soul. If you think me guilty of hyperbole or hysterics, consider the assessment of the noted French philosopher-historian Jacques Barzun. After coming to Columbia University to teach, Barzun wrote a Tocquevillian commentary on our nation entitled *God's Country and Mine*, in which he observed that "whoever wants to know the heart and mind of America had better learn baseball, the rules and realities of the game."

This is why criticism has been so intense; this is why you—a presumably well-intentioned priest of God—have been misrepresented and vilified by once-loyal PC alumni; this is why a majority of the Rhode Island community (for PC is Rhode Island's college) is angered or at least dismayed by your decision; and this is why the SAVE PC BASEBALL committee has given its time and money to persuade the administration to rethink its position in light of the foregoing facts and suggestions.

We are all familiar with the simile "As American as Baseball and Apple Pie." One feeds our spirit, the other our stomach—and not by pie alone does man live. The notable baseball philosopher Yogi Berra (who was not on that list of great intellectuals, although he has received an honorary doctorate from Roger Williams University) sagaciously observed that "It's not over 'til it's over." Our committee subscribes to that view. Prisoners condemned to death are reprieved or even pardoned when new evidence or new attitudes are applied to their situations. PC baseball not only deserves but demands such a reprieve.

George Brown, Rich McGeough, and I were grateful for the opportunity to meet with you and present our case. I found you to be patient. I am sure your demeanor was influenced by the knowledge that our efforts—though unauthorized, unorthodox, and abrasive—are animated by our concern for Providence College, especially its image, its betterment, and its long-range financial well-being.

Notes

1. Providence College publications mistakenly list 1921 as the first year the Friars fielded a baseball team. Even a meticulously researched typescript history of PC athletics from 1921 to 1938 by John Farrell (on which I heavily relied) makes this error. While conducing my research, I discovered references to the 1920 team in the college magazine, *The Alembic.* The archivist Jane Jackson and I uncovered the scorebook for the "lost" 1920 season in the papers of the team moderator, Father Ambrose Howley, O.P. On a more technical note, PC sports teams were not called the Friars until 1929; earlier nicknames included "Cardinals," "Dominicans," and the "Black and White."

2. At the end of Reynolds's public career, when he served as East Providence city manager, I wrote two budget messages for him, and he related to me the details of his glory days.

3. In the 1950s McElroy was my coach and mentor when I pitched for the Richardson Park team, the perennial champions of the Providence Recreation League.

4. In 1976 Bodington, Bellemore, Guy "Doc" Calise ('58), and I joined in a last hurrah, playing with a senior (over thirty-five) slow-pitch softball team to raise money for charity and to publicize the Bicentennial of American Independence. That squad, the ri76 Seniors, composed of former collegiate and local sandlot stars, became Rhode Island's first senior slow-pitch softball champion, compiling a record, against all-comers, of 72 and 19.

The four former Friars acquitted themselves well on this select squad. Bellemore, joined on the left side by All-World shortstop Joe Unsworth, led the team defensively; Bodington bashed a slew of homers, some clearing fences built for baseball; pitcher "Doc" Calise won about as many games as "Old Hoss" Radbourne; and I batted .514 through the first eighteen games before suffering a torn medial meniscus rounding second, an injury that ended, for me, yet another promising season.

5. I have seldom cited quantity records (e.g., most home runs, hits, wins, etc.) because of the great fluctuation in the number of games played per season, especially between pre-1973 teams and those from that season onward.

Rhode Island senior athletes from various sports pose for this 2001 promotional photo. Sportscaster Mike Lyons, a senior athlete himself and the volunteer director of the annual Rhode Island Senior Games, stands at left, his hand on my throwing shoulder.

These brief remarks were made in October 1999 at a State House send-off for the 106 senior (over fifty) athletes who had qualified to compete in the biennial National Senior Games. The talk was delivered in my capacity as captain of the Rhode Island delegation to the Senior Olympics, held in Orlando, Florida. I finished eighth (the final medal position) in the javelin event, competing against 39 qualifiers from around the nation. The honor of being team captain and the thrill of earning an Olympic ribbon were slightly diminished because my winning throw of 126 feet 3 inches was 20 inches short of the standard in my age category for designation as an All-American.

Rhode Island Senior Games director Mike Lyons, Lieutenant Governor Fogarty, fellow Olympians, Ladies and Gentlemen:

IT IS MY PRIVILEGE to address you on this special occasion in your athletic career. I feel that my designation as your team captain may be due more to my oratorical than to my dwindling athletic skills. Or, perhaps, it is because, like the Independent Man, I throw a spear. Whatever the reason, I cherish the honor.

Later this month we will compete with over eleven thousand senior athletes from around America at the Disney Sports Complex. How we fare against such formidable opposition is far less important than the fact that we engage in the competition. Sportswriter Grantland Rice said it best: "When the One Great Scorer comes to write against your name, he marks—not that you won or lost—but how you played the game." For us, who will meet the "Great Scorer" sooner rather than later, one might add "*if* we played the game"—and we did!

Rhode Island has a great sports tradition. Three natives—Hugh Duffy, Nap Lajoie, and Gabby Hartnett—are enshrined in the Baseball Hall of Fame. The Providence Grays won baseball's first-ever World Series in 1884, and the Providence Steam Roller were the champions of the National Football League in 1928. John L. Sullivan and Rocky Marciano used Rhode Island as a base in their successful quest for the heavyweight boxing championship of the world. From 1893 to 1934 the Herreshoffs of Bristol built six defenders of yachting's greatest prize, the America's Cup. Glenna Collett Vare of Providence dominated women's golf during the 1920s and 1930s, winning six U.S. championships—more than any golfer before or since.

Collegiate sports have also gained Rhode Island national fame, especially Brown's undefeated 1926 "Iron Men," coached by D. O. "Tuss" McLaughry; URI's "point-a-minute" basketball Rams of the 1930s and 1940s, coached by the legendary Frank Keaney; and the Providence College basketball teams of Joe Mullaney, Dave Gavitt, and Rick Pitino that twice reached the "Final Four" (1973 and 1987) and captured two NIT crowns (1961 and 1963).

For good reason, Rhode Island is home to the International Tennis Hall of Fame in Newport, the America's Cup Hall of Fame in Bristol, and the International Scholar-Athlete Hall of Fame at the University of Rhode Island. In sum, sports have been an important and colorful aspect of Rhode Island history, and we, as Senior Olympians, have become a small part of that tradition.

At the Olympic level, which interests us most as Senior Olympians, Norman Taber of Providence and Brown University won gold at Stockholm in 1912 in the 3000–meter team race and bronze in the metric mile. From 1915 to 1923 Taber held the world record in the mile run. Other Rhode Island Olympians who have brought home the gold include Brown University coach Archie Hahn, three sprint golds at St. Louis in 1904 and a repeat in the 100-meter dash at Athens in 1908; Aileen Riggin of Newport in women's springboard diving at Antwerp in 1920; Fred Tootell of URI fame in the hammer throw and John Spellman in freestyle wrestling at the 1924 Paris games; sprinter James Quinn of Cranston in the 4×100–meter relay at Amsterdam in 1928; Albina Osipowich of Pembroke College, the swimming star of the 1928 Olympics, earning gold in the 100–meter freestyle and the 4×100–meter freestyle relay; Geoffrey T. Mason of East

Providence, a member of the USA's five-man bobsled team at St. Moritz in 1928; swimmer Helen Johns (Carroll) of Pembroke in the 4×100–meter freestyle relay at Los Angeles in 1932; and track star Janet Moreau (Stone) in the 4×100–meter relay at Helsinki in 1952.

In the nearly half century since the Helsinki games, Olympic gold has become a scarce commodity for Rhode Island athletes. The only competitors to strike gold have been Providence native Harriet "Holly" Metcalf in the eight-oars with coxswain at Los Angeles in 1984, Lynne Jewell (Shore) of Newport in 470 sailing at Seoul in 1988, and, most notably, Mike Barrowman, who began a swimming career at the Cumberland-Lincoln Boys Club that carried him to such honors as World Swimmer of the Year in 1989 and 1990 and a gold medal in the 200–meter breaststroke at the Barcelona Olympics in 1992, where he broke his own world record in the victory. Most recently, Sarah DeCosta of Warwick and Providence College earned her piece of sports immortality as the goalie for the U.S. Women's Hockey Team at the 1998 Nagano, Japan, winter Olympics.

Although our athletic feats are infinitesimal compared to those whose litany I have just recited, we, too, are Olympians. Our efforts and aspirations are no less worthy. The luster of our national champion Little League team from Cranston is not diminished if no one from that squad ascends to the major leagues, nor is our 1999 Providence College baseball team, the Big East champions, in any way diminished by its inability to win the NCAA crown. Our perennial Rhode Island high school hockey kingpin, Mount St. Charles Academy, is no less impressive because it suffered a loss to a Massachusetts hockey power or because it would be outclassed by the Providence Bruins.

The examples are endless. All of us compete and strive in accordance with our age, our level of skill, our gender, and our physical capacities. The only thing that can and should be equal is our determination. Whether we are Special Olympians, Senior Olympians, regular Olympians, or professional superstars, victory is just as sweet and competition is just as intense.

In the manner that professional athletes are role models and a source of inspiration for the young, we senior athletes can be good examples for our aging peers. Competition encourages exercise, proper diet, and a healthful lifestyle. It recaptures, though imperfectly, the zeal and ardor of youth. It relieves tension, promotes a positive outlook, and delays our final rendezvous with the "Great Scorer."

Good luck to you in Florida, and, win or lose, congratulations for keeping your flame alive and burning brightly!

10

The Local Scene:
East Bay, West Bay,
All Around the State

This 1830s print shows the Blackstone River as it flowed into the industrial village of Pawtucket. The river's east bank (right) was in the state of Massachusetts until 1862; its west bank was in the town of North Providence until 1865. At Pawtucket Falls (right center), the fast-flowing, free-falling Blackstone becomes the placid Seekonk River.

The Blackstone Valley: Its River, Its Canal, and Its People

This talk was originally written for presentation at the 1977 "Conference on the Future of the Blackstone Valley Canal-River Area," sponsored by the Urban Field Center of the Cooperative Extension Service of the University of Rhode Island, directed by Dr. Marcia Marker Feld, and the Rhode Island Committee for the Humanities. This program helped to lay the groundwork for the creation of the Blackstone Valley National Corridor. I dedicated the piece reprinted here to Michael Cahalan (1839–1905), an Irish mule spinner of Central Falls via Tipperary, and his great-granddaughter Gail Cahalan-Conley.

i

THE BLACKSTONE RIVER has meandered for many centuries from its source in east central Massachusetts through northeastern Rhode Island to the sea. At Pawtucket Falls the river discards its maiden name, becoming the Pawtucket River. It then commingles with the Seekonk River, the Providence River, and Narragansett Bay before its waters reach the open ocean.

The Blackstone Canal, which sometimes paralleled and sometimes merged with its parent, the river, had a much shorter life. It began in 1796 as a seed in the mind of Providence merchant John Brown, who desired to siphon the trade of east central and northwestern Massachusetts away from Boston to the expanding Port of Providence.

The canal's period of gestation was long and uncertain; in fact, one historian, James B. Hedges, has suggested that the delay between conception and birth "made the canal obsolete before a shovelful of earth had been turned" because "the railway era was at hand." The Rhode Island General Assembly, anxious to gain access to the untapped resources of the Massachusetts portion of the valley of Blackstone, responded to Brown's plan immediately by incorporating the Providence Plantations Canal Company in 1796. The Massachusetts General Court, whose concurrence was essential to this interstate project, was persuaded by certain members, especially those representing the Boston mercantile establishment, that unless the canal with its Providence terminus was blocked, "Boston will be in a few years reduced to a fishing town." They submitted a counterpetition that a canal be constructed from Boston to Worcester, and then on to the Connecticut River. Neither canal gained approval, and the matter rested uneasily for more than a quarter of a century.

After the War of 1812, as the country set out to achieve economic self-sufficiency and embarked upon an extensive program of internal improvements, the neglected Blackstone Canal project was revived in response to the business climate, the economic spirit of the age, and the practical needs of Worcester County farmers and entrepreneurs desirous of cheap and ample access to the sea for their produce and their products. Promoters held meetings in Providence, Worcester, and several valley towns, and in early 1822 they appointed a committee of investigation and authorized a project survey. Benjamin Wright, who gained fame as chief engineer for the middle section of the Erie Canal, directed the study, and his assistant, Holmes Hutchinson, did the field work. Their report, completed in September 1822, discussed the grades, the towpath, the number, size, and location of canal locks (there would be sixty-two of them), the rainfall and evaporation, the possible feeders (i.e., ponds and streams), and the estimated cost ($323,919) for a canal 32 feet wide at the top, with a minimum depth of 3½ feet, that would descend 451½ feet in a 45-mile stretch from Worcester (population 3,650 in 1825) to Providence (population 15,941 in 1825). The projected route would adhere to the Blackstone River for much of its length, except for a divergence into the Moshassuck at Saylesville, Rhode Island, to connect more directly with port facilities in Providence harbor at the end of Canal Street (formerly known as North Water Street).

The enthusiasm and insistence of both Worcester County business and agrarian interests and Providence merchants carried the day. In March 1823 the legislature of Massachusetts authorized a canal corporation, and the Rhode Island General Assembly granted a similar charter in June. These corporations were merged in 1825 to form the Blackstone Canal Company, with three commissioners appointed from each state to supervise the construction and operation of the project.

The canal funding came from subscription, with Rhode Island merchants, manufacturers, and financiers—especially Nicholas Brown, Thomas P. Ives, Edward Carrington, Moses Brown Ives, Cyrus Butler, and Sullivan Dorr—providing most of the capital. Relying on the topographical survey, however, the investors underestimated their money requirements. Four thousand shares of stock at $100 a share were quickly subscribed, and many prospective investors were turned away, but when actual construction costs soared to over $700,000, the promoters had great difficulty raising the balance. Such devices as a new stock issue and loan certificates were used, as well as the creation of a so-called improvement bank—the Blackstone Canal Bank.

Excavation was begun in Rhode Island in 1824 by the laborious method of pick, shovel, and wheelbarrow, supplemented by horses and carts. Finally, on October 7, 1828, the *Lady Carrington* (named for the wife of Edward Carrington, a Providence merchant and canal commissioner who had made a fortune in the China trade) arrived in Worcester with much fanfare, becoming the first boat to traverse the length of the canal. On the following day the Worcester newspaper optimistically carried a feature section entitled "Ship News. For Port of Worcester."

The canal seemed an instant success: new impetus was given to industries along its course, land values rose, and the ditch brought an immediate savings to the Worcester merchant of $3.80 for every ton of freight shipped via the canal from the Port of Providence rather than hauled by team overland to be shipped from the Port of Boston.

Eventually the canal boasted a fleet of twenty freight barges and one passenger packet. An alarmed Boston businessman noted that a shipment of iron from New York to Boston, intended to be transported by land to Worcester, was shipped back to Providence for a journey up the Blackstone at a saving to its Worcester recipient of $2.28 per ton, despite its circuitous trip.

But Boston was not to be denied. This era of the 1820s and 1830s, which economic historian George Rogers Taylor has called the age of the "Transportation Revolution," spawned a development that would curb the canal-building boom of the postwar decade and divert the capital and energy of merchants and financiers to a more rapid, reliable, and efficient mode of transport. That development was the railroad, an all-weather carrier not nearly as subject to seasonal freeze-ups, floods, or drought as the cumbersome canal. The Boston and Worcester Railroad was completed in 1835, and it regained for Boston the economic ascendancy in Worcester County that it had so recently relinquished to Rhode Island.

After rising steadily from $8,606 in 1829 to a peak of $18,807 in 1832, canal tolls suffered an irreversible decline, culminating in the canal's ultimate demise on November 8, 1848, when the last toll was collected.

Nature contributed in several ways to the project's failure. First, a portion of the canal was located in the riverbed, where excessively high or low water detained boats for weeks at a time; second, the ditch was icebound for several months each winter; and finally, in time of drought, water was scarce for use in the locks.

Still another difficulty was the battle over water rights between the canal men and the mill owners who held water privileges along the Blackstone River. The canal corporation did not acquire full riparian rights, but only joint use, and such an arrangement was an invitation to contest the management of water resources. Boatmen claimed that mills diverted too much water, and mill managers countered with a similar charge. When the latter went so far as to dump boulders into the canal and damage the locks, the boatmen responded by threatening to sabotage or burn the mills.

The canal's death blow, however, was delivered by the railroad. The Boston and Worcester caused injury; the Providence and Worcester was the mortal wound to the moribund canal. Chartered in 1844, the P&W sent its first train between the two cities on October 25, 1847, making the canal an archaic facility. At a triumphant gathering of railroad investors held at Brinley Hall in Worcester two weeks later, the failure of the canal was noted in a toast offered by the exuberant railroaders: "The two Unions between Worcester and Providence—the first was *weak* as *water*; the last is *strong* as *iron*."

Massachusetts historians have noted that the short-lived canal had an important economic impact on the towns along its path, especially Uxbridge and Worcester, with the latter town's population nearly doubling from 1825 to 1835 (3,650 to 6,624). As the canal's first historian, Colonel Israel Plummer, observed in 1878:

> The Blackstone Canal proved more useful to the public than to the stockholders, as by building reservoirs it increased and equalized the volume of water very materially in the Blackstone River, and the power for hydraulic purposes was much increased, and more mills and manufactories were built, and villages sprung up and increased.... The manufactories on the line, or within ten miles, were nearly doubled, and Rhode Island was much benefitted. In particular did Providence receive great advantage; while Massachusetts, and particularly Worcester, were proportionately benefitted. An impetus was given to trade and manufactures.

ii

Though the canal was both a product and a victim of the Transportation Revolution, the Blackstone River just kept rolling along as it had done for many centuries before William Blackstone, an eccentric English clergyman, became the first white to settle on its banks in 1635. The river shared with Blackstone its beauty as he looked over its valley from his home on "Study Hill" (near Lonsdale), and he lent to the waterway his name. But the pragmatic Englishmen who followed Blackstone to this valley in the late seventeenth and eighteenth centuries were not content to view the river aesthetically; they wished to use it and the waterpower it generated in its 451-foot plunge from Worcester to Narragansett Bay as an economic resource. As the canal had locks, the river had falls, where the rapidly descending water could be diverted into trenches to drive the wheels, and later the turbines, that mechanized the mills along its banks.

From 1790 onward, Mother Nature and Yankee ingenuity transformed the Blackstone Valley into a succession of mill villages, teeming with factory hands drawn from the farms of Rhode Island, the factories of England and Scotland, the potato patches of Ireland, the fields of Quebec, Germany, and Scandinavia, and, eventually, the far-flung peasant villages of the Azores, continental Portugal, Italy, Poland, Ukraine, Romania, Russia, Greece, Syria, and Lebanon.

Political subdivisions, especially in the Rhode Island portion of the valley, were shaped in part by this influx as new towns and cities were created, at times to accommodate and at times to discriminate against these immigrants. The entire valley to a point just north of Woonsocket Falls ("Thunder Mist," as the Indians called it) had been conveyed by the Narragansett tribe to Roger Williams and his town of Providence by a series of deeds granted between 1637 and 1659.

The growth of population through the spread of agriculture prompted the General Assembly in 1731 to incorporate the outlands of Providence into the separate towns of Scituate, Glocester, and Smithfield, each much larger than its present size. Old Smithfield ran along the west bank of the Blackstone and embraced the land that present-day Central Falls, Lincoln, Smithfield, North Smithfield, and a portion of Woonsocket now occupy. In 1746/47 a boundary settlement with Massachusetts added several towns to eastern Rhode Island, including the Attleboro Gore on the east bank of the Blackstone directly across the river from Smithfield. This section, once part of the Wampanoag domain, was immediately incorporated as the town of Cumberland.

In 1765 Providence relinquished more territory to create another valley town, North Providence, which extended from the Woonasquatucket River to the Blackstone, embracing a large portion of present-day Pawtucket. During the industrial boom of the late nineteenth century, the legislature made further subdivisions and realignments in the valley. In 1862 the Massachusetts town of Pawtucket, lying on the east bank of the Blackstone, was annexed. This new Rhode Island municipality expanded across the river by securing a portion of North Providence in 1874.

In 1867 Cumberland relinquished the bulk of her population and her northern mill villages of Woonsocket Falls, Social, and Jenckesville to create the town of Woonsocket. The new municipality crossed the river to embrace the villages of Globe, Bernon, and Hamlet in 1871 when Old Smithfield was divided and greatly reduced in size. This 1871 division created the new valley towns of North Smithfield and Lincoln and excluded the new Smithfield from the river and the valley.

The final incidence of political mitosis came in 1895, when financial disputes, urban-rural antagonism, and native-immigrant rivalry prompted the General Assembly to slice 1.32 square miles from the southeast corner of Lincoln to create the river city of Central Falls. At this time three valley communities filled with foreign stock—Pawtucket (1886), Woonsocket (1888), and Central Falls (1895)—were among Rhode Island's five cities, a dubious blessing for those of low socioeconomic status, since residents could vote in city council elections only if they paid a property tax. This restriction, imposed in 1888 by Amendment VII to the Rhode Island Constitution (the Bourn Amendment), denied nearly 60 percent of the electorate the power to vote in council-manic elections at a time when Assembly-granted city charters made the mayor merely ceremonial and the council dominant in city government.

But political discrimination against the people of the Blackstone Valley had become a tradition by 1888. The industrial towns (or, more precisely, the mill villages) of the Blackstone had been centers of reform agitation in the generation preceding the Dorr Rebellion of 1842. In the early nineteenth century the towns of Providence, North Providence, Smithfield, and Cumberland objected to the governmental system under the still operative royal charter whereby a malapportioned Assembly, dominated by static or declining rural towns in the southern and western sectors of the state, imposed a landholding, or freehold, requirement for voting upon the landless factory hands in the industrial centers. Legislative resistance to these demands for reapportionment and "free suffrage" stiffened in the late 1830s as it became increasingly clear that this mounting industrial population would be composed of such dangerous elements as Irish Catholic immigrants.

When Thomas Wilson Dorr and his valley supporters like Jonah Titus, David Daniels, Ariel Ballou, and Metcalf Marsh attempted to achieve genuine reform, they were thwarted by a coalition of Whig merchant-industrialists and farmers from South County and the western hill towns. This faction—called the Law and Order party—drafted the present state constitution under pressure from the Dorrites. When it became operative in 1843, the constitution imposed a nativistic freehold requirement on foreign-born citizens and gave the farmers of the south and west a veto in the General Assembly by apportioning the Senate on a one-vote-per-town basis.

This arrangement left the valley's burgeoning industrial population, increasingly composed of naturalized Irish and French Canadians, at a distinct political disadvantage. When the freehold requirement for those of foreign birth was finally removed in 1888 by the Bourn Amendment, a new system of discrimination was instituted in city elections. The malapportionment of the Senate, modified by Amendment XIX in 1928, was not fully corrected, nor the valley people adequately represented, until 1965, when the Rhode Island General Assembly was forced to redistrict by the one–man, one–vote rulings of the United States Supreme Court.

iii

Who are the valley people? First, of course, were the Indians of the Narragansett and Wampanoag tribes who had hunted and fished in this beautiful, pristine land. After displacing the Wampanoag, the Narragansett sachems obligingly deeded the valley to the early English settlers, though they did not feel that by such grants they relinquished their own right to share its bounty. This generosity was often returned (albeit less in Rhode Island than elsewhere) with discrimination and ingratitude. The Indians reciprocated with a vengeance in King Philip's War. The bloody last stand of Captain Michael Pierce and his force of seventy on the riverbank near Central Falls and the subsequent atrocity in Cumberland at Nine Men's Misery were the most prominent examples in the Blackstone region of Indian-white hostility during this race war.

The Indian defeat in this violent conflict gave the English settlers and their Yankee descendants unchallenged supremacy in the Blackstone Valley. In the century and a half that followed, this pioneering English stock acquired the land along the river, gained water rights or privileges, and began the economic exploitation of this valuable natural resource.

The first entrepreneur at Pawtucket Falls was Joseph Jenks, Jr., a skilled ironworker, who began Pawtucket's rise as an industrial community in 1671, when he bought sixty acres of land on the west side of the falls for manufacturing purposes. Driven off by the Indian war, Jenks returned immediately after its conclusion to build a sawmill and forge. His descendants expanded these enterprises, and his eldest son, Joseph Jenks III, acquired enough wealth and influence to become Rhode Island's first non-Newport governor, serving from 1727 to 1732. Another important pre-Revolutionary era industrialist was Hugh Kennedy of northern Ireland, who established a variety of enterprises at Pawtucket Falls.

Upstream, the power furnished by Central Falls was gradually tapped from the 1750s onward by entrepreneurs such as the Jenks family and Charles Keene, who in the 1780s began the manufacture of scythes, other sharp-edged tools, and chocolate, giving Central Falls its early name of Chocolate Mills. This area did not emerge as an important industrial village, however, until the decade of the 1820s.

The famous Wilkinson family made its start during the eighteenth century further upstream in Smithfield. Israel Wilkinson built the Unity Furnace near Manville, and Oziel, father of David Wilkinson of Slater Mill fame, also operated a furnace in Smithfield, where he produced nails, anchors, spades, and other iron goods. This family, known for its mechanical and inventive genius, was the first to use the waterpower at Valley Falls.

Still farther north, the Arnold family began to develop Woonsocket Falls as an industrial site when it constructed a sawmill in 1698 and later added a grist and fulling mill. The early records also reveal that in 1698 John Balkam operated an ironworks at Woonsocket Falls. By the mid-eighteenth century other families—Aldrich, Logee, Gaskill, and Jillson, plus French Huguenots Ballou and Tourtelott—had settled in the area of present-day Woonsocket, and most were engaged in industry. In Massachusetts the valley town of Mendon (established in 1667) was an early center of business activity and dominated the upper reaches of the Blackstone.

It was at Pawtucket Falls on this historic river in 1790 that British immigrant Samuel Slater, a defector from the middle-management level of the English textile industry, assembled under the sponsorship of Moses Brown a working Arkwright system for spinning cotton yarn. This event—the most important single achievement in the history of early American industry (though too lavishly termed by some the beginning of America's Industrial Revolution)—set in motion a dramatic series of developments that helped transform the character of Rhode Island (and especially the towns of the Blackstone Valley) from rural and agrarian to urban and industrialized. In 1793 the Old Slater Mill was built, and up and down the valley—at Pawtucket, Central Falls, Valley Falls, Lonsdale, Albion, Berkeley, Ashton, Manville, Woonsocket Falls, Globe, Social, Bernon, Hamlet, and Jenckesville—mill villages grew in size and significance during the ensuing decades.

The Americans of English stock were the first immigrants to the valley, and since they owned the land, built the mills, and possessed the capital, they dominated the Blackstone region economically and politically well into the twentieth century. Newcomers worked for them, were sometimes recruited by them, often lived in their housing, and shopped at their company stores. The Yankee mill owners ruled the roost, and the newer immigrants adjusted to this basic fact of life.

iv

The first major non-English group to migrate to once homogeneous Rhode Island was the Catholic Irish. From the 1820s onward these Celts came to America to escape centuries of repression and subjugation at the hands of the English and to find economic opportunity. Their arrival coincided with the Transportation Revolution and the development of American industry.

The early Irish migrants to Rhode Island in the 1820s and 1830s were attracted by such projects as the building of Fort Adams, the construction of the Blackstone Canal, the railway boom, and the expansion of the textile, base-metals, and precious-metals industries. The Blackstone Canal project brought Michael Reddy and several fellow laborers to Woonsocket in 1826 as the area's first Irish Catholic settlers, and according to a local antiquarian, it brought the first Catholic Irishman to Uxbridge.

The textile industry and then the railroad lured many more Irishmen to the Providence-Pawtucket region, enough to necessitate the establishment of the state's second oldest Catholic parish—St. Mary's, Pawtucket, in 1829. Next, in 1841, the Catholics founded St. Patrick's in Providence to serve the spiritual needs of the Irish in the North End and the adjacent town of North Providence. It was situated just a few hundred feet west of the terminus of the Blackstone Canal.

The Woonsocket Irish community reached sufficient size in 1844 to create the parish of St. Charles Borromeo. S. C. Newman's census of 1846 listed 666 persons of Irish birth living in the area. From that time onward the Famine-spawned migration would increase the number of Irish dramatically in every Rhode Island industrial center.

For the remainder of the century the valley and its mills continued to attract Irish settlers. That fact is revealed in the establishment of new parishes created primarily to serve their spiritual and social needs: St. Patrick's, Valley Falls (1859); St. Joseph's, Ashton (1872); Sacred Heart, Pawtucket (1872); St. Joseph's, Pawtucket (1873); St. John's, Slatersville (1873); and Holy Trinity, Central Falls (1889).

The Irish impact on Rhode Island was enormous. By the first state census in 1865, nearly 3 out of every 8 Rhode Islanders were Irish. By the census of 1885, over 125,000 of Rhode Island's 304,000 inhabitants—41 percent of the total population—were of Irish stock. This figure is a rough estimate that attempts to embrace third-generation Irish and immigrants of Irish ancestry from England, Scotland, and Canada, of which there were many.

The next major ethnic element to arrive in the Blackstone Valley was the group destined to become numerically dominant in this region—the Franco-Americans. The trickle of what would become a flood of French Canadian immigrants to Rhode Island began in 1815. During that year Francis Proulx and his family settled in Woonsocket. Six years later the families of Prudent and Joseph Mayer chose northern Rhode Island as their new home. In 1846 S. C. Newman's "statistical survey of Woonsocket" revealed that 250 of the 4,856 inhabitants in the Woonsocket area were of French Canadian ancestry.

Most of the new arrivals were responding to what some have called "the lure of the loom." The continued expansion of the textile industry in Rhode Island, especially in the Blackstone Valley, prompted the mill owners to recruit the eager *habitants* of French Canada who were already experienced in the domestic production of textiles. With the coming of the Civil War, the need for manpower to replace those serving the Union cause became so acute that many New England manufacturers set up employment agencies in Quebec province.

By 1865 there were 3,384 foreign-born Rhode Islanders from "British America," and a substantial majority of this number were people of French descent from Quebec. Five years later the federal census recorded 10,242 immigrants from this source. Woonsocket continued to be the population and cultural center for the state's Franco-Americans, but the Blackstone Valley mill villages of Manville, Ashton, Albion, Slatersville, Central Falls, Pawtucket, and Marieville also attracted large numbers of *habitants*.

The devoutly religious Franco-American longed for his own national parish where his language and culture would be preserved. The establishment of these French national churches is an excellent indicator of the growth and influence of the Franco-American community. The mother parish was Precious Blood, Woonsocket, founded in 1872, with its imposing church completed in 1881. It was followed in rapid succession by Notre Dame, Central Falls (1873), founded by the noted Franco-American cleric Father Charles Dauray; St. James's, Manville (1874); St. John the Baptist, Pawtucket (1886); St. Ann's, Woonsocket (1890); and Our Lady of Consolation, Pawtucket (1895). Six additional French parishes were established in the valley by 1910.

Other immigrants who came to the valley in smaller but substantial numbers were the Germans and the Swedes. Most migrants from these countries bypassed Rhode Island and other industrial areas for the fertile farmlands or new cities of the Midwest. Much of the German immigration was spawned by economic factors, political discontent, and the dislocations associated with unification under militaristic Prussia; the Scandinavians suffered from a decline in the timber industry, general agricultural depression, and a devastating famine that hit Sweden in the late 1860s. The Swedes were mainly farmers, while many of the German migrants to Rhode Island were skilled craftsmen.

By the state census of 1895, Pawtucket was the only valley community with a sizable number of these ethnic groups. The city contained 644 residents of German stock and 380 Swedes. Those Germans who were Lutheran worshiped at St. Matthew's Evangelical Lutheran Church, while the Swedes attended the Swedish Episcopal Church. In 1902 the Pawtucket Swedish community organized the Barnadotte Lodge, Order of Vasa, to serve its social needs. A small Swedish congregation formed in heterogeneous Woonsocket in 1911 and built the Swedish-Finnish Lutheran church on Fairmount Street in 1917. In the 1960s the descendants of this group merged with a Swedish community established in 1893 in nearby Millville, Massachusetts, to form St. Mark Evangelical Lutheran Church on Harris Avenue. J. S. Osterberg, in his history of the Swedes in Rhode Island (*Svenskarna, Rhode Island*, 1915), also alludes to a few early Swedish settlers (ca. 1870) in the Cumberland villages of Valley Falls, Lonsdale, Albion, and Diamond Hill.

In the analysis of this pre-1890 migration to Rhode Island and the Blackstone Valley, the continuing influx of British immigrants should be noted. Migrants to Rhode Island from England, Scotland, Wales, and British Canada ranked behind only those from Ireland and Quebec during the course of the nineteenth century. Many of these arrivals had skills that were ideally suited to the industries of the valley. In the late sixties there began a large-scale exodus from England of Lancashire textile workers, followed shortly afterward by one of Yorkshire woolen operatives and a smaller migration of silk workers. As late as 1960, Lincoln and Pawtucket were the only towns in the state where more than 10 percent of the population was of British stock, though it is quite likely that a significant number of these Britishers (which in the 1960 census included persons from Northern Ireland) were of Irish ancestry.

v

Thus far in our ethnic profile of the Blackstone Valley we have examined the period up to the 1890s. Now we must consider the heterogeneous influx from 1890 to World War I, called by historians the "new immigration." Historians have contended that three distinct stages of migration to America marked the nineteenth and early twentieth centuries. The first, called the Celtic, began around 1830 and continued until 1860, reaching its crest in the years 1847–1854. It was spearheaded by the Catholic Irish. The next great wave of migration spanned the decades between 1860 and 1890, when English, Scandinavians, and north Germans from Prussia and Saxony predominated. This exodus was Teutonic in blood, in institutions, and in the basis of its language.

In the third wave, extending from 1890 to 1914, two new and distinct geographic regions sent a flood of migrants to America. One was Mediterranean and southern European in origin and was composed primarily of Italians, Greeks, Portuguese, and minorities from the Turkish Empire, including Armenians, Syrians, and Lebanese. The other was predominantly Slavic and eastern European in origin. This segment was composed mainly of minority or subject peoples within the Austro-Hungarian and Russian Empires, such as Poles, Lithuanians, Ukrainians, Serbs, Czechs, Slovaks, Slovenes, Ruthenians, and such non-Slavic groups as Hungarians, Austrians, Romanians, and Jews from Poland and Russia. This mass migration crested in the decade prior to 1914 and was temporarily and abruptly curtailed by the outbreak of World War I. This third movement was known as the new immigration, primarily because it flowed from southern and eastern Europe rather than from the traditional northern and western sectors of the continent.

Of the newer immigrant groups, several have figured prominently in the political, economic, and cultural life of the Blackstone Valley—notably the Portuguese, Italians, Jews, Poles, Syrian-Lebanese, Greeks, and Ukrainians—though none of these diverse groups approached the numerical strength in the valley of the Franco-Americans, the Irish, or the English. By the time these later immigrants arrived, the river had become less a source of power than an open sewer to carry industrial and residential waste, but the mills that lured them were bigger, busier, and more noisy than ever.

Although many Portuguese migrated to Rhode Island in the 1860s and 1870s, most of these pioneers were Azoreans associated with the whale fishery who settled in the seacoast communities such as Providence, Bristol, and Newport. Only after the dawn of the twentieth century was the Portuguese presence felt in the cities of Pawtucket and Central Falls and the Valley Falls section of Cumberland. In addition to the Azoreans, this region attracted comparatively large numbers of continental Portuguese, who began a major migration in 1910 during the revolutionary period surrounding the establishment of the Portuguese republic. These newcomers were aided in 1911 and after by the ships of the Fabre line, which stopped at both Lisbon and the Azores en route to the Port of Providence. According to the census of 1920, there were 1,102 Pawtucket inhabitants of Portuguese birth. In 1927 St. Anthony's Church in Pawtucket was founded as a Portuguese national parish, and in 1953 the Catholic diocese established Our

Lady of Fatima in Cumberland to serve the religious needs of that town's growing Portuguese community.

The Italians—especially the peasants, or *contadini*, of southern Italy—also experienced political turmoil and severe agricultural depression in the late nineteenth century. These conditions prompted a massive migration to America. Rhode Island, via the Fabre Line, was significantly affected by this outpouring. Curiously, the Italians concentrated in Providence, North Providence, and the adjacent towns to the south and west but did not settle heavily in the Blackstone Valley. In Pawtucket they constitute a relatively small but important percentage of the population centered around St. Maria Goretti Parish, established in Fairlawn in 1953. Of the state's sixteen Italian churches, only one other is located in the Blackstone Valley—the Church of St. Anthony, Woonsocket, founded in 1924 to serve a local community composed in 1920 of 1,328 people of Italian stock.

As significant numerically among the valley people as any "new" immigrant group are the Poles, who migrated from the turn of the century to World War I in reaction to foreign domination (by Germany, Russia, and Austria), overpopulation, and depressed conditions in agriculture and industry. A *Providence Journal* survey in 1907 enumerated 6,000 Poles in the state, including 1,500 in Central Falls and 1,000 in Woonsocket. There was a substantial increase in this number before migration from central Europe was shut off by World War I. By the 1915 census, for example, Woonsocket had 2,167 residents of Polish birth.

The Poles founded eight national parishes in Rhode Island, and four of these were in the valley: St. Stanislaus, Woonsocket (1905); St. Joseph's, Central Falls (1906); the Holy Cross Polish National Catholic Church, Central Falls (1919), which is not in communion with Rome; and the Church of Our Savior, which was founded in 1924 on Arnold Street, Woonsocket, as a Polish National Catholic Church, but which has since moved to Great Road and has become ethnically heterogeneous.

Both Pawtucket and Woonsocket have small but significant Jewish communities dating back to the late nineteenth century, when Russian persecutions (called pogroms) drove Jews from

Russia and Poland by the thousands. At that time some members of this perpetually persecuted group came to Woonsocket, where three small congregations were established. The one that endured and prospered was that of B'nai Israel, founded as the Lovers of Peace in 1893. The beautiful modern temple it occupies on Prospect Street reflects the success and upward mobility achieved by the Jews of Woonsocket. The Pawtucket Jewish community, which also dates back to the late nineteenth century, numbered nearly 3,000 members according to a 1963 survey conducted by the General Jewish Committee of Providence. It had grown significantly in the post-World War II era because of out-migration from the older Jewish neighborhood in Providence's North End section. Most of these Jews worshiped in Providence at nearby Temple Emanuel, Temple Beth El, or Temple Beth Sholom, reflecting their pattern of settlement, but Pawtucket had one Orthodox temple of its own.

The Syrian-Lebanese population, though ethnically Arab, shared a common experience with its Jewish neighbors. These Middle Eastern people fled to America to escape persecution inflicted upon them by certain Muslim sects because of their adherence to Christianity, and to escape the oppressive political restrictions imposed upon them by the Turkish Empire. Overpopulation, lack of employment, and economic hardship also contributed to their decision to leave their native lands.

Nearly 1,600 "Syrian" migrants came to Rhode Island between 1898 and 1914, and most of these settled in Providence, Pawtucket, Central Falls, and Woonsocket. In the 1980s the valley had four national churches ministering to its Syrian population: St. Basil's on Broad Street, Central Falls (1910), and St. Elias's, Woonsocket (1931), both of the Melkite Rite, in communion with the Church of Rome; the Syrian Orthodox Church of St. Mary's on High Street, Pawtucket (1910); and the Orthodox Church of St. Ephraim, Central Falls (1913).

The Greeks are another small but important ethnic group in the valley. Their exodus began after 1900 because of depressed agricultural conditions similar to those in Italy and Portugal. From 1898 to 1914 nearly 4,000 came from Greece to Rhode Island.

532

These newcomers settled in close-knit communities in Providence, Newport, and Pawtucket, and in each community they established a Greek Orthodox church to sustain themselves spiritually and culturally. The Church of the Assumption on Walcott Street, Pawtucket, became the center of Greek Orthodox worship and Hellenic culture in the lower Blackstone Valley.

The valley's final numerically important ethnic group from the pre-World War I migration is the Ukrainians. Their homeland in southeastern Europe has been long dominated by Russia. These Slavic people came to America to escape foreign rule and to improve their economic condition. Most of these immigrants to Rhode Island came from the extreme southwestern section of Ukraine known as Galicia, and they settled first in Cumberland Hill and then in Woonsocket during the first decade of this century. They have since established St. Michael's Ukrainian Catholic Church (1909), which is Uniat, or allied with Rome, and St. Michael's Orthodox Church (1926). The Ukrainians still form one of the most cohesive ethnic groups in the pluralistic city of Woonsocket—a community that also contains St. John the Baptist Romanian Orthodox Church. That Elbow Street house of worship near Social Pond became a cultural center for the city's small Romanian population.

The outbreak of World War I brought a dramatic halt to the new immigration (except from Portugal). When it began to revive in 1919 and 1920, nativists and immigration restrictionists, who felt that the peoples of southern and eastern Europe were ethnically inferior, imposed the discriminatory National Origins Quota System in 1921 and 1924 to curtail it. This measure, soon followed by worldwide economic depression and World War II, brought an end to the century of mass immigration (1824–1924).

In the post-World War II period the internal migration of black Americans from the South to the industrial cities of the North has added a new element to the population of the valley. According to the 1936 state census, Woonsocket contained only 9 blacks (down from 38 in 1925). By 1960 the number had risen to 337, and in 1980 it reached 944. Pawtucket, which had 248 blacks in

1936, had 453 in 1960 and 993 in 1980. Central Falls had only 87
black residents in the 1980 census count.

Two final developments have recently affected the ethnic diversity of the valley. The first is the revival of Portuguese immigration
after the repeal of the discriminatory National Origins Quota
System by the Immigration and Nationality Act of 1965. For the
past decade Portuguese newcomers have been arriving in the state
at the rate of 1,500 per year. They make up about half the total
number of annual immigrants, and many are coming to the Blackstone Valley.

The second development is the migration to Rhode Island and
the valley by Latin American or Spanish-speaking people from
Puerto Rico, Cuba, Venezuela, the Dominican Republic, Mexico,
and, especially, Colombia. The 1970 federal census listed 6,961
"persons of Spanish language" in Rhode Island, but that number
was understated and has increased dramatically since that tabulation, according to informed local observers. The Colombian impact on the communities of Pawtucket, Central Falls, and
Cumberland has been especially significant and gives still a new
ethnic dimension to the culturally pluralistic Blackstone region.
According to the 1980 census, Pawtucket had 2,502 residents of
Spanish origin; Central Falls had 1,769, and Woonsocket only 346.
The magnet for the Spanish—as for the French Canadians, the
Irish, and the English before them—is job opportunities in the
factories of the valley.

Economic development and population growth have proceeded
hand in hand. And while the landscape is sometimes unsightly,
the valley can boast at least one redeeming consequence: it is
adorned by a beautiful mosaic of diverse peoples in the best tradition of this nation of immigrants. Let us hope they will now unite
to revitalize their region—the valley that gave them sustenance—
and reclaim their heritage.

The Sprague Mansion (ca. 1790, with additions in 1864), at 1351 Cranston Street, Cranston, as it appeared in 1979 after its restoration

Save the Sprague Mansion! | 54

Written in March 1966, this letter to the *Cranston Herald* involved me in the successful campaign to save the Sprague Mansion for community use. When the effort was over, I became a member of the board of managers of the mansion, and then chairman of the Cranston Historic District Commission—my first history-related position in the public sector.

IN DECEMBER 1965 an incredible proposal was made by the Cranston Housing Authority. The agency expressed a desire to erect a ten-story apartment project on the site of the historic Sprague Mansion. Giving little thought to saving this important part of our heritage, the authority went ahead and invested $40,000 for site testing and preliminary plans.

The callousness of this public agency shocked the sensibilities of many cultured and aesthetic-minded citizens of Cranston, and Robert and Viola Lynch inaugurated a community effort to save the mansion.

I am in full sympathy with this cause. Our city has only a handful of prime historic sites, of which the Sprague Mansion is easily the most prominent. Would Pawtucket raze its Slater Mill? Would Newport allow the bulldozer to crush its Touro Synagogue? I think not.

Cranston's sister city, Providence, realizes the value of its cultural and historic heritage. For over a decade it has been engaged in a vigorous program of restoration and preservation. This successful rescue effort has been spearheaded by the Providence Preservation Society.

What has happened in our city? It appears that Mayor James DiPrete had advance notice of the Cranston Housing Authority's dispassionate plan to raze the Sprague Mansion. Why did he fail to nip these plans in the bud before $40,000 of taxpayers' money was expended in a project repugnant to the cultural sensibilities of our citizens? The widespread outburst of indignation brought the scheme to a temporary standstill and forced our mayor to reassess his earlier position. It is remarkable, however, that the political considerations which altered his course have not prompted him to use the moral weight of his office to help save the Sprague Mansion. I look to him to make a bold and vigorous statement on behalf of this worthy cause, which has now aroused the passions of preservationists within our community and around the state.

As a professional historian, I would like to be included in the ranks of those Cranstonians who value our city's heritage and who are fighting to save this historic structure. The Spragues of Cranston deserve to be remembered. The most illustrious member of their family, William Sprague (1830–1915), himself the nephew of a governor and senator, was governor of Rhode Island, United States senator, and the outfitter of the First Rhode Island Regiment—one of the first Northern volunteer units of the Civil War. In addition, Sprague, like his forebears, was a textile-manufacturing magnate as well as an investor in banking, railroading and horse-breeding enterprises. He was a friend of Garibaldi and a generous contributor to the cause of Italian unity, a fact that should endear him to the residents of nearby Knightsville. In 1864 Senator Sprague enlarged the original 1790 structure to give it the size and appearance befitting the status of its illustrious owner.

Let us hope that misguided municipal officials will not demolish this handsome early nineteenth-century home in the name of progress, for it stands as a tangible reminder of Rhode Island's most famous industrial empire.

My wish is that the Cranston Historical Society acquire the mansion, restore it faithfully, and make it a community resource and house museum much like the John Brown House in Providence. Let us transform the Housing Authority's blunder into a civic boon!

55

City Celebrates 150: Providence from Town to City

This public lecture was presented in the council chamber of Providence City Hall on October 1, 1982, as part of a series of events held to commemorate the sesquicentennial of Providence's 1832 incorporation as a city with a mayor-council form of government.

THIS YEAR PROVIDENCE IS COMMEMORATING 150 years of city government. It's a safe bet, though, that this year's excitement will be tame compared with the hubbub that Providence experienced in the fall of 1831. For an understanding of what happened in those fateful months, a sketch of the town's history is essential.

Providence was founded by Roger Williams in 1636 on lands granted to him by the Narragansett Indians after that tribe had seized them from the Wampanoag. The first settlers promptly laid out house lots stretching from the shoreline (i.e., the Moshassuck River and a now-filled saltwater cove) eastward up and over College Hill. These parcels extended from present-day Wickenden Street on the south to Olney Street on the north. They fronted on a narrow winding road called the Towne Street, which ran in a north-south direction following the shoreline.

For more than a century that street (now North and South Main) was Providence's major thoroughfare. The lands across the Great Salt River (the Providence River) in the present-day Downtown consisted of swamps, meadows, and farms. Not until the mid-eighteenth century did the so-called West Side develop, and not until that time did Providence begin to challenge larger Newport for economic and political supremacy.

Providence was a leader in the struggle for independence during the Revolution, but unlike vulnerable Newport, it escaped British occupation. When the war was over, Providence emerged, under the financial leadership of the Brown family, as Rhode Island's most populous and most important municipality.

Yet in the first federal census of 1790 Providence had only 6,380 residents. Of these, only adult male citizens who were landowners could vote or hold public office. These so-called "freemen" were less than six hundred in number—still a small enough group to participate directly in governing themselves through the traditional town meeting. That famed device, still used in the smallest Rhode Island towns, was direct democracy in action. As it operated in Providence and elsewhere in the state, the freemen assembled, elected a moderator, and then passed ordinances and approved budgets for the operation of their town. They also chose a town council, with only ministerial functions, to carry out their collective will.

As long as Providence remained small, homogeneous, and relatively peaceful, the town meeting was adequate to the task of governing. But in the early decades of the nineteenth century, Providence was growing and changing like an unruly adolescent. It was also increasingly diverse in its socioeconomic, class, and ethnic makeup.

During these early years of the republic, Providence was elbowing its way into the front rank of the nation's municipalities, first as a bustling port and then as an industrial and financial center. Providence merchants, especially the Browns, accumulated the money to sponsor experiments in manufacturing. Samuel Slater was their first important protégé.

The transition begun by Slater in 1790 was on its way to completion by 1830. By that date manufacturing had replaced maritime activity as the dynamic element in Providence's economy, and industry had become the principal outlet for investment capital and the primary source of wealth.

Providence's four major areas of manufacturing endeavor—base metals and machinery, cotton textiles, woolen textiles, and jewelry and silverware—were established by 1830, and for the next century they dominated the city's economy. They made Providence the industrial leader of the nation's most industrialized state. Providence owed this primacy to its superior financial resources and banking facilities, its position as the hub of southeastern New England's transportation network, and—especially—to its skilled work force and enterprising business leaders.

But all was not rosy in the early years of the nineteenth century. A smallpox epidemic in 1800 claimed about fifty lives, a major fire on South Main Street in January 1801 destroyed thirty-seven buildings, and the Great Gale of September 1815 left the entire waterfront in shambles. The War of 1812 brought hardship to commerce and apprehension to the residents of a port vulnerable to enemy attack, and a postwar depression (the panic of 1819) interrupted economic recovery.

Most serious, however, were the town's internal growing pains. In 1820 the population of Providence reached 11,745; by 1830 the number of inhabitants had jumped to 16,832, of whom 1,213, or 7.2 percent, were black. As Providence became more populated, as its older houses became less habitable, and as its factories darkened the landscape, tensions increased between the white working class and the black community. The fact that "citizens of color" were stripped of the right to vote in 1822 and were segregated by the public-school law of 1828 intensified their resentment.

Most blacks lived in an area called Hard-Scrabble (near present-day Moshassuck Square) or further to the northeast along Olney's Lane. In October 1824 a minor race riot occurred in Hard-Scrabble. Although it resulted in no deaths and only moderate damage, it shocked the citizenry and kindled debate not only on issues of race but also on those of law and order and governmental reform. The old town meeting system, said some, was no longer adequate for the administration and security of a community harboring nearly seventeen thousand socially and racially antagonistic residents.

In subsequent years the drive for a city form of government gained momentum because of the town's steady growth. In January 1830 the General Assembly granted Providence a city charter, subject to ratification by a three-fifths vote. When balloting was held the next month, 383 supported the proposed charter and 345 opposed it—a result short of the 60 percent approval requirement that the state legislature had imposed.

Here things stood until September 1831, when another race riot erupted, much more serious than that of 1824. It began with a clash between some rowdy white sailors and local blacks living on Olney's Lane. The four-day episode, in which five men died, was the final catalyst for municipal change.

In the aftermath of this incident, the town meeting appointed a fourteen-member committee to conduct an investigation and prepare a report. The committee's extensive findings can be summarized as follows (the quotations are from the report):

On Wednesday evening, September 21, five sailors headed from their boardinghouses to go "on a cruise" through Olney's Lane, a street where "houses of ill-fame" stood side by side with the dwellings of respectable citizens. Upon their arrival at 8:00 P.M. they met six or seven white mariners who had just brawled with local blacks. As a crowd gathered, the belligerent whites headed up Olney's Lane. Eventually a black homeowner confronted the group, defending his house with a gun and ordering the mob to "clear out." Someone defiantly shouted "Fire and be damned." A shot rang out, and sailor George Erickson fell mortally wounded. When the crowd down the lane became aware that a black man had shot a white, it went berserk, proceeded up the street, demolished two of the houses occupied by blacks, and broke windows in several others.

On Thursday news of the previous night's affair spread through Providence, and plans were made for a full-fledged raid on Olney's Lane and the neighboring section of Snow Town (near the Smith Street bridge over the Moshassuck River), where other blacks lived. Governor Lemuel Arnold and Providence County sheriff Henry G. Mumford got word of the impending raid and called out 25 militiamen of Providence's First Light Infantry as a precautionary measure to help the civil authorities. Seven disorderly persons were arrested early in the evening, when the mob was small, but as the crowd grew, it became bolder and totally unmanageable. "Brick-bats, stones and other missiles were thrown ... and a consultation between the governor and the sheriff resulted in a determination to withdraw the military from the ground, it being evident that nothing short of firing would produce any other effect than increased irritation and ferocity in the mob." At 3:00 A.M. the rioters finally disbanded.

Friday was somewhat quieter. The seven prisoners taken the previous night were examined. Four were discharged and three bound over for trial and then released on bail. Five local militia units, totaling 130 men, were mobilized. That evening a smaller mob demonstrated at the jail and made a menacing trip through the Snow Town section, but then dispersed.

On Saturday night—the time for the working class to howl— the rioting reached its violent conclusion. Despite the repeated presence of Governor Arnold, Sheriff Mumford, and the various militia companies, a "great crowd collected on Smith's Bridge." Soon the mob began to damage property, stone the militia, and scuffle with some of the troops.

At this tense point, Justice of the Peace William S. Patten was directed to read the riot act. The shouts of the crowd subsided temporarily as Patten, speaking in a loud, clear voice from the brow of the hill where the State House now stands, warned the unruly that the use of force against them by the militia and the civil authorities was authorized and imminent unless they ceased their vandalism, dispersed, and returned in peace to their homes.

The mob's collective response to Patten was a chorus of defiant shouts and jeers. Following this reaction the militia proceeded downhill towards the demonstrators. The First Light Infantry, Capt. James Shaw commanding, and the Providence Light Dragoons, under Col. William B. Thornton, crossed the bridge, waded through the crowd, and stopped at the corner of Smith Street and North Main. When the mob pelted them with rocks, the increasingly exasperated militia fired a volley into the air. This attempt at intimidation only angered their antagonists, who boldly surrounded the troops and threatened to breach their ranks. At this point, with several of the besieged militiamen falling to the ground or bleeding from stones or other missiles, a desperate Sheriff Mumford directed the soldiers to fire. One round was discharged into the menacing mob. Four men fell dead, and many others were wounded. A silence came upon the place. The riot at last was quelled.

In the aftermath of this tragedy an apprehensive town meeting decided, with only one dissenting vote, to petition the General Assembly again for a charter that would establish a city form of government, with a full-time chief executive to administer and enforce the laws and a two-chamber council to make them. The charter was promptly issued and then ratified by the voters, 459 to 188, in a November 1831 referendum.

In June 1832 Samuel Willard Bridgham, an attorney, became the first mayor of Providence. He died in office in December 1840.

In April 1832 the freemen of Providence chose Samuel W. Bridgham (1776–1840) as the new city's first mayor. With him they also chose a legislative branch consisting of six aldermen elected at large and twenty-four councilmen, four elected from each of six wards.

In his inaugural address on June 4, 1832, Mayor Bridgham stated what most citizens now realized: Providence, observed Bridgham, had become "too heterogeneous and unmanageable" to maintain the part-time government of the old town meeting system. Another stage in the history of Providence had passed.

According to urban historians Howard Chudacoff and Theodore Hirt, race was not the only factor in the disorders of 1824 and 1831. These incidents, they say, "fit within a larger context of urban growth and change. Increase in vice and disorganized violence; social breakdown of the old village sense of community; decline of the influence of the church; a rise in intemperance, plus an increasing awareness by middle and upper classes of need for reform"—all signified that the economic and social ferment of the early nineteenth century was undercutting old patterns of political and social authority.

In response, Providence upgraded and expanded its municipal services and streamlined its government. The city charter of 1832 by no means insured peace and harmony (as the Dorr Rebellion of 1842 would prove), but it was an innovation that heralded a new era in Providence's growth and development—and the commemoration of this milestone is why the "City Celebrates 150."

RHODE ISLAND REGIMENTS EMBARKING AT PROVIDENCE FOR NEW YORK AND WASHINGTON.

This April 1861 sketch at the Port of Providence depicts the Providence Marine Corps loading its light artillery pieces for shipment to the battlefront in Virginia.

Mother of Batteries, Matrix of Military History: The Providence Marine Corps of Artillery at Two Hundred

56

This oration was delivered in the rotunda of the State House on May 4, 2002, as part of the bicentennial observance of the founding of the Providence Marine Corps of Artillery.

Lieutenant Governor Fogarty, General Harold N. Read, Adjutant General Reginald Centracchio, General Richard Valente, General Everett Francis, Chaplain Lemoi, Distinguished Members of the Providence Marine Corps of Artillery and the 103rd Field Artillery Brigade, Distinguished Guests, Ladies and Gentlemen —Americans All!

EXCEPT FOR the Newport Artillery Company, founded in 1741, and the Bristol Train of Artillery (on whose board I serve), founded in 1776 and chartered in 1792, the Providence Marine Corps of Artillery is the parent organization of all current Rhode Island artillery units, or, as your great commanding officer General Harold R. Barker proudly called it, "the mother of batteries."

Having acknowledged their longer lineage, however, I do no historical disservice to the Newport and Bristol units (who elected in 1875 to retain their independent status) when I state that the Providence Marine Corps of Artillery has exerted by far the greatest influence upon Rhode Island's distinguished tradition in the artillery branch of the armed forces of our nation.

But like a caisson starting down a muddy trail, the corps started slowly and traversed its first four decades in a rut. It was an outgrowth of the Providence Marine Society, a fraternal organization created in 1798 by Providence ship captains to provide a pension and insurance program for their families and to compile "marine intelligence," so that accurate nautical charts and information could be disseminated to those actively engaged in maritime commerce. The prime movers in the creation of the PMS were John Updike, Seth Wheaton, and Edward Carrington, Providence's most prosperous China merchant.

Within three years the benevolent PMS was transformed into the PMCA, largely through the initiative of Seth Wheaton. Since there was no stigma attached to the designation PMS in 1801, we must look to other reasons for the establishment of the PMCA, and we need not probe too deep to find them.

American merchants from 1798 onward had navigated troubled waters. Caught in the rivalry between England and France, two of our principal trading partners, America found its commerce and its maritime rights victimized by both.

The creation of the PMS coincided with the outbreak of the quasi war with France, a limited naval conflict that vexed the administration of Federalist president John Adams. When Adams's principled conduct in that war contributed to his defeat by Thomas Jefferson in the bizarre election of 1800, a champion of the agrarian interest took the helm, a president who viewed a standing army and navy as a potential threat to liberty.

Jefferson and his penurious secretary of the treasury, Albert Gallatin, immediately announced plans to eliminate the national debt by sharp cuts in military and naval expenditures. Jefferson's preference for gunboats to defend America's harbors rather than a formidable seagoing navy caused some critics to contend that the Virginian believed his own navy was more to be feared than that of the enemy.

Against this immediate backdrop, Seth Wheaton perceived the need for "a corps of artillery in the town of Providence for the purpose of improving in the use of cannon, and in the tactics employed in the attack and defense of ships and batteries." So read the petition that fifty-nine PMS members presented to the General Assembly in 1801 in their successful quest for a charter that would constitute them as an independent, volunteer naval militia.

The charter was granted, and the PMCA organized in April 1802, electing Seth Wheaton its lieutenant colonel and first commander. According to the original bylaws, all officers had to be members of the PMS, and hence ships' masters.*

The first forty years need not detain us, for no battle streamers accumulated on the walls of a PMCA armory. There were no battles (at least with an enemy), and there was no armory either! There was, however, a war in which most of New England chose not to participate: "Mr. Madison's War," some unfairly called it, and no American conflict—not even Vietnam—generated such formidable domestic opposition.

The maritime states of Massachusetts, Connecticut, and, to a lesser extent, Rhode Island were notably noncompliant with the requests of the Madison administration to wage war against England, the Mistress of the Seas. By the time Congress declared the War of 1812, Seth Wheaton had long since relinquished his command to head a local bank, and Col. Amos Atwell, another charter member, led the unit.

Wheaton's legacy, however, significantly impacted the conduct of that war, not militarily but paternally. Despite its disapproval of the War of 1812, Rhode Island produced not only the foremost naval hero of that conflict, Oliver Hazard Perry, and its most successful privateer, the *Yankee*, sponsored primarily by Bristol's James De Wolf, but also one of the war's most persuasive legal defenders, Henry Wheaton (1785–1848), the son of your founder, Seth.

This jurist, diplomat, and expounder of international law graduated from Brown in 1802 and practiced law in Providence until 1812, when his legal defense of the policies of Jefferson and Madison prompted Democratic-Republicans in New York City to offer him the editorship of the *National Advocate*, their local party newspaper. Writing forcefully and with learning on the questions of international law growing out of the War of 1812, Wheaton was considered the mouthpiece of the Madison administration during

*An 1830 amendment allowed two officers to be nonmembers of the PMS. In May 1842, during the Dorr War, the restriction was removed completely.

his three-year wartime tenure with this paper. He was rewarded with the post of U.S. Supreme Court reporter in 1816, and after serving with distinction in that position until 1827, he embarked upon a long and successful diplomatic career.

548   Wheaton's most enduring achievement was his work as an expounder and historian of international law. His classic study *Elements of International Law* (1836) went through numerous editions and translations. Its excellence has prompted historians to rank Wheaton with John Marshall, James Kent, and Joseph Story as the major architects of the American legal system.

*   *   *

The first major campaign of the PMCA occurred in May and June of 1842, during a conflict known as the Dorr Rebellion. When the People's governor, Thomas Wilson Dorr, attempted to gain control of the state arsenal at the Dexter Training Grounds on the night of May 18, 1842, members of the PMCA were inside that building ready to defend it; and when Dorr retreated from the field, the PMCA advanced to Federal Hill to seize his headquarters, thereby quelling the disorder that convulsed Providence. Then, on June 27, 1842, the PMCA, led by Col. George C. Nightingale, marched with approximately twenty-five hundred fellow militiamen to Acote's Hill in Chepachet, where they seized Dorr's defensive fortifications and put the reformer to flight.

The most detailed account of the Chepachet campaign was compiled by William Rodman, the recording clerk of the PMCA, who later became mayor of Providence. When Acote's Hill was taken, Rodman exclaimed that the event "made the hills and valleys echo with the glad notes of joy—joy for the triumph of law over misrule and mobocracy—joy for the victory of truth over error—joy for the safety of our institutions, our laws, our privileges, our kindred, and our homes." Upon the PMCA's return to Providence, the unit marched triumphantly to Smith Hill, where they fired a twenty-six-gun salute in honor of what Rodman called "the triumph of law over wild and mad ambition, over the plans and schemes of one whose only attribute of greatness is an indomitable will."

My wife Gail and I view Dorr differently. In recently commissioning a statue of the People's governor to stand in the rotunda of the Heritage Harbor Museum, we assessed Dorr's character and achievements in a much different way.

Thomas Wilson Dorr is the pivotal figure in Rhode Island history, the bridge between early and modern Rhode Island, between old stock and new, and between the charter government that served Rhode Island for 180 years and the present constitutional order. But Dorr was not merely a force for constitutional change; he was the quintessential reformer of America's first great age of reformist activity. Among his causes were opposition to slavery, abolition of imprisonment for debt, banking regulation in the public interest, a myriad of improvements in free public education, mobilization of women as a political force, and the defense of the rights of Irish Catholic immigrants.

Optimistic, articulate, dedicated, concerned—these were among the qualities of Thomas Dorr. Liberty and equality were to him, as much as to any reformer of this remarkable age, the indispensable conditions of human activity.

As you can gather from this assessment, choosing me to comment on the role of the PMCA in suppressing the Dorr Rebellion is like having chosen Cornwallis to speak at George Washington's retirement ceremony, or selecting General Nathan Bedford Forrest to deliver the eulogy for John Brown.

Truth, like beauty, is often in the eye of the beholder!

*   *   *

The Dorr War campaign was PMCA's coming-out party. To prevent further domestic upheaval, the triumphant Law and Order faction subsidized the loyal militia; and PMCA members, having finally tasted confrontation (if not battle), sacrificed to build an armory of their own on Benefit Street. The castellated stone structure opened in March 1843 about two hundred yards south of its present site.

In 1847 the state honored a petition from the PMCA for new cannon. Instead of the two heavy brass fieldpieces for each Rhode

Island artillery unit stipulated by the militia act of 1843, the PMCA requested four light guns, which were much more mobile than the cumbersome cannon the unit lugged to Chepachet.

When the legislature responded positively, the PMCA reorganized as a battery of light, or "flying," artillery, becoming the first light battery to be organized in America outside the regular army. The Flying Artillery attracted great interest throughout southern New England, and the PMCA, under the command of Col. Joseph P. Balch, gave numerous exhibitions of its skill and prowess.

In 1856 William Sprague became commander of the PMCA. A nephew and namesake of a former Rhode Island governor and U.S. senator and the son of Amasa Sprague, a textile magnate who was the victim of Rhode Island's most famous murder, young William was a dashing military figure. He endowed the unit with two additional pieces of artillery to make it a six-gun battery, and he provided his men with handsome uniforms as well.

In 1860 Colonel Sprague was the successful fusionist candidate for governor. His victory over abolitionist Republican Seth Padelford (also a member of the PMCA) was made possible by the votes of moderate Republicans and Democrats. Sprague was inaugurated several months before his thirtieth birthday, making him the state's youngest chief executive ever.

In April 1861, immediately after the Southern shelling of Fort Sumter, the Civil War erupted. Governor Sprague promptly offered President Lincoln both political and military support, volunteering as an aide to Col. Ambrose Burnside, the commander of the Second Brigade, Second Division, Army of the Potomac.

Because of Sprague's zeal and initiative, the Providence Marine Corps of Artillery was one of the first units to respond to Lincoln's call for troops on April 15, 1861. A contingent of 142 officers and men headed south on April 18 as the First Light Battery, Rhode Island Volunteers, under the command of Capt. Charles H. Tompkins, who later became chief of artillery for the Sixth Army Corps. Another contingent left Providence on June 19, 1861, as the Second Light Battery (Battery A), under the command of Capt. William H. Reynolds. A third group organized in May 1862 as the Tenth Battery, Rhode Island Volunteers, and took the field for garrison duty to protect the national capital from the flanking movements of Lee's roving Army of Northern Virginia.

During the course of this bloody war, the PMCA trained and sent forth from its armory ten units: Batteries A through H of the First Regiment, Rhode Island Light Artillery, and the First and Tenth Light Batteries, Rhode Island Volunteers. In addition, the PMCA played a role in the transition of the Third Rhode Island Regiment from infantry to heavy artillery in December 1861. Only Rhode Island's final two heavy artillery regiments, the Fifth (transitioned from infantry in May 1863) and the Fourteenth (created in August 1863 with an Afro-American rank and file), were beyond the sphere of influence of the PMCA. Small wonder that the soubriquet "Mother of Batteries" became such a fitting description of the Providence Marine Corps of Artillery!

From First Bull Run through Antietam, Fredericksburg, Gettysburg, Cold Harbor, Petersburg, and Appomattox, the Rhode Island artillery was ever present, earning fifteen battle streamers. Symbolically, its Bull Run Gun now graces the lawn of the Squantum Club in East Providence, its Gettysburg Gun adorns our State House entrance, and the uniform of PMCA colonel Charles H. Tompkins is enshrined at the Antietam Visitors' Center as a relic of America's bloodiest day of battle. By war's end, nine light artillerymen were among the sixteen Rhode Island recipients of the newly created Congressional Medal of Honor, and Gen. Ambrose Burnside, commander of the Army of the Potomac, had been accorded an honorary membership in the PMCA, which he accepted with gratitude and enthusiasm.

In 1875 the legislature enacted a new statute to bring the militia into a consolidated regimental organization modeled on the federal system, a reform designed to reduce costs, increase efficiency, and heighten professionalism. The PMCA agreed to the reorganization, but most of Rhode Island's several independent chartered companies did not. Those chartered commands that opted to remain independent forfeited all state pay and allowances, but by accepting the provisions of the militia organization act of 1875, the PMCA was relegated to the status of a social auxiliary to Battery A, Rhode Island Militia.

In 1879 another realignment resulted in the creation of one Rhode Island state militia brigade composed of twenty companies of infantry, two companies of cavalry, one battery of light artillery (Battery A), and one machine-gun battery. The brigade's first commander was Brig. Gen. Elisha Hunt Rhodes, the now famous chronicler of the Civil War.

The outbreak of the Spanish-American War in April 1898 revived Rhode Island's long-dormant martial ardor. According to the computations of Governor (and former PMCA commander) Elisha Dyer, Jr., the state furnished a total of 1,780 volunteers. Rhode Island raised several military units—the First Regiment, Rhode Island Volunteer Infantry; Light Batteries A and B, First Rhode Island Volunteer Artillery; the Rhode Island Naval Militia; a contingent of hospital corpsmen; and twenty-five crewmen of the USS *Vulcan*, a repair ship. None of these saw combat in this brief conflict except the *Vulcan* crew.

Battery A enthusiastically volunteered for service and trained at the new Quonset Point facility (established in 1893) under the command of Capt. Edgar R. Barker, the head of the PMCA, but the call to action never came. Spain surrendered in July 1898 and Battery A, still at Quonset, was mustered out of service.

In 1903 a federal law pertaining to the militia formally established the National Guard as a consortium of the militia of the several states. The Dick Act (named for Maj. Gen. Charles Dick, its principal exponent) standardized the organization, structure, armaments, and training of this confederated volunteer force. The General Assembly voted to conform to the Dick Act in 1907, giving birth to the Rhode Island National Guard.

Despite this upgrade in status and operation, the long period of military inactivity since Appomattox had sapped the vitality from Battery A and other units of the state militia. In 1910 Lt. Pelham D. Glassford, the federal inspector assigned by the War Department to assess the performance of Battery A, noted problems in proficiency and morale severe enough to jeopardize the professional status of the unit.

Governor Aram Pothier addressed this threat by appointing

Ralph S. Hamilton, Jr., a former adjutant of the First Regiment of Infantry, to serve as the battery's captain and to oversee its reorganization, and Hamilton became the PMCA's commander. Help also came from within. Rush Sturges and Everette St. John Chaffee, both graduates of Yale University and Harvard Law School, came from the ranks of Battery A to offer their energy and support. The governor designated this trio "commissioners" and instructed them to recharge Battery A.

The turnaround was amazing. By 1916, when President Wilson mobilized the unit to secure the Mexican border against raids by Pancho Villa and other Mexican dissidents, Battery A was in such fine condition and in such a state of readiness that War Department inspectors ranked it number one among the eighty-five National Guard field artillery batteries stationed at the border.

For three months during the sweltering summer of 1916, Battery A, under the command of Captain Chaffee, manned a sector near El Paso. They were a part of the law west of the Pecos. By October 1916, when the threat of raids had subsided, the Rhode Islanders returned home, greeted by their cheering fellow citizens.

But soon a far greater threat emerged, one that made service on the Mexican border seem like a mere drill. In April 1917, at the urging of President Wilson, Congress declared war on Germany, and America entered World War I—a bloodbath that had been raging since the summer of 1914. On July 25, 1917, the president summoned the entire National Guard into service, and Battery A responded eagerly to the call. It became the nucleus of three field artillery batteries—A, B, and C of the 103rd Field Artillery of the Twenty-sixth Division of the Allied Expeditionary Force.

This famed "Yankee Division" would compile the longest combat record of any National Guard division in World War I, and the 103rd was in the thick of that combat. Under leaders such as Colonel Glassford (the former federal inspector), Colonel Chaffee, and Capt. Harold Barker (Edgar's son), the unit trained under experienced French officers at Camp de Coetquidan, an artillery camp in Brittany built by Napoleon in 1804. They practiced not on their light artillery guns, as had been the unit's custom since 1847, but on 155 mm howitizers with a nearly seven-mile range. The conditions of World War I had transformed Battery A and the 103rd into a heavy-artillery unit.

The Rhode Islanders performed amazingly well on the western front—and they were not quiet! In 1918 their guns roared at Toul, at the Second Battle of the Marne, on the St. Mihiel salient, and in the decisive Meuse-Argonne offensive that forced the Germans to surrender. The guns of the 103rd kept firing—"giving the enemy hell"—right up to the eleventh hour of the eleventh day of the eleventh month, when the armistice became effective. The 103rd heeded a poetic exhortation of Rudyard Kipling: "If you want to win your battles, take and work your blooming guns!"

Carrying six rainbow-colored battle streamers, Batteries A, B, and C of the 103rd returned home in the spring of 1919 to a heroes' welcome after their service in a brutal and devastating war. Then, in yet another postwar reorganization, guardsmen from Rhode Island joined their New England neighbors from Maine, Vermont, and Connecticut to form the Forty-third Division. Within this unit was the Sixty-eighth Field Artillery Brigade, a component of which was the 103rd Field Artillery Regiment, headed by Lieutenant Colonel Chaffee. This inspiring leader and superb drillmaster also served as commander of the Providence Marine Corps of Artillery from 1919 to 1924 before accepting a new challenge as the first superintendent of the Rhode Island State Police. His colleague, Col. Pelham Glassford, became a member of the PMCA and also took a post in law enforcement as chief of police for the District of Columbia.

During the 1920s and 1930s the Guard was called upon occasionally to quell labor unrest and to assist in coping with such natural disasters as the hurricane of 1938. Fortunately it maintained its preparedness, because "the war to end all wars" did not.

In September 1939 World War II erupted with the German invasion of Poland. By August 1940 President Roosevelt felt compelled to federalize the National Guard. Six months later the Forty-third Division traveled to Camp Blanding, Florida, for training. Included in this call-up was the Sixty-eighth Field Artillery Brigade, with its 103rd regimental component. The entire brigade was under the command of Brig. Gen. Harold R. Barker, a member of the PMCA and a winner of the Silver Star in World War I.

Within the Forty-third Division, another realignment placed most Rhode Islanders in either the 103rd or the 169th artillery battalions, and there they served throughout a Pacific campaign that included battles in New Georgia, New Guinea, and the Luzon invasion to reclaim the Philippines. On September 13, 1945, a month after Japan's surrender, the Forty-third Division landed near Tokyo. Two weeks later it departed for California and home, having earned four battle streamers for its World War II exploits.

The unit's commander, General Barker, won many decorations, including another Silver Star as well as a Bronze Star for "courageous and brilliant leadership" during the Philippine invasion. When a plaque in this hero's honor was dedicated at the State House in 1968, Barker, a citizen-soldier who had resumed his local business career, observed that "without the men whose names do not appear on this plaque, there would have been no history or record of achievement."

Barker became commander of the PMCA in 1946, succeeding Rush Sturges, the reorganizer of Battery A, who had been at the helm for twenty years. Barker led this distinguished organization until 1965, when he was replaced by Gen. Chester A. Files. The succession was appropriate; Files had been Barker's right-hand man in the Pacific campaign, and his service had earned Files both the Legion of Merit for his role in New Georgia and the Bronze Star for his leadership in the Philippines. General Files—a Brown University graduate, like so many members of the PMCA—had also succeeded Barker in 1946 as commander of the Forty-third Division Artillery.

During the period from 1945 to the present, the Forty-third Division Artillery has engaged in only one foreign tour of duty. In 1951, during the Korean War, the unit was dispatched to Augsburg, Germany, under the command of Col. Frederick Lippitt, to face off against the Russians as part of America's Cold War policy of deterrence. Since its return in 1953, protection of the home front in the wake of natural disasters such as hurricanes and blizzards, and now in anticipation of terrorism, has become the 103rd Regiment's principal function, though it is prepared for any military emergency.

The PMCA today continues its supportive role under the direction of Gen. Harold N. Read, a distinguished soldier in the tradition of Tompkins, Monroe, Hazard, Glassford, Chaffee, Barker, and Files. Included in General Read's World War II exploits were participation in the invasion of Normandy and the relief of Bastogne. Having succeeded General Files in 1973, General Read is by far the longest-serving commander in the illustrious two hundred-year history of the Providence Marine Corps of Artillery.

This honorable and much-honored organization, which now celebrates its bicentennial, has made contributions to Rhode Island more substantial than any volunteer group of comparable size. I have outlined its military heritage as the Mother of Batteries and nursery for artillery commanders, but there is much more to be said.

The PMCA has also been the cradle of civic leadership. From its ranks have emanated Governors Henry Bowen Anthony, William Sprague, Ambrose Burnside (all three of whom were also U.S. senators), Seth Padelford, Henry Howard, Henry Lippitt, and Elisha Dyer, Jr.; Chief Justices William Read Staples and Samuel Ames; and Providence mayors William M. Rodman, Jabez C. Knight, Thomas A. Doyle, and Elisha Dyer, Jr. The litany could be continued for a dozen lesser posts.

The PMCA has been the guardian, as well, of Rhode Island's military history and tradition. Most of the works written on that subject are in fact about the PMCA or its offspring, the 103rd, the 169th, or the Forty-third Division Artillery.

William Rodman, the PMCA's recording clerk, penned the most detailed account of the Chepachet campaign of 1842; Thomas Aldrich recounted the role of Battery A in the Civil War; and Harold Barker, in his *History of Rhode Island Combat Units in the Civil War* (1964), gave us a panorama of that tragic conflict.

Elisha Hunt Rhodes, who served as president of the Battery A Veterans Association, and whose revealing diary filmmaker Ken Burns used heavily in his classic PBS-TV documentary on the

Civil War, joined with PMCA historian Dr. George Peck in presenting the record of Rhode Island's exploits in the Civil War.

PMCA commander Elisha Dyer, Jr., compiled a volume called *Rhode Island in the War with Spain*, and Henry Stiness told the story of *Battery A on the Mexican Border*.

557

Fred McKenna compiled a book on *Battery A in France*, John Russell did the same for Battery D, and William F. Kernan and Henry F. Sampson collaborated to produce a World War I *History of the 103rd Field Artillery*.

Next, Harold Barker related the *History of the 43rd Division Artillery in World War II* (1960), and now, for the PMCA's bicentennial, Jane Lancaster and Cynthia Comery Ferguson have combined to write a comprehensive history of the PMCA and its leaders. Truly, this organization is not only the Mother of Batteries; it is also the Matrix of Rhode Island's Military Heritage.

The PMCA and its present offspring, the 103rd Field Artillery Brigade, exemplify the great American tradition of the volunteer citizen-soldier. Today their role on the home front is more essential than ever, for they are an integral part of our defense in the present war against terrorism. War is doubly terrible when it is waged by the terrorist who makes the home front the battlefront, but terrorism must fail when our civilians and our citizen-soldiers meet it with vigilance, tenacity, and the will to persevere—and the history of the Providence Marine Corps of Artillery is a lesson in perseverence for all Rhode Islanders. Happy two hundredth birthday, PMCA!

These three owner-occupied, single-family houses located at 183, 185, and 187 Ocean Street in South Providence have been built by Stop Wasting Abandoned Property, Inc. (SWAP), a nonprofit group dedicated to the goal of providing affordable housing for Providence residents. These neat, well-constructed homes stand on tax-reverted lots that I cleared and sold to SWAP for a reasonable price.

Housing in Providence: Recommendations and Reflections from a Reputed Land Baron

57

Written in 1990 during the depths of a severe recession, this paper was presented to a joint meeting of the Greater Providence Board of Realtors and the Greater Providence Chamber of Commerce. It was selected for inclusion in this volume to represent other facets of my career—real estate development and tax-title law—that have provided the funding for my publication efforts and allowed me the luxury of volunteerism. It also affords a historical snapshot of the Providence real estate market in the early stages of the city's so-called "renaissance."

Fellow Realtors and Providence Entrepreneurs:

IT IS WITH SURPRISE AND PLEASURE that I accept your invitation to address an issue important to us all—the basic need for shelter. Presumably I have been selected to discuss this topic because a recent list compiled by *Providence Business News* ranked me as Providence's largest private landowner in terms of the number of parcels held, or perhaps it was because a *Providence Journal* article has labeled me "The Titan of Titles," or maybe it was due to an October 1988 *Rhode Island Monthly* profile of me entitled "Dirt Rich." All three distinctions are overstated, but much more so is a reputation that I have acquired in Southside neighborhoods (where I was raised) as a "slumlord." Envy, to its object, is the most disheartening capital sin.

Therefore, prior to articulating noble housing goals, I feel the need to provide an *apologia pro negotia sua*—the refutation of an unfounded and totally inaccurate charge concerning my business activities as a real estate developer. I have never created a slum property, but I often buy vacant and deteriorated housing at collectors' sales for delinquent taxes. Within sixty days of such purchase, a deed is recorded on the land records listing me or one of my entities as the tax-title holder. Vigilant neighborhood groups, in their campaigns against blight, often inspect the land records, see my name on the title of a dilapidated property, and assume I was the cause of that condition. Actually, under state law a tax-sale purchaser cannot take possession or enter upon the parcel he has purchased until the expiration of one year from the date of sale, and so I have no right or power to correct any problem during that time or, in practice, until I file a petition in Superior Court to foreclose the former owner's right of redemption and receive a final decree. That judicial process takes several additional months.

When title is clear and vested in me, I invariably sell my vacant houses to owner-occupants and finance the transaction, after receiving a small deposit. When the property is renovated (usually by "sweat equity"), I arrange permanent financing for the new owner through regular commercial mortgage channels. By this process I actually eliminate slum property and create owner-occupants in houses that were owned by absentee investors at the time of the tax sale.

I have also been taken to task for the debris that has been dumped, without my knowledge or approval, on many vacant lots that I have acquired at tax sales during the decade of the 1980s. In fact, I have cleared title to those lots and made them marketable for development. Without my intervention, these parcels would not only be littered but also unusable for development purposes. The land on which the Omni Point housing facility and the Providence Housing Authority's 120-unit scattered-site low-income housing have been built, and much of the land occupied by Women and Infants' Hospital, were once in a dormant, tax-reverted state until I acquired these properties and cleared title. Only then could they be put to their present productive use.

Having thus clarified the record, I can ascend the pulpit to survey constructively the topic of housing in Providence. Since I am not only a real estate professional but also the former chief of staff to Mayor Vincent Cianci, many of my suggestions for reform will allude to the role that the city government can and should assume in our common quest for decent, affordable housing in the capital city.

* * *

A city's housing stock is one of its most critical commodities. Housing inventory directly affects a municipality's tax base, its livability, its population size, the stability of its neighborhoods, and its physical appearance. For every city, the quality of its housing must be a primary concern. When I served as chief of staff during the Cianci administration, housing was a priority. Millions of dollars (most of them federal) were channeled through the Mayor's Office of Community Development (MOCD) for home rehabilitation and repair and for painting the homes of our handicapped and senior citizens. These efforts directly affected and improved over five thousand Providence homes from 1975 through 1984.

Fueled by a booming regional economy and reckless real estate speculation (much of it by Boston-area investors), Providence housing prices skyrocketed during the mid-1980s. In 1986 and 1987, Providence far outstripped all other American cities in the rise of home prices. The appreciation in the cost of a single-family home in each of those years was just under 40 percent. The sale prices of many multifamily rental properties doubled or tripled during this orgy of speculation.

In accord with historically proven economic trends, the speculative boom has been followed by an equally pronounced economic bust in the local real estate market. The legacy of this episode is an affordability crisis in owner-occupied housing; burdensome rents; a recession in real estate, construction, and related fields; rising unemployment and homelessness; moderately high interest rates; and a surge in bank foreclosures of residential investment property. Yet housing prices remain stable, and the MLS Listing Book has become nearly as thick as the New York City telephone directory. With local economic forecasters predicting no upturn until the second quarter of 1992 at the earliest, the residents of Providence cannot afford (in either a literal or a figurative sense) continued inaction by city government.

To meet this current housing crisis in Providence, we should adopt a comprehensive housing strategy that addresses such concerns as (1) new affordable housing for owner-occupants; (2) rehabilitation assistance for existing housing, using rent-relief incentives for investment properties; (3) a vacant land use program; (4) public housing initiatives pertaining to security and cleanliness; (5) the homeless; and (6) major administrative reforms in city government involving those agencies that deal with housing. These reforms include the implementation of a rental-permit system; a restructuring of the Housing Court, with an enlargement of its powers; enactment of a new zoning ordinance; a streamlining of the cumbersome building-permit process; and the creation of a housing division in the Department of Planning.

AFFORDABLE HOUSING FOR OWNER-OCCUPANTS

During the 1980s two salient economic trends squeezed many Providence residents out of the housing market. Median family income in the city fell below 70 percent of the state average, while simultaneously the cost of single-family housing in Greater Providence rose more sharply than anywhere in America during the peak of the city's housing boom. On the East Side, the median price of a single-family home jumped from $93,000 in 1985 to $175,000 in 1986. For the remainder of the city, the corresponding increase was from $43,000 in 1985 to $83,000 by 1987.

These countervailing trends contributed to an acute shortage in "affordable housing," about which much has been spoken and little accomplished. Quite simply, the right to affordable housing is the right of our citizens to respectable shelter consistent with their means. By this definition it is clear that a mix of housing stock is needed to satisfy the respective needs of our residents. This mix should include subsidized rentals (both publicly and privately run), market-rate rentals, condominiums, owner-occupied multiunit structures, and detached owner-occupied single-family housing.

From the perspective of neighborhood stability, the last-mentioned form of housing is the most desirable. The key to neighborhood revitalization is the construction therein of single-family, owner-occupied housing. Providence has hundreds of buildable vacant lots suitable for such housing, especially in the South Side and the West End neighborhoods. Some are city-owned, but most are privately held. Yet owing to the run-down condition of the areas in which they are located and the lack of financial feasibility in developing them for market-rate housing, even those in private ownership are relatively inexpensive to acquire.

The city needs to take the initiative in converting these forlorn, litter-strewn liabilities into new homesites for our residents. Large-scale construction of single-family housing on such parcels is economically feasible only if the city can arrange a combination of subsidies, tax incentives, and low-interest financing to qualify a significant number of families to purchase these homes.

I propose a bond issue to fund the subsidies, with the city securing its advance by obtaining a performance contract and holding a second mortgage from the buyer. These guarantees will allow the city to curb speculation, exercise a mortgagee's control against waste or abuse, and maintain a degree of equity participation by which a part of the purchase subsidy will be recovered upon sale and used as a revolving fund for further housing construction. In this process I envision a role for nonprofit housing groups in funding and counseling prospective owners and in building some of the housing. Such public-private partnerships must be encouraged.

I also envision participation by the Rhode Island Housing and Mortgage Finance Corporation (RIHMFC) and local banks in providing low-interest financing for buyers. The legal responsibility of a private bank to participate in "meeting the credit needs of its entire community, including low- and moderate-income neighborhoods" (to use the language of federal and state community reinvestment acts), must be enforced, especially if such a bank also wishes to become a repository for municipal funds.

THE REHABILITATION OF EXISTING HOUSING

Most of Providence's housing stock is old. The bulk of it consists of two-, three-, and four-family units built (often inexpensively) between 1890 and 1930. The problem of maintaining this stock in habitable condition is a continuous one. A recent revaluation survey revealed that 5,336 structures out of a citywide total of 30,053 (or more than 1 in 6) are in below-average condition. Since federal community development dollars are less available now than in the

1960s or 1970s, the city must make policy adjustments to stem deterioration of existing structures. As part of a successful rehabilitation policy, I suggest the following initiatives: (1) using a housing bond issue (referred to above) to finance renovations and repairs (elderly, handicapped, and low-income homeowners could receive matching grants, while others could avail themselves of very low interest city loans secured by liens); (2) securing an agreement by owners of rental property who receive assistance whereby they consent to a temporary rent freeze in return for the city's assistance; (3) giving preference in awarding funds to those structures with code violations; (4) increasing the housing share of Community Development Block Grant money to 50 percent (a 1987 study showed that only one-fifth of the Community Development Block Grants were allocated to housing); (5) implementing existing laws that would allow an abandoned house to be turned over to non-profit developers for rehabilitation; (6) creating (as other cities have done) a Neighborhood Housing Rehabilitation Trust Fund to which corporations, foundations, and others could make tax-deductible contributions (this nonprofit agency could maintain a revolving fund to give low-interest loans to necessary yet non-bankable rehabilitation projects, such as those involving abandoned housing); and (7) lobbying as businessmen and realtors for the passage by Congress of the proposed Community Revitalization Act, a measure that would spur historic rehabilitation by allowing a taxpayer at least $20,000 in historic tax credits per year (up from the $7,000 limit of the Tax Reform Act of 1986).

The rehabilitation of existing rental properties is especially critical. As the June 1990 Winsor–Veri Housing Survey of Providence warns, in somewhat stilted prose: "Clearly there is a mismatch between what the housing market is able to provide and what the tenant can pay for. If the trends in rental housing loss, increases in rent, and [slower] increases in household income continue at a pace approximating the 1980s, and in the absence of more effective public and nonprofit sector housing initiatives, the housing crisis in Providence, particularly in the rental sector, will most certainly deepen."

A Vacant Land Use Program

Vacant residential land could be a great housing resource for Providence, but instead it has been a source of blight. Instituted in 1986, the city's vacant lot program (VLP), apart from its illegality and unconstitutionality, has been a failure. Under this misguided program (aimed at alleged speculators, like me), the city simply stockpiles vacant lots with no plan for their use. In effect, the VLP has placed a moratorium on the assignment of tax titles. In addition, the VLP has been arbitrarily administered, it has deprived the city of over a million dollars in tax revenue, and it has had an insignificant impact on the city's available housing stock. Existing state law (RIGL, Title 44, Chapter 9) contains an adequate mechanism for assigning and clearing title to tax-reverted parcels. The city should scrap the VLP (before a serious title problem regarding VLP land arises) and assign its tax-reverted land to those developers who will pay the back taxes to the city *and* agree to build affordable housing thereon within a specified time, under penalty of reverter.

The city must also increase the penalties for illegal dumping and enforce these new antidumping ordinances rigorously. Dumping is a serious offense: it diminishes property values; it hastens neighborhood decline; it poses a major health problem by establishing a breeding ground for rats and vermin; it creates a nuisance that threatens the safety of our children; it diverts the manpower of our Department of Public Works; and it generates huge cleanup costs for guiltless and unwitting lot owners.

Because of the varied social and economic evils that dumping causes, drastic measures are needed to bring this practice under control. The legislature must empower the city to strengthen the dumping ordinance (including the junking of cars) by allowing the city to impose a $1,000 fine upon violators for the first offense and $2,000, or an equivalent value in cleanup work, plus confiscation and sale of the offending truck or vehicle, for the second offense. The present fine of $300 actually provides an incentive for illegal dumping because the ordinance is almost never enforced, and if it is, the offender knows that it is cheaper to pay the fine than to pay the legal dumping fees at a remote landfill.

The present system makes the lot owner solely responsible for cleanup, either by forcing him to hire a private hauler to remove the debris or by incurring a cleanup lien placed on his property by the Department of Public Works. The owner is not the criminal, and we must stop regarding him as such. He is the victim of dumping and should be treated like any victim of a criminal act. (Please excuse the special pleading!)

Owners, of course, should be made to maintain their lots free of ordinary litter and plant overgrowth. However, the cleanup of dumped debris, placed on a parcel by someone in violation of the owner's rights, is the responsibility of the city, which has a duty to protect its taxpaying property owners by apprehending and punishing those who commit such crimes against property.

Since an ongoing, thorough, and comprehensive cleanup of vacant land would entail a significant expense for the Department of Inspection and Standards and the Department of Public Works, we should consider the imposition of surtax on vacant land that is lying fallow and unused. This levy would not only absorb the cost of cleanup (as would the higher dumping fines and penalties); it would also prod owners of unproductive vacant land to develop it. I believe this tax stimulant would induce owners of relatively inexpensive vacant land in the South Side and West End of Providence to construct affordable housing thereon or to sell the land to a developer who will build such needed homes.

Finally, I would expand the power (or the will) of the Housing Court to entertain suits by owners of vacant land to prevent squatters from establishing businesses thereon. The availability of prompt summary judgment, enforced by city police, is essential if we wish to stop the proliferation of unlicensed auto repair and body shops, storage operations, junk dealerships, and other unauthorized businesses on vacant land in residential zones. The debilitating impact of such abuses on the value of surrounding housing is enormous. For this reason, the rigorous enforcement of municipal licensing and zoning ordinances must be a priority. Nothing less than the image and future of our city is at stake.

Public Housing

Public housing in Providence is managed by the Providence Housing Authority (PHA), an independent agency, yet one having a close working relationship with city government. Since the federal government, through its Department of Housing and Urban Development (HUD), provides most of PHA funding, however, the tendency has been for the city to delay needed reforms in public housing until HUD's inept and labyrinthian bureaucracy responds. Given the expense of building and maintaining public housing, this policy of watchful waiting is unavoidable, but in certain ancillary areas, where costs are relatively small and needs great, the city must help the PHA cope.

Two such areas are the cleanliness of our public housing sites and the security of its residents, especially the defenseless elderly and handicapped. To achieve greater cleanliness, the Department of Public Works must supplement the PHA's overburdened maintenance crews, and dumping-law violators must be assigned community service cleanup work in public housing.

The more urgent need for greater safety in public housing can be achieved by the use of police academy graduate trainees as security officers, by the location of police posts or neighborhood substations in several of the elderly high-rise apartments, and by the use of foot and bicycle patrols in housing projects to supplement the efforts of PHA police.

Homelessness in Providence

Providence has not escaped the scourge of homelessness. In a 1987 survey conducted by the United States Conference of Mayors, it was determined that families with children constituted 65 percent of the homeless population in Providence, a 75 percent increase from the previous year. During that same period, Providence reported a 63 percent increase in the number of homeless single women. More disturbingly, Providence also reported that the demand for emergency shelter went unmet.

As a city, Providence must not fall victim to the temptation to ignore this problem, or to accept homelessness as a fact of life. We must never lose sight of the fact that people, not statistics, are sleeping on park benches, on street corners, in alcoves, and, as reported in the *Providence Journal* last July, in our abandoned bus terminal.

The war against homelessness must be waged on two fronts: first, we must care for those currently without homes; second, we must put into place preventive measures to stem the growth of the ever-increasing ranks of the homeless.

ADMINISTRATIVE REFORMS

To preserve and improve our housing policy, the city government must implement structural reforms. For these administrative adjustments, I offer the following recommendations:

A. A RENTAL-PERMIT SYSTEM SHOULD BE ESTABLISHED. All newly rented units in the city of Providence should be required to obtain a rental permit. City code enforcement officers should inspect each unit and record its condition in writing and by videotape. The combination of the tape and the written verification will become a record of the condition of the unit as of the date of inspection and can be used as a valuable tool in determining the cause of a later code violation.

This self-funding program will prevent good landlords from becoming the victims of the system when their tenants are at fault, and it will likewise spare good tenants from being forced to live in substandard conditions while being blamed by less-than-honest property owners for the condition of their units. Both landlords and tenants will have a stake in the maintenance and habitability of our rental housing.

B. THE HOUSING COURT SHOULD BE REORGANIZED. There is no need for a judicial entity separate from

Municipal Court, with its separate, part-time judges and separate staffs. Municipal Court should have full-time judges with a traffic division and a housing division. Stability and professionalism must replace our part-time, haphazard, patronage-prone municipal court system.

C. THE BUILDING-PERMIT PROCESS MUST BE STREAMLINED.
Accessibility and cooperation must become the guiding principles of the Department of Building Inspection. Presently the office is inconveniently located, some of the personnel are adversarial in dealing with the public, and the permitting process is time-consuming and inefficient. The city must also exert pressure on the Water Board and other public utilities whose bureaucratic delays unnecessarily burden developers and add greatly to their construction costs (which are passed on to buyers or tenants).

D. A HOUSING DIVISION SHOULD BE ESTABLISHED IN THE DEPARTMENT OF PLANNING AND DEVELOPMENT.
This division would administer home ownership and rehabilitation programs; compile housing information and data; manage city-owned residential land; coordinate housing programs with the private sector, including nonprofit corporations, neighborhood organizations, and banks; serve as a resource for the housing division of Municipal Court; and assess the feasibility for Providence of all proposals and blueprints generated by experts and consultants for meeting our city's housing needs.

E. A NEW ZONING ORDINANCE IS NEEDED.
We should promptly enact the new zoning ordinance proposed by the special study commission created for that purpose. The ordinance contains many desirable features, but especially noteworthy are the more carefully defined zoning districts it will create, especially as these districts pertain to the waterfront and open space and its provision to merge adjacent undersize lots having common ownership.

Decent shelter for our people is too basic a need to go unmet, especially when the achievement of this humanitarian goal also stabilizes our neighborhoods, deters crime, expands our tax base, and enhances our environment. Housing is a need that we can no longer afford to neglect. I believe that a joint public-private sector effort, such as I have outlined, is the best means of making Providence one of America's most livable cities—in every sense of that term.

Postscript

In the twelve years from mid-1990 to mid-2002, I have acquired at tax sale, cleared, and sold to owner-occupants, most of them recent Hispanic arrivals to Providence, approximately 120 vacant and abandoned houses throughout the city. I have also cleared the title of eighteen vacant lots that I sold to nonprofit SWAP (Stop Wasting Abandoned Property) as sites for affordable single-family houses, and another thirty vacant, tax-reverted lots on Bogman, Pilgrim, and Public Streets in South Providence, adjacent to the Community College of Rhode Island. Collectively, these latter parcels will form the bulk of the campus of the new Metropolitan Regional Career and Technical Center now being constructed on the site. In addition, my wife Gail and I donated fifty-eight scattered vacant lots to the Providence Redevelopment Agency in December 1997. These parcels, with a total fair market value of $608,500, have been used to relieve density in the neighborhoods and provide sites for new homes, parking, community gardens, and recreational facilities.

North Kingstown: A Tricentennial Survey of Its History

58

This talk was delivered before the North Kingstown Women's Club in June 1974 on the occasion of North Kingstown's tricentennial observance. Ironically, the presentation coincided with the closing of the Quonset Point Naval Air Station.

NORTH KINGSTOWN's earliest recorded history was intertwined with the activities of the famous Narragansett tribe of Indians, for the land upon which the community now rests was part of the Narragansett Country. This Indian domain corresponded roughly with present-day Washington County, except for Charlestown and Westerly, where Eastern Niantics and Pawcatuck Pequots prevailed. In that portion of their holdings that eventually became North Kingstown, the Narragansetts cultivated crops of beans, squash, tobacco, strawberries, and maize, or Indian corn. So proficient were these Indians as planters that they were reported by contemporaries to be "the best farmers among the aborigines along the Atlantic seaboard."

When English and Dutch merchants came to America, they soon found their way to the land of the Narragansetts, and a brisk trade in agricultural produce developed. This was carried on particularly in North Kingstown's fine natural harbor at Wickford Cove, an area the Indians called Cocumscussoc ("marshy meadows"). John Oldham, a Plymouth Colony trader who ventured many times to Narragansett waters in his brig, described the countryside in the area that was to become North Kingstown as treeless farmland, but "very stony and full of Indians."

In 1636 Roger Williams came to the region as a religious exile to establish the settlement of Providence at the head of Narragansett Bay. It is well known that Williams's Providence settlement, devoted to the great American principles of religious liberty and separation of church and state, was the earliest Rhode Island town. What is not generally known is that Williams had a role in the development of the Narragansett Country, and in the establishment of a permanent settlement in present-day North Kingstown.

When the popular litany of Rhode Island's early towns is recited, the emphasis has been on the four "original" incorporated towns—Providence (1636), founded by Williams; Portsmouth (1638) and Newport (1639), founded principally by William Coddington; and Warwick (1642), founded by Samuel Gorton. Those who are better versed in Rhode Island history are aware of the Pawtuxet community established by William Harris and his associates in 1638. But there are very few indeed who realize that the permanent settlement of North Kingstown also dates from this formative era, entitling this community to rank as one of Rhode Island's pioneer towns.

That settlement can be traced to the year 1637, when Roger Williams and Richard Smith each set up trading posts near Wickford Harbor. These establishments were ideally situated, with the bay to the eastward and, to the west, the Pequot Trail. This road was described as the great Indian thoroughfare through the Narragansett Country and "its one real artery of life." Portions of its meandering path in later years became the Old Post Road.

Williams, of course, made his fame and his reputation elsewhere, so it fell to Richard Smith, the first English settler of the Narragansett Country, to become North Kingstown's founding father. In 1641 Smith purchased from Canonicus and Miantonomi, renowned sachems of the Narragansett tribe, a tract of land north of Wickford Harbor. Shortly thereafter he built a blockhouse, part fort and part trading center, which became known as "Smith's Castle." Then he bought out the local trading rights of John Wilcox, another North Kingstown pioneer, and by 1651 he purchased Roger Williams's post, thus becoming the sole proprietor in the Cocumscussoc area.

Smith had trading contacts with the Dutch in New Netherlands, and his wife and family often journeyed there. On one such trip his daughter Catharine met Gysbert Op Dyck (Updike). The young couple married, and eventually, after the death of Richard Smith, Jr., in 1692, title to Cocumscussoc passed to their child Lodowick Updike. Thus began at Cocumscussoc an Updike dynasty that would endure until 1812.

Smith's Castle was burned in King Philip's War (1675–76), but it was rebuilt immediately thereafter by Richard Smith, Jr., to become "the focal point of the diverse forces and cross-currents—political, military, commercial, agricultural, and social—that shaped the uncertain destiny of the struggling colony." This assessment of its significance has been rendered by Dr. Carl Woodward, president emeritus of the University of Rhode Island and a noted student of American agricultural development, in his book *Plantation in Yankeeland* (1971).

Despite the success of the Smith clan, North Kingstown was beset by several problems during its formative years. The first controversy arose in 1659, when a group of land speculators known as the Atherton Company laid fraudulent claim to a large portion of the Narragansett Country. This attempted land grab was followed in 1662 by the issuance of Connecticut's royal charter, a document which granted to that colony all lands up to the western shore of Narragansett Bay. When the Atherton Company (with whom Richard Smith, Sr., collaborated) decided to support the Connecticut claim, Rhode Island's control of North Kingstown and the remainder of the Narragansett Country was placed in jeopardy. Fortunately, Rhode Island's royal charter of 1663 set the colony's boundary at the Pawcatuck River, thus superseding the Connecticut claim and preserving the Narragansett lands. The conflicting provisions of the two charters, however, set off a series of boundary disputes, and not until 1726 was North Kingstown's position as a Rhode Island town fully secured by royal decree.

Several important events transpired during that period of boundary strife. In 1674 a large portion of the Narragansett Country comprising the present communities of North Kingstown, South Kingstown, Narragansett, and Exeter was incorporated under the name Kings Towne. Since North Kingstown was the most populous community and the first of the four to be settled, it is regarded as the parent town, and we celebrate its incorporated history from that year.

Not long after its legal establishment, the town experienced further adversity. In 1675–76 it was ravaged in King Philip's War. No sooner had it recovered than Sir Edmund Andros and his Dominion of New England acquired jurisdiction over it and renamed the town Rochester. When the Dominion collapsed in 1689 after the fall of King James II, local autonomy was restored, and so was the name Kings Towne.

The eighteenth century brought to North Kingstown more prosperity and less adversity than had occurred during the formative years, albeit at the expense of the Narragansett tribe. The boundary disputes were settled, the Indians were subdued, population increased, commerce expanded, and agriculture prospered with the aid of black slaves. In some respects this era marked the high point of the town's influence in state affairs; it was North Kingstown's golden age. The rapid growth resulted in Kings Towne's subdivision. Because, as the General Assembly observed, the town was "very large and full of people," South Kingstown was carved from its southern sector in February 1722/23 and Exeter was created from its western portion in March 1742/43.

It was also during the eighteenth century that the village of Wickford (formerly called Updike's Newton) became a significant port and the town's political and economic center. Vessels sailed from its harbor to the West Indies, to the fishing grounds off the Grand Banks, and to other ports along the Atlantic coast, and entrepreneurs located shipbuilding facilities, a distillery, and other commerce-related industries in the village. Picturesque Wickford is now graced with the historic and stately homes of the colonial merchants who prospered during the village's commercial heyday. These structures serve as tangible reminders of Wickford's era of commercial prominence.

During its golden age, North Kingstown produced several native sons who achieved distinction in their respective spheres. One was Daniel Updike of Cocumscussoc, who served as state attorney general for twenty-five years (1722–32, 1743–58), the longest tenure of any attorney general in Rhode Island history. Another was Gilbert Stuart, who was born in a gambrel-roofed snuff mill a few miles below Wickford. Stuart's early years were spent in this still extant structure, and though his fame was made elsewhere as the great portrait painter of George Washington and other Founding Fathers, he remains North Kingstown's most illustrious native son.

The town also attracted some notable residents during the eighteenth century. Foremost among these were the Reverend James MacSparran and the Reverend Samuel Fayerweather, the successive Anglican rectors of North Kingstown's St. Paul's Church. Popularly known as "the Old Narragansett Church," St. Paul's was built in 1707 on "the Platform," four miles south of Wickford, but in 1800 it was moved to its present site on Church Lane in Wickford village. Under the guidance of MacSparran—a writer, teacher, and physician—and the learned Fayerweather, St. Paul's became the region's intellectual, cultural, and religious center. Fortunately its fascinating history has been preserved by the pens of Wilkins Updike and Daniel Goodwin.

When the American Revolution erupted in 1775, Rhode Island was in the vanguard of the movement for independence, and North Kingstown was a very active and willing participant in that struggle. Since its position on Narragansett Bay rendered it vulnerable to English attack, in 1777 its citizenry petitioned the state legislature for permission to form a military company, to be called the Newton Rangers. When permission was granted, the blacks of the town followed suit and formed a sizable military company of their own, officered, of course, by white men. Thus did the courageous blacks of North Kingstown unite to help the whites gain full political freedom, even though they themselves had been denied the most basic civil rights by the people to whose aid they came. Happily the Revolution generated a spirit of reform in Rhode Island, leading to the passage in 1784 of an act that provided for the gradual abolition of slavery.

George Babcock, whose name headed the petition for the charter of the Newton Rangers, became a successful commander of the

Revolutionary privateer *Mifflin*. This twenty-gun ship, manned by 130 men enlisted from North Kingstown and Exeter, took prize after prize from the English. Babcock and his men capped a remarkable career of privateering with the defeat and seizure of the twenty-six gun British vessel *Tartar* and its complement of 162 men off the Grand Banks of Newfoundland in 1779.

576

As the eighteenth century drew to a close, North Kingstown was clearly playing a very prominent role in Rhode Island's development: the state's sixth largest town, wielding considerable political weight, it was a leader in agriculture, an important if secondary commercial center, a place of cultural, religious, and intellectual vitality, and a town whose residents had performed courageously in the Revolutionary movement.

But this success and progress, at least in the material sphere, was not destined to endure. The opening of western farmlands adversely affected local agriculture, the port of Wickford declined, and Updike's Cocumscussoc plantation was subdivided, bringing the town's era of prosperity to an end. As manufacturing replaced commerce and agriculture as the backbone of the Rhode Island economy in the nineteenth century, this new source of wealth and importance centered not in North Kingstown but in Providence and the valleys of the Pawtuxet and the Blackstone Rivers.

For North Kingstown, these changes inaugurated a long period of economic stagnation and painfully slow growth. The federal census of 1790, a year approximating the end of the town's golden age, listed 2,907 inhabitants in North Kingstown, making it the state's sixth most populous community. In 1940, a century and a half later, its population had climbed only to 4,604, and its rank was twenty-third among the state's thirty-nine communities. In that same period Rhode Island's total population had increased more than tenfold.

Agriculture continued to predominate as North Kingstown's major activity during the nineteenth century, but for many local farmers it was not particularly lucrative. Their small holdings and rocky soil kept farming at the subsistence level.

Manufacturing, however, did make some inroads. A historian of the town, writing in 1878, noted "four cotton and eight woolen mills, with others in the process of construction." He also observed that these industries "represent an invested capital of between one and two million dollars, and the sound of factory bells assembles daily from five to six hundred operatives." Many of these workers were undoubtedly farmers who supplemented their income by toiling long hours in the mills.

577

Despite the limited nature of North Kingstown's industrial activity—far less than that of Providence, Pawtucket, or Woonsocket—manufacturing was not without its impact on the town. Along the banks of such local streams as the Pettaquamscutt and the Annaquatucket, on the Post Road, and on the Providence-Stonington Railroad line, small mill villages and mercantile hamlets sprang up, such as Allenton, Annaquatucket, Bellville, West Wickford, Hamilton, Kettle-Hole, Mount View, Lafayette, Wickford Junction, Narragansett, Oak Hill, Davisville, Silver Spring, Scrabbletown, Sandy Hill, and Slocum. Most of these tiny settlements were the products of the selective spread of industry in nineteenth-century North Kingstown, but despite their random creation, the general character of the town continued to be rural and agrarian, with the fashionable bayside summer resorts of Sanderstown and Plum Beach noteworthy exceptions.

This 1900 photo shows historic Main Street in Wickford, then (as now) North Kingstown's principal village.

The first four decades of the twentieth century wrought only slight change in the composition and size of the town. From 1900 to 1920 the population actually dropped, from 4,194 to 3,397, a loss that was probably attributable in part to the general decline in the Rhode Island textile industry. By 1940, however, the beginnings of the suburban movement brought about a mild revival, boosting the town's population to 4,604.

Then came the great economic and population boom. The United States Navy was the catalyst. Largely through the efforts of U.S. senator Theodore Francis Green, the federal government decided to locate major naval installations in the northeastern sector of the town. The sites the Navy chose were the hamlet of Davisville and nearby Quonset Point, a small peninsula on Narragansett Bay. Part of Quonset Point had become a summer resort, while another portion had served as a training camp for the Rhode Island militia and National Guard since the 1890s.

On May 25, 1939, President Franklin D. Roosevelt signed into law a bill appropriating one million dollars for the purchase of North Kingstown land. By July 12, 1941, the Quonset Naval Air Station was commissioned. Eleven thousand civilian laborers dramatically transformed the area in the interim, removing peat bogs, some as deep as 30 feet and 400 feet long; dynamiting nearly 45,000 cubic feet of ledge rock to provide room for a spur track railroad; laying millions of square feet of asphalt over the once grassy landscape; and extracting some 20 million cubic yards of fill from Narragansett Bay to add 200 man-made acres to the air station area.

The Naval Air Station and the adjoining base at Davisville, which serves as the home of the Atlantic Seabees (the Naval Construction Battalion), have had a remarkable impact on the town of North Kingstown, the state of Rhode Island, and the nation. Naval designers developed the famous Quonset hut here in 1941. During World War II, antisubmarine warfare patrols flew constantly from Quonset and auxiliary stations, pilots and crews were trained for carrier operations, and seven days a week, around the clock, the Overhaul and Repair Department's Navy-civilian team worked to "keep 'em flying."

Quonset played another major military role in the years following the war, this time in the operational development of carrier-
based jet aviation. The Navy's first all-jet fighter squadron was
formed and trained at Quonset Point. In recent years Quonset has
served as the home of the sub hunters and as a base of operations
for the Navy's Antarctic exploration. Throughout the station's
entire lifetime, Quonset's O & R Department, manned by many
residents of North Kingstown, has played a vital role in keeping
the Atlantic Fleet's aircraft and ordinance in ready condition.

Largely because of the naval bases at Quonset and Davisville,
the U.S. Navy became Rhode Island's largest single employer, and
the Navy's North Kingstown installations had a dramatic effect on
the economic and physical growth of the town. The community
that had gained only 1,697 inhabitants in the century and a half
from 1790 to 1940 increased its population by 10,206 during the
decade of the forties. The population leap from 4,604 to 14,810 was
a 221.7 percent increase, by far the highest growth rate in the state
for that ten-year period.

North Kingstown's remarkable development has continued from
1950 to the present (1974), primarily as a result of the suburban
exodus. In 1960 the town's population rose to 18,977, and by the
1970 census it had jumped to 27,673 — a growth rate of 45.8 percent
for the decade of the sixties. This population increase has been
accompanied by significant economic development, brought about
by the creation of many new local businesses and by the relocation
to North Kingstown of the large-scale industrial operation of the
Brown and Sharpe Manufacturing Company.

Indeed, the economic future seemed bright for North Kingstown until it was announced in 1973 that Quonset Naval Air
Station would be closed and Davisville would have its activities
curtailed. The immediate impact of this cutback on local wage
earners and merchants was severe. Ironically, as the town now celebrates its three hundredth anniversary, a more solemn ceremony
has been held — the formal closing of Quonset. Yet the future of
North Kingstown remains promising, for many firms — including
the Electric Boat Division of the General Dynamics Corporation — intend to locate their plants on Quonset land. If these eco-

nomic development plans are successful, large-scale private industry will more than offset the effect of the Navy's departure from North Kingstown.

History shows that the citizens of North Kingstown have always displayed an ability to overcome adversity, whether it be threats to their lives and property, as in the early years, or such later challenges to their livelihood as the decline of maritime activity or the demise of the textile industry. With such a record of tenacity and resiliency, the citizens of North Kingstown can scarcely fail to cope with their current economic crisis. Indeed, the history of this town should be a source of inspiration to its residents, providing them with the courage and determination to face the future and to shape it to their needs.

Bicentennial Commencement Address to the Graduates of Bristol High School

59

Written in 1976, this speech will remain my only commencement address. It is reproduced here not so much for its historical content as for its simple, didactic message to a young audience.

I AM HONORED to have been asked, in my capacity as state Bicentennial chairman, to address you on the occasion of this great milestone in your life: your graduation from Bristol High School as the Bicentennial class of 1976. To show my gratitude, I can promise you that my talk will have one virtue—brevity. As a student, I have sat (or perhaps suffered) through five commencement talks since my high school graduation. Each time I endured crowded conditions, sweltering heat, and the anxiety of waiting for postcommencement parties and celebrations. A commencement speaker is always faced with a dilemma and a problem: he is supposed to be formal, solemn, and inspirational when his audience—the successful students—are rightfully festive, happy, and in a mood to celebrate.

In this Bicentennial year, the two hundredth anniversary of Rhode Island and American Independence, it is most appropriate that we reflect on the history of our country, our state of Rhode Island, and your historic town of Bristol.

The Bicentennial should inspire patriotism in all Americans, young and old, but by *patriotism* I do not mean blind allegiance or uncritical acceptance of everything that our ancestors have said or done. Rather, patriotism and love of country must be intelligent,

582

critical, and based upon a knowledge of what has been wrong with America as well as upon what has been right and worthy of commendation. Our portrait of this nation must include the shadows, the warts, and the blemishes. It must not be retouched (like your yearbook photos) to eliminate the flaws. Only by a knowledge of what has been wrong with America, or what continues to be wrong, can we address ourselves to the task of correcting those faults and removing those inequities. That is the task that my generation will leave to you! How important it is, therefore, that you prepare yourself through education, civic improvement, and a knowledge of history for the duties that await you.

U.S. senator James De Wolf (1764–1837), an infamous slave trader as well as a successful merchant, shipowner, and manufacturer, was regarded as Bristol's leading citizen during the first third of the nineteenth century.

Let me illustrate what I mean by the importance of an informed yet critical knowledge of our past as a guide toward shaping a more perfect future. I will use examples from Bristol's history at hundred-year intervals, beginning in 1676. That year marked the conclusion of King Philip's War. Most of you have heard of that great conflict, which raged throughout New England just three centuries ago. When we reflect upon it, however, the usual emphasis is on the heroic Captain Benjamin Church of Bristol and Little Compton, the most distinguished military figure of that war, a man who reduced the power of the Narragansett Indians in the Great Swamp Fight in December 1675 and participated in the ultimate defeat and death of King Philip of the Wampanoag tribe at Mount Hope in August 1676. Many who commemorate that episode stress the romantic nature of the clash between Indian and white and praise the militaristic virtues of the combatants—their courage, tenacity, and endurance. Perhaps it should also be said that this was, in some respects, a race war marked by unbelievable cruelty and barbarism; that the Wampanoag tribe owned and lived upon this Bristol land and understandably resented its seizure by the white colonists from Plymouth Colony (of which Bristol was a part); and that the neutral Narragansetts, who had always shown friendliness to Roger Williams and other Rhode Island settlers, were the victims in this war of an unjustified preemptive attack.

In 1776 and throughout the Revolutionary era, your town of Bristol was a leader in the movements for independence and for the framing and adoption of the Constitution of the United States. Bristol furnished many ships and seamen for our young navy, and Bristol residents bravely endured a bombardment by the HMS *Rose* and raids by the enemy. Bristolians, like other colonists, fought with determination for their political, civil, and economic rights. These are facts which are being so ably commemorated by such enthusiastic and public-spirited groups as the Bristol Bicentennial Commission and the Bristol Fourth of July Committee.

Few people will recall, however, that a primary source of colonial Bristol's wealth and influence stemmed, according to town historian George Howe, from the slave trade—a detestable practice that is a prime historical example of man's inhumanity to his fellow man. Too few people admit that the Declaration of Independence, which Bristol so splendidly commemorates, contains the phrase "all men are created equal"—a phrase which was contradicted not only by the slave trade and the Constitution of 1787 but by two centuries of discrimination by white Americans against their black neighbors.

Three hundred years ago our history was marred by cruelty to Native Americans; two centuries ago it was blemished by injustice to blacks. In 1876, as Bristol County was caught up in America's impressive and highly successful Industrial Revolution, the immigrant laborers who came to this area from Ireland, Portugal, Italy, and French Canada were also subjected to discrimination or abuse because they were foreign in religion, ethnic background, culture, or language. Long hours, low pay, unsafe working conditions in the textile and rubber factories, and lack of job or retirement security characterized their lot in life.

While it is most proper and fitting that we praise the courageous veterans of King Philip's War, the visionary leaders of the

War for Independence, and the talented businessmen who managed the Industrial Revolution, like Bristolians Samuel P. Colt and Augustus O. Bourn, let us be mindful also that these and other illustrious figures in American history may have had a seamy, greedy, or inhumane side that must be known and shown if the seaminess is to remain just a thing of the past. Repeat the glories of our ancestors; avoid their sins!

We must not view our history through rose-colored glasses if we are to find there some clues to human betterment. We cannot improve society if we see no need for improvement. We cannot promote the cause of justice if we are blind to injustice. If we refuse to recognize racism, greed, injustice, and intolerance in our past—if our view of America is not a balanced one—then we will be oblivious to these evils, which still cry out for concern. As the philosopher George Santayana has succinctly stated, "A nation that does not know History is fated to repeat it." Another philosopher, Francis Bacon, observed in his evaluation of the various academic subjects that "Histories make men wise." He was referring, of course, to a balanced and objective analysis of the past and not to the one-sided whitewash which often characterizes our commemoration of famous historical events.

We may conclude, therefore, with this observation: *Commencement* is a word that means "beginning." Your education does not end here; it continues. Whether you go to college or to work, whether you enroll in adult-education programs later in your life or not, it is nonetheless your duty as a responsible citizen to learn, to experience, and to grow in knowledge and wisdom. History, if it is balanced and impartial, and patriotism, if it is informed and rational, will be your invaluable tools, as you, of the "Now Generation," undertake the task of making your town, your state, and your nation a better, fairer place for those who will succeed you.

CONGRATULATIONS; GOOD LUCK; THANK YOU.

60

Warren's Warriors for Freedom: The Town's Defenders of Liberty from Narragansett Bay to the Persian Gulf, 1775–1991

This oration was delivered on Veterans' Day, November 11, 2001, at the dedication of an honor roll dedicated to the town of Warren's veterans of all American wars. I was selected to give this address by childhood chum Ed Little and project chairman Dave McCarthy, both dedicated veterans.

Honored Veterans, Living and Dead; Congressman Kennedy; Chairman McCarthy; General Vallente; Council President McCanna; Senator Felag; Representative Malik; Reverend Behr and Other Distinguished Guests; Townspeople of Warren; Citizens of America:

To be chosen to deliver this address at such a moving and momentous event is to have conferred upon me both a great honor and a weighty responsibility. In several ways I feel unequal to the task. I am not a war veteran but only a cashiered ROTC cadet whose congenital blindness in my right eye rendered me unfit for combat service. I am not a resident of Warren; my roots are in South Providence, whence I moved to Cranston and then to Bristol, where I now reside. Apart from occasional antiquing and dining, I merely drive through Warren en route to home or work, albeit under the very watchful gaze of your vigilant police patrols. I am not a militarist, because as an American historian I have learned that not all of our nation's wars were both wise and just. And although this is a public ceremony, I am not a public official. The voters in their wisdom have consigned me to private life.

I come, therefore, not as a soldier but as a scholar, not as a warrior but as a writer, not as a rhetorician but as a reporter. Despite my lengthy resume, you—and I speak directly to those we honor—you are something that I am not. You are war veterans, and I regard your sacrifice with awe and admiration.

In a poem titled "The Soldier on Crutches," the popular poet Edgar A. Guest, writing during World War I, captured my feelings and the sentiments of those who have come to honor you. The poem reads in part:

> The tap of his crutch on the marble of white
> Caught my ear as I sat all alone there that night.
> I turned—and a soldier my eyes fell upon;
> He had fought for his country, and one leg was gone!
> As he entered, a silence fell over the place;
> Every eye in the room was turned up to his face.
> His head was up high and his eyes seemed aflame
> With a wonderful light, and he laughed as he came.
> He was young—not yet thirty—yet never he made
> One sign of regret for the price he had paid.
>
> Some day in the future in many a place
> More soldiers just like him we'll all have to face.
> We must sit with them, talk with them, laugh with them, too,
> With the signs of their service forever in view.
> And this was my thought as I looked at him then—
> Oh, God! Make me worthy to stand with such men.

As I look at this ceremony's agenda and observe the crowded quarters you must endure because of the great public participation this project has inspired, I am reminded of America's most famous memorial observance—the dedication of the national cemetery at Gettysburg. On that bright November day in 1863, the program committee welcomed the renowned orator Edward Everett of Massachusetts as the principal speaker. Among other achievements, Everett had been a clergyman, a prominent politician, a professor, and a former president of Harvard University. (In contrast, thanks to Ed Little, Warren had to settle for me!)

Everett delivered an eloquent two-hour address focusing on the specific details of America's greatest battle, fought on that site only twenty weeks before. Then it was President Lincoln's turn. The president was scheduled to make brief "remarks," and he did so in his high-pitched tenor voice and Kentucky accent. His 272-word address took three minutes to deliver. Today, who remembers Edward Everett?

There is much to be said for brevity. A famous preacher once told me that he never saved a soul after twenty minutes. Since I believe him, I wish I could say to you what Henry VIII told each of his six wives: "I won't be keeping any of you very long!" But Dave McCarthy has rendered that statement impossible for me to utter. Even the title of the topic he assigned me approaches in length the Gettysburg Address.

Edward Everett held forth for two hours because Americans of his era listened to three-hour sermons in church every week. Today we are more used to sound bites than to sermons, so I promise to improve on Everett's performance, if only in duration.

Here is your town's war story.

*   *   *

Warren's military history began before the town existed as a political unit, when the Wampanoag village of Sowams was located here. King Philip's War, the most devastating conflict in New England history, began on June 19, 1675, within the present bounds of Warren. This struggle, pitting Native Americans against aggressive and acquisitive immigrants from the British Isles, commenced with Indian raids in the south side of town. The area was at that time part of Swansea. (It was then part of Bristol until 1873, when Warren prevailed upon the General Assembly to extend its boundary one mile southward—from St. Mary's Church to the present town line—at Bristol's expense.)

In that bloody civil war, Warren's white and Indian settlers battled each other until Philip's ultimate defeat and death in August 1676 broke the power of the Wampanoag nation forever. Warren thus became an English settlement.

The East Bay, controlled by Plymouth Colony until 1691 and by Massachusetts thereafter, came under the jurisdiction of Rhode Island on February 17, 1746/47. Shortly after the transfer, the General Assembly incorporated Warren as a separate town. Its name was derived from Adm. Peter Warren of the Royal Navy, a leader in the 1745 amphibious assault upon the great French fortress of Louisbourg. The capture of that Cape Breton stronghold, with the aid of militia from Rhode Island, made Admiral Warren the hero of the day.

In view of this town's notable maritime and military history, it is fitting that an admiral was its namesake. The presence here of the U.S. Navy Band is thus appropriate and historically correct.

During the War for Independence rebel sentiment in Warren was strong, and the defiance of its citizens caused the British to raid the community. The town's travails during the Revolution were narrated in 1901 by Warren antiquarian Virginia Baker, whose detailed sixty–eight–page booklet should be consulted by those with a deep interest in that era. The highlights are these: In April 1775, in the aftermath of Lexington and Concord, the citizens of Bristol and Newport Counties promptly raised a regiment of troops whose second in command was Lt. Col. William Turner Miller, a leading citizen of Warren. The townspeople began to train as militia and organized a company of "alarm men." They also created a town watch under the direction of Capt. Ezra Ormsbee. This group of citizen-soldiers built a watch house on Burr's Hill to detect any pending British invasion by sea.

In February 1776 the town meeting voted to raise a company of artillery. Meanwhile, boatbuilders of Warren constructed several privateers, including the *General Stark*, to prey on enemy shipping, and all able-bodied men armed themselves with "two good firearms with bayonets" and cartridge boxes. At the time of this crisis the population of Warren totaled only 1,005, but its entire citizenry (except for one) mobilized for battle, both on land and on sea.

The British occupied the major port city of Newport in December 1776, and from that base they menaced the towns on Narragansett Bay. American troops, including men from Warren, sometimes skirmished with these British marauders. By far the most daring encounter was led by Col. William Barton, a native of the Touisset section of Warren. In 1777 Barton developed and carried out a scheme to capture British general Richard Prescott, whose occupation of Newport had been characterized by arrogance and harshness. On the evening of July 9, Barton's small handpicked force glided from Warwick Neck past three British frigates and landed near the Portsmouth-Middletown line. From the western shore of Aquidneck, Barton and his men advanced inland to the Overing House, where Prescott slept in the company of the widow Overing. After subduing the sentries, Barton captured the snoozing general and transported him, half-clothed, across the bay to Warwick. Later Prescott's freedom was purchased in an exchange for the captured American general Charles Lee. For his exploit, Barton was promoted to colonel by a grateful Continental Congress, and later to general by the State of Rhode Island.

Gen. William Barton (1748–1831) was Warren's most famous Revolutionary War soldier.

In 1778 the patriots formulated plans to lay siege to the British in Newport and force their surrender. In furtherance of this project, the people of Warren constructed seventy flatboats on the Kickemuit River to ferry the American army from the mainland to the northern part of Aquidneck Island, from where it could move southward towards Newport.

An informer—a Warren schoolmaster—relayed this intelligence to the new British commander, Gen. Robert Pigot, who soon dispatched a 500-man force of British and Hessians under Col. John Campbell to destroy the boats and punish Warren in the process. (With their tall headpieces and their wide boots, in which they carried their plunder, or "booty," the Hessians were particularly fearsome.) The raiders accomplished their mission. All but twelve boats were destroyed, the town was ransacked, its female residents were terrorized, and many of the male remnant of young boys and older men were taken prisoner. Some of these captives were later incarcerated in New York Harbor on the notorious prison ship *Jersey*, where at least one of them died. In addition, the marauders set ablaze the Baptist church and its parsonage, situated at the corner of present-day Main and Miller Streets. These structures had served as the cradle of Brown University when that famed institution was founded in Warren as Rhode Island College only fourteen years before.

When news of the sneak attack reached Colonel Barton in Providence, he raced southward on horseback with a small contingent, gathering volunteers en route. By the time he arrived, the enemy force had sacked Bristol and was heading back to its island base. The furious Barton caught them at the southern end of Bristol, but the ensuing skirmish failed to halt their departure and earned for Barton a severe gunshot wound in the right thigh that hobbled him for life.

Other tragedies affected Warren's freedom fighters in 1778. The year opened with an outbreak of smallpox, it was punctuated with a severe August hurricane that destroyed crops, and it ended with a bitter winter gale that sank the *General Stark* and condemned nineteen members of her crew to a frozen death.

The only bright and reassuring development in that dismal year of 1778 was the arrival in Warren of American forces after the conclusion of the indecisive Battle of Rhode Island. Gen. James Mitchell Varnum's brigade and Col. Israel Angell's regiment, both under the command of the youthful Marquis de Lafayette, encamped on Windmill Hill overlooking the Kickemuit. The dashing Frenchman was the toast of the town during his brief fall sojourn in Warren.

The year 1778 marked the darkness before the dawn. In October 1779 the British left Rhode Island as the theater of war shifted southward, and in July 1780 the friendly French under Count Rochambeau and Admiral Ternay arrived in Newport.

After meeting with Rochambeau in February 1781 to plan a joint offensive, George Washington stopped at Warren for lunch on

March 13, to the delight of the townspeople, as he headed for New York via Providence. Some members of the 6,000–man French army were quartered in Warren on the Windmill Hill campsite, and most passed through the town in June 1781 to keep their rendezvous with destiny at Yorktown.

Warren's William Turner Miller, in command of the schooner *Hunter*, hovered in Virginia's James River in the fall of 1781 as the British army under Lord Cornwallis attempted to withstand the combined military and naval forces of America and France. On September 19 Miller expressed his optimism to his wife Lydia in Warren: "I think from all circumstances that Cornwallis must fall"—and fall he did!

But Warren took a fall as well. Local historian Virginia Baker describes how hard that fall was:

> The condition of Warren at the end of the war was a most unhappy one. Business was almost entirely prostrated, and many families were impoverished. The town treasury was nearly depleted. The loss of shipping amounted to 1,090 tons. Household after household mourned the loss of dearly beloved members. Many a man who had gone forth to do service for his country in the full glory of vigorous manhood had returned the mere shadow of his former self. Young women had grown prematurely old under the too heavy burdens of anxiety, privation, and grief. The farms were neglected, the streets overgrown with grass, the ship-yards were deserted, the docks empty.
>
> But with the same courage and determination that had distinguished them in the darkest hours of adversity, the people instantly set about the bettering of their condition. The building of vessels was resumed, the farms were tilled, shops were re-opened, a new church built, and in less than a decade after the signing of the treaty of peace at Paris, Warren was once more a busy and prosperous maritime town.

Resilience has always been a cardinal American trait!

No other war, at least until now, has been fought on Warren soil. The second confrontation with England, begun in 1812, was more remote and lacking in citizen support. It was America's most unpopular foreign war. It is small wonder that the names of only eight veterans grace this honor roll, most of them from the naval service.

War was declared in June 1812 by a Democratic-Republican Congress at the request of President James Madison, who cited England's repeated violation of American maritime rights. Ironically, the commercially oriented Federalist party, strong in New England, opposed the declaration on the grounds that war with the Mistress of the Seas would bring destruction to American maritime trade and to our vulnerable coastal areas. Some extreme opponents of the war even advocated the secession of New England from the Union.

Despite local opposition to the War of 1812, Rhode Islanders participated, often for personal gain, in one phase of the conflict—privateering. Eighteen privately owned Rhode Island vessels secured commissions from the federal government to prey on British commerce. The most famous of these ships was the *Yankee*, owned principally by James De Wolf of Bristol. It was by far the most successful American privateer in history. The twelve-gun ship made six cruises, seizing forty-one prizes valued (in 1812 purchasing power) at more than three million dollars.

Though Bristol gets all the credit, the *Yankee* was refitted in the Warren boatyard of Caleb Carr and numbered Warren mariners among its daring hundred-man crews. The boatbuilders of Warren also constructed a privateer for De Wolf named the *MacDonough* after the hero of Lake Champlain, and with some of De Wolf's proceeds from the *Yankee*'s first cruise, they built another vessel, a 400-ton navy warship, in just fifty-seven days. Christened the *Chippewa*, this vessel was commissioned by Oliver Hazard Perry of Rhode Island, the great naval hero of the war.

Perry's contact with Warren went back many years. In 1798, during America's limited naval war with France, the Cromwell and Child shipyard constructed a huge 32-gun frigate named the *General Greene* for the United States Navy. To supervise construction, Capt. Christopher Perry moved to Warren with his son—

midshipman Oliver Hazard Perry. If Warren had made a category for the quasi war with France (1798–1800), the illustrious Perrys would grace your monument.

Unfortunately, the *General Greene*, the pride of the Warren boatbuilding industry, was at the Washington Navy Yard in 1814, when the British sacked and burned our capital. The trapped ship, alas, was scuttled to prevent its capture.

The 1840s witnessed a local political rebellion called the Dorr War and a conflict with Mexico. Warren responded to the first, but not the second. In 1842 local citizens formed the Warren Artillery to help the conservative charter government resist the challenge to its continued dominance posed by Thomas Wilson Dorr and the People's Constitution. For its efforts at the Providence armory and in Chepachet during this bloodless conflict, the state awarded the Warren unit two historic cannon that had been taken from the British at Saratoga in 1777 after the surrender of General Burgoyne. I will not comment on the valor of this unit, because my hero is the vanquished Thomas Dorr.

Although the Mexican War, fought between May 1846 and February 1848, was a major foreign conflict, it appears that Warren took no part in it. The campaigns were fought mainly by Texans, Tennessee volunteers, and other recruits from the South and West. Some northerners, like Whig congressman Abe Lincoln of Illinois, denounced the war as a southern attempt to extend the area of slavery. Wartime dissent seems as American as apple pie; even Lincoln did it! Far removed from the theater of battle and unmoved by President Polk's calls for expansion on the grounds of Manifest Destiny, Warren sat this conflict out.

No American was unmoved by the Civil War. It was our great national crisis. Warren sent 211 men—one out of every three of fighting age—to preserve the American Union and eliminate slavery in the process.

On August 25, 1861, a month after the Union disaster at First Bull Run, Alfred Luther became Warren's first enlistee. He was wounded in June 1862, losing his right arm. After serving as a POW, he returned to Warren to resume his life, like Edgar Guest's soldier who had lost a limb.

The Warren Artillery, activated as a unit in 1862, performed garrison duty to protect Washington, D.C., as part of Rhode Island's Ninth Regiment. Warren soldier Charles Sisson, of the Fifth Rhode Island Heavy Artillery, was captured during his regiment's North Carolina campaign and died of dysentery in that infamous Southern graveyard called Andersonville.

At the time of the Revolution, Warren had forty-four blacks, a third of whom were slaves. By 1861 the town's African Americans had long been free, but their number had dwindled. Of the few that remained, George and Joseph Gardner chose to fight to give their Southern brethren the freedom they enjoyed. Both served with the Fourteenth Colored Regiment, Rhode Island Heavy Artillery. Only one returned. Joseph died of consumption in the bayous of Louisiana; George came back to Warren, where he has lain buried and unremembered until now, when you have given him and all his comrades in arms one-line slivers of immortality on your honor roll.

In one encounter, the Civil War touched Warren directly. By 1864 the town's legendary whaling fleet—twenty-six vessels in number at its peak in the 1840s, when it was the largest in Rhode Island—had dwindled to one. That lone ship, the *Covington*, fell victim to the *Florida*, a ubiquitous Confederate commerce raider. The Civil War thus put the final nail in the coffin of Warren's most daring and colorful business enterprise.

When the war between the states was over, 618,000 Americans, North and South, lay dead; but we had proved, to paraphrase Lincoln, that this nation, conceived in liberty, could long endure.

The Spanish-American conflict of 1898 was a war of mixed motives—humanitarian concern over Spanish misrule in Cuba and the desire of expansionists like Teddy Roosevelt to create an American empire. Rhode Island produced 1,780 volunteers, 23 of whom hailed from Warren. The war was so poorly fought by Spain and so swiftly prosecuted by America that except for the 25-member crew of the repair ship USS *Vulcan*, it was over before any Rhode Islanders saw combat.

World War I was another matter. President Wilson's well-intentioned but inaccurate call to "make the world safe for democracy" was answered by 461 Warren men—about one in every four of fighting age. Their names, here inscribed, reveal the transformation that Warren had experienced from 1850 to 1917. Maritime pursuits had given way to industrialization; mills rather than docks now dominated the local economic landscape.

Manufacturing jobs attracted immigrant workers from Ireland, French Canada, Poland, Italy, Portugal, and the Middle East. These new Americans built churches—St. Mary's, St. Jean Baptist, St. Casimir, St. Alexander, and, later, St. Thomas—attesting to their love of God, and when the call to arms came in 1917, men like the McCanns, the Dions, the Goloskies, the Jannittos, and the Mellos, along with their fellow parishioners, demonstrated their love for America, thus earning a place on this Roll of Honor.

Alas, "the War to End All Wars" did not. Two decades later a united America's greatest crusade began, and a new, youthful generation met the challenge, fulfilling President Herbert Hoover's grim observation that "older men declare war, but it is youth that must fight and die."

Historians often observe that the times make the man. Brilliant responses to huge challenges equals greatness. Adm. Bull Halsey, a hero of the Pacific war, said it best: "There are no great men, just great circumstances, and how they handle those circumstances will determine the course of history." America's all-out response to the challenge of totalitarianism during World War II was nothing short of great. The most serious military threat to modern democracy since America launched that system of governance in the late eighteenth century was repelled. And this feat was accomplished not just by men under arms but by all Americans.

The war veterans—those we honor today—are the stars, but every winning team requires a supporting cast. A championship professional team, for example, not only needs great players; it is an organization that relies on such diverse talents as those of managers, coaches, trainers, scouts, a front office, investors, publicists, a grounds crew, a security force, stadium personnel, and the list goes on.

During World War II, more so than in any war since the Revolution, America got that team effort. You veterans were the stars.

There are 1,245 names of World War II servicemen and women on this honor roll. When you answered the call, Warren had a total population of only 8,158! Between 1941 and 1945, more than 15 percent of the total citizenry served in the armed forces of the United States, and about twenty families are represented by five or more members on your memorial—a litany much too long to recite here.

But although all veterans are patriots, not all true patriots are veterans. Those left behind were not idle, nor were they shirkers. The police kept Warren secure, and the firemen kept the home fires from burning out of control. Professionals attended to the medical, legal, political, and financial needs of the town. Workers in several Warren factories—including the huge Warren Manufacturing Company, Kleistone Rubber, Crown Fastener, and the Rains Company—won commendations from the Army or the Navy for excellence in producing products for use in the war effort.

Warren's historic maritime industry was especially productive. The Warren Boat Yard, under government contract, constructed two minesweepers, six coastal transports, and forty boats designed to service seaplanes. The Anchorage-Dyer boat company constructed more than two thousand small craft for a variety of military purposes. Both companies received commendations for the quality of their products and the high skill of their work force.

Who composed that talented work force during the war years? With 30 percent of all Warren males in the armed service and others guarding the home front as safety service personnel, that task fell mainly to Warren's women. During World War II they entered the work force in droves. It was their coming-out party, but instead of cotillion dresses and bonnets, they wore work clothes and hard hats. "Rosie the Riveter" became the national symbol of women in the workplace, and the active involvement of females there and in the military changed the role of women in America forever.

Because of the great national effort it demanded and the noble, universal ideals for which it was fought, World War II has been called "the good war." But for the twenty-seven Warren veterans who died fighting it, this war, like all wars, was tragic and violent.

Our recollections of war are sometimes rosy, but war itself is always thorny. When nostalgia drives us to depict World War II as a time of busy and cheerful production, team spirit, righteous zeal, and patriotism, we obscure the real suffering that took place and we lose sight of the fact that war is inherently destructive and wasteful of human and natural resources. Was it not William Tecumseh Sherman, one of the greatest and most consistently successful of American generals, who succinctly described war as hell?

The unified response of soldier and civilian alike to the great global crisis of the 1940s inspired journalist Tom Brokaw to dub Americans of that era "The Greatest Generation." There is merit to that description as it applies to the American people, on both the battlefront and the home front. Applied to World War II veterans alone, however, it diminishes those who came after, those who fought in Korea, Vietnam, and Iraq.

In some ways it is more difficult to fight a "police action," as our involvement in Korea was euphemistically called, or to wage a limited war with sharply circumscribed objectives. The task becomes even more difficult and discouraging when part of the support system at home is either indifferent, as in the Korean War; hostile, as in the Vietnam War; or has a business-as-usual attitude, such as that which marked our brief but brilliant foray into the Persian Gulf.

While the dangers may be equal, I believe that it is more psychologically difficult and more taxing on morale to fight a limited war, like those in Korea and the Persian Gulf, or to do battle in a conflict like Vietnam, where the civilian support system is resistant, than it is to fight an all-out war in response to an attack upon the United States. Our last three wars, in which 507 citizens of Warren answered the call of their country, were not the result of direct aggression against America. They were caused by attacks on our allies in areas of the globe far distant from Warren. My heart goes out to the veterans of those thankless conflicts. Through their sacrifice and service in wars that inspired no great national crusade, they have personified the highest ideals of the American military tradition—Duty, Honor, Country!

All war veterans are, at the least, on call to make the ultimate sacrifice. All are deserving of equal respect, honor, and praise from their fellow Americans. Let that be the lesson of this splendid memorial. Warren's 2,646-person honor roll makes no special distinction for race, religion, gender, ethnicity, or wealth; no distinction for branch of service, rank, or war fought. In this respect it is the perfect embodiment of the American spirit of equality that each of these Warren veterans fought to secure and protect.

I firmly believe that a nation or a town reveals itself not only by those people it produces but also by those it honors and remembers. By that standard, Warren is a great town indeed!

In conclusion, permit me a final word as we move from the Persian Gulf to the present, for today we are actively engaged in a new kind of war—one that can hit Warren on the home front for the first time since May 1778, when the British and Hessians left this ravaged town and marched southward with Colonel Barton at their heels.

As early as 1796, when the ink on our Constitution was scarcely dry, Thomas Jefferson warned Americans that "we are likely to preserve the liberty we have obtained only by unremitting labors and perils." A generation later Daniel Webster, the great apostle of Union, observed that "God grants liberty only to those who love it, and are always ready to guard and defend it"; and defend it now we must!

Ironically, Jefferson and Webster were more concerned with internal threats than with a foreign foe, but today we are faced with internal dangers *from* a foreign foe. Let us not only resist but retaliate, taking our encouragement from the words of Franklin Roosevelt when he reassured another generation of Americans faced with domestic distress that "we have nothing to fear but fear itself."

War is doubly terrible when it is waged by the terrorist who makes the home front the battlefront, but terrorism must fail when met by vigilance, tenacity, and the will to persevere.

I shall read you a letter that must dictate our response to the fanatics who attack us. That missive reads as follows: "We are pressed on every side but not crushed; perplexed but not in despair; persecuted but not abandoned; struck down but not destroyed." Would it surprise you to learn that these words of hope were penned by St. Paul in his Letter to the Corinthians? Would it be offensive to remind you that we are a nation under God? Would it be presumptuous of me to predict that with persistence and prayer, we shall prevail? God Bless America!

Built from my designs in 1999–2000 by general contractor Harold Brown and several skilled craftsmen, the library at my Bristol home, Gale Winds, now contains my personal book collection of more than seven thousand volumes.

Patrick T. Conley
A Bibliography

(In chronological order within each category)

Books

Proceedings of the Rhode Island Constitutional Convention of 1973. Providence: Oxford Press, 1973.

Catholicism in Rhode Island: The Formative Era (with Matthew J. Smith). Providence: Diocese of Providence, 1976.

Democracy in Decline: Rhode Island's Constitutional Development, 1776–1841. Providence: Rhode Island Historical Society, 1977.

Providence: A Pictorial History (with Paul R. Campbell). Norfolk, Va.: Donning Company, 1982.

The Aurora Club of Rhode Island: A Fifty-Year History (with Paul R. Campbell). Providence: privately printed, 1982.

Rhode Island Profile. Providence: Rhode Island Publications Society, 1982.

Fires and Firefighters in Providence, 1754–1984: A Pictorial History of the Providence Fire Department (with Paul R. Campbell). Providence: Rhode Island Publications Society, 1985. Revised edition (1754–2001), 2002.

The Irish in Rhode Island: A Historical Appreciation. Providence: Rhode Island Heritage Commission, 1986.

An Album of Rhode Island History, 1636–1986. Norfolk, Va.: Donning Company, 1986. Reprinted with additions, 1992 and 2000.

First in War, Last in Peace: Rhode Island and the Constitution, 1786–1790. Providence: Rhode Island Bicentennial Foundation, 1987.

The Colony and State Houses of Rhode Island: An Architectural and Historical Study (with Robert O. Jones and William McKenzie Woodward). Providence: Rhode Island Historical Society, 1988.

The Constitution and the States: The Role of the Original Thirteen in the Framing and Adoption of the Constitution (with John P. Kaminski). Madison, Wis.: Madison House Publishers, 1988. Winner of the 1993 Fraunces Tavern Museum Book Award from the Sons of the American Revolution.

The Bill of Rights and the States: The Colonial and Revolutionary Origins of American Liberties (with John P. Kaminski). Madison, Wis.: Madison House Publishers, 1992. Winner of the 1993 Fraunces Tavern Museum Book Award from the Sons of the American Revolution.

Liberty and Justice: A History of Law and Lawyers in Rhode Island, 1636–1998. Providence: Rhode Island Publications Society, 1998.

Neither Separate nor Equal: Legislature and Executive in Rhode Island Constitutional History. Providence: Rhode Island Publications Society, 1999.

Rhode Island in Rhetoric and Reflection: Public Addresses and Essays. Providence: Rhode Island Publications Society, 2002.

ARTICLES

"A Clear Dichotomy" (with Jay S. Goodman). *National Civic Review* 56 (September 1967): 447–52, 469. The local government article of the proposed Rhode Island constitution.

"The Dorr Rebellion." Rhode Island Yearbook, 1967, H80-H88.

"The Real Ichabod Crane." *American Literature* 40 (March 1968): 70–71.

"Rhode Island Constitutional Development, 1636–1775: A Survey."
Rhode Island History 27 (April–June 1968): 49–63, 74–94.
Reprinted in *Rhode Island Bar Annual* 5 (1968): 62–91.

"Rhode Island's Paper Money Issue and *Trevett* v. *Weeden* (1786)."
Rhode Island History 30 (August 1971): 95–108. Reprinted in
abridged form in *Rhode Island Reports* 116 (1976): 964–74.

"The Dorr Rebellion: Rhode Island's Crisis in Constitutional
Government." *American Chronicle: A Magazine of History* 1
(January 1972): 48–53.

"Brooks Adams' Law of Civilization and Decay." *Essex Institute
Historical Collections* 108 (April 1972): 89–98.

"Rhode Island in Disunion, 1787–1790." *Rhode Island History* 31
(November 1972): 99–115.

"The Supreme Court on Abortion: A Dissenting Opinion" (with
R. J. McKenna). *Catholic Lawyer* 19 (Winter 1973): 19–28.
Reprinted without documentation in *Review for Religious* 32
(May 1973): 473–81. Published also in *Providence Visitor*,
February 23, 1973. Reprinted in Glenn A. Phelps and Robert
A. Porier, eds., *Contemporary Debates on Civil Liberties:
Enduring Constitutional Questions* (Lexington, Mass.: D. C.
Heath & Co., 1985), pp. 204–10.

"State Restrictions on Local Government Debt with Special
Reference to Rhode Island," "State Restrictions on the Taxing
Powers of Local Government with Special Reference to
Rhode Island," and "An Annotated Bibliography of Works
Relating to the Development of Local Government in Rhode
Island, 1636–1972." In Robert W. Sutton, Jr., ed., *Rhode Island
Local Government: Past, Present, Future*, pp. 70–77, 78–82,
153–66. Kingston, R.I.: URI Bureau of Government
Research, 1974.

"Rhode Island's Latin Americans—An Historical Profile"
(with John Carpenter). *Providence Visitor*, August 9, 16, and
23, 1974.

"State Aid to Rhode Island's Private Schools: A Case Study of *DiCenso* v. *Robinson*" (with Fernando S. Cunha). *Catholic Lawyer* 22 (Autumn 1976): 329–43.

"Rhode Island Constitutional Issues during the Early National Period." In Linda L. Levin, ed., *Federal Rhode Island: The Age of the China Trade*, pp. 1–37. Providence: Rhode Island Historical Society, 1978.

"Ethnic Politics in Rhode Island: The Case of the Franco-Americans." In Marcel P. Fortin, ed., *Woonsocket, R.I.: The Americanization of a Foreign City*, pp. 11–13. Providence: Rhode Island Committee for the Humanities, 1981. Reprinted in *Old Rhode Island*, June 1993, pp. 16–22.

"Rhode Island." In *Worldmark Encyclopedia of the States*, ed. Moshe Y. Sachs et al., pp. 481–86. New York: Worldmark Press, 1981.

"Rhode Island." In *Encyclopedia Americana* (1983), 23:472–86.

"Death Knell for the Death Penalty: The Gordon Murder Trial and Rhode Island's Abolition of Capital Punishment." *Rhode Island Bar Journal* 34 (May 1986): 11–15. Winner of the First Annual Writing Contest of the Rhode Island Bar Association. An earlier version published in *Providence Visitor*, July 6, 1973.

"Rhode Island History—An Outline." In *Rhode Island Manual* for 1985–1986, prepared by Secretary of State Susan L. Farmer, pp. 131–75.

"Rhode Island's Crisis in Constitutionalism: The Dorr Rebellion and the Origins of the Present State Constitution." *Rhode Island Bar Journal* 35 (October 1986): 12–15, 19–22.

"First in War; Last in Peace: Rhode Island and the Constitution, 1786–1790." *Rhode Island Bar Journal* 35 (May 1987): 11–19.

"Civil Rights and Civil Wrongs in Rhode Island: Church, State, and the Constitution, 1636–1986." *Rhode Island Bar Journal* 35 (June-July 1987): 14–19.

"Anne Hutchinson—Founding Mother." East Bay Newspapers, August 18, 1988 (Portsmouth 300th anniversary commemorative issue).

"Thomas Wilson Dorr," "Henry Bowen Anthony," "Nelson Wilmarth Aldrich," and "Charles Ray Brayton." In *Encyclopedia of American Political Parties and Elections*, ed. Louis Maisel. New York, 1990.

"Rhode Island." In *The Encyclopedia of Colonial and Revolutionary America*, ed. John Mack Faragher, pp. 368–70. New York, 1990.

"The Irish of Bristol." In *Bristol Heritage and Discovery Celebration: Commemorative Book, 1492–1992* (1992). Reprinted as "The Irish in Rhode Island and the Bristol Connection" in *Old Rhode Island*, March 1993, pp. 7–13.

"No Tempest in a Teapot: The Dorr Rebellion in National Perspective." *Rhode Island History* 50 (August 1992): 67–100.

"The Biography of Nelson W. Aldrich (November 6, 1841-April 16, 1915)." *Old Rhode Island*, September 1992, p. 20.

"The Biography of Charles R. Brayton," *Old Rhode Island*, October 1992, pp. 16–17.

"The Dorr Rebellion and American Constitutional Theory: Popular Constituent Sovereignty, Political Questions, and the Case of *Luther* v. *Borden*." *Rhode Island Bar Journal* 41 (November 1992): 19–25. Simultaneously published in Joyce M. Botelho, ed., *Right and Might: The Dorr Rebellion and the Struggle for Equal Rights*, pp. 79–90. Providence: Rhode Island Historical Society, 1992.

"Thomas Wilson Dorr (November 5, 1805-December 27, 1854)." *Old Rhode Island*, December 1992–January, 1993, pp. 61–62.

"Rhode Island Profiles: Famed Irish Leaders from Rhode Island's Past." *Old Rhode Island*, March 1993, pp. 18–20.

"Ethnic Politics in Rhode Island: The Decisive Role of the Franco-Americans." *Old Rhode Island*, June-July 1993, pp. 16–22.

"The Last Shall Be First: Rhode Island's Statehood Stamp." *Old Rhode Island*, January-February 1995, pp. 18–20.

"Separation of Powers in Rhode Island." *Rhode Island Bar Journal* 44 (October 1995): 9–11.

"Matthew Harkins: Catholic Bishop and Educator." *Rhode Island History* 53 (August 1995): 70–89.

"Andersonville and the Civil War Prison System." *Bristol Phoenix*, March 7, 1996, pp. 17, 20; March 14, 1996, pp. 21–22. A review of the Turner Network Television documentary film on Andersonville.

"Rhode Island." An essay prepared for a CD-ROM production entitled *New England Business and Pleasure Guide*, by John Chaffee, 1996.

"Rhode Island." An article prepared for the 1997 edition of the Microsoft *Encarta Encyclopedia*.

"*State of Rhode Island* v. *The Rev. Ephraim K. Avery* (1833): The Legal and Geographical Setting." *Rhode Island Bar Journal* 47 (May 1999): 5–7, 32–35. Published in an earlier abbreviated version in *Bristol Phoenix*, November 18, 1998, pp. 8–9.

"Rhode Island [Irish]." In *The Encyclopedia of the Irish in America*, ed. Michael Glazier, pp. 803–8. Notre Dame, Ind.: University of Notre Dame Press, 1999.

"Charles Ray Brayton" and "Thomas Wilson Dorr." In *American National Biography*, ed. John A. Garraty and Mark C. Carnes, 3:447–48, 6:759–61. New York, 1999.

"Revising the Revisionists: A Review Essay." *Rhode Island Bar Journal* 48 (November 1999): 17–19, 40–42. The Supreme Court advisory opinion on separation of powers.

"Joseph R. Weisberger: A Life in Law." *Rhode Island Bar Journal* 49 (February 2001): 5–9, 32–42.

"Founding Lawyers: Doing Justice to the Legal Architects of Rhode Island Statehood." *Rhode Island Bar Journal* 50 (March/April, 2002): 15–17, 33–35.

"Popular Sovereignty or Public Anarchy? America Debates the Dorr Rebellion." *Rhode Island History* 60 (Summer 2002): 71–91.

Essays

"A Statement in Defense of the Proposed Rhode Island Constitution." *Rhode Island Bar Journal* 16 (January 1968): 3, 9–13. Reprinted in *Providence Visitor*.

"Reflections on Writing the History of the Diocese" (with Matthew J. Smith). *Providence Visitor*, November 3, 1972.

"Reflections on the Bicentennial Observance." *Woonsocket Call*, September 29, 1976.

"The 1986 State Constitutional Convention: The Salient Issues." *Rhode Island Bar Journal* 33 (May 1985): 10–12.

Pamphlets

North Kingstown: An Historical Sketch. Providence: Rhode Island Publications Society, 1976. 11 pp.

The Dorr Rebellion: Rhode Island's Crisis in Constitutional Government. Providence: Rhode Island Publications Society, 1976. 13 pp.

The Blackstone Valley: A Sketch of Its River, Its Canal, and Its People. Providence: Rhode Island Publications Society, 1982. 18 pp.

Providence: From Town to City. Providence: Rhode Island Publications Society, 1982. 6 pp.

Rhode Island Catholicism: A Historical Guide. Providence: Rhode Island Publications Society, 1984. 24 pp.

Rhode Island's Road to Liberty. Providence: Rhode Island Publications Society, 1987., 24 pp.

Posterity Views the Founding: General Published Works Pertaining to the Creation of the Constitution: A Bibliographic Essay. Providence: Rhode Island Publications Society, 1988. Offprint from *The Constitution and the States.* 36 pp.

The Bill of Rights and Rhode Island. Providence: Rhode Island Publications Society, 1991. Offprint from *The Bill of Rights and the States.* 39 pp.

MISCELLANEOUS

Sixteen research reports for the 1964–68 Rhode Island constitutional convention. Conley Collection, Providence College Archives.

Series of eight 16-page brochures on the eight Rhode Island Community Action Programs. Rhode Island Department of Community Affairs, 1971.

Report of the Cranston Charter Review Commission, 1973. 36 pp.

Foreword. *Rhode Island Bar Journal* 34 (May 1986). Historical issue commemorating the 350th anniversary of the founding of Rhode Island, Patrick T. Conley, guest editor.

Rhode Island Ethnic Heritage Fact Sheets (1980–84), 40 pp. Reprinted with introduction, Rhode Island Publications Society, 2000.

A Brief History of the Bicentennial Council of the Thirteen Original States and Its Successor, the U.S. Constitution Council. Providence: privately printed, 1988. 25 pp.

Foreword to William R. Staples, *The Documentary History of the Destruction of the Gaspee,* ed. Richard M. Deasy, pp. vii–x. Providence: Rhode Island Publications Society, 1990.

"Rhode Island in the Revolutionary Era, 1764–1790" (with John Kaminski). 1990. Instructional historical poster.

The Rhode Island Ratification Celebration by the Rhode Island Bicentennial Foundation. Providence: Rhode Island Bicentennial Foundation, 1990. 18 pp.

A Blueprint for Providence in the 1990s. Providence: privately printed, 1990. The position papers of Vincent A. Cianci, Jr., on crime, the drug problem, education, neighborhoods and human services, municipal finance and taxation, minorities, economic development and jobs, and housing. 108 pp.

Introduction to *The Broadsides of the Dorr Rebellion*, comp. Russell J. DeSimone and Daniel C. Schofield, pp. 1–13. Providence: Rhode Island Publications Society, 1992.

The History of Gale Winds: One Bristol Point Road (with James J. Mullen). Providence: Rhode Island Publications Society, 2001. 57 pp.

Eminent Rhode Islanders: Biographical Profiles of the Inductees into the Rhode Island Heritage Hall of Fame, 1965–2000 (with Manuel Gorriaran, Jr.). Providence: Rhode Island Publications Society, 2001. 56 pp.

Scholarly Book Reviews

Review of James Madison's *Notes of Debates in the Federal Convention of 1787*, with an introduction by Adriennne Koch. *Catholic Historical Review* 55 (October 1969): 536–37.

Review of Madison's "Advice to My Country," by Adrienne Koch. *Catholic Historical Review* 55 (October 1969): 540–42.

Review of *Rhode Island and the Union, 1774–1795*, by Irwin H. Polishook. *New England Quarterly* 43 (December 1970): 678–80.

Review of *Lopez of Newport: Colonial American Merchant Prince*, by Stanley F. Chyet. *New England Quarterly* 44 (June 1971): 346–48.

Review of *Plantation in Yankeeland: The Story of Cocumscussoc, Mirror of Colonial Rhode Island*, by Carl Woodward. *New England Quarterly* 44 (March-December 1972): 597–99.

Review of *The Churches Militant: The War of 1812 and American Religion*, by William Gribben. *Review for Religious* 32 (1973): 1187–88.

Review of *The Dorr Rebellion: A Study in American Radicalism, 1833–1849*, by Marvin E. Gettleman. *New England Quarterly* 47 (March 1974): 143–45.

Review of *Fat Mutton and Liberty of Conscience: Society in Rhode Island, 1636–1690*, by Carl Bridenbaugh. *New England Quarterly* 49 (March 1976): 136–38.

Review of *Colonial Rhode Island: A History*, by Sydney V. James. *Journal of American History* 64 (December 1977): 755–56.

Review of *Brotherly Love: Murder and the Politics of Prejudice in Nineteenth-Century Rhode Island*, by Charles Hoffman and Tess Hoffman. *New England Quarterly* 68 (September 1995): 506–9. Reprinted in *Rhode Island Bar Journal* 44 (February 1996): 23, 25.

Edited Works (with editor's introduction)

Rhode Island Ethnic Pamphlet Heritage Series
(Published jointly by The Rhode Island Heritage Commission and The Rhode Island Publications Society):

The Portuguese in Rhode Island, by M. Rachel Cunha et al. 1985.

The Armenians in Rhode Island, by Ara Arthur Gelenian. 1985.

The Germans in Rhode Island, by Raymond L. Sickinger and John K. Primeau. 1985.

The Jews in Rhode Island, by Geraldine Foster. 1985.

The Irish in Rhode Island, by Patrick T. Conley. 1986.

The Arabic-Speaking People in Rhode Island, by Eleanor A. Doumato. 1986.

The French in Rhode Island, by Albert K. Aubin. 1988.

The Ukrainians in Rhode Island, by Rt. Rev. John J. Mowatt. 1988.

The Southeast Asians in Rhode Island, by Louise Lind. 1989.

The Italians in Rhode Island, by Carmela E. Santoro. 1990.

The Cape Verdeans in Rhode Island, by Waltraud Berger Coli and Richard A. Lobban. 1990.

The Lithuanians in Rhode Island, by Rev. William Wolkovich-Valkavicius. 1992.

The Greeks in Rhode Island, by Stephen Kyriakou and Venetia B. Georas. 1994.

A Rhode Island Ethnic Group: Polish Americans, by Stanislaus A. Blejwas. Published by the Rhode Island American Polish Cultural Exchange Commission, 1995.

General Editor, RHODE ISLAND REVOLUTIONARY HERITAGE SERIES:

Silas Downer: Forgotten Patriot, by Carl Bridenbaugh. Providence: Rhode Island Bicentennial Foundation, 1974.

The Rights of Colonies Examined, by Stephen Hopkins, introduced and edited by Paul Campbell. Providence: Rhode Island Bicentennial Foundation, 1974.

Diary of a Common Soldier in the American Revolution, 1775–1783: An Annotated Edition of the Military Journal of Jeremiah Greenman, ed. by Robert C. Bray and Paul E. Bushnell. Dekalb, Ill.: Northern Illinois University Press, 1978.

Rhode Islanders Record the Revolution: The Journals of William Humphrey and Zuriel Waterman, introduced and edited by Nathaniel N. Shipton and David Swain. Providence: Rhode Island Publications Society, 1984

Building Early American Warships: The Journal of the Rhode Island Committee for Constructing the Continental Frigates Providence *and* Warren, *1775–1777*, Introduced by John Fitzhugh Millar. Williamsburg, Va.: Thirteen Colonies Press; Providence: Rhode Island Publications Society, 1988.

The Documentary History of the Destruction of the Gaspee, by
William R. Staples, introduced and supplemented by
Richard M. Deasy. Providence: Rhode Island
Publications Society, Rhode Island Bicentennial
Foundation, and Rhode Island Supreme Court Historical
Society, 1990.

POETRY

"A Lesson for Lamenters," "The Legacy," "The Forgotten," "The
Fleeting Scepter," "Thoughts at Twilight," and "Song to
Spring." *Alembic* (Providence College literary magazine) 33
(1959): 47, 48–49, 59, 60, 63–64, 64.

DOCTORAL DISSERTATIONS DIRECTED

Robert W. Hayman, "Catholicism in Rhode Island and the
Diocese of Providence, 1780–1886." 1977.

William J. Jennings, Jr., "The Prince of Pawtucket: A Study
of the Politics of Thomas P. McCoy." 1985.

D. Scott Molloy, "Motormen, Moguls, and the Machine:
Urban Mass Transit in Rhode Island, 1864–1902." 1991.

John C. Fredericksen, "Niagara, 1814: The United States
Army's Quest for Tactical Parity in the War of 1812 and
Its Legacy." 1993.

LONG SCHOLARLY UNPUBLISHED TREATISES

"The Military Legislation of the First and Second Sessions of
the Thirteenth Congress [1812–13]: A Study in War-Time
Leadership." Doctoral research paper, University of Notre
Dame, 1963. 123 pp.

"Christopher Dawson's Concept of World History." Doctoral
research paper, University of Notre Dame, 1963. 54 pp.

Publications Concerning Patrick T. Conley

Matthew J. Smith and Jane M. Jackson, comps. *Inventory to the Conley Collection of the Rhode Island Constitutional Convention, 1964–1968.* Providence, 1973.

Wayne Worcester. "Dirt Rich." *Rhode Island Monthly*, October 1988, pp. 46–49, 87–88, 91, 93–96, 98, 101–2.

The Reverend Cornelius Philip Forster, O.P. (1919–1993)
Neminem quod tetigit non ornavit.
(He touched no one he did not enrich.)

Cornelius P. Forster, O.P., Channel of Grace: The Quintessential Dominican

Dr. Donna T. McCaffrey

Dr. Donna McCaffrey, the author of this moving remembrance, was my former graduate student and the niece of Father Forster. She now teaches history at Providence College, where she holds the rank of assistant professor and performs several administrative roles.

RUEFULLY THE SAINTLY WALTER FARRELL, O.P., shook his head. Having entertained a series of questions on the limits of a priest's responsibilities, he once again replied, "No, even then, it is not enough." Finally, with a gentle exasperation, Father Farrell explained: "Now, son, a Dominican priest can never do enough. In all he does, in all he says, every day of his life, a Dominican must be a channel of grace, a passage through which God's love, God's grace, must be moved to do God's work on earth."

Among the aspirants to the Dominican Order present over a half century ago in Walter Farrell's studium classroom was young Cornelius Philip Forster, O.P. He listened and heeded Walter Farrell's dictum and made it a lifelong guiding principle. The character, intellect, prudence, courage, self-sacrifice, and docility prerequisite to accepting this challenge had long been in formation. Many forces had shaped this handsome, six-foot-two, powerfully built competitive athlete with the leonine head of jet black curly hair, dark expressive eyebrows, large brown vibrant eyes, and warm deep voice.

A New Yorker of Anglo-Celtic stock, descendant of the staunch Jacobite Fenwick and Forster clans of Northumbria, England,

Cornelius Aloysius Forster, Jr., was born October 27, 1919, in New York City. He was the third child of Cornelius A. Forster, Sr., fireman, master electrician, and devout man who prayed his daily rosary, hand in pocket, to and from work on the subway. His mother, Mary Catherine Collins, was a former foreign buyer for Bloomingdale's, an accomplished singer and pianist, as well as a staunch advocate of women's rights through suffrage. The formative years of young Neil (called Bus at home) laid the bedrock for this channel of grace.

Cornelius A. Forster, Jr., was nurtured in a loving home with his siblings William A. (Bill), Virginia T. (Tine), and Francis X. (Frank). His parents were people of great faith who had a special devotion and Third Order affiliation with the Dominicans. Married by the Dominican archbishop John T. McNicolas, O.P., Neil Sr. and Mamie Collins early introduced young Neil to the Dominicans. Baptized by Dominican artist J. J. Sullivan, O.P., Neil later began grade school with the Dominican Sisters at St. Catherine of Siena. Neil's maternal grandfather, Patrick Francis Collins, lived with the family. Himself a devout charter member of New York's Holy Name Society, Patrick not only quizzed his precocious grandson on facts of history (Bus could recite all the U.S. presidents in order by age five!) but also taught Neil the great Catholic prayers. "Daddy" Collins was also a creative Irish storyteller who early engendered in Neil a love for literature, Ireland, and precision in the expression of thought.

Neil's character was shaped in his early family life. In addition to virtue and love of truth, Neil's father gave Neil an enduring life principle. Neil Sr. insisted that his sons be gentlemen. When young Bus quipped as to the nature of this beast, Cornelius Sr. replied, "Always do and say the kindest thing in the kindest way."

Neil's mother gave Neil a love for music and goodness, but it was her acute concern for his character growth that was so influential. Neil turned ten two days before the October 29, 1929, stock market crash that ushered in the Great Depression. Times were hard. Yet, Neil's mother refused several lucrative Hollywood film and child-model contracts for her talented and handsome son. Mrs. Forster believed that to achieve fortune from the whimsical accident of good looks would not bode well for the character of Neil. One must work hard and utilize the talents given by God to the best of one's ability. Indeed, Neil took a small paper route of thirty customers for the *Bronx Home News*, and he built it into over 130 accounts. The earnings generated one-third of the family income during the Depression.

Neil's academic life progressed. After taking a competitive exam, Neil entered the freshman class of Cathedral Boy's High School on full scholarship in 1933. His scholastic achievement was superior, and he observed talented religious men engaged in the serious business of Catholic education.

A versatile student, Neil Forster won countless academic awards and medals as well as citywide recognition in debate, football, baseball, swimming, and other competitive high school sports. He accepted recognition graciously but never sought it. Only in one instance was he genuinely pleased. Foreshadowing his later historical talent, in May 1937 he won a coveted national first place award in *The New York Times* U.S. Constitution Essay Contest. He presented his father and mother with the handsome check.

In September 1937, Neil Forster entered the handpicked Fordham University Hundredth Anniversary Class of 1941. The Jesuit impact on his life began. A structured curriculum mandated course work in both philosophy and theology each semester. Neil's encounter with the great thinkers, the Church Doctors and Fathers, dogma, and scripture complemented his major course work in history under the tutelage of renowned historians Jeremiah O'Sullivan, Charles C. Tansill, Ross Hoffman, and others.

As a freshman, Neil competed and won a spot on Fordham's fabulous football team. He took the field with the famous "blocks of granite" in the opening game. He performed too well. On Monday morning following the weekend triumph, he was summoned by the Jesuit academic dean. "Mr. Forster, was that your name I heard so frequently on the loudspeaker this past Saturday?"

"Yes, Father."

"May I point out to you, young man, that you are here on a full four-year academic scholarship, not an athletic scholarship. Please choose."

Neil Forster acquiesced and, at the dean's insistence, resigned from the Fordham varsity. Yet, he was convinced that the athlete learns the transferable skills of discipline, teamwork, and integrity from competition. Rather than upset the dean, he joined a semi-professional New York City football league which fed the professional leagues. He later declined two professional contract offers. All his adult life he supported competitive collegiate athletics and rarely missed a PC basketball game.

As a student at Fordham, Neil was fascinated with political history, thought, and theory. He found 1930s European political developments riveting. He stayed up all night September 1, 1939, anxiously listening to the dramatic radio reports of Hitler's invasion of Poland, precipitating World War II. He predicted then the massive changes this would bring. Strong new leaders would be needed.

Neil fomulated future career plans: military service if the U.S. entered the war, a graduate degree in history, law school, and, ultimately, political life, culminating as a Catholic govenor of New York. These were his goals. Despite the fact that it was unheard of for a commuter, he ran for class office and won. He perfected other skills for the future. He joined Fordham's Debate Club, competed statewide, and garnered more awards. He joined Fordham's Dramatic Club, acted, directed, and in 1940 coauthored a play, *Lee of Virginia*, with fellow student R. L. McCarthy.

At Fordham, Neil Forster observed the keen intelligence, constant scholarship, priestly concern, and sophisticated intellect of his Jesuit professors. Again, he admired the dedication of religious men engaged in the work of Catholic education, while realizing the grave difficulties they faced in a largely anti-Catholic society.

Neil also developed enduring friendships, as well as a profound loyalty to Fordham University. Although he joined a rival order, Fordham's president invited him to say a private Mass in the Fordham chapel when he was first ordained. For his fortieth anniversary, he was editor of *Fordham, 1981 Reunion*, and he rejoiced as a Golden Ram for his fiftieth and Fordham's 150th anniversary in 1991.

In senior year, Neil won and accepted a full academic scholarship for Fordham's Graduate School in history. War in Europe might intervene, but his political career was planned. Yet, other channels of grace flowed into Neil's life.

On a canoe/camping trip with classmates Tom Doyle and Paul
Smith, a freak summer squall raged across Lake George. In a matter of minutes, powerful waves and wind overturned the canoe. The three classmates started to swim for shore, putting the smallest, Paul, between the two stronger swimmers. A series of huge waves and whirling undertow swamped the three. Paul and Tom went under. Neil dove, found and pulled Tom to shore, but Paul had disappeared. Neil swam back and repeatedly dove, searching for the missing Paul Smith, but his friend was gone.

In the spring of 1941, Tom Doyle was accepted as a candidate for the Dominican Novitiate and told Neil about it. Shortly after, Tom died of a brain tumor. As a pallbearer for Tom, Neil met the handsome, dignified Iowan T. S. McDermott, O.P., Dominican provincial. Father McDermott asked Neil if he had considered taking Tom's place in the Dominican Order. Neil replied that he had not.

Yet the formative influences of his life—the loving staunch Catholic family, the Dominican priests and nuns of his youth, the Christian Brothers and Jesuit Fathers engaged in Catholic education—bore fruit. Neil Forster was called, and he chose to answer yes.

In August 1941, Cornelius Forster entered the Dominican Novitiate at St. Rose Priory, Springfield, Kentucky, with the intention of serving as a Dominican missionary to the Fukien province in China. Here at St Rose, he met his superiors: Fathers L. P. Johansen, L. P. Thornton, and H. J. McManus. Neil also met his talented, spirited classmates: Thomas H. McBrien, Thomas L. Fallon, William D. Moriarty, Raymond Smith, Steven B. Jurasko, and Louis R. Durell. Neil began his Dominican life and his aspiration to be a channel of grace.

His first challenge came within four months of entering, with the U.S. suffering the bombing of Pearl Harbor on December 7,

1941. Torn between patriotism and his Dominican vocation, on August 23, 1942, Cornelius A. Forster, Jr., made his first profession as Brother Philip. He worked at his vocation, trusted in God, and prayed for the safety of his family members in service. His brothers returned safely, but Brother Philip's cousin George, son of his beloved godfather, John Concannon, was shot down over France shortly after D-Day.

Brother Philip strove to imitate his spiritual father, St. Dominic Guzman, and master the writings of his intellectual father, St. Thomas Aquinas. On August 24, 1945, in Ocean City, Maryland, Brother Philip made his solemn profession under superior Matthew Hanley, O.P.

Philip's spiritual life was nurtured by many, especially his beloved teacher, John Stephen McCormick, O.P., who inculcated another enduring life principle in Philip's student days: The Dominican Pope, St. Pius V (1566–1572), warned his brethren that a Dominican who fails to spend at least four hours daily in study approaches mortal sin. Brother Philip embarked on his life as a Dominican scholar.

On June 3, 1948, C. P. Forster was ordained a Dominican priest by Bishop John M. McNamara in Washington. In the Dominican tradition, Father Forster remained at the Dominican House of Studies to complete a final year of study. With three years of philosophy and four years of theology completed, he earned the S.T.L. (Licentiate) and S.T.Lr. (Lectorate of Sacred Theology) from the Pontifical Faculty of the Dominican College of the Immaculate Conception in 1949. Simultaneously, he completed his master's degree in history at the Catholic University of America under renowned historian Friedrick Engel-Janosi and also served as chaplain at a Washington prison and at Mt. Alto Naval Hospital.

By 1949, Mao Tse-tung and his Communist armies won victory after victory over Chiang Kai-shek's Nationalist government. Mao tortured and killed or ousted foreign missionaries. By December 1949, Mao was substantially in control of continental China. With the fate of the Dominican Mission at Fukien unknown, Father McDermott tabled Father Forster's request for a missionary assignment to China and temporarily sent him to Providence College as an instructor in history and dormitory prefect (head resident, until 1966). Here, for the next forty-four years, C. P. Forster, O.P., served as a channel of grace. His labors were many: Dominican priest, preacher, educator, scholar, teacher, author, administrator, archivist, mentor, model, and inspiration to thousands.

Although his assignment was only temporary, Father Forster dove into the work. Responding to the provincial's request in 1951, he volunteered as a military chaplain for Korea. Father McDermott had other plans, and told Father Forster he would prefer him to apply, pack his bags, and pursue his doctorate at Oxford University. The young Dominican obeyed, but the regent of studies intervened and insisted that Father Forster stay at PC, teach a full course load, and pursue the doctorate at Fordham University.

From 1954 to 1963, Father Forster taught full-time, perfected or retained fluency in seven foreign languages, traveled to New York each weekend for Friday night and Saturday morning graduate classes, heard confessions on Saturday afternoons, and said Sunday Masses at various area parishes. Summers he pursued graduate work and research full-time but exercised his priestly ministry after summer school in various parish assignments in New York, Massachusetts, and Florida. For one summer, he was given permission to pursue his research in London, and he completed his dissertation, "Charles Townshend: A Study of His Political Conduct," under the demanding direction of Dr. Ross Hoffman. Father Forster earned his Ph.D. from Fordham University in 1963.

At PC, his Dominican life was nurtured by Fathers Robert Slavin, Cyril Dore, Steve McCormick, Damien Schneider, Dan Reilly, Dick McAvey, Sandy McGregor, and countless other brethren. Faithful to his prayer life, Father Forster daily said his office and developed a deeper devotion to the rosary of the Blessed Mother. In the classroom, he was an exemplary teacher. Thorough in preparation, master of his subject, he presented lectures that were often riveting. His mastery of understatement belied a wry humor and sophisticated analysis of critical, complex material. When describing some political reprobate's passing, Father was fond of quipping, "And so he went to his eternal meeting with St. Peter, and we can only speculate on the outcome." Father Forster engendered a love for history in countless students. In forty-four years, he taught over 210 courses and at least 6,561 students, approximately 22 percent of Providence College's 30,000 alumni.

Father Forster rose through the academic ranks and by 1958 was a full professor of history. Succeeding Father Daniel Reilly from 1962 to 1992, he served as chairman of the history department. Concerned with the whole development of the student, he was always kind, supportive, quick to praise and encourage, generous with his time, and ever the channel of grace for each student he taught.

In 1963, President Cyril Dore, O.P., approved Father Forster's proposal to offer graduate studies at PC. Father founded the Graduate School of Arts and Sciences and became the first dean in 1965, a position he held until his death. Since 1964, over 4,000 students were awarded graduate diplomas bearing the signature of Cornelius P. Forster, O.P.

Philip Forster, O.P., also chaired countless committees, the results of which enriched the academic life of the PC community. From feasibility committees emerged the Graduate School and programs in English, education, history, and business, the M.B.A., and the Oxford Junior Year Abroad.

Father Forster never thought himself unique, nor did he ever feel that his workload was too great. Modest, never self-aggrandizing, he merely imitated the labors of those Dominican brethren before him. Most of his contemporaries shared his energy and commitment to pursue excellence for Providence College. He mentored younger Dominicans and encouraged their priestly and scholarly endeavors.

When Thomas R. Peterson, O.P., became PC's ninth president (1971–85), Father Forster assumed additional administrative roles. Frugal watchdog of the college budget, Father Forster was executive vice president from 1982 to 1985 and acting president during Father Peterson's illness in the summer of 1982. Walter Heath, O.P., dubbed Fathers Reg Peterson, Alan Morris, Hugh McBrien, and Phil Forster "The Steak Club." These Dominicans, W. J. Heath said, "worked hard, laughed harder, and undertook all jobs with bustling energy, superior talent, and unparalleled success."

Heath identified their ascendancy as the "Halcyon Years" of the college's development.

Although Father Forster's administrative and teaching roles were demanding, he never allowed either his priestly or scholarly life to diminish. Lauded for an exceptionally moving homily on one occasion, he looked genuinely surprised at the praise and gently replied, "Dear Lord, it's not my doing; it's the work of the Holy Spirit."

At a historical convention in Moscow long before *glasnost*, Father Forster was approached covertly to say Mass for Russian Catholics whose priest had mysteriously disappeared. He was warned of the severity of penalties attached to any such action. Twice at night he went by varied routes to an old basilica packed with believers. He celebrated Mass, preaching in Latin and the Russian he had studied for his trip. Approached by a young Muscovite interested in the priesthood, Father Forster later made contact arrangements for him with a vocation director. Neither threats of Lubyanka Prison nor Siberian internment could diminish Father Forster's missionary ardor.

Father Forster continued to publish scholarly articles, papers, book reviews, and books and contributed over forty publications to historical scholarship. The Council of Trent, Martyrs of The Paris Commune, Dominican figures, Lord Acton, Charles Townshend, and Dominican history were just a few of the topics to which he took pen and, later, his computer. At his death, he was engaged in research and writing for several books and articles, and he was serving as archivist for the Dominican Province of St. Joseph.

Father Forster's interest in politics had not waned. His enduring research and teaching interest in eighteenth- and nineteenth-century British history produced several treatises: *Lord Acton and the Papacy; Charles Townshend: A Study of His Political Conduct*; and the acclaimed critical political biography, *The Uncontrolled Chancellor: Charles Townshend and His American Policy*. In his scholarly studies he was a master of the political vagaries, strategies, and subtleties of the eighteenth-century Age of George III. At one New England Conference on British Studies, a young history department colleague was politely elbowed away from his side when other eighteenth-century specialists vied for Father's attention. On the fringe of the crowd, one specialist commented, "You may not realize it, but Father Forster is the best eighteenth-century British specialist on this side of the Atlantic, and some think on both Atlantic shores."

Father Forster was also an innovator. In addition to the Graduate School and Oxford Junior Year Abroad Program, Father introduced student/professor evaluations within the history department; invited competent women to the graduate faculty long before PC went coed; supported the admission of women students to the undergraduate school in 1971; advocated gender equity in education and legal rights for women; mentored junior faculty in both teaching techniques and publication efforts; and mandated permanent department records for all history majors.

An iron fist in a velvet glove, Father hounded history department faculty and other scholars to finish their doctorates, to publish, to research. Father critiqued countless articles, papers, and theses for colleagues and always encouraged their contributions to the college. Channel of grace, he was the first to pen a note of comfort in time of bereavement or illness, or a note of congratulations for some accomplishment.

Father Forster always held a special place in his heart for the history faculty, graduate assistants, and history majors. He hired most of the department, many of whom were his exemplary undergraduate students. Committed to excellence and the pursuit of truth, he wanted the best. His leadership inspired them to their best effort. His mentorship was a constant.

All his life, Cornelius P. Forster remained devoted to his family and friends. He constantly renewed the connection with classmates from Cathedral and Fordham. He was a channel of grace for both. As a priest, he brought sacramental grace. He baptized the next two Forster generations, performed all the marriages, and celebrated special Eucharistic liturgies. He was the rock from which they gathered strength and renewed their faith.

Father Forster asked little for himself, embraced his vow of poverty with joy, usually got Christmas gifts that didn't fit, attended all the birthday parties, laughed, and sang. His love for family and friends knew no bounds. Father Forster dedicated his Townshend biography "To my Mother and Father (in memoriam) who taught me to love truth, and to my sister and brothers who have encouraged me in the pursuit of it." For his family and friends, he was the channel of grace, the conduit of God's abiding love, the ultimate truth.

In 1989, one year after the death of his beloved classmate Father McBrien, Father Forster was diagnosed with lymphoma. No stranger to pain, he patiently bore the various treatments. He lamented only the time wasted sitting in the doctors' offices, which kept him from more productive work. He believed that "Dominicans do not retire," and that although the vineyards are many, the laborers are few. He spared those who knew and loved him by saying little about his condition. He taught his last class of graduate students on October 18, 1993. He informed Father McGonigle that he would step down as dean of the Graduate School in June 1994, and was pleased to be asked to join the search committee for his successor. He would remain dean emeritus.

God had other plans for this channel of grace. Weak, dizzy, and in pain, he consented to his admission to Fatima Hospital on November 1, 1993. From here he continued to be involved in the work of the college.

On November 18, 1993, Father John Peterson, Lois Auld, Sister Mary Frances McDonald, and his family—Bill, Frank, Ginger, Ray, and Donna—joined in prayer, and Cornelius P. Forster, O.P., went home to his God at 2:40 P.M.

To the hospital, to the wake, to the moving Mass of Resurrection, Father Forster's family, friends, students, and Dominican brothers and sisters came from all corners of the U.S. Two generations of Forsters and history students were pallbearers and ministers of the Word. His last classmate, Tom Fallon, O.P., his close friend, Alan Morris, O.P., and his homilist, Thomas R. Peterson, O.P., concelebrated Mass with uncounted Dominican and diocesan priests. Bishop Louis Gelineau gave the last blessing at Father Forster's last earthly liturgy.

After his death, many encomiums flowed into the graduate

office. Former student and history department colleague Richard Deasy poignantly summed the universal consensus: "Father Cornelius Forster was the consummate Providence College Dominican. He had the organizational genius of Dominic Guzman, the willingness to experiment of Albert the Great, the devotion to truth of Thomas Aquinas, the respect for law of Francis Vitoria, the zeal for justice of Anthony Montesinos, the appreciation for other cultures of Bartholomew de las Casas, the charity for all people of Peter Claver, and the love of God of Catherine of Siena. He truly was 'to honor bound, to love and virtue sworn.'" Yet, Father Forster's eulogy may have been written over two hundred years ago. What Edmund Burke said of Charles Townshend may have prophetically eulogized Townshend's biographer. Was Burke not referring to Father Forster when he proclaimed, "On the opposite quarter of the heavens arose another luminary, and for his hour became lord of the ascendant." Surely, Edmund Burke described Father Forster as "the charm of every private society which he honored with his presence."

Yet, unlike Burke's lament of Townshend that "this light too is passed and set forever," channel of grace Cornelius P. Forster, O.P., all those whose lives you touched now walk more closely with their God because of your priesthood. In faith, we are assured that the outcome of your meeting with St. Peter was fruitful, the goal for which you lived your quintessential Dominican life.

Illustration Credits

Cover: Photo of The Independent Man by moonlight, Patrick T. Conley photo collection, Providence College Archives (PTC).

Chapter 1: The Independent Man, photo by Lou Notarianni, 1976.

Chapter 2A: Williams Monument, photo from *Official Chronicle and Tribute Book of Rhode Island and Providence Plantations* (1936), p. 9.

Chapter 2B: Title page of *Key into the Language of America*, Rhode Island Historical Society (RIHS).

Chapter 2C: Map from John H. Cady, *Rhode Island Boundaries, 1636–1936* (1936).

Chapter 3A: Anne Hutchinson, sculpture by Cyrus Dallin, PTC.

Chapter 3B: Map of Portsmouth 1638–42, RIHS.

Chapter 4: Charter of 1663, RIHS.

Chapter 5: John Clarke, likeness attributed to Dutch artist Guilliam de Ville, courtesy of the Redwood Library, Newport.

Chapter 6: Smith's Castle, photo by Laurence Tilley, courtesy of the Cocumscussoc Association.

Chapter 7: Aaron Lopez, portrait from Stanley F. Chyet, *Lopez of Newport: Colonial American Merchant Prince* (1970), courtesy of the American Jewish Historical Society.

Chapter 8: Abraham Whipple, portrait by Edward Savage, courtesy of the U.S. Naval Academy.

Chapter 9A: William Ellery, portrait by Samuel Bell Waugh after John Trumbull, PTC.

Chapter 9B: Nathanael Greene, portrait courtesy of Independence National Historical Park, Philadelphia.

Chapter 10: Stephen Hopkins, sketch courtesy of the Frick Art Reference Library. For an authoritative and convincing analysis of the origins and identity of the Hopkins sketch, consult Irma B. Jaffe, *Trumbull: The Declaration of Independence* (New York, 1976), pp. 79, 81–2, 84, 87. The standing man with the Quaker hat in the Trumbull painting is not Hopkins (as previously believed) but John Dickinson of Pennsylvania. The purported portrait of Hopkins that hangs in the Rhode Island State House is inaccurate, based as it is on an erroneous attribution.

Chapter 29: Precious Blood Church, photo from *History of the Catholic Church in Woonsocket*, by James W. Smyth (1903), p. 114.

Chapter 30: Irish Famine Memorial in progress, photo courtesy of Raymond J. McKenna.

Chapter 31: Aram Pothier, photo from *Debuts de la Colonie Franco-Américaine de Woonsocket, R.I.*, by Marie-Louise Bonier (1920).

Chapter 32: *Venezia*, PTC.

Chapter 33: Louis W. Cappelli, photo from *Rhode Island Manual*, 1963–64, opp. p. 490.

Chapter 34: Two St. Michael's Churches, photos by Brian Ducharme and David Barnett, from *Woonsocket, Rhode Island: A Centennial History, 1888–1988*, ed. Marcel P. Fortin (1988), p. 91.

Chapter 35A: St. George's Church, photo from *The Arabic-Speaking People of Rhode Island*, by Eleanor A. Doumato (1986), p. 25, courtesy of Father Paul Mouawad.

Chapter 35B: Father Timothy Jock and the 1934 First Communion class of St. Basil's in Central Falls, photo from Doumato, *Arabic-Speaking People*, p. 23, courtesy of Rose Poole.

Chapter 36: Ramon Guiteras, photo from *Tercentenery of New England Families, 1620–1928* (1928), courtesy of Joan Prescott.

Chapter 37: Cathedral of SS. Peter and Paul, watercolor by Robert Pailthorpe, original owned by PTC.

Chapter 38: Matthew Harkins, PTC.

Chapter 39: St. Joseph's Hospital, engraving by J. J. Ryder from *Official Souvenir of the St. Joseph's Hospital, Containing a Complete History from Its Inception* (1894), p. 21.

Chapter 40: Act of 1719, from the Digest of 1719, Rhode Island State Archives.

Chapter 41: Henry B. Anthony, RIHS.

Chapter 42: Charles R. Brayton, RIHS.

Chapter 43: Nelson Aldrich, RIHS.

Chapter 44: Jim Kiernan, from *Rhode Island Manual*, 1937–38, opp. p. 112.

Chapter 45: Mary Brennan and Patrick Conley, photo by Lou Notarianni, 1976, PTC.

Chapter 46: Lloyd Griffin, photo courtesy of the Providence Journal Company.

629

Chapter 47: Colony House, Newport, PTC.

Chapter 48: State House, Providence, courtesy of the Rhode Island Department of Economic Development.

Chapter 49A: Charles E. Gorman, photo from *The History of the State of Rhode Island and Providence Planatations* (1920), by Thomas W. Bicknell, biographical volume (Lister to Traver), opp. p. 201.

Chapter 49B: Ku Klux Klan, photo courtesy of the Providence Journal Company.

Chapter 50: Pat Abbruzzi, photo courtesy of the Providence Journal Company.

Chapter 51: Charlie Reynolds and Jack Flynn, Providence College Archives.

Chapter 52: Senior athletes, photo by Joy Brown, PTC.

Chapter 53: Blackstone River at Pawtucket, engraving by J. S. Lincoln, RIHS.

Chapter 54: Sprague Mansion, photo ca. 1979, from *Cranston, Rhode Island: Statewide Historical Preservation Report, P-C-1*, by Robert E. Freeman (1980), p. 20.

Chapter 55: Samuel Bridgham, engraving, RIHS.

Chapter 56: Departure of the Providence Marine Corps of Artillery, April 1861, engraving by J. H. Schell, from *Frank Leslie's Illustrated Weekly Magazine*, PTC.

Chapter 57: Ocean Street houses, photo courtesy of SWAP, Inc., and Carla Young.

Chapter 58: Main Street, Wickford (ca. 1900), photo from *Old Wickford: The Venice of America*, by Mrs. F. Burge Griswold (1900), opp. p. 58.

Chapter 59: James De Wolf, watercolor on ivory, artist unknown, RIHS.

Chapter 60: William Barton, oil on canvas, artist unknown, RIHS.

Appendix I: Conley Library, pen-and-ink sketch by Marjorie J. Vogel.

Appendix II: Cornelius P. Forster, O.P., photo by D. A. Gunning Studio, courtesy of the Providence College Archives.

INDEX

DR. PATRICK T. CONLEY holds an A.B. from Providence College, an M.A. and Ph.D. from the University of Notre Dame, and a J.D. from Suffolk University Law School. He has published sixteen books, including *Catholicism in Rhode Island: The Formative Era* (1976), *Democracy in Decline: Rhode Island's Constitutional Development 1775–1841* (1977), *An Album of Rhode Island History, 1636–1986* (1986), *The Constitution and the States* (1988), *The Bill of Rights and the States* (1992), and *Liberty and Justice: A History of Law and Lawyers in Rhode Island, 1636–1998* (1998), as well as more than a score of scholarly articles in history, law, and political science. The youngest person ever to attain the rank of full professor at Providence College, Dr. Conley also practices law, runs a used- and rare-book firm, and manages a real estate development business. He has served as chairman of the Rhode Island Bicentennial Commission (ri76), chairman and founder of the Providence Heritage Commission, chairman and founder of the Rhode Island Publications Society, and general editor of the Rhode Island Ethnic Heritage Pamphlet Series. In 1977 he founded the Rhode Island Heritage Commission as a successor organization to ri76. Dr. Conley was also chairman of the Rhode Island Bicentennial [of the Constitution] Foundation and chairman of the U.S. Constitution Council. In May 1995 he was inducted into the Rhode Island Heritage Hall of Fame—one of a handful of living Rhode Islanders who have been accorded that honor.